ESSENTIAL ECONOMICS FOR BUSINESS

Pearson

At Pearson, we have a simple mission: to help people make more of their lives through learning.

We combine innovative learning technology with trusted content and educational expertise to provide engaging and effective learning experiences that serve people wherever and whenever they are learning.

From classroom to boardroom, our curriculum materials, digital learning tools and testing programmes help to educate millions of people worldwide – more than any other private enterprise.

Every day our work helps learning flourish, and wherever learning flourishes, so do people.

To learn more, please visit us at **www.pearson.com/uk**

ESSENTIAL ECONOMICS FOR BUSINESS

Sixth edition

John Sloman
Economics Network
Visiting Professor, University of the West of England

Elizabeth Jones
Professor of Economics and Director of Undergraduate Studies,
University of Warwick

 Pearson

Harlow, England • London • New York • Boston • San Francisco • Toronto • Sydney
Dubai • Singapore • Hong Kong • Tokyo • Seoul • Taipei • New Delhi
Cape Town • São Paulo • Mexico City • Madrid • Amsterdam • Munich • Paris • Milan

PEARSON EDUCATION LIMITED
KAO Two
KAO Park
Harlow CM17 9SR
United Kingdom
Tel: +44 (0)1279 623623
Web: www.pearson.com/uk

First published 2005 (print)
Second published 2008 (print)
Third published 2011 (print)
Fourth edition published 2014 (print and electronic)
Fifth edition published 2017 (print and electronic)
Sixth edition published 2020 (print and electronic)

ISBN: 978-1-292-30453-3 (print)
      978-1-292-30456-4 (PDF)
      978-1-292-30458-8 (ePub)

British Library Cataloguing-in-Publication Data
A catalogue record for the print edition is available from the British Library

Library of Congress Cataloging-in-Publication Data
Names: Sloman, John, 1947- author. | Jones, Elizabeth, 1984- author.
Title: Essential economics for business / John Sloman, Economics Network
   Visiting Professor, University of the West of England, Elizabeth Jones,
   Principal Teaching Fellow and Dean of Students, University of Warwick.
Description: Sixth edition. | Harlow, England : Pearson, 2020. | Includes
   bibliographical references and index. | Summary: "Welcome to the sixth
   edition of Essentials Economics for Business. If you are a student on a
   business or management degree or diploma course and taking a module
   which includes economics, then this book is written for you. Such
   modules may go under the title of Business Environment or Business
   Context, or they may simply be called Introduction to Economics or
   Introduction to Business Economics. Alternatively, you may be studying
   on an MBA and need a grounding in basic economic concepts and how they
   apply to the business environment"-- Provided by publisher.
Identifiers: LCCN 2019030563 (print) | LCCN 2019030564 (ebook) | ISBN
   9781292304533 (paperback) | ISBN 9781292304564 (pdf) | ISBN
   9781292304588 (epub)
Subjects: LCSH: Managerial economics. | Economics. | Business. | Industrial
   management.
Classification: LCC HD30.22 .S58 2020 (print) | LCC HD30.22 (ebook) | DDC
   330--dc23
LC record available at https://lccn.loc.gov/2019030563
LC ebook record available at https://lccn.loc.gov/2019030564

10 9 8 7 6 5 4 3 2 1
19

Cover image: Peter Barritt / robertharding / Alamy Stock Photo
All Part and Chapter opener images © John Sloman

Print edition typeset in Sabon MT Pro 10pt by SPi Global
Print edition printed in Slovakia by Neografia

NOTE THAT ANY PAGE CROSS REFERENCES REFER TO THE PRINT EDITION

Brief contents

Preface   *ix*
Publisher's acknowledgements   *xiv*

Part A — INTRODUCTION

1   Business and the economic environment   2

Part B — MARKETS, DEMAND AND SUPPLY

2   The working of competitive markets   26
3   Demand and the consumer   55
4   Supply decisions in a perfectly competitive market   81

Part C — THE MICROECONOMIC ENVIRONMENT OF BUSINESS

5   Pricing and output decisions in imperfectly competitive markets   110
6   Business growth and strategy   145
7   Multinational corporations and business strategy in a global economy   175
8   Labour and employment   196
9   Government, the firm and the market   221

Part D — THE MACROECONOMIC ENVIRONMENT OF BUSINESS

10   The economy and business activity   258
11   National macroeconomic policy   293
12   The global trading environment   325
13   The global financial environment   354

Websites appendix   *W:1*
Key ideas   *K:1*
Glossary   *G:1*
Index   *I:1*

Contents

Preface   ix
Publisher's acknowledgements   xiv

PART A INTRODUCTION

1 Business and the economic environment   2

1.1   The business organisation   6
1.2   The external business environment   11
1.3   The economist's approach to business   20
Box 1.1 A perfect partnership   3
Box 1.2 The airline industry   13
Box 1.3 The changing nature of business   19
Questions   24
Part end – additional case studies and relevant websites 24

PART B MARKETS, DEMAND AND SUPPLY

2 The working of competitive markets   26

2.1   Business in a perfectly competitive market   26
2.2   Demand   28
2.3   Supply   32
2.4   Price and output determination   35
2.5   Elasticity of demand and supply   42
Box 2.1 Stock market prices   38
Box 2.2 UK house prices   40
Box 2.3 Shall we put up our price?   47
Box 2.4 Speculation   49
Box 2.5 Market intervention   51
Questions   53

3 Demand and the consumer   55

3.1   Demand and the firm   55
3.2   Understanding consumer behaviour   56
3.3   Behavioural economics   63
3.4   Estimating and predicting demand   66
3.5   Stimulating demand   71
Box 3.1 Rogue traders   59
Box 3.2 Problems for unwary insurance companies   62
Box 3.3 Using policy to change behaviour   66
Box 3.4 Global advertising trends: a new world   72
Box 3.5 Advertising and the long run   78
Questions   80

4 Supply decisions in a perfectly competitive market   81

4.1   Production and costs in the short run   82
4.2   Production and costs: long run   89
4.3   Revenue   98
4.4   Profit maximisation   100
Box 4.1 Diminishing returns and business   83
Box 4.2 Understanding your fixed costs   87
Box 4.3 Lights, camera, action   94
Box 4.4 Minimum efficient scale   96
Box 4.5 Cost, revenue and profits   99
Box 4.6 E-commerce   104
Questions   106
Part end – additional case studies and relevant websites 107

PART C THE MICROECONOMIC ENVIRONMENT OF BUSINESS

5 Pricing and output decisions in imperfectly competitive markets   110

5.1   Alternative market structures   110
5.2   Monopoly   116
5.3   Oligopoly   121
5.4   Game theory   127
5.5   Alternative aims of the firm   134
5.6   Setting price   139
Box 5.1 A fast food race to the bottom   114
Box 5.2 Premier league football: the sky is the limit   120
Box 5.3 Market power in oligopolistic industries   125
Box 5.4 The prisoners' dilemma   130
Box 5.5 The Hunger Games   132
Box 5.6 Behavioural economics and the firm   137
Questions   143

6 Business growth and strategy   145

6.1   Strategic analysis   145
6.2   Strategic choice   149
6.3   Growth strategy   155
6.4   Financing growth and investment   165
6.5   Starting small   168
Box 6.1 Business strategy the Samsung way   150
Box 6.2 The ratios to measure success   153
Box 6.3 Strategies in uncertain times   161

Box 6.4 Hotel Chocolat   172
Questions   173

7 Multinational corporations and business strategy in a global economy   175

7.1 The globalisation debate   176
7.2 Multinational corporations   177
7.3 Business strategy in a global economy   183
7.4 Problems facing multinationals   190
7.5 Multinationals and the host state   191
Box 7.1 Cross-border merger activity   181
Box 7.2 Attracting foreign investors   187
Box 7.3 Grocers go global   189
Box 7.4 Investing in Africa   193
Questions   194

8 Labour and employment   196

8.1 Market-determined wage rates and employment   196
8.2 Power in the labour market   202
8.3 Minimum wages   207
8.4 The flexible firm and the market for labour   210
8.5 The labour market and incentives   215
Box 8.1 New ways of working   198
Box 8.2 What do post, airlines, bins, buses and universities have in common?   205
Box 8.3 Does gender inequality still exist?   212
Box 8.4 Education, earnings, productivity and talent   218
Questions   220

9 Government, the firm and the market   221

9.1 Market failures   222
9.2 Firms and corporate responsibility   228
9.3 Government intervention in the market   233
9.4 Environmental policy   235
9.5 Competition policy and business behaviour   244
9.6 The regulation of business   250
Box 9.1 The problem of free-riders   226
Box 9.2 The Body Shop   232
Box 9.3 A Stern rebuke   237
Box 9.4 The problem of urban traffic congestion   241
Box 9.5 Google 'Google'   247
Questions   253
Part end – additional case studies and relevant websites   254

PART D THE MACROECONOMIC ENVIRONMENT OF BUSINESS

10 The economy and business activity   258

10.1 The key macroeconomic objectives   258
10.2 Business activity and the circular flow of income   260
10.3 The determination of business activity   264
10.4 The business cycle   271
10.5 Money, interest rates and business activity   275

10.6 Unemployment   280
10.7 Inflation   284
Box 10.1 Doing the sums   268
Box 10.2 The economics of playing host   268
Box 10.3 Sentiment and spending   274
Box 10.4 Inflation and unemployment: how costly?   286
Box 10.5 Airlines and the macroeconomy   289
Questions   291

11 National macroeconomic policy   293

11.1 Fiscal policy   295
11.2 Monetary policy   304
11.3 Supply-side policy   314
Box 11.1 The fiscal framework in the eurozone   301
Box 11.2 The central banks of the USA and the eurozone   309
Box 11.3 The credit crunch and its aftermath   311
Box 11.4 Japan's volatile past and present   315
Box 11.5 Productivity   321
Questions   323

12 The global trading environment   325

12.1 International trade   326
12.2 Trade restrictions   333
12.3 The world trading system and the WTO   341
12.4 The European Union and the single market   345
12.5 Brexit   349
Box 12.1 The changing face of comparative advantage   330
Box 12.2 Strategic trade theory   335
Box 12.3 Beyond bananas   338
Box 12.4 Preferential trading   343
Box 12.5 In or out?   347
Questions   353

13 The global financial environment   354

13.1 The balance of payments   355
13.2 The exchange rate   358
13.3 The growth of global financial flows   368
13.4 Economic and monetary union in the EU   370
13.5 International economic policy: managing the global economy   375
Box 13.1 The importance of international financial movements   361
Box 13.2 Exchange rate uncertainty and the plight of business   364
Box 13.3 The euro/dollar seesaw   365
Box 13.4 Global problems. global answers?   377
Questions   379
Part end – additional case studies and relevant websites   380

Websites appendix   W:1
Key ideas   K:1
Glossary   G:1
Index   I:1

Preface

Welcome to the sixth edition of *Essentials Economics for Business*. If you are a student on a business or management degree or diploma course and taking a module which includes economics, then this book is written for you. Such modules may go under the title of Business Environment or Business Context, or they may simply be called Introduction to Economics or Introduction to Business Economics. Alternatively, you may be studying on an MBA and need a grounding in basic economic concepts and how they apply to the business environment.

The book covers the core economics that you will need as a business student, but it also covers various business-related topics not typically covered in an introductory economics textbook. These topics include elements of business organisation and business strategy.

As well as making considerable use of business examples throughout the text, we have included many case studies in boxes (60 in all). These illustrate how economics can be used to understand particular business problems or aspects of the business environment. Many of these case studies cover issues that you are likely to read about in the newspapers. Some cover general business issues; others look at specific companies. There are also an additional 112 case studies on the book's companion website. These, along with references to various useful websites, are listed at the end of each of the four parts of the book.

We hope that, in using this book, you will share our fascination for economics. It is a subject that is highly relevant to the world in which we live. You only have to look at global events and the news to see its importance: from economic growth, to levels of business investment, to interest rates, to employment issues, to the prices firms charge, to the rise of online shopping, to Brexit, to the rise of populist governments and policies. Many of our needs are served by business – whether as employers or as producers of the goods and services we buy. After graduating, you will prob-ably take up employment in business. A grounding in economic principles and how they relate to the world of business should prove invaluable in the business decisions you may well have to make.

The aim throughout the book is to make this intriguing subject clear for you to understand and as relevant as possible to you as a student of business.

The written style is direct and straightforward, with short paragraphs to aid rapid comprehension. Definitions of all key terms are given in the margin, with defined terms appearing in bold. We have high-lighted 29 Key Ideas, which are fundamental to 'thinking like an economist'. We refer back to these every time they recur throughout the book. This helps you to see how the subject ties together, and also helps you to develop a toolkit of concepts that can be used in a whole host of different contexts.

Summaries ('Recaps') are given at the end of each section of each chapter. These should help you in reviewing the material you have just covered and in revising for exams. Each chapter finishes with a series of questions, as does each of the boxes. These can be used to check your understanding of the chapter and help you to see how its material can be applied to various business problems. Each of the boxes also includes a student activity (new for this edition), which can be done individually or in groups.

There are also questions interspersed throughout the text in 'Pause for thought' panels. These encour-age you to reflect on what you are learning and to see how the various ideas and theories relate to different issues. Answers to these questions are given on the book's companion website.

We hope you enjoy the book and come to appreci-ate the crucial role that economics plays in all our lives and, in particular, in the practice of business.

Good luck and enjoy. Perhaps this will be just the beginning of a life-long interest in economic issues and how they apply to the world of business – and in your own personal life too!

TO LECTURERS AND TUTORS

The aim of this book is to provide a short course in economic principles as they apply to the business environment. It is designed to be used by first-year undergraduates on business studies degrees and diplomas where economics is taught from the business perspective, either as a separate one-semester module or as part of a business environment module. It is also suitable for students studying economics on MBA, CMS, DMS and various professional courses.

In addition to covering core economic principles, various specialist business topics are also covered that do not appear in conventional introductory economics textbooks. The following are some examples of these additional topics:

- Business organisations
- Industrial structure
- STEEPLE analysis (as an extension of PEST analysis)
- The structure–conduct–performance paradigm and its limitations
- The control of prices
- The multinational corporation
- Globalisation and business
- Marketing the product
- Strategic analysis and choice
- Principal–agent analysis and the problem of asymmetric information as applied to various business situations
- The problems of adverse selection and moral hazard
- Application of game theory to business situations
- Porter's five forces model
- Growth strategy
- Business strategy in a recession
- Transactions cost analysis
- Ratio analysis to measure firms' success (new to this edition)

- Alternative aims of firms
- Pricing in practice
- The product life cycle
- The small-firm sector
- Flexible labour markets and firms
- The economics of entrepreneurship
- Business ethics and corporate responsibility
- Government and the firm, including competition policy and regulation
- The macroeconomic environment of business, including the impact of macroeconomic policy on business
- Analysis of global policy responses to the credit crunch and the impact on business (new to this edition)
- The competitive advantage of nations
- Trading blocs including the effect of the single European market on business
- Monetary union, the crisis in the eurozone and its impact on business
- Brexit and its impact on business
- The implications of exchange rate movements and international capital flows for business.

The text is split into four parts containing a total of 13 chapters. Each chapter could be covered in a week, giving enough material for a semester. Each chapter is divided into discrete sections, each with its own summary, providing an ideal coverage for a single study session for a student. Chapters finish with review questions, which can be used for seminars or discussion sessions.

The first nine chapters cover microeconomics and its relation to business. The final four cover the macroeconomic environment of business, both national and international. This higher weighting for microeconomics reflects the structure of many economics for business or business environment modules.

SPECIAL FEATURES

The book contains the following special features:

- *A direct and straightforward written style,* with short paragraphs to aid rapid comprehension. The aim all the time is to provide maximum clarity.
- *Attractive full-colour design.* The careful and consistent use of colour and shading makes the text more attractive to students and easier to use by giving clear signals as to the book's structure.
- *Figures with captions.* Most diagrams have captions to explain their properties and to highlight key features.

- *Key Ideas* highlighted and explained where they first appear. There are 29 of these ideas, which are fundamental to the study of economics on business courses. Students can see them recurring throughout the book. Showing how ideas can be used in a variety of contexts helps students to 'think like an economist' and to relate the different parts of the subject together. All 29 Key Ideas are defined in a special section at the end of the book.
- *Pause for thought* questions integrated throughout the text. These encourage students to reflect on

what they have just read and make the learning process a more active and reflective one. Answers to these questions appear on the student website. This new edition contains additional 'Pause for thought' questions.

■ *Part opening sections* for each of the four parts of the book, setting the scene and introducing the material to be covered.

■ *Chapter opening sections* that identify key business issues to be covered in that chapter.

■ *All technical terms are highlighted and clearly defined in the margin* on the page they appear. This feature is especially useful for students when revising.

■ *A comprehensive index,* including a *glossary* with reference to all defined terms. This enables students to look up a definition as required and to see it used in context.

■ *Many boxes with additional applied material.* Additional applied material to that found in the text can be found in boxes, typically four or five per chapter. The extensive use of applied material makes learning much more interesting for students and helps to bring the subject alive. This is particularly important for business students who need to relate economic theory to their other subjects and to the world of business generally. The boxes are current and include discussion of a range of companies and business topics. They are ideal for use as case studies in class.

■ *Box questions.* Each box contains questions allowing students to assess their own understanding. Answers to these questions can be found on the lecturer website, which lecturers can make available to students if they choose.

■ *Student activities.* New to this edition, each box contains an activity designed to develop important

skills around research, data analysis and the communication of economic ideas and principles. These skills are not only of use to students while at university but also in the world of work. They are frequently identified by employers as being especially valuable. Hence, undertaking the activities in the boxes helps students to increase their employability.

■ *Additional case studies appearing on the companion website.* These are referred to at the end of each of the four Parts of the book. Most of these 112 cases contain questions for students to reflect on and answers can be found on the lecturer site, which can be distributed to students as you wish. As with the boxes, for this edition there is student activity given at the end of each case study.

■ *Detailed summaries appear at the end of each section.* These allow students not only to check their comprehension of a section's contents, but also to get a clear overview of the material they have been studying.

■ *Review questions at the end of each chapter.* These are designed to test students' understanding of the chapter's salient points. These questions can be used for seminars or as set work to be completed in the students' own time. Answers can be found on the lecturer site

■ *A list of relevant websites given at the end of each part.* Details of these websites can be found in the Web Appendix at the end of the book. You can easily access any of these sites from the book's Economics News website (at www.pearsoned.co.uk/sloman). When you enter the site, click on Hotlinks. You will find all the sites from the Web Appendix listed. Click on the one you want and the hyperlink will take you straight to it.

SUPPLEMENTS

Economics News site

■ Search 'Sloman Economics News' and visit the book's news blog site. This contains several posts each month. Each post considers a topic in the news that relates to economics, with an introduction to and description of the news item, links to newspaper articles from around the world, videos, podcasts and data. There are questions on each item and references to the relevant chapter(s) of the book. There is a powerful search feature that lets you search news items by chapter of the book, topic or month.

■ There are also hotlinks to a range of websites, including each of those referred to at the end of each of the four Parts of the book.

Student website

The book's companion website (see www.pearsoned.co.uk/sloman) provides a comprehensive set of online resources. The site is open and does not require a password. Resources on the website include:

■ Animations of key models with audio explanations ('audio animations') in MP4 files. These can be viewed on phones, tablets, laptops, etc.

- 112 case studies in Word®, with questions for self-study and student activities, ordered Part-by-Part and referred to in the text
- Updated list of over 250 hotlinks to sites of use for economics
- Answers in Word® to all in-chapter (pause for thought) questions
- Hotlinks to the websites referred to at the end of each Part of the book
- Glossary
- Flashcards of key terms
- Access to articles from the News site relevant to any given chapter of the book

Website for lecturers and tutors

There are many resources for lecturers and tutors that can be downloaded from the book's lecturer site. These have been thoroughly revised and redesigned for the sixth edition. These include:

- *PowerPoint® slide shows* in full colour for use with a data projector in lectures and classes. These can also be made available to students by loading them on to a local network. There are several types of slideshows:
  - *All figures from the book and most of the tables.* Each figure is built up in a logical sequence, thereby allowing tutors to show them in lectures in an animated form. There is also a static version for printing onto acetate for use with a conventional OHP.
  - *Customisable lecture plans.* These are a series of bullet-point lecture plans. There is one for each chapter of the book. Each one can be easily edited, with points added, deleted or moved, so as to suit particular lectures. A consistent use of colour is made to show how the points tie together. They come in various versions:
    - Lecture plans with integrated diagrams. These lecture plans include animated diagrams, charts and tables at the appropriate points.
    - Lecture plans with integrated diagrams and questions. These are like the above but also include multiple-choice questions, allowing lectures to become more interactive. They can be used with or without an audience response system (ARS). A specific ARS version is available for TurningPoint® and is ready to use with appropriate 'clickers' or internet-enabled devices, such as phones, tablets or laptops. There is also a 'show of hands' version for use without clickers.
    - Lecture plans without the diagrams. These allow you to construct your own diagrams on the blackboard or whiteboard, or use an OHP or visualiser.

- *Case studies.* These 112 cases in Word®, also available on the companion website for students, can be reproduced and used for classroom exercises or for student assignments. Answers are also provided (not available on the student site).
- *Workshops.* There are 13 of these, each one covering a specific chapter. They are in Word® and can be reproduced for use with large groups (up to 200 students) in a lecture theatre or large classroom. Suggestions for use are given in an accompanying file. Answers to all workshops are given in separate Word® files.
- *Economic experiments.* These are simulations that can be used in class and cover topics such as markets, price controls, taxes and public goods.
- *Business videos:* interviews with senior managers in a number of firms and other organisations discussing various economic issues that affect them. Accompanying questions test students' understanding of the topics covered.
- *Teaching/learning case studies.* There are 20 of these. They examine various approaches to teaching introductory economics and ways to improve student learning.
- *Answers to all:*
  - end-of-chapter questions
  - pause for thought questions
  - questions in boxes
  - questions in the case studies
  - the 13 workshops.

  These are in Word® and can be distributed to students as you wish.

ACKNOWLEDGEMENTS

First, many thanks to Elizabeth for all her work in helping to prepare this new edition and for adding lots of new content. Many thanks too to all the reviewers of the text, who, as with the previous edition, have given us valuable advice for improvements. Thanks also to the team at Pearson, and especially Catherine Yates and Carole Drummond.

Finally, thanks to all my family and especially, as always, to my wife Alison for her continued patience, love and support.

John Sloman

Once again, my thanks go to John Sloman for giving me this wonderful opportunity to co-author my fourth edition of this textbook and to the team at Pearson for their continued support. I am forever grateful to my family and in particular my parents, whose unfailing love and support have made this possible.

Elizabeth Jones

Publisher's acknowledgements

Text

4 John Lewis Partnership: http://www.johnlewispartnership.co.uk/about/john-lewis.html 4 RetailTimes.co.uk: Fiona Briggs, 'John Lewis improves online customer experience with Oracle Commerce', Retail News (24 September 2015) 5 Katy Perceval: Katy Perceval, 'Material World', JLP e-Zine (21 May 2010) 5 John Lewis Partnership: The John Lewis Partnership Annual Report and Accounts 2009 6 John Lewis Partnership: Company Annual Reports and Accounts 13 International Air Transport Association: 'Healthy passenger demand continues in 2018 with another record load factor', The International Air Transport Association Press Release (7 February 2019) 13 Business Insider: Will Martin, 'What brought down Monarch, the UK's biggest ever airline collapse', Business Insider (3 October 2017) 14 International Civil Aviation Organization: 'About ICAO', ICAO website 16 Crown Copyright: Based on data in Time series data, series KKD5, KKD9, KKI7, KKK9 and KKJ7 (ONS, 2019) 16 Crown Copyright: Based on Labour Market Statistics data, series DYDC, JWR5, JWR6, JWR7, JWR8, JWR9, JWT8, JWS2 (ONS, 2019) 17 Houghton Mifflin: Adapted from Industrial Market Structure and Economic Performance, 3rd edn, New York: Houghton Mifflin (Scherer, F. M. and Ross, D. 1990) Houghton Mifflin, From SCHERER. SPB – SCHERER IND MKT STR&ECON PERF, 3E. © South-Western, a part of Cengage Learning, Inc. Reproduced by permission. www.cengage.com/permissions. 19 Publications Office of the European Union: Innovation Management and the Knowledge-driven Economy, European Commission, Directorate-general for Enterprise (ECSC-EC-EAEC Brussels-Luxembourg, 2004) 40 Markit Group Ltd: Based on data in Halifax House Price Index (Lloyds Banking Group) 49 CoinMarketCap: https://coinmarketcap.com/currencies/bitcoin/historical-data/ 50 CoinMarketCap: https://coinmarketcap.com/currencies/bitcoin/ 51 Guardian News & Media: Denis Campbell, 'Minimum alcohol pricing cuts serious crime, study reveals', The Observer (28 June 2015) 52 Guardian News & Media: Rupert Neate and Lisa O'Carroll, 'New York's rent controls: essential for the future of the city', The Guardian (19 August 2015) 61 Grant Broadcasters: Christine Flatley, 'Townsville flood insurance bill hits $80m', Star News (6 February 2019) 64 Crown Copyright: 'Celebrities pledge to clean up their act on social media', Press Release, Competition and Markets Authority (23 January 2019) 66 Guardian News & Media: Richard Reeves, 'Why a nudge from the state beats a slap', Observer; (20 July 2008). 72 eMarketer inc: eMarketer, March 2018 73 Zenith: Global intelligence: Data & insights for the new age of communication, Q1: 2018, Zenith, The ROI agency (27 April 2018) 73 Zenith: Global intelligence: Data & insights for the new age of communication, Q1: 2018, Zenith, The ROI agency (27 April 2018) 79 The Globe and Mail: Susan Krashinsky, 'How a big bet on 'Batman v Superman paid off for Turkish Airlines', The Globe and Mail (16 May 2018) 91 Ship & Bunker: 'Drewry Warns Mega Ships Could Diminish Economies of Scale', Ship & Bunker (10 March 2016) 94 Michael E Porter: M.E. Porter and C.H.M. Ketels, UK competitiveness: moving to the next stage, DTI and ESRC (May 2003), p. 5. 97 Publications Office of the European Union: Pratten, C. F. 'A survey of the economies of scale', in Research on the 'Costs of Non-Europe', Volume 2 (Luxembourg: Office for Official Publications of the European Communities, 1988). © 1988 European Communities 97 Publications Office of the European Union: European Commission/Economists Advisory Group Ltd, 'Economies of scale', in The Single Market Review, Subseries V, Volume 4 (Luxembourg: Office for Official Publications of the European Communities, 1997). © 1997 European Communities 105 Crown Copyright: Based on series J4MC from Time Series Data (National Statistics). 115 Latin Post: K. J. Mariño, 'Fast Food competition intensifies as Burger King, McDonald's, Wendy's fight for cheapest meal deal', Latin Post (5 January 2016) 115 BBC: Bryan Lufkin, 'How can a fast food chain ever make money from a $1 burger?', BBC Capital (23 February 2018) 115 BBC: Bryan Lufkin, 'How can a fast food chain ever make money from a $1 burger?', BBC Capital

(23 February 2018) 125 Kantar: Based on data from Kantar Worldpanel 131 Cengage Learning: Thomas J. Nechyba, Microeconomics: an Intuitive Approach with Calculus, Cengage (2010) 146 Simon & Schuster: Porter, Michael E. Competitive Strategy: Techniques for Analyzing Industries and Competitors (The Free Press, 1980) 146 Simon & Schuster: Porter, Michael E. Competitive Strategy: Techniques for Analyzing Industries and Competitors (The Free Press, 1980) 161 Microsoft: John-Paul Ford Rojas, 'HSBC sees UK business weaken amid Brexit uncertainty', MSN Money (19 February 2019) 162 ITV plc: Angus Walker, 'Nissan hits out at Brexit 'uncertainty' as it confirms new X-Trail to be made in Japan not Sunderland', ITV News (2 February 2019) 162 Bloomberg L.P.: Benjamin D Katz and Joe Mayes, 'Airbus Threat to Quit U.K. Over Brexit Adds to Risk of Exodus', Bloomberg (24 January 2019) 162 Open Door Media Publishing: Pedro Gonçalves, 'Aviva to move £9bn in assets to Dublin as Brexit looms', International Investment (22 February 2019) 162 Lloyd's: 'Lloyd's Brussels: Our base in the heart of Europe', Lloyd's Press Release (June 2018) 162 ITV plc: Angus Walker, 'Nissan hits out at Brexit 'uncertainty' as it confirms new X-Trail to be made in Japan not Sunderland', ITV News (2 February 2019) 168 European Commission: What is an SME?, Internal Market, Industry, Entrepreneurship and SMEs, European Commission 170 Global Entrepreneurship Research Association: After Global Entrepreneurship Monitor 2018/19 Permission to reproduce a figure from the GEM 2018/19 Global Report, which appears here, has been kindly granted by the copyright holders 176 Organisation for Economic Co-operation and Development: Angel Gurría, Managing globalisation and the role of the OECD, OECD (20 September 2006). 176 International Monetary Fund: IMF staff, Globalization: A Brief Overview, IMF (May 2008). 179 United Nations Conference on Trade and Development: Based on data from World Investment Report 2018: Annex Tables (UNCTAD, Annex Table 1) 180 United Nations Conference on Trade and Development: Based on data from World Investment Report 2018: Annex Tables (UNCTAD) 182 United Nations Conference on Trade and Development: 'Net Cross-Border M&As', World Investment Report Annex Tables (UNCTAD, June 2018), Tables 5 and 7 183 United Nations Conference on Trade and Development: 'Cross Border Mergers & Acquisitions' World Investment Report Annex Tables (UNCTAD, June 2018), Tables 5 and 7 187 Milken Institute: Based on Global Opportunity Index, IFM Milken Institute (2019). 189 Bloomberg L.P.: 'Tesco stumbles with Wal-Mart as China shoppers buy local', Bloomberg (19 October 2012) 189 Bloomberg L.P.: 'Tesco stumbles with Wal-Mart as China shoppers buy local', Bloomberg (19 October 2012) 192 Guardian News & Media: Prem Sikka, 'Shifting profits across borders', The Guardian (12 February 2009) 193 Boston Consulting Group: Patrick Dupoux, Lisa Ivers, Stefano Niavas and Abdeljabbar Chraïti, Pioneering one Africa, Boston Consulting Group, (4 April 2018) 194 Boston Consulting Group: Patrick Dupoux, Lisa Ivers, Adham Abouzied, Abdeljabbar Chraïti, Fatymatou Dia, Hamid Maher and Stefano Niavas, Dueling with Lions: Playing the new game of business success in Africa, Boston Consulting Group, (10 November 2015) 199 Chartered Institute of Personnel and Development: 'Selection methods', CIPD Factsheet, Chartered Institute of Personnel and Development (2013) 205 Crown Copyright: Based on Time series Data, series BBFW (ONS) 207 Organisation for Economic Co-operation and Development: Based on data from OECD.Stat (OECD, 2018) 212 Crown Copyright: Annual Survey of Hours and Earnings: 2018 Provisional Results, Tables 1.1a, 1.10a, 1.11a, and 14.6a ONS (25 October 2018) 213 Organisation for Economic Co-operation and Development: Based on data from StatExtracts (OECD) 216 High Pay Centre: 'It's "Fatcat Friday" – CEO pay for 2019 surpasses the amount the average UK worker earns all year', HPC blog, High Pay Centre (3 January 2019) 217 High Pay Centre: RemCo Reform: governing successful organisations that benefit everyone, High Pay Centre and CIPD (January 2019) http://highpaycentre.org/files/report_for_website.pdf 217 Financial Times: Andrew Hill, 'Bonuses are bad for bankers and even worse for banks', Financial Times (25 January 2016) 219 Crown Copyright: International comparisons of productivity, Tables 1 and 2, ONS (April 2018) 228 BlackRock, Inc: Larry Fink's 2019 letter to CEOs BlackRock 229 Forbes Media LLC: The World's Most Reputable Companies for Corporate Responsibility 2018, Forbes and the Reputation Institute (11 October 2018) 229 Reputation Institute: 2018 and 2017 Global CSR 100 RepTrack Data Reputation Institute 230 Forbes Media LLC: Vicky Valet, 'The World's most reputable companies for Corporate Responsibility 2018', Forbes (11 October 2018) 232 Startups.co.uk: 'Q & A with The Body Shop's Dame Anita Roddick', Success Stories, Startups (4 September 2007) 232 US Environment Protection Agency: US Environment Protection Agency to help bring an end to animal testing and in March 2013 233 Guardian News & Media: Sarah Butler, 'L'Oréal to sell Body Shop to Brazil's Natura in €1bn deal', The Guardian (9 June 2017) 237 Crown copyright: Stern Review in the Economics of Climate Change: Executive Summary, HM Treasury (30 October 2006) 237 The Intergovernmental Panel on Climate Change: Climate

Change 2014: Impacts, Adaptation, and Vulnerability, from Working Group II of the IPCC (IPCC, 2014) 241 INRIX RESEARCH: Trevor Reed and Joshua Kidd, Global Traffic Scorecard, INRIX Research (February 2019) 243 INRIX RESEARCH: Trevor Reed and Joshua Kidd, 2018 Global Traffic Scorecard, INRIX Research (February 2019) 243 Crown copyright: Road Traffic Estimates: Great Britain 2017, op.cit. (p. 6) 247 Margrethe Vestager: Margrethe Vestager 247 Margrethe Vestager: Margrethe Vestager 247 FairSearch: 'FairSearch: European Commission Android decision will foster competition', FairSearch: Google Android Decision press pack (18 July 2018) 247 The New York Times Company: James Stewart, 'Why Trump is right about the EU's penalty against Google', The New York Times (26 July 2018) 248 European Union: 'Antitrust: Commission takes further steps in investigations alleging Google's comparison shopping advertised-related practices breach EU rules', European Commission Press Release (14 July 2016) 268 The New York Times Company: Binyamin Appelbaum, 'Does hosting the Olympics actually pay off', The New York Times Magazine, (5 August 2014) 270 CNBC LLC: Holly Ellyatt, 'The World Cup will give Russia's economy a boost – just don't expect it to last', CNBC (14 June 2018) 270 The New York Times Company: Binyamin Appelbaum, 'Does hosting the Olympics actually pay off', The New York Times Magazine, (5 August 2014) 272 International monetary Fund: Based on data in World Economic Outlook Database, IMF (April 2019) 274 European Union: Based on data in AMECO Database (European Commission, DGECFIN) 275 European Union: Based on data in AMECO Database (European Commission, DGECFIN) 283 International monetary Fund: Based on data in World Economic Outlook Database, IMF (April 2019) 285 International monetary Fund: Based on data in World Economic Outlook Database, IMF (April 2019) 290 The World Bank Group: Data from Air transport, passengers carried, The World Bank (2019) 291 IATA: Economic performance of airline industry, IATA (12 December 2018) 291 European Union: Based on data in AMECO Database (European Commission, DGECFIN) 296 European Union: Based on data from AMECO database, Tables 16.3 and 18.1 (European Commission, DG ECFIN) 297 Crown copyright: Public Finances Databank (Office for Budget Responsibility, 25 March 2019) 302 Crown copyright: Economic and Fiscal Outlook, Charts and tables, Chart 5.4, OBR (March 2016) 303 Crown copyright: Economic and Fiscal Outlook, March 2019, Chart 5.4 (Office for Budget Responsibility) 301 European Union: Based on data in Statistical Annex to the European Economy (European Commission). 308 Bank of England: Inflation Report (Bank of England, February 2019) 319 Crown copyright: Office for Budget Responsibility 321 National Statistics: Based on data in International Comparisons of Productivity (National Statistics, 2019) 321 Organisation for Economic Co-operation and Development: Gross Domestic Spending on R&D (OECD, 2019) 326 World Trade Organization: WTO Statistics Database, WTO (April 2019) 328 World Trade Organization: Based on data in World Trade Statistical Review 2018, (WTO, 2018), statistical table A4 330 World Scientific: Paul Krugman, 'Increasing Returns in a Comparative Advantage World', p45, in Robert M. Stern, Comparative Advantage, Growth, and the Gains from Trade and Globalization, Chapter , World Scientific (2011) 331 Harvard Political Review: Lauren Dai, 'The Comparative Advantage of nations: How global supply chains change our understanding of comparative advantage', Harvard Political Review (25 June 2013) 331 The Washington Post: Jia Lynn Yang, 'China's manufacturing sector must reinvent itself, if it's to survive', The Washington Post (23 November 2012) 338 European Union: 'EC fact sheet on Caribbean bananas and the WTO', EC Press Release, memo/97/28 (18 March 1997) 339 Financial Times: Sylvia Pfeifer et al., 'WTO rules US failed to stop unfair tax break to Boeing', Financial Times (28 March 2019) 340 European Union: 'EU adopts rebalancing measures in reaction to US steel and aluminium tariffs', European Commission News Archive (20 June 2018) 342 World Trade Organization: Documents from the negotiating chairs, WTO (21 April 2011) 342 World Trade Organization: In December 2013, agreement was reached on a range of issues at the WTO's Bali Ministerial Conference 342 World Trade Organization: 'WTO members secure "historic" Nairobi Package for Africa and the world', WTO News Items, WTO (19 December 2015) 344 Shinzo Abe: The Japanese Prime Minister, Shinzo Abe, invited the UK to consider joining the CPTPP 345 European Union: In 2012, the European Commission published 20 Years of the European Single Market, 349 Crown copyright: The government's negotiating objectives for exiting the EU: PM speech, Prime Minister's Office, 10 Downing Street, Department for Exiting the European Union, and The Rt Hon Theresa May MP (17 January 2017) 347 Organisation for Economic Co-operation and Development: The economic consequences of Brexit: a taxing decision, OECD (27 April 2016) 350 European Union: Draft negotiating guidelines were unanimously adopted by the European Council and the UK government set out its negotiating objectives 350 European Union: Draft Withdrawal Agreement on the withdrawal of the United Kingdom of Great

Britain and Northern Ireland from the European Union and the European Atomic Energy Community, European Commission (28 February 2018) 350 Parliamentary Copyright: UK/EU Future Economic Partnership: Speech by the Prime Minister, Theresa May to the House of Commons', Hansard, vol. 637 (5 March 2018) 350 David Davis: David Davis, the Brexit Secretary and key negotiator for the UK 351 Michel Barnier: House of Commons, Michel Barnier made a statement 355 Crown copyright: Balance of Payments: 2018 Q4, Office for National Statistics (March 2019) 357 International monetary Fund: Based on data in World Economic Outlook database (IMF, April 2019) 359 Crown copyright: Based on data in Time Series Data (ONS) 369 European Union: Treaty of the Functioning of the European Union (TFEU) 374 International monetary Fund: Based on data in World Economic Outlook, IMF (April 2019) 377 International monetary Fund: International Monetary Fund

Photographs

All Part and Chapter opener Images courtesy © John Sloman

Introduction

In this book we will be looking at the economic environment in which firms operate and how economic analysis can be used in the process of business decision making. In doing so, you will gain an insight into how economists think and the sorts of concepts they use to analyse business problems.

But what particular aspects of business does the economist study? Firms are essentially concerned with using inputs to make output. Inputs cost money and output earns money. The difference between the revenue earned and the costs incurred constitutes the firm's profit. Firms will normally want to make as much profit as possible or, at the very least, to make satisfactory profits and certainly to avoid a decline in profits. Although it is important to note, and as we shall see, there are other objectives that firms can pursue.

In order to meet the firm's objectives, managers must make choices: choices of what types of output to produce, how much to produce and at what price; choices of what techniques of production to use; what types and how many workers to employ; what suppliers to use for raw materials, equipment, etc. In each case, when weighing up alternatives, managers will want to make the best choices for their firm. Business economists study these choices. They study economic decision making by firms.

All these choices will be affected by the environment in which the firm operates. If the firm is in a stable market with a well-established customer base, the choices may be relatively simple. The choices will be very different if firms are in a rapidly changing market, with lots of competition and new products and processes being developed.

The decisions of the firm are also affected by the much broader national and international environment. Is the economy expanding or contracting? What is happening to interest rates and taxes? Is there competition from other countries? Are other countries more or less open to trade? At the time of writing, Brexit remains one of the main topics of discussion, following the defeat of the Conservative government's Withdrawal Agreement and growing expectations that there may be a 'No deal Brexit'. Trade relations with the USA and other nations remain strained; demand from China for many products is declining due to an economic slowdown and the eurozone economy continues to struggle.

The local, national and international economic and political environments all crucially influence a firm's decisions. We will be looking at these influences as the book progresses.

Business and the economic environment

Business issues covered in this chapter

- Which factors influence a firm's behaviour and performance?
- How are businesses organised and structured?
- What are the various legal categories of business and how do different legal forms suit different types of business?
- What are the aims of business?
- Will owners, managers and other employees necessarily have the same aims? How can the decision makers in a firm be persuaded to achieve the objectives of the owners and hence their employers?
- How are businesses influenced by their national and global market environment?
- How are different types of industry classified in the official statistics?
- How do economists set about analysing business decision taking?

What are the core economic concepts that are necessary to understand the economic choices that businesses have to make, such as what to produce, what inputs and what technology to use, where to locate their production and how best to compete with other firms?

The business environment has been somewhat uncertain over the past decade, with many economic and political changes occurring. Uncertainty has come from many quarters: how much Chinese economic growth will slow; what will happen to the price of oil and various other commodities; the future of the EU and the euro; the UK's relationship with the EU; how American politics will affect the US and world economies; the changing state of international relations between many economies; the ability of the global banking system to withstand various shocks; and many more. These uncertainties affect business confidence and business plans.

What is more, the world economy has undergone many other changes in recent decades, and these changes have had profound effects on businesses across the world.

Most countries have embraced the 'market' as the means of boosting prosperity. Privatisation of state industry has occurred; until recently, trade barriers have been lowered; governments have pursued policies to promote competition and attract inward investment; global financial markets have grown and developed. A consequence has been the growth of multinational businesses seeking the best market opportunities and the cheapest sources of supply. This has also contributed towards an increasing interdependence between nations, which has both good and bad consequences, as we will discuss in Part D.

Other important influences on businesses around the world have included the development of faster and smaller computers, easier access to and more widespread use of the Internet globally and improvements in transport and communication systems. These technological advances have provided both opportunities and threats to businesses. Firms have had to adapt to them to maintain their competitiveness, but these developments have also allowed businesses to take advantage of growing market opportunities.

Today, for many firms the world is their market. Their business environment is global. This is obviously the case with large multinational companies, such as McDonald's, Sony, VW, HSBC, Nestlé and Shell. But many small and medium-sized enterprises (SMEs) and even individual traders also have global reach, selling their products in various countries, often via the Internet, and buying their supplies from wherever in the world they get the best deal. Clearly, the terms of access to such markets is crucial and we need only look at the debate within the UK Parliament regarding access to European markets for evidence of this. For example, for companies based in the UK or trading with the UK, the terms of the withdrawal deal and the final trade agreement between the UK and the rest of the EU may be key in determining the success of their business.

For other firms, however, their market is much more local. Take a restaurant or firm of heating engineers – in fact, use a search engine to look for any service in a given area and you will see a host of companies serving a market whose radius is no more than a few miles. But these firms can also be affected by the global environment, either in terms of where their supplies are sourced and/or if they face competition from global companies. A local shop is likely to face competition from a supermarket, such as Tesco or Aldi, both of which have shops around the world and source their supplies from across the globe.

In this chapter, we take an overview of the types of environment in which firms operate and of the role of the economist in business decision taking. We start by looking at the internal environment of the firm – the organisation and aims of the business. We then look at the external environment in which the firm operates – the nature of competition it faces, the type of industry in which it operates, the prices of its inputs, the general state of the economy (e.g. whether growing or in recession), the actions of the government and other authorities that might affect the firm (e.g. changes in taxes or interest rates or changes in competition legislation) and the global environment (e.g. the extent to which the company operates internationally and how it is influenced by global market opportunities and the state of the world economy). Finally, we look at the approach of the economist to analysing the business environment and business decision taking.

Box 1.1 introduces many of the topics that you will be covering in this book by taking the case of John Lewis and seeing how it is affected by its environment.

BOX 1.1   **A PERFECT PARTNERSHIP**

Making the best of your business environment

John Spedan Lewis created John Lewis in 1864 with the opening of a single shop on Oxford Street, London. In 1937, it bought Waitrose, which at the time had 10 shops. However, prior to this, in 1929, the first Trust Settlement was created making the John Lewis Partnership legal. Since then the Partnership has grown to include 51 John Lewis shops across the UK, 37 department stores, 12 John Lewis at home, shops at St Pancras International, Birmingham New Street and Heathrow Terminal 2, 349 Waitrose supermarkets, an online and catalogue business, a production unit and a farm.

The John Lewis Partnership has over 83 000 permanent staff and they own the business. The interests of these employees are the first priority of the John Lewis Partnership and they benefit if the company does well. They share in the profits and their opinions are taken into account in decision-making, creating a democratic and transparent business. The Partnership has annual gross sales of over £11.5 billion and provides a wide range of goods and services. John Lewis itself has over 350 000 lines available in store and more than 280 000 lines available online. In addition, it offers other services, such as credit cards, insurance and broadband, to name a few.

The John Lewis Partnership is a unique one, with an organisational structure that puts its employees at its heart. Despite this very different focus, the Partnership has been a success, expanding its reach over the past century. But how

has it continued to be successful? What lessons are there for other businesses? How has its performance been affected by its business environment – by consumer tastes, by the actions of its rivals, by the state of the national and world economies and by government policy?

So let's take a closer look at the John Lewis Partnership and relate its business in general to the topics covered in this book.

The market environment

To be successful, it is important for the John Lewis Partnership to get its product right. This means understanding the markets that it operates in and how consumer demand responds to changes in prices and to the other services being offered. For example, in 2008, John Lewis responded to challenging conditions by increasing the number of products available for national delivery, prioritising customer service and introducing free delivery across the UK. Its investment in customer service clearly achieved its goal, helping John Lewis to rank as the best company in the 2009 UK Customer Satisfaction Survey.

It has maintained good customer service since then, for example, winning awards for Customer Satisfaction in 2014 and 2015. In the GlobalData Customer Satisfaction Awards 2018, it won Best Multichannel Retailer and the Best Clothing and Furniture Retailer.

►

Waitrose has also been recognised in various awards, such as the Best Food & Grocery Retailer in 2015[1] and the Grocer Gold Award for Consumer Initiative of the Year for its 'Pick your Own Offers'. Then in 2018, it received the highest score in the sector in the UK Customer Satisfaction Index.

John Lewis also enforced its commitment to being 'Never Knowingly Undersold', which helped the company to maintain its market share. It added lines such as Jigsaw to its fashion ranges to continue meeting customer demand and keep up with the fast-moving women's fashion industry. Waitrose has continued to adapt to changing market conditions, with initiatives designed to maintain high levels of customer satisfaction.

We look at how markets work in general in Chapter 2 and then look specifically at consumer demand and methods of stimulating it in Chapter 3.

To stay successful, the Partnership must respond to changes in the global economic environment, changing tastes and fashions and, to some extent, set fashion. Given the legal structure of its business, it must also balance its competitive position with its objective of 'giving every Partner a voice in the business they co-own'. To quote from the John Lewis Partnership website, 'We build relationships with our customers, suppliers and each other based on honesty, respect and encouragement.'[2]

The store 'John Lewis' operates in a highly competitive market, facing competition in its fashion departments from firms such as Debenhams, Selfridges, Next, etc. and in other departments from firms such as Currys and DFS. The products it sells are crucial for its success, but the prices charged are equally important. Consumers will not be willing to pay any price, especially if they can buy similar products from other stores. Thus, when setting prices and designing products, consideration must be given to what rival companies are doing. John Lewis' prices must be competitive to maintain its sales, profitability and its position in the global market. In 2018, a key competitor, House of Fraser, had to be rescued from collapse by Mike Ashley's Sports Direct and Debenhams issued profit warnings. It is thus a testament to John Lewis' understanding of and response to the changing retail environment that its sales have remained robust.

With the emergence of the Internet and online shopping, John Lewis has had to adapt its strategy and consider which markets to target. In 2011, John Lewis expanded its online market to continental Europe, as part of a £250 million investment programme. This decision to expand was partly influenced by record Christmas sales in 2010/11 and online sales that were also significantly higher in 2010. John Lewis has invested more money to improve its online experience through Oracle Commerce, a platform that makes it easier for customers to search and this has led to improved customer conversion rates. David Hunn, Director of IT Delivery at John Lewis said:

> Our on-going customer commitment includes adopting new technology to enable us to better serve customer needs and meet their expectations for convenience, choice and experience . . . This latest Oracle deployment is driving growth online and supporting our aim to deliver a true omni-channel experience.[3]

Over the past few years, John Lewis has continued to add to its online presence and online sales have expanded rapidly, with year-on-year growth of 9.9 per cent in 2017/18. Click and Collect overtook home delivery in 2014/15[4] and this trend has continued. John Lewis extended the cut-off for Christmas Click and Collect to 8pm on 23 December, aiming to cater to last-minute shopping and increase sales, as customers could then collect parcels until Christmas Eve.

Waitrose was also the first supermarket to trial fully automated, temperature-controlled, grocery Click and Collect lockers across the transport network and its online presence has also expanded, with year-on-year sales growth in 2017/18 of 10.9 per cent.

The John Lewis Partnership has typically been UK based, but Waitrose ventured into the Channel Islands in 2011, following approval by the Jersey Competition Regulatory Authority (JCRA) in August 2010 for it to purchase five Channel Island supermarkets.[5] In 2015, John Lewis made its first venture into Europe, with a presence in seven Dutch stores. If the Partnership were to think about expanding further into the global market place, such as into the USA and Asia, careful consideration would need to be given to the competitors in these nations and to the tastes of consumers. Tesco, for example, had little success in its foray into the United States. The factors behind this would be something that the Partnership would need to consider before making any significant global move.

Strategic decisions such as growth by expansion in the domestic and global economy are examined in Chapters 6 and 7, respectively.

Production and employment

Being a profitable business depends not just on being able to sell a product, but on how efficiently the product can be produced. This means choosing the most appropriate technology and deploying the labour force in the best way. John Lewis and Waitrose, as with other companies, must decide on how many workers to employ, what wage rates to pay and what the conditions of employment should be. We explore production and costs in Chapter 4 and the employment of labour in Chapter 8.

The John Lewis Partnership has over 83 000 permanent members of staff employed in a variety of areas. However, despite rising sales in difficult trading conditions, in 2013 John Lewis cut over 300 managerial positions, the biggest cut seen since 2009 when hundreds of call-centre workers lost their jobs. Workers typically have involvement in decisions given the nature of the organisational structure, but these enforced job cuts came as a shock, especially given the good Christmas trading when sales were 13 per cent up on the same period the previous year. However, it appears as though much of these sales came from its online trading, further suggesting a change in the way we shop and a need for companies to adapt. This is reinforced by the collapse of companies such as HMV (twice), which are facing increased competition from online companies, including Amazon.

[1] http://www.johnlewispartnership.co.uk/about/john-lewis.html

[2] http://www.johnlewispartnership.co.uk/about/the-partnership-spirit.html

[3] Fiona Briggs, 'John Lewis improves online customer experience with Oracle Commerce', *Retail News* (24 September 2015).

[4] https://www.johnlewispartnership.co.uk/content/dam/cws/pdfs/financials/interim-reports/john_lewis_partnership_interim_report_2015.pdf/

[5] John Whiteaker, 'Waitrose invades Channel Islands', *Retail Gazette* (26 August 2010).

On the production side, the Partnership is a vertically integrated company, with a production unit and a farm. John Lewis makes its own-brand textiles in Lancashire and also has a small fabric weaving operation creating thousands of products for its stores every week. Its efficient operations also allow John Lewis to operate a seven-day delivery system on orders of products such as curtains. However, the growth in this area has required changes, as the Managing Director Ron Bartram pointed out:

> To support that growth we've had to change the way we work . . . We need to expand our output in every area but our factory is very tight for space. . . We have to be flexible to handle the peaks and troughs of demand, and many Partners have been cross-trained so they can help out in different areas of the factory.[6]

In addition to selling its own-brand items in both John Lewis and Waitrose, numerous other brands are sold. As an organisation which prides itself on its ethical stance, this does create a need for an awareness of how its suppliers treat the environment, their employees, their own suppliers and their customers. This is an example of a more general point about the Partnership's 'corporate social responsibility'. We examine these broader social issues in Chapter 9, along with government policies to encourage, persuade or force firms to behave in the public interest.

The Partnership has been active in diversifying its suppliers and creating opportunities for small and medium-sized enterprises (SMEs) to access their supply chain, creating wider social benefits. Waitrose became the first supermarket to commit to stocking 100% own-label British dairy, helping it to win the 'Best Buy' Award in 2015 and, given growing consumer awareness over the source of and ingredients in products, this has brought it many benefits.

It has also focused on various ethical aspects in its business model and this has been recognised through Waitrose's Italian continental meat supplier being awarded the Good Pig Award 2016 due to its focus on raising animal welfare standards in farms. It is also phasing out hard-to-recycle plastics from its own-label food packaging. It removed black plastic by the end of 2019, which was earlier than any other supermarket, and pledged to remove polystyrene and laminated card by 2023. It is also eliminating unnecessary plastic. As the Waitrose site states: 'We no longer provide disposable coffee cups in our stores, have stopped selling packs of disposable plastic drinking straws, and have switched our plastic stem cotton buds to paper. We were also the first supermarket to stop selling products containing microbeads. In our fruit and veg aisles we are replacing loose plastic bags with bags that can go in the home compost or be used as a food waste caddy liner.'[7]

The members of the John Lewis Partnership remain a success story of Britain's high streets and it has been hailed by the government as a 'model of responsible capitalism'.

The economy

So do the fortunes of The John Lewis Partnership and other companies depend solely on their policies and those of their competitors? The answer is no. One important element of a company's business environment is largely beyond its control: the state of the national economy and, for internationally trading companies, of the global economy.

When the world economy is booming, sales and profits are likely to grow without too much effort by the company. However, when the global economy declines or various events, such as Brexit, occur, it means that uncertainty is created and trading conditions become much tougher.

Since the global financial crisis of 2007–9, the national and global economies have been in a relatively vulnerable position, with many economic and political changes and this has led to many companies closing down, such as Woolworths, Comet and Blockbuster, or having to be rescued from administration, such as Jessops, House of Fraser and Patisserie Valerie.

In the Annual Report by the John Lewis Partnership from 2009, its Chairman said:

> As the economic downturn gained momentum, the focus of the Partnership has been to achieve the right balance between continuing to meet the needs and expectations of our customers and Partners while making sufficient profit to support our growth plans, by controlling our costs tightly and managing our cash efficiently.[8]

John Lewis experienced a slowdown in its sales of large purchases in its home market as the effects of the 2008 financial crisis began to spread. This decline in sales was largely driven by the collapse of the housing market. The Partnership's net profit (i.e. after tax) fell by 47 per cent in the financial year 2009/10 compared with the previous financial year (from £580.0 million to £303.6 million). Since then, its profits have fluctuated.

Nevertheless, the John Lewis Partnership has become one of the beacons on a declining high street. In all but one of the past 12 years, its sales have increased. Black Friday in 2018 gave the company its biggest sales week in history. Gross sales for the John Lewis Partnership increased by 1.8 per cent in 2017/18, reaching £10.2 billion.[9]

But, despite the rise in sales, price competition, especially from online sales, has reduced profits (see chart). This is made more challenging by John Lewis's pledge to be 'never knowingly undersold'. In 2017/18, pre-tax-and-bonus profit fell by 77 per cent, from £452.2 million to £103.9 million. For the six-month period to 28 July 2018, it fell by 99 per cent compared with the same period the previous year – to a mere £1.2 million.[10]

In the past few years, the supermarket industry has become increasingly competitive, with low-cost retailers, such as Aldi and Lidl, posing a very real threat to the major supermarkets. Consumers have tended to become more willing to shop around, getting different products in different supermarkets. Thus, people who previously would do all their shopping in Waitrose may now just use it for more speciality products and buy the more basic lines in a cheaper supermarket. This was the experience of the Partnership in 2013/14 and 2014/15, as pre-tax profits fell. Waitrose's response was to cut prices on the more basic lines. However, with a focus on product

---

[6] Katy Perceval, 'Material World', *JLP e-Zine* (21 May 2010).

[7] 'Plastics and Packaging', *Waitrose.com*

[8] *The John Lewis Partnership Annual Report and Accounts 2009*.

[9] 'John Lewis Partnership Christmas trading statement for seven weeks to 5 January 2019' *John Lewis Press Release* (10 January 2019).

[10] 'John Lewis profits slump 99% in "challenging times"', *BBC News* (13 September 2018).

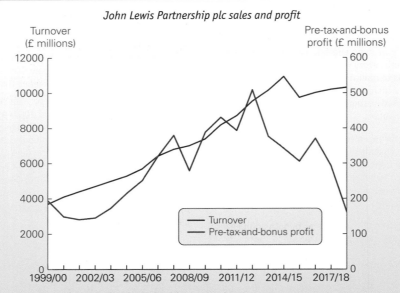

John Lewis Partnership plc sales and profit

Note: Financial years run from beginning February to end January
Source: Company Annual Reports and Accounts

differentiation, new promotions and excellent customer service, sales at Waitrose have seen moderate growth.[11]

Thus, despite the more difficult conditions that have prevailed in the economy, the Partnership has nevertheless continued to increase its market share and in most years to deliver healthy profits.[12]

Prior to 2009, John Lewis' advertising investment seemed largely ineffective and part of its strategy to boost demand was the use of a new approach to advertising. Their highly emotive TV advertising campaigns stimulated interest in the brand and it led to increased numbers of shoppers visiting their stores and increased sales. According to the Institute of Practitioners in Advertising (IPA), the emotive campaigns generated £1074 million of extra sales and £261 million of extra profit in just over two years. In 2012, John Lewis was the Grand Prix winner, receiving the Gold Award in the IPA's Effectiveness Awards. Its emotive Christmas advertising has continued and the John Lewis Christmas advert is certainly one of the things that people look out for in the weeks leading up to Christmas. That in itself is a testament to the company.

So, it is certainly possible for companies to grow and even benefit from challenging trading conditions, especially if, like the John Lewis Partnership, companies are responsive to consumer demand and to the changing economic environment. The continued success of the John Lewis Partnership will depend on the Partnership's internal organisation and crucially on the external environment.

We examine the national and international business environment in Part D. We also examine the impact on business of government policies to affect the economy – policies such as changes in taxation, interest rates, exchange rates and customs duties.

What challenges is John Lewis likely to face in the coming years?

Choose a well-known company that trades globally and do a Web search to find out how well it has performed in recent years and how it has been influenced by various aspects of its business environment.

---

[11] 'John Lewis Partnership plc Interim results for the half year ended 1 August 2015', *John Lewis Press Release* (10 September 2015).

[12] The John Lewis Partnership *Annual Report and Accounts 2011*.

1.1 THE BUSINESS ORGANISATION

There are many factors that affect the behaviour of firms, and here we focus on three key things:

- the legal status of the business;
- the way in which the firm is organised – whether as a simple top-down organisation or as a more complex multi-department or multi-division organisation;

- the aims of the firm – is profit maximisation the objective of the firm, or are there other aims?

The firm as a legal entity

In a small firm, the owner(s) is likely to play a major part in running the business. Such businesses will normally be one of two types.

The sole proprietor. Here, the business is owned by just one person. Owners of small shops, builders and farmers are typical examples. Such businesses are easy to set up and may require only a relatively small initial capital investment. However, they suffer two main disadvantages:

- *Limited scope for expansion*. Finance is limited to what the owner can raise personally, for example through savings or a bank loan. Also, there is a limit to the size of an organisation that one person can effectively control.
- *Unlimited liability*. The owner is personally liable for any losses that the business might make. This could result in the owner's house, car and other assets being seized to pay off any outstanding debts, should the business fail.

The partnership. This is where two or more people own the business. In most partnerships, there is a legal limit of 20 partners. Partnerships are common structures for solicitors, accountants, surveyors, etc. Whilst partnerships do mean a loss of control, as decision making is now shared, with more owners there is scope for expansion. Extra finance can usually be raised and as partners can specialise in and control different areas of the business, a larger organisation can become more viable.

Since 2001, limited liability partnerships have been possible. However, many firms still retain unlimited liability. This problem could be very serious, as the mistakes of one partner could jeopardise the personal assets of all the other partners.

Where large amounts of capital are required and/or when the risks of business failure are relatively high, partnerships are not generally an appropriate form of organisation. In such cases it is best to form a company (or *joint-stock company*, to give it its full title).

Companies

A company is legally separate from its owners. This means that it can enter into contracts and own property. Any debts are its debts, not the owners'.

The owners are the shareholders. Each shareholder receives his or her share of the company's distributed profit: these payments are called 'dividends'. The owners have only *limited liability*. This means that if the company goes bankrupt, the owners will lose the amount of money they have invested in the company, but no more – their cars, houses, etc. belong to them and not to the company. This has the advantage of encouraging people to become shareholders, thereby providing more finance to businesses and creating greater scope for expansion.

Shareholders often take no part in the running of the firm. They may elect a board of directors which decides broad issues of company policy. The board of directors in turn appoints managers who make the day-to-day decisions. This can create problems in terms of the divorce of ownership (by shareholders) from control (by managers), as we will see on page 9.

There are two types of company: public and private.

Public limited companies (plc). These are companies that can offer new shares publicly: by issuing a prospectus, they can invite the public to subscribe to a new share issue. In addition, many public limited companies are quoted on the Stock Exchange (see section 6.4), where existing shares can be bought and sold. A public limited company must hold an annual shareholders' meeting. Examples of well-known UK public limited companies are Marks & Spencer, BP, Barclays, BSkyB and Tesco.

Private limited companies (Ltd). Private limited companies cannot offer their shares publicly. Shares have to be sold privately. This makes it more difficult for private limited companies to raise finance, and consequently they tend to be smaller than public companies. However, they are easier to set up than public companies. One of the most famous examples of a private limited company is Manchester United Football Club, which, until it was bought out by the Glazer family in 2005, was a public limited company. It then became a public limited company again in August 2012 when 10 per cent of its shares were floated on the New York Stock Exchange.

Co-operatives

There are also two types of co-operatives

Consumer co-operatives. These are officially owned by the consumers, although they play no part in running the business.

Producer co-operatives. These are owned by the firm's workers, who share in the firm's profits. The John Lewis Partnership is a prime example of such an organisation, as we discussed in Box 1.1.

The internal organisation of the firm

The internal operating structures of firms are frequently governed by their size. Small firms tend to be

---

Definitions

Joint-stock company A company where ownership is distributed between shareholders.

Limited liability Where the liability of the owners for the debts of a company is limited to the amount they have invested in it.

centrally managed, with decision making operating through a clear managerial hierarchy. In large firms, however, the organisational structure tends to be more complex. Technology also influences a firm's structure, with technological change forcing many organisations to reassess the most suitable organisational structure for them.

U form

In small to medium-sized firms, the managers of the various departments – marketing, finance, production, etc. – are normally directly responsible to a chief executive, whose function is to co-ordinate their activities: relaying the firm's overall strategy to them and being responsible for interdepartmental communication. We call this type of structure *U (unitary) form* (see Figure 1.1).

When firms expand beyond a certain size, a U-form structure is likely to become inefficient. This inefficiency arises from difficulties in communication, co-ordination and control, as the chief executive's office receives too much information to make efficient decisions and so it becomes too difficult to manage the whole organisation from the centre.

M form

To overcome these organisational problems, the firm can adopt an *M (multi-divisional) form* of managerial structure (see Figure 1.2).

This suits larger firms. The firm is divided into a number of 'divisions'. Each division could be responsible for a particular stage of production, a particular product or group of products, or a particular market (e.g. a specific country). The day-to-day running and even certain long-term decisions of each division would be the responsibility of the divisional manager(s). This leads to the following benefits:

- reduced length of information flows;
- the chief executive being able to concentrate on overall strategic planning;
- an enhanced level of control, with each division being run as a mini 'firm', competing with other

divisions for the limited amount of company resources available.

The flat organisation

One of the major problems with M-form organisations is that they can become very bureaucratic with many layers of management. Recent technological innovations, however, especially in respect to computer systems such as e-mail and management information systems, have enabled senior managers to communicate easily and directly with those lower in the organisational structure. As a result, some companies have moved back towards simpler structures. These *flat organisations*, as they are called, dispense with various layers of middle management and so can speed up communication.

The holding company

As many businesses have expanded their operations, often on a global scale, more complex forms of business organisation have evolved. One such organisation is the **H-form** *or* **holding company**. A holding company (or parent company) is one that owns a controlling interest in other subsidiary companies.

Definitions

U-form business organisation One in which the central organisation of the firm (the chief executive or a managerial team) is responsible both for the firm's day-to-day administration and for formulating its business strategy.

M-form business organisation One in which the business is organised into separate departments, such that responsibility for the day-to-day management of the enterprise is separated from the formulation of the business's strategic plan.

Flat organisation One in which technology enables senior managers to communicate directly with those lower in the organisational structure. Middle managers are bypassed.

Figure 1.1	U-form business organisation

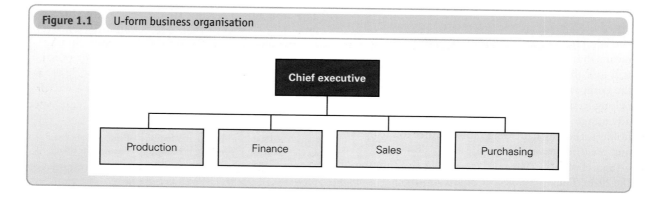

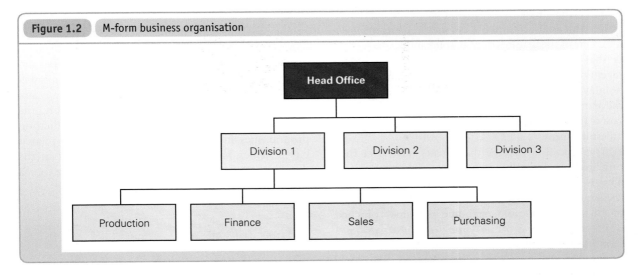

Figure 1.2 M-form business organisation

These subsidiaries, in turn, may also have controlling interests in other companies. There may thus be a complex web of interlocking holdings. While the parent company has ultimate control over its various subsidiaries, typically both tactical and strategic decision making is left to the individual companies within the organisation. A good example of such an organisation would be the Walt Disney Company.

The aims of the firm

Economists have traditionally assumed that firms want to maximise profits. The 'traditional theory of the firm', as it is called, shows how much output firms should produce and at what price in order to make as much profit as possible. But do firms necessarily want to maximise profits?

One question arises over the time period in which they may want to maximise profits. For example, if a business adopts a strategy of growth, more must be spent on investment in machinery and advertising to increase both production and sales. These large expenditures will reduce the profit in the short run, but profits in the long run may be maximised. In this case, what is inconsistent with short-run profit maximisation may be wholly consistent with long-run profit maximisation.

A more fundamental criticism of the assumption of profit maximisation, however, is that in large companies it is the managers and not the owners that make the decisions about how much to produce and at what price. In such cases, other objectives may be pursued by these decision makers.

The divorce of ownership from control

As we saw in our discussion of public limited companies, the shareholders are the owners and they elect directors. Directors in turn employ professional managers who often have considerable discretion in making decisions on things such as pricing, advertising, costing, etc. There is therefore a separation between the ownership and control of a firm.

The owners (shareholders) may want to maximise profits to increase their dividends, but what are the objectives of the managers? They too will probably want to pursue their own interests, such as a higher salary, greater power or prestige, greater sales, better working conditions or greater popularity with their subordinates. Indeed, different managers in the same firm may well pursue different aims. The point is that these aims may conflict with the aim of maximum profit.

> **Pause for thought**
>
> *Make a list of four possible aims that a manager of a McDonald's restaurant might have. Which of these might conflict with the interests of McDonald's shareholders?*

Managers will still have to ensure that *sufficient* profits are made to keep shareholders happy, but that may be very different from maximising profits. Alternative theories of the firm to those of profit maximisation, therefore, tend to assume that large firms are profit 'satisficers'. That is, managers strive hard for a minimum target level of profit, but are less interested in profits above this level.

The principal–agent relationship

Can the owners of a firm ever be sure that their managers will pursue the business strategy most appropriate to achieving the owners' goals (i.e. profit maximisation)? This is an example of the *principal–agent problem*. One of the features of a complex modern economy is that people (principals) have to employ others (agents) to carry out their wishes. If you want to go on holiday, it is easier to go to a travel agent to sort out the arrangements than to do it all yourself. Likewise, if you want to sell a house, it is more convenient to go to an estate agent.

The crucial advantage that agents have over their principals is specialist knowledge and information. This is usually why we employ agents. For example, owners employ managers for their specialist knowledge of a market or their understanding of business practice. But this situation of *asymmetric information* – that one party (the agent) knows more than the other (the principal) – means that it will be very difficult for the principal to judge in whose interest the agent is operating. Are the managers pursuing their own goals, rather than the goals of the owner? It is the same in other walks of life. The estate agent may try to convince you that it is necessary to accept a lower price, while the real reason may be to save the agent time, effort and expense.

 KEY IDEA 1 *The principal–agent problem.* Where people (principals), as a result of a lack of knowledge (asymmetric information), cannot ensure that their best interests are served by their agents. Agents may take advantage of this situation to the disadvantage of the principals.

Principals may attempt to reconcile the fact that they have imperfect information, and are thus in an inherently weak position, in the following ways.

- *Monitoring* the performance of the agent. Shareholders could monitor the performance of their senior managers through attending annual general meetings. The managers could be questioned by shareholders and ultimately replaced if their performance is unsatisfactory.
- Establishing a series of *incentives* to ensure that agents act in the principals' best interest. For example, managerial pay could be closely linked to business performance, through schemes such as profit sharing. Although this can be useful in encouraging managers (agents) to act in the owners' (principals') interests, this is likely to be more effective the larger the incentive: e.g. the larger the share in company profits. But this could prove costly from the owners' point of view.

Within any firm there will exist a complex chain of principal–agent relationships – between workers and managers, between junior managers and senior managers, between senior managers and directors, and between directors and shareholders. All groups will hold some specialist knowledge which they may use to further their own distinct goals. Predictably, the development of effective monitoring and evaluation programmes and the creation of performance-related pay schemes have been two central themes in the development of business practices in recent years – a sign that the principal is looking to fight back!

Pause for thought

Identify a situation where you, as a consumer, are in a principal–agent relationship with a supplier. How can you minimise the problem of asymmetric information in this relationship?

Staying in business

Aiming for profits, sales, salaries, power, etc. will be useless if the firm does not survive! Trying to *maximise* any of the various objectives may be risky. For example, if a firm tries to maximise its market share by aggressive advertising or price cutting, it might invoke a strong response from its rivals. The resulting war may drive it out of business. Concern with survival, therefore, may make firms cautious.

However, being cautious does not guarantee survival and could even lead to the demise of a business, as market share may be lost to more aggressive competitors. Ultimately, if a firm is concerned with survival, it must be careful to balance caution against keeping up with competitors, ensuring that the customer is sufficiently satisfied and that costs are kept sufficiently low by efficient management and the introduction of new technology.

Definitions

Principal–agent problem One where people (principals), as a result of lack of knowledge, cannot ensure that their best interests are served by their agents.

Asymmetric information A situation in which one party in an economic relationship knows more than another.

RECAP

1. There are several types of legal organisation of firms: the sole proprietorship, the partnership, the private limited company, the public limited company and co-operatives. In the first two cases, the owners have unlimited liability. With companies, however, shareholders' liability is limited to the amount they have invested. This reduced risk encourages people to invest in companies, providing scope for expansion.

2. As firms grow, so they tend to move from a U-form to an M-form structure. In recent years, however, with the advance of information technology, many firms have adopted a flatter organisation – a return to U-form structure. Multinational companies often adopt relatively complex forms of organisation. Many multinationals adopt a holding company (H-form) structure.

3. Typically, owners of firms will seek to maximise profits. With large companies, however, there is a divorce of ownership from control. Control is by managers, who might pursue goals other than profit.

4. The problem of managers not pursuing the same goals as the owners is an example of the *principal–agent problem*. Agents (the managers) may not always carry out the wishes of their principals (the owners). Because of asymmetric information, managers can pursue their own aims, as long as they produce results that satisfy the owners. The solution for owners is for there to be a better means of monitoring the performance of managers, and incentives for the managers to behave in the owners' interests.

1.2 THE EXTERNAL BUSINESS ENVIRONMENT

The decisions and performance of a firm are affected not just by its internal organisation and aims; they are also affected by the external environment in which the firm operates.

Dimensions of the external business environment

It is normal to identify various dimensions to the external business environment. These include political, economic, social/cultural and technological factors.

Political factors. Firms are directly affected by the actions of government and other political events. These might be major events affecting the whole of the business community, such as the problems in Syria and Iraq, the tensions between Russia and the UK, the USA, etc., Brexit or a change of government. Alternatively, they may be actions affecting just one part of the economy. For example, the charge on plastic carrier bags affects the retail sector; the ban on smoking in pubs and restaurants affected the tobacco industry; environmental reports about the impact of diesel cars affects the car industry, with certain manufacturers, such as Jaguar Land Rover being particularly affected.

Economic factors. Businesses are affected by a whole range of economic factors, such as a rise in the cost of raw materials, a price cut by a rival firm, new taxes, movements in interest rates and changes in domestic or foreign economic policy. A firm must constantly take such factors into account when devising and implementing its business strategy.

It is normal to divide the economic environment into two levels:

- *The microeconomic environment.* This includes all the economic factors that are *specific* to a particular firm operating in its own particular market. Thus one firm may be operating in a highly competitive market, whereas another may not; one firm may be faced by rapidly changing consumer tastes (e.g. a designer clothing manufacturer), while another may be faced with a virtually constant consumer demand (e.g. a potato merchant); one firm may face rapidly rising costs, while another may find that costs are constant or falling.

- *The macroeconomic environment.* This is the *national* and *international* economic situation in which a business as a whole operates. Business in general will fare much better if the economy is growing than if it is in a recession, like that following the financial crisis of 2008. In examining the macroeconomic environment, we will also be looking at the policies that governments adopt in their attempt to steer the economy, since these policies, by affecting things such as taxation, interest rates and exchange rates, will have a major impact on firms.

Social/cultural factors. This aspect of the business environment concerns social attitudes and values. These include attitudes towards working conditions and the length of the working day, equal opportunities for different groups of people (whether by ethnicity, gender, physical attributes, etc.), the nature and purity of products, the use and abuse of animals, and images portrayed in advertising. The social/cultural environment also includes social trends, such as an increase in the average age of the population, or changes in attitudes towards seeking paid employment while bringing up small children. In recent times, various ethical issues, especially concerning the protection of the environment, have had a big impact on the actions of business and the image that many firms seek to present.

Technological factors. Over the past 30 years, there has been rapid technological change. This has had a huge impact not only on how firms produce, advertise and sell products, but also on how their business is organised. The use of robots and other forms of computer-controlled production has changed the nature of work for many workers. It has also created a wide range of new opportunities for businesses, many of which have yet to be realised. The information-technology revolution is also enabling much more rapid communication and making it possible for many workers to do their job from home, while travelling, or from another country. The growth in online shopping has enabled firms to reach truly global markets, creating many opportunities, but it has also presented problems for other high-street retailers.

The division of the factors affecting a firm into political, economic, social and technological is commonly known as a ***PEST analysis***. More recently, three more elements of the business environment have been added to give what is known as ***STEEPLE analysis***. The extra elements are:

Environmental (ecological) factors. The environment has become an increasingly important issue in politics and business, with many firms aiming to take a greener approach to business or being forced to do so by changes in government policy, such as 'naming and shaming' large polluters. While 'greener business activities' can increase a firm's costs, having a greener image can also help to drive sales as consumers have become more environmentally aware. It can also provide more finance for firms from the government and those investors seeking to improve their image. Business attitudes towards the environment are examined in section 9.4.

Legal factors. Businesses are affected by the legal framework in which they operate. Examples include industrial relations legislation, product safety standards, regulations governing pricing in the privatised industries and laws preventing collusion between firms to keep prices up. We examine some of these laws in sections 9.3–9.6.

Ethical factors. Corporate responsibility is a major concern for many firms, whether in terms of working conditions, the safety and quality of their products, truthful advertising or concern for local residents. With growing consumer awareness and government pressure, many companies have found themselves in difficulties over 'suspect' business practices, such as Volkswagen and its 'defeat device' in diesel engine cars to cheat emissions tests; the sexual harassment allegations against Harvey Weinstein, the film director, which adversely affected Weinstein Co.; and a variety of scandals that hit Uber. Business ethics and corporate responsibility are examined in section 9.2.

 KEY IDEA 2 *The behaviour and performance of firms is affected by the business environment.* The business environment includes social/cultural (S), technological (T), economic (E), ethical (E), political (P), legal (L) and environmental (E) factors. The mnemonic STEEPLE can be used to remember these.

> ## Pause for thought
>
> 1. *Under which heading of a PEST or STEEPLE analysis would you locate training and education?*
> 2. *Identify at least one factor under each of the STEEPLE headings facing an electricity generating company.*

The PEST or STEEPLE framework is widely used by organisations to audit their business environment and to help them establish a strategic approach to their business activities. It is nevertheless important to recognise that there is a great overlap and interaction among these sets of factors. Laws and government policies reflect social attitudes; technological factors determine economic ones, such as costs and productivity; technological progress often reflects the desire of researchers to meet social or environmental needs; and so on.

> ## Definition
>
> **PEST (or STEEPLE) analysis** Where the political, economic, social and technological factors shaping a business environment are assessed by a business so as to devise future business strategy. STEEPLE analysis also takes into account ethical, legal and environmental factors.

To be successful, a business needs to adapt to changes in its business environment and, wherever possible, take advantage of them. Ultimately, the better business managers understand the environment in which they operate, the more likely they are to be successful, either in exploiting ever-changing opportunities or in avoiding potential disasters.

The business environment has become more global, with many firms competing in a world market and this has added both opportunities and threats to each aspect of the business environment. We will consider some of the aspects of the globalisation debate and what it means for businesses in Chapter 7 and also look at the macroeconomic effects of a globalised world in Chapters 12 and 13.

Although we will consider the different dimensions of the STEEPLE framework, especially if they affect the economic environment, it is the economic factors that will be our main focus throughout the book.

Pause for thought

Give one example within each dimension of the STEEPLE framework that demonstrates the impact of a more global business environment. For example, a technological factor might be that Skype means that businesses and consumers can talk to people half way around the world.

BOX 1.2 THE AIRLINE INDUSTRY

In Box 1.1, we considered the John Lewis Partnership and looked at some of the influences on its decision-making, its finances and how it runs its business. In this box, we look at a whole industry – the airline industry – and begin to consider some of its key microeconomic features and the factors that create both threats and opportunities for the firms within this industry. We will revisit the airline industry in later boxes to consider particular firms within it and how they behave and also the macroeconomic factors that influence it.

A growing demand in a shrinking world

Few industries have made such progress or become such a big and important part of society, whether it is for business or pleasure, as the airline industry. This industry has transformed our way of life, reducing the size of the world by making the transport of goods, services, capital and people increasingly easy. It has created more opportunities for businesses and consumers, changing the way that we work and conduct business and is an industry that we rely on every day. Globalisation has, therefore, had an important effect, opening up new routes to airlines and in many ways, increasing the pressures on them to become ever-more responsive to changing global circumstances.

Passenger demand has grown strongly in recent years, with the exception of 2009, when it fell by 1.2 per cent. Since then, passenger numbers have increased each year by between 5.3 and 8.0 per cent. This is considerably more than the global rate of growth in output ('gross national product' or 'GDP'), which from 2010–19 averaged 3.8 per cent. By 2018, the airline industry was transporting 4.3 billion passengers.

Growth in passenger demand has varied across the world. For example, according to the International Air Transport Association (IATA) passenger numbers on Asian and Pacific airlines increased by 7.3 per cent in 2018, while for European operators it was up by 6.6 per cent and for Middle Eastern operators by 4.2 per cent. Latin American and African airlines experienced growth in numbers of 6.9 and 6.5 per cent respectively, and North America-based airlines experienced their fastest growth since 2011 of 5.0 per cent. However, in all but North America and Africa, growth in passenger demand in 2018 was down on that in 2017 and the Director General of IATA did warn that: 'Slowing growth in the second half of 2018, coupled with concerns over issues, including Brexit and US–China trade tensions, are creating some uncertainty.'[1]

The trend is similar in domestic markets, with average annual growth in 2018 of 7.0 per cent and all markets showing growth, led particularly by China and India. Despite the concerns about Brexit, political conflict, geopolitical tensions, security concerns and trade issues, the industry outlook is still positive.

Its business environment

Just like any other industry, the airline industry is affected by its business environment and we can consider the various factors that influence its performance.

The political environment has influenced the industry, with conflict in certain parts of the world dictating which countries aircraft should avoid both in terms of flying across and as a destination. We have seen terror attacks in various countries, which have had significant negative impacts on certain airlines, if those destinations had formerly been popular ones. For example, Monarch, a British airline, had focused on providing flights to slightly different destinations, including Tunisia and Sharm el Sheikh in Egypt. As a result of terrorist activities in such locations and subsequent travel bans and travel advice from the UK government, Monarch saw demand for its flights begin to decline. Insolvency lawyer, Tim Symes noted:

> A higher terrorism threat has proved to be difficult for trading conditions; Egypt and Turkey provided a key chunk of revenue for [Monarch] and subsequent terror attacks left the airline deprived from the resulting weaker demand.[2]

[1] 'Healthy passenger demand continues in 2018 with another record load factor', *The International Air Transport Association Press Release* (7 February 2019).
[2] Will Martin, 'What brought down Monarch, the UK's biggest ever airline collapse', *Business Insider* (3 October 2017).

Another key influence on the airline industry is the environment. With demand for flights for business and pleasure increasing, noise and air pollution is becoming more problematic, such that the environmental damage caused by the industry is considered unsustainable by many analysts.

Airlines are under increasing pressure to do more to protect the environment, such as ensuring planes are operating at efficient capacity; improving fuel efficiency and emissions; investing in research and development and carefully considering the times at which flights start and end. One of the key issues concerns noise pollution. While planes flying at 30 000 feet are unobtrusive, it is the taking off and landing that creates noise pollution. With more flights taking off and landing every day, the demand for runway capacity is growing and this has led to many issues in terms of building new runways and the best locations, such that the adverse impact on local residents is minimised.

Various ethical issues are also apparent, some related to the environmental impact, but others linked to the economic determinants. With growing pressure to cut costs, as we shall see in the next section, there are concerns that safety is being compromised, through less training of pilots and cabin crew, older aircraft or even the use of regional carriers.

The economic influences

The industry is typically divided into two areas: short-haul and long-haul flights. Each country has airlines that specialise in these areas, with thousands of planes and millions of flights each year. The industry is therefore highly competitive both within nations and between nations. Even airlines based in a particular nation have numerous competitors in countries around the world.

Over the years, the industry structure has seen significant change and the short-haul market, in particular, has become an over-crowded market and, as such, it is not surprising that we have seen the demise of several airlines, such as Monarch (UK), Primera (Iceland/Denmark) and Air Berlin (Germany). In the USA, de-regulation of the airline industry led to an influx of 'no-frills' airlines, which provided significant competition for the big three airlines (American, Delta and United). The low prices on offer forced the established airlines to cut their prices and customer service inevitably fell, as they aimed to protect profit margins. It has been over 40 years since this de-regulation occurred and the intense competition has meant that the failure rate in this industry is ten times that of businesses in general.[3]

One of the biggest influences on any given airline is therefore the actions of its competitors: which routes they fly; how many and what type of aircraft they have; what prices are charged; how much luggage customers can take; which country they are based in. All of these factors can lead to airlines behaving in quite different ways. We shall see the importance of taking into account the actions of competitors in Chapter 5.

Airlines are also very sensitive to costs, including fuel, labour, borrowing costs and other raw materials. Rising oil prices mean higher fuel prices and potentially a negative impact on profits. As we shall see in Chapter 4, there are certain features of the airline industry that make it particularly vulnerable to changes in market conditions and thus make the operators

economically vulnerable. As airlines are therefore so susceptible to external factors, it implies that airlines are always looking for ways to cut their costs through internal measures, which can possibly lead to safety concerns.

Demand for airline travel is very dependent on the strength of the macroeconomy. In times of economic growth, when household and business incomes are rising, people tend to travel abroad more often. The opposite then happens during harsher economic times, as we saw in 2009. Families were more inclined to delay a holiday or remain in their own country and so airlines that offered flights abroad saw demand fall. We consider the macroeconomic influences on the industry in part D.

Similarly, those airlines that are less diverse in terms of the destinations of their flights can be very susceptible to changes in demand. Adverse or favourable weather conditions in particular parts of the world, political conflict, terror attacks, government warnings, etc. can all change consumer preferences when it comes to holiday destinations.

Monarch again is a good example of an airline that focused on flights to specific destinations and suffered the consequences when terror attacks occurred in nearby locations.

Industry regulation

International regulation

Much of the regulation that affects the aviation industry is harmonised across the world, with safety standards and consumer protection laws in place. The International Civil Aviation Organisation (ICAO) and European Aviation Safety Agency are there to ensure that high safety standards are met; that consumers are protected and treated fairly; that risks are managed and that the industry works to improve environmental standards, including a reduction in CO_2 emissions. ICAO currently has five strategic objectives: safety; air navigation capacity and efficiency; security and facilitation; economic development of air transport and environmental protection.

The ICAO has 192 members and aims to 'reach consensus on international civil aviation Standards and Recommended Practices (SARPs) and policies in support of a safe, efficient, secure, economically sustainable and environmentally responsible civil aviation sector.'[4] There are over 12 000 SARPS and five Procedures for Air Navigation (PANS), which are constantly being developed and updated, as changes occur in technology and the global business environment. However, the adoption of new SARPS or PANS takes approximately 2 years, so airlines do have quite some time to adapt to potential changes that are coming into force.

National regulation

As well as the international regulatory bodies, countries also have their own regulations affecting airlines operating or flying into/out of their country. US airlines are facing increasing pressure to improve service and there are widespread concerns about the lack of true competition in the US market.

The UK Civil Aviation Authority does not regulate fairs but can take action against airlines which do not comply with things

---

[3] Milton Ezrati, 'Airlines face more regulation, even from this administration', *Forbes* (29 January 2018).

[4] 'About ICAO', ICAO website.

such as consumer protection, including compensation paid to passengers. Furthermore, things such as Air Passenger Duty are set by the government (HM Treasury) and so the industry is subject to intervention.

The Civil Administration Aviation of China provides a similar role, focusing on safety and security, developing standards and policies and regulating prices and taxes.

With the world becoming more globalised, passenger demand for air travel is only going to go in one direction. More and more people are going on holiday; business travel is growing and airlines are increasingly being used for transporting goods. Estimates from IATA suggest that the industry will see an Eastward shift, with growing demand in countries like India and China and that this will continue to mean growing demand worldwide. Forecasts

indicate that passenger numbers in 20 years will be double what they are today. This means that capacity must increase and so continued investment in this sector and continued monitoring of the environmental impact will be essential.[5]

? *What challenges is the airline industry likely to face in the coming years?*

Q *Choose another industry, such as the biotechnology industry; cars; film and television; construction or mobile phones, or any other industry you like, and consider the determinants of its business environment.*

[5] '20 Year Passenger Forecast', IATA website.

Classifying industries

One of the most important elements of the economic environment of a firm is the nature of the industry in which it operates and the amount of competition it faces. Knowledge of the structure of an industry is therefore crucial if we are to understand business behaviour and its likely outcomes.

In this section we will consider how the production of different types of goods and services are classified and how firms are located into different industrial groups.

Classifying production

When analysing production it is common to distinguish three broad categories.

- *Primary production.* This refers to the production and extraction of natural resources such as minerals and sources of energy. It also includes output from agriculture.
- *Secondary production.* This refers to the output of the manufacturing and construction sectors of the economy.
- *Tertiary production.* This refers to the production of services, and includes a wide range of sectors such as finance, the leisure industry, retailing, tourism and transport.

Figures 1.3 and 1.4 show the share of output (or *gross domestic product (GDP)*) and employment of these three sectors in 1974 and 2017. They illustrate how the tertiary sector has expanded rapidly. In 2017, it contributed 79.2 per cent to total output (up from 54.9 per cent in 1974) and employed 83.1 per cent of all workers (up from 54.7 per cent). By contrast, the share of output and employment of the secondary sector has declined. In 2017, it accounted for only

20.2 per cent of output (down from 42.3 percent in 1974) and 15.8 per cent of employment (down from 41.9 per cent).

This trend is symptomatic of a process known as *deindustrialisation* – a decline in the share of the secondary sector in GDP. Many commentators argue that this process of deindustrialisation is inevitable and that the existence of a large and growing tertiary sector in the UK economy reflects its maturity. As people become richer, so a growing proportion of their consumption is of services such as leisure activities.

It is possible to identify part of the tertiary sector as a fourth or 'quarternary' sector. This refers to the knowledge-based part of the economy and includes services such as education, information generation and sharing, research and development, consultation, culture and parts of government. This sector tends to grow as a proportion of the tertiary sector (see Box 1.3).

Definitions

Primary production The production and extraction of natural resources, plus agriculture.

Secondary production The production from manufacturing and construction sectors of the economy.

Tertiary production The production from the service sector of the economy.

Gross Domestic Product (GDP) The value of output produced within the country over a 12-month period.

Deindustrialisation The decline in the contribution to production of the manufacturing sector of the economy.

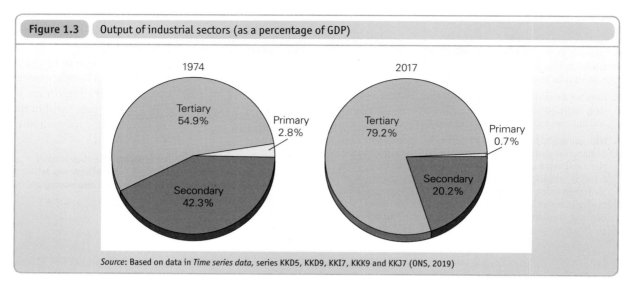

Figure 1.3   Output of industrial sectors (as a percentage of GDP)

Source: Based on data in *Time series data,* series KKD5, KKD9, KKI7, KKK9 and KKJ7 (ONS, 2019)

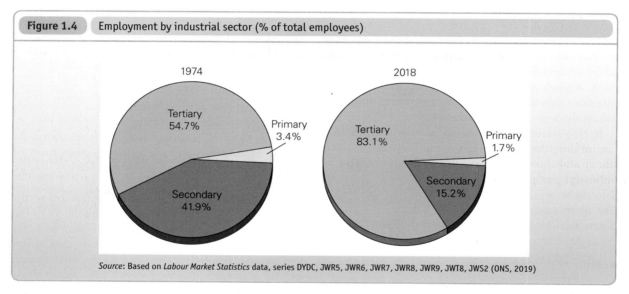

Figure 1.4   Employment by industrial sector (% of total employees)

Source: Based on *Labour Market Statistics* data, series DYDC, JWR5, JWR6, JWR7, JWR8, JWR9, JWT8, JWS2 (ONS, 2019)

Pause for thought

Into which of the three sectors would you put (a) the fertiliser industry; (b) a marketing agency serving the electronics industry?

The classification of production into primary, secondary and tertiary (or even quarternary) sectors allows us to consider broad changes in the economy. However, if we require a more comprehensive analysis of the structure of industry and its changes over time, then such a general classification is of little value. What we need to do is to classify firms into particular industries.

Classifying firms into industries

An *industry* refers to a group of firms that produce a particular category of product. Thus we could refer to the electrical goods industry, the tourism industry, the aircraft industry or the insurance industry. Industries can then be grouped together into broad *industrial sectors*, such as manufacturing industry, or mining and quarrying, or construction, or transport.

Classifying firms into industrial groupings and subgroupings has a number of purposes. It helps us to analyse various trends in the economy and to identify areas of growth and areas of decline. It helps to identify parts of the economy with specific needs, such as

Definitions

Industry A group of firms producing a particular product or service.

Industrial sector A grouping of industries producing similar products or services.

training or transport infrastructure. Perhaps most importantly, it helps economists and businesspeople to understand and predict the behaviour of firms that are in direct competition with each other. In such cases, however, it may be necessary to draw the boundaries of an industry quite narrowly.

To illustrate this, take the case of the vehicle industry. The vehicle industry produces cars, lorries, vans and coaches. The common characteristic of these vehicles is that they are self-propelled road transport vehicles. In other words, we could draw the boundaries of an industry in terms of the broad physical or technical characteristics of the products it produces. However, the problem with this type of categorisation is that these products may not be substitutes in an *economic* sense. If you need to buy a new vehicle to replace your car, you're hardly likely to consider buying a coach or a lorry! Lorries are not in competition with cars. If we are to group together products which are genuine competitors for each other, we will want to divide industries into more narrow categories. For example, we could classify cars into several groups according to size, price, function, engine capacity, etc.: e.g. luxury, saloon (of various size categories), estate (again of various size categories), seven-seater and sports.

On the other hand, if we draw the boundaries of an industry too narrowly, we may end up ignoring the effects of competition from another closely related industry. For example, if we are to understand the pricing strategies of electricity supply companies in the household market, it might be better to focus on the whole domestic fuel industry.

Thus how narrowly or broadly we draw the boundaries of an industry depends on the purposes of our analysis. If the issue is one of *consumer demand* we might want to focus on the market and group goods together that are in direct competition with each other (e.g. particular types of car). If, however, the issue is one of *supply* – of *production* and *costs* – we might want to group products that are produced in the same companies (e.g. vehicle manufacturers).

Standard industrial classification

The formal system under which firms are grouped into industries is known as the *Standard Industrial Classification (SIC)*. It is divided into 21 sections, such as Manufacturing, Transport and Storage, Real Estate Activities and Education and each section has its own divisions, such as Manufacturing being divided into divisions such as manufacture of food products, or textiles or basic metals. These divisions are then divided into groups, then into classes and even subclasses, as you can see in Case Study A.3 on the student website.

Changes in the structure of the UK economy

Over the past 70 years, new products and industries have emerged and revisions have been made to the SIC to reflect this, allowing us to consider how UK industry has changed over time, in terms of output and employment. It can often be very important to look at changes in output and employment within the sub-divisions of the SIC in order to identify whether whole sectors are experiencing changes or if changes are affecting specific parts of a sector.

For example, in the UK, there has been significant growth in the output of the services industries, including financial services, though some parts of the retail banking sector have seen a decline in employment due to technological change (fewer counter staff are required in high-street banks, given the growth in cash machines, credit cards, etc.). Figure 1.4 shows that manufacturing has seen a general decline in employment, though some sub-divisions within manufacturing have seen growth, such as instruments and electrical engineering.

We can also use the SIC to consider which sectors of the economy are particularly susceptible to the strength of the economy. For example, construction and real estate tend to experience significant growth in employment during periods of economic growth and falls in employment during periods of economic decline.

The SIC also allows us to consider wider issues, such as *industrial concentration*. This provides business economists with information about the structure of an industry, in terms of whether it is dominated by a few large firms (those employing 250 or more people), such as the electricity, gas and mining sectors, or if an industry is comprised of lots of small and medium-sized enterprises (SMEs). Such information is an important determinant of firm behaviour.

Structure–conduct–performance

As we shall see throughout the book, business performance is strongly influenced by the market structure within which the firm operates. This is known as the *structure–conduct–performance paradigm* and is illustrated in Figure 1.5.

The structure of an industry depends on a number of basic factors. Some concern consumer demand,

> **Definition**
>
> **Standard Industrial Classification (SIC)** The name given to the formal classification of firms into industries used by the government in order to collect data on business and industry trends.

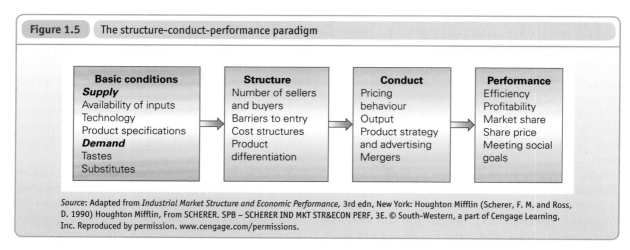

Figure 1.5   The structure-conduct-performance paradigm

Source: Adapted from *Industrial Market Structure and Economic Performance*, 3rd edn, New York: Houghton Mifflin (Scherer, F. M. and Ross, D. 1990) Houghton Mifflin, From SCHERER. SPB – SCHERER IND MKT STR&ECON PERF, 3E. © South-Western, a part of Cengage Learning, Inc. Reproduced by permission. www.cengage.com/permissions.

such as consumer tastes and whether there are close substitute products. Others concern production (supply), such as technology and the availability of resources.

Such conditions will influence whether the market structure is highly competitive or dominated by just a few producers who are able to erect various barriers to the entry of competitors into the market. A business operating in a highly competitive market structure will conduct its activities differently from a business in a market with relatively few competitors. For example, the more competitive the market, the more aggressive the business may have to be in order to sell its product and remain competitive. The less competitive the market structure, the greater the chance that collusion between producers might be the preferred strategy, as this reduces the excesses and uncertainties that outright competition might produce.

Such conduct will in turn influence how well businesses perform. Performance can be measured by several different indicators, such as efficiency in terms of cost per unit of output, current or long-term profitability, market share or growth in market share, changes in share prices or share prices relative to those of other firms in the industry or to other firms in general, to name some of the most commonly used.

Throughout the book, and particularly in Chapter 5, we shall see how market structure affects business conduct, and how business conduct affects business performance. It would be wrong, however, to argue that business performance is entirely shaped by external factors such as market structure. In fact, the internal aims, organisation and strategy of business may be very influential in determining success. We examine business strategy and the factors determining business competitiveness in Chapter 6.

Pause for thought

Why is a firm facing little competition from rivals likely to have higher profits, but also higher costs, than a firm facing intense competition?

RECAP

1. The external business environment is commonly divided into four dimensions: political, economic, social and technological (PEST analysis); or into seven dimensions, where the additional three are environmental, legal and ethical (STEEPLE analysis).

2. The economic dimension of the business environment is divided into two: the microeconomic environment and the macroeconomic environment. The micro environment refers to the particular market in which the firm operates. The macro environment refers to the national and international economy in which all firms operate.

3. The increasingly global market place means that many companies must consider an international dimension within their external business environment.

4. Production is divided into primary, secondary or tertiary sectors. The contribution to output of these different sectors of production has changed over time. Over the years the tertiary sector has grown, while the secondary sector has contracted.

5. Firms are classified into industries and industries into sectors. Such classification enables us to chart changes in industrial structure over time and to assess changing patterns of industrial concentration.

BOX 1.3	THE CHANGING NATURE OF BUSINESS

Knowledge rules

In the knowledge-driven economy, innovation has become central to achievement in the business world. With this growth in importance, organisations large and small have begun to re-evaluate their products, their services, even their corporate culture in the attempt to maintain their competitiveness in the global markets of today. The more forward-thinking companies have recognised that only through such root and branch reform can they hope to survive in the face of increasing competition.[1]

Knowledge is fundamental to economic success in many industries and, for most firms, key knowledge resides in skilled members of the workforce. The result is a market in knowledge, with those having the knowledge being able to command high salaries and often being 'head hunted'. The 'knowledge economy' is fundamentally changing the nature, organisation and practice of business.

The traditional limited company was based around five fundamental principles:

- Individual workers needed the business and the income it provided more than the business needed them. After all, employers could always find alternative workers. If a worker loses his job, the opportunity cost to that worker is much bigger than the opportunity cost to the firm. As such, the company was the dominant partner in the employment relationship.
- Employees tended to be full time and depended upon this work as their sole source of income.
- The company was integrated, with a single management structure overseeing all the various stages of production. This was seen as the most efficient way to organise productive activity.
- Suppliers, and especially manufacturers, had considerable power over the customer by controlling information about their product or service.
- Technology relevant to an industry was often developed within the industry.

In more recent times, with the advent of the knowledge economy, the principles above have all but been turned on their heads.

- The key resource in a knowledge economy is knowledge itself, and the workers that hold such knowledge. Without such workers, the company is unlikely to succeed. As such, the balance of power between the business and the specialist worker in today's economy is far more equal.
- Even though the vast majority of employees still work full time, the development of the flexible firm, which has created more diversity in employment contracts, such as part-time and short-term contracts and consultancy, means that full-time work is not the only option.

(We examine this in section 8.5.) The result is an increasing number of workers offering their services to business in non-conventional ways: e.g. as consultants.

- As companies are increasingly supplying their products to a complex global marketplace, so many find they do not have the necessary expertise to do everything themselves – from production through all its stages, research and development, adapting their products to specific markets, to marketing and sales etc. With communication costs that have become insignificant, businesses are likely to be more efficient and flexible if they outsource and de-integrate. Not only are businesses outsourcing various stages of production, but many are employing specialist companies to provide key areas of management, such as HRM (human resource management) – hiring, firing, training, benefits, etc.
- Whereas in the past, businesses controlled information to their customers, today access to information via sources such as the Internet means that power is shifting towards the consumer.
- Today, unlike in previous decades, technological developments are less specific to industries. Knowledge developments are diffused and cut across industry boundaries. What this means for businesses, in a knowledge-driven economy, is that they must look beyond their own industry if they are to develop and grow. We frequently see partnerships and joint ventures between businesses that cut across industry types and technology.

What is clear from the above is that the dynamics of the knowledge economy require a quite fundamental change in the nature of business. Organisationally it needs to be more flexible, helping it to respond to the ever-changing market conditions it faces. Successful companies draw upon their core competencies to achieve market advantage, and thus ultimately specialise in what they do best. For other parts of their business, companies must learn to work with others, either through outsourcing specialist tasks, or through more formal strategic partnerships.

Within this business model, the key assets are the specialist people in the organisation – its 'knowledge workers'. Businesses need to find ways of attracting, motivating and retaining such workers.

How is the development of the knowledge economy likely to affect the distribution of income in the economy? Will it become more equal or less equal? (Clue: think about the effects of specialist knowledge on the wage rates of specialists.)

Choose a particular industry and find out how it has been affected and is likely to be affected in the future by the development of the knowledge economy.

[1] *Innovation Management and the Knowledge-driven Economy,* European Commission, Directorate-general for Enterprise (ECSC-EC-EAEC Brussels-Luxembourg, 2004).

1.3 THE ECONOMIST'S APPROACH TO BUSINESS

Economics is all around us and whether as individuals, businesses or governments, we constantly face economic decisions. With events such as the financial crisis of 2007–8, the UK's vote to leave the EU, changes in US politics, calls for greater protectionism, growing environmental concerns and questions of inequality, interest in economics has grown. This means that if you are studying economics, you are doing so at incredibly interesting, if not turbulent, times. Economics offers valuable insights into many important issues and helps to answer crucial questions in all areas of life. For example:

- Why do some businesses spend huge amounts of money on advertising certain products, while other products are rarely seen in adverts?
- When you go shopping, what should you buy?
- Why have some high-street retailers collapsed, at the same time as others are expanding?
- Should governments devote more money to protecting country borders to prevent the movement of goods, services, capital and people?
- Why are many drugs illegal? Would it be more effective if governments legalised drugs and then taxed and closely regulated them?
- What is the justification for paying football players such high wages?

As well as these important questions, economics can also help us to answer some more obscure questions! For example:

- Why do you decide to have a lie in, while your flatmate gets up early?
- Should you spend more time working on your microeconomic or macroeconomic assignment? Or perhaps you should get someone else to write it? Or not do it at all?
- U2 gave away a free album on iTunes. Why would U2 and Apple do this, especially when there had been a significant crackdown on illegal downloading of music?

All of these questions are economic questions and they can be answered by applying many of the economic concepts that we will consider in this book. Hopefully, you can already see the breadth of the subject and why it is so interesting and helpful no matter who you are! Throughout the book, we will be looking specifically at some of the economic problems that businesses face and how economists can analyse them and help to recommend solutions. However, before we do this, we first need to think about the fundamental concept that economists study. What is it that makes the above problems *economic* problems?

Tackling the problem of scarcity

There is one central problem faced by all individuals, businesses, governments and more generally by all societies, no matter how rich they are. This is the problem of *scarcity* and it is this concept that provides the foundation of economics. So, what is scarcity and why is it a problem?

Would you like more money? More clothes or more expensive clothes? A bigger house; better healthcare; more time? What about more music; a better mobile phone; a faster car; more savings? Your answer to many of these questions will probably be 'Yes'. Most of us would like more money, as that means we can buy more goods and services or bigger and better ones. And it doesn't matter how wealthy you are: almost everyone will answer yes!

Some people, especially those in African countries, have very limited (or no) access to things like education and healthcare, or even food and water, and so their wants may be food, water, education and healthcare. For you, it may be that you already have access to a good education system and receive good healthcare, but I'm sure you would like even better education and healthcare. You might want to go to a more expensive supermarket or go out to dinner more often. Therefore, while you have food and water, you want more, better or different types of food and drink. This means that even when some of your consumer wants are satisfied, more are created! Consumer wants are virtually unlimited.

Satisfying wants

The question then is, how do we satisfy those wants? The production of goods and services involves the use of inputs, or *factors of production*, as they are often called. However, unlike consumer wants, these inputs are not limitless. There are three broad types of inputs:

- Human resources: *labour*.
- Natural resources: *land and raw materials*.

Definitions

Factors of production (or resources) The inputs into the production of goods and services: labour, land and raw materials, and capital.

Labour All forms of human input, both physical and mental, into current production.

Land and raw materials Inputs into production that are provided by nature: e.g. unimproved land and mineral deposits in the ground.

- Manufactured resources: *capital*. Capital consists of all those inputs that themselves have had to be produced in the first place.

All of these resources are limited or finite. There are only so many people of working age and so the labour force is limited in number, but also in skills: i.e. there are only so many doctors, or teachers. The world's land area is limited. In some large countries, this may not seem to be a problem, but even then, perhaps huge sections of land cannot be used to produce goods and services. Raw materials are also finite – there is a limited amount of oil, minerals, etc., hence the significant investment in renewables. The world also has a limited stock of capital: a limited supply of factories, machines, transportation and other equipment. The productivity of that capital is also limited by the state of technology.

By combining the unlimited wants of consumers and the limited resources in the world, we are faced with the problem that, at any one time, the world can produce only a limited amount of goods and services. This is therefore the reason for *scarcity*, which we define as 'the excess of human wants over what can actually be produced'.

Of course, we do not all face the problem of scarcity to the same degree. A poor person unable to afford enough to eat or a decent place to live will hardly see it as a 'problem' that a rich person cannot afford a second Ferrari. But economists do not claim that we all face an *equal* problem of scarcity. The point is that people, both rich and poor, want more than they can have and this will cause them to behave in certain ways. Economics studies that behaviour.

Two of the key elements in satisfying wants are *consumption* and *production*. As far as consumption is concerned, economics studies how much the population spends; what the pattern of consumption is in the economy; and how much people buy of particular items. The business economist, in particular, studies consumer behaviour; how sensitive consumer demand is to changes in prices, advertising, fashion and other factors; and how the firm can seek to persuade the consumer to buy its products.

As far as production is concerned, economics studies how much the economy produces in total; what influences the rate of growth of production; and why the production of some goods increases and that of others falls. The business economist tends to focus on the role of the firm in the production process: what determines the output of individual businesses, the range of products they produce, the techniques and inputs they use and why, the amount they invest and how many workers they employ.

Having read the above, you should already be able to see that economics therefore studies choice and behaviour on both the consumption and production side. It is the problem of scarcity that requires choices to be made and the business economist analyses those choices.

Demand and supply

We said that economics is concerned with consumption and production. Another way of looking at this is in terms of *demand* and *supply*. It is quite likely that you already knew that economics had something to do with demand and supply. In fact, demand and supply and the relationship between them lie at the very centre of economics. But what do we mean by the terms, and what is their relationship with the problem of scarcity?

Demand is related to wants. If goods and services were free, people would simply demand whatever they wanted. Such wants are virtually boundless: perhaps only limited by people's imagination. *Supply*, on the other hand, is limited. It is related to resources. The amount that firms can supply depends on the resources and technology available.

Given the problem of scarcity, and that human wants exceed what can actually be produced, *potential* demands will exceed *potential* supplies. Society therefore has to find some way of dealing with this problem. Somehow it has to try to match demand and supply. This applies at the level of the economy overall: *aggregate* demand will need to be balanced against *aggregate* supply. In other words, total spending in the economy must balance total production. It also applies at the level of individual goods and services. The demand and supply of cabbages must balance, and so must the demand and supply of laptops, books, cars and houses.

But if potential demand exceeds potential supply, how are *actual* demand and supply to be made equal?

Either demand has to be curtailed, or supply has to be increased, or a combination of the two. Economics studies this process. It studies how demand adjusts to available supplies, and how supply adjusts to consumer demands.

The business economist studies the role of firms in this process: how they respond to demand, or, indeed, try to create demand for their products; how they combine their inputs to achieve output in the most efficient way; how they decide the amount to produce and the price to charge their customers; and how they make their investment decisions. In this, firms are affected by the economic environment in which they operate. In section 1.2, we saw how we can divide the economic environment into microeconomics and macroeconomics. At a *microeconomic* level, firms are affected by their competitors, by technology and by changing consumer tastes. At a *macroeconomic* level they are affected by the state of the economy, by government macroeconomic policies and by the global economy.

> ## Pause for thought
>
> *When you go into a supermarket, the shelves are normally well stocked. Does this mean that the problem of scarcity has been solved?*

Making choices

Resources are scarce and so choices must be made. There are three main categories of choice that must be made in any society.

- *What* goods and services are going to be produced and in what quantities, given that there are not enough resources to produce all the things that people desire? How many cars, how much wheat, how much insurance, how many rock concerts, etc. will be produced?
- *How* are things going to be produced, given that there is normally more than one way of producing things? Which resources will be used and in what quantities? What techniques of production are going to be adopted? Will cars be produced by robots or by assembly-line workers? Will electricity be produced from coal, oil, gas, nuclear fission, renewable resources or a mixture of these?
- *For whom* are things going to be produced? In other words, how is the nation's income going to be distributed? After all, the higher your income, the more you can consume of the nation's output. What will be the wages of farm workers, printers, cleaners and accountants? How much will pensioners receive? How much profit will owners of private companies receive or state-owned industries make?

All societies have to make these choices, whether they are made by individuals, by business or by the government.

Choice and opportunity cost

Choice involves sacrifice. The more food you choose to buy, the less money you will have to spend on other goods. The more food a nation produces, the fewer resources there will be for producing other goods. In other words, the production or consumption of one thing involves the sacrifice of alternatives. This sacrifice of alternatives in the production (or consumption) of a good is known as its *opportunity cost*.

 KEY IDEA 3 *Opportunity cost.* The opportunity cost of something is what you give up to get it/do it. In other words, it is cost measured in terms of the best alternative forgone.

If a tailor can produce either 100 jackets or 200 pairs of trousers, then the opportunity cost of producing one jacket is the two pairs of trousers foregone. The opportunity cost of you buying this textbook is the new pair of jeans you also wanted that you have had to go without! The opportunity cost of working overtime is the leisure you sacrifice.

Rational choices

Economists often refer to *rational choices*. This simply means the weighing up of the *costs* and *benefits* of any activity, whether it be firms choosing what and how much to produce, workers choosing whether to take a particular job or to work extra hours, or consumers choosing what to buy.

Imagine you are shopping and want to buy some baked beans. Do you buy expensive Heinz baked beans or do you buy the cheaper alternatives, such as the supermarket's own 'value' brand? To make a rational (i.e. sensible) decision, you will need to weigh up the costs and benefits of each alternative. Heinz baked beans may taste better to you and thus will give you a lot of enjoyment, but they have a high opportunity cost: because they are more expensive, you will need to sacrifice quite a lot of consumption of other goods if you decide to buy them. If you buy the cheaper alternatives, although you may not enjoy them as much, you will have more money left over to buy other things: they have a lower opportunity cost.

> ## Definitions
>
> **Opportunity cost** The cost of any activity measured in terms of the best alternative foregone.
>
> **Rational choices** Choices that involve weighing up the benefit of any activity against its opportunity cost.

Thus rational decision making, as far as consumers are concerned, involves choosing those items that give you the best value for money, i.e. the *greatest benefit relative to cost*. One person's choice of which product to buy may not be the same as another's, yet both decisions could still be rational.

The same principles apply to firms when deciding what to produce. For example, should a car firm open up another production line? A rational decision will again involve weighing up the benefits and costs. The benefits are the revenues that the firm will earn from selling the extra cars. The costs will include the extra labour costs, raw material costs, costs of component parts, etc. It will be profitable to open up the new production line only if the revenues earned exceed the costs entailed: in other words, if it earns a profit.

In the more complex situation of deciding which model of a mobile phone to produce, or how many of each model, the firm must weigh up the relative benefits and costs of each: i.e. it will want to produce the most profitable product mix.

Marginal costs and benefits

In economics we argue that rational choices involve weighing up *marginal costs* and *marginal benefits*. These are the costs and benefits of doing a little bit more or a little bit less of a given activity. They can be contrasted with the *total* costs and benefits of the activity. For example, a mobile phone manufacturer will weigh up the marginal costs and benefits of producing mobiles – in other words, it will compare the costs and revenue of producing *additional* mobile phones. If additional phones add more to the firm's revenue than to its costs, it will be profitable to produce them.

KEY IDEA 4

Rational decision making involves weighing up the marginal benefit and marginal cost of any activity. If the marginal benefit exceeds the marginal cost, it is rational to do the activity (or to do more of it). If the marginal cost exceeds the marginal benefit, it is rational not to do it (or to do less of it).

Pause for thought

1. *Assume that you have an assignment to write. How would you make a rational choice about whether to work on it today or whether to do something else?*
2. *Assume that you are looking for a job and are offered two. One is more pleasant to do but pays less. How would you make a rational choice between the two jobs?*

Choices and the firm

We will look at the choices of how much to produce, what price to charge the customer, how many inputs to use and in what combination. Firms must also make decisions that have longer term effects, such as whether to expand the scale of their operations; merge with or take over another company; diversify into other markets or whether it should export more.

The right choices (in terms of best meeting the firm's objectives) will vary according to the type of market in which the firm operates, its predictions about future demand, its degree of market power, the actions and reactions of competitors, the degree and type of government intervention, the current tax regime, the availability of finance, and so on. In short, we will be studying the whole range of economic choices made by firms and in a number of different scenarios.

In all these cases, the owners of firms will want the best possible choices to be made, i.e. those choices that best meet the objectives of the firm. As we have seen, making the best choices will involve weighing up the marginal benefits against the marginal opportunity costs of each decision.

Definitions

Marginal costs The additional cost of doing a little bit more (or 1 unit more if a unit can be measured) of an activity.

Marginal benefits The additional benefits of doing a little bit more (or 1 unit more if a unit can be measured) of an activity.

RECAP

1. The central economic problem is that of scarcity. We have endless wants, but there is a limited supply of resources. As such, it is impossible to provide everybody with everything they want. Potential demands exceed potential supplies.

2. Because resources are scarce, people have to make choices. Society has to choose by some means or other what goods and services to produce, how to produce them and for whom to produce them. Microeconomics studies these choices.

3. Rational choices involve weighing up the marginal benefits of each activity against its marginal opportunity costs. If the marginal benefit exceeds the marginal cost, it is rational to choose to do more of that activity.

4. Businesses are constantly faced with choices: how much to produce, what inputs to use, what price to charge, how much to invest, etc. We will study these choices.

QUESTIONS

1. Compare and contrast the relative strengths and weaknesses of unlimited liability partnerships with public limited companies.

2. Explain why the business objectives of owners and managers are likely to diverge. How might owners attempt to ensure that managers act in their interests and not in the managers' own interests?

3. What is the Standard Industrial Classification (SIC)? In what ways might such a classification system be useful? Can you think of any limitations or problems such a system might have over time?

4. Choose a country other than the UK and investigate the changes in its industrial structure. Are the changes similar to or different from those in the UK?

5. Outline the main determinants of business performance. In each case, explain whether it is a micro- or macroeconomic issue.

6. Virtually every good is scarce in the sense we have defined it, but are water and air exceptions? If they are not scarce, explain whether it would be possible to charge for them. Does the way in which you define water and air determine whether they are scarce or abundant?

7. Which of the following are macroeconomic issues, which are microeconomic ones and which could be either depending on the context?
   (a) Inflation.
   (b) Low wages in certain service industries.
   (c) The rate of exchange between the pound and the euro.
   (d) Why the price of cabbages fluctuates more than that of cars.
   (e) The rate of economic growth this year compared with last year.
   (f) The decline of traditional manufacturing industries.
   (g) Britain's referendum about whether to exit the EU.

8. Make a list of three things you did yesterday. What was the opportunity cost of each?

9. How would you use the principle of weighing up marginal costs and marginal benefits when deciding whether to (a) buy a new car; (b) study for an extra hour? How would a firm use the same principle when deciding whether to (a) purchase a new machine; (b) offer overtime to existing workers?

ADDITIONAL PART A CASE STUDIES ON THE *ESSENTIAL ECONOMICS FOR BUSINESS* WEBSITE (www.pearsoned.co.uk/sloman)

A.1 **Minding the Gap.** An investigation into Gap and the business and economic issues it faces.

A.2 **The UK defence industry.** A PEST analysis of the changes in the defence industry in recent years.

A.3 **A Lidl success story.** An investigation into Lidl and the business and economic issues it faces in challenging the Big Four supermarkets and its direct rival Aldi.

A.4 **Standard industrial classification.** An analysis of the structure of UK industry and its changes over time.

A.5 **Scarcity and abundance.** If scarcity is the central economic problem, is anything truly abundant?

A.6 **Global economics.** This examines how macroeconomics and microeconomics apply at the global level and identifies some key issues.

A.7 **The opportunity cost of studying at university.** An examination of the costs of being a student, using the concept of opportunity cost.

A.8 **Positive and normative statements.** A crucial distinction when considering matters of economic policy.

WEBSITES RELEVANT TO PART A

Numbers and sections refer to websites listed in the Web Appendix and hotlinked from this book's website at **www.pearsoned.co.uk/sloman/**

■ For a tutorial on finding the best economics websites see site C8 (Internet for Economics).

■ For news articles relevant to Part A, Google the Sloman Economics News site.

■ For general economics news sources see websites in section A of the Web Appendix at the end of the book, and particularly A1–9, 11, 12, 18–25, 35 and 36. See also links to newspapers worldwide in A38, 39, 43 and 44 and the news search feature in Google at A41.

■ For business news items, again see websites in section A of the Web Appendix at the end of the book, and particularly A1–4, 20–26, 35, 36.

■ For sources of economic and business data, see sites in section B and particularly B1–5, 27–29, 32, 36, 39, 41, 43 and 48.

■ For general sites for students of economics for business, see sites in section C and particularly C1–7.

■ For sites giving links to relevant economics and business websites, organised by topic, see section I and particularly sites I7, 11, 12, 16, 18.

Markets, demand and supply

One of the key determinants of a business's profitability is the price of its products. Many firms have the option of changing their prices in order to increase their profits. Sometimes, a cut in price might be in order, if the firm anticipates that this will generate a lot more sales. At other times, a firm may prefer to raise its prices, believing there will be little effect on sales – perhaps it believes that its competitors will follow suit; or, perhaps, there are no close competitors, making it easy for the firm to get away with raising prices.

For some firms, however, the prices of the products they sell are determined not by them, but by the market. The 'market' is the coming together of buyers and sellers – whether in a street market, a shop, an auction, a mail-order system, the Internet or whatever. Thus, we talk about the market for apples, the market for oil, for cars, for houses, for televisions and so on. As we shall see, market prices are determined by the interaction of demand (buyers) and supply (sellers).

When the price is determined by the market, the firm is called a *price taker*. It has to accept the market price as given. If the firm attempts to raise the price above the market price, it will simply be unable to sell its product; it will lose all its sales to its competitors. Take the case of farmers selling wheat. They have to accept the price as dictated by the market. If individually they try to sell above the market price, no one will buy from them.

Competitive markets also imply that consumers are price takers. In fact, this is typically the case when you buy things, whether or not the seller is operating in a competitive market. For example, when you get to the checkout at a supermarket, you don't start negotiating with the member of staff over the price of the products in your trolley. Instead, you take the prices as given.

So how does a competitive market work? How are prices determined in such markets? We examine this question in Chapter 2.

In Chapter 3 we look more closely at demand and at firms' attempt to understand demand and the behaviour of consumers. Then in Chapter 4 we look at supply and ask how much a profit maximising firm will produce at the market price.

2

The working of competitive markets

Business issues covered in this chapter

- ■ How do markets operate?
- ■ How are market prices determined and what causes them to rise or fall?
- ■ Under what circumstances do firms have to accept a price given by the market rather than being able to set the price themselves?
- ■ What are the influences on consumer demand?
- ■ How responsive is consumer demand to changes in the market price? How responsive is it to changes in consumer incomes and to the prices of competitor products?
- ■ How is a firm's sales revenue affected by a change in price?
- ■ What factors determine the amount of supply coming onto the market?
- ■ How responsive is business output to changes in price?

2.1 BUSINESS IN A PERFECTLY COMPETITIVE MARKET

As we saw in Chapter 1, one of the key objectives of firms is to make a profit and one of the key determinants of profit is the price at which a firm sells its products.

Most firms have discretion over what prices to charge. But should a firm raise its prices, lower them or keep them the same? The answer to this question depends on the market conditions in which it is operating. If the market is buoyant and growing, increasing the price may be a good strategy. However, if the market is in decline, the firm may need to cut prices and begin to think about diversifying into another market. The market environment is therefore a key determinant of a firm's behaviour and performance.

For many small firms, prices are determined not by them, but by the market and it is in this scenario where we begin our analysis.

The price mechanism under perfect competition

In a *free market*, individuals can make their own economic decisions. Consumers are free to decide what to buy with their incomes: free to make demand decisions. Firms are free to choose what to sell and what production methods to use: free to make supply decisions.

Definition

Free market One in which there is an absence of government intervention. Individual producers and consumers are free to make their own economic decisions.

For simplicity we will examine the case of a *perfectly competitive market*. This is where both producers and consumers are too numerous to have any control over prices: a situation where everyone is a *price taker*. In such markets, the demand and supply decisions of consumers and firms are transmitted to each other through their effect on *prices*: through the *price mechanism*. The prices that result are the prices that firms have to accept.

The effect of changes in demand and supply

One of the key roles of the price mechanism is to eliminate *shortages* and *surpluses*. After all, the pattern of consumer demand and of supply changes over time. For example, people may decide they want more holidays abroad and fewer at home; advances in technology may allow the mass production of microchips at lower cost, while the production of hand-built furniture becomes relatively expensive.

A shortage of a product causes its market price to rise and this, as we shall see, eliminates the shortage. A surplus causes price to fall and this eliminates the surplus. As demand and supply change, prices will therefore be affected and these act as signals and incentives. Let us see why.

If consumers decide they want more of a good at the current price or if producers decide to cut back supply, demand will exceed supply. (This is exactly what happened in the case of pencils following a 'craze' for adult colouring and also in the case of butter. You can read about these cases in the *Independent*[1] and *Business Insider*.[2]) The resulting *shortage* encourages sellers to *raise* the price of the good. This creates an incentive for producers to supply more, since production of each unit will now be more profitable. On the other hand, it discourages consumers from buying so much: *The price will continue rising until the shortage has thereby been eliminated.*

If, on the other hand, consumers want less of a good at the current price (or if producers decide to produce more), supply will exceed demand. The resulting *surplus* will cause sellers to *reduce* the price of the good. This will act as a disincentive to producers, who will supply less, since production of each unit will now be less profitable. At the same time, it will encourage consumers to buy more. *The price will continue falling until the surplus has thereby been eliminated.*

This price, where demand equals supply, is called the *equilibrium price*. By *equilibrium* we mean a point of balance or a point of rest, i.e. a point towards which there is a tendency to move. It is the price mechanism that works to find this equilibrium price.

The same analysis can be applied to labour (and other input) markets, except that here the demand and supply roles are reversed. Firms are the demanders of labour; individuals are the suppliers.

If an industry expands, so that the demand for a particular type of labour exceeds its supply, the resulting shortage will drive up the wage rate (i.e. the price of labour) as employers compete with each other for labour. The rise in the wage rate will curb firms' demand for that type of labour and encourage more workers to take up that type of job. Wages will continue rising until demand equals supply, thereby eliminating the shortage.

If an industry declines, so that there is a surplus of a particular type of labour, the wage rate will fall until demand equals supply, as you can see in a BBC News article.[3] As with price, the wage rate where the demand for labour equals the supply is known as the *equilibrium* wage rate.

The response of demand and supply to changes in price illustrates a very important feature of how economies work: people respond to incentives.

> **KEY IDEA 5**
>
> *People respond to incentives, such as changes in prices or wages.* It is important, therefore, that incentives are appropriate and have the desired effect.

Definitions

Perfectly competitive market A market in which all producers and consumers of the product are price takers. (There are other features of a perfectly competitive market; these are examined in Chapter 4.)

Price taker A person or firm with no power to be able to influence the market price.

Price mechanism The system in a market economy whereby changes in price, in response to changes in demand and supply, have the effect of making demand equal to supply.

Equilibrium price The price where the quantity demanded equals the quantity supplied; the price where there is no shortage or surplus.

Equilibrium A position of balance. A position from which there is no inherent tendency to move away.

[1] Alexandra Sims, 'Adult colouring book craze prompts global pencil shortage', *Independent* (21 March 2016).

[2] Oscar Williams-Grut, 'The butter market is going crazy', *Business Insider* (30 October 2017).

[3] Matthew West, 'No wage rises until jobless rate falls to 5% says MPC member', *BBC News* (18 June 2014).

KEY IDEA 6 *Changes in demand or supply cause markets to adjust.* Whenever such changes occur, the resulting 'disequilibrium' will bring an automatic change in prices, thereby restoring 'equilibrium' (i.e. a balance of demand and supply).

Let us now turn to examine each side of the market – demand and supply – in more detail.

RECAP

1. A firm is greatly affected by its market environment. The more competitive the market, the less discretion the firm has in determining its price. In the extreme case of a perfect market, the price is entirely outside the control of the firm and consumers. The price is determined by demand and supply in the market, and both sides of the market have to accept this price: they are price takers.

2. In a perfect market, price changes act as the mechanism whereby demand and supply are balanced.

3. If there is a shortage, price will rise until the shortage is eliminated. If there is a surplus, price will fall until that is eliminated.

2.2 DEMAND

The relationship between demand and price

The headlines announce, 'Major crop failures in Brazil and East Africa: coffee prices soar.' Shortly afterwards you find that coffee prices have doubled in the shops. What do you do? Presumably you will cut back on the amount of coffee you drink. Perhaps you will reduce it from, say, six cups per day to two. Perhaps you will give up drinking coffee altogether.

This is simply an illustration of the general relationship between price and consumption: *when the price of a good rises, the quantity demanded will fall.* This relationship is known as the *law of demand* and there are two reasons behind it:

- People feel poorer. They are not able to afford to buy so much of the good with their money. The purchasing power of their income (their *real income*) has fallen. This is called the *income effect* of a price rise.
- The good is now dearer relative to other goods. People thus switch to alternative or 'substitute' goods. This is called the *substitution effect* of a price rise.

In our example of the increase in the price of coffee, we will not be able to afford to buy as much as before (the income effect), and we will probably drink more tea, hot chocolate, cola, fruit juices or even water instead (the substitution effect).

Similarly, when the price of a good falls, the quantity demanded will rise. People can afford to buy more (the income effect), and they will switch away

from consuming alternative goods (the substitution effect).

A word of warning: be careful about the meaning of the words *quantity demanded*. They refer to the amount consumers are willing and able to purchase at a given price over a given time period (e.g. a week, or a month). They do *not* refer to what people would simply *like* to consume. You might like to own a luxury yacht, but your demand for luxury yachts will almost certainly be zero at current prices!

The demand curve

Consider the hypothetical data in Table 2.1. The table shows how many kilos of potatoes per month would be purchased at various prices.

Definitions

Law of demand The quantity of a good demanded per period of time will fall as the price rises and rise as the price falls, other things being equal (*ceteris paribus*).

Income effect The effect of a change in price on quantity demanded arising from the consumer becoming better or worse off as a result of the price change.

Substitution effect The effect of a change in price on quantity demanded arising from the consumer switching to or from alternative (substitute) products.

Quantity demanded The amount of a good that a consumer is willing and able to buy at a given price over a given period of time.

Table 2.1	The demand for potatoes (monthly)			
	Price (pence per kg) (1)	Tracey's demand (kg) (2)	Darren's demand (kg) (3)	Total market demand (tonnes: 000s) (4)
A	50	28	16	700
B	100	15	11	500
C	150	5	9	350
D	200	1	7	200
E	250	0	6	100

Figure 2.1 Market demand curve for potatoes (monthly)

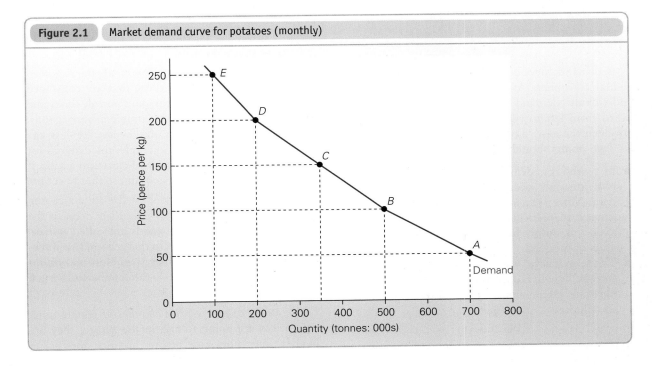

Columns (2) and (3) show the *demand schedules* for two individuals, Tracey and Darren. Column (4), by contrast, shows the total *market demand schedule*. This is the total demand by all consumers. To obtain the market demand schedule for potatoes, we simply add up the quantities demanded at each price by *all* consumers, i.e. Tracey, Darren and everyone else who demands potatoes. (This is known as horizontal summation.) Notice that we are talking about demand *over a period of time* (not at a *point* in time). Thus, we would talk about daily demand or weekly demand, etc.

The demand schedule can be represented graphically as a *demand curve*. Figure 2.1 shows the market demand curve for potatoes corresponding to the schedule in Table 2.1. The price of potatoes is plotted on the vertical axis. The quantity demanded is plotted on the horizontal axis.

Definitions

Demand schedule for an individual A table showing the different quantities of a good that a person is willing and able to buy at various prices over a given period of time.

Market demand schedule A table showing the different total quantities of a good that consumers are willing and able to buy at various prices over a given period of time.

Demand curve A graph showing the relationship between the price of a good and the quantity of the good demanded over a given time period. Price is measured on the vertical axis; quantity demanded is measured on the horizontal axis. A demand curve can be for an individual consumer or a group of consumers, or more usually for the whole market.

Point *E* shows that at a price of 250p per kilo, 100 000 tonnes of potatoes are demanded each month. When the price falls to 200p we move down the curve to point *D*. This shows that the quantity demanded has now risen to 200 000 tonnes per month. Similarly, if price falls to 150p, we move down the curve again to point *C*: 350 000 tonnes are now demanded. The five points on the graph (*A–E*) correspond to the figures in columns (1) and (4) of Table 2.1. The graph also enables us to read off the likely quantities demanded at prices other than those in the table.

> ### Pause for thought
>
> *Referring to Figure 2.1, what tonnage of potatoes would be purchased per month if the price were 175p per kg?*

A demand curve could also be drawn for an individual consumer. As with market demand curves, individuals' demand curves generally slope downward from left to right: the lower the price of the product, the more a person is likely to buy.

Two points should be noted at this stage:

- In textbooks, demand curves (and other curves too) are only occasionally used to plot specific data. More frequently they are used to illustrate general theoretical arguments. In such cases the axes will simply be price and quantity, with the units unspecified.
- The term 'curve' is used even when the graph is a straight line! In fact, when using demand curves to illustrate arguments we frequently draw them as straight lines – it's easier.

Other determinants of demand

Price is not the only factor that determines how much of a good people will buy. Think about your own consumption of any good or service – which other factors would cause you to buy more or less of it? Take the case of travel. With numerous terrorist attacks taking place in different countries, some people have been put off travelling abroad, as discussed in a *Reuters* article,[4] which looks at Thomas Cook passengers. Here are some other factors that might affect your demand for a product:

Tastes. The more desirable people find the good, the more they will demand. Your tastes are probably affected by advertising, fashion, observing what others

buy, such as your friends, considerations of health and your experiences from consuming the good on previous occasions. Taste for dairy is rising quickly in China, which is affecting the dairy market, as discussed in an article from *New Food*.[5] Take another example: studies indicate that for our own health and the future of the planet, we should all become vegetarians or preferably vegans, or at least certainly eat less meat. Looking at the demand for meat and typical vegan foods over the coming decades may tell us how much this report influenced our demand.

The number and price of substitute goods (i.e. competitive goods). The higher the price of *substitute goods*, the higher will be the demand for this good as people switch from the substitutes. For example, the demand for coffee depends on the price of tea. If tea goes up in price, the demand for coffee will rise.

The number and price of complementary goods. Complementary goods are those that are consumed together: coffee and milk, cars and petrol, shoes and polish. The higher the price of complementary goods, the fewer will be bought and hence the less the demand for this good. For example, the demand for electricity depends on the price of electrical goods. If the price of electrical goods goes up, so that fewer are bought, the demand for electricity will fall.

Income. As people's incomes rise, their demand for most goods will rise. Such goods are called *normal goods*. There are exceptions to this general rule, however. As people get richer, they spend less on *inferior goods*, such as supermarkets' value lines and switch to better quality goods.

Expectations of future price changes. If people think that prices are going to rise in the future, they are likely to buy more now before the price does go up and so demand will increase. Think about the housing market. If people expect the price of houses to increase, they try to buy now before that happens.

> ### Definitions
>
> **Substitute goods** A pair of goods which are considered by consumers to be alternatives to each other. As the price of one goes up, the demand for the other rises.
>
> **Complementary goods** A pair of goods consumed together. As the price of one goes up, the demand for both goods will fall.
>
> **Normal goods** Goods whose demand rises as people's incomes rise. They have a positive income elasticity of demand. Luxury goods will have a higher income elasticity of demand than more basic goods.
>
> **Inferior goods** Goods whose demand falls as people's incomes rise. Such goods have a negative income elasticity of demand.

---

[4] Sarah Young, 'Thomas Cook holiday demand falls as wary customers delay booking', *Reuters* (22 March 2016).

[5] George Smith, 'Research reveals global consequences of China's growing taste for dairy', *New Food* (19 February 2018).

Figure 2.2   An increase in demand for good X

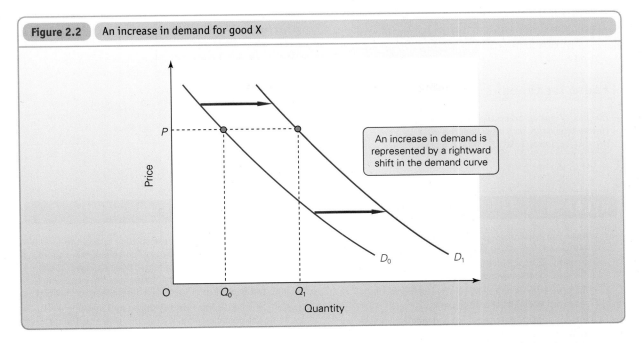

You can find countless examples on the Internet of factors affecting the demand for particular products. These include the introduction of a charge on plastic bags[6] in the UK in 2016 and a change in the demand for beef,[7] following the publication of a report[8] prepared for the Cattlemen's Beef Board in January 2018.

Pause for thought

Can you think of any other factors that affect (a) your demand for goods and services and (b) the market demand for goods and services?

KEY IDEA 7   *People's actions are influenced by their expectations.* People respond not just to what is happening now (such as a change in price), but to what they anticipate will happen in the future.

Movements along and shifts in the demand curve

A demand curve is constructed on the assumption that 'other things remain equal' (*ceteris paribus*). In other words, it is assumed that none of the determinants of demand, other than price, change. The effect of a change in price is then simply illustrated by a movement along the demand curve, e.g. from point *B* to point *D* in Figure 2.1 when price rises from 40p to 80p per kilo.

6 Rebecca Morelle, 'Plastic bag use plummets in England since 5p charge', *BBC News* (30 July 2016).

7 National Cattlemen's Beef Association, 'NCBA Study: Many Factors Impacting Domestic Beef Demand', *Drovers* (1 February 2018).

8 Glynn T. Tonsor, Jayson L. Lusk and Ted C. Schroeder, *Assessing Beef Demand Determinants*, Cattlemens' Beef Board (18 January 2018).

KEY IDEA 8   ***Partial analysis: other things remaining equal (ceteris paribus).*** In economics it is common to look at just one determinant of a variable such as demand or supply and see what happens when the determinant changes. For example, if price is taken as the determinant of demand, we can see what happens to quantity demanded as price changes. In the meantime, we have to assume that other determinants remain unchanged. This is known as the 'other things being equal' assumption (or, using the Latin, the '*ceteris paribus*' assumption). Once we have seen how our chosen determinant affects our variable, we can then see what happens when another determinant changes, and then another, and so on.

What happens, then, when one of these other determinants changes? The answer is that we have to construct a whole new demand curve; the curve shifts. Consider a change in one of the determinants of your demand for books, excluding price: say your income rises. Assuming books are a normal good, this increase in income will cause you to buy more at any price: the whole curve will shift to the right. Thus in Figure 2.2 at a price of *P*, a quantity of Q_0 was originally demanded. But now, after the increase in demand, Q_1 is demanded. (Note that D_1 is not necessarily parallel to D_0.)

If a change in a determinant other than price causes demand to fall, the whole curve will shift to the left. Less will be demanded at each price than before.

To distinguish between shifts in and movements along demand curves, it is usual to distinguish between a change in *demand* and a change in the *quantity demanded*. A shift in demand is referred to as a *change in demand*, whereas a movement along the demand curve, as a result of a change in price, is referred to as a *change in the quantity demanded*.

Definitions

Change in demand The term used for a shift in the demand curve. It occurs when a determinant of demand *other* than price changes.

Change in the quantity demanded The term used for a movement along the demand curve to a new point. It occurs when there is a change in price.

RECAP

1. When the price of a good rises, the quantity demanded per period of time will fall. This is known as the 'law of demand'. It applies both to individuals' demand and to the whole market demand.

2. The law of demand is explained by the income and substitution effects of a price change.

3. The relationship between price and quantity demanded per period of time can be shown in a table (or 'schedule') or as a graph. On the graph, price is plotted on the vertical axis and quantity demanded per period of time on the horizontal axis. The resulting demand curve is downward sloping (negatively sloped).

4. Other determinants of demand include tastes, the number and price of substitute or complementary goods, income and expectations of future price changes. You are a consumer, so anything that influences the goods you buy, and how much of them, is a determinant of demand.

5. If price changes, the effect is shown by a movement along the demand curve. We call this effect 'a change in the quantity demanded'.

6. If any other determinant of demand changes, the whole curve will shift. We call this effect 'a change in demand'. A rightward shift represents an increase in demand; a leftward shift represents a decrease in demand.

2.3 SUPPLY

Supply and price

Imagine you are a farmer deciding what to do with your land. Part of your land is in a fertile valley. Part is on a hillside where the soil is poor. Perhaps, then, you will consider growing vegetables in the valley and keeping sheep on the hillside.

Your decision will depend to a large extent on the price that various vegetables will fetch in the market, and likewise the price you can expect to get from sheep and wool. As far as the valley is concerned, you will plant the vegetables that give the best return. If, for example, the price of potatoes is high, you will probably use a lot of the valley for growing potatoes. If the price gets higher, you may well use the whole of the valley, perhaps being prepared to run the risk of potato disease. If the price is very high indeed, you may even consider growing potatoes on the hillside, even though the yield per hectare is much lower there. In other words, the higher the price of a particular crop, the more you are likely to grow in preference to other crops.

This illustrates the general relationship between supply and price: *when the price of a good rises, the quantity supplied will also rise*. There are three reasons for this.

■ As firms supply more, they are likely to find that, beyond a certain level of output, costs rise more and more rapidly. Only if price rises will it be worth producing more and incurring these higher costs.

   In the case of the farm we have just considered, once potatoes have to be grown on the hillside, the costs of producing them will increase. Also if the land has to be used more intensively, say by the use of more and more fertilisers, again the cost of producing extra potatoes is likely to rise quite rapidly. It is the same for manufacturers. Beyond a certain level of output, costs are likely to rise rapidly as workers have to be paid overtime and as machines approach their full capacity. If higher output involves higher costs of production, producers will need to get a higher price if they are to be persuaded to produce extra output. This concept is considered further in Chapter 4.

■ The higher the price of the good, the more profitable it becomes to produce. Firms will thus be encouraged to produce more of it by switching from producing less profitable goods.

■ Given time, if the price of a good remains high, new producers will be encouraged to set up in production. Total market supply thus rises.

Figure 2.3 Market supply curve of potatoes (monthly)

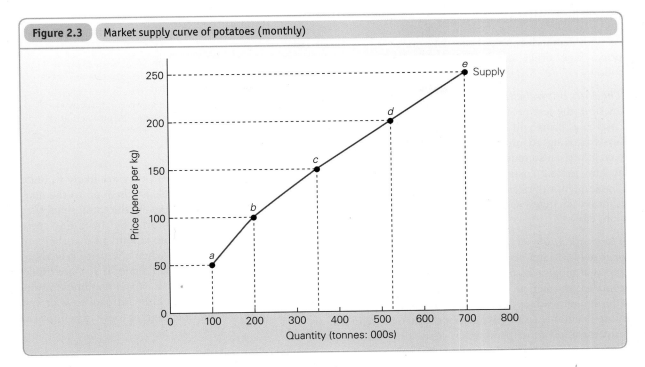

The first two determinants affect supply in the short run. The third affects supply in the long run. We distinguish between short-run and long-run supply at the end of section 2.5 (see page 48).

The supply curve

The amount that producers would like to supply at various prices can be shown in a *supply schedule*. Table 2.2 shows a hypothetical monthly supply schedule for potatoes, both for an individual farmer (farmer X) and for all farmers together (the whole market).

The supply schedule can be represented graphically as a *supply curve*. A supply curve may be an individual firm's supply curve or a market supply curve (i.e. that of the whole industry).

Figure 2.3 shows the *market* supply curve of potatoes. As with demand curves, price is plotted on the vertical axis and quantity on the horizontal axis. Each of the points *a–e* corresponds to a figure in Table 2.2. Thus, for example, a price rise from 150p

per kilogram to 200p per kilogram causes a movement along the supply curve from point *c* to point *d*: total market supply rises from 350 000 tonnes per month to 530 000 tonnes per month.

Not all supply curves are upward sloping (positively sloped). Sometimes they are vertical, or horizontal, or even downward sloping. This depends largely on the time period over which the response of firms to price changes is considered. (This question is examined on page 48.)

Pause for thought

1. *How much would be supplied at a price of 175p per kilo?*
2. *Draw a supply curve for farmer X. Are the axes drawn to the same scale as in Figure 2.3?*

Definitions

Supply schedule A table showing the different quantities of a good that producers are willing and able to supply at various prices over a given time period. A supply schedule can be for an individual producer or group of producers, or for all producers (the market supply schedule).

Supply curve A graph showing the relationship between the price of a good and the quantity of the good supplied over a given period of time.

Table 2.2 The supply of potatoes (monthly)

	Price of potatoes (pence per kg)	Farmer X's supply (tonnes)	Total market supply (tonnes: 000s)
a	50	50	100
b	100	70	200
c	150	100	350
d	200	120	530
e	250	130	700

Other determinants of supply

As with demand, supply is not determined simply by price. The other determinants of supply are as follows.

The costs of production. The higher the costs of production, the less profit will be made at any price. As costs rise, firms will cut back on production, probably switching to alternative products whose costs have not risen so much. As such, less will be supplied at any price. Costs could change as a result of changing input prices, changes in technology,[9] organisational changes within the firm, changes in taxation, etc.

The profitability of alternative products (substitutes in supply). Many firms produce a range of products and will move resources from the production of one good to another as circumstances change. If some alternative product (a **substitute in supply**) becomes more profitable to supply, perhaps due to a rise in its price or a fall in its production costs, producers are likely to switch from the first good, thus cutting its supply, to this alternative. For example, if the price of carrots goes up, or the cost of producing carrots comes down, farmers may decide to cut down potato production in order to produce more carrots. The supply of potatoes is therefore likely to fall.

The profitability of goods in joint supply. Sometimes when one good is produced, another good is also produced at the same time. These are said to be **goods in joint supply**. An example is the refining of crude oil to produce petrol. Other grade fuels will be produced as well, such as diesel and paraffin. If more petrol is produced, due to a rise in demand, then the supply of these other fuels will rise too.

Nature, 'random shocks' and other unpredictable events. In this category we would include the weather and diseases affecting farm output, wars affecting the supply of imported raw materials, the breakdown of machinery, industrial disputes, earthquakes, floods, fire, and so on.

The aims of producers. A profit-maximising firm will supply a different quantity from a firm that has a different aim, such as maximising sales. We considered the aims of the firm in section 1.1.

Expectations of future price changes. If price is expected to rise, producers may temporarily reduce

the amount they sell. Instead they are likely to build up their stocks and only release them on to the market when the price does rise. At the same time, they may plan to produce more, by installing new machines, or taking on more labour, so that they can be ready to supply more when the price has risen. Consider the housing market again. If you are thinking of selling your house, but expect that house prices will soon be higher, it would be rational to wait and put your house on the market only when prices have risen.

Movements along and shifts in the supply curve

The principle here is the same as with demand curves. The effect of a change in price is illustrated by a movement along the supply curve: e.g. from point *d* to point *e* in Figure 2.3 when price rises from 200p to 250p. Quantity supplied rises from 530 000 to 700 000 tonnes.

If any other determinant of supply changes, the whole supply curve will shift. A rightward shift illustrates an increase in supply. More will be supplied at any given price. A leftward shift illustrates a decrease in supply. A movement along a supply curve is often referred to as a *change in the quantity supplied*, whereas a shift in the supply curve is simply referred to as a *change in supply*.

---

[9] Ashley Armstrong; 'Marks & Spencer ramps up cost-cutting with technology overhaul', *The Telegraph* (9 January 2018).

RECAP

1. When the price of a good rises, the quantity supplied per period of time will usually also rise. This applies both to individual producers' supply and to the whole market supply.

2. There are two reasons in the short run why a higher price encourages producers to supply more: (a) they are now willing to incur the higher costs per unit associated with producing more; (b) they will switch to producing this product and away from now less profitable ones. In the long run there is a third reason: new producers will be attracted into the market.

3. The relationship between price and quantity supplied per period of time can be shown in a table (or schedule) or as a graph. As with a demand curve, price is plotted on the vertical axis and quantity per period of time on the

horizontal axis. The resulting supply curve is upward sloping (positively sloped).

4. Other determinants of supply include the costs of production, the profitability of alternative products, the profitability of goods in joint supply, random shocks and expectations of future price changes.

5. If price changes, the effect is shown by a movement along the supply curve. We call this effect 'a change in the quantity supplied'.

6. If any determinant *other* than price changes, the effect is shown by a shift in the whole supply curve. We call this effect 'a change in supply'. A rightward shift represents an increase in supply; a leftward shift represents a decrease in supply.

2.4 PRICE AND OUTPUT DETERMINATION

Equilibrium price and output

We can now combine our analysis of demand and supply. This will show how the actual price of a product and the actual quantity bought and sold are determined in a free and competitive market.

Let us return to the example of the market demand and market supply of potatoes, and use the data from Tables 2.1 and 2.2. These figures are given again in Table 2.3.

What will be the price and output that actually prevail? If the price started at 50p per kilogram, demand would exceed supply by 600 000 tonnes ($A - a$). Consumers would be unable to obtain all they wanted and would thus be willing to pay a higher price. Producers, unable or unwilling to supply enough to meet the demand, will be only too happy to accept a higher price. The effect of the shortage, then, will be to drive up the price. The same would happen at a price of 100p per kilogram. There would still be a shortage; price would still rise. But as the price rises, the quantity demanded falls and the quantity supplied rises. The shortage is progressively eliminated.

What would happen if the price started at a much higher level: say at 250p per kilogram? In this case, supply would exceed demand by 600 000 tonnes ($e - E$). The effect of this surplus would be to drive down the price as farmers competed against each other to sell their excess supplies. The same would happen at a price of 200p per kilogram. There would still be a surplus; price would still fall.

In fact, only one price is sustainable. This is the price where demand equals supply: namely 150p per kilogram, where both demand and supply are 350 000 tonnes. When supply matches demand the market is said to *clear*. There is no shortage and no surplus.

As we saw on page 27, the price where demand equals supply is called the *equilibrium price*. This is the same as the market clearing price. In Table 2.3, if the price starts at other than 150p per kilogram, there will be a tendency for it to move towards 150p. The equilibrium price is the only price at which producers' and consumers' wishes are mutually reconciled, where the producers' plans to supply exactly match the consumers' plans to buy.

Table 2.3	The market demand and supply of potatoes (monthly)	
Price of potatoes (pence per kg)	Total market demand (tonnes: 000s)	Total market supply (tonnes: 000s)
50	700 (*A*)	100 (*a*)
100	500 (*B*)	200 (*b*)
150	350 (*C*)	350 (*c*)
200	200 (*D*)	530 (*d*)
250	100 (*E*)	700 (*e*)

KEY IDEA 9

Equilibrium is the point where conflicting interests are balanced. Only at this point is the amount that demanders are willing to purchase the same as the amount that suppliers are willing to supply. It is a point which will be automatically reached in a free market through the operation of the price mechanism.

Definition

Market clearing A market clears when supply matches demand, leaving no shortage or surplus. The market is in equilibrium.

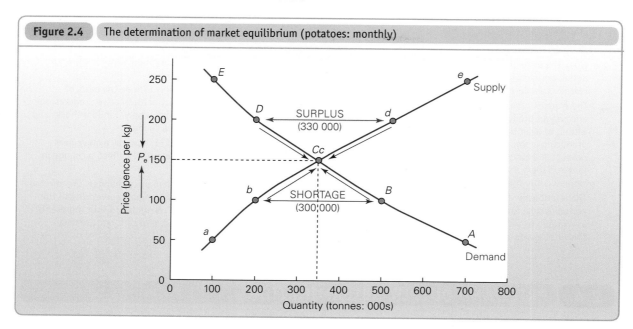

Figure 2.4   The determination of market equilibrium (potatoes: monthly)

Demand and supply curves

The determination of equilibrium price and output can be shown using demand and supply curves. Equilibrium is where the two curves intersect.

Figure 2.4 shows the demand and supply curves of potatoes corresponding to the data in Table 2.3. Equilibrium price is P_e (150p) and equilibrium quantity is Q_e (350 000 tonnes).

At any price above 150p, there would be a surplus. Thus at 200p there is a surplus of 330 000 tonnes $(d - D)$. More is supplied than consumers are willing and able to purchase at that price. Thus a price of 200p fails to clear the market. Price will fall to the equilibrium price of 150p. As it does so, there will be a movement along the demand curve from point D to point C, and a movement along the supply curve from point d to point c.

At any price below 150p, there would be a shortage. Thus at 100p there is a shortage of 300 000 tonnes $(B - b)$. Price will rise to 150p. This will cause a movement along the supply curve from point b to point c and along the demand curve from point B to point C.

Point Cc is the equilibrium: where demand equals supply.

Movement to a new equilibrium

The equilibrium price will remain unchanged only so long as the demand and supply curves remain unchanged. If either of the curves shifts, a new equilibrium will be formed.

A change in demand

If one of the determinants of demand changes (other than price), the whole demand curve will shift. This will lead to a movement *along* the *supply* curve to the new intersection point.

Pause for thought

What would happen to price and quantity if the demand curve shifted to the left? Draw a diagram to illustrate your answer.

For example, in Figure 2.5(a), if a rise in consumer incomes led to the demand curve shifting to D_2, there would be a shortage of $h - g$ at the original price P_{e1}. This would cause price to rise to the new equilibrium P_{e2}. As it did so there would be a movement along the supply curve from point g to point i, and along the new demand curve (D_2) from point h to point i. Equilibrium quantity would rise from Q_{e1} to Q_{e2}.

The effect of the shift in demand, therefore, has been a movement *along* the supply curve from the old equilibrium to the new: from point g to point i.

A change in supply

Likewise, if one of the determinants of supply changes (other than price), the whole supply curve will shift. This will lead to a movement *along* the *demand* curve to the new intersection point.

For example, in Figure 2.5(b), if costs of production rose, the supply curve would shift to the left: to S_2. There would be a shortage of $g - j$ at the old price of P_{e1}. Price would rise from P_{e1} to P_{e3}. Quantity would fall from Q_{e1} to Q_{e3}. In other words, there would be a movement along the demand curve from point g to point k, and along the new supply curve (S_2) from point j to point k.

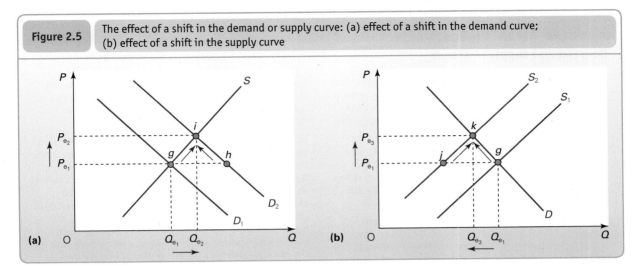

Figure 2.5 The effect of a shift in the demand or supply curve: (a) effect of a shift in the demand curve; (b) effect of a shift in the supply curve

To summarise: a shift in one curve leads to a movement along the other curve to the new intersection point.

Sometimes a number of determinants might change. This may lead to a shift in *both* curves. When this happens, equilibrium simply moves from the point where the old curves intersected to the point where the new ones intersect. If this is the case, it is a good idea to consider each effect separately, rather than immediately trying to find the new equilibrium.

Search for the following blogs on the Sloman Economics News site for some examples of supply and demand in action: *One little piggy went to market . . .* (pork markets), *£1 per litre* (the price of petrol) and *When will wine run out?* (the market for fine wine).

Pause for thought

Referring to Figure 2.4 and Table 2.3, what would happen to the equilibrium price of potatoes if there were a good harvest and the monthly supply of potatoes rose by 300 000 tonnes at all prices?

RECAP

1. If the demand for a good exceeds the supply, there will be a shortage. This will result in a rise in the price of the good.

2. If the supply of a good exceeds the demand, there will be a surplus. This will result in a fall in the price.

3. Price will settle at the equilibrium. The equilibrium price is the one that clears the market, such that demand equals supply. This is shown in a demand and supply diagram by the point where the two curves intersect.

4. If the demand or supply curves shift, this will lead either to a shortage or to a surplus. Price will therefore either rise or fall until a new equilibrium is reached at the position where the supply and demand curves *now* intersect.

BOX 2.1 STOCK MARKET PRICES

Demand and supply in action

Firms that are quoted on the stock market (see page 166) can raise money by issuing shares. These are sold on the 'primary stock market' (see section 6.4). People who own the shares receive a 'dividend' on them, normally paid six-monthly. The amount varies with the profitability of the company.

People or institutions that buy these shares, however, may not wish to hold on to them for ever. This is where the 'secondary stock market' comes in. It is where existing shares are bought and sold. There are stock markets, primary and secondary, in all the major countries of the world.

There are 2089 companies (as of February 2019) whose shares and other securities are listed on the London Stock Exchange and trading in them takes place each weekday. The prices of shares depend on demand and supply. For example, if the demand for Tesco shares at any one time exceeds the supply on offer, the price will rise until demand and supply are equal. Share prices fluctuate throughout the trading day and sometimes price changes can be substantial.

To give an overall impression of share price movements, stock exchanges publish share price indices. The best known one in the UK is the FTSE 100, which stands for the 'Financial Times Stock Exchange' index of the 100 largest companies' shares. The index represents an average price of these 100 shares. The chart shows movements in the FTSE 100 from 1995 to 2019. The index was first calculated on 3 January 1984 with a base level of 1000 points and it has increased by an average of 7 per cent per year since. Despite the consistent increases, there have been some significant variations in share prices, with peaks of 6930 points on 30

December 1999 and 7104 points on 27 April 2015. However, there have also been some significant lows, particularly a drop to 3512 points in March 2009, in the midst of the financial crisis (see chart).

In early 2016, the FTSE 100 had fallen down to around 6000 points, but despite the shock of the Brexit vote in June 2016, the FTSE 100 recovered and rose back to 7000 by the end of the year and finished 2017 at 7688. Part of the reason for this was the fall in the sterling exchange rate that occurred because of the uncertainty over the nature of the Brexit deal. With many of the FTSE 100 companies having assets denominated in dollars, a falling sterling exchange rate meant that these dollar assets were now worth more pounds. The rise also reflected a general buoyancy in stock markets around the word, which, in fact, in most major countries rose faster than the FTSE 100. In August 2018, the FTSE 100 was around the 7700 mark, but by the end of the year, with continued uncertainty over the Withdrawal Agreement, it had fallen to 6700.

But what causes share prices to change? Search for a blog entitled *The Shanghai Stock Exchange: a burst bubble?* on the Sloman Economics News Site to see how changes in supply and demand caused share prices quoted on that exchange to decline dramatically in 2015. The answer as to why share prices change lies in the determinants of the demand and supply of shares.

Demand

There are five main factors that affect the demand for shares.

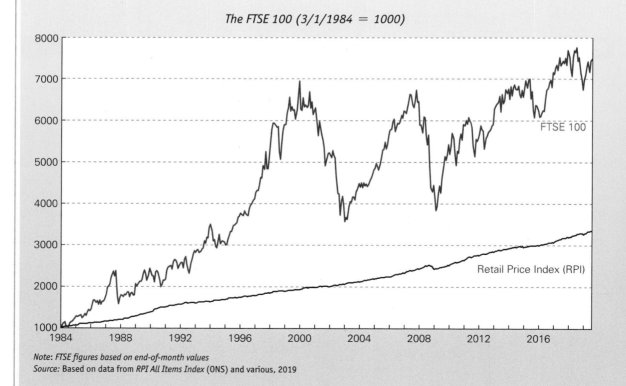

The FTSE 100 (3/1/1984 = 1000)

Note: *FTSE figures based on end-of-month values*
Source: Based on data from *RPI All Items Index* (ONS) and various, 2019

The dividend yield. This is the dividend on a share as a percentage of its price. The higher the dividend yields on shares the more attractive they are as a form of saving. High profits and high dividends caused stock market prices to rise between 2003 and 2007 and once again in the recovery after the financial crisis. By contrast, the financial crisis and slowdown in the world economy helped to explain the falling profits and dividends of companies from 2007 and the consequent decline in share prices.

The price of and/or return on substitutes. The main substitutes for shares in specific companies are other shares. Thus if, in comparison with other shares, Tesco shares are expected to pay high dividends relative to the share price, people will buy Tesco shares. As far as shares in general are concerned, the main substitutes are other forms of saving. Thus if the interest rate on savings accounts in banks and building societies fell, people with such accounts would be tempted to take their money out and buy shares instead.

Another substitute is property. If house prices are rising, as they did from the late 1990s to 2007, people switch to buying property in anticipation of even higher prices and so demand for shares tends to fall. In cases, where both house prices and share prices fall, as we saw in the financial crisis and global slowdown, investors looked for other substitutes, such as gold and government debt, as they were seen as much safer bets.

Incomes. If the economy is growing rapidly and people's incomes are thus rising rapidly, they are likely to buy more shares. Thus in the mid to late 1990s, when UK incomes were rising at an average annual rate of over 3 per cent, and again when incomes rose between 2003 and 2007 and between 2012 and mid-2015, share prices rose rapidly (see chart). As growth rates fell in the early 2000s and again from 2007, so share prices fell. Slower growth in some of the Chinese and other Asian economies has also negatively affected share prices.

Wealth. 'Wealth' is people's accumulated savings and property. Wealth rose in the 1990s and many people used their increased wealth to buy shares. The growth in wealth was halted by the financial crisis and many people looked to 'cash in' their shares and this depressed share prices.

Expectations. From 2003 to 2007, people expected share prices to go on rising. They were optimistic about continued growth in the economy and as people responded to this optimism by buying shares, this pushed their prices up even more. This fuelled further speculation that they would go on rising, encouraging further share buying.

In the early 2000s, confidence was shaken as growth began to slow and this was further exacerbated by other factors, including the 11 September 2001 attack on the World Trade Center and a range of corporate scandals. Combined, these factors caused share prices to plummet and, as people anticipated further price falls, so they held back from buying, thereby pushing prices even lower. A similar thing occurred with the global banking crisis in 2007–8. It was only when confidence started to return that share prices begin to rise once more.

Uncertainty once again emerged in the global economy in 2018, not only with the UK's impending exit from the EU without a deal, but also with slower growth rates in many Asian nations, such as China.

The rise and fall in share prices associated with expectations mirror those seen in the housing market and are discussed in Box 2.2

Supply

The factors affecting supply are largely the same as those affecting demand, but in the opposite direction.

If the return on alternative forms of saving falls, people with shares are likely to hold on to them, as they represent a better form of saving. The supply of shares to the market will fall. If incomes or wealth rises, people again are likely to want to hold on to their shares.

As far as expectations are concerned, if people believe that share prices will rise, they will hold on to the shares they have. Supply to the market will fall, thereby pushing up prices. If, however, they believe that prices will fall, as they did in 2008, they will sell their shares now before prices do fall. Supply will increase, driving down the price.

Share prices and business

Companies are crucially affected by their share price. If a company's share price falls, this can indicate that 'the market' is losing confidence in the company, as we saw with Tesco during the latter part of 2014 and with companies such as easyJet from June 2016 to February 2017. Such falls in share prices make it more difficult for companies to raise finance, not only by issuing additional shares in the primary market, but also from banks.

It can also make the company more vulnerable to a takeover bid. This is where one company seeks to buy out another by offering to buy all its shares. A takeover will succeed if the owners of more than half of the company's shares vote to accept the offered price. Shareholders are more likely to agree to the takeover if the company's shares have not been doing very well recently.

Many factors, therefore, influence share prices and can be attributed to changes in demand and/or supply. Getting a good understanding of the factors that shift each curve and in which direction is an absolutely essential part of applying economics to any industry or market.

If the rate of economic growth in the economy is 3 per cent in a particular year, why are share prices likely to rise by more than 3 per cent that year?

Find out what has happened to the FTSE 100 index over the past 12 months (see site B27 on the hotlinks part of the website)? Can you explain the reasons behind the data?

BOX 2.2 — UK HOUSE PRICES

The ups and downs of the housing market

If you are thinking of buying a house sometime in the future, then you may well follow the fortunes of the housing market with some trepidation. This market is very important to consumers, firms and government, with households spending more on housing as a proportion of their income than on anything else, and movements in the market are rarely out of the news. This is not only because nominal (actual) prices are increasing over the longer term but, more significantly, because they are increasing in real terms too. This means that house prices are increasing *relative* to general prices. The average UK house price in January 1970 was a little over £3900. By November 2018, it had risen to around £231 000, an increase of nearly 6000 per cent.

As you can see from the chart, while house prices have increased significantly over the past 50 years, there has also been volatility in the market – more so than in general prices across the economy. For example, house prices doubled between 1984 and 1989, leading to many people buying houses, hoping that prices would continue to rise. However, prices then fell by 12.2 per cent over the next 6 years, sending many households into *negative equity*. This occurs when the size of a household's mortgage is greater than the value of the house, meaning that if they sold their house, they would still owe money. Many people, therefore, found themselves in a situation where they were unable to move house.

House prices also boomed between 1996 and 2007, rising by 26 per cent per year at the peak (in the 12 months to January 2003). They rose again in late 2013, with the UK's annual house price inflation reaching 11.7 per cent. Such periods of house price growth mean that for many low-income households, owning a home has become increasingly difficult, as even by 2007, the average price of a house was more than 5 times the size of a first-time buyer's income, compared to just twice the size in the mid-1990s.

We also saw a big fall in house prices as a consequence of the financial crisis of 2007–8. This led to further falls, as people postponed buying, believing that prices would continue to fall and by 2009, prices were falling at an annual rate of 17.5 per cent. First-time buyers had more chance of buying their first home, but were still reluctant to buy, fearing a return of the problem of negative equity.

House prices also affect the rental sector (see the blog, *The rental sector,* on the Sloman Economics News site) and despite various trends in house prices in the UK, significant regional variations do exist (see the blog, *House price variations: a regional story,* on the Sloman Economics News site).

The determination of house prices

House prices are determined by demand and supply. If demand rises (i.e. shifts to the right) or if supply falls (i.e. shifts to the left), the equilibrium price of houses will rise. Similarly, if demand falls or supply rises, the equilibrium price will fall.

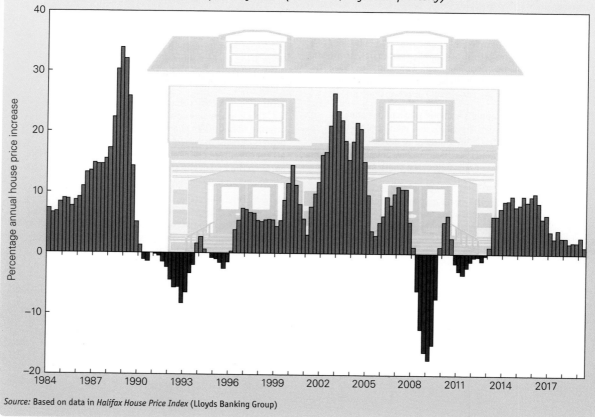

House price inflation (annual %, adjusted quarterly)

Source: Based on data in *Halifax House Price Index* (Lloyds Banking Group)

So why did house prices rise so rapidly in the 1980s, late 1990s, 2000s and from 2014 to 2016, but fall in the early 1990s, late 2000s and after the EU referendum of 2016? The answer lies primarily in changes in the *demand* for housing. Let us examine the various factors that affected the demand for houses.

Incomes (actual and anticipated). The second half of the 1980s, 1996 to 2007 and 2013 to 2016 were periods of rising incomes. The economy was experiencing an economic 'boom' or recovery as in the latter case. Many people wanted to spend their extra incomes on housing, either buying a house for the first time, or moving to a better one. What is more, many people thought that their incomes would continue to grow, and were thus prepared to stretch themselves financially in the short term by buying an expensive house, confident that their mortgage payments would become more and more affordable over time.

The early 1990s and late 2000s, by contrast, were periods of recession or low growth, with rising unemployment and flat or falling incomes. People had much less confidence about their ability to afford large mortgages. Similarly, in 2017, rising inflation rates caused real incomes to fall and this, together with uncertainty about the future of the UK outside of the EU, had a negative impact on demand for housing.

The cost of mortgages. Most people need a mortgage to buy a house. If mortgages become more affordable (longer repayment periods or lower interest rates), people tend to borrow more and this fuels the demand for houses and drives up their prices.

During the second half of the 1980s, mortgage interest rates were generally falling. Although they were still high compared with rates today, in *real* terms they were negative! In other words, even if you paid back none of the mortgage and simply accumulated the interest owed, your house would be rising faster in price than your debt; your 'equity' in the house (i.e. the value of the house minus what you owe on it) would be rising.

In 1989, however, this trend was reversed. Mortgage interest rates were now rising. Many people found it difficult to maintain existing payments, let alone to take on a larger mortgage. From 1996 to 2003 mortgage rates were generally reduced again, once more fuelling the demand for houses. Even with gently rising interest rates from 2003 to 2007, mortgages were still relatively affordable. Between 2009 and 2017 interest rates remained at an all-time low, which reduced the cost of mortgage repayments.

However, due to continued uncertainty following the financial crisis and lenders remaining cautious, housing demand did not start to increase significantly until around 2013. However, uncertainty has returned to the market since the UK's referendum.

The availability of mortgages. In the late 1980s and early and mid-2000s, mortgages of several times a person's annual income were readily available and only small deposits were required. Indeed, in the mid-2000s, some mortgage lenders were willing to lend more than 100 per cent of the value of the property. By contrast, in the early 1990s and late 2000s banks and building societies were much more cautious about granting mortgages. They were aware that with the banking crisis and a global recession contributing to rising

unemployment, as well as falling house prices and hence a growing problem of negative equity, there was a growing danger that borrowers would default on payments.

Furthermore, the problem in the late 2000s was compounded by the financial crisis, which meant that banks had less money to lend. Credit criteria remained tight into the early 2010s so that purchasers had to find historically large deposits. Many mortgage lenders were asking for deposits of at least 25 per cent – over £40 000 for an average house in the UK. This reduced significantly the number of first-time buyers.

The deposit requirement eased a little through 2013 and 2014 and government-backed 'Help to Buy' schemes were introduced to help borrowers get a mortgage with a 5 per cent deposit. The easing of credit constraints contributed towards an increase in house prices once again.

Speculation. In the 1980s and from 1997 to 2007, people generally believed that house prices would continue rising. This encouraged people to buy as soon as possible, and to take out the biggest mortgage possible, before prices went up any further. There was also an effect on supply. Those with houses to sell held back until the last possible moment in the hope of getting a higher price. The net effect was a rightward shift in the demand curve for houses and a leftward shift in the supply curve. The effect of this speculation, therefore, was to help bring about the very effect that people were predicting (see Box 2.4).

In the early 1990s and late 2000s, the opposite occurred. People thinking of buying houses held back, hoping to buy at a lower price. People with houses to sell tried to sell as quickly as possible before prices fell any further. Again, the effect of this speculation was to aggravate the change in prices – this time a fall in prices.

The impact of speculation has also been compounded by a growth in the 'buy-to-let' industry, with mortgage lenders entering this market in large numbers. There was a huge amount of media attention on the possibilities for individuals to make very high returns.

Demographics. The general rise in house prices over the whole period since 1983 has been compounded by demographics: population has grown more rapidly than the housing stock. There are also more single households and more workers coming to the UK and these factors have caused demand to grow more rapidly than supply over the long term.

1. Draw supply and demand diagrams to illustrate what was happening to house prices (a) in the second half of the 1980s and from the late 1990s to 2007; (b) in the early 1990s and 2008–12; (c) in London and South East England from 2014.
2. Are there any factors on the supply side that contribute to changes in house prices? If so, what are they?
3. Find out what has happened to house prices over the past three years. Attempt an explanation of what has happened.

Undertake an Internet search to find out what forecasters are predicting for house prices over the next year and attempt to explain the role played by demand and supply in their forecasts.

2.5 ELASTICITY OF DEMAND AND SUPPLY

Price elasticity of demand

When the price of a good rises, the quantity demanded will fall. That much is fairly obvious. But in most cases firms and economists want to know just *how much* the quantity demanded will fall. In other words, we want to know how *responsive* demand is to a rise (or fall) in price.

Take the case of two products: petrol and broccoli. In the case of petrol, a rise in price is likely to result in only a slight fall in the quantity demanded. If people want to continue driving, they have to pay the higher prices for fuel. A few may turn to riding bicycles, and some people may try to make fewer journeys, but for most people, a rise in the price of petrol and diesel will make little difference to how much they use their cars.

In the case of broccoli, however, a rise in price may lead to a substantial fall in the quantity demanded. The reason is that there are alternative vegetables that people can buy. Many people, when buying vegetables, are very conscious of their prices and will buy whatever is reasonably priced.

We call the responsiveness of demand to a change in price the *price elasticity of demand*. If we know the price elasticity of demand for a product, we can predict the effect on price and quantity when the *supply* curve for that product shifts.

Definition

Price elasticity of demand A measure of the responsiveness of quantity demanded to a change in price.

KEY IDEA 10

Elasticity. The responsiveness of one variable (e.g. demand) to a change in another (e.g. price). This concept is fundamental to understanding how markets work. The more elastic variables are, the more responsive is the market to changing circumstances.

Figure 2.6 shows the effect of a shift in supply with two quite different demand curves (D and D'). Curve D' is more elastic than curve D over any given price range. In other words, for any given change in price, there will be a larger change in quantity demanded along curve D' than along curve D.

Assume that initially the supply curve is S_1, and that it intersects with both demand curves at point *a*, at a price of P_1 and a quantity of Q_1. Now supply shifts to S_2. What will happen to price and quantity? In the case of the less elastic demand curve D, there is a relatively large rise in price (to P_2) and a relatively small fall in quantity (to Q_2): equilibrium is at point *b*. In the case of the more elastic demand curve D', however, there is only a relatively small rise in price (to P_3) but a relatively large fall in quantity (to Q_3): equilibrium is at point *c*.

Defining price elasticity of demand

What we want to compare is the size of the change in quantity demanded of a given product with the size of the change in its price. Price elasticity of demand does just this. It is defined as follows:

$$P\varepsilon_D = \frac{\text{Proportionate (or Percentage)}}{\text{Proportionate (or Percentage) change in price}}$$

$$P\varepsilon_D = \frac{\text{change in quantity demanded}}{\text{Proportionate (or Percentage) change in price}}$$

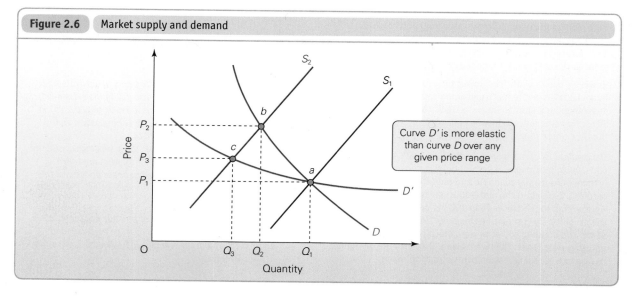

Figure 2.6 Market supply and demand

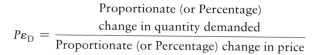

Curve D' is more elastic than curve D over any given price range

If, for example, a 20 per cent rise in the price of a product causes a 10 per cent fall in the quantity demanded, the price elasticity of demand will be:

$$-10\%/20\% = -0.5$$

Three things should be noted about the figure that is calculated for elasticity.

The use of proportionate or percentage measures. Elasticity is measured in proportionate or percentage terms because this allows comparison of changes in two qualitatively different things, which are thus measured in two different types of unit, i.e. it allows comparison of quantity changes (quantity demanded) with monetary changes (price).

It is also the only sensible way of deciding *how big* a change in price or quantity is. Take a simple example. An item goes up in price by £1. Is this a big increase or a small increase? We can answer this only if we know what the original price was. If a can of beans goes up in price by £1 that is a huge price increase. If, however, the price of a house goes up by £1, that is a tiny price increase. In other words, it is the percentage or proportionate increase in price that we look at in deciding how big a price rise it is.

The sign (positive or negative). If price increases (a positive figure), the quantity demanded will fall (a negative figure). If price falls (a negative figure), the quantity demanded will rise (a positive figure). Thus price elasticity of demand will be negative: a positive figure is being divided by a negative figure (or vice versa).

The value (greater or less than 1). If we now ignore the sign and just concentrate on the value of the figure, this tells us whether demand is elastic or inelastic.

- *Elastic demand* ($\varepsilon > 1$). This is where a change in price causes a proportionately larger change in the quantity demanded. In this case the price elasticity of demand will be greater than 1, since we are dividing a larger figure by a smaller figure.
- *Inelastic demand* ($\varepsilon < 1$). This is where a change in price causes a proportionately smaller change in the quantity demanded. In this case the price elasticity of demand will be less than 1, since we are dividing a smaller figure by a larger figure.
- *Unit elastic demand* ($\varepsilon = 1$). This is where the quantity demanded changes proportionately the same as price. This will give an elasticity equal to 1, since we are dividing a figure by itself.

The determinants of price elasticity of demand

The price elasticity of demand varies enormously from one product to another. But why do some products have a highly elastic demand, whereas others have a highly *in*elastic demand? What determines price elasticity of demand?

The number and closeness of substitute goods. This is the main determinant of price elasticity of demand. The more substitutes there are for a good and the closer they are as substitutes, the greater will be the price elasticity of demand. The reason is that people will be able to switch to the substitutes when the price of the good rises. The more numerous the substitutes and the closer they are, the more people will switch: in other words, the bigger will be the substitution effect of a price rise.

The price elasticity of demand for a product in general will be relatively low compared to the price elasticity of demand for a more narrowly defined product. For example, a number of international meta-studies have found that alcohol has a relatively inelastic demand of around -0.4.[10] This is to be expected, given that there are few substitutes for alcohol and we know that alcohol is an addictive substance – people are still willing to buy, even if price rises.

However, if we look at a more specific product, such as beer, it has a more elastic demand, as there are other substitutes – not only substitutes for alcohol in general, but also substitutes for beer, such as wine and spirits. Typical estimates for the price elasticity of beer vary between -0.98 and -1.27.[11] This means that when the price of alcohol rises, demand for it will fall, but when the price of a particular type of alcohol rises, demand will fall by more, as there are substitutes for this drink. We would expect the price elasticity of demand for particular types of beer to be even higher and for particular brands to be higher still.

The proportion of income spent. The higher the proportion of our income we spend on a good, the more

---

[10] João Sousa, 'Estimate of price elasticities of demand for alcohol in the United Kingdom', *HMRC Working Paper 16*, HM Revenue & Customs (December 2014).

[11] Y. Meng et al., 'Estimation of own and cross price elasticities of alcohol demand in the UK – A pseudo-panel approach using the Living Costs and Food Survey 2001–2009', *Journal of Health Economics* 34, White Rose Research Online (2014).

Definitions

Elastic demand If demand is (price) elastic, then any change in price will cause the quantity demanded to change proportionately more. (Ignoring the negative sign) it will have a value greater than 1.

Inelastic demand If demand is (price) inelastic, then any change will cause the quantity demanded to change by a proportionately smaller amount. (Ignoring the negative sign) it will have a value less than 1.

Unit elasticity When the price elasticity of demand is unity, this is where quantity demanded changes by the same proportion as the price. Price elasticity is equal to -1.

we will have to reduce our consumption of it following a rise in price: the more elastic will be the demand. Think about salt – the amount we spend on it accounts for a tiny proportion of our income and so if its price doubles, it makes little difference to our overall expenditure: the income effect of a price rise is very small – estimates suggest it is about −0.1.[12] However, a car accounts for a much larger proportion of our income and so if the price of cars double, there would be a larger income effect.

The time period. When price rises, people may take time to adjust their consumption patterns and find alternatives. The longer the time period after a price change, the more elastic is the demand likely to be.

The Office for Budget Responsibility estimates that the price elasticity of demand for road fuel is −0.07 in the short run and −0.13 in the medium term. Research from America on the price elasticity of electricity demand finds a 1-year figure of −0.14, a 3-year figure of −0.29 and a long-run figure of between −0.29 and −0.39[13] and research from Korea estimates short-run and long-run price-elasticity figures of −0.36 and −0.55 for diesel demand.[14] In each of these cases, we observe more elastic demand in the long run, when people have time to shop around (for alternative means of transport in the case of road fuel), than we do in the short run.

Pause for thought

Think of two products and estimate which is likely to have the higher price elasticity of demand. Explain your answer.

Price elasticity of demand and consumer expenditure
One of the most important applications of price elasticity of demand concerns its relationship with the total amount of money consumers spend on a product. *Total consumer expenditure (TE)* is simply price multiplied by quantity purchased:

$$TE = P \times Q$$

For example, if consumers buy 3 million units (Q) at a price of £2 per unit (P), they will spend a total of £6 million (TE).

Total consumer expenditure is the same as the *total revenue (TR)* received by firms from the sale of the product (before any taxes or other deductions).

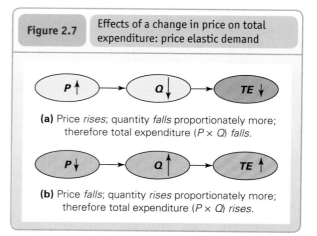

| Figure 2.7 | Effects of a change in price on total expenditure: price elastic demand |

(a) Price *rises*; quantity *falls* proportionately more; therefore total expenditure ($P \times Q$) *falls*.

(b) Price *falls*; quantity *rises* proportionately more; therefore total expenditure ($P \times Q$) *rises*.

What will happen to consumer expenditure, and hence firms' revenue, if there is a change in price? The answer depends on the price elasticity of demand.

Elastic demand. As price rises, so quantity demanded falls, and vice versa. When demand is elastic, quantity changes proportionately more than price. Thus the change in quantity has a bigger effect on total consumer expenditure than does the change in price. This is summarised in Figure 2.7. In other words, total expenditure and total revenue change in the same direction as quantity.

This is illustrated in Figure 2.9(a). The areas of the rectangles in the diagram represent total expenditure (and total revenue). Why? The area of a rectangle is its height multiplied by its length. In this case, this is price multiplied by quantity purchased, which is total expenditure. Demand is elastic between points *a* and *b*. A rise in price from £4 to £5 (25 per cent) causes a proportionately larger fall in quantity demanded: from 20m to 10m units (−50 per cent). Total expenditure *falls* from £80m (the green shaded area) to £50m (the red striped area).

When demand is elastic, then, a rise in price will cause a fall in total expenditure and hence the total revenue earned by the firms selling the product. A reduction in price, however, will result in consumers spending more, and hence firms earning more. Two cases where the elasticity of demand has been

Definitions

Total consumer expenditure (TE) (per period) The price of the product multiplied by the quantity purchased: $TE = P \times Q$.

Total revenue (TR) (per period) The total amount received by firms from the sale of a product, before the deduction of taxes or any other costs. The price multiplied by the quantity sold: $TR = P \times Q$.

[12] Patrick L. Anderson et al., *Price Elasticity of Demand*, Mackinac Center for Public Policy (13 November 1997).

[13] Tatyana Deryugina, Alexander MacKay and Julian Reif, *The Long-Run Elasticity of Electricity Demand: Evidence from Municipal Electric Aggregation* (16 December 2016).

[14] Kyoung-Min Lim, Myunghwan Kim, Chang Seob Kim and Seung-Hoon Yoo, 'Short-run and long-run elasticities of diesel demand in Korea', *Energies* 2012, 5 (28 November 2012).

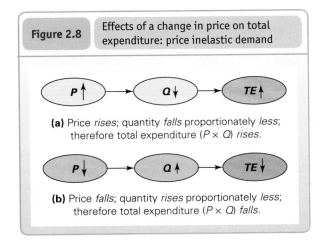

Figure 2.8 Effects of a change in price on total expenditure: price inelastic demand

(a) Price *rises*; quantity *falls* proportionately *less*; therefore total expenditure ($P \times Q$) *rises*.

(b) Price *falls*; quantity *rises* proportionately *less*; therefore total expenditure ($P \times Q$) *falls*.

important are discussed on the Sloman Economics News Site in the blogs: *Price changes for travellers in Bristol* and *Morrisons Brand: 'Milk for Farmers'*.

So far, we have been looking at the *market* demand curve. If we take the demand curve for a single firm, however, which is also a price taker, its demand curve will be perfectly elastic (i.e. horizontal). The price elasticity of demand is $-\infty$. In other words, being a price taker, it can sell as much as it likes at the given market price. Any increase in its output and sales necessarily results in an increase in its total revenue, since it is selling a higher quantity at the *same* price. (When firms are not price takers, they face a downward-sloping demand curve. We consider such firms in Chapter 5.)

Inelastic demand. When demand is inelastic, price changes proportionately more than quantity. Thus the change in price has a bigger effect on total

expenditure than does the change in quantity. This is summarised in Figure 2.8. In other words, total expenditure changes in the same direction as price.

This effect is illustrated in Figure 2.9(b). Demand is inelastic between points *a* and *c*. A rise in price from £4 to £8 (100 per cent) causes a proportionately smaller fall in quantity demanded: from 20m to 15m units (-25 per cent). Total revenue *rises* from £80m (the green shaded area) to £120m (the red striped area). In this case, firms' revenue will increase if there is a rise in price, and fall if there is a fall in price.

In the extreme case of a totally inelastic demand curve, this would be represented by a vertical straight line. No matter what happens to price, quantity demanded remains the same and so the price elasticity of demand will be zero. It is obvious that the more the price rises, the bigger will be the level of consumer expenditure.

Pause for thought

1. *If the price of petrol goes up, what will happen to a firm's total revenue? Does your answer change if it is only the price of Esso petrol that increases?*
2. *Can we determine the impact on a firm's profits following a price fall if it faces (a) an elastic demand and (b) an inelastic demand? Explain.*

Unit elastic demand. With unitary elastic demand (where the value for elasticity $= -1$), the proportionate changes in price and quantity are equal. Any rise in price will be exactly offset by a fall in quantity, which means that total revenue and total expenditure

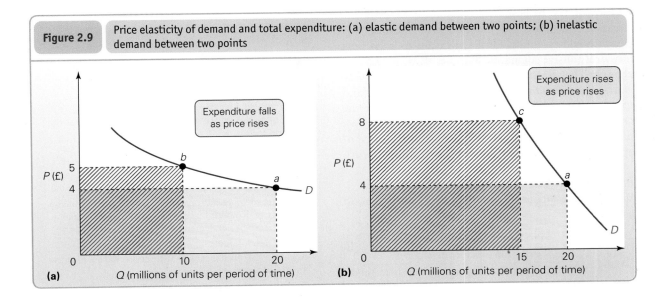

Figure 2.9 Price elasticity of demand and total expenditure: (a) elastic demand between two points; (b) inelastic demand between two points

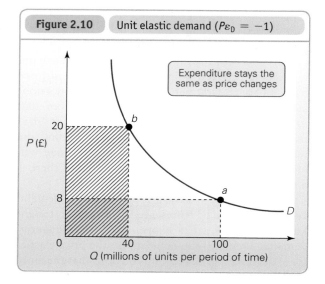

Figure 2.10 Unit elastic demand ($P\varepsilon_D = -1$)

Expenditure stays the same as price changes

will remain unchanged. In Figure 2.10 the red striped area is exactly equal to the green shaded area: in both cases total revenue and expenditure are £800 million. The shape of a demand curve that has unit elastic demand is known as a rectangular hyperbola.

Other elasticities

As we already know, demand is affected by many factors besides price and so firms are interested to know the responsiveness of demand to a change in these other variables. They might want to know how responsive demand will be to increased expenditure on a particular advertising campaign or how demand will be affected by more ethically sourced products. Of course, as with many aspects of business, the figures will only be estimates, as we can never guarantee that past behaviour will be the same as future behaviour.

Two of the biggest determinants of demand are consumer incomes and the prices of substitute or complementary goods. Firms will want to know just how responsive demand will be if these factors change. That is: they will want to know the *income elasticity of demand* – the responsiveness of demand to a change in consumers' incomes (Y) – and the *cross-price elasticity of demand* – the responsiveness of demand for their good to a change in the price of another good (whether a substitute or a complement).

Income elasticity of demand ($Y\varepsilon_D$)

We define the income elasticity of demand for a good as follows:

$$Y\varepsilon_D = \frac{\text{Proportionate (or Percentage) change in quantity demanded}}{\text{Proportionate (or Percentage) change in income}}$$

For example, if a 2 per cent rise in consumer incomes causes an 8 per cent rise in a product's demand, then its income elasticity of demand will be:

$$8\%/2\% = 4$$

Note that in the case of a normal good, the figure for income elasticity will be positive: a *rise* in income leads to a *rise* in demand (a positive figure divided by a positive figure gives a positive answer).

The major determinant of income elasticity of demand is the degree of 'necessity' of the good. Typically, the demand for luxury goods expands rapidly as people's incomes rise, whereas the demand for more basic goods such as bread will only rise a little. If your income rises, you are unlikely to buy a lot more bread or milk, but you may buy more football tickets or foreign holidays. Thus items such as foreign holidays or cars have a high income elasticity of demand, whereas items such as potatoes and bus journeys have a low income elasticity of demand.

In the case of inferior goods such as many of the 'value' products in supermarkets, as income rises, demand *falls*. As people earn more, they switch to the supermarket's superior lines or to branded products and hence the demand for the 'value' product falls. Unlike **normal goods**, which have a positive income elasticity of demand, **inferior goods** have a negative income elasticity of demand: a *rise* in income leads to a *fall* in demand (a negative figure divided by a positive figure gives a negative answer).

Income elasticity of demand is an important concept to firms considering the future size of the market for their product. If the product has a high-income elasticity of demand, sales are likely to expand rapidly as national income rises, but may also fall significantly if the economy moves into recession.

Definitions

Income elasticity of demand The responsiveness of demand to a change in consumer incomes: the proportionate change in demand divided by the proportionate change in income.

Cross-price elasticity of demand The responsiveness of demand for one good to a change in the price of another: the proportionate change in demand for one good divided by the proportionate change in price of the other.

Normal goods Goods whose demand increases as consumer incomes increase. They have a positive income elasticity of demand. Luxury goods will have a higher income elasticity of demand than more basic goods.

Inferior goods Goods whose demand decreases as consumer incomes increase. Such goods have a negative income elasticity of demand.

BOX 2.3   SHALL WE PUT UP OUR PRICE?

Competition, price and revenue

When you buy a can of drink on a train, or an ice-cream in the cinema, or a bottle of wine in a restaurant, you may well be horrified by its price. How can they get away with it?

The answer is that these firms are *not* price takers. They can choose what price to charge. We will be examining the behaviour of such firms in Chapter 5, but here it is useful to see how price elasticity of demand can help to explain their behaviour.

Take the case of the can of drink on the train. If you are thirsty, and if you haven't brought a drink with you, then you will have to get one from the train's bar, or go without. There is no substitute. What we are saying here is that the demand for drinks on the train is inelastic at the normal shop price. This means that the train operator can put up the price of its drinks, and food too, and earn *more* revenue, because demand will be relatively unresponsive.

Generally, the less competition a firm faces, the lower will be the elasticity of demand for its products, since there will be fewer substitutes (competitors) to which consumers can turn. The lower the price elasticity of demand, the higher is likely to be the price that the firm charges.

When there is plenty of competition, it is quite a different story. Petrol stations in the same area may compete fiercely in terms of price. One station may hope that by reducing its price by 1p or even 0.1p per litre below that of its competitors, it can attract customers away from them. With a highly elastic demand, a small reduction in price may lead to a substantial increase in their revenue. The problem is, of course, that when they *all* reduce prices, no firm wins. No one attracts customers away from the others! In this case it is the customer who wins.

1. *Why might a restaurant charge very high prices for wine and bottled water and yet quite reasonable prices for food?*
2. *Why are clothes with designer labels so much more expensive than similar 'own brand' clothes from a chain store, even though they may cost a similar amount to produce?*

Individually or in pairs, go around a supermarket and try to identify products that have a very high price relative to their cost of production. In each case, try to establish why this is the case.

Students could then report back to their groups and compare notes. The groups could also discuss whether there any other products not sold in supermarkets – either goods or services – that are similarly highly priced relative to their costs of production. Are there any common factors in each case?

Firms may also find that some parts of their market have a higher income elasticity of demand than others, and may thus choose to target their marketing campaigns on this group. For example, middle income groups may have a higher income elasticity of demand for high-tech products than lower income groups (who are unlikely to be able to afford such products even if their incomes rise somewhat) or higher income groups (who can probably afford them anyway, and thus would not buy much more if their incomes rose). For this reason, changes in the distribution of income can be an important factor for firms to consider when making decisions about what to sell.

Cross-price elasticity of demand ($C\varepsilon_{Dab}$)

This is often known by its less cumbersome title of *cross elasticity of demand*. It is a measure of the responsiveness of demand for one product to a change in the price of another (either a substitute or a complement). It enables us to predict how much the demand curve for the first product will shift when the price of the second product changes. For example, knowledge of the cross elasticity of demand for Coca-Cola with respect to the price of Pepsi would allow Coca-Cola to predict the effect on its own sales if the price of Pepsi were to change.

We define cross-price elasticity as follows:

$$C\varepsilon_D = \frac{\text{Proportionate (or Percentage) change in quantity demand for good A}}{\text{Proportionate (or Percentage) change in price of good B}}$$

If good B is a *substitute* for good A, A's demand will *rise* as B's price rises. For example, the demand for bicycles will rise as the price of public transport rises. In this case, cross elasticity will be a positive figure. If B is *complementary* to A, however, A's demand will *fall* as B's price rises and thus as the quantity of B demanded falls. For example, the demand for petrol falls as the price of cars rises. In this case, cross elasticity will be a negative figure.

The major determinant of cross elasticity of demand is the closeness of the substitute or complement. The closer it is, the bigger will be the effect on the first good of a change in the price of the substitute or complement, and hence the greater will be cross elasticity – either positive or negative.

Pause for thought

If Good A had a cross-price elasticity of demand of zero with respect to Good B, would Good B be a substitute or a complement for Good A, or neither?

Firms will wish to know the cross elasticity of demand for their product when considering the effect on the demand for their product of a change in the price of a rival's product (a substitute). If firm B cuts its price, will this make significant inroads into the sales of firm A? If so, firm A may feel forced to cut its prices too; if not, then firm A may keep its price unchanged. The cross-price elasticities of demand between a firm's product and those of each of its rivals are thus vital pieces of information for a firm when making its production, pricing and marketing plans.

Similarly, a firm will wish to know the cross-price elasticity of demand for its product with any complementary good. Car producers will wish to know the effect of petrol price increases on the sales of their cars.

Price elasticity of supply (Pε_S)

Just as we can measure the responsiveness of demand to a change in a determinant of demand, we can also measure the responsiveness of supply to a change in a determinant of supply. The *price elasticity of supply* refers to the responsiveness of supply to a change in price. We define it as follows:

$$Pε_S = \frac{\text{Proportionate (or Percentage) change in quantity supplied}}{\text{Proportionate (or Percentage) change in price}}$$

Thus if a 15 per cent rise in the price of a product causes a 30 per cent rise in the quantity supplied, the price elasticity of supply will be:

$$30\%/15\% = 2$$

In Figure 2.11 curve S_2 is more elastic between any two prices than curve S_1. Thus, when price rises from P_0 to P_1 there is a larger increase in quantity supplied with S_2 (namely, Q_0 to Q_2) than there is with S_1 (namely, Q_0 to Q_1).

There are two main determinants of the price elasticity of supply.

The amount that costs rise as output rises. The less the additional costs of producing additional output, the more firms will be encouraged to produce for a given price rise; the more elastic will supply be.

Supply is thus likely to be elastic if firms have plenty of spare capacity, if they can readily get extra supplies of raw materials, if they can easily switch away from producing alternative products and if they can avoid having to introduce overtime working

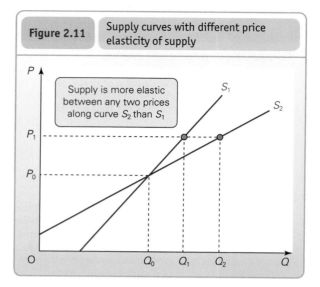

| Figure 2.11 | Supply curves with different price elasticity of supply |

Supply is more elastic between any two prices along curve S_2 than S_1

(at higher rates of pay). If all these conditions hold, costs will be little affected by a rise in output and supply will be relatively elastic. The less these conditions apply, the less elastic will supply be.

Time period.

- Immediate time period. Firms are unlikely to be able to increase supply by much immediately. Think about a market stall selling fresh vegetables: supply is virtually fixed, or can vary only according to available stocks. Supply is highly inelastic.
- Short run. If a slightly longer time period is considered, some inputs can be increased (e.g. raw materials), while others will remain fixed (e.g. heavy machinery). Supply can increase somewhat and so is more elastic.
- Long run. In the long run, there will be sufficient time for all inputs to be increased and for new firms to enter the industry. Supply, therefore, is likely to be highly elastic. In some circumstances the supply curve may even slope downwards. (See the section on economies of scale in Chapter 4, pages 89–92.)

Pause for thought

If you were the owner of a clothes shop, how would you set about deciding what prices to charge for each garment at the end-of-season sale?

Definition

Price elasticity of supply The responsiveness of quantity supplied to a change in price: the proportionate change in quantity supplied divided by the proportionate change in price.

BOX 2.4 SPECULATION

Bubble, bubble, toil and trouble

In a world of shifting demand and supply curves, prices are constantly moving. If prices are expected to change in the near future, this can affect the behaviour of buyers and sellers *now*. For example, in early December, you might consider buying a new winter coat, but decide to delay purchasing one until the after-Christmas sales. Then, when the sales do come, you may decide to buy a summer jacket and not wait until summer for fear that it will be more expensive then. The opposite applies to sellers, who will delay selling if they think prices will soon rise but will sell now if they think prices are likely to fall.

Thus a belief that prices will go up will cause people to buy now and to delay selling; a belief that prices will come down will cause people to delay their purchases, but will encourage sellers to sell now. This behaviour of looking into the future and making buying and selling decisions based on your predictions is called *speculation*.

Speculation is often based on current trends in price behaviour. If prices are currently rising, people may try to decide whether they are about to peak and go back down again, or whether they are likely to go on rising. Having made their prediction, they will then act on it. This speculation will thus affect demand and supply, which in turn will affect price.

Speculation tends to be *self-fulfilling*, as the actions of speculators often bring about the very effect on prices that speculators had anticipated. For example, if speculators believe that the price of BP shares is about to rise, they will buy more of them. The demand curve for BP shares shifts to the right. Those owning BP shares and thinking of selling will wait until the price has risen. In the meantime, the supply curve shifts to the left. The result of these two shifts is that the share price does rise. In other words, the prophecy has become self-fulfilling. Speculation is commonplace in many markets: the stock market (see Box 2.1), the foreign exchange market and the housing market (see Box 2.2) are three examples.

One consequence of speculation can be speculative bubbles and while you may be familiar with some examples, such as in housing, the Internet (the dotcom bubble of the early 2000s) and various financial commodities, there are some other more unusual cases!

Tulips

One of the earliest recorded bubbles occurred in the Netherlands and involved tulips. Tulips were a new flower for the Dutch and, following a virus that had the effect of creating new vibrant colours on the petals, demand for them began to increase.

More and more people began to trade in tulips, with different varieties (affected differently by the virus) fetching different prices. The market was seen as having no limits; and so began a wave of speculation that fuelled prices. With more and more people buying tulips, demand increased, as shown in Figure (a).

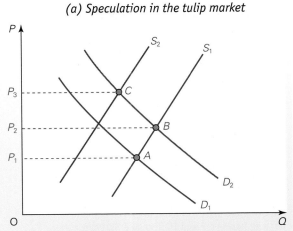

(a) Speculation in the tulip market

At the same time, suppliers (those growing the tulips) had to replenish their stock for the summer, as they would always do. This, however, reduced supply on the market and made tulip bulbs scarcer.

As supply shifted leftwards and demand shifted to the right, prices climbed upwards – speculation was destabilising, as everyone thought prices would keep going up. The higher the prices went, the more people began to trade in tulips, hoping to make their millions by selling tulips to unwitting foreigners.

Between November 1636 and February 1637, there was a 20-fold increase in the price of tulip bulbs, such that a skilled worker's annual salary would not even cover the price of one bulb. Some were even worth more than a luxury home! But, only three months later, their price had fallen by 99 per cent. Some traders refused to pay the high price and others began to sell their tulips. Prices began falling. This dampened demand (as tulips were seen to be a poor investment) and encouraged more people to sell their tulips. Soon the price was in freefall, with everyone selling – another case of destabilising speculation, as everyone thought prices would just go on falling. The bubble had burst (see Figure (b)).[1]

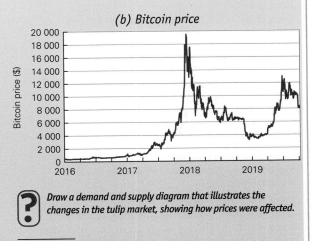

(b) Bitcoin price

Definitions

Speculation This is where people make buying or selling decisions based on their anticipations of future prices.

Self-fulfilling speculation The actions of speculators tend to cause the very effect that they had anticipated.

? *Draw a demand and supply diagram that illustrates the changes in the tulip market, showing how prices were affected.*

[1] Andrew Beattie, 'Market Crashes; The tulip and bulb craze', *Investopedia* (14 November 2017).

The ups and downs of bitcoin

Created in 2009, bitcoin is an electronic currency that has seen huge price volatility, a bubble that burst and ongoing speculation about its future price.

The supply of national currencies is typically controlled by central banks and the banking sector. In the case of bitcoin, however, its supply is determined by 'mining', whereby individuals/groups solve complicated mathematical problems in exchange for new 'blocks' of bitcoins. The maximum number of bitcoins that can be supplied is restricted to ₿21 million, though this number is not expected to be mined until sometime in the next century. However, 99 per cent should have been mined by around 2032, as the number of bitcoins generated per block is halved for every 210 000 blocks created. By February 2019, ₿17.5 million had been created.

The price of bitcoin had risen from under $300 in October 2015 to a peak of over $19 000 at the end of 2017, increasing between September and December 2017 by just under 600 per cent. But the price has not risen consistently. In fact, it has exhibited significant volatility. For example, it fell by 22 per cent between 7 and 10 December 2017, but then recovered within a few hours by 18 per cent. By the start of February 2018, it had plummeted by 56 per cent from its December 2017 high. It then recovered by the start of March. Since March 2018, the price has exhibited a downward trend, falling to approximately $3000 by the end of 2018 and remaining at a similar price in the first months of 2019.

What has caused its price to rise and fall so significantly? In order to answer this question, we need to refer to our old friends – demand and supply.

As we have discussed, the supply of bitcoin is growing (at around 150 per hour), but, as we have seen, it is growing at an increasingly slower rate. Given the relatively stable supply increase, the initial rise in bitcoin must be down to the demand-side.

Although it can be used for transactions in some places, especially on the 'Dark Web', most legitimate vendors do not accept this 'currency' and so the demand for it has come from those viewing it as an investment. They are speculating that the price of bitcoin will rise and want to put their money into this asset, in the hopes of selling it in the future for a significantly higher price.

Bitcoin has therefore been subject to *destabilising speculation*, as the more that people have expected its price to go up, the more people have bought bitcoin, which pushes up prices further. This then encourages even more people to buy and as continued demand pushes up the price, so we begin to see the emergence of a bubble. The price of bitcoin at its peak, therefore, reflected not the actual value of bitcoin, but the enthusiasm of buyers.

A bitcoin bubble?

One thing that we know about bubbles is that they tend to burst, which we saw on 10 December 2017, albeit temporarily, and also at the start of 2018. As a cryptocurrency, bitcoin is very susceptible to media announcements, especially about its future as a currency and any regulations that might emerge.

At the start of 2018, there was much discussion about the future regulation of bitcoin, which deterred investors from buying and hence reduced demand, thus cutting price. Similar results were observed after India's Minister of Finance announced that the Indian government did not view electronic currencies, such as bitcoin, as legal tender and would be aiming to eliminate them, especially given their potential role in criminal activities. Facebook announced that it would be banning adverts for cryptocurrencies.

Many officials have issued warnings, including RBS Chairman, Sir Howard Davies, who told Bloomberg: 'All the authorities can do is put up the sign from Dante's Inferno – "abandon hope all ye who enter here"'.[2] These and other similar announcements by high profile commentators and government officials caused the demand curve for bitcoin to shift to the left and thus depressed the price, as investors became more uncertain about the future of the currency.

Interpreting the bursting of the bitcoin bubble

When a bubble bursts, it is always important to consider how a price fall is interpreted. If people think it is a permanent price fall (or at least a price fall that will be sustained over a long time period) and that further falls will come, then they will rush to sell their bitcoin before it falls any lower. However, this action, an increase in supply, will push prices down further and when these next lot of price falls are observed, more people decide to sell and so it continues. Speculation is destabilising as people believe that prices will continue to fall.

On the other hand, people may view the bubble bursting as a temporary blip – perhaps some are selling to cash in and the expectation is that a new bubble will soon emerge. In this case, when the price does fall, investors do not rush to sell their bitcoin; indeed, some may take the opportunity to invest in it at the slightly lower price. Speculation now is *stabilising*, as the actions help to stabilise the price.

It is impossible to predict when a bubble will burst and how investors will respond to it. It all depends on people's expectations – what do they think will happen? But this, in turn, depends on what people think others are going to do. My expectations depend on other people's expectations, which in turn depend on other people's expectations, which depend on. . .

This is known as a 'Keynesian beauty contest' and, as the name suggests, the future price of bitcoin is very uncertain! The concept of a Keynesian beauty contest is explained in the blog, *A stock market beauty contest of the machines,* on the Sloman Economics News site.

 Find out what has happened to the price of bitcoin over the past year. Have there been more bubbles and if so, have they burst? In each case, think about whether speculation has played a role and whether it was destabilising or stabilising.

[2] See also: https://coinmarketcap.com/currencies/bitcoin/

Definitions

Destabilising speculation A situation where the actions of speculators cause demand and/or supply curves to shift further in the direction they are currently shifting. This amplifies price changes.

Stabilising speculation A situation where the actions of speculators cause demand and/or supply curves to shift in the opposite direction from which they have recently shifted. This causes price to change back again.

BOX 2.5 **MARKET INTERVENTION**

How might governments set about changing the price of a product?

Over the decades, there has been a general shift across the world to free markets. However, sometimes the free-market price may not be seen as the 'best' price and governments may wish to adjust that price. Here, we look at some ways in which governments around the world have intervened either to lower the price of a particular product or to raise it.

Minimum pricing

If the government feels that the current price is too low, it may set a *minimum price* (or price floor) *above* the equilibrium price. This will create a surplus, as illustrated in Figure (a). Normally, a surplus would be eliminated by a fall in price, but with the price not allowed to fall, the surplus remains.

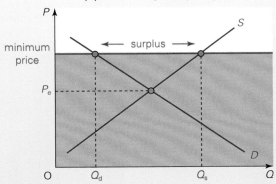

(a) Minimum price: price floor

Minimum unit pricing for alcohol

One market where a system of minimum price controls has been extensively discussed is that of alcohol, but only a few countries have implemented one, including Canada and more recently Scotland. In Canada, different provinces have different policies, but the empirical evidence analysing the effects from this minimum pricing policy is very positive. In Saskatchewan, evidence suggests that a 10 per cent rise in alcohol prices leads to an 8 per cent fall in consumption.[1] Many other pieces of research also indicate the benefits of a minimum price, including a paper that considered 33 studies, which found that 'price-based alcohol policy interventions such as MUP are likely to reduce alcohol consumption, alcohol-related morbidity and mortality'.[2]

Minimum pricing on alcohol had been discussed for many years in the UK, with estimates by the Royal College of Physicians suggesting that the total cost of excessive drinking is £6 billion, half of which is directly related to higher costs for the NHS. Following the Scottish government's successful legal battle in 2017, the UK Supreme Court ruled that a minimum price on alcohol was legal and on 1 May 2018, a 50p per unit minimum price was imposed in Scotland. It is still too early to tell the effect of this minimum price, but NHS Scotland will be evaluating it on an ongoing basis, though many are already suggesting that 50p is too low.

1 Nick Triggle, 'The Battle over alcohol pricing', *BBC News* (30 January 2013).

2 Denis Campbell, 'Minimum alcohol pricing cuts serious crime, study reveals', *The Observer* (28 June 2015).

Critics of the minimum price policy continue to argue that it will be ineffective, because those at whom it is primarily aimed (binge drinkers) will be largely unresponsive to the higher price, due to their inelastic demand. Instead, it would be the 'sensible' drinkers who suffer from having to pay a higher price on alcohol. Furthermore, there are concerns that it will adversely affect pubs and small supermarkets. It will take time to see how effective the minimum price in Scotland will be and what impact, if any, it has on the drinks industry.

Maximum pricing

When a price is set below the equilibrium, it is known as a *maximum price* (or price ceiling). In this case, a shortage will emerge, as the quantity demanded will exceed the quantity supplied, as shown in Figure (b). Again, the shortage will remain, as the price is not allowed to rise to eliminate the shortage.

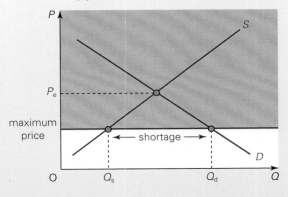

(b) Maximum price: price ceiling

The housing market

One market where we have seen maximum prices is housing and particularly in the rental sector, where governments intervene to keep rents below a particular level. In 1943, New York City introduced rent controls and although the number of properties where this policy still applies has fallen, it remains the longest running rent control policy in the USA, with approximately 38 000 apartments and 2 million residents affected.

A key objective of this policy is to ensure that the stock of affordable housing is maintained and to prevent landlords

Definitions

Minimum price A price floor set by the government or some other agency. The price is not allowed to fall below this level (although it is allowed to rise above it).

Maximum price A price ceiling set by the government or some other agency. The price is not allowed to rise above this level (although it is allowed to fall below it).

▶

from exploiting low-income tenants. Carl Weisbrod, Chairman of the New York City planning commission, said:

> . . . [rent regulation] is essential for the future of the city, for its economic goals, for social equality to make a city attractive and available for all, rich, poor and middle class.[3]

Berlin became the first city in Germany to make rent controls a reality for new and existing tenants. Landlords are not permitted to charge more than 10 per cent above the local average rental value. This policy aimed to address housing shortages in the market and keep the city affordable for low-income households.[4]

Critics of such rent controls argue that they interfere with the efficient allocation of resources by reducing the quantity and quality of housing and removing the incentive for landlords to make improvements. In terms of Figure (b), keeping the rent below the equilibrium creates a shortage of rental accommodation.

Taxes on goods

If governments want to increase prices, another option is to impose a tax. When a tax is imposed it shifts the supply curve upwards by the amount of the tax, since the tax is a cost to the producers. This, in turn, causes a movement up along the demand curve, pushing up price. This is illustrated in Figure (c).

(c) A tax on a product

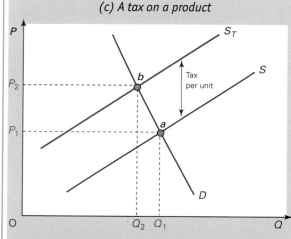

Assume that the tax is a fixed amount per unit. This is shown by the vertical distance between the original supply curve (S) and the supply curve after the imposition of the tax (S_T). The tax pushes price up from P_1 to P_2. Notice, however, that price does not rise by the full amount of the tax, because the demand curve is downward sloping. In other words, not all of the tax will

be passed on to consumers – the producers will have to absorb some of it. The more elastic the demand, the less the price will rise, and the more producers will have to absorb the tax.

Fat and sugar taxes

With the growing problem of obesity and over-consumption of fatty and sugary products, countries have been considering how best to address such issues. In October 2011, Denmark introduced a 'fat tax' designed to reduce consumption of products high in saturated fat (see the blog post, *Taxing fatty products,* on the Sloman Economics News site).

Although the tax did raise more revenue than expected, this also meant that consumption of the fatty products continued, with many consumers simply buying the products from Germany and Sweden. Furthermore, the tax was administratively costly and approximately 1300 Danish jobs were lost. The tax was also controversial, as it hurt the poor more than the rich and was thus 'regressive' and so after only 15 months, the controversial policy was abolished.[5]

In April 2018, the UK introduced a tax on sugary drinks[6] which increased the price per litre on drinks containing above 5g of sugar per 100ml (see the blog, *A soft target for a tax,* on the Sloman Economics News site). This policy meant that the UK joined a select group of nations with similar taxes, such as Mexico, France and Norway.

When the tax was announced in 2016, many soft-drink manufacturers were unhappy with the policy, claiming that it would be the consumers who would suffer with higher prices. The tax was forecast to raise £500 million, but following drink-manufacturers reducing the sugar content in advance of the tax, the forecast tax revenue was more than halved. According to HMRC, from its introduction up to October 2018, the tax has raised £153.8 million.[7] The impact on the consumption of high-sugar drinks and the eventual impact on obesity will take much more time to observe.

1. What methods could be used by the government to deal with:
   (a) the surpluses that result from minimum price controls?
   (b) the shortages that result from maximum price controls?

2. How are price elasticity of demand and supply relevant in the context of minimum/maximum price controls and taxes?

Undertake desktop research to examine moves in various countries to introduce minimum unit pricing for alcohol. How do the measures, or proposals, compare? Discuss which are likely to be more effective.

[3] Rupert Neate and Lisa O'Carroll, 'New York's rent controls: essential for the future of the city', *The Guardian* (19 August 2015).
[4] Ruby Russell, 'Berlin becomes first Germany city to make rent cap a reality', *The Guardian* (1 June 2015).
[5] Christopher Snowdon, 'Denmark's fat tax disaster – the proof of the pudding' *Institute of Economic Affairs* (25 May 2013).
[6] 'Sugar tax surprise in Budget, but growth forecasts cut', *BBC News* (16 March 2016).
[7] 'Soft Drinks Industry Levy Statistics'; HMRC (October 2018).

RECAP

1. Price elasticity of demand measures the responsiveness of the quantity demanded to a change in price. It is defined as the proportionate (or percentage) change in quantity demanded divided by the proportionate (or percentage) change in price.

2. Given that demand curves are downward sloping, price elasticity of demand will be negative.

3. If quantity demanded changes proportionately more than price, the figure for elasticity will be greater than 1 (ignoring the sign): it is elastic. If the quantity demanded changes proportionately less than price, the figure for elasticity will be less than 1: it is inelastic. If they change by the same proportion, the elasticity has a value of 1: it is unit elastic.

4. Demand will be more elastic the greater the number and closeness of substitute goods, the greater the proportion of income spent on the good and the longer the time period that elapses after the change in price.

5. When the demand for a firm's product is price elastic, a rise in price will lead to a reduction in consumer expenditure on the good and hence to a reduction in the total revenue of producers.

6. When demand is price inelastic, however, a rise in price will lead to an increase in total expenditure and revenue.

7. Income elasticity of demand measures the responsiveness of demand to a change in income. For normal goods it has a positive value. Demand will be more income elastic the more luxurious the good.

8. Cross-price elasticity of demand measures the responsiveness of demand for one good to a change in the price of another. For substitute goods the value will be positive; for complements it will be negative. The cross-price elasticity will be greater the closer the two goods are as substitutes or complements.

9. Price elasticity of supply measures the responsiveness of supply to a change in price. It has a positive value. Supply will be more elastic the less costs per unit rise as output rises and the longer the time period.

QUESTIONS

1. Referring to Table 2.1, assume that there are 200 consumers in the market. Of these, 100 have schedules like Tracey's and 100 have schedules like Darren's. What would be the total market demand schedule for potatoes now?

2. Refer to the list of determinants of demand (see page 30). For what reasons might the demand for sofas from a particular outlet, such as DFS, fall? Is the slow recovery from recession relevant here?

3. Why do the prices of fresh strawberries fall when they are in season? Could an individual producer prevent the price from falling?

4. Refer to the list of determinants of supply (see pages 33–4). For what reasons might (a) the supply of potatoes fall; (b) the supply of leather rise?

5. This question is concerned with the supply of oil for central heating. In each case consider whether there is a movement along the supply curve (and in which direction) or a shift in it (and whether left or right): (a) new oil fields start up in production; (b) the demand for central heating rises; (c) the price of gas falls; (d) oil companies anticipate an upsurge in the demand for central heating oil; (e) the demand for petrol rises; (f) new technology decreases the costs of oil refining; (g) all oil products become more expensive.

6. The price of cod is much higher today than it was 30 years ago. Using demand and supply diagrams, explain why this should be so.

7. What will happen to the equilibrium price and quantity of butter in each of the following cases? You should state whether demand or supply or both have shifted and in which direction: (a) a rise in the price of margarine; (b) a rise in the demand for yoghurt; (c) a rise in the price of bread; (d) a rise in the demand for bread; (e) an expected increase in the price of butter in the near future; (f) a tax on butter production; (g) the invention of a new, but expensive, process of removing all cholesterol from butter, plus the passing of a law which states that butter producers must use this process. In each case assume that other things remain the same.

8. The weekly demand and supply schedules for red dresses (in millions) in a free market are as follows:

    (a) What is the equilibrium price and quantity?
    (b) If there is a change in fashion that causes demand for red dresses to rise by 4 million at each price, what will be the new equilibrium price and quantity? Has the equilibrium quantity risen by as much as the increase in demand? Explain why or why not.

Price (£)	8	7	6	5	4	3	2	1
Quantity demanded	6	8	10	12	14	16	18	20
Quantity supplied	18	16	14	12	10	8	6	4

9. Why does price elasticity of demand have a negative value, whereas price elasticity of supply has a positive value?

10. Rank the following in ascending order of elasticity: jeans, black Levi jeans, black jeans, black Levi 501 jeans, trousers, outer garments, clothes.

11. Will a general item of expenditure like food or clothing have a price elastic or inelastic demand? Explain.

12. Assume that an iPhone currently sells for £200 and at this quantity, 10 million units are purchased. The price now falls to £170. If the price elasticity of demand (using the formula: percentage change in quantity demanded/percentage change in price) is calculated to be −1.5, by how many units will the quantity demanded increase?

13. Explain which of these two pairs is likely to have the higher cross-price elasticity of demand: two brands of coffee, or coffee and tea?

14. Would a firm want demand for its brand to be more or less elastic? How might a firm achieve this?

15. Why are both the price elasticity of demand and the price elasticity of supply likely to be greater in the long run?

Demand and the consumer

If a business is to be successful, it must be able to predict the strength of demand for its products and be able to respond quickly to any changes in consumer tastes. It will also want to know how its customers are likely to react to changes in its price or its competitors' prices, or to changes in income. In other words, it will want to know the price, cross-price and income elasticities of demand for its product. The better the firm's knowledge of its market, the better will it be able to plan its output to meet demand, and the more able it will be to choose its optimum price, product design, marketing campaigns, etc.

3.1 DEMAND AND THE FIRM

In Chapter 2, we saw how prices are determined by the interaction of demand and supply. We distinguished between those markets where firms are price takers and those where firms have some discretion in choosing their price. In perfectly competitive markets, although the *market* demand curve is downward sloping, the demand curve faced by the individual firm will be horizontal. This is illustrated in Figure 3.1.

The market price is P_m. The individual firm can sell as much as it likes at this market price, but it is too small to have any influence on the market – it is a price taker. It will not force the price down by producing more because, in terms of the total market, this extra output would be an

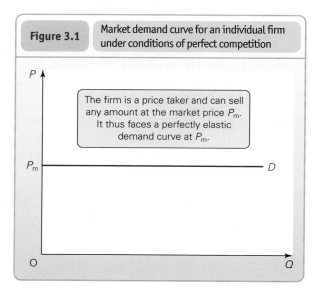

Figure 3.1 Market demand curve for an individual firm under conditions of perfect competition

The firm is a price taker and can sell any amount at the market price P_m. It thus faces a perfectly elastic demand curve at P_m.

infinitesimally small amount. If an individual farmer doubled the output of wheat sent to the market, it would be far too tiny an increase to affect the world price of wheat!

In practice, however, most firms are not price takers; they have some discretion in choosing their price. Such firms face a downward-sloping demand curve. If they raise their price, they will sell less; if they lower their price, they will sell more, as we saw in section 2.2. But firms don't just want to know in which direction quantity will move; they want to know just *how much* the quantity demanded will change and hence they want to know the price elasticity of demand, as we considered in the previous chapter.

It is in a firm's interest to make the demand for its product less elastic, as this gives it greater flexibility to change its price, knowing that demand is relatively unresponsive to a price change. Firms will generally try to do this by attempting to differentiate their product from those of their rivals. If they can produce a product that consumers feel does not have a close substitute, then demand will be relatively inelastic. Success here will depend partly on designing and producing a product that is clearly different, and partly on achieving an effective marketing and advertising programme.

3.2 UNDERSTANDING CONSUMER BEHAVIOUR

In this section, we examine the nature of consumer behaviour and in particular relate consumer demand to the amount of satisfaction that consumers get from products.

Marginal utility

When you buy something, it is normally because you want it. You want it because you expect to get pleasure, satisfaction or some other sort of benefit from it. This applies to everything from chocolate bars, to bus journeys, to calculators, to jeans, to insurance. Economists use the term 'utility' to refer to the benefit or satisfaction we get from consumption. As an illustration, you can read about the utility from watching football in the blog, *The Leicester effect: the impact on the preparedness to pay to watch the EPL*, on the Sloman Economics News site.

An important concept for helping understand the nature of demand is *marginal utility (MU)*. This is the additional utility you get from consuming an *extra* unit of a product. For example, we might refer to the marginal utility (or extra satisfaction) that a consumer gains from a second slice of pizza or a fifth slice. Clearly, the nature and amount of utility that people get varies from one product to another, and from one person to another, but there is a simple rule that applies to virtually all people and all products: *the principle of diminishing marginal utility* (Key idea 11). For example, the second cup of tea in the morning gives you less additional satisfaction than the first cup. The third cup gives less still.

KEY IDEA 11 *The principle of diminishing marginal utility.* As you consume more of a product, and thus become more satisfied, so your desire for additional units of it will decline.

Pause for thought

Are there any goods or services where consumers do not experience diminishing marginal utility? If so, give some examples. If not, then explain why.

This rule states that the marginal utility will fall as we consume more of a product over a given period of time. This doesn't mean that the *total utility (TU)* you get from consuming all units of a commodity falls, but that each *additional* unit adds less and less to your total satisfaction.

Definitions

Marginal utility (*MU*) The extra satisfaction gained from consuming one extra unit of a good within a given time period.

Total utility (*TU*) The total satisfaction a consumer gets from the consumption of all the units of a good consumed within a given time period.

But how do we measure utility? You would need to know this to understand how much of a good consumers should buy in order to make the best use of their limited income. But measuring utility is problematic. After all, we cannot get inside each other's heads to find out just how much pleasure we are getting from consuming a product!

One way round the problem is to measure marginal utility in money terms, i.e. the amount that a person would be prepared to pay for one more unit of a product. Thus if you were prepared to pay 70p for an extra packet of crisps per week, then we would say that your marginal utility from consuming it is 70p. As long as you are prepared to pay more (or the same) as the actual price, you will buy an extra packet. If you are not prepared to pay that price, you will not.

Consumer surplus

The demand curve shows how much consumers are prepared to pay for a given quantity of a good. Yet, quite often, we do not have to pay that full amount. For example, if a packet of crisps costs 60p, but you were prepared to pay 70p, you don't offer the shop-keeper 70p, but pay the 60p to buy the crisps. You then benefit from having 10p left in your pocket! The difference between what you were willing to pay (70p) and the price you actually paid (60p) is known as the *consumer surplus* (10p, in this case).

Marginal utility and the demand curve for a good

We can now see how marginal utility relates to a downward-sloping demand curve. As the price of a good falls, it is worth buying extra units, as the price will now be below the amount you are prepared to pay: i.e. price is less than your marginal utility.

But as you buy more, your marginal utility from consuming each extra unit will get less and less. How many extra units do you buy? You will stop when the marginal utility has fallen to the new lower price of the

good: when $MU = P$. Beyond that point it is not worth buying any more. This represents the optimal consumption point, as *rational* consumers will aim to maximise their consumer surplus. Many factors will affect an individual's utility, as is discussed in the blog from the Sloman Economics News site: *Peak stuff*.

An individual's demand curve

Individuals' demand curves for any good are the same as their marginal utility curves for that good, measured in money.

This is demonstrated in Figure 3.2, which shows the marginal utility curve for a particular person and a particular good. The downward-sloping nature of the curve illustrates diminishing marginal utility.

If the price of the good were P_1, the person would consume Q_1: where $MU = P$. Thus point *a* would be one point on that person's demand curve. If the price fell to P_2, consumption would rise to Q_2, since this is where $MU = P_2$. Thus point *b* is a second point on the demand curve. Likewise, if price fell to P_3, Q_3 would be consumed. Point *c* is a third point on the demand curve.

Thus, as long as individuals aim to maximise consumer surplus and so consume where $P = MU$, their demand curve will be along the same line as their marginal utility curve.

The firm's demand curve

The firm's demand curve will simply be the (horizontal) sum of all individuals' demand curves for its product.

The shape of the demand curve. The price elasticity of demand will reflect the rate at which MU diminishes. If there are close substitutes for a good, it is likely to have an elastic demand, and its MU will diminish slowly as consumption increases. The reason is that increased consumption of this product will be accompanied by

Definitions

Consumer surplus The difference between how much a consumer is willing to pay for a good and how much they actually pay for it.

Rational consumer behaviour When consumers weigh up the marginal utility they expect to gain from a product they are considering purchasing against the product's price (i.e. the marginal cost to them). By buying more of a product whose marginal utility exceeds the price and buying less of a product whose price exceeds marginal utility, the consumer will maximise consumer surplus.

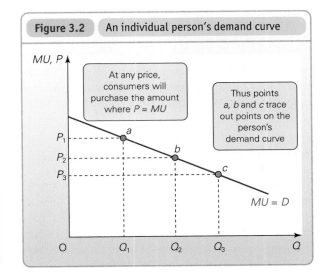

| Figure 3.2 | An individual person's demand curve |

At any price, consumers will purchase the amount where $P = MU$

Thus points *a*, *b* and *c* trace out points on the person's demand curve

$MU = D$

decreased consumption of the alternative product(s). Since total consumption of this product plus the alternatives has increased only slightly (if at all), the marginal utility will fall only slowly.

For example, the demand for a given brand of petrol is likely to have a fairly high price elasticity, since other brands are substitutes. If there is a cut in the price of Esso petrol (assuming the prices of other brands stay constant), consumption of Esso will increase a lot. The *MU* of Esso petrol will fall slowly, since people consume less of other brands. Petrol consumption *in total* may be only slightly greater and hence the *MU* of petrol only slightly lower.

Shifts in the demand curve. How do *shifts* in demand relate to marginal utility? For example, how would the marginal utility of (and hence demand for) margarine be affected by a rise in the price of butter? The higher price of butter would cause less butter to be consumed. This would increase the marginal utility of margarine, since if people are using less butter, their desire for margarine is higher. The *MU* curve (and hence the demand curve) for margarine thus shifts to the right.

The problem of imperfect information

So far, we have assumed that when people buy goods and services, they know exactly what price they will pay and how much utility they will gain. In many cases this is a reasonable assumption. When you buy a bar of chocolate, you clearly do know how much you are paying for it and have a very good idea how much you will like it. But what about a television, medicine, a car, a washing machine, or any other *consumer durable*? In each of these cases you are buying something that will last you a long time and/or that you only buy occasionally; and the further into the future you look, the less certain you will be of its costs and benefits to you. The problem of imperfect information is considered in the blog, *When it's a pain choosing the right painkiller* on the Sloman Economics News site.

Consider buying a laptop, costing you £400. If you pay cash, your immediate outlay involves no uncertainty: it is £400. But laptops can go wrong. After a couple of years, you could have a repair bill of £100.

This cannot be predicted and yet it is a price you will have to pay, just like the original £400. In other words, when you buy the laptop, you are uncertain as to the full 'price' it will entail over its lifetime.

Just as the costs of the laptop are uncertain, so too are the benefits. You might have been attracted to buy it by an online advert or by a salesperson in the shop. When you have used it for a while, however, you will probably discover things you had not anticipated. Perhaps it takes a long time to download files, struggles to find internet connections or keeps restarting. Or perhaps it has unexpected positive features, such as good speakers. The market does work to provide information, for example through customer feedback on websites, but while this can help to reduce customer uncertainty, it will not eliminate it.

Buying consumer durables thus involves uncertainty. So too does the purchase of assets, whether a physical asset such as a house or financial assets such as shares. In the case of assets, the uncertainty is over their future *price*. If you buy shares in a currently profitable company, what will happen to their price in the future? Will they shoot up in price, thus enabling you to sell them at a large profit, or will they fall? You cannot know for certain. A lot depends on the company's future performance and what other people think that performance is likely to be.

At this point, it is useful to distinguish between uncertainty and risk. *Risk* is where an outcome may or may not occur, but where the *probability* of it occurring is known. *Uncertainty* is where the probability is not known.

Insurance: a way of removing risks

Insurance is a means of eliminating, or at least reducing, risk for people. If, for example, you could lose your job if you are injured, you can remove the risk of loss of income by taking out an appropriate insurance policy. Typically, people don't like risk and so most people are willing to pay to take out insurance.

But why is it that the insurance companies are prepared to shoulder the risks that their customers were not? Do they simply love risk? Definitely not! The answer is that the insurance company is able to *spread its risks*.

Definitions

Consumer durable A consumer good that lasts a period of time, during which the consumer can continue gaining utility from it.

Risk This is when an outcome may or may not occur, but where the probability of its occurring is known.

Uncertainty This is when an outcome may or may not occur and where the probability of its occurring is not known.

Spreading risks (for an insurance company) The more policies an insurance company issues and the more independent the risks of claims from these policies are, the more predictable will be the number of claims.

BOX 3.1	ROGUE TRADERS

Buyer beware!

Markets are usually an efficient way of letting buyers and sellers exchange goods and services. However, this does not stop consumers making complaints about the quality of the goods or services they receive. Furthermore, particular sectors seem to receive a significantly higher number of complaints and seem to be more vulnerable to 'rogue traders'. According to the Ombudsman Service's 2017 Annual Review, the retail sector received the largest share of complaints (25%), followed by so-called 'grudge purchases' (i.e. things you have to have), such as energy (12%), telecoms (11%) and transport (9%).[1]

Between 1 July and 20 September 2018, econsumer.gov received 7941 complaints from around the world and of these, 4794 (over 60%) related to shop at home/catalogue sales, followed by 615 (8%) to imposters from government or business.[2] The data also indicate that American consumers are the most likely to complain, followed by consumers in France and India and it is Chinese companies which receive the most complaints, with US and UK ones in second and third place.

But, why do markets, which you would think would need to be responsive to consumer wishes, give rise to consumer complaints? Why is it that rogue traders can continue in business?

Adverse selection and moral hazard

The concepts of adverse selection and moral hazard provide answers to these questions. In both cases, the problem is essentially one of 'information asymmetries' and is an example of the 'principal–agent problem' (see pages 9–10). The buyer (the 'principal') has poorer information about the product than the agent (the 'seller').

Information asymmetries. The potential for an information 'gap' between buyers and sellers, and hence for more complaints, is far greater in the market for some types of goods than others. For example, I know what different types of bread should look and taste like and how much I like them. If I buy a loaf from a market trader, but then return it if it is mouldy, I am likely to get a refund, otherwise the trader's sales will be affected by bad publicity. Here information asymmetries are minimal.

However, where the product is more complex or it is an 'experience good', such as eating out in a restaurant, going on holiday, or studying a degree at university, there may be a significant 'information gap'. This creates greater scope for deception and fraud, allowing rogue traders to thrive. In these situations, the number of consumer complaints increases.

Consider the sale of a conservatory. A product such as this involves an expensive outlay for consumers, but they may have very limited information about the price of materials and labour, as well as the method of building a conservatory.

Assume that there is a standard-sized conservatory and that a high-quality seller would be prepared to supply this product at a price of £10 000. Such a price would reflect the quality of their work and would keep them in the business of selling high-quality products. On the other hand, assume that a poor-quality supplier, a 'rogue trader', could provide this conservatory at £5000.

Given information asymmetry, let us assume that consumers are not aware of who is a high-quality or low-quality seller. As a result, rogue traders offer to supply a standard conservatory for, say, £9000.

Adverse selection. This price of £9000, however, is not enough to cover the costs of high-quality sellers, and so they will not want to offer their services to build high-quality conservatories. On the other hand, 'rogue traders' will find this price very profitable and it will attract a higher than normal number of such sellers into the market. Of course, if consumers know that the only sellers in the market are likely to be 'rogue traders', they will not buy conservatories and the market will collapse.

The problem just described is an example of *adverse selection*. In this case a group of sellers ('rogue traders') have been attracted to the market by prices considerably greater than their costs even before any transactions have taken place.

> **KEY IDEA 12**
>
> *Adverse selection.* Where information is imperfect, high-risk/poor-quality groups will be attracted to profitable market opportunities to the disadvantage of the average buyer (or seller).

Although information is imperfect, things aren't as bad as the above suggests. Consumers do try to find out about sellers before they buy and most consumers get a good product. However, 'rogue traders' also make sales. The poorer the information on the part of consumers, the more adverse will be their selection: the worse the likely quality of the products they buy.

George Akerlof published a paper in the 1970s that considered the problem of asymmetric information in the market for used-cars in his paper entitled 'The Market for Lemons'.[3] In this paper, he set out the problem that asymmetric information presents to consumers. He demonstrated how it can, in extreme circumstances, lead to the total unravelling of a market, as second-hand car dealers consistently try to sell poor quality cars (or 'lemons') as 'reliable' ones and as consumers, unable to distinguish poor quality cars from good ones, become increasingly mistrustful.

Moral hazard. This is another problem that arises from asymmetric information. This occurs once a contract has been

> ### Definition
>
> **Adverse selection** Where information is imperfect, high-risk/poor-quality groups will be attracted to profitable market opportunities to the disadvantage of the average buyer (or seller).

---

[1] 'Making a difference together', *Annual Review 2017*, Ombudsman Services.

[2] 'Top complaint categories for econsumer.gov: July 1–30 September 2018', econsumer.gov

[3] G. Akerlof, 'The Market for "Lemons": Quality, Uncertainty and the Market Mechanism', *The Quarterly Journal of Economics* vol. 84, no. 3. (August 1970).

►

signed and is known as ***moral hazard***. In our example, the rogue trader might initially agree to supply and install the conservatory to meet particular high standards of quality for a particular price. However, unless the buyer has full information about the construction of conservatories or can keep a constant watch over the work, defective materials or poor-quality workmanship may be supplied. But the buyer will not know this until a later date when problems start to appear with the conservatory!

Moral hazard results because the seller has acted inappropriately (immorally) and to the detriment of the buyer. The 'hazard' arises because of imperfect information on the part of the consumer. Rogue traders are tempted to supply an inferior product, believing that they can get away with it.

KEY IDEA 13

Moral hazard. Following a deal, if there are information asymmetries (see pages 9–10), it is likely that one party will engage in problematic (immoral and/or hazardous) behaviour to the detriment of the other. In other words, lack of information by one party to the deal may result in the deal not being honoured by the other party.

Usually, the process of law would work in favour of the buyer because a contract had been established, but in many cases involving rogue traders the business has been declared bankrupt or the costs to buyers of pursuing a legal case are too great.

Solutions

So how can sellers signal to buyers that they offer high-quality products? And how can consumers trust this information? A number of methods exist.

Establishing a reputation. A single firm can establish a reputation for selling high-quality goods, usually over a number of years, by word of mouth or, perhaps, by creating a valued brand name through advertising. Many online sites now exist where consumers can rate their satisfaction with various services, such as TripAdvisor, Yelp and Angie's List. Other companies, such as eBay and Amazon have built-in feedback mechanisms for customers, and their success is, in part, attributable to this feature.

A survey commissioned by the Competition and Markets Authority[4] found that 54 per cent of adults read on-line reviews. It estimated that £23 billion of consumer spending in the UK was influenced by these reviews. A 2017 study in the USA[5] found that 97 per cent of customers read on-line reviews when choosing a local business.

Definition

Moral hazard Following a deal, if there are information asymmetries (see page 10), it is likely that one party will engage in problematic (immoral and/or hazardous) behaviour to the detriment of the other. In other words, lack of information by one party to the deal may result in the deal not being honoured by the other party.

Guarantees and warranties. Firms can offer guarantees and warranties on their products; if the product goes wrong, the company will repair, replace or refund you. By offering such warranties, the seller is signalling to consumers that they are selling a high-quality product, as they don't believe that the product will be returned.

Rogue traders are unlikely to offer such guarantees, as their lower-quality product is much more likely to develop a problem, which will be costly for them.

Trade associations and other third parties. Firms can also band together collectively and establish a trade association. Examples include the Federation of Master Builders or the Association of British Travel Agents (ABTA). The trade association may provide guarantees for consumers. For example, if one firm provides a poor-quality product, then consumers may get compensation via the association. ABTA, for example, guarantees to make sure customers will complete their holiday, or obtain a refund, if they have purchased it from a member that has gone bankrupt. By encouraging consumers to purchase from member firms, both consumers and firms gain.

Trade associations are a means by which firms can demonstrate that they regulate themselves rather than have governments impose rules on them.

Government intervention. On the whole, recent governments have not liked to intervene in particular industries, preferring a sector to regulate itself or requiring the creation of an ombudsman by law, such as the Financial Ombudsman and the Legal Ombudsman. However, in the case of the financial services industry, the government has directly intervened because the impact of the industry on consumers in recent times has been widespread and financially devastating. Following a number of financial scandals, including the mis-selling of pensions and mortgages, the government replaced ineffective self-regulation in 2000 with the Financial Services Authority (FSA), an independent industry regulator with statutory powers, whose Board was appointed by and accountable to the Treasury. In this instance the level of product complexity and information asymmetry between buyer and seller was viewed to be too great for the industry to control itself.

However, the FSA was widely criticised for failing to do anything to curb the lending boom which led to the financial crisis in 2007 and was abolished in April 2013 and replaced by the Financial Conduct Authority (FCA) and the Prudential Regulation Authority (PRA) (a division of the Bank of England), which between them have greater powers. (See section 9.5 for a more general discussion of competition policy and regulation.)

1. *If a car manufacturer offers a full warranty, could this action actually create a problem of moral hazard and/ or adverse selection?*
2. *What are the disadvantages of trade associations?*
3. *The communications sector is one area that receives a high number of complaints. Can we use the concepts of moral hazard and adverse selection to explain why this might be the case?*

Consider a product or service that you have purchased which at some point involved adverse selection or moral hazard. Explain how this influenced your behaviour. Compare your findings with those of other students.

4 *On-line Reviews and Endorsements,* Competition and Markets Authority (June 2015).
5 *Local Consumer Review Survey* (BrightLocal, 2017).

The spreading of risks

If there is a one in ten thousand chance of your house burning down each year, although it is only a small chance it would be so disastrous that you are simply not prepared to take the risk. You thus take out home insurance and are prepared to pay a premium of *more than* 0.01 per cent (one ten thousandth) of the value of your house.

The insurance company, however, is not just insuring you. It is insuring many others at the same time. If your house burns down, there will be approximately 9999 others that do not. The premiums the insurance company has collected will be more than enough to cover the insurance pay-out it must make to the unlucky homeowner. The more houses it insures, the smaller will be the variation in the proportion that actually burn down each year.

This is an application of the *law of large numbers*. What is unpredictable for an individual becomes highly predictable in the mass. The more people the insurance company insures, the more predictable is the total outcome.

What is more, the insurance company will be in a position to estimate just what the risks are. It can thus work out what premiums it must charge in order to make a profit. With individuals, however, the precise risk is rarely known. Do you know your chances of living to 80? Almost certainly you do not. But a life assurance company will know precisely the chances of a person of your age, sex and occupation living to 80! It will have the statistical data for an average person to show this information. In other words, an insurance company will be able to convert your *uncertainty* into their *risk*.

> ### Pause for thought
> *Explain why an insurance company could not pool the risk of flooding in a particular part of the country. Does your answer imply insurance against flooding is unobtainable?*

The spreading of risks does not just require that there should be a large number of policies. It also requires that the risks should be *independent*. If any insurance company insured 1000 houses *all in the same neighbourhood,* and then there was a major fire in the area, the claims would be enormous. The risks of fire were not independent. The company would, in fact, have been taking a gamble on a single event. If, however, it provides fire insurance for houses scattered all over the country, the risks *are* independent.

An example of the problem presented by risks which are *not* independent is the widespread flooding experienced in the UK in 2012 and 2015 and in Townsville, Australia, in January/February 2019, as discussed in a *Brisbane Times* article.[1] Damage assessment reports identified 2063 properties with minor damage, 1101 with moderate damage and 135 with severe damage. Shortly after the Townsville flood, some 14 000 insurance claims had been lodged, amounting to AU$165 million, and hardship payments totalling over $4 million had been made to over 23 000 residents. Many policyholders faced uncertainty as to whether the insurance companies would pay out, due to issues with what is covered under their policy. Further concerns related to future premiums and whether they would now have to rise in response to the flood. The problem is that the risks of flood damage are *dependent*: if one household in an area prone to flooding claims for flood damage, the probability of other houses in that area also claiming is pretty high, if not certain. The Mayor of Townsville, Jenny Hill said that '. . . north Queenslanders would not accept unfair premium rises following the floods', but the ICA Communications Manager noted that 'Any talk of premium rises is premature'.[2]

> ### Pause for thought
> *How would an insurance company establish a 'fair' premium for flood damage?*

Insurance companies also tend to offer a diverse range of insurance (houses, cars, travel, health, life) and this *diversification* allows the company to spread its risk: this time across many products. The more types of insurance a company offers, the greater is likely to be the independence of the risks.

> ### Definitions
> **Law of large numbers** The larger the number of events of a particular type, the more predictable will be their average outcome.
>
> **Independent risks** Where two risky events are unconnected. The occurrence of one will not affect the likelihood of the occurrence of the other.
>
> **Diversification** Where a firm expands into new types of business.

---

[1] Felicity Caldwell, 'Insurance companies are urged to treat flood victims with compassion', *Brisbane Times* (10 February 2019).
[2] Christine Flatley, 'Townsville flood insurance bill hits $80m', *Star News* (6 February 2019).

BOX 3.2 PROBLEMS FOR UNWARY INSURANCE COMPANIES

'Adverse selection' and 'moral hazard'

In Box 3.1, we saw how consumers may suffer from adverse selection and from moral hazard on the part of suppliers. Adverse selection and moral hazard can also apply the other way around. Insurance companies may incur higher costs from adverse selection and moral hazard on the part of certain policyholders. These higher costs are then likely to be passed on to other policyholders.

Adverse selection

This occurs where the people taking out insurance are those who pose the highest risk.

For example, suppose that a company offers medical insurance. It surveys the population and works out that the average person requires £200 of treatment per year. The company thus sets the premium at £250 (the extra £50 to cover its costs and provide a profit). But it is likely that the people most likely to take out the insurance are those most likely to fall sick: those who have been ill before, those whose families have a history of illness, those in jobs that are hazardous to health, etc. These people on average may require £500 of treatment per year, but the insurance company doesn't know this. The insurance company would soon make a loss.

But cannot the company then simply raise premiums to £550 or £600? It can, but the problem is that it will thereby be depriving the person of *average* health of reasonably priced insurance and thus may discourage some people from taking out insurance. Those who drop out are likely to be the healthier people and hence the insurance company is left insuring a less healthy group of people. Perhaps now the average person taking out insurance requires £250 of treatment per year and thus premiums must rise to £300. This discourages more people from taking out insurance and again the healthier drop out, meaning premiums must rise once more. And so it goes on, with the less healthy consumers 'adversely selecting' into the market, pushing up premiums and, in extreme cases, causing markets to disappear.

The answer is for the company to discriminate more carefully between people. You may have to fill out a questionnaire so that the company can assess your own particular risk and set an appropriate premium. There may need to be legal penalties for people caught lying!

1. *What details does an insurance company require to know before it will insure a person to drive a car?*

Moral hazard

This occurs where having insurance makes you less careful and thus increases your risk to the insurance company. For example, if your bicycle is insured against theft, you may be less concerned to go through the hassle of chaining it up each time you leave it.

Again, if insurance companies work out risks by looking at the *total* number of bicycle thefts, these figures will understate the risks to the company because they will include thefts from *uninsured* people who are likely to be more careful.

The problem of moral hazard occurs in many other walks of life. A good example is that of debt. If someone else is willing to pay your debts (e.g. your parents) it is likely to make you less careful in your spending! This argument has been used by some rich countries for not cancelling the debts of poor countries.

2. *How will the following reduce moral hazard?*
   (a) *A no-claims bonus.*
   (b) *Your having to pay the first so much of any claim.*
   (c) *Offering lower premiums to those less likely to claim (e.g. lower house contents premiums for those with burglar alarms).*

First, research the various types of insurance products available. Second, identify possible adverse selection and moral hazard issues arising with these various types of insurance and the ways in which insurers attempt to address them.

RECAP

1. Economists call consumer satisfaction 'utility'. Marginal utility diminishes as consumption increases over any given period of time.

2. People will consume more of a good as long as its marginal utility to them (measured in terms of the price they are prepared to pay for it) exceeds its price. They will stop buying additional amounts once MU has fallen to equal the price. The difference between what they are willing to pay for a product and what they actually pay for it is called the consumer surplus.

3. An individual's demand curve lies along the same line as the individual's marginal utility curve, when a consumer maximises consumer surplus. The market demand curve is the sum of all individuals' marginal utility curves.

4. When people buy consumer durables, they may be uncertain of their benefits and any additional repair and maintenance costs. When they buy financial assets, they may be uncertain of what will happen to their price in the future. Buying under these conditions of imperfect knowledge is therefore a form of gambling. When we take such gambles, if we know the odds we are said to be operating under conditions of *risk*. If we do not know the odds we are said to be operating under conditions of *uncertainty*.

5. Insurance is a way of eliminating risks for policyholders. People are prepared to pay premiums in order to obtain insurance and avoid risk. Insurance companies are prepared to take on these risks because they can spread them over a large number of policies. According to the law of large numbers, what is unpredictable for a single policyholder becomes highly predictable for a large number of them, provided that their risks are independent.

3.3 BEHAVIOURAL ECONOMICS

Up to now we have assumed that consumers behave rationally – trying to get the best value for money by making choices between products that will maximise their consumer surplus (see page 57). However, a moment's thought leads to examples of behaviour that do not appear 'rational'. For example, have you ever bought something simply because others were buying it? The answer is probably 'yes'! 'Behavioural economics' relaxes the rationality assumption and looks at the way people *actually* behave.

Behavioural economics recognises that people are subject to emotions and impulses, which can result in 'errors' and biases in their decision making. By understanding how people actually behave, firms can target their marketing strategies to influence this behaviour. Irrational shopping is discussed in the blog *Are impulses irrational?* on the Sloman Economics News site. This field of economics has developed rapidly over the past twenty-five years and in October 2017 Richard Thaler won the Nobel Prize in Economics for his work in the area.[3]

Explaining 'irrational' consumer choices

How options are framed

Traditional economic theory assumes that presenting the same choice to consumers, but in different ways, should have no impact on the outcome of the decision. However, behavioural economics shows us that the choices people make are indeed influenced by the context in which they are made; people will often make different choices when they are presented, or framed, in different ways. For example, people will buy more of a good when it is flagged up as a special offer than they do if there is no mention of an offer, even though the price is the same. This principle has led to the development of 'nudge' theory, which underpins many marketing techniques. We look at it in more detail in Box 3.3 below.

Too much choice

Choice is generally thought to be a good thing and this is what standard economic theory tells us. But can we have too much choice? Choice should allow us to maximise our utility by making 'better' decisions. Yet this does not always seem to be the case. Too much choice can be confusing and hinder decision making, thereby reducing consumers' utility and reducing the likelihood of a purchase being made.

One famous experiment that considered this idea was conducted by Sheena Ivengar and Mark Lepper.[4]

They set up a jam tasting stall in a supermarket and shoppers were invited to sample the jams, encouraged by a $1 voucher towards the purchase of any of the jams they had tasted. Every few hours, the number of varieties of jam was switched from six to 24 and back again. The authors were aiming to see whether shoppers who visited the stall when there were 24 varieties of jam were more or less likely to use the voucher (and hence buy jam) than those who had just six varieties. The experiment found that approximately 30 per cent of shoppers who visited the stall with just six varieties used the vouchers, as opposed to just 3 per cent who visited it when there were 24 varieties. In this case, more choice led to significantly fewer purchases.

Bounded rationality

A person might want to maximise consumer surplus, but faces complex choices and imperfect information. Sometimes it *would* be possible to obtain better information, but the individual decides it is not worth the time and effort, and perhaps expense, of getting more information. This problem inevitably grows with more choice. People's ability to be 'rational' is thus limited or **bounded** by the situation in which they find themselves.

So they may resort to making the best guess, or to drawing on past experiences of similar choices that turned out to be good or bad. It is important for firms to understand the different assumptions people make and their different responses in situations of bounded rationality.

This use of past experience, or rules of thumb or trial and error is known as *heuristics*. The decision is not guaranteed to be optimal, but it might be the best bet given the limited information or time available.

Behavioural economics attempts to identify these heuristics and the systematic errors they sometimes cause. Such methods are useful to those in advertising and marketing, as they provide information as to the most effective ways of influencing people's spending

---

> ### Definitions
>
> **Bounded rationality** When the ability to make rational decisions is limited by lack of information or the time necessary to obtain such information.
>
> **Heuristics** People's use of strategies that draw on simple lessons from past experience when they are faced with similar, although not identical, choices.

---

[3] 'The Prize in Economic Sciences 2017', *Press Release*, The Nobel Prize organisation (9 October 2017).

[4] Sheena S. Ivengar and Mark R. Lepper, 'When choice is demotivating: can one desire too much of a good thing?', *Journal of Personality and Social Psychology* 79, no. 6 (2000), pp. 995–1006.

decisions. For example, a field experiment conducted by Wansink, Kent and Hoch[5] found that people purchased 3.3 cans of soup on average from a grocery store. However, when the researchers placed a sign stating 'There is a limit of 12 per person', the average number of cans purchased increased to seven. The limit appears to have influenced consumers' decisions even though it was irrelevant. Taking advantage of such behaviour can be an effective tool for firms aiming to increase sales.

> **Pause for thought**
>
> *Why might different people respond differently from each other in otherwise similar circumstances?*

Relativity matters

If I am making a choice about buying a car, traditional economics says my demand will derive from a number of factors: my income; my tastes for driving and for particular cars; the prices of the car I am considering and of the alternatives; and the associated costs of motoring. Yet I might also be highly influenced by the car my sister drives; if she chooses an Audi, perhaps I would like a more expensive car – a Mercedes possibly. If she switches to a Jaguar, then perhaps I will opt for a Porsche. I want a better (or faster or more expensive) car than my sister; I am concerned not only with my choice of car but with my *relative* choice.

This does not disprove that our choices depend on our perceived utility. But it does demonstrate that our satisfaction often depends on our consumption *relative* to that of other people, such as our peers. This is something about which the advertising industry is only too aware. Adverts often try to encourage you to buy a product by showing that *other* people are buying it.

Celebrities, in particular, influence what people buy. Recently, there has been much attention on this issue and whether celebrities that post photos or views about a product are actually posting their personal views or if they are being paid to do so. The Competition and Markets Authority (CMA) has received commitments from a number of high-profile celebrities to ensure that they clearly label which products they have been paid to endorse. Andrea Coscelli, the CMA's Chief Executive, said that 'Influencers can have a huge impact on what their fans decide to buy. People could, quite rightly, feel misled if what they thought was a recommendation from someone they admired turns out to be a marketing ploy'.[6]

Herding and 'groupthink'

Being influenced by what other people buy, and thus making relative choices, can lead to herd behaviour. A fashion might catch on; people might grab an item in a sale because other people seem to be grabbing it as well; people might buy a particular share on the stock market because other people are buying it.

Now part of this may simply be bounded rationality. Sometimes it may be a good rule of thumb to buy something that other people want, as they might know more about it than you do. But there is a danger in such behaviour: other people may also be buying it because other people are buying it, and this builds a momentum. Sales may soar and the price may be driven well above a level that reflects the utility that people will end up gaining.

> **Pause for thought**
>
> *Give some examples of mental short-cuts/heuristics that you use when choosing a product or service? Why do you use them?*

Sunk costs

When buying products, 'rational' consumers will weigh up the *additional* benefits and costs of their purchases (i.e. the utility gained against the money spent on the products). This must imply that costs already incurred in the past are irrelevant. These are called sunk costs. Yet when we look at how people actually behave, they do seem to be influenced by sunk costs.

Take the case of a person who spends a lot on a car, which subsequently turns out to be unreliable and requires a lot spending on it to keep it on the road. The rational person would ask whether the large amount spent on repairs and maintenance is worth it and whether it would be better to sell it and buy a new car. But many people would decide not to sell it as they had paid a lot in the first place (a sunk cost) and would rather spend money keeping it on the road.

The point is, if consumers were behaving rationally, they would ignore these sunk costs. They cannot be recouped. Yet many people do behave as if they were *continuing* to pay these costs.

[5] Brian Wansink, Robert J. Kent and Stephen J. Hoch, 'An anchoring and adjustment model of purchase quantity decisions', *Journal of Marketing Research* vol. 35 (February 1998), pp. 71–81.

[6] Celebrities pledge to clean up their act on social media', *Press Release*, Competition and Markets Authority (23 January 2019).

Present bias and self-control

In many cases, the experience of the emotion of desire when contemplating buying something, such as a bar of chocolate, is merely an aid to rational behaviour. You imagine the pleasure you will receive, something that is borne out when you do actually eat the chocolate. Similarly, the emotion of displeasure at the thought of paying for the product helps you to be cautious and think of the cost of buying the product: what will you have to sacrifice? These issues, however, can lead to irrational behaviour, especially if the costs and benefits of purchasing the good occur in different time periods.

For example, many consumers buy things on credit, where the benefits of having the good are immediate, but the cost of paying for it only occurs in the future. This means that many people downplay the costs of the items they buy and are even encouraged to buy things they would never otherwise have bought. No wonder many shops like to offer credit.

Other examples include our purchases of chocolate bars and fatty products: we derive pleasure from them today, but the adverse health effects occur in the future. Going to the gym incurs costs today (the effort), but the health benefits don't occur until the future.

Evidence suggests that the majority of people tend to be impatient most of the time. Traditional models of economic behaviour capture this idea but also predict something else: if someone plans to do something at some point in the future, they will do so when the time arrives. For example, if a consumer plans to shop around for a new energy supplier or a new mobile phone contract when their current deal expires, then they will do it. If they plan to start a diet tomorrow, they do so when tomorrow arrives. This is called **time consistency.**

The only reason time-consistent people would change their mind is if new information became known about the relative size of the costs and benefits of their decisions. For example, you plan to shop around for a new energy supplier, but when your current deal actually expires, the current supplier offers a much better deal than you anticipated. This is still time-consistent behaviour, as the only reason you changed your mind is that information changed. The cost of not switching supplier is much smaller than you thought it was going to be before the current deal expired.

Time consistency seems to predict and explain behaviour reasonably well when all the costs and benefits of a decision occur at the same time, whether now or in the future. A consumer's plan of action often remains the same with the passage of time as long as none of the costs and benefits occur immediately. For example, at 9.00am today you may plan to eat a healthy lunch tomorrow: i.e. you plan to eat a piece of fruit instead of a chocolate muffin. The plan remains the same throughout today and tomorrow morning. However, when lunchtime finally arrives you do not stick to the plan and eat the chocolate muffin instead. What has changed? When lunchtime finally arrives, the costs of not eating the chocolate muffin are now immediate – missing out on the greater enjoyment – but the health benefits are still in the future. Once the time arrives to experience the costs or benefits of a decision, many people have a tendency to change their minds. They act in a time inconsistent manner and suffer from self-control problems.

Behavioural economists refer to this as **present bias.** If people are impatient, they weight costs and benefits that occur sooner more heavily than those that occur later. However, present bias is different from simple impatience. The theory predicts that once any of the costs and benefits are immediate, the relative weighting of these pay-offs over those that occur later becomes much greater. In the previous example, the costs of not eating the chocolate muffin appear to be much greater when it is in front of a consumer! This theory predicts that a consumer can appear both patient when making a decision about the future (i.e. planning to eat healthily when all the costs and benefits occur in the future) and very impatient when making the same decision about a present action (i.e. eating unhealthily now).

Read and van Leeuwen[7] (1998) tested this idea by conducting a field experiment. They approached over 200 employees in their normal place of work and informed them they would return a week later to be given a selection of free snacks. The employees simply had to choose in advance whether they wanted a healthy snack (e.g. a piece of fruit) or an unhealthy snack (e.g. a chocolate bar or a packet of crisps). Seventy-four per cent chose the healthy option.

When the researchers returned a week later with the snacks, the employees were asked for their decision again. However, this was now for immediate consumption and they did not have to stick with the same decision they had made the week before. Seventy per cent of the employees now opted for the unhealthy snack.

Present bias helps to explain why many people have difficulty in sticking to commitments. Think of how many people make and then very quickly break New Year's resolutions!

---

7 Daniel Read and Barbara van Leeuwen, 'Predicting hunger: The effects of appetite and delay on choice', *Organizational Behavior and Human Decision Processes* vol. 76, no. 2 (November 1998), pp. 189–205.

| BOX 3.3 | USING POLICY TO CHANGE BEHAVIOUR |

Nudging people

One observation of behavioural economists is that people make many decisions out of habit. They use simple rules or heuristics, such as: 'I'll buy the more expensive item because it's bound to be better'; or 'I'll buy this item because it's on offer'; or 'I'm happy with Brand X, so why should I change brands?'; or 'Other people are buying this, so it must be worth having'.

Given that people behave like this, how might they be persuaded to change their behaviour? Governments might want to know this when designing policy. What policies will encourage people to stop smoking, or save energy, or take more exercise or eat more healthy food? Firms too will want to know how to sell more of their products or to motivate their workforce. Any successful policy or campaign will therefore need to include appropriate incentives, but what is appropriate depends on how people respond to them. In order to know this, policymakers and firms need to understand people's behaviour. This is one area where behavioural economics has an important role to play.

According to Richard Thaler and Cass Sunstein,[1] people can be 'nudged' to change their behaviour. For example, healthy food can be placed in a prominent position in a supermarket or healthy snacks at the checkout. For many years, chocolate bars, crisps and other unhealthy products were prominently displayed at the supermarket checkout and shoppers would spontaneously pick one up without weighing up the costs and benefits. If fashion houses ceased to use ultra-thin models, it could reduce the incentive for many girls to under-eat. If kids at school are given stars or smiley faces for turning off lights or picking up litter, they might be more inclined to do so. You can read about 'nudging' in the blogs *Nudging for better or for*

worse and *Nudging mainstream economics* on the Sloman Economics News site.

Opting in versus opting out

An interesting example within behavioural economics and how we can influence behaviour concerns 'opting in' versus 'opting out'. In some countries, with organ donor cards, or many company pension schemes or charitable giving, people have to opt in. In other words, they have to make the decision to take part. Many as a result do not, partly because they never seem to find the time to do so, even though they might quite like to. With the busy lives people lead, it's too easy to think, 'Yes, I'll do that some time', but never actually get around to doing it.

With an 'opt-out' system, people are automatically signed up to the scheme, but can freely choose to opt out. Thus, it would be assumed that organs from people killed in an accident who had not opted out could be used for transplants. If you did not want your organs to be used, you would have to join a register. It could be the same with charitable giving. Some firms add a small charitable contribution to the price of their products (e.g. airline tickets or utility bills), unless people opt out. Similarly, under UK pension arrangements introduced from 2012, firms automatically deduct pension contributions from employees' wages unless they opt out of the scheme.

> Opt-in schemes have participation rates of around 60 per cent, while otherwise identical opt-out funds retain between 90 and 95 per cent of employees. It is no wonder that Adair Turner, in his report on pensions, urged legislation to push pension schemes to an opt-out default position and that policy is moving in this direction.[2]

[1] Richard H. Thaler and Cass R. Sunstein, *Nudge: Improving Decisions about Health, Wealth, and Happiness* (Yale University Press, 2008).

[2] Richard Reeves, 'Why a nudge from the state beats a slap', *Observer* (20 July 2008).

RECAP

1. Traditional economics is based on the premise that consumers act rationally, weighing up the costs and benefits of the choices open to them. Behavioural economics acknowledges that real-world decisions do not always appear rational; it seeks to understand and explain what economic agents actually do.

2. A number of effects can explain why rational decision-making may fail to predict actual behaviour. These include: the roles of framing, relativity and groupthink;

individuals failing to disregard sunk costs and being confused by too many choices; and the problem of present bias and self-control. Research undertaken by behavioural economists is bringing together aspects of psychology and economics in order to understand fully how we behave.

3. Government policy is increasingly focused on behavioural economics and introducing appropriate incentives to 'nudge' people to behave in certain ways.

3.4 ESTIMATING AND PREDICTING DEMAND

If a business is to be successful, it must have a good understanding of its market. How might a business set about discovering the wants of consumers and hence the intensity of demand? The more effectively a business can identify such wants, the more likely it is

to increase its sales and be successful. The clearer idea it can gain of the rate at which the typical consumer's utility will decline as consumption increases, the better estimate it can make of the product's price elasticity. Also, the more it can assess the relative

Following the move to automatic enrolment, participation rates in large companies rose from 61 to 83 per cent.

This type of policy can improve the welfare of those who make systematic mistakes (i.e. suffer from present bias), while imposing very limited harm on those who act in a time consistent manner. If it is in the interests of someone to opt out of the scheme, they can easily do so. Policies such as these are an example of what behavioural economists call 'soft paternalism'.

The UK Behavioural Insights Team

Understanding people's behaviour and then adjusting incentives, often only very slightly, can nudge people to behave differently. Politicians are increasingly looking at ways of nudging people to behave in ways that they perceive as better, whether socially, environmentally or simply personally. In the UK, the Coalition government established the Behavioural Insights Team (BIT) (unofficially known as the 'Nudge unit') for this purpose. BIT was partially privatised in 2014 and is now equally owned by the UK Government, the innovation charity, Nesta and the Teams' employees.

A major objective of this team is to use ideas from behavioural economics to design policies that enable people to make better choices for themselves. However, it is not simply a behavioural economics unit. BIT uses research findings from a number of different subject areas such as psychology and marketing science to inform its policy recommendations. In many cases, very simple principles have led to significant changes in behaviour.

For example, things that require less effort will get a higher take-up, as will contacting people in the right way and at the right time. Sending text messages just before a payment is due or just before a form needs to be submitted will increase the response rate. Making it attractive or more social to change behaviour is also a simple principle that informs policy recommendations. When people were informed by HMRC that most people pay their taxes on time, payment rates increased by as much as 5 percentage points. When letters to non-payers of car tax included a picture of the offending vehicle, payment rates rose from 40 to 49 per cent.

For government, nudging people to behave in ways that accord with government objectives can be both low-cost and effective. For this and other reasons, the role of behavioural economics in policy making is growing in importance.

1. *How would you nudge members of a student household to be more economical in the use of electricity?*
2. *How could the government nudge people to stop dropping litter?*
3. *In the 2011 UK Budget, George Osborne announced that charitable giving in wills would be exempt from inheritance tax. Do you think this was an effective way of encouraging more charitable donations?*

Visit the website of the Behavioural Insights Team (BIT). Search for Policy Publications and then write a short summary of the suggested approaches or interventions contained within one of the publications relating to a policy area of interest to you. What behavioural ideas are the motivation for the team's recommendations?

utility to the consumer of its product compared with those of its rivals, the more effectively it will be able to compete by differentiating its product from theirs.

Although gathering information on consumer behaviour can be costly and time-consuming and is never going to be perfect, it is usually better to rely on the imperfect information rather than on hunches when forming business strategy.

In this section, we therefore start by examining methods for gathering data on consumer behaviour and then see how firms set about forecasting changes in demand over time.

Methods of collecting data on consumer behaviour

There are three general approaches to gathering information about consumers. These are: *observations of market behaviour*, *market surveys* and *market experiments*.

Market observations

The firm can gather data on how demand for its product has changed over time. Virtually all firms will have detailed information on their sales broken down by week, month, year, etc. They will also tend to have information on how sales have varied from one part of the market to another.

Definitions

Observations of market behaviour Information gathered about consumers from the day-to-day activities of the business within the market.

Market surveys Information gathered about consumers, usually via a questionnaire, that attempts to enhance the business's understanding of consumer behaviour.

Market experiments Information gathered about consumers under artificial or simulated conditions. A method used widely in assessing the effects of advertising on consumers.

In addition, the firm will need to obtain data on how the various determinants of demand (such as price, advertising and the price of competitors' products) have themselves changed over time. Firms are likely to have much of this information already, e.g. the amount spent on advertising and the prices of competitors' products. Other information might be relatively easy to obtain by paying an agency to do the research.

Having obtained this information, the firm can then use it to estimate how changes in the various determinants have affected demand in the past, and hence what effect they will be likely to have in the future.

Even the most sophisticated analysis based on market observations, however, will suffer from one major drawback. Relationships that held in the past will not necessarily hold in the future. Consumers are human, and humans change their minds. Their perceptions of products change (something that the advertising industry relies on!), tastes change and technology changes. It is for this reason that many firms turn to market surveys or market experiments to gather more information about the future.

Market surveys

It is not uncommon to be stopped in a city centre, or to have a knock at the door, a postal questionnaire or a phone call, and be asked whether you would kindly answer the questions of some market researcher. A vast quantity of information can be collected in this way. It is a relatively quick and cheap method of data collection. Questions concerning all aspects of consumer behaviour might be asked, such as those relating to present and future patterns of expenditure, or how people might respond to changing product specifications or price, both of the firm in question and of its rivals.

A key feature of the market survey is that it can be targeted at distinct consumer groups, thereby reflecting the specific information requirements of a business. For example, businesses selling luxury goods will be interested only in consumers falling within higher income brackets. Other samples might be drawn from a particular age group or gender, or from those with a particular lifestyle, such as eating habits.

The major drawback with this technique concerns the accuracy of the information acquired. Accurate information requires various conditions to be met. These include a randomly selected sample of consumers to ensure unbiased results; clear, unambiguous questions to avoid misleading respondents; the avoidance of leading questions, so as not to encourage the respondent to give the answer the firm wants to hear; and it also requires truthful answers.

Even if all of these conditions are met, the information gathered may still be inaccurate, as, by the time the product is launched or the changes to an existing product are made, time will have elapsed. The information may then be out of date. Consumer demand may have changed, as tastes, fashions and technology have shifted, or as a result of the actions of competitors.

Market experiments

Rather than asking consumers questions and getting them to *imagine* how they *would* behave, the market experiment involves observing consumer *behaviour* under simulated conditions. It can be used to observe consumer reactions to a new product or to changes in an existing product and so this method is particularly useful when information is scarce.

A simple experiment might involve consumers being asked to conduct a blind taste test for a new brand of toothpaste. The experimenter will ensure that the same amount of paste is applied to the brush, and that the subjects swill their mouths prior to tasting a further brand. Once the experiment is over, the 'consumers' are quizzed about their perceptions of the product.

More sophisticated experiments might include a *laboratory shop* that simulates a real shopping experience. People could be given a certain amount of money to spend in the 'shop' and their reactions to changes in prices, packaging, display, etc. could be monitored.

The major drawback with such 'laboratories' is that consumers might behave differently because they are being observed. For example, they might spend more time comparing prices than they would otherwise, simply because they think that this is what a *good*, rational consumer should do. With real shopping, however, it might simply be habit, or something 'irrational' such as the colour of the packaging, that determines which product they select. If you are in a rush, you may simply grab the first brand of orange juice you find, irrespective of its price (see Box 3.3).

Another type of market experiment involves confining a marketing campaign to a particular town or region. The campaign could involve advertising, or giving out free samples, or discounting the price, or introducing an improved version of the product, but each confined to that particular locality. Sales in that area are then compared with sales in other areas in order to assess the effectiveness of the various campaigns.

Pause for thought

Identify some other drawbacks in using market experiments to gather data on consumer behaviour.

Forecasting demand

Businesses are not just interested in knowing the current strength of demand for their products and how demand is likely to be affected by changes in its determinants, such as product specifications and the price of competitors' products. They are also interested in trying to predict *future* demand. After all, if demand is going to increase, they may well want to invest *now* so that they have the extra capacity to meet the extra demand. But it will be a costly mistake to invest in extra capacity if demand is not going to increase.

We now, therefore, turn to examine some of the forecasting techniques used by business.

Simple time-series analysis

Simple time-series analysis involves directly projecting from past sales data into the future. Thus if it is observed that sales of a firm's product have been growing steadily by 3 per cent per annum for the past few years, the firm can use this to predict that sales will continue to grow at approximately the same rate in the future. Similarly, if it is observed that there are clear seasonal fluctuations in demand, as in the case of holidays, ice cream or winter coats, then again it can be assumed that fluctuations of a similar magnitude will continue into the future.

Using simple time-series analysis assumes that demand in the future will continue to behave in the same way as in the past. The problem is that it may not. Just because demand has followed a clear pattern in the past does not necessarily mean that it will

continue to exhibit the same pattern in the future. After all, the determinants of demand may have changed: consumers do change their minds! Successful forecasting, therefore, will usually involve a more sophisticated analysis of trends.

The decomposition of time paths

One way in which the analysis of past data can be made more sophisticated is to identify different elements in the time path of sales. Figure 3.3 illustrates one such time path, the (imaginary) sales of woollen jumpers by firm X. It is shown by the continuous green line, labelled 'Actual sales'. Four different sets of factors normally determine the shape of a time path like this.

Trends. These are increases or decreases in demand over a number of years. In our example, there is a long-term decrease in demand for this firm's woollen jumpers up to year seven and then a recovery in demand thereafter.

Trends may reflect factors such as changes in population structure, or technological innovation or longer-term changes in fashion. Thus, if wool were to become more expensive over time compared with other fibres, or if there were a gradual shift in tastes away from woollen jumpers and towards acrylic or cotton jumpers, or towards sweatshirts, this could explain the long-term decline in demand up to year seven. A gradual shift in tastes back towards natural fibres, and to wool in particular, or a gradual reduction in the price of wool, could then explain the subsequent recovery in demand.

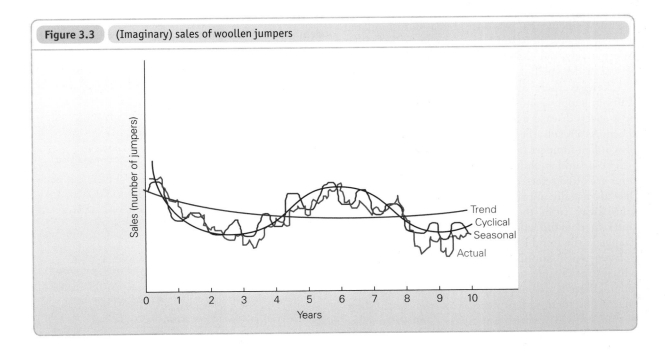

| Figure 3.3 | (Imaginary) sales of woollen jumpers |

Alternatively, trends may reflect changes over time in the structure of an industry. For example, an industry might become more and more competitive, with new firms joining. This would tend to reduce sales for existing firms (unless the market was expanding very rapidly).

Cyclical fluctuations. In practice, the level of actual sales will not follow the trend line precisely. One reason for this is the cyclical upswings and downswings in business activity in the economy as a whole. In some years, incomes are rising rapidly and thus demand is buoyant. In other years, the economy will be in recession, with incomes falling. In these years, demand may well also fall. In our example, in boom years people may spend much more on clothes (including woollen jumpers), whereas in a recession, people may make do with their old clothes. The cyclical variations line is thus above the trend line in boom years and falls below the trend line during a recession.

Seasonal fluctuations. The demand for many products also depends on the time of year. In the case of woollen jumpers, the peak demand is likely to be as winter approaches or just before Christmas. Thus, the seasonal variations line is above the cyclical variations line in winter and below it in summer.

Short-term shifts in demand or supply. Finally, the actual sales line will also reflect various short-term shifts in demand or supply, causing it to diverge from the smooth seasonal variations line.

There are many reasons why the demand curve might shift. A competitor might increase its price, or there may be a sudden change in fashion, caused, say, by a pop group deciding to wear woollen jumpers for their new video: what was once seen as unfashionable by many people now suddenly becomes fashionable! Alternatively, there may be an unusually cold or hot, or wet or dry spell of weather.

Likewise, there are various reasons for sudden shifts in supply conditions. For example, there may be a sheep disease which ruins the wool of infected sheep. As a result, the price of wool goes up, and sales of woollen jumpers fall.

These sudden shifts in demand or supply conditions are often referred to as 'random shocks' because they are usually unpredictable and temporarily move sales away from the trend. (Note that *long-term* shifts in demand and supply will be shown by a change in the trend line itself.)

Even with sophisticated time-series analysis, which breaks time paths into their constituent elements, there is still one major weakness: time-series analysis is merely a projection of the *past*. Most businesses will want to anticipate *changes* to sales

trends – to forecast any deviations from the current time path. One method for doing this is *barometric forecasting*.

Barometric forecasting

Assume that you are a manager of a furniture business and are wondering whether to invest in new capital equipment. You would only want to do this if the demand for your product was likely to rise. You will probably, therefore, look for some indication of this. A good barometer of future demand for furniture would be the number of new houses being built. People will tend to buy new furniture some months after the building of their new house has commenced.

Barometric forecasting involves the use of *leading indicators*, such as housing starts, when attempting to predict the future. In fact, some leading indicators, such as increased activity in the construction industry, rises in Stock Exchange prices, a rise in the rate of exchange and a rise in industrial confidence, are good indicators of a general upturn in the economy. In other words, firms use these indicators to predict what is likely to happen to their own demand.

Barometric forecasting suffers from two major weaknesses. The first is that it only allows forecasting a few months ahead – as far ahead as is the time lag between the change in the leading indicator and the variable being forecast. The second is that it can give only a general indication of changes in demand. It is simply another form of time-series analysis. Just because a relationship existed in the past between a leading indicator and the variable being forecasted, it cannot be assumed that exactly the same relationship will exist in the future.

Normally, firms use barometric forecasting merely to give them a rough guide as to the likely changes in demand for their product, i.e. whether it is likely to expand or contract, and by how much. Nevertheless, information on leading indicators is readily available in government or trade statistics.

Pause for thought

What might be a good leading indicator of the demand for a particular brand of printer ink?

Definitions

Barometric forecasting A technique used to predict future economic trends based upon analysing patterns of time-series data.

Leading indicators Indicators that help predict future trends in the economy.

RECAP

1. Businesses seek information on consumer behaviour so as to predict market trends and improve strategic decision making.

2. One source of data is the firm's own information on how its sales have varied in the past with changes in the various determinants of demand, such as consumer incomes and the prices of competitors' products.

3. Another source of data is market surveys. These can generate a large quantity of cheap information. Care should be taken, however, to ensure that the sample of consumers investigated reflects the target consumer group.

4. Market experiments involve investigating consumer behaviour within a controlled environment. This method is particularly useful when considering new products where information is scarce.

5. It is not enough to know what will happen to demand if a determinant changes. Businesses will want to forecast what will actually happen to demand.

6. Time-series analysis bases future trends on past events. Time-series data can be decomposed into different elements: trends, seasonal fluctuations, cyclical fluctuations and random shocks.

7. Barometric forecasting involves making predictions based upon changes in key leading indicators.

3.5 STIMULATING DEMAND

For most firms, selling their product is not simply a question of estimating demand and then choosing an appropriate price and level of production. In other words, they do not simply take their market as given. Instead they will seek to *increase* demand. They will do this by developing their product and differentiating it from those of their rivals, and then marketing it by advertising and other forms of product promotion. This will make their product more price inelastic.

What firms are engaging in here is *non-price competition*. In such situations, the job of the manager can be quite complex, involving strategic decisions about product design and quality, product promotion and the provision of various forms of after-sales service.

Product differentiation

Central to non-price competition is *product differentiation*. Most firms' products differ in various ways from those of their rivals. Take the case of washing machines. Although all washing machines wash clothes, and as such are close substitutes for each other, there are many differences between brands. They differ in price, in their capacity, their styling, their range of

programmes, their economy in the use of electricity, hot water and detergent, their reliability, their noise, their after-sales service, etc.

Firms attempt to design their product so that they can emphasise its advantages (real or imaginary) over the competitor brands. By doing this, a firm is advertising its product's unique selling point (USP): what it is that makes their product different from its competitors' products. Just think of the specific features of particular models of car, tablet computers or brands of cosmetic, and then consider the ways in which these features are stressed by advertisements. In fact, think of virtually any advertisement and consider how it stresses the features of that particular brand. It doesn't even have to be a high-tech product: look at men's razors. There is constant innovation, with each competitor advertising any new feature that differentiates its product from those of its rivals.

Features of a product

A product has many dimensions, and a strategy to differentiate a product may focus on one or more of these. Dimensions include:

- *Technical standards.* These relate to the product's level of technical sophistication: how advanced it is in relation to the current state of technology. This would be a very important product dimension if, for example, you were purchasing a laptop or tablet.
- *Quality standards.* These relate to aspects such as the quality of the materials used in the product's construction and the care taken in assembly. These will affect the product's durability and reliability. The purchase of consumer durables, such as televisions, furniture and toys, will be strongly influenced by quality standards.

Definitions

Non-price competition Competition in terms of product promotion (advertising, packaging, etc.) or product development.

Product differentiation Where a firm's product is in some way distinct from its rivals' products. In the context of growth strategies, this is where a business upgrades existing products or services so as to make them different from those of rival firms.

BOX 3.4　GLOBAL ADVERTISING TRENDS: A NEW WORLD

The changing face of advertising

Advertising is both lucrative and expensive. As we briefly discussed in Chapter 1, globalisation is changing the way that firms and consumers behave and advertising is affected by this. Firms selling in global markets now have to reach global audiences and so it is important to take a global perspective on the nature of advertising. Has global advertising expenditure risen? Are some countries seeing faster increases than others? We know that online and digital advertising is increasing rapidly, but will it continue and what are the implications for the more traditional mediums of advertising?

Global growth

Research from eMarketer found that worldwide expenditure on advertising increased to £628.63 billion in 2018, a growth of 7.4 per cent. This follows previous years of similarly high growth rates on the back of a relatively healthy global economy. Given the relationship between advertising expenditure and GDP, this should mean a steady growth in the demand for goods and services. The table below shows the growth in advertising expenditure across the world.

Despite all regions showing growth in advertising expenditure, the rate of growth is forecast to slow. Furthermore, certain regions have experienced, and are forecast to have, much faster growth than others. There has been double-digit growth in advertising expenditure in Central and Eastern Europe and the Asia–Pacific regions, particularly in Central Asia. The Asia–Pacific region will account for 33.5 per cent of worldwide spending by 2022 (just behind North America's 37 per cent), with the Chinese market driving this and accounting for 45.5 per cent of the region's advertising market.[1]

While the double-digit growth in the Asia–Pacific region and Central and Eastern Europe is unlikely to continue, it is evidence that new regions are seeing the benefits of advertising. According to Zenith, the Philippines and Ireland are two of the advertising hot spots for market growth and thanks to some unexpectedly strong growth in China in early 2018, adspend here is now expected to grow faster than forecast. However, Zenith still estimates that in 2020,

advertising expenditure in the USA will be more than twice that in China.[2] This means that global companies which are focused on selling to the US market do have plenty of scope for expansion in the coming years, but the data also indicate that there are plenty of new avenues to explore, both in domestic and international markets.

How are firms advertising?

Facing competition in both domestic and international markets and with many industries being overcrowded, advertising the unique characteristics of products has become more important for firms aiming to increase market share. With customers located throughout the world, finding the best means of reaching them must be a key part of any firm's advertising strategy. This, together with technological progress, means that the ways firms are advertising is changing.

Many decades ago, newspapers and magazines were one of the key forms of advertising and, although the share of advertising spend that they account for has declined significantly and is expected to continue in that direction, they still represent an important source of demand. Research from NewsMediaWorks in 2016, showed that the first person in a social group to try a new product was a newspaper reader 75 per cent of the time. Furthermore, some surveys indicate that newspapers remain the most trusted advertising format by consumers, especially for those below the age of 35.[3]

Despite this, Zenith's *Global Intelligence Report* highlights the continued weakness of traditional media, with many companies diverting advertising budgets from television, magazines and newspapers towards online video and digital advertising. The share of advertising in newspapers and magazines is expected to decline by 4–6 cent per year between 2017 and 2020, with television and radio advertising expected to show modest growth of 1.2 and 1.1 per cent, respectively.

---

[1] Michael Del Gigante, 'Global advertising trends every marketer should watch', *MDG Advertising* (10 July 2018).

[2] *Global intelligence: Data & insights for the new age of communication, Q1: 2018*, Zenith, The ROI agency (27 April 2018).

[3] '10 reasons why you should be advertising in newspapers', *NewsMediaWorks* (17 November 2017).

Total Media Advertising Expenditure Worldwide by Region, 2017–22

	2017	2018	2019	2020	2021	2022
	Total media advertising expenditure ($ billions) and growth (% change)					
North America	$218.16 (7.2%)	$232.48 (6.6%)	$248.09 (6.7%)	$263.53 (6.2%)	$276.12 (4.8%)	$289.04 (4.7%)
Asia–Pacific	$190.05 (11.4%)	$210.43 (8.7%)	$232.14 (10.3%)	$253.87 (9.4%)	$274.34 (8.1%)	$293.67 (7.0%)
Western Europe	$101.68 (2.8%)	$104.57 (2.8%)	$107.35 (2.7%)	$109.82 (2.3%)	$112.22 (2.2%)	$114.76 (2.3%)
Latin America	$35.01 (8.7%)	$38.04 (8.7%)	$40.05 (5.3%)	$41.61 (3.9%)	$43.07 (3.5%)	$44.35 (3.0%)
Middle East & Africa	$23.77 (4.6%)	$24.91 (4.8%)	$25.99 (4.3%)	$27.02 (4.0%)	$28.05 (3.8%)	$29.03 (3.5%)
Central & Eastern Europe	$16.77 (7.0%)	$18.19 (8.5%)	$19.32 (6.2%)	$20.36 (5.4%)	$21.29 (4.5%)	$22.40 (5.2%)
Worldwide	$585.45 (7.7%)	$628.63 (7.4%)	$672.94 (7.0%)	$716.21 (6.4%)	$755.09 (5.4%)	$793.25 (5.1%)

Source: eMarketer, March 2018

At the same time, online advertising budgets are forecast to grow and account for greater and greater shares of total advertising budgets for companies. Zenith forecast that 'advertisers will spend 40.5% of their budgets on online advertising in 2018, up from 37.6% in 2017.'[4] Some countries, such as China, Sweden and the UK, have already broken the 50 per cent mark when it comes to the share of advertising that now occurs online and growth looks set to continue.

In the USA, just under 50 per cent of all advertising is now digital, with almost 16 per cent growth in 2017, and social media now accounts for almost one quarter of digital spending. In the EU, there was a 93 per cent growth in online advertising between 2011 and 2016, and 2018 saw online advertising growth in the UK of 10.8 per cent.

The chart compares the share of global advertising expenditure by medium in 2017 and as forecast in 2020. Even in this short period of time, you can see by how much the mediums are expected to change.

Social media

As you might expect, with such growth in online advertising, there has been even faster growth in advertising technology. Firms are demanding new ways of reaching their customers and advertising technology ('ad tech') companies have responded with record amounts of research and development (R&D). The *Global Intelligence Report* found that '. . . the revenues of 14 listed ad tech companies between 2010 and 2016. . . grew five times faster than online revenues over this time.'[5]

The two giants of digital media, Facebook and Google, are continuing to change the face of global media and communication. Facebook has seen year-on-year growth of 48 per cent in advertising revenues, with 89 per cent of this coming from mobile phones. It now reaches over 50 per cent of all internet users globally. Google has seen year-on-year growth of 43 per cent for its 'paid clicks' and has a global reach of 74.1 per cent, with much of its growth coming from YouTube and mobile searches.

Both companies have been investing in advertising technology, with Google making its mobile shopping experience easier, including integrating it with Google Pay and introducing AdSense Auto ads, 'which use machine learning to improve the yield of ads by optimising when and where they appear'. Facebook has invested in providing more ad tech to small businesses, such as the Value Optimisation tool, which enables them to target their adverts to those consumers that Facebook believes have a greater chance of buying their product. This means that smaller businesses are now on more of an even playing field and are able to compete more effectively with big business.[6]

Companies are increasingly using social media to support their advertising activity on the television and support long-running campaigns. One of the clearest examples of this approach was implemented by the price comparison website *Compare the Market*. In January 2009, the company launched its 'Compare the Meerkat' advert on the television. This centred on a CGI animated Russian Meerkat, Aleksandr Orlov, complaining about the confusion between the 'Compare the Meerkat' and the *'Compare the Market'* websites. The company launched a real 'Compare the Meerkat' website in order to promote its brand further.

The impact was immediate, with Internet searches for 'meerkat' increasing by 817% the week following its first broadcast. Within nine weeks, the requested number of

---

[4] *Global intelligence: Data & insights for the new age of communication, Q1: 2018,* Zenith, The ROI agency (27 April 2018).

[5] Ibid.

[6] Ibid.

Global share of adspend by medium (%)

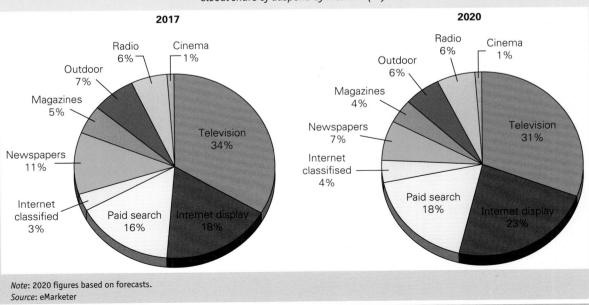

Note: 2020 figures based on forecasts.
Source: eMarketer

insurance quotes via the *Compare the Market* website increased by 80 per cent and the company quickly saw the potential, creating a Facebook page and Twitter account for Aleksandr Orlov. These now have over half a million fans and over 60 000 followers! Further adverts have continued to follow Aleksandr's life and new products and promotions have continued on the back of the success, including a 'Meerkat Movies' promotion, wallpapers, ringtones, text alerts, a novel about Aleksandr Orlov's life and a Meerkat cuddly toy!

1. *Global advertising confidence is rising and this has led to an upward revision of forecasts of advertising expenditure and revenue. What factors might explain this?*
2. *Choose a country and research the trends in advertising expenditure. Do they follow the same pattern as those observed globally?*

Choose a product that is advertised on social media and find data on sales. Assess the effectiveness of the advertising campaign.

- *Design characteristics*. These relate to the product's direct appeal to the consumer in terms of appearance or operating features. Examples of design characteristics are colour, style and even packaging. The demand for fashion products such as clothing will be strongly influenced by design characteristics. A major reason for the success of Apple's iPhone has been its design and appearance – something that Samsung has tried to match in recent years with various models of its Galaxy series of smartphones.
- *Service characteristics*. This aspect is not directly concerned with the product itself, but with the support given to the customer after the product has been purchased. Servicing, product maintenance and guarantees fall under this heading. When purchasing a new car, the quality of after-sales service might strongly influence the choice you make.

Market segmentation

Different features of a product will appeal to different consumers. Where features are quite distinct, and where particular features or groups of features appeal to a particular category of consumers, it might be useful for producers to divide the market into segments. Taking the example of cars again, the market could be divided into luxury cars, large, medium and small family cars, sports cars, multi-terrain vehicles, seven-seater people carriers, etc. Each type of car occupies a distinct market segment and each segment will have cars that are of a different quality and that cater to differing tastes.

When consumer tastes change over time, or where existing models do not cater for every taste, a firm may be able to identify a new segment of the market – a *market niche*. Having identified the appropriate market niche for its product, the marketing division within the firm will then set about targeting the relevant consumer group(s) and developing an appropriate strategy for promoting the product.

Marketing the product

There is no universally accepted definition of marketing, but it is generally agreed that it covers the following activities: establishing the strength of consumer demand in existing parts of the market, and potential demand in new niches; developing an attractive and distinct image for the product; informing potential consumers of various features of the product; fostering a desire by consumers for the product; and, in the light of all these, persuading consumers to buy the product.

Product/market strategy

Once the nature and strength of consumer demand (both current and potential) have been identified, the business will set about meeting and influencing this demand. In most cases it will be hoping to achieve a growth in sales. To do this, one of the first things the firm must decide is its *product/market strategy*. This will involve addressing two major questions:

- Should it focus on promoting its existing product, or should it develop new products?
- Should it focus on gaining a bigger share of its existing market, or should it seek to break into new markets?

These choices can be shown in a *growth vector matrix*. This is illustrated in Figure 3.4. The four cells show the possible combinations of answers to the above questions: cell A – *market penetration* (current product, current market); cell B – *product development* (new product, current market); cell C – *market development* (current product, new market); cell D – *diversification* (new product, new market).

Market penetration. In the market penetration strategy, the business will seek not only to retain existing customers, but to expand its customer base with current products in current markets. Of the four strategies, this is generally the least risky: the business will be able to play to its product's strengths and draw on its knowledge of the market. The business's marketing strategy will tend

Definitions

Market niche A part of a market (or new market) that has not been filled by an existing brand or business.
Growth vector matrix A means by which a business might assess its product/market strategy.

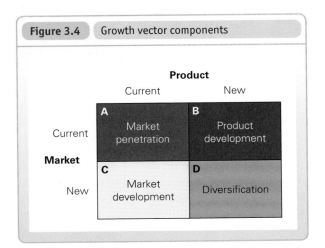

Figure 3.4 Growth vector components

to focus upon aggressive product promotion and distribution. Such a strategy, however, is likely to lead to fierce competition from existing business rivals, especially if the overall market is not expanding and if the firm can therefore gain an increase in sales only by taking market share from its rivals.

Product development. Product development strategies will involve introducing new models and designs in current markets. It could include the introduction of an upgrade or a completely new model. This strategy may be adopted in fast-moving markets where competitors frequently launch new products.

Market development. With a market development strategy, the business will seek increased sales of current products by expanding into new markets. These may be in a different geographical location (e.g. overseas), or new market segments. Alternatively, the strategy may involve finding new uses and applications for the product. Such a strategy is likely if the current market has become saturated and hence sales are beginning to slow.

Pause for thought

What unknown factors is the business likely to face following a diversification strategy?

Diversification. A diversification strategy will involve the business expanding into new markets with new products. This strategy can prove to be highly profitable, but of all the strategies, this is the most risky given the unknown factors that the business is likely to face.

Once the product/market strategy has been decided upon, the business will then attempt to devise a suitable *marketing strategy*. This will involve looking at the marketing mix.

The marketing mix

In order to differentiate the firm's product from those of its rivals, there are four variables that can be adjusted. These are as follows:

- product;
- price;
- place (distribution);
- promotion.

The particular combination of these variables, known as 'the four Ps', represents the business's *marketing mix*, and it is around a manipulation of them that the business will devise its marketing strategy.

Product considerations. These involve issues such as quality and reliability, as well as branding, packaging and after-sales service.

Pricing considerations. These involve not only the product's basic price in relation to those of competitors' products, but also opportunities for practising price discrimination (the practice of charging different prices in different parts of the market; see section 5.6), offering discounts to particular customers, and adjusting the terms of payment for the product.

Place considerations. These focus on the product's distribution network, and involve issues such as where the business's retail outlets should be located, what warehouse facilities the business might require, and how the product should be transported to the market.

Promotion considerations. These focus primarily upon the amount and type of advertising the business should use. In addition, promotion issues might also include selling techniques, special offers, trial discounts and various other public relations 'gimmicks'.

Every product is likely to have a distinct marketing *mix* of these four variables. Thus we cannot talk about an ideal value for one (e.g. the best price), without considering the other three. What is more, the most appropriate mix will vary from product to product and from market to market. Ferrari is unlikely to see sales rise by offering free promotional gifts!

What the firm must seek to do is to estimate how sensitive demand is to the various aspects of marketing. The greater the sensitivity (elasticity) in each case, the more the firms should focus on that particular

Definition

Marketing mix The mix of product, price, place (distribution) and promotion that will determine a business's marketing strategy.

aspect. It is important for a firm to make sure that the four Ps do not come into conflict with each other, which is possible when one element of the marketing mix is adjusted.

Advertising

One of the most important aspects of marketing is advertising. The major aim of advertising is to sell more products, and businesses spend a vast quantity of money on advertising to achieve this goal. Through advertising, a business is not only making consumers aware of the product and its features, but is purposefully trying to persuade the consumer to buy the good.

In fact, there is a bit more to it than this. Advertisers are trying to do two things:

■ Shift the product's demand curve to the right.
■ Make it less price elastic.

This is illustrated in Figure 3.5. D_1 shows the original demand curve with price at P_1 and sales at Q_1. D_2 shows the curve after an advertising campaign. The rightward shift allows an increased quantity (Q_2) to be sold at the original price. If, at the same time, the demand is made less elastic, the firm can also raise its price and still experience an increase in sales. Thus in the diagram, price can be raised to P_2 and sales will be Q_3 – still substantially above Q_1. The total gain in revenue is shown by the shaded area.

How can advertising bring about this new demand curve?

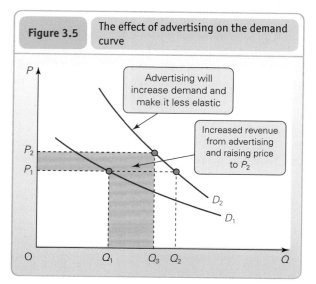

| Figure 3.5 | The effect of advertising on the demand curve |

Shifting the demand curve to the right. This will occur if the advertising brings the product to more people's attention and if it increases people's desire for the product, such that they want to purchase more at any given price.

Making the demand curve less elastic. This will occur if the advertising creates greater brand loyalty. People must be led to believe (rightly or wrongly) that competitors' brands are inferior. This will allow the firm to raise its price above that of its rivals with no significant fall in sales. There will be only a small substitution effect of this price rise because consumers have been led to believe that there are no close substitutes.

The more successful an advertising campaign is, the more it will shift the demand curve to the right and the more it will reduce the price elasticity of demand.

We often see some of the most well-known brands being advertised in the middle of big sporting events and the impact on sales of such products is clearly affected by the success of the host nation, as we discuss in the blog, *The Economic downs of Rugby*, on the Sloman Economics News site.

Assessing the effects of advertising

While there are many examples of excellent adverts and parts of section 3.5 have considered what advertising aims to do, here we provide a brief overview of the pros and cons of advertising.

A brief case for. Advertising plays a key role in providing information to consumers about the products that are available. It also helps firms to develop and introduce new products and hence can be a crucial tool for firms aiming to break into new markets. In this way, it can be a good means of reducing the barriers to entry of new firms into markets and boosting competition, as we discuss in Chapter 5. This growth in competition can be good for quality, as consumers are more aware of the substitutes available.

By providing information to consumers about the choices that are available and the special features of products, it can encourage price competition, especially if the product's price is one of the 'special features'. This can therefore bring significant benefits to society. Advertising in itself is a huge market and provides countless job opportunities and, as we shall see, it can make a significant contribution to the economy.

Finally, advertising's main role is to boost sales and, if successful, this will obviously be of benefit to the company. But, if advertising helps a firm to generates more sales, this revenue can be used for the development of new products, or it can help a firm gain economies of scale (see section 4.2), which in turn can help to keep prices down and thus also benefits consumers and society.

A brief case against. Although there is regulation of the content of adverts, sometimes advertising can be misleading, as it is aiming to persuade people to buy a product. Although adverts provide information, consumers do not have perfect information and may be misled into purchasing goods whose qualities may be inferior to goods which are not advertised.

Advertising can be very costly and some argue that the money spent on campaigns could be better spent elsewhere, e.g. on product innovation, greater efficiency or sustainability. Although advertising can generate sales, firms may need to fund the campaign by raising prices – not something that consumers would wish. Furthermore, advertising aims to shift the demand curve to the right, and so directly creates wants. Therefore, perhaps it increases the problem of scarcity. Also, if the company cannot meet the higher demand, then excess demand could emerge and this again may mean higher prices.

Successful advertising campaigns can reduce barriers to entry, but they can also establish brand loyalty, making it difficult for new firms to enter a market. It can therefore result in markets dominated by one or two firms, which can mean higher prices and less innovation. Finally, we face adverts everywhere. Some of them may be welcome, but many people find them annoying, tasteless and confusing. Thus, advertising can impose costs on society in general beyond those faced by the firm.

Advertising and the state of the economy

One final thing to consider is the impact of booms and recessions on marketing and advertising. Marketing expenditure can be a huge expense for a firm, and so varying the amount spent on advertising as the state of the economy changes can be a sensible strategy.

For example, in the UK, advertising expenditure fell in real terms by 6.3 per cent in 2008 and 14.4 per cent in 2009 when the economy was in recession. According to the Advertising Association, advertising expenditure was then fairly stable between 2010 and 2014 at between £14.5 billion and £16 billion and it has since increased every year by an average by 6 per cent. Quarter 3 of 2018 saw the highest expenditure since 2015, with the 21st consecutive quarter of growth. Total advertising expenditure for 2018 is estimated at £23.5 billion, up from £22 billion in the previous year. Despite the uncertainty surrounding Brexit, the industry is expecting growth of 4.6 per cent throughout 2019.

Similar trends have been observed in the USA, with advertising expenditure falling by 2.6 per cent in 2008 relative to 2007 and then by 12.3 per cent in 2009. Since then, advertising expenditure has grown year on year.

However, is cutting back on advertising and marketing in a recession the right thing to do? Maintaining, or even increasing, expenditure on marketing during a recession might enable a firm to take advantage of weaker competitors. Increasing market share during a down-turn may mean higher profits when demand recovers.

According to research from the Open University that looked at previous recessions, advertising during weak economic times can increase sales, market share and brand reputation in the long run, as Domino's UK, the pizza company, found when its advertising during 2009–10 led to excellent sales and profits growth.[8] This included using social media and launching a smartphone app. Other media-savvy companies also maintained their advertising, despite the recession. But in many cases they switched to the Internet, as a cheaper and perhaps more far-reaching means of promoting their product, as we saw in Box 3.4.

There are close links between the state of the economy and advertising expenditure, but it is not just in one direction. Advertising expenditure can be a key stimulant to an economy.

A report published in 2014[9] by Deloitte and the Advertising Association found that for every £1 spent on advertising in the UK, £6 is generated for the wider economy, thus adding to gross domestic product (GDP) and creating many jobs. Data from the Creative Industries indicated that in 2017, advertising added £120 billion to UK GDP. A report in January 2017 from Deloitte found that in 2014, €92 billion was spent on advertising and this accounted for 4.6% of EU GDP.[10] Furthermore, data from the Interactive Advertising Bureau found that for every €1 invested in advertising, €7 of GDP is created, and that advertising creates 5.8 million jobs.[11]

---

[8] Sean Farrell, 'The rise and rise of Domino's pizza', *The Guardian* (9 January 2014).

[9] *Advertising Pays: How Advertising Fuels the UK Economy,* Advertising Association and Deloitte (2013).

[10] *The Economic Contribution of Advertising in Europe,* Deloitte (January 2017).

[11] *Value of Advertising Infographic: The Economic Contribution of Advertising in Europe,* Interactive Advertising Bureau (16 January 2017).

BOX 3.5 ADVERTISING AND THE LONG RUN

Promoting quality

It is relatively straightforward to measure the short-term impact of an advertising campaign; a simple before and after assessment of sales will normally give a good indication of the advertising's effectiveness. But what about the medium and longer-term effects of an advertising campaign? How will sales and profits be affected over, say, a five-year period?

The typical impact of advertising on a product's sales is shown in Figure (a). Assume that there is an advertising campaign for the product between time t_1 and t_2. There is a direct effect on sales while the advertising lasts and shortly afterwards. Sales rise from S_1 to S_2. After a while (beyond time t_3), the direct effect of the advertising begins to wear off, and wears off completely by time t_4. This is illustrated by the dashed line. But the higher level of sales declines much more slowly, given that many of the new customers continue to buy the product out of habit. Sales will eventually level off (at point t_5). It is likely, however, that sales will not return to the original level of S_1: there will be some new customers who will stick with the product over the long term. This long-term effect is shown by the increase in sales from S_1 to S_3.

But just what is this long-term effect? One way to explore the impact of advertising over the long run is to evaluate how advertising and profitability in general are linked. Figure (b) shows how advertising shapes the image of the product and its perceived quality, which the customer then compares with price to determine the product's value. The more that advertising can enhance the perceived quality of a product, the more it will increase the product's profitability.

How this benefits the business over the longer term can be illustrated with some examples.

Nike

Founded in 1964, this American company was mainly known for selling to marathon runners. As more and more people began to 'get fit' in the 1980s, the marketing team at Nike took advantage of this trend and in 1988, they introduced the world-famous advertising campaign 'Just Do It'. Between 1988 and 1998, its sales increased from $800 million to over $9.2 billion, and its market share of the North American domestic sport-shoe business rose from 18 to 43 per cent. By 2018, its worldwide revenue was $36.4 billion.

Audi

This prestige car company was one of the winners of the 2011 and 2018 Institute of Practitioners in Advertising (IPA) Effectiveness Awards. Audi initially received praise for its campaign's focus on design, performance and innovation and its success in moving from the understated alternative to Mercedes and BMW, to the fastest growing prestige car brand. Between 2000 and 2010, its share of the UK car market increased from 1.5 to 5.3 per cent. Since then, its advertising has focused on communicating 'the desirability and technical innovation of its cars to higher spending users' and this has led Audi to become the top company for desirability among the prestige audience, with UK sales growing three times faster than the UK market itself and its market share rising to 8.21 per cent.[1]

PG Tips

This tea brand has dominated the UK market since 1958, with over 25 per cent of the tea market. While other traditional competitors, such as Tetley, have seen a decline in market share, especially with the growth in popularity of fruit and herbal teas, PG Tips has maintained its position of strength.

In 1956, PG Tips broadcast its first TV advert in black and white, featuring the famous 'chimps'. Since then, the chimp adverts, the Aardman T-Birds and the Monkey and Johnny Vegas adverts have established a clear brand image, enabling

---

[1] *IPA Effectiveness Awards: Winners 2018* (Institute of Practitioners in Advertising, 2018).

(a) Advertising and the long run

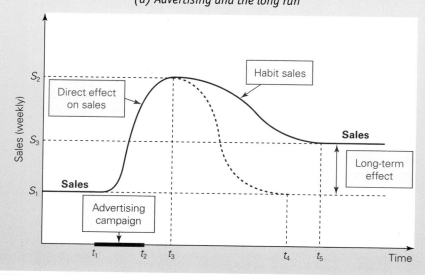

(b) Advertising, profit margins and company growth

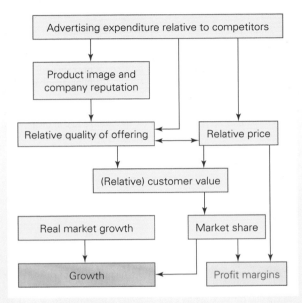

PG Tips to hold its ground in a highly competitive market and charge a price premium. Market analysis shows that PG Tips has a price elasticity of demand of -0.4 compared with its nearest rival, Tetley, which has an elasticity of -1.4. It is estimated that between 1980 and 2000 advertising the PG Tips brand cost £100 million but generated in the region of £2 billion in extra sales. Not a bad return!

PG Tips has constantly responded to changing consumer tastes, introducing the first tea bag in 1960 and responding to the 'mug revolution' in the 1980s, by introducing a tea bag with a string. In 2013, PG Tips introduced 'Special Moments', an innovation focusing on the black tea market, supported by a multi-million pound marketing campaign. It is continuing to expand the range of tea it offers, with the recent introduction of 'Gold' and 'Dairy Free' ranges.

Turkish Airlines

In Box 1.2, we considered how the business economist might analyse the airline industry and one aspect that warrants attention is advertising, especially given the crowded nature of the market. Turkish Airlines increased its marketing budget by hundreds of millions of dollars, especially after 2011, aiming to become a household name and be seen as more than just a 'regional carrier'.

In 2013, Lionel Messi and Kobe Bryant starred in their advert, aiming to take the most impressive selfies, and this advert attracted 140 million views. YouTube named it as its best advert of its first decade as a video sharing service. The airline's International Corporate Sales and Marketing Manager, Mr Ertugrul Aktan said:

They really paid off for us, in terms of revenue . . . People talked about it, and showed it to their family and friends, retweeted it, shared it through links. This eventually causes [people to] wonder: Who is this Turkish Airlines? It really worked for us and increased our passenger potential.[2]

The campaign worked in enabling Turkish Airlines to expand globally, increasing its destinations from 132 international and 42 domestic locations in 2010 to 236 international and 49 domestic ones by 2018.

Since then, Turkish Airlines has continued to 'go big', focusing on brand awareness. It had been voted 'Europe's Best Airline' for six consecutive years and won the Gold prize in Epica Awards for its 'Batman v. Superman' advertising campaign in 2016. The main aim of the campaign was to inform consumers about its innovative movie-themed experiences and advertise two new fictional routes, taken from the movie. By linking its adverts with the blockbuster film 'Batman v. Superman: Dawn of Justice', Turkish airlines was able to reach a global audience and the campaign led to 125 million earned media impressions and its YouTube ads initially reached over 30 million people, with now over 50 million views.[3]

The advertising appears to have done its job, with Turkish Airlines becoming a globally recognised name; its destinations increasing markedly; and revenues rising substantially. In the first half of 2018, total revenue increased by 30 per cent compared to the same time in 2017, reaching $6 billion. Its net operating profit also rose from $17 million to $258 million, despite the increases in fuel prices. Thus, despite some significant advertising bills, its advertising appears to have paid off.

The message is that advertising should seek to promote a product's quality and be memorable. This is the key to long-term sales and profits. What is also apparent is that successful brands have advertising campaigns, which have been consistent over time. A brand image of quality is not created overnight and if investment and innovation are not maintained, brand loyalty can suffer in the long run. However, with continuous market research and innovative campaigns it is possible for brands to endure and yield profits over the longer term.

1. How are long-run profits and advertising linked?
2. Why does quality 'win out' in the end?
3. How would you advise the owner of the PG Tips brand (Unilever) on a pricing strategy?

Research some recent advertising campaigns. Identify what characteristics or attributes the advertising was attempting to highlight and what perceptions it was trying to influence. Where possible, examine the impact of the campaign so far.

---

[2] Susan Krashinsky, 'How a big bet on Batman v Superman paid off for Turkish Airlines', *The Globe and Mail* (16 May 2018).

[3] Ibid.

RECAP

1. When firms seek to differentiate their products from those of their competitors, they can adjust one or more of four dimensions of the product: its technical standards, its quality, its design characteristics, and the level of customer service.

2. Marketing involves developing a product image and then persuading consumers to purchase it.

3. A business must choose an appropriate product/market strategy. Four such strategies can be identified: market penetration (focusing on existing product and market); product development (new product in existing market); market development (existing product in new markets); diversification (new products in new markets).

4. The marketing strategy of a product involves the manipulation of four key variables: product, price, place and promotion. Every product has a distinct marketing mix.

5. The aims of advertising are to increase demand in the short and long run and make the product less price elastic.

6. Supporters of advertising claim that it provides information, introduces new products and helps their development, encourages new competitors and enhances price competition; generates economies of scale and brings benefits to the wider economy through economic growth and job creation.

7. Critics of advertising claim that it can mislead consumers, worsens the scarcity problem and can push up prices; can create barriers to entry and problems for society in general.

QUESTIONS

1. How would marginal utility and market demand be affected by a rise in the price of (a) a substitute good, (b) a complementary good?

2. How can marginal utility be used to explain the price elasticity of demand for a particular brand of a product?

3. Why are insurance companies unwilling to provide insurance against losses arising from war or 'civil insurrection'? Name some other events where it would be impossible to obtain insurance.

4. Why might premiums for home insurance for those houses that have been flooded and remain at risk of flooding rise? Which factors have caused this change? Is there a role for the government to intervene in this market?

5. How does behavioural economics differ from standard economic theory?

6. Can you think of any studying decisions where students often change their mind with the passage of time once the costs or benefits become immediate?

7. What are the relative strengths and weaknesses of using (a) market observations, (b) market surveys and (c) market experiments as a means of gathering evidence on consumer demand?

8. You are working for a recording company which is thinking of signing up some new artists. What market observations, market surveys and market experiments could you conduct to help you decide which artists to sign?

9. You are about to launch a new range of cosmetics, but you are still to decide upon the content and structure of your advertising campaign. Consider how market surveys and market experiments might be used to help you assess consumer perceptions of the product. What limitations might each of the research methods have in helping you gather data?

10. Imagine that you are an airline attempting to forecast demand for seats over the next two or three years. What do you think could be used as leading indicators?

11. How might we account for the growth in non-price competition within the modern developed economy?

12. Consider how the selection of the product/market strategy (market penetration, market development, product development and diversification) will influence the business's marketing mix. Choose a particular product and identify which elements in the marketing mix would be most significant in developing a successful marketing strategy for it.

13. Think of some advertisements that deliberately seek to make demand less price elastic. How do they do this?

14. Imagine that 'Sunshine' sunflower margarine, a well-known brand, is advertised with the slogan, 'It helps you live longer' (the implication being that butter and margarines high in saturates shorten your life). What do you think would happen to the demand curve for a supermarket's *own* brand of sunflower margarine? Consider both the direction of shift and the effect on elasticity. Will the elasticity differ markedly at different prices? How will this affect the pricing policy and sales of the supermarket's own brand? Could the supermarket respond other than by adjusting the price of its margarine?

15. On balance, does advertising benefit (a) the consumer; (b) society in general?

Supply decisions in a perfectly competitive market

- ■ What do profits consist of?
- ■ What is the relationship between inputs and outputs in both the short and long run?
- ■ What do we mean by costs and how do they vary with output?
- ■ What are 'economies of scale' and 'diseconomies of scale' and what are the reasons for each?
- ■ What are 'transactions costs' and how do these vary with the degree of vertical integration of the firm?
- ■ How does a business's sales revenue vary with output?
- ■ What do we mean by a price-taking firm?
- ■ How do we measure profits?
- ■ At what output will a firm maximise its profits?
- ■ Why do conditions of perfect competition make being in business a constant battle for survival?

In this chapter we turn to supply. In other words, we focus on the amount that firms produce at different prices. In Part C we shall see how the supply decision is affected by the microeconomic environment in which a firm operates, and in particular by the amount of competition it faces. However, in this chapter, we assume that the firm is a price taker. We also assume that the firm seeks to maximise profits.

Profit is made by firms earning more from the sale of goods than the goods cost to produce. A firm's total profit ($T\Pi$) is thus the difference between its total sales revenue (TR) and its total costs of production (TC).

In order, then, to discover how a firm can maximise its profit, or even make a profit at all, we must first consider what determines costs and revenue. Sections 4.1 and 4.2 examine costs. Section 4.3 considers revenue, and then section 4.4 puts costs and revenue together to examine profit.

4.1 PRODUCTION AND COSTS IN THE SHORT RUN

The cost of producing any level of output depends on the amount and mix of inputs used and the price that the firm must pay for them. Let us first focus on the quantity and mix of inputs used.

Short-run and long-run changes in production

If a firm wants to increase production, it will need more inputs, but how easy and quick is it to acquire them? This will vary from input to input. For example, a manufacturer can increase output by switching on spare machines and hence using more electricity, but it might take a long time to increase output further by obtaining and installing more machines, and longer still to build a second or third factory.

If, then, the firm wants to increase output in a hurry, it will only be able to increase the quantity of certain inputs and so the input mix will be adjusted. It can use more raw materials, more fuel, more tools and possibly more labour (by hiring extra workers or offering overtime to its existing workforce). But it will have to make do with its existing buildings and most of its machinery.

The distinction we are making here is between *fixed inputs* and *variable inputs*. A *fixed* input is an input that cannot be increased within a given time period (e.g. buildings). A *variable* input is one that can.

The distinction between fixed and variable inputs allows us to distinguish between the short run and the long run.

The short run
The *short run* is a time period during which at least one input is fixed. This means that in the short run output can be increased only by using more variable inputs. For example, if a shipping line wanted to carry more passengers in response to a rise in demand, it could accommodate more passengers on existing sailings if there was space. It could increase the number of sailings with its existing fleet, by hiring more crew and using more fuel. But in the short run it could not buy more ships; there would not be time for them to be built.

The long run
The *long run* is a time period long enough for all of a firm's inputs to be varied. Thus in the long run, the shipping company could have a new ship built to cater for the increase in demand.

The short run and long run are not set periods of time and they will be different from firm to firm. Thus if it takes a farmer a year to obtain new land, buildings and equipment, the short run is any time period up to a year

and the long run is any time period longer than a year. But if it takes a shipping company three years to obtain an extra ship, the short run is any period up to three years and the long run is any period longer than three years.

For this section we will concentrate on *short-run* production and costs. We will look at the long run in section 4.2.

> ### Pause for thought
>
> *How will the length of the short run for the shipping company depend on the state of the shipbuilding industry?*

Production in the short run: the law of diminishing returns

Production in the short run is subject to *diminishing returns*, which is a concept we first alluded to in section 2.3 (page 32). You may well have heard of 'the law of diminishing returns', it is one of the most famous of all 'laws' of economics. To illustrate how this law underlies short-run production, let us take the simplest possible case where there are just two inputs: one fixed and one variable.

Take the case of a farm. Assume the fixed input is land and the variable input is labour. Since the land is fixed in supply, output per period of time can be increased only by employing extra workers. But imagine what would happen as more and more workers crowded on to a fixed area of land. Workers will begin to get in each other's way and the land simply cannot go on yielding more and more output indefinitely. After a point the additions to total output from each extra worker will begin to diminish.

We can now state the *law of diminishing (marginal) returns*.

> ### Definitions
>
> **Fixed input** An input that cannot be increased in supply within a given time period.
>
> **Variable input** An input that can be increased in supply within a given time period.
>
> **Short run** The period of time over which at least one input is fixed.
>
> **Long run** The period of time long enough for all inputs to be varied.
>
> **Law of diminishing (marginal) returns** When one or more inputs are held fixed, there will come a point beyond which the extra output from additional units of the variable input will diminish.

KEY IDEA 14

The law of diminishing marginal returns. When increasing amounts of a variable input are used with a given amount of a fixed input, there will come a point when each extra unit of the variable input will produce less extra output than the previous unit.

A good example of the law of diminishing returns is given in Case Study B.20 on the book's website. The case looks at diminishing returns to the application of nitrogen fertiliser on farmland. There is also an article on the Sloman Economics News site titled *Tackling diminishing returns in food production* which provides another good application of this core concept.

Opportunity cost

When measuring costs, economists always use the concept of *opportunity cost*. As we saw in section 1.3, opportunity cost is the cost of any activity measured in terms of the sacrifice made in doing it,

i.e. the cost measured in terms of the opportunities forgone. If a car manufacturer can produce 10 small saloon cars with the same amount of inputs as it takes to produce 6 large saloon cars, then the opportunity cost of producing 1 small car is 0.6 of a large car. If a taxi and car hire firm chooses to use all of its cars as taxis, then the opportunity cost includes not only the cost of employing taxi drivers and buying fuel, but also the sacrifice of rental income from hiring its vehicles out.

Measuring a firm's opportunity costs

To measure a firm's opportunity cost, we must first discover what inputs it has used. Then we must measure the sacrifice involved in using them. To do this it is necessary to put inputs into two categories.

Inputs not owned by the firm: explicit costs. The opportunity cost of those inputs not already owned by the firm is simply the price that the firm has to pay for them. Thus if the firm uses £100 worth of

---

BOX 4.1   DIMINISHING RETURNS AND BUSINESS

What can managers do?

Everywhere you look in business you can see diminishing returns. It applies to both giant multinational corporations and the corner shop; to manufacturing, farming, mining and services. Let us take some examples.

A car manufacturer. In the short run, a company such as Toyota or Ford will have a particular number of factories. If it wants to increase output in the short run, there will not be enough time to build a new one. Instead, it will have to use its existing plants more intensively. For example, it could increase the length of shifts or use machines more intensively. But, workers may become more tired; machines may break down or require more maintenance and so output per worker or per machine is likely to fall.

Eventually, no matter how many extra people are employed, the factory will reach full capacity. At this point any additional workers would produce no extra output whatsoever. Returns from additional labour have diminished to zero.

The convenience store. Go into a shop and see what fixed inputs you can see. There will be the shelving, the tills, the warehouse space at the back and the floor space itself. At busy times the shop may take on more workers, but will each additional worker be able to serve the same number of customers? Probably not. Assume, for example, that there are two tills. Once they are fully in use, taking on more workers will not allow more customers to be served. True, additional workers can make sure the shelves are stocked, collect the trolleys, and so on; but diminishing returns to labour are obvious. Each additional worker is permitting fewer and fewer *extra* customers to be served.

The problem applies similarly to supermarkets. At busy times, queues at the tills get longer and crowding in the shop slows down your progress around it.

The arable farm. In the short run, farmers have a fixed amount of land. They can increase crop yields by applying more fertiliser. However, beyond a certain quantity of fertiliser per hectare, diminishing returns to fertiliser will set in. Additional bags will yield less and less additional output. Case B.19 on the book's website looks at some evidence on diminishing returns to the application of nitrogen fertiliser on farmland.

Professionals. In many occupations, even non-physical ones, there is only so much work you can do before you get tired and become less efficient. Each additional hour worked beyond a certain level is likely to result in lower productivity.

The student. Which brings us to you! You have no doubt experienced diminishing returns to study time. Working that extra hour late at night may result in little if any extra learning!

1. *Give some other examples of diminishing returns to inputs other than labour (such as the fertiliser example above).*
2. *If all inputs were variable (as they are in the long run), would expanding output result in diminishing marginal returns? (We examine this question later when we consider the long run.)*

Investigate a department store or other large shop. Identify any cases of diminishing returns. Consider what the shop could do to reduce these diminishing returns. Is it necessarily desirable for the shop to do so?

If this is done as a group exercise, the investigations could be done individually or in pairs of different shops. The group could then compare the findings of the individual students or pairs. It could also discuss whether online retailers experience the same types of diminishing returns and with what implications.

electricity, the opportunity cost is £100. The firm has sacrificed £100 which could have been spent on something else.

These costs are called *explicit costs* because they involve direct payment of money by firms.

Inputs already owned by the firm: implicit costs. When the firm already owns inputs (e.g. machinery) it does not as a rule have to pay out money to use them. Their opportunity costs are thus *implicit costs.* They are equal to what the inputs could earn for the firm in some alternative use, either within the firm or hired out to some other firm.

Here are some examples of implicit costs:

■ Say you own a house. The opportunity cost of living in your house is the rental income you could have earned had you chosen to rent it out to a tenant.
■ A firm withdraws £100 000 from the bank in order to invest in a new plant and equipment. The opportunity cost of this investment is not just the £100 000 (an explicit cost), but also the interest it thereby forgoes (an implicit cost).
■ The owner of the firm could have earned £30 000 per annum by working for someone else.

This £30 000 is the opportunity cost of the owner's time.

If there is no alternative use for an input, as in the case of a machine designed to produce a specific product, and if it has no scrap value, the opportunity cost of using it is *zero*. In such a case, if the output from the machine is worth more than the cost of all the *other* inputs involved, the firm might as well use the machine rather than let it stand idle.

What the firm paid for the machine – its *historic cost* – is irrelevant. Not using the machine will not bring that money back. It has been spent. These are sometimes referred to as 'sunk costs'.

 KEY IDEA 15 | *Sunk costs and the bygones principle.* The principle states that sunk (fixed) costs should be ignored when deciding whether to produce or sell more or less of a product. Only variable costs should be taken into account.

Likewise, the *replacement cost* is irrelevant. That should be taken into account only when the firm is considering replacing the machine.

Costs and inputs

As a firm changes its output, its costs will change. We can look at the growth of some companies, such as Google and see how its costs have varied as the company has grown. A firm's costs of production will depend on the inputs it uses. The more inputs it uses,

the greater will its costs be. More precisely, this relationship depends on two elements:

■ The productivity of the inputs. The greater their physical productivity, the smaller will be the quantity of them that is needed to produce a given level of output, and hence the lower will be the cost of that output.
■ The price of the inputs. The higher their price, the higher will be the costs of production.

In the short run, some inputs are fixed in supply. Therefore, the total costs (*TC*) of these inputs are fixed and thus do not vary with output. Consider a piece of land that that a firm rents: the rent it pays will be a *fixed cost*. Whether the firm produces a lot or a little, its rent will not change.

The cost of variable inputs, however, does vary with output. The cost of raw materials is a *variable cost*. The more that is produced, the more raw materials are needed and therefore the higher is their total cost. *Total cost* is thus total fixed cost (*TFC*) plus total variable cost (*TVC*).

Average and marginal cost

In addition to the total cost of production (fixed and variable) there are two other measures of cost which are particularly important for our analysis of profits. These are average and marginal cost.

Definitions

Explicit costs The payments to outside suppliers of inputs.

Implicit costs Costs which do not involve a direct payment of money to a third party, but which nevertheless involve a sacrifice of some alternative.

Historic costs The original amount the firm paid for inputs it now owns.

Replacement costs What the firm would have to pay to replace inputs it currently owns.

Fixed costs Total costs that do not vary with the amount of output produced.

Variable costs Total costs that do vary with the amount of output produced.

Total cost (*TC*) (per period) The sum of total fixed costs (*TFC*) and total variable costs (*TVC*): $TC = TFC + TVC$.

Average cost (AC) is cost per unit of production:

$$AC = TC/Q$$

Thus if it costs a firm £2000 to produce 100 units of a product, the average cost would be £20 for each unit (£2000/100).

As with total cost, average cost can be divided into the two components, fixed and variable. In other words, average cost equals *average fixed cost* (AFC = TFC/Q) plus *average variable cost* (AVC = TVC/Q):

$$AC = AFC + AVC$$

Marginal cost (MC) is the *extra* cost of producing *one more unit*, i.e. the rise in total cost per one unit rise in output. Note that all marginal costs are variable, since, by definition there can be no extra fixed costs as output rises.

$$MC = \frac{\Delta TC}{\Delta Q}$$

where Δ means 'a change in'.

For example, assume that a firm is currently producing 1 000 000 boxes of matches a month. It now increases output by 1000 boxes (another batch): $\Delta Q = 1000$. Assume that as a result its total costs rise by £30: $\Delta TC = £30$. What is the cost of producing *one* more box of matches? It is:

$$MC = \frac{\Delta TC}{\Delta Q} = \frac{£30}{1000} = 3p$$

Table 4.1 shows costs for an imaginary firm, firm X, over a given period of time (e.g. a week). The table shows how average and marginal costs can be derived from total costs. It is assumed that total fixed costs are £12 000 (column 2) and that total variable costs are as shown in column 3.

The figures for *TVC* have been chosen to illustrate the law of diminishing returns. Initially, *before* diminishing returns set in, TVC rises less and less rapidly as more variable factors are added. For example, in the case of a factory with a fixed supply of machinery, initially as more workers are taken on, the workers can do increasingly specialist tasks and make a fuller use of the capital equipment. Extra workers are producing more and more extra output. However, above a certain output (3 units in Table 4.1), diminishing returns set in. Given that extra workers (the extra variable factors) are producing less and less extra output, the extra units of output they do produce will be costing more and more in terms of wage costs. Thus TVC rises more and more rapidly. You can see this by examining column 3.

> **Pause for thought**
>
> Use the figures in the first three columns of Table 4.1 to plot TFC, TVC and TC curves (where costs are plotted on the vertical axis and quantity on the horizontal axis). Mark the point on each of the TVC and TC curves where diminishing returns set in. What do you notice about the slope of the two curves at this output?

The figures in the remaining columns in Table 4.1 are derived from columns 1 to 3. Look at the figures in each of the columns and check how the figures are derived. Note the figures for marginal cost are plotted between the lines to illustrate that marginal cost

> **Definitions**
>
> **Average (total) cost (AC)** Total cost (fixed plus variable) per unit of output: $AC = TC/Q = AFC = AVC$.
>
> **Average fixed cost (AFC)** Total fixed cost per unit of output: $AFC = TFC/Q$.
>
> **Average variable cost (AVC)** Total variable cost per unit of output: $AVC = TVC/Q$.
>
> **Marginal cost (MC)** The cost of producing one more unit of output: $MC = \Delta TC/\Delta Q$.

Output (Q) (1)	TFC (£000) (2)	TVC (£000) (3)	TC (TFC + TVC) (£000) (4)	AFC (TFC/Q) (£000) (5)	AVC (TVC/Q) (£000) (6)	AC (TC/Q) (£000) (7)	MC (ΔTC/ΔQ) (£000) (8)
0	12	0	12	–	–	–	
1	12	10	22	12	10	22	10
2	12	16	28	6	8	14	6
3	12	21	33	4	7	11	5
4	12	28	40	3	7	10	7
5	12	40	52	2.4	8	10.4	12
6	12	60	72	2	10	12	20
7	12	91	103	1.7	13	14.7	31

Table 4.1 Costs for firm X

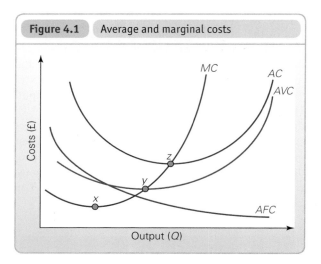

Figure 4.1 Average and marginal costs

The relationship between average cost and marginal cost. The shape of the AC curve depends on the shape of the MC curve. As long as new units of output cost less than the average, their production must pull the average cost down. That is, if MC is less than AC, AC must be falling. Likewise, if new units cost more than the average, their production must pull the average up. That is, if MC is greater than AC, AC must be rising. Therefore, the MC curve crosses the AC curve at its minimum point (point z in Figure 4.1). If you find this concept difficult, then try inserting some data for AC, MC and TC at different levels of output.

For example, say 4 units of output cost £5 each to produce. Total cost = £20 (4 × 5) and average cost = £5 (20/4). If output is increased by 1 unit and this unit costs an extra £5 to produce, (the same as the average cost) then the average cost simply remains at £5 (Average cost = TC/Q = 25/5 = £5). However, now assume that the marginal cost of this fifth unit is £6 (MC > AC). Total costs for 6 units are now £26 and the average cost is: AC = TC/Q = 26/5 = £5.20. The average cost has been pulled up by the higher marginal cost. The opposite will happen if marginal cost is lower than average cost.

The relationship described here is just one illustration of the relationship that applies between all average and marginal variables.

Average variable cost (AVC). Since AVC = AC − AFC, the AVC curve is simply the vertical difference between the AC and the AFC curves. Again, note that as AFC falls, the gap between AVC and AC narrows. Since all marginal costs are variable, the same relationship holds between MC and AVC as it did between MC and AC. That is, if MC is less than AVC, AVC must be falling, and if MC is greater than AVC, AVC must be rising. Therefore, as with the AC curve, the MC curve crosses the AVC curve at its minimum point (point y in Figure 4.1).

Although the AVC, AC, TVC, MC and TC curves are typically drawn in the ways described, it should be noted that they do not always have to be drawn like this. As we vary the assumptions about how output changes in response to increasing inputs, the impact on a firm's costs will change. This means that the shape of the cost curves will also vary.

represents the increase in costs as output increases from one unit to the next.

We can use the data in Table 4.1 to draw MC, AFC, AVC and AC curves (see Figure 4.1).

Marginal cost (MC). The shape of the MC curve follows directly from the law of diminishing returns. Initially, in Figure 4.1, as more of the variable input is used, extra units of output cost less than previous units. This means that MC initially falls.

Beyond a certain level of output, however, diminishing returns set in. This is shown as point x. Thereafter MC rises. Additional units of output cost more and more to produce, since they require ever-increasing amounts of the variable input.

Average fixed cost (AFC). This falls continuously as output rises, since total fixed costs are being spread over a greater and greater output. If a firm finds that its fixed costs represent a large proportion of its total costs, expanding output can be a good strategy to adopt, as average fixed costs will begin to fall.

Average (total) cost (AC). This is the vertical sum of the average fixed cost and the average variable cost curves. As you can see from Figure 4.1, as AFC falls, the gap between AVC and AC decreases.

Pause for thought

Before you read on try to explain why the marginal cost curve will always cut the average cost curve at its lowest point?

RECAP

1. Production in the short run is subject to diminishing returns. As greater quantities of the variable input(s) are used, so each additional unit of the variable input will add less to output than previous units, i.e. output will rise less and less rapidly.

2. When measuring costs of production, we should be careful to use the concept of opportunity cost. In the case of inputs not owned by the firm, the opportunity cost is simply the explicit cost of purchasing or hiring them: it is the price paid for them. In the case of inputs already owned by the firm, it is the implicit cost of what the factor could have earned for the firm in its best alternative use.

3. As some factors are fixed in supply in the short run, their total costs are fixed with respect to output. In the case of

variable factors, their total cost increases as more output is produced and hence as more of them are used. Total cost can be divided into total fixed and total variable cost.

4. Marginal cost is the cost of producing one more unit of output. It will typically fall at first but will start to rise when diminishing returns set in.

5. Average cost, like total cost, can be divided into fixed and variable costs. Average fixed cost will decline as more output is produced. The reason is that the total fixed cost is being spread over a greater and greater number of units of output. Average variable cost will tend to decline at first, but once the marginal cost has risen above it, it must then rise. The same applies to average cost.

BOX 4.2   **UNDERSTANDING YOUR FIXED COSTS**

The effect of changing output

The distinction between fixed and variable costs has profound implications for the behaviour of any business. In the short run, if a firm increases its output, total variable costs will increase; total fixed costs will not. Put another way, average variable costs may well rise, but average fixed costs will fall (as Figure 4.1 illustrates).

So why is this so important for business? The answer is that no firm will want to have its fixed inputs underused, except for short periods of time. After all, using more of them incurs no extra fixed costs – by definition. The larger the proportion of fixed costs to variable costs, the more important this becomes. It becomes especially important when a business has more than one production plant and where the ratio of fixed and variable costs vary between them.

The case of electricity generation

Let's take the example of electricity generation and compare a gas-fired power station with a nuclear one. There is a similar average cost of generating electricity from each type of station (around £80 to £100 per megawatt/hour), yet the proportion of fixed and variable costs is very different. A nuclear power station has low variable costs (mainly fuel), but is very expensive to build, maintain and decommission and so has very high fixed costs; average fixed cost at full capacity is around 91 per cent of average cost. In comparison, gas-fired power stations are relatively cheap to build, but more expensive to run, such that average fixed cost at normal capacity account for only around 16 per cent of average cost.

The implication of these differences is that nuclear power stations should be kept working near to full capacity, because when output increases, average fixed costs are spread over more units and so the lower average fixed cost pulls down average costs. However, if less output is produced in a gas-fired power station with its lower fixed costs, this will not significantly increase its average fixed cost.

As electricity cannot be stored and demand fluctuates with the time of day, it is necessary to have spare capacity to meet surges in demand and so gas-fired power stations with their lower fixed costs can fill this role. Thus, the output of nuclear power stations is virtually constant, while the output of gas-fired stations fluctuates with demand.

1. *On a diagram similar to Figure 4.1, sketch the AFC, AVC, AC and MC curves for (a) a nuclear power station and (b) a gas-fired power station. For simplicity assume that both stations would produce the same amount of electricity at full capacity.*

Economic vulnerability

Type 1 vulnerability: to changes in demand. Although many firms have a U-shaped average cost curve, the rate at which average costs fall and then rise as output increases will vary between firms. This explains why some firms are more vulnerable than others to changes in demand.

Consider two firms, A and B. Each firm's average cost curve is shown in Figure (a). Assume, for simplicity, that each firm achieves minimum average cost at point x, namely at the same output Q_0 and at the same average cost, AC_0. Now consider what would happen if there was a recession, such that both firms experience a fall in demand and cut output to Q_1.

With a U-shaped AC curve, per unit costs begin to rise, but firm A's costs rise significantly faster than firm B's, because firm A has a steeper AC curve. The same fall in quantity pushes firm A's average costs up from AC_0 to AC_1 (point a) but only causes firm B's costs to increase to AC_2 (point b) as firm B's AC curve is relatively flat.

Returning to point x, now assume that there is an expansion in demand. Both firms consequently increase output. Again, firm A's costs rise more rapidly than firm B's, because of the shape of the AC curves.

Therefore, firm A is much more susceptible to any change in demand, as this will have a greater effect on its costs and hence on its profit margin and profits, making it a much more vulnerable firm.

What are the factors that affect the steepness of the AC curve and hence make one firm more vulnerable than another?

■ If a firm has a high ratio of fixed factors to variable factors then it is likely to face a steeper AC curve. Total fixed costs do not change with output and hence, if output falls, it implies that its high fixed costs are spread over fewer and fewer units of output and this causes average costs to rise rapidly.

▶

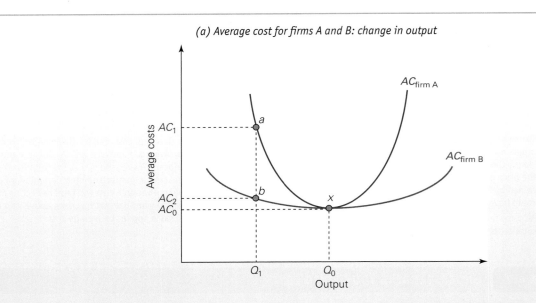

(a) Average cost for firms A and B: change in output

- If a firm is relatively inflexible in its use of inputs, it may find that a cut in production means that efficiency goes down and average costs rise rapidly. Similarly, if it wishes to expand output beyond Q_0, it may find it difficult to do so without incurring considerable extra costs, for example by employing expensive agency staff or hiring expensive machinery.

2. *Conduct some research on a firm of your choice, looking into its data on costs and decide whether or not you think this firm would be economically vulnerable due to its fixed costs.*

Type 2 vulnerability: to changes in input prices. Another way in which firms can be vulnerable is if they have heavy reliance on external or bought-in inputs. For example, some firms may be heavily dependent on oil or other raw materials and if the price of these change, it can have a very big effect on the firm's costs of production, its profit margins and profit. During an economic boom or a period of high growth, production tends to increase, and the demand for oil and other raw materials often rises, thus pushing up these prices. The more dependent a firm is on

such inputs, the greater the effect on its costs and the bigger the upward vertical shift in its *AC* curve. If a firm is less reliant on these raw materials or has alternative inputs it can turn to, such a change in global prices will cause only a small shift in the firm's *AC* curve.

In Figure (b), assume both firms X and Y have the same *AC* curve, given by AC_1. But let us also assume that firm X is very dependent on oil, whereas firm Y is not.

Assume that oil prices now rise. This will lead to a large upward shift in firm X's *AC* curve from AC_1 to AC_2, but a smaller upward shift in firm Y's *AC* curve from AC_1 to AC_3. There is a much larger cost penalty imposed on firm X than on firm Y, due to its reliance on oil as a factor of production.

In 2010, oil prices rose significantly, so firms that were big users of oil, either directly into the production process or for transporting their inputs and produce, saw their costs rise and their profits eroded. However, from late 2014 into early 2016, oil prices fell considerably and so those firms that were heavily dependent on oil saw their *AC* curves shift downwards significantly, thereby helping to increase their profits. Other firms that were less reliant on oil, however, did not benefit so much from low global prices for oil.

(b) Average cost for firms X and Y: change in costs

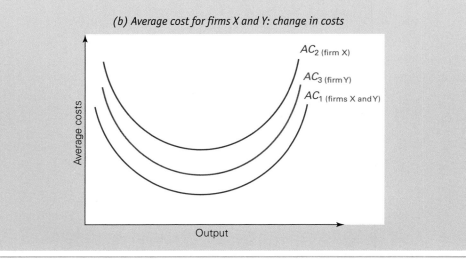

? 3. *Now look at some data on a firm of your choice and decide whether or not you think this firm would be vulnerable from too much reliance on bought-in or external inputs. Is it the same firm as you discussed in the previous question? If your data suggests the firm would be vulnerable in both ways, what might this mean for the firm?*

An application to Monarch

If a firm is vulnerable to a change in output due to both its fixed costs and its reliance on external inputs, then any change in economic circumstances can cause serious problems. It will suffer from both type 1 and type 2 vulnerability.

Type 1 vulnerability. Airlines are notorious for having high fixed costs, including costs of purchasing planes, salaries, aircraft maintenance, airport charges, aviation taxes and insurance. These costs do not vary whether a plane is full or has just one passenger. Monarch, a British airline, had even higher fixed costs than a typical airline, because it had agreed to high leasing costs for its planes. It also tended to pay staff higher salaries than competitor airlines, such as Ryanair. It wanted to retain pilots and was prepared to allow staff to belong to unions – something that Ryanair resisted. Monarch also invested more in training. The implication was that Monarch was particularly vulnerable to any decline in passenger numbers.

And passenger numbers did decline. Monarch flew to a number of previously popular holiday destinations in the middle east, such as Egypt, which experienced terrorist attacks (see Box 1.2). Revenue declined and fixed costs had to be spread over fewer passengers. Profits thus took a big hit.

Type 2 vulnerability. Airlines are also an example of firms that are vulnerable to changes in external costs – in this case oil, because of their reliance on fuel, which is priced in dollars. Any movement in oil prices creates significant changes in an airline's costs and thus impacts profits.

In the case of Monarch, it was also affected by the fall in the value of sterling, which occurred after the UK voted to leave the EU in June 2016. Monarch had to purchase dollars on the foreign exchange market in order to buy a given quantity of fuel and so with the fall in the value of sterling, Monarch needed to buy more and more dollars in order to purchase the same quantity of fuel. This fact, combined with the higher cost of aircraft leases and also priced in dollars, led to Monarch's costs increasing by £50 million and so again its profits were hit.

The combination of these two types of vulnerability therefore had a significantly negative impact on Monarch's profits and contributed to its demise in 2017.

The structure of the firm is thus a key determinant of how vulnerable it is to reductions in demand or increases in input prices. Understanding this can help managers devise strategies to insulate themselves from such fluctuations.

Q *Choose a particular company and assess the extent to which it faces type 1 and type 2 vulnerability. Students could then compare their assessments of their chosen companies.*

4.2 PRODUCTION AND COSTS: LONG RUN

In the long run *all* inputs are variable. There is time for the firm to install new machines, to use different techniques of production or to build a new factory (maybe in a different part of the country), and in general to combine its inputs in whatever proportion and in whatever quantities it chooses.

Therefore, when planning for the long run, a firm will have to make a number of decisions about the scale of its operations and the techniques of production it will use. These decisions will affect the firm's costs of production and can be completely irreversible, so it is important to get them right.

The scale of production

If a firm were to double all of its inputs – something it could only do in the long run – would this cause its output to double? Or would output more than double or less than double? We can distinguish three possible situations.

Constant returns to scale. This is where a given percentage increase in inputs leads to the same percentage increase in output.

Increasing returns to scale. This is where a given percentage increase in inputs leads to a larger percentage increase in output.

Decreasing returns to scale. This is where a given percentage increase in inputs leads to a smaller percentage increase in output.

Notice the terminology here. The words 'to scale' mean that *all* inputs increase by the same proportion. Decreasing returns to *scale* are therefore quite different from *diminishing* marginal returns (where only the *variable* input increases). The differences between marginal returns to a variable input and returns to scale are illustrated in Table 4.2.

In the short run, input 1 is assumed to be fixed in supply (at 3 units). Output can be increased only by using more of the variable input (input 2). In the long run, however, both inputs are variable.

In the short-run situation, diminishing returns can be seen from the fact that as input 2 is increased, output increases at a decreasing rate (25 to 45 to 60 to 70 to 75). In the long-run situation, the table illustrates increasing returns to scale. As both inputs are

Table 4.2		Short-run and long-run increases in output			
Short run			**Long run**		
Input 1	Input 2	Output	Input 1	Input 2	Output
3	1	25	1	1	15
3	2	45	2	2	35
3	3	60	3	3	60
3	4	70	4	4	90
3	5	75	5	5	125

increased, output increases at an *increasing* rate (15 to 35 to 60 to 90 to 125).

Economies of scale

The concept of increasing returns to scale is closely linked to that of *economies of scale*. A firm experiences economies of scale if costs per unit of output fall as the scale of production increases. Clearly, if a firm is getting increasing returns to scale from its inputs, then as it produces more, it will be using smaller and smaller amounts of inputs per unit of output. Other things being equal, this means that it will be producing at a lower unit cost.

There are several reasons why firms are likely to experience economies of scale. Some are due to increasing returns to scale, some are not:

Specialisation and division of labour. In large-scale plants, workers can do more simple repetitive jobs. With this *specialisation and division of labour*, less training is needed; workers can become highly efficient in their particular job, especially with long production runs; there is less time lost in workers switching from one operation to another; each worker only needs one set of tools, thereby cutting costs; supervision is easier. Workers and managers who have specific skills in specific areas can be employed and this may improve productivity.

Indivisibilities. Some inputs are of a minimum size. They are indivisible. The most obvious example is machinery. Take the case of a combine harvester. A small-scale farmer could not make full use of one. They only become economical to use, therefore, on farms above a certain size. The problem of *indivisibilities* is made worse when different machines, each of which is part of the production process, are of a different size. Consider a firm that uses two different machines at different stages of the production process: one produces a maximum of 6 units a day, the other can package a maximum of 4 units a day. Therefore, if all machines are to be fully utilised, a minimum of 12 units per day will have to

be produced, involving two production machines and three packaging machines.

The 'container principle'. Any capital equipment that contains things (blast furnaces, oil tankers, pipes, vats, etc.) will tend to cost less per unit of output the larger its size. This is due to the relationship between a container's volume and its surface area. A container's cost will depend largely on the materials used to build it and hence roughly on its *surface area*. Its output will depend largely on its *volume*. Large containers have a bigger volume relative to surface area than small containers. For example, a container with a bottom, top and four sides, with each side measuring 1 metre, has a volume of 1 cubic metre and a surface area of 6 square metres (6 surfaces of 1 square metre each). If each side were now to be doubled in length to 2 metres, the volume would be 8 cubic metres and the surface area 24 square metres (6 surfaces of 4 square metres each). Therefore a fourfold increase in the container's surface area and thus an approximate fourfold increase in costs has led to an eightfold increase in capacity.

Greater efficiency of large machines. Large machines may be more efficient, in the sense that more output can be gained for a given amount of inputs. For example, whether a machine is large or small, only one worker may be required to operate it. Also, a large machine may make a more efficient use of raw materials.

By-products. With production on a large scale, firms may produce sufficient waste products to enable them to make some by-product, thereby spreading costs over more units of output.

Multi-stage production. A large factory may be able to take a product through several stages in its manufacture. This saves time and cost moving the semifinished product from one firm or factory to another. For example, a large cardboard-manufacturing firm may be able to convert trees or waste paper into cardboard and then into cardboard boxes in a continuous sequence.

Definitions

Economies of scale When increasing the scale of production leads to a lower cost per unit of output.

Specialisation and division of labour Where production is broken down into a number of simpler, more specialised tasks, thus allowing workers to acquire a high degree of efficiency.

Indivisibilities The impossibility of dividing an input into smaller units.

All the above are examples of *plant economies of scale*. They are due to an individual factory or workplace or machine being large. There are other economies of scale that are associated with the business itself being large – perhaps with many factories.

Organisational. With a large business, individual plants can specialise in particular functions. There can also be centralised administration of the plants. Often, after a merger between two firms, savings can be made by *rationalising* their activities in this way.

Spreading overheads. Some expenditures, such as research and development, are economic only when the *business* is large; only a large business can afford to set up a research laboratory. For example, in the biotechnology industry in the USA and France, over 80 per cent of R&D comes from larger companies. This is another example of indivisibilities, only this time at the level of the whole business rather than the plant. The greater the business's output, the more these *overhead costs* are spread and this helps to cut average fixed costs. Similarly, it is much better for an airline to have full or nearly full flights rather than half empty ones, as these mean they are able to spread the costs of operating the flight over more passengers.

Financial economies. Large businesses may be able to obtain finance at lower interest rates than small ones, as they are seen as a lower risk or have the power to negotiate a better deal. Indeed, during the financial crisis many small businesses did find that banks were unwilling to lend to them at competitive rates of interest. Larger firms may also be able to obtain certain inputs more cheaply, by purchasing in bulk. This relates to the concept of opportunity cost. The larger is a business's order of raw materials, the more likely it is that the supplier will offer a discount, as the opportunity cost of losing the business is relatively high. This helps to reduce the cost per unit.

Economies of scope. Often a business is large because it produces a range of products. This can result in each individual product being produced more cheaply than if it was produced in a single-product firm. The reason for these *economies of scope* is that various overhead costs and financial and organisational economies can be shared between the products. For example, a firm that produces a whole range of CD players, BluRay players and recorders, games consoles, TVs and so on can benefit from shared marketing and distribution costs and the bulk purchase of electronic components. Producing a range of products also allows a business to spread its risks and hence insulate itself against a fall in demand for one of its products.

Many companies will experience a variety of economies of scale and you can find examples in practice from a variety of sources. On the Sloman Economics News site, you will find blogs that discuss economies of scale, such as those experienced by companies using cloud computing (*Operating in a cloud*) and whether big supermarkets can use economies of scale to their advantage (*Supermarket wars: a pricing race to the bottom*). An article in *The Economist* discusses the economies of scale that occur with one of the world's most prized aquarium fish.[1] The economies of scale for large cloud providers is also discussed in numerous articles, including an article by Randy Bias[2] and another that considers the case of Microsoft.[3]

Diseconomies of scale

When businesses get beyond a certain size, costs per unit of output may start to increase and in this article from *Ship & Bunker*,[4] there is an interesting analysis of the problem of diseconomies of scale in the case of large vessels. There are several reasons for such *diseconomies of scale*:

- Management problems of coordination may increase as the business becomes larger and more complex, and as lines of communication get longer. There may be a lack of personal involvement by management. We saw the emergence of this problem with growing U-form organisations in section 1.1.
- Workers may feel 'alienated' if their jobs are boring and repetitive, and if they feel an insignificantly small part of a large organisation. Poor motivation may lead to shoddy work.

Definitions

Plant economies of scale Economies of scale that arise because of the large size of the factory.

Rationalisation The reorganising of production (often after a merger) so as to cut out waste and duplication and generally to reduce costs.

Overheads Costs arising from the general running of an organisation, and only indirectly related to the level of output.

Economies of scope When increasing the range of products produced by a firm reduces the cost of producing each one.

Diseconomies of scale Where costs per unit of output increase as the scale of production increases.

---

[1] 'Economies of scale: Why Asia is obsessed with arowanas', *The Economist*, Asia (13 September 2018).
[2] Randy Bias, 'Understanding Cloud Datacenter economies of scale', *Cloudscaling Blog* (4 May 2010).
[3] Charles Babcock, 'Microsoft: "Incredible economies of scale" Await Cloud Users', *InformationWeek* (11 May 2011).
[4] 'Drewry Warns mega ships could diminish economies of scale', *Ship & Bunker* (10 March 2016).

- Industrial relations may deteriorate as a result of these factors and also as a result of the more complex interrelationships between different categories of worker.
- Production line processes and the complex interdependencies of mass production can lead to great disruption if there are hold-ups in any one part of the business.

> ### Pause for thought
>
> *Which of the economies of scale we have considered are due to increasing returns to scale and which are due to other factors?*

Whether businesses experience economies or diseconomies of scale will depend on the conditions applying in each individual business.

The size of the whole industry

As an *industry* grows in size, this can lead to *external economies of scale* for its member firms. This is where a firm, whatever its own individual size, benefits from the *whole industry* being large. For example, the firm may benefit from having access to specialist raw material or component suppliers, labour with specific skills, firms that specialise in marketing the finished product, sharing research and development, and banks and other financial institutions with experience of the industry's requirements. What we are referring to here is the *industry's infrastructure*: the facilities, support services, skills and experience that can be shared by its members.

> ### Pause for thought
>
> *Would you expect external economies of scale to be associated with the concentration of an industry in a particular region? Explain.*

When industries form a cluster in an area, external economies are likely to be experienced. In the long run, a firm can change its location and this can help clusters to develop in certain areas, typically dictated by the availability, suitability and cost of the factors of production in that location. We examine one such industrial cluster in Box 4.3.

The member firms of a particular industry might, however, experience *external diseconomies of scale*. For example, as an industry grows larger, this may create a growing shortage of specific raw materials or skilled labour. This will push up their prices, and hence the firms' costs. If the industry grows larger in a particular region, the price of land could increase and there may be increased pollution and congestion in the surrounding area.

Long-run average cost

We turn now to *long-run* cost curves. Since there are no fixed inputs in the long run, there are no long-run fixed costs. For example, a firm may rent more land in order to expand its operations. Its rent bill will therefore rise as it expands its output. All costs, then, in the long run are variable costs.

Although it is possible to draw long-run total, marginal and average cost curves, we will concentrate on *long-run average cost (LRAC) curves*. These can take various shapes, but a typical one is shown in Figure 4.2.

It is often assumed that as a firm expands, it will initially experience economies of scale and thus face a downward-sloping *LRAC* curve. But while it is possible for a firm to experience a continuously decreasing *LRAC* curve, in most cases, after a certain point, all such economies will have been achieved and thus the curve will flatten out. Then (possibly after a period of constant *LRAC*), the firm will get so large that it will start experiencing diseconomies of scale and thus a rising *LRAC*. At this stage, production and financial economies begin to be offset by the managerial problems of running a giant organisation. There is evidence to show that this is the case within growing businesses, but there is less evidence to indicate that technical diseconomies of scale exist.

Assumptions behind the long-run average cost curve

We make three key assumptions when constructing long-run average cost curves:

Input prices are given. At each output, a firm will face a given set of input prices. If input prices *change*, therefore, both short- and long-run cost curves will shift. Thus an increase in wages would shift the curves upwards.

However, input prices might be different at *different* levels of output. For example, one of the

> ### Definitions
>
> **External economies of scale** Where a firm's costs per unit of output decrease as the size of the whole industry grows.
>
> **Industry's infrastructure** The network of supply agents, communications, skills, training facilities, distribution channels, specialised financial services, etc. that support a particular industry.
>
> **External diseconomies of scale** Where a firm's costs per unit of output increase as the size of the whole industry increases.
>
> **Long-run average cost curve** A curve that shows how average cost varies with output on the assumption that all factors are variable.

Figure 4.2 A typical long-run average cost curve

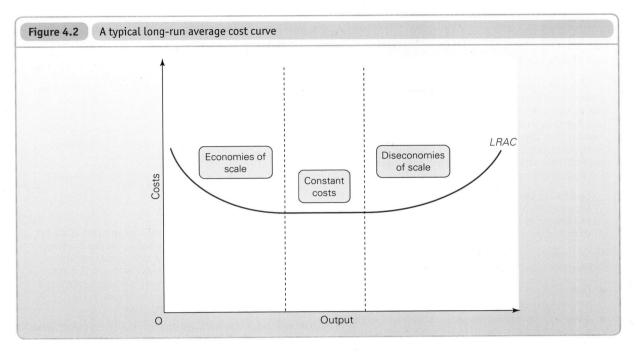

economies of scale that many firms enjoy is the ability to obtain bulk discount on raw materials and other supplies. In such cases the curve does *not* shift. The different input prices are merely experienced at different points along the curve, and are reflected in the shape of the curve. Input prices are still given for any particular level of output.

The state of technology and input quality are given. These are assumed to change only in the *very* long run. If a firm gains economies of scale, it is because it is able to exploit *existing* technologies and make better use of the existing availability of inputs, thus shifting the curve downwards.

Firms operate efficiently. The assumption here is that firms operate efficiently: that they choose the cheapest possible way of producing any level of output. If the firm did not operate efficiently, it would be producing at a point above the *LRAC* curve.

Transactions costs

So far we have concentrated largely on production costs: the cost of the inputs used in the production process. There is another category of costs, however, that businesses will need to take into account when considering the scale and scope of their organisation. These are *transactions costs*: costs associated with the process of buying or selling. There are four main categories of transactions costs:

Search costs. In many cases, inputs can be obtained from a large number of suppliers and a firm will incur costs in searching out the best supplier in terms of

price and/or quality. The problem here is that the firm starts with imperfect information and it takes time and money to obtain that information. It may employ a *logistics* company to seek out the best sources of supply, but obviously the logistics company will charge for its services. What is more, the firm may well run into the principal–agent problem unless it can monitor the behaviour of the logistics company – i.e. its agent (see pages 9–10).

Contract costs. When a supplier is found, time and effort may be incurred in bargaining over price and quality. If the supplier is to continue supplying over a period of time, then a contract will probably be negotiated. There will be costs in drawing up such contracts, including legal costs and the time of specialists to ensure that specifications are correct.

Monitoring and enforcement costs. When a contract has been drawn up, it is unlikely to cover every eventuality. To use the jargon, it is 'incomplete'. For example, if a logistics company is contracted to provide transportation of a manufacturing firm's products, the contract may specify maximum times for

Definitions

Transactions costs The costs associated with exchanging products. For buyers it is the costs over and above the price of the product. For sellers it is the costs over and above the costs of production.

Logistics The business of managing and handling inputs to and outputs from a firm.

BOX 4.3 LIGHTS, CAMERA, ACTION

Location, Location, Location

Globalisation means that it is easy to source inputs and products from anywhere in the world and this would suggest that location is becoming less important. It is no longer vital for a firm to be located near raw materials or places where they have a competitive cost advantage, as it can buy from and sell to anywhere. Yet, location is still one of the most important factors in determining both firm and industry competitiveness and much of this is driven by the formation of *clusters*.

> Clusters are geographically proximate groups of interconnected companies, suppliers, service providers, and associated institutions in a particular field, linked by commonalties and complementarities.[1]

Porter suggests that clusters are vital for competitiveness in three crucial respects:

- Clusters improve productivity. The close proximity of suppliers and other service providers enhances flexibility.
- Clusters aid innovation. Interaction among business within a cluster stimulates new ideas and aids their dissemination.
- Clusters contribute to new business formation. Clusters are self-reinforcing, in so far as specialist factors such as dedicated venture capital, and labour skills, help reduce costs and lower the risks of new business start-up.

Clusters are also one of the key things that create competition between rivals, as they compete for both customers and inputs and this competitiveness is a crucial ingredient for a successful cluster.

Porter's view is that economic development is achieved through a series of stages.

[1] M. E. Porter and C. H. M. Ketels, *UK competitiveness: moving to the next stage*, DTI and ESRC (May 2003), p. 5.

- The factor-driven stage identifies factors of production that are plentiful in supply, as the basis of competitive advantage.
- The investment-driven stage of development focuses upon efficiency and productivity as the key to competitive success.
- The third stage is achieved through the production of innovative products and services.

One highly successful cluster will be familiar to everyone: Hollywood.

The success of Hollywood

In the early 1900s, movie companies began to move to what we now know as Hollywood, attracted by the good weather and the cheaper labour costs. The industry was initially dominated by major studios, such as Paramount Pictures, which controlled all aspects of movie production, but also owned the cinemas where the films were shown. They, therefore, also controlled consumption.[2]

A legal case helped to break up the major studios and created smaller specialist firms which, by clustering around Hollywood, were still able to receive the benefits of a large studio, without many of the issues experienced by a large

Definition

(Business or industrial) cluster A geographical concentration of related businesses and institutions.

[2] M. Gupta, R. Jacobi, J. F. Jamet and L. Malik, 'The LA Motion Picture Industry Cluster', *The Microeconomics of Competitiveness: Firms, clusters and economic development*, Harvard Business School (May 2006).

---

delivery. The manufacturing firm is then likely to incur costs in ensuring that the logistics firm sticks to the contract – and in taking action if it does not. What is more, there is a moral hazard involved (see pages 59–62). If the logistics firm *could* deliver items more quickly than specified in the contract, it will have no incentive to do so, even though it would have been in the manufacturer's interests.

Transport and handling costs. The more firms rely on buying components from other firms, rather than making them in-house, the greater will be the costs of transporting and handling these materials.

KEY IDEA 16

Transactions costs. The costs associated with exchanging products. For buyers it is the costs over and above the price of the product. For sellers it is the costs over and above the costs of production. Transactions costs include search costs, contract costs, monitoring and enforcement costs, and transport and handling costs.

Pause for thought

What transactions costs do you incur when (a) going to the supermarket to do a regular shop; (b) buying a new laptop?

Transactions costs and the scale and scope of the firm
One way of reducing transactions costs is for the firm to produce more *within* the firm rather than buying inputs from other firms or supplying to other firms. What we are describing here is a *vertically integrated firm*. This is where a firm is involved in several stages of the production of a good, such as component production, assembly and wholesale and retail distribu-

Definition

Vertically integrated firm A firm that produces at more than one stage in the production and distribution of a product.

firm. It also meant that consumption and production were separated, creating a more competitive environment.

Another factor that required the companies to adapt was the growing demand and the emergence of new technologies. Firstly, television ownership began to expand and then technology that allowed households to have entire films to watch at their leisure emerged (VHS – the pre-cursor to DVDs!). Such innovations required the industry to adapt, seeing these new forms of entertainment not as a potential threat to the industry, but as a new opportunity to generate revenue.[3]

Making the most of the competitive advantage that Hollywood had already established, the industry quickly grew. Data from 2013 show that the creative industries contributed $504 billion to US GDP, and Hollywood and the video industry together employed 310 000 workers – more than any other industry in California.

Reasons for the success of the Hollywood cluster
So, what is behind the cluster's success? Its location is certainly crucial, having all the geographical features that could be required in a film, together with a climate suitable for filming all year. The growth of Hollywood led many related industries to relocate there and this brought many significant benefits to the whole cluster, including cost advantages.

It attracted huge amounts of human capital, which is a key input for any successful cluster. Aspiring actors and actresses moved to Hollywood, as did those working in production, marketing and distribution, etc. It became the place to be for success in this industry.

---
[3] R. Kumar, J. Zwirbulis, A. Narko, M Goszczycki and E. Ersöz, *Hollywood Movie Cluster Analysis*, Warsaw School of Economics, Microeconomics of Competitiveness (January 2014).

As technology developed and movie production became more complex, so Hollywood attracted more and more industries: electronics, IT, special effects and animation, to name a few. This, together with the location playing home to thousands of movie stars, created a huge tourism industry, generating millions of dollars each year and providing another key contributing factor to the cluster's success: capital investment.

The film industry in Hollywood has always sought to move with the times, creating the most technologically advanced films that are always in high demand. The local rivalry between studios has been a key factor in driving competitiveness and fostering innovation, for example through special effects and animations: explosions have to be bigger and better. The cluster's success has also been driven by government support, as both state and federal government provide incentives to aid in the growth of the cluster, such as tax credits to support film production and to help cut costs.

One big downside of Hollywood's success is the growing cost of film production. Despite the government incentives that keep costs down, the popularity of Hollywood as a place to live and work has inflated property prices and wages. Movie making in this successful cluster generates huge revenues, but is also experiencing some of the adverse effects of its own success.

What other examples of clusters can you find and how have they evolved to be a success?

Choose another industrial cluster and assess how successful clustering has been for the firms involved.

---

tion. The energy sector is an example of an industry with a considerable degree of vertical integration and you can read some of the articles concerning this in two blogs on the Sloman Economics News site: *The Big Six: for how much longer?* and *Making UK energy supply more competitive.*

Firms may expand their operations vertically by integrating backwards down the *supply chain* or forwards up it. *Backward integration* is where a firm itself produces the inputs it needs. Thus a car manufacturer may itself produce components such as body panels, engines and trimmings. *Forward integration* is where a firm itself moves into producing stages closer to the end consumer. Thus a manufacturer of building materials may move into construction or become a builder's merchant.

Through vertical integration, a firm is able to avoid many of the costs discussed above. For example, a firm will not need to compare different suppliers, so will not incur search costs. As components are produced in-house, they do need to be transported

from one location to another and so transport and handling costs will fall. As no contracts exist between the firm and any supplier, legal fees will not be an issue and nor will the problem of monitoring and enforcing any contract. We return to this in section 6.2, where we will take a closer look at some other reasons why firms may vertically integrate, as well as the disadvantages of it.

Definitions

Supply chain The flow of inputs into a finished product, from the raw materials stage, through manufacturing and distribution, right through to the sale to the final consumer.

Backward integration Where a firm expands backwards down the supply chain to earlier stages of production.

Forward integration Where a firm expands forward up the supply chain towards the sale of the finished product.

BOX 4.4　MINIMUM EFFICIENT SCALE

The extent of economies of scale in practice

Two of the most important studies of economies of scale have been those made by C. F. Pratten[1] in the late 1980s and by a group advising the European Commission[2] in 1997. Both studies found strong evidence that many firms, especially in manufacturing, experienced substantial economies of scale.

In a few cases, long-run average costs fell continuously as output increased. For most firms, however, they fell up to a certain level of output and then remained constant.

The extent of economies of scale can be measured by looking at a firm's *minimum efficient scale (MES)*. The *MES* is the size beyond which no significant additional economies of scale can be achieved; in other words, the point where the *LRAC* curve flattens off. In Pratten's studies he defined this level as the minimum scale above which any possible doubling in scale would reduce average costs by less than 5 per cent (i.e. virtually the bottom of the *LRAC* curve). In the diagram *MES* is shown at point *a*.

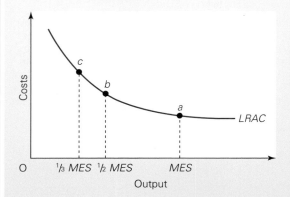

The *MES* can be expressed in terms either of an individual factory or of the whole firm. Where it refers to the minimum efficient scale of an individual factory, the *MES* is known as the *minimum efficient plant size (MEPS)*.

The *MES* can then be expressed as a percentage of the total size of the market or of total domestic production. Table (a), based on the Pratten study, shows *MES* for plants and firms in various industries. The first column shows *MES* as a percentage of total UK production. The second column shows *MES* as a percentage of total EU production. Table (b), based on the 1997 study, shows *MES* for various plants as a percentage of total EU production.

Expressing *MES* as a percentage of total output gives an indication of how competitive the industry could be. In some industries (such as footwear and carpets), economies of scale were exhausted (i.e. *MES* was reached) with plants or firms that were still small relative to total UK production and even smaller relative to total EU production. In such industries there would be room for many firms and thus scope for considerable competition.

In other industries, however, even if a single plant or firm were large enough to produce the whole output of the industry in the UK, it would still not be large enough to experience the full potential economies of scale; the *MES* is greater than 100 per cent. Examples from Table (a) include factories producing cellulose fibres, and car manufacturers. In such industries there is no possibility of competition. In fact, as long as the *MES* exceeds 50 per cent there will not be room for more than one firm large enough to gain full economies of scale. In this case the industry is said to be a *natural monopoly*. As we shall see in the next few chapters, when competition is lacking consumers may suffer by firms charging prices considerably above costs.

A second way of measuring the extent of economies of scale is to see how much costs would increase if production were reduced to a certain fraction of *MES*. The normal fractions used are 1/2 or 1/3 *MES*. This is illustrated in the diagram. Point *b* corresponds to 1/2 *MES*; point *c* to 1/3 *MES*. The greater the percentage by which *LRAC* at point *b* or *c* is higher than at point *a*, the greater will be the economies of scale to be gained by producing at *MES* rather than at 1/2 *MES* or 1/3 *MES*. For example, in the table there are greater economies of scale to be gained from moving from 1/2 *MES* to *MES* in the production of electric motors than in cigarettes.

The main purpose of the studies was to determine whether a single EU market is big enough to allow both economies of scale and competition. The tables suggest that in all cases, other things being equal, the EU market is large enough for firms to gain the full economies of scale *and* for there to be enough firms for the market to be competitive.

The second study also found that 47 of the 53 manufacturing sectors analysed had scope for further exploitation of economies of scale.

With the EU having expanded significantly since these two studies and with the use of the Internet growing all the time, firms across the EU are part of an increasingly large market. Further studies that consider the MES across different industries, especially in the EU, are vital to determine whether continued expansion will bring benefits in terms of falling *LRAC* and thus economies of scale or if continued enlargement could lead to diseconomies of scale. *MES* studies

---

[1] C. F. Pratten, 'A survey of the economies of scale', in *Research on the 'Costs of Non-Europe'*, Volume 2 (Luxembourg: Office for Official Publications of the European Communities, 1988). Copyright © 1988 European Communities.

[2] European Commission/Economists Advisory Group Ltd, 'Economies of scale', in *The Single Market Review*, Subseries V, Volume 4 (Luxembourg: Office for Official Publications of the European Communities, 1997). Copyright © 1997 European Communities.

Table (a)

Product	MES as % of production		% additional cost at half MES
	UK	EU	
Individual plants			
Cellulose fibres	125	16	3
Rolled aluminium semi-manufactures	114	15	15
Refrigerators	85	11	4
Steel	72	10	6
Electric motors	60	6	15
TV sets	40	9	9
Cigarettes	24	6	1.4
Ball-bearings	20	2	6
Beer	12	3	7
Nylon	4	1	12
Bricks	1	0.2	25
Tufted carpets	0.3	0.04	10
Shoes	0.3	0.03	1
Firms			
Cars	200	20	9
Lorries	104	21	7.5
Mainframe computers	>100	n.a.	5
Aircraft	100	n.a.	5
Tractors	98	19	6

Sources: see footnote 1

Table (b)

Plants	MES as % of total EU production
Aerospace	12.19
Tractors and agricultural machinery	6.57
Electric lighting	3.76
Steel tubes	2.42
Shipbuilding	1.63
Rubber	1.06
Radio and TV	0.69
Footwear	0.08
Carpets	0.03

Source: see footnote 2

could be used to address the question: how big is too big when it comes to the EU? The European Commission has agreed to fund such investigations, but no research is available at present.

1. Why might a firm operating with one plant achieve MEPS and yet not be large enough to achieve MES? (Clue: are all economies of scale achieved at plant level?)
2. Why might a firm producing bricks have an MES which is only 0.2 per cent of total EU production and yet face little effective competition from other EU countries?

Conduct a short literature search looking into the relationship between international trade and economies of scale. Summarise your findings and the theories behind this relationship.

RECAP

1. In the long run, a firm is able to vary the quantity of all its inputs. There are no fixed inputs and hence there are no fixed costs.

2. If it increases all inputs by the same proportion, it may experience constant, increasing or decreasing returns to scale.

3. Economies of scale occur when costs per unit of output fall as the scale of production increases. This can be due to a number of factors, some of which are directly caused by increasing (physical) returns to scale. These include the benefits of specialisation and division of labour, the use of larger and more efficient machines, and the ability to have a more integrated system of production. Other economies of scale arise from the financial and administrative benefits of large-scale organisations.

4. Typically, *LRAC* curves are drawn as L-shaped or as saucer-shaped. As output expands, initially there are economies of scale. When these are exhausted, the curve will become flat. When the firm becomes very large, it may begin to experience diseconomies of scale. If this happens, the *LRAC* curve will begin to slope upwards again.

5. Transactions costs are the costs associated with exchanging products. They include search costs, the costs of drawing up and monitoring contracts and transport and handling costs. The more firms rely on other firms as suppliers or buyers, the larger these costs are likely to be. Vertical integration is one way of reducing such transactions costs.

4.3 REVENUE

Remember that we defined a firm's total profit as its total revenue minus its total costs of production. In the last two sections we have examined costs. We now turn to revenue.

As with costs, we distinguish between three revenue concepts: total revenue (*TR*), average revenue (*AR*) and marginal revenue (*MR*).

Total, average and marginal revenue

Total revenue (TR)

Total revenue is the firm's total earnings per period of time from the sale of a particular amount of output (*Q*).

For example, if a firm sells 1000 units (*Q*) per month at a price of £5 each (*P*), then its monthly total revenue will be £5000: in other words, £5 $\times$ 1000 ($P \times Q$). Thus:

$$TR = P \times Q$$

Average revenue (AR)

Average revenue is the amount the firm earns per unit sold. Thus:

$$AR = TR/Q$$

So if the firm earns £5000 (*TR*) from selling 1000 units (*Q*), it will earn £5 per unit. But this is simply the price! Thus:

$$AR = P$$

Marginal revenue (MR)

Marginal revenue is the extra total revenue gained by selling one more unit (per time period). So if a firm sells an extra 20 units this month compared with what it expected to sell, and in the process earns an extra £100, then it is getting an extra £5 for each extra unit sold: *MR* = £5. Thus:

$$MR = \Delta TR/\Delta Q$$

We now need to see how revenue varies with output. We concentrate on average and marginal revenue. We can show this relationship graphically in the same way as we did with costs.

The relationship will depend on the market conditions under which a firm operates. The revenue curves we look at in this section are for a price-taking firm: a firm that faces a horizontal demand curve (see section 3.1). When firms face a downward-sloping demand curve and thus have some choice in setting price, they will face different revenue curves. We look at such curves in the next chapter.

Average and marginal revenue curves

Average revenue. We are assuming in this chapter that the firm has such a small share of the market that it is a price taker. That is, it has to accept the price

Definitions

Total revenue (*TR*) (per period) The total amount received by firms from the sale of a product, before the deduction of taxes or any other costs. The price multiplied by the quantity sold: $TR = P \times Q$.

Average revenue (*AR*) Total revenue per unit of output. When all output is sold at the same price, average revenue will be the same as price: $AR = TR/Q = P$.

Marginal revenue (*MR*) The extra revenue gained by selling one or more units per time period: $MR = \Delta TR/\Delta Q$.

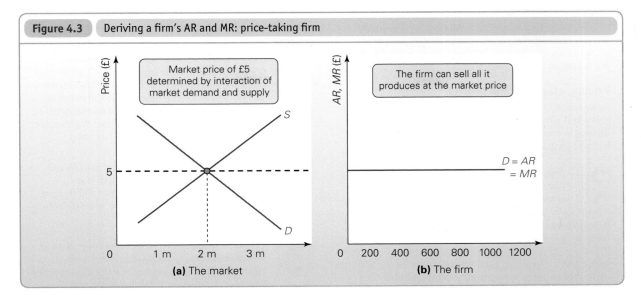

Figure 4.3 Deriving a firm's AR and MR: price-taking firm

(a) The market

(b) The firm

given by the intersection of demand and supply in the whole market. At this price, it can sell as much as it is capable of producing, but if it increases the price, it would lose all its sales to competitors. Furthermore, it would be irrational to reduce price below the equilibrium. This is illustrated in Figure 4.3.

Figure 4.3(a) shows market demand and supply. Equilibrium price is £5. Figure 4.3(b) looks at the demand for an individual firm which is tiny relative to the whole market. (Look at the difference in the scale of the horizontal axes in the two diagrams.)

Being so small, any change in the firm's output will be too insignificant to affect the market price. The

firm thus faces a horizontal demand 'curve' at this price. It can sell any output up to its maximum capacity without affecting this £5 price.

Average revenue is thus constant at £5. The firm's average revenue curve must therefore lie along exactly the same line as its demand curve.

Marginal revenue. In the case of a horizontal demand curve, the marginal revenue curve will be the same as the average revenue curve, since selling one more unit at a constant price (*AR*) merely adds that amount to total revenue. If an extra unit is sold at a constant price of £5, an extra £5 is earned.

BOX 4.5 COST, REVENUE AND PROFITS

Increased revenue – increased profits?

Increasing profits will nearly always be important for a firm. As a firm's profit depends on costs and revenue, focusing on the best strategy to increase profits is vital to success. In 2013, Starbucks implemented a strategy to boost profits, as is discussed in an article by Tucker Dawson[1] and a travel agency in the Northeast of the UK also changed its strategy in a bid to increase profits, as discussed in an article by Jonathan Manning.[2]

In the past two chapters, we have looked at ways in which firms can increase revenues and cut costs, but what is the impact on profit? Here we consider the uncertain effects on a firm's profits.

Firms may use market research to develop new products or markets, such as Apple's expansion into Asian markets and

the expansion by many Japanese companies into South East Asia, as discussed in a PwC blog.[3] Firms also use advertising to distinguish their product from others, thereby persuading consumers to buy it. Assuming these strategies are a success, a firm's revenue should rise, though it may take some time for the full effects to occur. But, will profits also rise?

Advertising, product innovation and market research require time, resources and money and so increase a firm's costs. Furthermore, the increase in costs will occur as soon as work starts on the process of product differentiation or market research, or at the beginning of an advertising campaign. This means that a firm is initially likely to experience rising costs, while revenues remain fairly constant. Thus profits will decline until the sales figures respond to the firm's strategy. Even after revenue responds to the firm's strategy, the impact

---

[1] Tucker Dawson, 'How Starbucks uses pricing strategy for profit maximization' *Price Intelligently blog* (30 June 2013).

[2] Jonathan Manning, 'Hays travel sees profits soar as expansion strategy begins to take off', *Chronicle Live* (19 March 2018).

[3] Arie Nakamura, 'The continuous expansion of Japanese companies in South East Asia', Growth Market Centre blog, PwC (25 August 2017).

▶

on profits is still unknown as, while total revenue might increase, total costs also rise. This means that, unless we know the relative increase in total revenue and total costs, the impact on profits is uncertain.

Pricing, elasticity and profits

As we saw in Chapter 2, changing the price of a product will also affect a firm's total revenue and the price elasticity of demand is crucial in determining the impact. But what happens to profit following a price change?

 1. *How will total revenue be affected by (a) a price rise and (b) a price fall if demand for the product is relatively elastic?*

If firms face an elastic demand, then cutting price will boost revenue, as the quantity demanded rises proportionately more than the price falls. Yet, the increased demand may require production to rise and so the firm's total variable and average costs will rise (although average fixed costs will fall). If, however, the firm has sufficient stocks to satisfy the higher demand, then the impact on costs may be less severe. With elastic demand, the impact on profit depends on whether total revenue increases by more or less than total costs.

What about the situation where a product has an inelastic demand? This time it is an *increase* in price that will boost total revenue, as the resulting fall in quantity will be proportionately smaller than the rise in price. If production is reduced by even a small amount, it will reduce the firm's demand for raw materials and in doing so cut its variable costs. In this case, the impact on profit is somewhat more predictable, as total revenue is increasing, while total costs are falling.

There are many factors that can influence profitability and whenever a firm considers a change in strategy, it is important to consider the impact on both costs and revenue and the timing of such changes. This may make the difference between a company's success and failure.

2. *Consider a firm that introduced a new policy of using only environmentally friendly inputs and locally sourced products in its production process. Analyse the impact of this strategy on the firm's costs and revenue. How do you think profits will be affected?*

RECAP

1. Total revenue (*TR*) is the total amount a firm earns from its sales in a given time period. It is simply price multiplied by quantity: $TR = P \times Q$.

2. Average revenue (*AR*) is total revenue per unit: $AR = TR/Q$. In other words, $AR = P$.

3. Marginal revenue is the extra revenue earned from the sale of one more unit per time period: $MR = \Delta TR/\Delta Q$.

4. The *AR* curve will be the same as the demand curve for the firm's product. In the case of a price taker, the demand curve and hence the *AR* curve will be a horizontal straight line and will also be the same as the *MR* curve.

4.4 PROFIT MAXIMISATION

We are now in a position to put costs and revenue together to find the output at which profit is maximised, and also to find out how much that profit will be. At this point, you may find an article by Renee O'Farrell[5] interesting: it considers the advantages and disadvantages of pursuing a strategy of profit maximisation.

First, we need to look a little more precisely at what we mean by the term 'profit'.

The meaning of 'profit'

One element of cost is the opportunity cost to the owners of the firm incurred by being in business. This is the minimum return that the owners must make on their capital in order to prevent them from eventually deciding to close down and perhaps move into some alternative business. It is a *cost* since, just as with wages, rent, etc., it has to be covered if the firm is to continue producing. This opportunity cost to the owners is sometimes known as *normal profit*, and is included in the cost curves.

What determines this normal rate of profit? It has two components. First, someone setting up in business invests capital in it. There is thus an opportunity cost, which is the interest that could have been earned

Definition

Normal profit The opportunity cost of being in business. It consists of the interest that could be earned on a riskless asset, plus a return for risk taking in this particular industry. It is counted as a cost of production.

[5] Renee O'Farrell, 'Advantages & disadvantages of profit maximization', *Small Business*Chron.com* (Houston Chronicle, 24 June 2011).

by lending the capital in some riskless form (e.g. by putting it in a savings account in a bank). Nobody would set up a business unless they expected to earn at least this rate of profit. Running a business is far from riskless, however, and hence a second element is a return to compensate for risk. Thus:

Normal profit (%) = rate of interest on a riskless loan + a risk premium

The risk premium varies according to the line of business. In those with fairly predictable patterns, such as food retailing, it is relatively low. Where outcomes are very uncertain, such as mineral exploration or the manufacture of fashion garments, it is relatively high. Thus if owners of a business earn normal profit, they will (just) be content to remain in that industry.

Any excess of profit over normal profit is known as *supernormal profit*. If firms earn supernormal profit, they will clearly prefer to stay in this business. Such profit will also tend to attract new firms into the industry, since it will give them a better return on capital than elsewhere. If firms earn *less* than normal profit, however, then after a time they will consider leaving and using their capital for some other purpose.

Short-run profit maximising

In the *short run under perfect competition*, we assume that the number of firms in an industry cannot be increased: there is simply not time for new firms to enter the market.

Figure 4.4 shows short-run equilibrium for an industry and the profit-maximising position for a firm under perfect competition. Both parts of the diagram have the same scale for the vertical axis. The horizontal axes have totally different scales, however. For example, if the horizontal axis for the firm were measured in, say, thousands of units, the horizontal axis for the whole industry might be measured in millions or tens of millions of units, depending on the number of firms in the industry.

Let us examine the determination of price, output and profit in turn.

Price. The price is determined in the industry by the intersection of demand and supply. The firm faces a horizontal demand (or average revenue) 'curve' at this price. It can sell all it can produce at the market price (P_e), but nothing at a price above P_e and we know it would not be rational to sell at a price below P_e.

Output. The firm will maximise profit where marginal cost equals marginal revenue ($MR = MC$), at an output of Q_e. In fact this *profit-maximising rule* will apply to firms in all types of market, as long as we assume that the objective of the firm is to maximise profits, so it is very important to understand.

But why are profits maximised when $MR = MC$? The simplest way of answering this is to see what the position would be if MR did not equal MC.

Referring to Figure 4.4, at a level of output below Q_e, MR exceeds MC. This means that by producing more units there will be a bigger addition to revenue (MR) than to cost (MC). Total profit will *increase*. *As long as MR exceeds MC, profit can be increased by increasing production.*

Definitions

Supernormal profit The excess of total profit above normal profit.

Short run under perfect competition The period during which there is too little time for new firms to enter the industry.

Profit-maximising rule Profit is maximised where marginal revenue equals marginal cost.

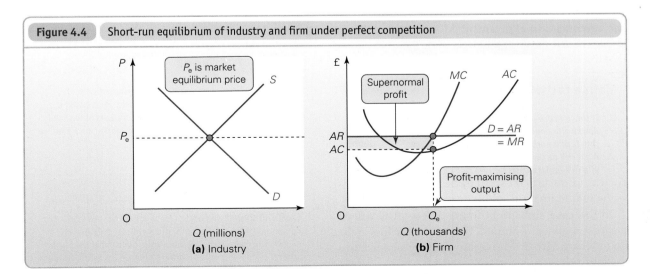

Figure 4.4 Short-run equilibrium of industry and firm under perfect competition

At a level of output above Q_e, MC exceeds MR. All levels of output above Q_e thus add more to cost than to revenue and hence *reduce* profit. *As long as MC exceeds MR, profit can be increased by cutting back on production.*

Profits are thus maximised where $MC = MR$: at an output of Q_e.

Students worry sometimes about the argument that profits are maximised when $MR = MC$. Surely, they say, if the last unit is making no profit, how can profit be at a *maximum*? The answer is very simple. If you cannot add anything more to a total, the total must be at the maximum. Take the simple analogy of going up a hill. When you cannot go any higher, you must be at the top.

Profit. Once the profit-maximising output has been discovered, we now use the average curves to measure the *amount* of profit at the maximum. Remember that normal profit is included in the AC curve. If, therefore, $AC = AR$, just normal profit will be made. For example, if the price (AR) were £8 and AC were also £8, then the firm would be earning enough revenue to cover all its costs and still earn normal profit, but no supernormal profit.

If the firm's average cost (AC) curve dips below the average revenue (AR) 'curve', as in Figure 4.4, the firm will earn supernormal profit. Supernormal profit per unit at Q_e is the vertical difference between AR and AC at Q_e. So if AR (= P) were £10 and AC were £8, then supernormal profit per unit would be £2.

Total supernormal profit at Q_e is found by multiplying supernormal profit per unit $(AR - AC)$ by the total number of units sold (Q_e). This is given by the area of the shaded rectangle in Figure 4.4. The reason is that the area of a rectangle is found by multiplying its height $(AR - AC)$ by its width (Q_e).

Loss minimising. Sometimes there may be no output at which the firm can make even normal profit. Such a situation is illustrated in Figure 4.5. With the average revenue 'curve' given by AR_1, the AC curve is above the AR curve at all levels of output.

Pause for thought

1. If the industry under perfect competition faces a downward-sloping demand curve, why does an individual firm face a horizontal demand curve?
2. What will be the effect on firm's profit-maximising output of a rise in fixed costs?

In this case, the output where $MR = MC$ will be the loss-minimising output. The amount of loss at the point where $MR = MC$ is shown by the shaded area in Figure 4.5.

Whether or not to produce. If a firm is making a loss, however, should it shut down? To answer this, we need to return to our distinction between fixed and variable costs. Fixed costs have to be paid even if the firm is producing nothing at all. Rent has to be paid, business rates have to be paid, and so forth. Providing, therefore, that the firm is more than covering its *variable* costs, it can go some way to paying off these fixed costs and therefore will continue to produce.

Therefore, the firm will shut down if the loss it would make from doing so (i.e. the fixed costs that must still be paid) is less than the loss it makes from continuing to produce. That is, a firm will shut down if it cannot cover its variable costs, as shown in Figure 4.5, where the price (AR) is below AR_2. This situation is known as the *short-run shut-down point* and is shown by point S.

The long-run equilibrium of the firm

Under perfect competition, we assume that there are no barriers to entry for new firms and in the long run we assume that there is time for firms to enter the industry. This will occur if typical firms are making supernormal profits. Likewise, if existing firms can make supernormal profits by increasing the scale of their operations, they will do so, since all inputs are variable in the long run.

The effect of the entry of new firms and/or the expansion of existing firms is to increase industry supply. This is illustrated in Figure 4.6.

The industry supply curve shifts to the right. This in turn leads to a fall in price. Supply will go on increasing, and price falling, until firms are making just normal profits. This will be when price has fallen to the point where the demand 'curve' for the firm just touches the bottom of its long-run average cost curve. This is shown as curve D_L. Q_L is thus the long-run equilibrium output of the firm, with P_L the long-run equilibrium market price. This long-run equilibrium is productively efficient, as the firm is producing at the minimum average cost. If the firm is unable to cover its long-run average costs, it will shut down and exit the industry.

Pause for thought

Consider a perfectly competitive market where losses are being made in the short run by a given firm. By drawing a diagram to illustrate this, use the same analysis as we used above to explain what will happen in this market such that we arrive at a long run equilibrium.

Definition

Short-run shut-down point This is where the AR curve is tangential to the AVC curve. The firm can only just cover its variable costs. Any fall in revenue below this level will cause a profit-maximising firm to shut down immediately.

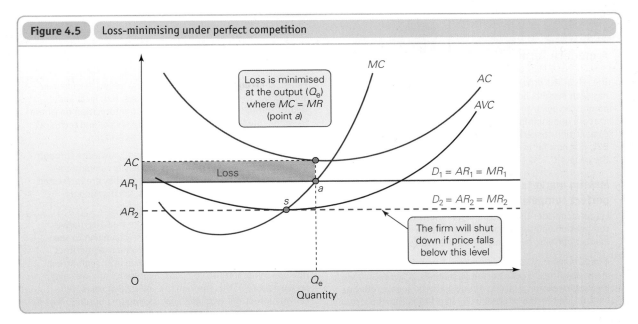

Figure 4.5 Loss-minimising under perfect competition

Loss is minimised at the output (Q_e) where $MC = MR$ (point a)

The firm will shut down if price falls below this level

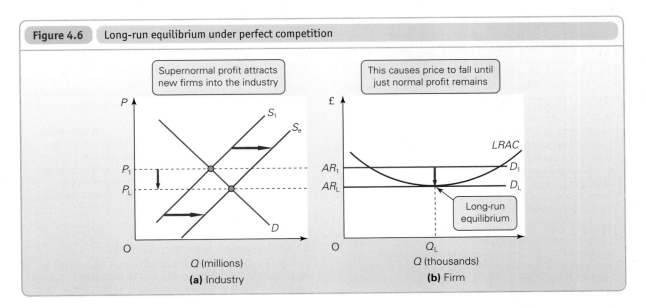

Figure 4.6 Long-run equilibrium under perfect competition

Supernormal profit attracts new firms into the industry

This causes price to fall until just normal profit remains

Long-run equilibrium

(a) Industry

(b) Firm

Do firms and consumers benefit from perfect competition?

Under perfect competition the firm faces a constant battle for survival. If it becomes less efficient than other firms, it will make less than normal profits and be driven out of business. If it becomes more efficient, it will earn supernormal profits, but they will not last for long. Soon other firms, in order to survive themselves, will be forced to copy the more efficient methods of the new firm, which they can do because of the assumption of perfect knowledge. In the long run, therefore, as we have seen, firms will produce at minimum average cost and hence will be productively efficient.

A similar battle for survival happens with product development. If a firm produces a new popular product, it will gain a temporary advantage over its rivals. It may make supernormal profits in the short run, but these will not last. Competitor firms will have to respond in order to avoid making a loss and being driven from the market. They too will have to develop this new product themselves. Total supply of it will rise. This will drive down the price and eliminate the supernormal profits.

Effect on consumers

Firms are encouraged to invest in new improved technology to ensure survival and in the long run, they must also produce at the least cost output to ensure

BOX 4.6　E-COMMERCE

A modern form of perfect competition?

The relentless drive towards big business in recent decades has seen markets become more concentrated and increasingly dominated by large producers. However, forces are at work that are undermining this dominance, and bringing more competition to markets. One of these forces is *e-commerce*. But, just how far is e-commerce going in returning 'power to the people'?

Moving markets back towards perfect competition?

Let us reconsider three of the assumptions of perfect competition and the impact of e-commerce on them: a large number of firms; freedom of entry; and perfect knowledge.

A large number of buyers and sellers. E-commerce has allowed many new firms to set up small businesses, often selling via their own websites or using online markets, such as eBay or Amazon. At the end of 2018, eBay had 179 million buyers and over 25 million sellers, while Amazon had 2 million third-party sellers (accounting for approximately 50 per cent of sales volume), reaching 310 million customers. The global reach of the Internet increases the number of buyers and sellers that can trade with each other. Firms must now compete with others across the world, as consumers have access to the global marketplace. They must keep an eye on the prices and products of competitors worldwide and be aware of the continual emergence of new smaller businesses.

Freedom of entry. The costs of starting a business have often been a key obstacle for firms, but e-commerce has created a low-cost marketplace. Internet companies tend to have lower start-up costs, as they are often run from much smaller premises, including owners' homes and only require a computer and access to the Internet. With advanced search algorithms, new businesses can also minimise marketing costs, by ensuring their website is easily located by consumers on search engines.

Many of the new online companies focus on specialist products and rely on Internet 'outsourcing' (buying parts, equipment and other supplies through the Internet), rather than making everything themselves. Small businesses also tend to use other companies for transport and distribution, all of which help to keep costs down, thus making more businesses viable.

All of these factors, together with the speed with which a new firm can set up a website and hence a business, mean that the market has never been more open to new competitors. The benefit of e-commerce has therefore been to open up the marketplace and this has had spill-over effects on existing firms, which have been forced to become more efficient and, consequently, markets have become more price competitive. Demand curves have tended to become more elastic and we now see a growing range of innovative products. We have also seen a blurring of the line between firms and consumers, given the ease with which people can start a business.

Perfect knowledge. The Internet has also added to consumer knowledge. There are some obvious ways, e.g. facts and figures through sites such as Wikipedia, information on where to eat or stay through sites such as Tripadvisor and technical information on products on sites such as Amazon.

However, it has also improved consumer knowledge through greater transparency. Consumers can easily compare the prices and other features of the products they are interested in purchasing by using search engines, such as Google Shopping, NexTag and PriceGrabber.

You can also use comparison websites to find alternative suppliers and their prices. It is now fairly common to see people in shops on the high street browsing competitors' prices on their mobile phones. This has placed high-street retailers under intense competitive pressure and we have seen evidence of this through the collapse of some well-known high-street retailers, such as Maplins, Borders, Toys R Us and BHS.

Although the competitive pressures seem to have increased in 'B2C' (business-to-consumers) e-commerce, the impact may be even greater in 'B2B' (business-to-business) e-commerce. Many firms are constantly searching for cheaper sources of supply, and the Internet provides a cheap and easy means of conducting such searches.

?

1. Give three examples of products that are particularly suitable for selling over the Internet and three that are not. Explain your answer.
2. Before reading ahead, consider your own shopping and buying habits – how much shopping do you do online? What do you think are the limits to e-commerce? Compare your answers with a friend and try to determine the key factors that explain any differences between you and what might be the limits to e-commerce.

What does the future hold?

A continued growth in online sales

Statista recorded global online retail sales at $1.3 trillion in 2014. By 2017, this had grown to $2.3 trillion, with predictions that it will reach $4.9 trillion by 2021.[1] The chart shows the growth in UK online retail sales since 2007. The year 2018 saw an increase in UK online sales of 13.9 per cent, bring the proportion of total retail sales to 20.0 per cent. This compares with an increase of just 2.7 per cent in total retail sales and a fall of 0.9 per cent of in-store sales. The Centre of Retail Research believes that its growth will continue, with a potential to reach 25 per cent by 2025.[2]

---

[1] *Retail e-commerce Sales Worldwide from 2014 to 2021 (in billion US dollars)*, Statista (accessed June 2019).

[2] *Peak e-commerce* (Centre for Retail Research, 2019).

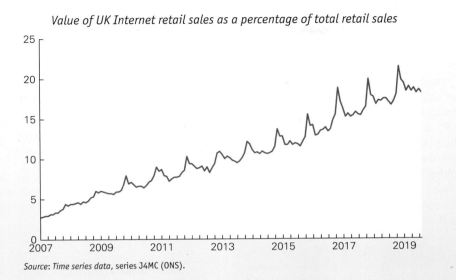

Value of UK Internet retail sales as a percentage of total retail sales

Source: Time series data, series J4MC (ONS).

If e-commerce is developing so quickly and costs are much lower for firms by trading online, why do so many big firms retain a physical presence on our high streets and have even increased their number of stores? Why are high-street retailers still prepared to pay an extremely high price for a prime location in cities, despite sales in UK stores falling by an estimated 2.5 per cent in 2017 and nearly 1 per cent in 2018?

'Shop shopping' still plays a key role in society; people are able to see, touch and try the good. Behavioural economics tells us that being able to see something and take possession of it immediately is something we are prepared to pay a price for, even with next-day or even same-day delivery available to us. Many people (though not all) also like the experience of shopping and the other activities that complement it and hence are prepared to pay a 'premium'. Therefore, a physical presence is still important, especially in some markets where location really does matter.

However, an online presence has never been more important, with firms investing huge sums of money on their websites and expansion of online ordering and advertising to compete more effectively. With technology improving every day and reducing the problems of slow internet speeds, busy sites and failures in logistics, online shopping is likely to go in just one direction. But are there any downsides?

Some downsides of e-commerce

Although greater price transparency should increase competition, there are some concerns that it may actually reduce the incentive for firms to lower prices. Firms can now observe and instantly respond to their rivals cutting prices. Thus the previous advantage that firms might have gained from cutting price are now removed very quickly such that it may remove the incentive, and even encourage firms to collude and charge higher prices, something we consider in section 5.3.

Comparison sites earn revenue by charging a fee every time a customer is referred to a listed firm's website via the price comparison website. These are additional costs and thus firms may push up prices to maintain profitability.

While it is certainly easier and cheaper than ever before to set up a business, it is likely that established firms are also benefiting from the lower costs that technology and online marketplaces bring. Amazon has invested heavily in automating its distribution centres using Kiva robots. However, this type of capital investment will only reduce a firm's average costs if it sells a large volume of products, which is unlikely for new businesses. Furthermore, while search engines can make new businesses more visible to customers, it will still tend to be the more established firms which appear at the top of searches. These factors can lead to the growth of already large firms and make it harder for smaller firms to compete.

Generally, however, the marketplace is becoming more competitive with e-commerce, and more opportunities do now exist for firms and customers to interact in a global market.

3. Why may the Internet work better for replacement buys than for new purchases?
4. As eBay and Amazon have grown in size, they have acquired substantial power in the market, while simultaneously increasing competition. How can both be true?

normal profits are made. This idea is known as *productive efficiency*. Producing at the minimum cost and making only normal profits mean that prices are kept to a minimum, which is beneficial to consumers.

Under perfect competition, we also see firms producing exactly the right amount of the product and they do this by producing where *price equals marginal cost*. But, why is this desirable?

Consider what would happen if price and marginal cost were not equal. If price were greater than marginal cost, this would mean that consumers were putting a higher value (P) on the production of extra units than they cost to produce (MC). Therefore, more ought to be produced. If price were less than marginal cost, consumers would be putting a lower value on extra units than they cost to produce. Therefore, less ought to be produced. When they are equal, $MC = P$, production levels are just right and this is referred to as *allocative efficiency*.

Perfect competition is often used as a benchmark to assess the effectiveness of actual markets. However, we should be careful when talking about a 'perfectly' competitive market, as it would not necessarily be an ideal environment for promoting new products and new technologies, as an article from the Mises Institute,[6] a pro-free-market organisation, argues.

Definitions

Productive efficiency A situation where firms are producing the maximum output for a given amount of inputs, or producing a given output at the least cost.

Allocative efficiency A situation where the current combination of goods produced and sold gives the maximum satisfaction for each consumer at their current levels of income.

---

[6] F. A. Hayek, 'The meaning of competition'; *Mises Daily Articles*, Mises Institute (15 March 2010).

Pause for thought

Why is it highly unlikely that an industry where firms can gain substantial economies of scale can also be perfectly competitive?

RECAP

1. Normal profit is the minimum profit that must be made to persuade a firm to stay in business in the long run. It is counted as part of the firm's costs. Supernormal profit is any profit over and above normal profit.

2. The maximum profit output is where marginal revenue equals marginal cost. Having found this output, the level of maximum (supernormal) profit can be found by finding the average (supernormal) profit ($AR - AC$) and then multiplying it by the level of output.

3. For a firm that cannot make a profit at any level of output, the point where $MR = MC$ represents the loss-minimising output. In the short run, a firm will close down if it cannot cover its variable costs. In the long run, it will close down if it cannot make normal profits.

4. In the short run, there is not time for new firms to enter the market, and thus supernormal profits can persist. In the long run, however, any supernormal profits will be competed away by the entry of new firms.

QUESTIONS

1. Are all explicit costs variable costs? Are all variable costs explicit costs?

2. Roughly how long would you expect the short run to be in the following cases?

   (a) A mobile wedding DJ;
   (b) Electricity power generation;
   (c) A small grocery retailing business;
   (d) 'Superstore Hypermarkets plc'.
   In each case, specify your assumptions.

3. The following are some costs incurred by a shoe manufacturer. Decide whether each one is a fixed cost or a variable cost or has some element of both.

   (a) The cost of leather;
   (b) The fee paid to an advertising agency;
   (c) Wear and tear on machinery;
   (d) Business rates on the factory;
   (e) Electricity for heating and lighting;
   (f) Electricity for running the machines;
   (g) Basic minimum wages agreed with the union;
   (h) Overtime pay;
   (i) Depreciation of machines as a result purely of their age (irrespective of their condition).

4. Why does the marginal cost curve pass through the bottom of the average cost curve and the average variable cost curve?

5. Does the marginal value of a variable (such as cost, revenue or profit) determine the average value of the variable, or does the average value of the variable determine the marginal value? Explain your answer.

6. What economies of scale is a large department store likely to experience? What about Google?

7. Why are many firms likely to experience economies of scale up to a certain size and then diseconomies of scale after some point beyond that?

8. Normal profits are regarded as a cost (and are included in the cost curves). Explain why.

9. What determines the size of normal profit? Will it vary with the general state of the economy?

10. A firm will continue producing in the short run even if it is making a loss, providing it can cover its variable costs. Explain why. Just how long will it be willing to continue making such a loss?

11. Would it ever be worthwhile for a firm to try to continue in production if it could not cover its *long-run* average (total) costs?

12. The price of tablet computers and digital cameras fell significantly in the years after they were first introduced and at the same time demand for them increased substantially. Use cost and revenue diagrams to illustrate these events. Explain the reasoning behind the diagram(s) you have drawn.

13. Illustrate on a diagram similar to Figure 4.6 what would happen in the long run if price were initially below P_L.

14. In 2017 and 2018, M&S, a food and clothing retailer in the UK, made some big decisions to close a number of its stores, reassess and reduce its planned expansions, overhaul its clothing and home outlets and focus more of its shop space on food-only outlets, where demand remains relatively high. The hope was to boost sales and increase profits. If it meets these targets, what is likely to have happened to its total costs, total revenue, average costs and average revenue? Give reasons for your answer.

ADDITIONAL PART B CASE STUDIES ON THE *ESSENTIAL ECONOMICS FOR BUSINESS* WEBSITE (www.pearsoned.co.uk/sloman)

B.1 The interdependence of markets. A case study of the operation of markets, examining the effects on a local economy of the discovery of a large shale oil deposit.

B.2 Coffee prices. An examination of the coffee market and the implications of fluctuations in the coffee harvest for growers and coffee drinkers.

B.3 The measurement of elasticity. This examines how to work out the value for elasticity using the 'mid-point' method.

B.4 Any more fares? Pricing on the buses: an illustration of the relationship between price and total revenue.

B.5 Elasticities of demand for various foodstuffs. An examination of the evidence about price and income elasticities of demand for food in the UK.

B.6 Adjusting to oil price shocks. A case study showing how demand and supply analysis can be used to examine the price changes in the oil market since 1973.

B.7 The role of the speculator. This assesses whether the activities of speculators are beneficial or harmful to the rest of society.

B.8 The demand for lamb. An examination of a real-world demand function.

B.9 Markets where prices are controlled. This examines what happens if price is set either above or below the equilibrium.

B.10 The Common Agricultural Policy of the EU. This case study looks at the various forms of intervention in agriculture that have been used in the EU. It looks at successes and problems and at various reforms that have been introduced.

B.11 Rent control. This shows how setting (low) maximum rents is likely to lead to a shortage of rented accommodation.

B.12 Agriculture and minimum prices. This shows how setting (high) minimum prices is likely to lead to surpluses.

B.13 The fallacy of composition. An illustration from agricultural markets of the fallacy of composition: 'what applies in one case will not necessarily apply when repeated in all cases'.

B.14 What we pay to watch sport. Consideration of the demand for season tickets to watch spectator sports such as football.

B.15 Brands and own brands. An examination of the nature of competition between branded products and supermarkets' own-brand varieties that led to the rise, fall and rise again of own-label brands.

B.16 The characteristics approach. An approach to analysing consumer behaviour and how consumers choose between products.

B.17 Diminishing returns in the bread shop. An illustration of the law of diminishing returns.

B.18 Dealing in futures markets. How buying and selling in futures markets can reduce uncertainty.

B.19 Short-run production. An analysis of how output varies with increases in the quantity of variable inputs used.

B.20 Diminishing returns to nitrogen fertiliser. This case study provided a good illustration of diminishing returns in practice by showing the effects on grass yields of the application of increasing accounts of nitrogen fertiliser.

B.21 The fallacy of using historic costs. A demonstration of how it is important to use opportunity costs and not historic costs when working out prices and output.

B.22 The relationship between averages and marginals. An examination of the rules showing how an average curve relates to a marginal curve.

B.23 Short-run cost curves in practice. Why *AVC* and *MC* curves may have a flat bottom.

B.24 Deriving cost curves from total physical product information. This shows how total, average and marginal costs can be derived from a total product information and the price of inputs.

B.25 Division of labour in a pin factory. This is the famous example of division of labour given by Adam Smith in his *Wealth of Nations* (1776).

B.26 The logic of logistics. How efficient logistics can drive down a firm's costs and increase its revenue.

WEBSITES RELEVANT TO PART B

Numbers and sections refer to websites listed in the Web Appendix and hotlinked from this book's website at **www.pearsoned. co.uk/sloman/**

- For news articles relevant to Part B, Google the Sloman Economics News site.

- For general news on markets, demand and supply see websites in section A of the Web Appendix, and particularly sites A1–12, 18–25, 35 and 36. See also links to newspapers worldwide in A38, 39, 42, 43 and 44 and the news search feature in Google at A41.

- For links to sites on markets, see section I, the relevant parts of B1, I7, 13–15, 23.

- For data, information and sites on products and marketing, see sites B1, 3, 14, 27.

- For data on commodities, see site B29.

- For data on advertising, see site E37.

- For data on stock markets, see section B, sites B14, 27 and 32; see also sites A1, 3 and F18.

- For data on the housing market, see section B, sites B7–11.

- For a case study examining costs, see site D2.

- For student resources relevant to Part B, see section C, sites C1–7, 9, 10, 14 and 19.

- For games and simulations, see section D, sites D3, 6–9, 12–14, 16–20.

- For sites favouring the free market, see site C17 and E34.

The microeconomic environment of business

Whatever the aims of firms, they must take account of the environment in which they operate if they are to be successful. In Part C we look at the microeconomic environment of firms, i.e. the market conditions that firms face in their particular industry.

Most firms are not price takers; they can choose the prices they charge. But in doing so they must take account of the reactions of their rivals. We look at pricing and output decisions in Chapter 5 and see how the aims of a firm affect these decisions.

Firms must also take account of rivals in planning their longer-term strategy – in making decisions about developing and launching new products, how quickly and how much to expand, the methods of production to use, their supply chain, the balance of what should be produced in-house and what should be 'outsourced' (i.e. bought in from other firms), their sources of finance, and whether to target international markets or to confine themselves to producing and selling domestically. These strategic decisions are the subject of Chapters 6 and 7.

In Chapter 8, we turn to the labour market environment of business. What power does the firm have in setting wages; what is the role of trade unions; how flexibly can the firm use labour? These issues all affect the profitability of business, its organisation and its choice of techniques.

Finally, in Chapter 9 we look at the impact of government policy towards business and how this in turn affects firms' decision making. How much does government legislation constrain business activity? Do we need governments to force firms to behave in the interests of society or will firms choose to take a socially responsible attitude towards things such as ethical trading, the environment, product standards and conditions for their workforce?

Pricing and output decisions in imperfectly competitive markets

5.1 ALTERNATIVE MARKET STRUCTURES

In the previous chapter we looked at price-taking firms, which face a perfectly elastic demand curve. In this chapter we examine firms that face a downward-sloping demand curve. This gives them some 'market power', such that they can raise their price without losing *all* of their customers.

The degree of market power that firms have affects the competitiveness of an industry. This, in turn, can affect the prices charged to consumers and paid to suppliers, how much profit firms make, and the incentives to invest and innovate. In particular, it affects firms' behaviour in a multi-

tude of ways and can help us to answer many questions, such as:

- Why do some markets have many competitors while others have only a few?
- Why do we see constant advertising and innovation in some products while others are rarely promoted and see little development?
- Why do prices fall in some industries and rise in others?
- To what extent do firms act in the public interest and is there a need for governments or regulators to intervene?

■ Why is government more concerned with the behaviour of firms in just some industries?

The degree of competition in different markets

The importance of competition. Most markets have a number of firms competing against each other. Go into your local town or city and look around. If you want to buy shoes, there are probably many shops, all selling shoes of different types, quality and price. Alternatively, you could go online and there will be a very high number of suppliers. If you want lunch or a cup of coffee, there are lots of cafés providing choice. The same thing applies for birthday cards, wrapping paper, food, electronic devices and many other products, including services.

If you need a haircut, there are many salons. When writing this section, I (Elizabeth) used Google to search for hairdressers in St. Ives (a small town in Cornwall with a population around 10 000, though a popular tourist destination and covering an area of less than 11 km^2). I found over 15 salons advertised online and there are many others without websites. Expanding the search area only slightly, gave me a huge list of hairdressers – some practically next door to others. If you need a cleaner, gardener or builder, I imagine you could find several people advertising their services in the relevant area.

Markets where there are few competitors. In practice, most markets have a number of competitors, each trying to gain customers, though how they do it and the market outcomes, can vary significantly. However, in some markets, there are very few competitors, sometimes just two or three – or occasionally just one firm with no competitors. Or there might be lots of small firms, but with a few big ones dominating.

Let us consider a product that everyone needs: food. There are many places selling food, whether it is your local corner shop, a farm shop, households selling eggs and freshly grown vegetables or Amazon. But for many people, it is in supermarkets that they do the bulk of their food shopping.

Together, the four largest British supermarkets (Tesco, Sainsbury's, Asda and Morrisons) account for just under 70 per cent of sales in the food industry.[1] Therefore, while the market has many competitors, it is actually dominated by four big firms, all of whom are in a constant battle to gain and retain customers. If you turn on the TV or radio, you will often see adverts from these supermarkets, advertising price cuts, savings, promotions and deals, all of which aim to gain you as a customer.

The supermarkets each have a sufficiently large share of the market that, if one of them cuts prices, it would cause many customers to switch and buy from the cheaper supplier – after all, the cabbage you buy from Tesco is pretty similar to the one sold in Asda. This means that we do not just see one supermarket advertising its latest price cuts, but we see all of them doing this – they are constantly responding to each other. For example, watch adverts from a range of supermarkets, such as Tesco, Asda, Aldi and Morrisons. This characteristic is called *interdependence,* which we will discuss further in section 5.3.

Another related industry where this occurs is fast food restaurants. In the USA, there has been a high degree of advertising and price cutting from chains such as McDonalds, Burger King and Wendy's. Although it is a market with many competitors, there are several bigger chains, all of which respond to the tactics employed by their rivals. You can read more about the latest rivalry in Box 5.1.

We see similar things happening with mobile phones, energy companies, petrol stations, razors, cars and other consumer durables, such as sofas: a few big firms constantly advertising price cuts or offers and responding to the actions of each other. This is a form of *imperfect competition* that economists call *oligopoly.* We examine oligopoly in detail in section 5.3.

Markets with many competitors. There are countless places you can go to buy clothes: Next, Tesco, Top Shop, Selfridges, John Lewis, Bloomingdales, Burton and many, many more. As with shoes, we can then divide the market into different types or quality of clothing, but even then, there are many places you could buy a pair of jeans, a shirt, or a dress.

Although clothing retailers do compete on price, it is not a market where we see as much television advertising, with one retailer telling us that it has cut the price of scarves and another saying that it has slashed the price of jumpers. Retailers here compete in other areas, such as the quality of the product and are less responsive to the strategies employed by their rivals as, although we still see some big firms, there are many more of them, each with a smaller share of the market. For example, M&S is the UK's biggest clothing retailer, but it has only a 9.7 per cent share of the market – significantly lower than Tesco's almost 28 per cent of the food market in the UK.

There are other markets with a similar degree of competition to that of clothing: hairdressers, restaurants, builders, plumbers and many more. Economists call this market structure *monopolistic competition* and, again, it is the structure of the industry which helps to explain the outcomes we see, as we shall discuss throughout this chapter.

---

[1] 'Market share of grocery stores in Great Britain', Statista (accessed June 2019).

> ### Pause for thought
>
> *Think of five different products or services and estimate roughly how many firms there are in the market and what share of the market is accounted for by the biggest four or five firms. You will need to decide whether 'the market' is a local one, a national one or an international one. In what ways do the firms compete in each of the cases you have identified?*

By analysing the particular characteristics of each industry's structure and its competitiveness, we can gain a better understanding of how firms behave and why they do so and then use this to explain their overall performance and the outcomes for them, their customers and their suppliers, such as the prices consumers pay and the prices suppliers receive. It helps to explain the amount of profits that firms make and whether they can be sustained and also whether firms need to innovate, advertise or respond in any other ways to their rivals.

Factors affecting the degree of competition

So what influences the degree of competition in an industry? There are four key determinants:

- The number of firms
- The freedom of entry and exit of firms into the industry
- The nature of the product
- The shape of the demand curve

We will consider each determinant to establish exactly what impact it has on the degree of competition within a market and then look at how these features vary between different market structures. We should then be able to place different industries into one of four key market structures.

The number of firms. The more firms there are competing against each other, the more competitive any market is likely to be, with each firm trying to steal customers from its rivals. Though there are many ways by which this can be done, one strategy will be to keep prices low. This will generally be in the consumer's interest.

If, however, there are only a few firms in the market, there may be less intense price competition, though as we shall see, this is not always the case. Sometimes, there may be only two or three firms in the industry and yet they are constantly trying to undercut each other's prices to gain greater market share.

The freedom of entry and exit of firms into the industry. A key factor that will affect the number of firms in an industry is how easy it is for a new firm to set up in competition. In some markets, there may be barriers to entry (see page 116–7) which prevent new firms from entering and this then acts to restrict the number of competing firms in the market. A key question here is, just how great are the barriers to the entry of new firms?

There is also the question of how costly it is to leave an industry. If the costs of exit are low, firms may be more willing to enter in the first place.

> ### Pause for thought
>
> 1. *Consider a situation where you have set up a business selling a brand-new product, which is not available anywhere else. As the only seller of this product, what could you do in terms of price?*
> 2. *Why could the ease with which a firm can leave an industry be a factor that determines the degree of competition within that industry?*

The nature of the product. If firms produce an identical product – in other words, if there is no product differentiation within the industry – there is little a firm can do to gain an advantage over its rivals. If, however, firms produce their own particular brand or model or variety, this may enable them to charge a higher price and/or gain a larger market share from their rivals.

The shape of the demand curve. Finally, the degree of competition is related to the price elasticity of demand. The less elastic is the demand for a firm's product, the greater will be its control over the price it charges – the less will sales fall as it raises its price. Thus the less elastic the demand for its product, the greater will be a firm's market power.

> **KEY IDEA 17**
>
> ***Market power benefits the powerful at the expense of others.*** When firms have market power over prices, they can use this to raise prices and profits above the perfectly competitive level. Other things being equal, the firm will gain at the expense of the consumer. Similarly, if consumers or workers have market power they can use this to their own benefit.

Market structures

Traditionally, we divide industries into categories based on the factors above, which determine the degree of competition that exists between the firms. There are four such categories.

At the most competitive extreme is *perfect competition*, which we examined in the last chapter. Each firm is so small relative to the whole industry that it has no power to influence market price. It is a price taker.

Table 5.1	Features of the four market structures			
Type of market	Number of firms	Freedom of entry	Examples of product	Implication for demand curve for firm's product
Perfect competition	Very many	Unrestricted	Fresh fruit and vegetables, shares, foreign exchange (approximately)	Horizontal. The firm is a price taker
Monopolistic competition	Many/several	Unrestricted	Builders, restaurants, hairdressers	Downward sloping, but relatively elastic. The firm has some control over price
Oligopoly	Few	Restricted	Cars, petrol, banking, razors	Downward sloping, relatively inelastic, but depends on reactions of rivals to a price change
Monopoly	One	Restricted or completely blocked	Local water company, many prescription drugs	Downward sloping; more inelastic than oligopoly. Firm has considerable control over price

At the least competitive extreme is *monopoly*. This is where there is just one firm in the industry, and hence no competition from within the industry. Normally the monopolist will have effective means of keeping other firms out of the industry. We look at monopoly in section 5.2.

In the middle there are two forms of *imperfect competition*: monopolistic competition and oligopoly. Under imperfect competition firms still face a downward-sloping demand curve, but have varying degrees of market power. The vast majority of firms in the real world operate under imperfect competition.

The more competitive of the two is *monopolistic competition* (not to be confused with monopoly). This involves quite a lot of firms competing and there is freedom for new firms to enter the industry in the long run, if for example they see that existing firms are making supernormal profits. Thus, as under perfect competition, this will have the effect of driving down profits to the normal level.

Examples of monopolistic competition can be found by a quick search online for businesses of a particular type in a given area. Taxi companies, restaurants, small retailers, small builders, plumbers, electrical contractors, etc. all normally operate under monopolistic competition – as does busking, which is discussed on the *Freakonomics* blog.[2] As a result of the high degree of competition, firms' profits are kept down. However, competition is not perfect, as the firms are all trying to differentiate their product or service from their rivals'. They have *some* power over prices: their demand curve, whilst relatively elastic, is not horizontal.

The other type of imperfect competition is *oligopoly*, where there are only a few firms and where the entry of new firms is difficult. Some or all of the existing firms

will be dominant – that is, they will tend to have a relatively high market share and can influence prices, advertising, product design, etc. As under monopoly, the entry of new firms is restricted. We examine oligopoly in section 5.3.

Table 5.1 summarises the features of the four different types of market structure.

Pause for thought

Give one more example in each of the four market categories in Table 5.1.

Market structure and the conduct and performance of firms

The market structure under which a firm operates will determine its behaviour. Firms under perfect competition behave quite differently from firms that

Definitions

Monopoly A market structure where there is only one firm in the industry.

Imperfect competition The collective name for monopolistic competition and oligopoly.

Monopolistic competition A market structure where, like perfect competition, there are many firms and freedom of entry into the industry, but where each firm produces a differentiated product and thus has some control over its price. (Not to be confused with a monopoly or monopolist!)

Oligopoly A market structure where there are few enough firms to enable barriers to be erected against the entry of new firms.

---
[2] Daniel Hamermesh, 'The economics of busking', *Freakonomics* (21 May 2012).

are monopolists, which behave differently again from firms under oligopoly or monopolistic competition.

This behaviour (or 'conduct') will in turn affect the firm's performance: its prices, profits, efficiency, etc. In many cases it will also affect other firms' performance: their prices, profits, efficiency, etc. The collective conduct of all the firms in the industry will affect the whole industry's performance.

Some economists thus see a causal chain running from market structure to the performance of that industry. This paradigm was first considered in section 1.2:

Structure → Conduct → Performance

This does not mean, however, that all firms operating in a particular market structure will behave in exactly the same way. For example, some firms under oligopoly may be highly competitive, whereas others may collude with each other to keep prices high. This conduct may then, in turn, influence the development of the market structure. For example, the interaction between firms may influence the development of new products or new production methods, and may encourage or discourage the entrance of new firms into the industry.

It is also important to remember that some firms with different divisions and products may operate in more than one market structure. As an example, consider the case of Microsoft. Its Edge browser (which replaced Internet Explorer) competes with more successful rivals, such as Chrome and Firefox and, as a result, has little market power in the browser market. Its Office products, by contrast, have a much bigger market share and dominate the word processor, presentation and spreadsheet markets.

Also, some firms under oligopoly are highly competitive and may engage in fierce price cutting, while others may collude with their rivals to charge higher prices. It is for this reason that government policy towards firms – known as 'competition policy' – prefers to focus on the *conduct* of individual firms, rather than simply on the market structure within which they operate. Regulators focus on aspects of conduct such as price fixing and other forms of collusion. Indeed, competition policy in most countries accepts that market structures evolve naturally (e.g. because of economies of scale or changing consumer preferences) and do not necessarily give rise to competition problems.

Nevertheless, market structure still influences firms' behaviour and the performance of the industry, even though it does not, in the case of oligopoly and monopoly, rigidly determine it.

> ## BOX 5.1   A FAST FOOD RACE TO THE BOTTOM
>
> ### Measuring the degree of competition
>
> In the USA, in 2015, industry analysis found that there were over 200 000 fast food restaurants, employing over 4 million people. Despite having thousands of firms, the market is dominated by a few big chains, including McDonalds, Burger King and Wendy's and hence has some of the characteristics of an oligopoly. A similar structure exists in many other countries.
>
> When analysing an industry, it is important to look not just at the number of firms as an indicator of the degree of competition, as in doing that, we could come to misleading conclusions. Another key indicator that should be considered is the level of 'concentration' of firms. This is the market share of the largest so many firms, e.g. the largest three, or five, or 15, etc. This gives the '3-firm', '5-firm' or '15-firm' concentration ratio. The resulting figures can be used to assess whether or not the largest firms in an industry dominate the market.
>
> For example, in the case of British supermarkets, we saw that the 4-firm concentration ratio was approximately 70 per cent. The concentration ratio in the US fast food industry is not as high, but estimates put the 3-firm concentration ratio at approximately 40 per cent – still quite a high figure. This means that, despite the market having over 200 000 firms, a significant portion is dominated by three chains, creating a nice example of an oligopoly.
>
> While in some oligopolies, firms can collude with each other and fix prices, in other cases, we observe a highly
>
> competitive market. It is the latter that applies to the fast food industry.
>
> 1. *What are the advantages and disadvantages of using a 5-firm concentration ratio rather than a 10-firm, 3-firm or even a 1-firm ratio?*
>
> ### Price competition
>
> Fast food outlets have always focused on cheaper meals, but over the past few years, the level of price competition has intensified and it has moved beyond the typical hamburger outlets, hitting places like Pizza Hut.
>
> In early 2012, a pizza price war developed in New York. The 6th Avenue Pizza Company was selling slices for $1.50, but two new competitors (Joey Pepperoni's Pizza and the 2 Bros pizza chain) began pricing a slice at $1. Not to be outdone, the 6th Avenue Company first matched the price and then undercut it to $0.79. 2 Bros then undercut this price to sell at $0.75 and was soon matched by 6th Avenue. Neither was willing to concede, with 6th Avenue suggesting it may begin selling at $0.50 and 2 Bros saying it may begin 'selling' slices for free! In the end, further cuts were not needed, as the chains' imminent demise, together with potential legal problems, encouraged both pizza places to agree to end the price war, with slices returning to $1.50![1]
>
> ---
>
> [1] Matt Flegenheimer, '$1 pizza slice is back after a sidewalk showdown ends two parlor's price war', *The New York Times* (5 September 2012).

In 2016, McDonalds launched its promotion, 'McPick 2' (choose two items from a selection including McChicken and McDouble for $2). In response, Wendy's launched its '4 for $4' (where customers can choose four items from a selection for $4) and soon after, Burger King announced its promotion of a five-item meal for $4. Pizza Hut joined the party, offering a seven-item menu for just $5.

Within just a few days, the biggest fast food chains in the USA had responded to each other and were creating new deals at budget prices. The chains freely admitted that they were 'aggressively pursuing value-conscious customers looking for the cheapest meal deals'.[2] The outlets were aiming to be the best value chain, while still making profits. This price war has continued.

In 2018, McDonald's launched a new deal, called the '$1$2 $3 Menu', allowing customers to choose items from three price points. As demand for fast food is relatively elastic, demand for McDonald's products would have increased significantly, if its competitors had not responded. Customers are price sensitive and hence respond to small price changes and thus we saw McDonald's rivals responding immediately to its new promotion. Wendy's added 20 things onto its menu, all priced at just $1; JACK announced plans for promotions focused on products within the $1 to $5 bracket and Taco Bell then began to sell $1 nacho fries, together with announcing plans for a range of other $1 offers. Analysis from Credit Suisse suggested that McDonald's closest competitors could see sales affected by around 1 per cent following un-matched price changes.[3]

This competitive market has therefore seen falling prices and more products offered at a given price. There is, of course, a danger from this race to the bottom for prices, as firms will need to ensure that the price at which they sell each burger is sufficient to cover the costs of producing it. With prices on a downward spiral, this difference is getting smaller and, in some cases, has turned negative. Why are firms continuing to cut prices if it means their profit margins are falling?

Competitors choose their promotions carefully, focusing on those with more elastic demand, as this is what attracts customers and increases sales. They then hope that customers will spend money on other products, such as drinks, sides or desserts, that will tend to be more profitable. Professor Patricia Smith from the University of Michigan said:

> McDonald's will make money selling burgers for a buck if it can make the burger for less than $1 and sell *lots* and *lots* of burgers . . . Part of the strategy is to attract consumers in to the store and then entice them to buy more than just the burger – fries, drinks, desserts.[4]

Product differentiation

There have been price wars in the UK too, with many outlets offering highly competitive deals, though certainly not at the same level as those in the USA. In mainland Europe, price competition is less intense again, but we see another characteristic of an oligopoly here, as well as in the UK and USA: namely, product differentiation.

The big chains are constantly innovating with new products, deals and variations to make their burger or pizza just a bit different, including extra cheese, bacon, fries and toys in meal deals. In doing this, firms are attempting to make demand for their products less elastic. The fast food outlets know how competitive the market is and that, without product differentiation, they would lose customers, sales and hence profits. In the UK and Europe, similar things occur, but we have also seen a different type of product differentiation, focusing on customer demands.

Customers are increasingly conscious of sustainability, locally sourced produce and ethical consumerism, as we will discuss in section 9.2. Food outlets have responded to this by differentiating their products, not with extra food or toys, but with advertising the local source of their food and its use of sustainable sources, including in the European branches of McDonald's. Martin Caraher, from City University, London, has noted that any significant cuts in prices in Europe would negatively affect McDonald's reputation amongst its customers who are more focused on ethical consumerism, saying:

> In order to lower their prices, they would have to break a lot of their marketing initiatives that they've implemented here in Europe. They've positioned themselves in a different level of the market'.[5]

In the UK, McDonald's aims to make all of its coffee 'ethically sourced' by 2020.

Therefore, although the fast food industry does always seem to be dominated by a few big firms, indicating an oligopoly, the actions of the competitors are different across the world. They all focus on strategies to gain customers, reflecting the competitiveness of the market, but the way in which they attract and keep customers does vary. In each case, they focus on the key things that customers respond to and in doing this, they aim to maintain market share.

2. *Explain how fast food outlets are changing the shape of their demand curve by engaging in product differentiation.*

3. *How can fast food outlets sell a burger at $1, when the person making it is earning say $10 and still make profits?*

Choose another industry under oligopoly and select two companies. Find out what competitive strategies they use and why.

---

[2] K. J. Mariño, 'Fast Food competition intensifies as Burger King, McDonald's, Wendy's fight for cheapest meal deal', *Latin Post* (5 January 2016).

[3] 'McDonald's Corp: Assessing impact of LCD's new value menu . . .', *Americas/United States, Equity Research, Restaurants,* Credit Suisse (19 December 2017).

[4] Bryan Lufkin, 'How can a fast food chain ever make money from a $1 burger?' *BBC Worklife* (23 February 2018).

[5] Ibid.

> ## RECAP
>
> 1. The structure of an industry will affect the way in which firms behave and this in turn will affect the performance of that industry. This is known as the structure–conduct–performance paradigm.
>
> 2. There are four market structures. In ascending order of firms' market power, they are: perfect competition, monopolistic competition, oligopoly and monopoly.

5.2 MONOPOLY

What is a monopoly?

This may seem a strange question because the answer seems obvious. A monopoly exists when there is only one firm in the industry.

But whether an industry can be classed as a monopoly is not always clear. It depends on how narrowly the industry is defined. For example, a textile company may have a monopoly on certain types of fabric, but it does not have a monopoly on fabrics in general. The consumer can buy fabrics other than those supplied by the company. A rail company may have a monopoly over rail services between two cities, but it does not have a monopoly over public transport between these two cities. People can travel by coach or air, or use private transport. When you went to an adventure playground as a child, your parents may have refused to buy you an ice cream, because they were too expensive. The ice cream seller had a local monopoly, but it was obviously not the only seller of ice creams in the UK! Consider the following blog from the Sloman Economics News site, which asks: *Is Amazon a monopolist?*

To some extent, the boundaries of an industry are arbitrary. What is more important for a firm is the amount of market power it has, and that depends on the closeness of substitutes produced by rival industries. Before 2006, Royal Mail had a monopoly over the delivery of letters in the UK, but still faced competition in communications from telephone, faxes and e-mail (and more recently from social media). Since the government opened the market to competitors, Royal Mail has complained about the 'unfair' competition it faces from other firms, such as Whistl, which delivers mail, packets and parcels but only in certain areas. An article from *Post&Parcel*[3] considers this competition to Royal Mail.

Barriers to entry

For a firm to maintain its monopoly position, there must be barriers to the entry of new firms. Barriers also exist under oligopoly, but in the case of monopoly they must be high enough to block the entry of new firms. Barriers can take various forms:

Economies of scale. If the monopolist's costs per unit go on falling significantly up to the output that satisfies the whole market, the industry may not be able to support more than one producer. This case is known as *natural monopoly*. It is particularly likely if the market is small and/or the industry has relatively high capital/infrastructure costs (i.e. fixed costs) and relatively low marginal costs. For example, two bus companies might find it unprofitable to serve the same routes, each running with perhaps only half-full buses, whereas one company with a monopoly over the routes could make a profit. Electricity transmission via a national grid is another example of a natural monopoly. The following blogs: *Fair Fares?* and *BT, Openreach and Ofcom* from the Sloman Economics News site consider the bus and communications industry, respectively.

Even if a market could support more than one firm, a new entrant is unlikely to be able to start up on a very large scale. Thus the monopolist, which is already experiencing economies of scale, can charge a price below the cost of the new entrant and drive it out of business. If, however, the new entrant is a firm already established in another industry, it may be able to survive this competition. For example, Amazon entered the UK online grocery market in 2016.

Economies of scope. These are the benefits in terms of lower average costs of production, because a firm produces a range of products. For example, a large pharmaceutical company producing a range of drugs and toiletries can use shared research, marketing, storage and transport facilities across its range of products. These lower costs make it difficult for a

> ### Definition
>
> **Natural monopoly** A situation where long-run average costs would be lower if an industry were under monopoly than if it were shared between two or more competitors.

[3] 'Royal Mail's challenger, TNT Post UK, to rebrand as "Whistl"', *Post&Parcel* (15 September 2014).

new single-product entrant to the market, since the large firm will be able to undercut its price and drive it out of the market.

Product differentiation and brand loyalty. If a firm produces a clearly differentiated product, where the consumer associates the product with the brand, it will be very difficult for a new firm to break into that market. Rank Xerox invented and patented the plain paper photocopier. After this legal monopoly ran out, people still associated photocopiers with Rank Xerox. It was not unusual to hear someone say that they are going to 'Xerox the article' or, for that matter, 'Hoover their carpet' or, more recently, 'Google it'. The monopolist may also have access to superior technology, helping to distinguish its product from the competition. For example, Google's search ranking algorithm set it apart from its rivals, as many people found Google's search engine more useful than any others.

Lower costs for an established firm. An established monopoly is likely to have developed the most efficient way of producing and marketing its product and this may be very difficult for other competitors to replicate. It is also likely to be aware of the cheapest suppliers and have access to cheaper finance. This implies that it is likely to be operating on a lower average total cost curve, making it difficult for new entrants to compete on price.

Ownership of, or control over, key inputs or outlets. In some markets the monopolist might be able to obtain access to key inputs on more favourable terms for a certain period of time. For example, if there was a supplier that provided a much higher quality input than its rivals, the monopolist could either sign a long-term exclusive contract with this firm or take ownership via a merger. For example, in 2012 Amazon purchased Kiva Systems. This company was the leading supplier of robotics for a number of warehouse operators and retailers. After the takeover, Kiva only supplied Amazon and was renamed Amazon Robotics in 2015.

In more extreme cases, the monopolist may gain complete control of a market if there is only one supplier of that input. For many years, the De Beers group owned both the majority of the world's diamond mines and the major distribution system.

Similarly, if a firm controls the outlets through which the product must be sold, it can prevent potential rivals from gaining access to consumers. For example, approximately 50 per cent of public pubs in the UK operate on tenancy contracts known as the 'tied lease model'. This is effectively an exclusive supply contract, which means that landlords of such pubs have to purchase almost all of their beverages from the pub company (e.g. Enterprise Inns, Punch Taverns and J D Wetherspoon) that owns the pub.

Legal protection. The firm's monopoly position may be protected by patents on essential processes, by copyright, by various forms of licensing (allowing, say, only one firm to operate in a particular area) and by tariffs (i.e. customs duties) and other trade restrictions to keep out foreign competitors. Examples of monopolies protected by patents include most new medicines developed by pharmaceutical companies (e.g. anti-AIDS drugs), Microsoft's Windows operating systems and agro-chemical companies, such as Monsanto, with various genetically modified plant varieties and pesticides. While patents do help monopolists to maintain their market power, they are also essential in encouraging new product innovation, as R&D is very expensive. Patents allow firms that engage in R&D to reap the rewards of that investment.

Mergers and takeovers. The monopolist can put in a takeover bid for any new entrant. The sheer threat of takeovers may discourage new entrants.

Retained profits and aggressive tactics. An established firm is likely to have some retained profits behind it. If a new firm enters the market, the established firm could reduce prices and thus start a price war, or start a massive advertising campaign, knowing that it could sustain losses until the new entrant leaves the market. The threat of this can act as a barrier to entry.

> ## Pause for thought
>
> *Do you think that if customers incur switching costs when moving products or changing suppliers, this could act as a barrier to entry and hence give a firm some monopoly power?*

Profit maximising under monopoly

The rule for profit maximisation is the same under any market structure. It should produce the output where marginal cost equals marginal revenue. The cost curves for a monopolist will look similar to those for a firm under perfect competition, although, due to economies of scale, they could be lower. The revenue curves, however, will look different, as the firm is no longer a price taker.

Average and marginal revenue

Compared with other market structures, demand under monopoly will be relatively inelastic at each price. The monopolist can raise its price and consumers have no alternative supplier to turn to within the

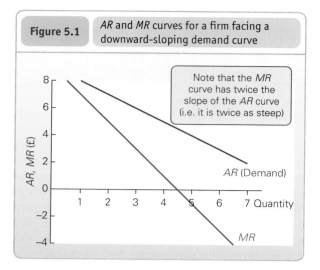

| **Figure 5.1** | *AR* and *MR* curves for a firm facing a downward-sloping demand curve |

Note that the *MR* curve has twice the slope of the *AR* curve (i.e. it is twice as steep)

| **Table 5.2** | Revenue for a monopolist |

Q (units)	P = AR (£)	TR (£)	MR (£)
1	8	8	8
2	7	14	6
3	6	18	4
4	5	20	2
5	4	20	0
6	3	18	−2
7	2	14	−4

industry. They either pay the higher price, or go without the good altogether. This price-making power is beneficial for the firm, as is discussed in an article from Harvard Business School.[4]

Because the firm faces a downward-sloping demand curve, its average and marginal revenue curves will also be downward sloping. This is illustrated in Figure 5.1, which is based on Table 5.2.

Note that, as in the case of a price-taking firm, the demand curve and the *AR* curve lie along exactly the same line. The reason for this is simple: $AR = P$, and thus the curve relating price to quantity (the demand curve) must be the same as that relating average revenue to quantity (the *AR* curve).

When a firm faces a downward-sloping demand curve, marginal revenue will be less than average revenue, and may even be negative. But why?

While a monopolist can set its price, it is still constrained by its (and hence the industry) demand curve. If a firm wants to sell more per time period, it must lower its price (assuming it does not advertise). This will mean lowering the price not just for the

extra units it hopes to sell, but also for those units it would have sold had it not lowered the price.

Thus the marginal revenue is the price at which it sells the last unit, minus the loss in revenue it has incurred by reducing the price on those units it could otherwise have sold at the higher price. This can be illustrated with Table 5.2.

Assume that price is currently £7. Two units are thus sold. If the firm wants to sell an extra unit, it must lower the price, say to £6. It gains £6 from the sale of the third unit, but loses £2 by having to reduce the price by £1 on the two units previously sold at £7. Its net gain is therefore $£6 − £2 = £4$. This is the marginal revenue: the extra revenue gained by the firm from selling one more unit.

Profit-maximising output and price

We can now put cost and revenue curves together on one diagram. This is done in Figure 5.2. Profit is maximised at an output of Q_m, where $MC = MR$. The price is given by the demand curve. Thus at Q_m the price is $AR = P$ (point *a* on the demand curve). Average cost (*AC*) is found at point *b*. Supernormal profit per unit is $AR − AC$ (i.e. *a* − *b*). Total supernormal profit is shown by the shaded area.

These profits will tend to be larger the less elastic is the demand curve (and hence the steeper is the *MR* curve), and thus the bigger is the gap between *MR* and price (*AR*). The actual elasticity will depend on whether reasonably close substitutes are available in other industries. The demand for a rail service between two places will be much less elastic (and the potential for profit greater) if there is no bus service running between those same destinations.

Under both monopolistic and perfect competition, any supernormal profits made in the short run will be competed away in the long run, as new firms are able to enter the industry. Significant barriers to entry under monopoly, however, will enable the firm to maintain its supernormal profits in the long run.

Comparing monopoly with perfect competition

Because it faces a different type of market environment, the monopolist will produce a quite different output and at a quite different price from a perfectly competitive industry. Typically a monopolist will charge a price above the market price of an equivalent industry under perfect competition. There are three main reasons for this:

■ Under perfect competition price equals marginal cost (see Figure 4.4 on page 101). Under monopoly, however, price is above marginal cost (see Figure 5.2). The less elastic the demand curve, the higher will price be above marginal cost.

---

[4] Benson P. Shapiro, 'Commodity busters: be a price maker, not a price taker', *Working Knowledge*, Harvard Business School (10 February 2003).

Figure 5.2 Profit maximising under monopoly

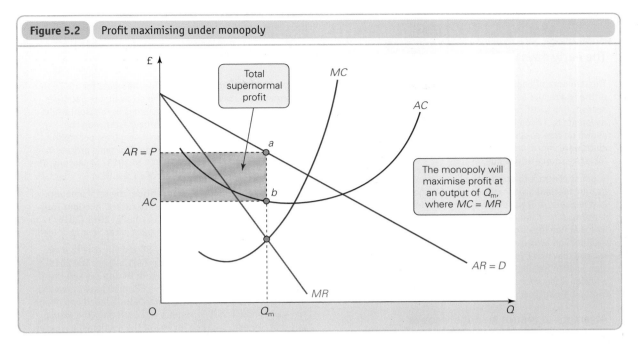

- Since there are barriers to the entry of new firms, a monopolist's supernormal profits will not be competed away in the long run. There is no competition to drive down the price. The monopolist is not forced to operate at the bottom of the *LRAC* curve. Thus, other things being equal, long-run prices will tend to be higher, and hence output lower, under monopoly.
- The monopolist's cost curves may be higher. The sheer survival of a firm in the long run under perfect competition requires that it uses the most efficient known technique. The monopolist, however, sheltered by barriers to entry, can still make large profits even if it is not using the most efficient technique. It has less incentive, therefore, to be efficient.

Pause for thought

If the shares in a monopoly (such as a water company) were very widely distributed among the population, would the shareholders necessarily want the firm to use its monopoly power to make larger profits?

It is possible, however, that a monopolist will operate with lower costs than an equivalent industry under perfect competition. The monopoly may be able to achieve substantial economies of scale due to larger plant size, centralised administration and the avoidance of unnecessary duplication (e.g. a monopoly water company would eliminate the need for several sets of rival water mains under each street).

If this results in an *MC* curve substantially below that of the same industry under perfect competition, the monopoly may even produce a higher output at a lower price. However, if the monopolist continues to maximise profits, it will still charge a price above marginal cost and thus be inefficient.

Another reason why a monopolist may operate with lower costs is that it can use part of its supernormal profits for research and development and investment. This may provide the firm with more opportunities to cut its costs relative to a smaller perfectly competitive firm.

The promise of supernormal profits, protected perhaps by patents, may also encourage the development of new (monopoly) industries producing new products. It is this chance of making monopoly profits that encourages many people to take the risks of going into business.

Although a monopoly faces no competition in the goods market, it may face an alternative form of competition in financial markets. A monopoly, with potentially low costs, which is currently run inefficiently, is likely to be subject to a takeover bid from another company. This *competition for corporate control* may thus force the monopoly to be efficient in order to prevent it being taken over.

Definition

Competition for corporate control The competition for the control of companies through takeovers.

BOX 5.2   PREMIER LEAGUE FOOTBALL: THE SKY IS THE LIMIT

The early days of Sky

The structure of English football changed with the formation of the FA Premier League (EPL) for the 1992/3 football season. One justification for this was the promise of higher payments by TV companies. Live league football had been shown on free-to-air television throughout the 1980s and the clubs were very aware that this was potentially a very lucrative source of revenue.

The first contract to acquire the live and exclusive FA Premier League football broadcasting rights for the United Kingdom and Republic of Ireland was worth £191 million over five seasons. A consequence of Sky being awarded the contract was that live top-flight English league football was no longer available on terrestrial and free-to-air television. Those who wanted to watch live football matches on television had to sign up with Sky, buying both a basic package and the additional Sky sports channels; Sky thus had a monopoly on football broadcasts.

Attempts to reduce monopoly power

Both the Premier League and Sky's coverage proved to be hugely successful with viewers and advertisers and this was reflected in the price paid for subsequent packages. The one starting in 1997 cost Sky £670 million for four seasons, while in 2003 BSkyB, as the company was now formally known, paid over £1 billion for exclusive rights for three seasons.

However, over this period the European Commission expressed increasing concern about the extent of Sky's monopoly. The Commission started legal proceedings in 2002, filing a statement of objections, but it was thwarted when the League agreed a new contract with Sky before ironing out an EC-approved deal.

At this time Sky did agree to sub-license up to eight 'top quality Premier League matches' each season to another broadcaster in order to win European approval. The Commission trumpeted this pledge as meaning 'that for the first time in the history of the Premier League free-to-air television will have a realistic opportunity to show live Premier League matches'. These hopes were dashed, however, when no rival broadcaster met the asking price set by Sky.

Auctioning the TV rights to the EPL

In 2005, the European Commission announced that Sky's monopoly would be broken. From 2007, the next set of rights, for a three-season period, would be sold in six 'balanced' packages of 23 games per season, with no broadcaster allowed more than five packages. The Commission claimed the deal would give fans 'greater choice and better value'.

However, concern was expressed about the impact on incomes of the Premiership clubs. While some commentators expected a more competitive process to result in roughly the same total income as was paid by Sky in 2003 (just over £1 billion), others suggested that Sky had originally paid a premium for the guarantee that it would be the sole broadcaster and that the introduction of competitive bidding would result in a fall in the revenues paid to clubs.

In May 2006 the bidding process for the rights for 2007–10 was completed. Sky won four of the six available packages and showed 92 live Premiership matches per season, while Setanta, an Irish-based satellite broadcaster, won the remaining two packages and showed 46 games per season. Between them, they paid £1.7 billion. The same process was undertaken in 2009 for the 2010/11 to 2013/14 seasons. This time the rights fetched just short of £1.8 billion.

Despite the opening up of 'competition' the total amount paid for domestic EPL TV rights was to rocket. Auctions took place in 2012 (2013/14 to 2015/16) and in 2015 (2016/17 to 2018/19) with BT now entering market, after Setanta folded.

In 2012, the total amount paid by BT and Sky rose to over £3 billion and then in 2015 to over £5.1 billion. The 2015 auction was acutely competitive. Both BT and Sky saw the securing of the rights to screen live EPL matches as a means by which it could sell highly profitable broadband and phone services bundled with its respective TV offering. The result was that Sky paid £4.17bn for five of the auctioned packages of matches (£11.047 million per game) while BT paid £960 million for two packages (£7.619 million per game).

Prior to the 2018 auction (in February), Sky and BT struck a deal to carry each other's content on their TV platforms. For some, this marked the end to what had been an aggressive battle for domination of the UK pay-TV market. BT had struggled to make inroads against Sky's strong position in the market. This was then reflected in the 2018 auction for rights to screen live EPL matches from 2019/20 to 2022/23. The initial announcement revealed that Sky and BT had paid £4.464 billion for five of the seven auctioned packages, with Sky paying £3.579 billion (£9.3 million per game) and BT £885 million (£9.22 million per game).

The final two packages, largely a mix of midweek and bank holiday fixtures, were not initially allocated, having failed to meet the reservation price. There has been some suggestion that the remaining 40 fixtures could be packaged together with other rights, but this would prevent Sky from bidding, given the auction rules. It looked likely, therefore, that these matches would remain unsold until the summer, as the Premier League aimed to secure the best deal.

1. *What other examples of monopoly power exist in football? Could this power be reduced?*
2. *Assess the impact of the broadcasters' emergence since the establishment of the English Premier League on (a) football fans, (b) other viewers.*
3. *What are the challenges that would face another telecommunications company wishing to enter the market?*

Undertake desktop research on the allocation of rights to broadcast live top-flight football in another European league. Compare the approach with that used to allocate rights to screen live English Premier League matches and assess its impact on the revenues raised, TV viewers and football fans.

RECAP

1. A monopoly is where there is only one firm in an industry. Whether a monopoly exists depends on how narrowly an industry is defined.

2. Barriers to the entry of new firms will normally be necessary to protect a monopoly from competition. Such barriers include economies of scale (making the firm a natural monopoly or at least giving it a cost advantage over new, smaller, competitors), control over supplies of inputs or over outlets, patents or copyright, and tactics to eliminate competition (such as takeovers or aggressive advertising).

3. The demand curve (*AR* curve) for a monopolist is downward sloping. The *MR* curve is below it and steeper.

4. Profits for the monopolist (as for other firms) are maximised where $MC = MR$.

5. If demand and cost curves are the same in a monopoly and a perfectly competitive industry, the monopoly will produce a lower output and at a higher price than the perfectly competitive industry.

6. Economies of scale for a monopolist may lead to lower prices, and the monopolist's high profits may be used for research and development and investment, which in turn may lead to better products at possibly lower prices.

5.3 OLIGOPOLY

Oligopoly occurs when just a few firms share a large proportion of the industry. Examples include some of the best-known companies, such as Ford, Coca-Cola, Apple and Tesco. Most oligopolists produce differentiated products (e.g. cars, soap powder, soft drinks, electrical appliances), but some may produce almost identical products (e.g. metals, petrol). Much of the competition between such oligopolists is in terms of the marketing of their particular brand. On the Sloman Economics News site, you will find many blogs written about different oligopolies and it is both useful and interesting to compare the conduct and performance of the firms involved. Some examples of powerful oligopolies are the market for toothbrushes (*Wobbly answer to oligopoly*), supermarkets (*Will the Big 4 become the Big 3?* and *An oligopoly price war*) and energy (*CMA referral for energy sector*).

As with monopoly, there are barriers to the entry of new firms (see pages 116–7). The size of the barriers, however, varies from industry to industry. In some cases, entry is relatively easy; in others it is virtually impossible.

Interdependence of the firms

With only a few firms under oligopoly, each firm is likely to have a relatively large market share, and so its actions will affect the other firms in the industry and it, in turn, will be affected by their actions. As such, before a firm makes any decisions, it will have to take account of the behaviour of these other firms. This means that they are mutually dependent: they are *interdependent*. It is this interdependence that differentiates oligopolies from the other market structures.

If a firm changes the price or specification of its product or the amount of its advertising, the sales of its rivals will be affected. The rivals may then respond by changing their price, specification or advertising.

A blog on the Sloman Economics News site, *Pizza price war*, illustrates this concept of interdependence under oligopoly.

> **KEY IDEA 18**
>
> ***People often think and behave strategically.*** How you think others will respond to your actions is likely to influence your own behaviour. Firms, for example, when considering a price or product change will often take into account the likely reactions of their rivals.

It is impossible, therefore, to predict the effect on a firm's sales of, say, a change in its price without first making some assumption about the reactions of other firms. Different assumptions will yield different predictions about how firms will respond to a given market situation and thus there are multiple theories of oligopoly.

Competition and collusion

The interdependence of oligopolists means firms are pulled in two different directions:

■ The interdependence of firms may make them wish to *collude* with each other. If they can club together and act as if they were a monopoly, they could jointly maximise industry profits and then split these maximum profits between them.

Definition

Interdependence (under oligopoly) This is one of the two key features of oligopoly. Each firm is affected by its rivals' decisions and its decisions will affect its rivals. Firms recognise this interdependence and take it into account when making decisions.

■ On the other hand, they will be tempted to *compete* with their rivals to gain a bigger share of industry profits for themselves.

These two policies are incompatible. The more fiercely firms compete to gain a bigger share of industry profits, the smaller these industry profits will become! For example, price competition drives down the average industry price, while competition through advertising raises industry costs. Either way, industry profits fall.

Sometimes firms will collude. Sometimes they will not. The following sections examine first *collusive oligopoly*, where we consider both formal agreements and tacit collusion, and then *non-collusive oligopoly*.

Collusive oligopoly

When firms under oligopoly engage in collusion, they may agree on prices, market share, advertising expenditure, etc. Such collusion reduces the uncertainty they face. It reduces the fear of engaging in competitive price cutting or retaliatory advertising, both of which could reduce total industry profits and thus a firm's share of them.

A cartel

A formal collusive agreement is called a **cartel**. The cartel will maximise profits by acting like a monopolist: behaving as if they were a single firm. This is illustrated in Figure 5.3.

The total market demand curve is shown with the corresponding market MR curve. The cartel's MC curve is the horizontal sum of the MC curves of its members (since we are adding the output of each of the cartel members at each level of marginal cost). Profit for the whole industry is maximised at Q_1

where $MC = MR$. The cartel must therefore set a price of P_1 (at which Q_1 will be demanded).

But, having agreed on price, how will the resulting output (Q_1) be divided between the cartel members? The members may simply compete against each other using non-price competition to gain as big a share of resulting sales (Q_1) as they can.

Alternatively, the cartel members may somehow agree to divide the market between them. Each member would be given a *quota*. These quotas could be the same for every firm, or they might be allocated based on the market share of the firm. Whatever the method of allocation, the sum of all the quotas must add up to Q_1. If the quotas exceeded Q_1, either there would be output unsold if price remained fixed at P_1, or the price would have to fall.

In many countries, cartels are illegal, seen by government as a means of driving up prices and profits and acting against the public interest. Government policy towards cartels is examined in section 9.5.

The most famous example of a cartel is OPEC, which was set up in 1960 by the five major oil-exporting

Definitions

Collusive oligopoly When oligopolists agree (formally or informally) to limit competition between themselves. They may set output quotas, fix prices, limit product promotion or development, or agree not to 'poach' each other's markets.

Non-collusive oligopoly When oligopolists make no agreement between themselves – formal, informal or tacit.

Quota (set by a cartel) The output that a given member of a cartel is allowed to produce (production quota) or sell (sales quota).

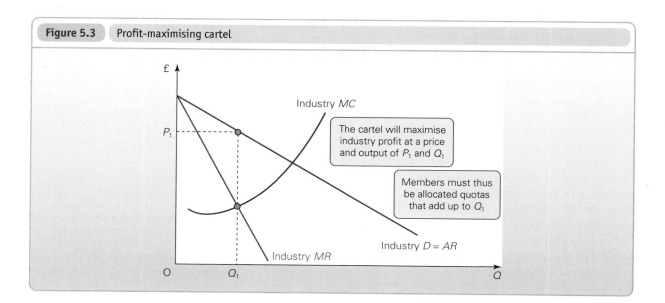

| Figure 5.3 | Profit-maximising cartel |

The cartel will maximise industry profit at a price and output of P_1 and Q_1

Members must thus be allocated quotas that add up to Q_1

countries, Iran, Iraq, Kuwait, Saudi Arabia and Venezuela, and now consists of 13 member countries. You may want to investigate the behaviour of OPEC and how it has influenced oil prices. There are numerous blogs on the Sloman Economics News site that consider this most famous of cartels and how it has managed oil price changes. See, for example the blog from January 2018, *OPEC's juggling act*, another from December 2016, *OPEC deal pushes up oil prices*, another from February 2016, *Will there be an oil price rebound?*, another from 2015, *The price of oil in 2015 and beyond*, and another from 2012, *OPEC cartel faces lawsuit for price fixing*. See also Case Study C.8 on the book's website.

Pause for thought

1. Which countries are members of the OPEC cartel and what are its objectives?
2. How has OPEC's behaviour affected oil prices and have the problems of a typical cartel been experienced by OPEC?

Tacit collusion

Where open collusion is illegal, firms may simply break the law, or find ways to get round it. Alternatively, firms may stay within the law, but still tacitly collude by watching each other's behaviour. Firms may tacitly 'agree' to avoid price wars or aggressive advertising campaigns.

One form of *tacit collusion* is where firms keep to the price that is set by an established leader. Such *price leadership* is more likely when there is a dominant firm in the industry, normally the largest.

Other forms include having an established set of rules that everyone follows, such as adding a certain percentage on top of average costs for profit. Alternatively, there are certain benchmark prices, which firms follow, such as goods priced at £9.99, rather than at £10.13.

A good example of price fixing can be found in the petrol retailing industry in Melbourne, Australia, in 2009. The ACCC (Australian Competition and Consumer Commission) studied the pricing decisions of a number of petrol stations in the same area and in 49 of the 53 weeks studied, when one of the big three petrol stations changed its price, the industry followed these movements exactly (see the blog on the Sloman Economics News site, *Price-fixing oligopolies*). Whilst there was no formal collusive agreement in place, this is an example of tacit collusion. Price fixing agreements of this nature are often very difficult to prosecute and in this case, no action was taken against the petrol stations.

Factors favouring collusion

Collusion between firms, whether formal or tacit, is more likely when firms can clearly identify with each other or some leader and when they trust each other not to break agreements. It will be easier for firms to collude if the following conditions apply:

- There are only very few firms, all well known to each other.
- They are open with each other about costs and production methods.
- They have similar production methods and average costs, and are thus likely to want to change prices at the same time and by the same percentage.
- They produce similar products and can thus more easily reach agreements on price.
- There is a dominant firm.
- There are significant barriers to entry and thus there is little fear of disruption by new firms.
- The market is stable. If industry demand or production costs fluctuate wildly, it will be difficult to make agreements, partly due to difficulties in predicting market conditions and partly because agreements may frequently have to be amended. There is a particular problem in a declining market where firms may be tempted to undercut each other's price in order to maintain their sales.
- There are no government measures to curb collusion.

In some oligopolies, there may be only a few (if any) factors favouring collusion. In such cases, the likelihood of price competition is greater.

Elements of competition under collusive oligopoly

Even when oligopolists collude over price, they may compete intensively though product development and marketing. As we saw in section 3.4, such 'non-price competition' can make the job of the manager quite complex, involving strategic decisions about product design and quality, product promotion and the provision of various forms of after-sales service.

Although non-price competition assumes that price is given in the short run, price may well be affected over the longer term. Industries with intensive non-price competition are likely to face higher

---

Definitions

Tacit collusion When oligopolists follow unwritten 'rules' of collusive behaviour, such as price leadership. They will take care not to engage in price cutting, excessive advertising or other forms of competition.

Price leadership When firms (the followers) choose the same price as that set by one of the firms in the industry (the leader). The leader will normally be the largest firm.

marketing costs, and this can result in a higher collusive price.

Even if there is collusion, for example to fix price, firms will always have an incentive to cheat, by undercutting the cartel price or selling more than their allocated quota. Whilst the firm can gain from this action, there is a danger of retaliation, which might lead to a price war, such that in the long run the firm could lose out. However, as long as the firm that undercuts the cartel price is confident of winning any price war, this may be a good strategy to follow. We consider this idea further in section 5.4.

Non-collusive oligopoly

In some oligopolies, there may be only a few (if any) factors favouring collusion. In such cases, the likelihood of price competition is greater. There are many theories of oligopoly, but one of the most famous theories of oligopoly was developed simultaneously on both sides of the Atlantic: in the USA by Paul Sweezy and in Britain by R. L. Hall and C. J. Hitch.

The kinked demand curve
Economists noted that even when oligopolists did not collude over price, the prices charged across the industry often remained relatively stable. The *kinked demand curve model* was developed to explain this observation and it rests on two key assumptions:

■ If a firm cuts its price, its rivals will feel forced to follow suit and cut theirs, to prevent losing customers to the first firm.
■ If a firm raises its price, however, its rivals will *not* follow suit since, by keeping their prices the same, they will thereby gain customers from the first firm.

On these assumptions, the oligopolist's perceived demand curve is kinked at the current price and output (see Figure 5.4). It believes that if it raises its price, its rivals will not follow and so there will be a large fall in sales as customers switch to the now relatively lower-priced rivals. With an elastic demand above the kink, therefore, the firm will be reluctant to raise its price. On the other hand, it believes that if it reduces price, its rivals will feel forced to cut their prices too to avoid losing market share and so few consumers will switch, giving the firm only a modest increase in sales. With, therefore, a relatively inelastic demand below the kink, the firm will also be reluctant to reduce its price.

Oligopoly and the consumer

If oligopolists act collusively and jointly maximise industry profits, they are in effect acting as a monopoly. In such cases, prices may be very high. This is clearly not in the best interests of consumers.

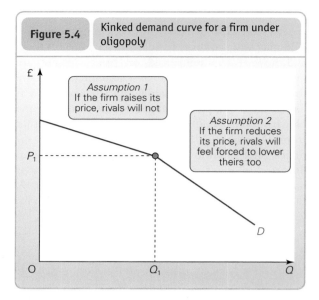

Figure 5.4 Kinked demand curve for a firm under oligopoly

Furthermore, in two respects, oligopoly may be more disadvantageous than monopoly:

■ Depending on the size of the individual oligopolists, there may be less scope for economies of scale and hence lower costs to mitigate the effects of market power.
■ Oligopolists are likely to engage in much more extensive advertising and marketing than a monopolist. Consumers may benefit from product development and better information about the product's characteristics. However, advertising and marketing are costly and may result in higher prices, so the consumer could lose out.

These problems will be less severe, however, if oligopolists do not collude, if there is some degree of price competition and if barriers to entry are weak.

Indeed, in some respects, oligopoly may be more beneficial to the consumer than other market structures:

■ Oligopolists, like monopolists, can use part of their supernormal profit for research and development. Unlike monopolists, however, oligopolists will have a considerable *incentive* to do so. If the product design is improved, this may allow the

Definition

The kinked demand curve model The theory that oligopolists face a demand curve that is kinked at the current price: demand being significantly more elastic above the current price than below. The effect of this is to create a situation of price stability.

firm to capture a larger share of the market, and it may be some time before rivals can respond with a similarly improved product.

■ Non-price competition through product differentiation may result in greater choice for the consumer. Take the case of tablets or mobile phones. Non-price competition has led to a huge range of different products of many different specifications, each meeting the specific requirements of different consumers.

It is difficult to draw any general conclusions about the outcomes in this market structure, since oligopolies differ so much in their behaviour and performance. Although an oligopoly is closer to the non-competitive end of the spectrum, it can still be a highly competitive market structure.

BOX 5.3 · MARKET POWER IN OLIGOPOLISTIC INDUSTRIES

Three examples

Faced with a choice between competition and collusion, firms under oligopoly can behave very differently. Just how they behave is often of interest to the competition authorities, which are on the look-out for anti-competitive practices. We consider competition policy in section 9.5.

Supermarkets

In the UK, the largest four supermarkets have a combined market share of just under 70 per cent (69.5%), as shown in the chart. Although this has fallen in the past few years, it still represents market dominance by a few firms – a key characteristic of oligopoly.

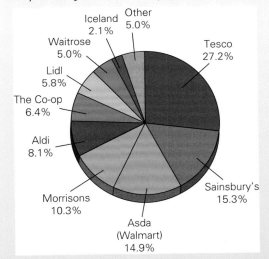

UK supermarket food market share (12 weeks to 14/7/2019)

Iceland 2.1%
Other 5.0%
Waitrose 5.0%
Lidl 5.8%
The Co-op 6.4%
Aldi 8.1%
Morrisons 10.3%
Asda (Walmart) 14.9%
Sainsbury's 15.3%
Tesco 27.2%

Source: Based on data from *Kantar Worldpanel*

The industry has faced major enquiries by the UK competition authorities and the big four have been accused of restricting competition and consumer choice at the local and national level by erecting barriers to entry (see the blog on the Sloman Economics News site, *Will the Big 4 become the Big 3?*). These include buying up tracts of land to prevent rival supermarkets setting up there or taking advantage of large economies of scale to make it impossible for new firms to compete on price. There have also been accusations of 'shadow pricing', which is a form of tacit collusion whereby firms observe each other's prices and sell at similar levels – often similarly high levels rather than similarly low levels. This limits true price competition and the resulting high prices have seen profits grow.

However, we have still seen a fairly high degree of price competition, which has grown in recent years, especially with the emergence of Aldi and Lidl.[1] But intense price competition does tend to be over more basic items, such as the own-brand 'value' products. To get to these competitively priced 'value' products, shoppers have to pass the more luxurious, higher priced products that also have higher profit margins. Here behavioural economics provides an insight (see section 3.3), as supermarkets rely on shoppers making impulse buys of these more expensive lines.

Although the four-firm concentration ratio has fallen, it remains a classic example of an oligopoly. However, firms in the supermarket industry use their dominant position not only in selling products, but also in buying them. Supermarkets have been accused of using 'heavy-handed tactics' to increase their buying power, driving down costs by forcing suppliers to offer discounts. The problem is that if a wholesale manufacturer of ready-meals, a supplier of sausages, or a farmer wants to reach a wide customer base, it is very likely that it will need to deal with one of the big four. A market such as this where there are just a few large *buyers* is known as an *oligopsony*.

Various practices have been identified, such as retrospectively changing contracts, forcing suppliers to fund special offers such as 'buy one, get one free' and having to make large payments to be included on 'preferred supplier' lists. In order to protect suppliers, a 'Groceries Code Adjudicator' (GCA) was appointed in 2016 to make sure that supermarkets were complying with the Grocery Supplies Code of Practice (GSCP), which was introduced in 2009.

1. *In what forms of tacit collusion are supermarkets likely to engage?*
2. *Explain why manufacturers of food products continue to supply supermarkets, despite concerns that they are not always treated fairly.*

Definition

Oligopsony A market with just a few buyers. This will give such firms power to drive down the prices they pay to suppliers. It can also refer to employers with market power in employing labour.

---

[1] 'Aldi and Lidl double market share in three years', *BBC News* (17 November 2015).

Who has the energy to switch?

Another UK oligopoly is the energy sector, with the 'Big Six' energy suppliers[2] selling to over 75 per cent of UK households. You can find many articles about the energy sector on the Sloman News site, which consider, among other things, the barriers to entry to the industry (*Energising the energy market*), the referral to the Competition and Markets Authority (CMA) (*An energy price cap*) and the savings that are possible from switching suppliers (*Do people have the energy to switch*).

A key problem is the existence of barriers to entry. In this industry, there is both vertical and horizontal integration within firms (see pages 156–61), with the big six energy suppliers being involved in both generation of power and the local distribution of it (vertical integration) and offer 'dual-fuel' deals, where customers can receive a discount from buying electricity and gas from the same supplier (horizontal integration).

The vertical integration, in particular, has made it difficult for smaller suppliers to enter the market, as they have had to buy wholesale from one of the Big Six. Furthermore, this may give smaller suppliers less favourable terms of access, thus pushing up their costs and necessitating higher prices for customers, raising barriers to entry and growth, thereby leading to less effective competition. Thus a key focus of the industry regulator, Ofgem (the Office of Gas and Electricity markets), has been how to reduce the barriers to entry to make the market more competitive and keep prices down.

3. Does vertical integration matter if consumers still have a choice of supplier and if generators are still competing with each other?

Behavioural economics can help us to explain another problem that appears in the energy market and that is a type of brand loyalty. In investigating this oligopoly, the UK competition regulator, the Competition and Markets Authority (CMA), noted that consumers do pay more than they would in a more competitive market and that part of the problem is that customers are reluctant to switch suppliers.[3] There are many tariffs available to domestic consumers and so faced with too much choice, customers are too confused to switch, leading to inertia in the market and making it difficult for new entrants to attract customers. The suppliers were accused of exploiting these 'loyalty' customers and limiting competition.

Various measures have been taken to break down the barriers to entry in the industry that arise from inertia, including a requirement to publish simple 'per-unit' prices to allow customers to compare tariffs more easily and to publish prices up to two years in advance to ensure more effective competition. More customers are now switching and the market is becoming more competitive, with new suppliers entering, but concern remains that the Big Six retain a more than 75 per cent share of the market and hence continued monitoring of their behaviour will be vital.

US Airlines?

In the USA, the domestic airline industry is controlled by four main airlines: American Airlines, Delta Air Lines, Southwest Airlines and United Airlines (a subsidiary of Continental Airlines) and together they account for approximately 80 per cent of all passenger numbers. This is a classic example of an oligopoly. But how did the industry get there?

Airlines have high fixed costs and so achieving relatively full planes, or high 'load factors', is important. In order to gain customers, one strategy is for airlines to undercut prices and to continue to do so until competitors are driven out of the market. This may seem like a good outcome for customers, benefiting from low prices, but once just a few carriers remain, each with significant market power, they can then push up prices. Moreover, they may be able to allocate routes to each other, giving them a natural monopoly on certain routes.

This potential outcome was foreseen by US legislators, and regulation from the 1930s aimed to address it. Routes were allocated to airlines, price competition was forbidden and airlines were required to offer a certain level of service. However, this regulation was abandoned in 1978 and so began a more competitive period in US aviation. No-frills airlines entered the market, forcing the larger carriers to compete on price, and in order to protect profit margins, airlines reduced the level of service offered. This competition intensified and led to many airlines failing. Indeed, since deregulation, over 160 airlines have entered and exited the US market – which brings us to the present-day oligopoly.[4]

Up until 2015, the US industry had received a vast number of complaints from passengers about the quality of service and many commentators put this down to the market power of the big four. Although some argued that they were formally colluding, evidence for this was minimal. Instead, it appeared to be another case of tacit collusion. However, rather than adopting common prices, it seemed more likely that the four airlines had tacitly given each other *monopolies* on certain routes. This meant that even though there were four big airlines competing for domestic passengers, when flying between two destinations, customers often had only one option and that airline could therefore set the monopoly price.

Growth of the small carrier

However, since 2015, there has been a change in the market. The number of small carriers has grown, providing more competition to the big four on some routes and this has had an effect on prices.

At the same time, some of the local monopoly routes that the big four had benefited from have begun to disappear, with the largest US airlines growing by increasing passenger capacity on flights to and from cities or 'hubs' that were previously monopolised by one airline. One good example is the Boston-Akron/Cleveland city pairing. In 2007, Continental Airlines (United Airlines) had a passenger share of 63 per cent, with AirTran having 30 per cent of the market. By 2018, there were five main airlines competing over this route, with market shares as follows: jetBlue (48%), United (25%), Spirit (15%), Delta (5%), American Airlines (5%). The impact has been for passenger numbers to rise by 23 per cent, while real fares have fallen by 20 per cent.[5]

Despite some positive changes, issues of a natural monopoly remain. Towards the end of 2017, airline executives felt the wrath of both houses of Congress in response to the service they provide. Both Republicans and Democrats complained

[2] British Gas, EDF Energy, E.ON UK, npower, ScottishPower and SSE.

[3] *Energy market investigation: Summary of final report*, Competition & Markets Authority (24 June 2016).

[4] Milton Ezrati, 'Airlines face more regulation, even from this administration', *Forbes* (29 January 2018).

[5] *Airlines for America: Industry Review and Outlook*, Airlines for America (25 February 2019).

about the lack of competition and poor service. Airlines responded by arguing that it was difficult to improve service as low prices had already eroded profit margins.

However, airlines in North America are expected to make a net profit of $16.6 billion in 2019, with those in Europe forecast to make less than half that at $7.4 billion. They are clearly serving very different markets, but the degree of competition between airlines in America and Europe does appear to be a factor. For example, between 2014 and 2016, the global price of jet fuel had fallen from $120 to $40 per barrel and had only risen back to $80 by 2019. In Europe the

fall in fuel prices led to a price war between the airlines. In the USA, however, ticket prices remained fairly rigid. US airlines were not forced into a competitive price war, in many cases being able to rely on their local monopoly.[6]

🔍 *Consider the airline industry in your own country or region. What type of market structure does it have and what does this mean for prices and profits?*

_____

[6] 'A lack of competition explains the flaws in American aviation', *The Economist* (22 April 2017).

RECAP

1. An oligopoly is where there are just a few firms in an industry with barriers to the entry of new firms. Firms recognise their interdependence and each must consider the reactions of rivals to any changes it makes.

2. Whether oligopolists compete or collude depends on the conditions in the industry. They are more likely to collude if there are few of them; if they are open with each other; if they have similar products and cost structures; if there is a dominant firm; if there are significant entry barriers; if the market is stable; and if there is no government legislation to prevent collusion.

3. A formal collusive agreement is called a 'cartel'. A cartel aims to act as a monopoly. It can set a price and leave the members to compete for market share, or it can assign quotas. There is always a temptation for cartel members to 'cheat' by undercutting the cartel price if

they think they can get away with it and not trigger a price war.

4. Rather than having a formal collusive agreement, firms may collude tacitly. This can take the form of price leadership, or firms can follow an 'agreed' set of rules.

5. When firms do not collude, prices may still be relatively stable. One reason for this is that firms face a kinked demand curve, such that they are reluctant either to raise or to lower prices.

6. Whether consumers benefit from oligopoly depends on the particular oligopoly and how competitive it is; whether the firms engage in extensive advertising and of what type; whether product differentiation results in a wide range of choice for the consumer; and how much of the profits are ploughed back into research and development.

5.4 GAME THEORY

The interdependence between oligopolists requires firms to think strategically, making assumptions about rivals' behaviour before taking decisions. *Game theory* is used by economists to examine the best strategy that a firm can adopt and how this may affect market outcomes.

This section will focus on how game theory can be used to provide some useful insights into firms' behaviour. It allows us to assess the various strategies that firms might use for dealing with their rivals, for example in response to price changes, the launch of a new advertising campaign or product.

However, it is worth bearing in mind that game theory can be applied to a huge range of other areas. For example, the BBC News article, 'What exactly is "game theory"?',[5] examines the application of game theory by Greek Finance Minister Yanis Varoufakis in 2015 in his approach to negotiations over Greek

debt. Game theory can also be applied to negotiations over the UK's exit from the European Union.

Simultaneous one-shot games

When a firm is competing against others, its profit-maximising strategy (under non-collusive oligopoly) depends, in part, on how it thinks its rivals will react to its decisions on prices, new products, advertising, etc. It also depends on whether it expects the competition to be a one-off event (such as firms competing for a specific contract) or repeated.

Definition

Game theory (or the theory of games) The study of alternative strategies that oligopolists may choose to adopt, depending on their assumptions about their rivals' behaviour.

_____

[5] Chris Stokel-Walker, 'What exactly is "game theory"?', *BBC News Magazine* (18 February 2015).

We focus firstly on competition that is a one-off event. In the case of firms bidding for a specific contract, each firm will make its decision independently (i.e. submit its bid price); then all the bids will be considered. The contract will be awarded – probably to the lowest bidder; then the game ends. In this case, each firm 'moves' just once and it is therefore modelled as a *single-move or one-shot game*. As both firms are making their decisions at the same time, or without observing the decision of each other, it is also a *simultaneous game*.

Dominant strategy games

Consider a market where there are just two firms with identical costs, products and demand. They are both considering which of two alternative prices to charge. Figure 5.5 shows typical profits they could each make.

Let us assume that at present both firms (X and Y) are charging a price of £2 and that they are each making a profit of £10 million, giving a total industry profit of £20 million. This is shown in the top left-hand cell (A).

Now assume they are both (independently) considering reducing their price to £1.80. Given the interdependence between them, firm X will need to consider what firm Y might do and the impact this will have. Firm Y must do the same. Let us consider X's position. In our simple example there are just two things that its rival, firm Y, might do. Either Y could cut its price to £1.80, or it could leave its price at £2. What should X do?

To answer this question, we need to take each of firm Y's two possible actions and look at firm X's best response to each. If we assume that firm Y chooses a price of £2, firm X could keep its price at £2 giving it £10m in profit. This is shown by cell A. Alternatively, firm X could cut its price to £1.80 and

earn £12m in profit, in cell B. Firm X's best response is therefore to cut price to £1.80, preferring a profit of £12m to one of £10m.

What happens if we now assume that firm Y charges £1.80 – how should firm X best respond? If firm X charged £2, we would end up in cell C and firm X would earn only £5m in profits. On the other hand, firm X could also cut its price to £1.80, moving us to cell D and it would earn £8m in profits. By comparing these two profit outcomes, we can see that firm X's best response is again to cut price to £1.80, preferring a profit of £8m to a profit of £5m. Note that firm Y will argue along similar lines, cutting price to £1.80 as well, whatever it assumes firm X will do.

This game is called a *dominant strategy game*, since the firm's best response is always to play the same (dominant) strategy (namely, cutting price to £1.80). The result is that the firms will end up in cell D, with each firm earning a profit of £8 million.

Nash equilibrium. The equilibrium outcome of a game where there is no collusion between the players (cell D in the above game) is known as a *Nash equilibrium*. Each firm does what is best for itself, given the assumptions about its rival's behaviour and neither firm has any incentive to change its behaviour. It is named after John Nash, a US mathematician who introduced the concept in 1951. The Oscar-winning film, 'A Beautiful Mind' depicts the life story of John Nash and you can watch the famous scene where he begins to formulate the famous Nash equilibrium on YouTube.[6] You may also like to look at the blog on the Sloman Economics News site, *Death of a Beautiful Mind*, following John Nash's death on 23 May 2015.

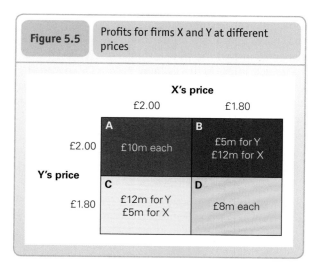

Figure 5.5	Profits for firms X and Y at different prices

X's price

		£2.00	£1.80
Y's price	£2.00	**A** £10m each	**B** £5m for Y £12m for X
	£1.80	**C** £12m for Y £5m for X	**D** £8m each

---

[6] Nash Equilibrium, *YouTube* (available at: https://www.youtube.com/watch?v=2d_dtTZQyUM).

KEY IDEA 19

Nash equilibrium. The position resulting from everyone making their optimal decision based on their assumptions about their rivals' decisions. Such an outcome, however, is unlikely to maximise the collective benefit. Nevertheless, without collusion in this 'game', whether open or tacit, there is no incentive to move from this position.

The prisoners' dilemma. In the previous game in Figure 5.5, it is important to note that the profits earned by each firm in the Nash equilibrium (cell D) are lower than they would have been had the firms colluded and charged the higher price (cell A). Each firm would have earned £10 million.

But even with collusion, both firms would be tempted to cheat and cut prices. This is known as the *prisoners' dilemma*. The prisoners' dilemma is examined in Box 5.4.

Pause for thought

If firms were to collude, how could they avoid the prisoners' dilemma?

More complex simultaneous one-shot games

More complex 'games' can be devised with more than two firms, many alternative prices, differentiated products and various forms of non-price competition (e.g. advertising). We may also see 'games', where the best response for each firm depends on the assumptions made, meaning there is no dominant strategy. Consider the payoff matrix in Figure 5.6.

If firm X assumes that firm Y will charge £20, then firm X will either earn £5m in profit if it charges £25 or £4m in profit if it charges £19. Firm X's best response would be to charge £25. However, if it

assumes that firm Y will charge £15, then firm X's best response will now be to charge £19, preferring £7m in profit (cell D) to £3m in profit (cell C). We no longer have a dominant strategy. Firm X's best response depends on its assumption about Y's price. However, firms X and Y are still both choosing their best response, given the assumptions they make about their rival's behaviour and hence we can still arrive at a Nash equilibrium.

Pause for thought

What is firm Y's best response to each of firm X's possible choices in the game shown in Figure 5.6? Does it have a dominant strategy in this game?

In many situations, firms will have a number of different options open to them and a number of possible reactions by rivals. Such games can become highly complex and predicting your rivals' behaviour can be crucial in ensuring the best possible outcome. It now becomes possible to have multiple Nash equilibria.

The better the firm's information about (a) its rivals' costs and demand, (b) the likely reactions of rivals to its actions and (c) the effects of these reactions on its own profit, the better the firm's 'move in the game' is likely to be. It is similar to a card game: the more you know about your opponents' cards and how your opponents are likely to react to your moves, and the better you can calculate the effects of their moves on you, the better your moves in the game are likely to be.

Repeated simultaneous games

Although one-shot games do occur and not just in business scenarios, many firms will actually compete with each other on a continuous basis. In our earlier example of firms bidding for a contract, once each firm had set its price, the game ended. But, what happens if the game does not end there? Supermarkets and fast food restaurants are frequently amending their prices; Apple and Samsung launch new versions of their mobile phones on an annual basis.

Definition

Prisoners' dilemma Where two or more firms (or people), by attempting independently to choose their best strategy given the assumptions they make about their rivals' behaviour, end up in a worse position than if they had co-operated in the first place.

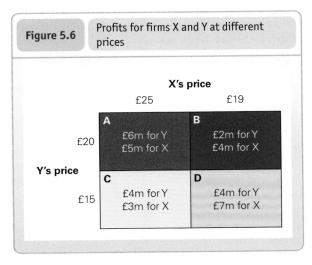

Figure 5.6	Profits for firms X and Y at different prices

X's price

	£25	£19
£20	**A** £6m for Y £5m for X	**B** £2m for Y £4m for X
£15	**C** £4m for Y £3m for X	**D** £4m for Y £7m for X

Y's price

BOX 5.4 THE PRISONERS' DILEMMA

When confession may be the best strategy

A famous non-economic example of game theory is the origin of the term 'prisoners' dilemma'. Consider Nigel and Amanda who have been arrested for a joint crime of serious fraud. Each is interviewed separately and given the following alternatives:

- If they say nothing, the court has enough evidence to sentence both to a year's imprisonment.
- If either Nigel or Amanda *alone* confesses, he or she will get only a three-month sentence but the partner would get ten years.
- If both confess, they get three years each.

Let us consider Nigel's dilemma. If he believes that Amanda will confess, then he should also confess, preferring three years in prison to ten years. If he believes that Amanda will not confess, then he should still confess, as by doing so he gets only three months, as opposed to one year. Nigel's best response, then, is always to confess.

Amanda is in the same dilemma and so the result is simple. When both prisoners do what is best for themselves, given how they think the other will behave, they both confess and end up with relatively long prison terms. Only when they collude and both deny will they end up with relatively short sentences, but neither has an incentive to do this, as the more certain they are that their compatriot will deny, the greater the incentive for them to confess!

Of course, the police know this and will do their best to prevent collusion, keeping the prisoners separate and trying to persuade each that the other is bound to confess.

> 1. Devise a box diagram for the above case, similar to that in Figure 5.5. Why is this a dominant strategy game?
> 2. How would Nigel's choice of strategy be affected if he had instead been involved in a joint crime with Nikki, Kim, Paul and Dave, and they had all been caught?

Some other examples of the prisoners' dilemma

Standing at concerts

When people go to a concert or a match, they often stand to get a better view. But once people start standing, everyone is likely to do so: after all, if they stayed sitting, they would not see at all. In this Nash equilibrium, most people are worse off, since, except for tall people, their view is likely to be worse and they lose the comfort of sitting down. But once everyone is standing, nobody has an incentive to sit down, because then you won't see anything. Thus we arrive at a Nash equilibrium.

Too much advertising

Why do firms spend so much on advertising? If they are aggressive, they probably do so to get ahead of their rivals. If they are cautious, they probably do so for fear of their rivals increasing their advertising. Although in both cases it may be in the individual firm's best interests to increase advertising, the resulting Nash equilibrium is likely to be one of excessive advertising: the total spent on advertising (by all firms) is not recouped in additional sales.

> 3. Give some other examples (economic and non-economic) of the prisoners' dilemma.

> Individually or in small groups arrange a meeting with a manager in a company that clearly competes with rivals. Formulate a series of questions to determine the extent to which the company takes a strategic approach to pricing, advertising and other forms of marketing and the ways in which it (a) tries to anticipate what its rivals will do; (b) how it responds to its rivals' actions; (c) how its rivals respond to its actions. Write a brief report on your findings. It might be appropriate to present this in class.

In these cases, we do not have a one-shot game, as the 'players' have to make decisions, over and over again. Such games are now *repeated games*. The big difference is that now each firm or 'player' can see its rivals' actions in previous periods/rounds of the game, even though firms are playing simultaneously in each period. Players can use this information to inform their own strategy and hence it creates a scenario whereby a player's actions in period one may have an impact on its rivals' actions and its own profits in subsequent periods. Firms may face a trade-off between the short run and the long run.

Consider the prisoners' dilemma game from Box 5.4, which was a one-shot game. Even though both Nigel and Amanda would have been better off colluding, neither had an incentive to do so and thus the Nash equilibrium was for both to confess. If we now think of this as a repeated game, will the

predicted outcome change? Is there a way in which Nigel and Amanda can be encouraged to co-operate with each other so that they both deny the charges and end up with the most efficient outcome for each of them: they each get one year.

Infinitely repeated games

Perhaps Nigel and Amanda are a modern version of Bonnie and Clyde and are constantly committing crimes, but getting caught! They therefore find themselves having to decide between 'confess' and 'deny' on a weekly basis. This is a repeated game and now our two criminals may have an incentive to collude. Before, neither player could be convinced to collude and choose 'deny', because if their partner confessed, they would then receive up to ten years in prison. But now, there is an incentive to collude. Let us consider Amanda's decision.

The grim trigger strategy. Assume that Nigel and Amanda have agreed that they will 'deny' if they are ever caught. However, when they are caught for the first time, Amanda changes her mind under questioning and confesses (persuaded by the shorter sentence). Once the sentences are served and they play the game again (commit the next crime and get caught), Nigel may now decide to punish Amanda for breaking their agreement. That is, he may now play 'confess' in all future rounds of the game. This strategy employed by Nigel is known as the ***grim trigger strategy***.

It means that Amanda benefits in round one by confessing, as she only gets three months in jail (Nigel did as promised and denied). However, in all future rounds of the game, Nigel and Amanda now both play 'confess' and hence Amanda suffers in the long run, from repeatedly getting three years in jail. She trades off three months in jail in round one, but then suffers from three years in jail in every other round of the game.

If Amanda had not changed her mind and instead played 'deny' in round one, she would have received one year in jail (worse than the three months she served by confessing in period one), but then in all future rounds, both of them would have continued to deny. Thus, every future round of the game would lead to just one year in jail for Amanda, rather than three.

In this repeated game, both players have an incentive to co-operate with each other from the start, as they want to avoid their partner punishing them in all future rounds. This means that as long as both players believe they will 'play' again and they value their future payoffs (as little time in jail as possible), we can see a situation where neither player will choose the Nash equilibrium. Instead, both will choose to collude and 'deny'. Through co-operation the most efficient strategy has now been achieved.

The tit-for-tat strategy. You may think that the grim trigger strategy is rather extreme! Another strategy that might be played is what game theorists have found to be the most successful strategy in a repeated game, called the ***tit-for-tat strategy***. Just as with the grim trigger strategy, tit-for-tat can also encourage players to co-operate.

In this strategy, each player observes the action of its rival in one period and then copies that action in the next period. Therefore, if Nigel chose to play the tit-for-tat strategy, then after Amanda confessed in round one, Nigel would confess in round two. If Amanda confessed in round two, Nigel would confess in round three. But, if Amanda denied in round two, then Nigel would deny in round three.

This strategy therefore still incorporates the 'punishment' from the grim trigger strategy, but it also introduces the idea of forgiveness. That is: if you confessed in the last round, I'll punish you this round by confessing, but if you change your mind and deny, I'll forgive your earlier transgression and will deny next time too! A comment from a Microeconomics textbook by Thomas Nechyba[7] nicely summarises the idea behind it. He says, 'Play nice with the other kids. . . but if someone hits you, you hit them back until they start being nice again'.

In the context of pricing, a tit-for-tat strategy might be for a firm not to be the first to cut prices, but if one of its rivals cuts its price, this firm will cut its price too. The hope of this first firm is that the other firm will realise this and, not wanting to trigger a price war, will decide not to cut its price. This could be seen as a form of tacit collusion: the implicit threat of retaliation prevents firms from cutting prices (or from launching an advertising campaign, etc.).

Finitely repeated games

An important thing to consider with repeated games is just how many rounds there will be. In our previous scenario, we didn't consider the last round of the game. That is, we assumed it was an infinitely repeated game and hence there was always a chance that the players would meet again.

If instead, the game is a finitely repeated game, i.e. there are a certain number of rounds, say ten, the outcome of the game reverts to the one-shot game. The reason is that in the final tenth round, both players know that they will never be in this position again and thus the incentive they had to collude has now disappeared. Both players will revert to playing 'confess' in this final period. If, in the ninth period, both players realise that they cannot influence what their

---

Definitions

Repeated games Games that involve two or more moves. Games can either be repeated an infinite number of times or can be repeated a set number of times.

Grim trigger strategy Once a player observes that its rival has broken some agreed behaviour, it will never again co-operate with them again.

Tit-for-tat strategy A strategy where you copy whatever your rival does. Thus, if your rival cuts price, you will too. If your rival does not, neither will you. If the rival knows this, it will be less likely to make an initial aggressive move.

---

7 Thomas J. Nechyba, *Microeconomics: An Intuitive Approach with Calculus* (Cengage, 2010).

partner will do in the tenth period, then they have no incentive to collude in the ninth period. And hence no incentive to collude in the eighth period, or the seventh, etc. The Nash equilibrium of 'confess, confess' returns.

This process of working backwards from the last period to think about outcomes in earlier periods is called *backwards induction*.

> ### Pause for thought
>
> *Consider the game from Figure 5.5, but this time extend it beyond one time period. Explain whether either firm has an incentive to keep the price at £2.00 and hence if co-operation can be sustained. (Hint: consider both an infinitely and finitely repeated game.)*

Sequential games

Most decisions by firms are made by one firm at a time rather than simultaneously by all firms. In Box 5.1, we saw McDonald's move first by announcing its new prices and deals and then other firms responded. This is an example of a 'sequential game', where the 'order of play' is important and firms can now observe the decisions of their rivals.

Take the case of a new generation of large passenger aircraft which can fly further without refuelling. Assume that there is a market for a 500-seater version of this type of aircraft and a 400-seater version, but that the individual markets for each aircraft are not big enough for the two manufacturers, Boeing and Airbus, to share them profitably. Let us also assume that the 400-seater market would give an annual profit of

> ### Definition
>
> **Backwards induction** A process by which firms consider the decision in the last round of the game and then work backwards through the game, thinking through the most likely outcomes in earlier rounds.

BOX 5.5   THE HUNGER GAMES

To sleep or not to sleep

Suzanne Collins published the first book of the trilogy, *The Hunger Games* in 2008 and it has been made into four films. It follows Katniss Everdeen, living in a future time where a country has been divided into Districts. The wealthy Capitol rules the other 12 other Districts. Each year, a girl and boy from every District are chosen randomly to compete to the death against each other in The Hunger Games, which is set in a dangerous and very public arena. Katniss volunteers in place of her younger sister and enters the arena with Peeta, the male 'Tribute' and so the use of strategic thinking and game theory begins, until just one 'Tribute' remains.[1]

The Games can last for weeks and so survival relies on avoiding being killed by another 'Tribute' and getting enough sleep to sustain yourself. The problem is, when you are asleep there is the chance of a stealth attack by another competitor, but if you don't sleep, you become more susceptible to future attacks, due to sleep deprivation.

  1. Try constructing a matrix and determine the Nash equilibrium in this game.

Many stabs in the dark

In the Games, a coalition is formed between some Tributes, who agree to work together, but still know they are competing against each other and hence at some point, will have to try to kill their rivals. They are camping together and so within that group, they know where everyone is.

2. Does the Nash equilibrium in the game change if we are now thinking about the decision of one member of the Coalition, given the possible responses of the other members of the Coalition?

Looking at the matrix you constructed and perhaps making some assumptions about the relative value of sleep versus progress, the likely outcome seems to be 'Don't sleep' for everyone. After all, being sleep deprived is better than being dead. So, why do the members of the Coalition get any sleep?

The Hunger Games goes on for many nights, so it is an infinitely repeated game, as no player knows when their last night will be. The members of the Coalition have to make the sleep decision every night, knowing that every night they don't sleep they may make progress, but will become more vulnerable to other attacks. Furthermore, as there are multiple members of the Coalition, each member will become less trustworthy if others are killed during the night. So, perhaps the best response in this infinitely repeated game is for the Coalition to co-operate from the start, so everyone gets some sleep. However, if one night a member is killed, then the next night would probably see each player once again best responding by remaining awake. Perhaps there would be a 'tit-for-tat' strategy, until a winner emerges.

Search for the gameshow 'Golden Balls' on YouTube and watch a clip of the very last part of the game '£66,885 Split or Steal?'[2] Try constructing a matrix for this game and working out what the Nash equilibrium is.

---

[1] See: Samuel Arbesman, 'Probability and Game Theory in The Hunger Games', *Wired* (4 October 2012).

[2] See: https://www.youtube.com/watch?v=yM38mRHY150

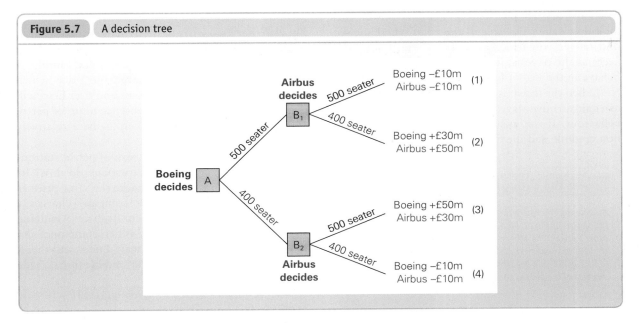

Figure 5.7 A decision tree

£50 million to a single manufacturer and the 500-seater would give an annual profit of £30 million, but that if both manufacturers produced the same version, they would each make an annual loss of £10 million.

Assume that Boeing announces that it is building the 400-seater plane. What should Airbus do? The choice is illustrated in Figure 5.7. This diagram is called a *decision tree or game tree* and shows the sequence of events. The small square at the left of the diagram is Boeing's decision point (point A). If it had decided to build the 500-seater plane, we would move up the top branch. Airbus would now have to make a decision (point B_1). If it too built the 500-seater plane, we would move to outcome 1: a loss of £10 million for both manufacturers. Clearly, with Boeing building a 500-seater plane, Airbus would choose the 400-seater plane: we would move to outcome 2, with Boeing making a profit of £30 million and Airbus a profit £50 million. Airbus would be very pleased!

Boeing's best strategy at point A, however, would be to build the 400-seater plane. We would then move to Airbus's decision point B_2. In this case, it is in Airbus's interests to build the 500-seater plane. Its profit would be only £30 million (outcome 3), but this is better than a £10 million loss if it too built the 400-seater plane (outcome 4). With Boeing deciding first, the Nash equilibrium will thus be outcome 3.

There is clearly a *first-mover advantage* here. Once Boeing has decided to build the more profitable version of the plane, Airbus is forced to build the less profitable one. Naturally, Airbus would like to build the more profitable one and be the first mover. Which company succeeds in going first depends on how advanced they are in their research and development and in their production capacity.

More complex decision trees. The aircraft example is the simplest version of a decision tree, with just two companies and each one making only one key decision. In many business situations, much more complex trees could be constructed. The 'game' would be more like one of chess, with many moves and several options on each move. If there were more than two companies, the decision tree would be more complex still.

Pause for thought

Give an example of decisions that two firms or 'players' could make in sequence, each one affecting the other's next decision.

Credible threats and promises

In sequential games, firms may threaten (or promise) that they will act in a certain way as a means of influencing the outcome of the game. The key question is whether the threat or promise is *credible*.

We often see threats being made by the second mover in a game, as it tries to convince the first mover

Definitions

Decision tree (or game tree) A diagram showing the sequence of possible decisions by competitor firms and the outcome of each combination of decisions.

First-mover advantage When a firm gains from being the first to take action.

Credible threat (or promise) One that is believable to rivals because it is in the threatener's interests to carry it out.

to choose a particular action. The first mover must look down the game tree to the point where the second mover will make its decision and, taking into account the payoffs, it must ask, will the firm really behave in the way it has threatened? If the answer is 'yes', then the threat is credible and the second mover can gain an advantage by influencing the first mover's behaviour. If the answer is 'no', then the threat is non-credible and the firm will ignore it.

> **Pause for thought**
>
> *Assume that there are two major oil companies operating filling stations in an area. The first promises to match the other's prices. The other promises to sell at 1p per litre cheaper than the first. Describe the likely sequence of events in this 'game' and the likely eventual outcome. Could the promise of the second company be seen as credible?*

Take the simple situation where a large oil company, such as Esso, states that it will match the price charged by any competitor within a given radius.

Assume that competitors believe this 'price promise' but also that Esso will not try to undercut their price. In the simple situation where there is only one other petrol station in the area, what price should it charge? Clearly it should charge the price which would maximise its profits, assuming that Esso will charge the same price. In the absence of other petrol stations in the area, this is likely to be a relatively high price.

Now assume that there are several petrol stations in the area. What should the company do now? Its best response is probably to charge the same price as Esso and hope that no other company charges a lower price and forces Esso to cut its price. Assuming that Esso's threat is credible, other companies are likely to respond in a similar way. Prices will therefore be kept high, because of the credible threat made by Esso.

The economic crisis in Greece in 2015–16 saw many applications of game theory, most involving both threats and promises, and you can read about this in articles from *The Conversation*,[8] *Bloomberg*[9] and *City A.M.*[10]

> **RECAP**
>
> 1. Game theory examines various strategies that firms or 'players' can adopt when the outcome for each player depends on the choices made by others and thus is not certain.
>
> 2. The simplest type of 'game' is a simultaneous one-shot game. Many games of this kind have predictable outcomes, as a player's best response does not depend on the assumptions made about the other players' behaviour. These are dominant strategy games with a single Nash equilibrium. However, in such games, it is possible that both players could do better by co-operating or colluding.
>
> 3. Other simultaneous one-shot games can be more complex, where a firm's best response does depend on the assumptions it makes about its rivals' behaviour. The Nash equilibrium is a useful way to predict the most likely outcome in any of these games.
>
> 4. If a simultaneous game is repeated, players can be encouraged to co-operate. The outcome will depend on whether the game is infinite or finite and hence whether players know when the last round will be and on how much they value future payoffs versus short-term gains.
>
> 5. In sequential games, play is passed from one 'player' to the other and we can use a decision or game tree to illustrate the decisions and outcomes of the game. In many instances, a firm can gain a strategic advantage over its rival by being the first mover.
>
> 6. Firms will respond not only to what firms do, but what they say they will do. To this end, a firm's threats or promises must be credible, if they are to influence rivals' decisions.

5.5 ALTERNATIVE AIMS OF THE FIRM

The traditional profit-maximising theories of the firm have been criticised for being unrealistic. They assume that it is the *owners* of the firm that make price and output decisions. It is reasonable to assume that owners will want to maximise profits: this much most of the critics of the traditional theory accept. But as we saw in Chapter 1, a separation of ownership and control (see page 9) may mean this does not happen.

Alternative theories of the firm typically make one or other of two assumptions: either that managers attempt to maximise some other aim (such as growth

[8] Partha Gangopadhyay, 'How game theory explains Grexit and may also predict Greek poll outcome' *The Conversation* (1 July 2015).

[9] Mohamed A. El-Erian, 'John Nash's Game Theory and Greece', *Bloomberg* (29 May 2015).

[10] Paul Ormerod, 'Against the grain: What Yanis Varoufakis can learn from a real game theory master – Nicola Sturgeon' *City A.M.* (24 June 2016).

in sales); or that they pursue a *number* of aims, which might possibly conflict. In either case, they must still make sufficient profits (the aim of *profit satisficing*) in order to keep shareholders happy. Otherwise they risk being taken over and/or losing their job.

We now examine these two alternative assumptions in turn.

Alternative maximising aims

Sales revenue maximisation

Perhaps the most famous of all alternative theories of the firm is the theory of *sales revenue maximisation*. So why should managers want to maximise their firm's sales revenue? The answer is that the success of managers, and especially sales managers, may be judged according to the level of the firm's sales. Sales figures are an obvious barometer of the firm's health. Managers' salaries, power and prestige may depend directly on sales revenue. The firm's sales representatives may be paid commission on their sales. Thus sales revenue maximisation may be a more dominant aim in the firm than profit maximisation, particularly if it has a dominant sales department.

Total sales revenue (TR) will be maximised at a higher output and lower price than will profits. This is illustrated in Figure 5.8. Profits are maximised at output Q_1 and price P_1, where $MC = MR$. Sales revenue, however, is maximised at the higher output Q_2 and lower price P_2, where $MR = 0$. The reason is that if MR equals zero, nothing more can be added to total revenue (TR) by producing extra and thus TR must be at the maximum. Indeed, by producing above Q_2, MR would be negative and thus TR would fall.

Sales revenue maximisation tends to involve more advertising than profit maximisation. Ideally the profit-maximising firm will advertise up to the point where the marginal revenue of advertising equals the marginal cost of advertising (assuming diminishing returns to advertising). The firm aiming to maximise sales revenue will go beyond this, since further advertising, although costing more than it earns the firm, will still add to total revenue. The firm will continue advertising until surplus profits above the minimum have been used up.

Growth maximisation

Rather than aiming to maximise short-run revenue, managers may take a longer-term perspective and aim for *growth maximisation* in the size of the firm. They may gain directly from being part of a rapidly growing 'dynamic' organisation; promotion prospects are greater in an expanding organisation, since new posts tend to be created; large firms may pay higher salaries; managers may obtain greater power in a large firm.

Growth is probably best measured in terms of a growth in sales revenue, since sales revenue (or 'turnover') is the simplest way of measuring the size of a business. An alternative would be to measure the capital value of a firm, but this will depend on the ups and downs of the stock market and is thus a rather unreliable method.

If a firm is to maximise growth, it needs to be clear about the time period over which it is setting itself this objective. For example, maximum growth over the next two or three years might be obtained by running factories at maximum capacity, cramming in as many machines and workers as possible, and backing this up with massive advertising campaigns and price cuts. Such policies, however, may not be financially sustainable in the longer run. A longer-term perspective (say, 5–10 years) may therefore require the firm to 'pace' itself, and perhaps to direct resources away from current production and sales into the development of new products that have a potentially high and growing long-term demand.

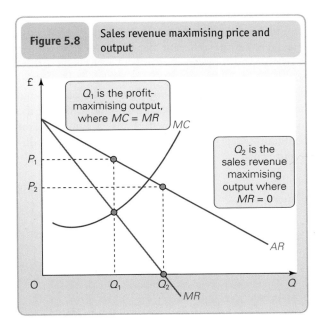

| Figure 5.8 | Sales revenue maximising price and output |

Q_1 is the profit-maximising output, where $MC = MR$

Q_2 is the sales revenue maximising output where $MR = 0$

Definitions

Profit satisficing Where decision makers in a firm aim for a target level of profit rather than the absolute maximum level.

Sales revenue maximisation An alternative theory of the firm which assumes that managers aim to maximise the firm's short-run total revenue.

Growth maximisation An alternative theory which assumes that managers seek to maximise the growth in sales revenue (or the capital value of the firm) over time.

Equilibrium for a growth-maximising firm. What will a growth-maximising firm's price and output be? Unfortunately, there is no simple formula for predicting this.

In the short run, the firm may choose the profit-maximising price and output, as this will provide the greatest funds for investment. On the other hand, it may be prepared to sacrifice some short-term profits in order to mount an advertising campaign to boost longer-term sales. Thus the price and output depend on the strategy it considers most suitable to achieve growth.

In the long run, prediction is more difficult still. The policies that a firm adopts will depend crucially on the assessments of market opportunities made by managers. Different managers may judge a situation differently.

> ### Pause for thought
>
> *How will competition between growth-maximising firms benefit the consumer?*

One prediction can be made. Growth-maximising firms are likely to diversify into different products, especially if their existing markets become saturated. We considered the Growth Vector Matrix in section 3.4 and will go on to analyse alternative growth strategies in Chapter 6.

Multiple aims

Behavioural theories of the firm: satisficing and the setting of targets

A major advance in alternative theories of the firm has been the development of **behavioural theories**.[11] Rather than setting up a model to show how various objectives could in theory be achieved, behavioural theories of the firm are based on observations of how firms *actually* behave.

Large firms are often complex institutions with several departments (sales, production, design, purchasing, personnel, finance, etc.). Each department is likely to have its own specific set of aims and objectives, which may come into conflict with those of other departments. In such cases all the aims cannot be maximised. Instead a 'satisficing' approach must be taken (see page 135).

This will normally involve setting targets for production, sales, profit, stock holding, etc. If, in practice, target levels are not achieved, a 'search' procedure will be started to find what went wrong and how to rectify it. If the problem cannot be rectified, managers will probably adjust the target downwards. If, on the other hand, targets are easily achieved, managers may adjust them upwards. Thus the targets to which managers aspire depend to a large extent on the success in achieving previous targets.

Targets are also influenced by expectations of demand and costs, by the achievements of competitors and by expectations of competitors' future behaviour. For example, if it is expected that the economy is likely to move into recession, sales and profit targets may be adjusted downwards.

When setting targets, firms will also need to take into account the interests of various *stakeholders*, such as shareholders, workers, customers, creditors, and the local and national communities. Those who support a 'stakeholder economy' argue that *all* interest groups should have a say in a firm's decisions. For example, trade unions could be on decision-making bodies or boards of directors. Banks or other lenders could be included in investment decisions, as often happens in Germany, where banks tend to finance a large proportion of investment. Supporters also argue that local communities should have a say in projects that affect them, such as new airport terminals, or railway lines and that consumers should have much more power and protection over the quality of, and information about, products. If representation by interest groups is not possible then they argue that companies should be regulated by government.

Given the number and variety of stakeholders and other factors that companies must consider, it is hardly surprising that targets will often conflict. In such cases, the conflict will often be settled by a bargaining process. Sometimes this will be between the managers of the different departments where their departmental objectives conflict with each other. Sometimes it will be between managers and various stakeholder groups. The outcome of the bargaining, however, will depend on the power and ability of the individual groups concerned. Thus, a similar set of conflicting targets may be resolved differently in different firms.

> ### Definition
>
> **Stakeholders (in a company)** People who are affected by a company's activities and/or performance (customers, employees, owners, creditors, people living in the neighbourhood, etc.). They may or may not be in a position to take decisions, or influence decision taking, in the firm.

---

[11] A major early work in this field which spawned a lot of further research was: R. M. Cyert and J. G. March, *A Behavioural Theory of the Firm* (Prentice Hall, 1963).

Behavioural theories of the firm: organisational slack

Since changing targets often involves search procedures and bargaining processes and is therefore time-consuming, and since many managers prefer to avoid conflict, targets tend to be changed fairly infrequently. Business conditions, however, often change rapidly. To avoid the need to change targets, therefore, managers will tend to be fairly conservative in their aspirations. This leads to the phenomenon known as *organisational slack.*

When the firm does better than planned, it will allow slack to develop. This slack can then be taken up if the firm does worse than planned. For example, if the firm produces more than it planned, it will build up stocks of finished goods and draw on them if production subsequently falls. It would not, in the meantime, increase its sales target or reduce its production target. If it did, and production then fell below target, the production department might not be able to supply the sales department with its full requirement.

Thus keeping targets fairly low and allowing slack to develop allows all targets to be met with minimum conflict.

Organisational slack, however, adds to a firm's costs. If firms are operating in a competitive environment, they may be forced to cut slack in order to survive. In the 1970s, many Japanese firms succeeded in cutting slack by using *just-in-time methods* of production. These involve keeping stocks to a minimum and ensuring that inputs are delivered as required. Clearly, this requires that production is tightly controlled and that suppliers are reliable. Many firms today have successfully cut their warehouse costs by using such methods. These methods are examined in section 8.5.

The consumer's interest

We have seen how firms that have multiple goals are likely to be satisficers and how this can lead to conflicts and organisational slack. But, what does this mean for consumers?

Such firms are less likely to be able to respond to changing market conditions, such as adjustments in consumer demand or in costs. This would then have an adverse effect on their efficiency. However, these firms, unlike profit-maximising firms, will be less concerned with pushing up prices, engaging in aggressive advertising or simply exploiting their market power. This may, therefore, be in the public interest. The overall impact on consumers will depend on factors such as the extent and type of competition a firm faces and how it responds to its rivals. For example, the more a firm is concerned with its own performance compared to that of its rivals, the more responsive it is likely to be to consumer wishes.

Definitions

Organisational slack When managers allow spare capacity to exist, thereby enabling them to respond more easily to changed circumstances.

Just-in-time methods Where a firm purchases supplies and produces both components and finished products as they are required. This minimises stock holding and its associated costs.

| BOX 5.6 | BEHAVIOURAL ECONOMICS AND THE FIRM |

Understanding how firms behave in various situations

In Chapter 3, we considered the role of behavioural economics with regards to consumer choice and here we look at some further insights that it can provide for the study of firms.

Using rules of thumb to profit

In order to deal with the increasingly complex business environment, firms use various heuristics (rules of thumb/mental short-cuts) to simplify things. For example, some firms observe the actions and profits made by their rivals and follow an imitation strategy by copying the most profitable business in the market. In oligopolies, this strategy can create intense competition and lower prices. Research indicates that this strategy is at least as successful as traditional profit maximisation.

Alternatively, rather than maximising profits, firms may aim to make more profits than their competitors and hence focus on relative rather than absolute profit. In this way, success is judged relative to competitors, with growth in market share, product design and technology often being more important than growth in sales or profit. Such strategies can create price wars and reduce a firm's profits, but this may be acceptable as long as rivals' profits fall by more.

Can firms benefit from 'irrational' consumers?

Profit-maximising firms can use behavioural economics if their customers use heuristics, make systematic mistakes or simply behave irrationally. Indeed, there is evidence that firms have used some of its principles for many years, such as marketing strategies tailored to consumers' irrational preferences, including loyalty points or 'buy one, get one free'.

Traditional economic theory predicts that different ways of presenting the same price should not impact consumer behaviour, but evidence indicates that consumers do respond to the way in which prices are presented and so firms can exploit that to boost profits.

Sometimes you may see a product with its price shown, but with other prices visible alongside it, such as competitor

▶

prices, recommended retail prices, or the manufacturer's suggested price. This is known as *reference pricing*. You may see adverts that the current price is only available until a certain date or only if you buy another product. Such strategies are aiming to take advantage of some irrational consumer behaviour.

Another example is *partitioned* or *drip pricing*. Here, rather than presenting one total combined price, firms split the product's price into components, such as a base price, plus fees for handling, administration, postage, etc. Partitioned pricing occurs when the different elements of the price are displayed simultaneously, whereas drip pricing is where consumers discover additional fees as they move through the buying process. Drip pricing is commonly used in online markets and is often used to lure consumers with an apparently low headline price.

For example, in 2013, the consumer group *Which?* carried out a mystery shopping investigation[1] into ticket prices for music, comedy and theatre events. In 76 out of 78 cases additional booking charges and delivery fees were added towards the end of the transaction. In some instances, these were up to a third of the advertised ticket price.

Evidence on the impact

Is there any evidence that partitioned or drip pricing has an impact on consumer behaviour? Morwitz, Greenleaf and Johnson (1998)[2] carried out an auction experiment and found that when a 15 per cent surcharge was separated from the base price, the participants were willing to pay more. Hossain and Morgan (2006)[3] conducted a field experiment on auctions for CDs and Xbox games on eBay. They found that the sales price in auctions was always greater when a low reserve price was displayed with high shipping/handling costs as opposed to a high reserve price with low shipping/handling costs. In a laboratory experiment, Huck and Wallace

[1] 'Play-fair-on-ticket-fees', *Which press release* (17 December 2013).

[2] V. G. Morwitz, E. A. Greenleaf and E. J. Johnson, 'Divide and prosper: Consumers' reactions to partitioned prices', *Journal of Marketing Research* vol. 35, pp. 453–63 (1998).

[3] Tanjim Hossain and John Morgan, '. . . Plus Shipping and Handling: Revenue (Non) equivalence in Field Experiment on eBay', *Advances in Economic Analysis and Policy* vol. 6, pp. 1–26 (2006).

(2015) found that drip pricing reduced consumer surplus (see page 57) by 22 per cent.[4]

What explains these results?

Consumers are often anchored to the base price of the product, believing that to be the most important piece of information and simply fail to take account of, or adjust to, other elements, causing them to underestimate the product's total price.

It can also be the case that, having seen the advertised price and decided that they are going to buy a product, consumers begin to value it more, almost believing that they already own it. Thus, when they then see additional fees, they are willing to pay them to avoid having to give up the purchase.

Understanding workers and competitors

Since, for most firms, labour is a major input, it will be important to account for the motivation of employees – to ensure that they work hard and that their actions are aligned with the interests of the firm. Mechanisms of reward, (and possibly punishment) may be most effective if the behaviour of workers and their preference for fairness is fully understood.

A crucial factor for firms is the behaviour of other firms. Behavioural economics of the firm is thus important not just for economists and policy makers in analysing the motivation and decisions of managers; it is important too for firms in understanding and predicting the behaviour of their competitors and suppliers.

Thus, firms can certainly make use of behavioural economics to boost sales and profits, though competition authorities from around the world have started to investigate some of the implications of these pricing strategies for consumer welfare.

 Is 'Black Friday' an example of any of the pricing strategies discussed in this Box?

Choose a company and, by looking at its marketing and pricing strategy, consider the extent to which it is 'nudging' the consumers of its products.

[4] Steffan Huck and Brian Wallace, 'The impact of price frames on decision making: Experimental evidence', *UCL Working paper* (October 2015).

RECAP

1. In large companies, aims may conflict due to the separation of ownership from control. This can lead to profit 'satisficing', where managers aim to achieve sufficient profits to keep shareholders happy, but this is a secondary aim to one or more alternative aims.

2. Managers may seek to maximise sales revenue. The output of a sales-revenue-maximising firm will be higher than that of a profit-maximising one. Its level of advertising will also tend to be higher.

3. Many managers aim for maximum growth of their organisation, believing that this will help their salaries, power, prestige, etc. It is difficult, however, to predict the price and output strategies of a growth-maximising firm.

4. Firms can make use of behavioural economics in deciding business strategy and setting prices.

5. In large firms, decisions are taken or influenced by a number of different people, including various managers and other stakeholders. If interests conflict, a satisficing approach will generally be adopted. This involves setting consistent targets, which will be adjusted in the light of experience and may involve a process of bargaining.

6. Life is made easier for managers if conflict can be avoided. This will be possible if slack is allowed to develop in various parts of the firm. If targets are not being met, the slack can then be taken up without requiring adjustments in other targets.

5.6 SETTING PRICE

How are prices determined in practice? Is there actually an equilibrium price? In many cases, probably not. Do firms construct marginal cost and marginal revenue curves (or equations) and find the output where they are equal? Do they then use an average revenue curve (or equation) to work out the price at that output?

The problem is that firms often do not have the information to do so, even if they wanted to. In practice, firms look for rules of pricing that are relatively simple to apply.

Cost-based pricing

One approach is *average cost or mark-up pricing*. Here producers work out the price by simply adding a certain percentage (mark-up) for profit on top of average costs (average fixed costs plus average variable costs).

$$p = AFC + AVC + \text{Profit mark-up}$$

Choosing the mark-up

The size of the profit mark-up on top of average cost will depend on the firm's aims, the likely actions of rivals and their responses to changes in this firm's price and how these responses will affect demand.

> ### Pause for thought
>
> *If a firm has a typical-shaped average cost curve and sets prices 10 per cent above average cost, what will its supply curve look like?*

Figure 5.9 Choosing the output and profit mark-up

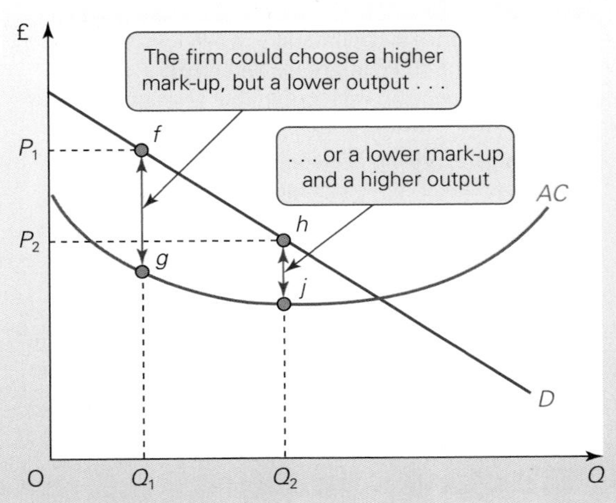

If a firm could estimate its demand curve, it could then set its output and profit mark-up at levels to avoid a shortage or surplus. Thus in Figure 5.9 it could choose a lower output (Q_1) with a higher mark-up (fg), or a higher output (Q_2) with a lower mark-up (hj). If a firm could not estimate its demand curve, then it could adjust its mark-up and output over time by a process of trial and error, according to its success in meeting profit and sales aims.

> ### Pause for thought
>
> *If the firm adjusts the size of its mark-up according to changes in demand and the actions of competitors, could its actions approximate to setting price and output where MC = MR?*

Variations in the mark-up

In most firms, the mark-up is not rigid. In expanding markets, or markets where firms have monopoly/oligopoly power, the size of the mark-up is likely to be greater. In contracting markets, or under conditions of rising costs and constant demand, a firm may well be forced to accept lower profits and thus reduce the mark-up.

Firms producing a range of products are likely to apply varying mark-ups to their different products. Those products with a less elastic demand can have a higher mark-up imposed on them, as any increase in price will have a relatively small effect on demand. Such products can thus make a larger contribution towards a firm's overhead costs.

The firm is likely to take account of the actions and possible reactions of its competitors, as we saw under the model of oligopoly. It may well be unwilling to change prices when costs or demand change, for fear of the reactions of competitors (see the kinked demand curve theory on page 124). If prices are kept constant and yet costs change, either due to a movement along the *AC* curve in response to a change in demand or due to a shift in the *AC* curve, the firm must necessarily change the size of the mark-up.

All this suggests that, whereas the mark-up may well be based on a target profit, firms are often prepared to change their target and hence their mark-up.

> ### Definition
>
> **Average cost or mark-up pricing** Where firms set the price by adding a profit mark-up to average costs.

Price discrimination

Up to now we have assumed that a firm will sell its output at a single price. However, rather than producing where $MC = MR$ in the market and charging everyone the same profit-maximising price, a firm might be able to make higher profits, by varying the price charged to different customers. This is known as *price discrimination*. The reason why this is possible is that some customers value a product more highly than others and thus have a higher willingness to pay for it.

The best scenario for the firm would be to charge every consumer a price equal to their marginal willingness to pay. However, this is very difficult, if not impossible, to achieve, as normally only the consumer knows (or thinks they know) how much they value the product. There is a problem for the firm, therefore, of asymmetric information – the consumer knows more than the firm. However, recent developments in big data may change this as firms gain more and more information about the preferences of individual consumers.[12] Also, it will be impractical with most products to charge different prices to each consumer, except in auctions or other bargaining situations, or in various street or online markets.

But, what if a firm can charge different prices to different *groups* of consumers based on its assumptions about the willingness to pay of each group? This is the most common type of price discrimination and is called *third-degree price discrimination*.

Conditions necessary for price discrimination to operate

In order for a firm to engage in third-degree price discrimination, three conditions must be met:

- The firm must be able to set its price, meaning that it must have some degree of market power. Price discrimination is therefore impossible under perfect competition, where firms are price takers.
- It must be possible to split consumers into separate markets and there must not be any possibility of resale between the markets. Consumers in the low-priced market must not be able to resell the product in the high-priced market. For example, children must not be able to resell a half-priced child's cinema ticket for use by an adult.
- Willingness to pay and hence demand elasticity must differ in each market. The firm will charge the higher price in the market where demand is less elastic, and thus less sensitive to a price rise.

Examples in practice

Many consumer characteristics can be used to create separate groups of consumers, each with a different willingness to pay.

For example, airlines and train companies charge much higher prices to late bookers for identical seats on the same journey, as they know late bookers place a higher valuation on the product and so will pay more: see the blog on the Sloman Economics News site, *Easy or not so easyPricing?* In the blog, *A sexist surcharge*, we consider the differing prices for products for men and women. In an archaeological site in India and a museum in Russia, even nationality was used to separate customers![13] Signs were in Hindi or Russian, respectively, and in English. However, the instructions in each language for how to get to the entrance were different. The Hindi/Russian sign pointed to one entrance and the English sign to another. Following the English directions took you to an entrance where you were charged a higher price. They were assuming that tourists have more inelastic demand and are willing to pay more. Similar things are done at Disney World in the USA or the Eden Project in Cornwall – locals can buy an annual pass that cuts their entry price.

Inter-temporal pricing. In this case, the price elasticity of demand for a product varies over time. For example, new books are often first published in hard-back and at a high price. Consumers who are desperate to read the book have inelastic demand and are prepared to pay this high price. After a few months, a paper-back edition is released at a much lower price and those with more elastic demand will then buy it. By varying prices over time, the publisher can increase revenue.

Peak-load pricing. In this type of price discrimination, consumers are charged a higher price if they travel at peak times. I (Elizabeth) often take the train from Coventry to London. If I need a certain train

---

[12] See: Anna Bernasek and DT Mongan, 'Big data is coming for your purchase history - to charge you more money', *The Guardian* (29 May 2015).

[13] See, for example: Mark Perry, 'Price discrimination: Russians get a discount', *Carpe Diem*, AEIdeas (31 July 2007).

during peak times, I typically have to pay well over £100. However, if I am willing to travel at off-peak times, the price I pay can be less than £20 for a return. And I, John, often have to travel from Bristol to London, where a peak return costs £218, while a super off-peak return costs £61.40. Commuters who need to travel at peak times have an inelastic demand and, with little option but to pay a high price, this is what they are charged. Those with more flexibility benefit from a lower off-peak price.

Advantages to the firm

By charging different groups of customers different prices, third-degree price discrimination allows a firm to earn higher revenue from any given level of sales and this generates higher profits. This is illustrated in Figure 5.10, which shows a firm's overall demand curve. If it is to sell 200 units without price discrimination, it must charge a price of P_1. The total revenue it earns is shown by the green area. If, however, it can practise price discrimination by selling 150 of those 200 units at the higher price of P_2, it will gain the mauve area in addition to the green area.

Another advantage to the firm of price discrimination is that it may be able to use it to drive competitors out of business. If a firm has monopoly power in one market (e.g. the home market), it may be able to charge a high price due to the relatively inelastic nature of the demand curve, and thus make high profits. If it is operating under oligopoly conditions in another market (e.g. the export market), it may be able to use the high profits in the first market to subsidise a very low price in the oligopolistic market, thus forcing its competitors out of business. This, of course, could have negative consequences for consumers.

It may also provide the firm with opportunities to enter new markets. Again, if the firm has high profits in its established market, it may be able to use them to cover the costs of entering another market. It could also use them to help it survive a price war with established firms in this new market, should one emerge. In this way, price discrimination could actually help to increase competition.

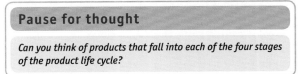

> **Pause for thought**
>
> *To what extent do consumers gain or lose from price discrimination?*

Pricing and the product life cycle

Price is a key variable for all firms, whatever degree of competition they face and although most firms do have the ability to set their prices, most products do go through a life cycle and the price will change accordingly. Brand new products are launched; then sales expand, perhaps rapidly; they then become established in the market; perhaps they are then replaced by more up-to-date products and possibly eventually they will become obsolete. The product life cycle therefore has four stages:

1. Introduction: the product is launched
2. Growth: a rapid growth in sales
3. Maturity: a levelling off in sales
4. Decline: sales begin to fall as the market becomes saturated or the product becomes obsolete

> **Pause for thought**
>
> *Can you think of products that fall into each of the four stages of the product life cycle?*

As you can imagine, at each stage of the product life cycle, firms face very different market conditions, in terms of demand and competition from rivals and this in turn influences the firm's pricing strategy.

The launch stage

In this stage the firm will probably have a monopoly (unless there is a simultaneous launch by rivals).

Given the lack of substitutes, the firm may be able to exploit its first-mover advantage (see page 133) and charge very high prices, thereby making large profits. This will be especially true if it is a radically new product – like the ballpoint pen, the home computer, the mobile phone and the iPod were.

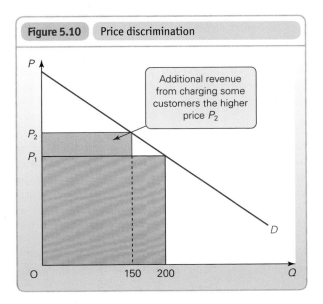

| Figure 5.10 | Price discrimination |

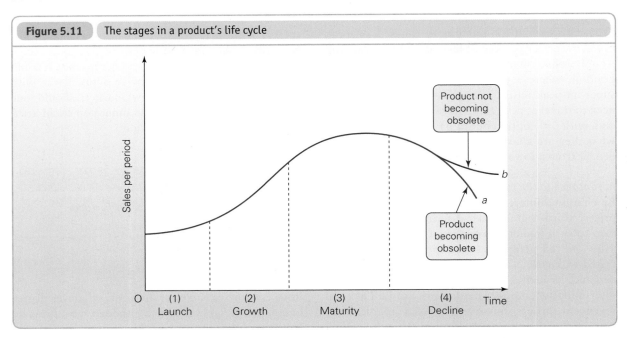

Figure 5.11 The stages in a product's life cycle

Such products are likely to have a rapidly expanding and price-inelastic demand.

The danger of a high-price policy is that the resulting high profits may tempt competitors to break into the industry, even if barriers are quite high. As an alternative, then, the firm may go for maximum 'market penetration' (see the growth vector matrix on pages 74–5): keeping the price low to get as many sales and as much brand loyalty as possible, before rivals can become established.

Pause for thought

If entry barriers are high, should a firm always charge a high price during this launch phase?

Which policy the firm adopts will depend on its assessment of its current price elasticity of demand and the likelihood of an early entry by rivals.

The growth stage

Unless entry barriers are very high, the rapid growth in sales will attract new firms. The industry becomes oligopolistic.

Despite the growth in the number of firms, sales are expanding so rapidly that all firms can increase their sales. Some price competition may emerge, but it is unlikely to be intense at this stage. New entrants may choose to compete in terms of minor product differences, while following the price lead set by the original firm.

The maturity stage

Now that the market has grown large, there are many firms competing. New firms – or, more likely, firms diversifying into this market – will be entering to get 'a piece of the action'. At the same time, the growth in sales is slowing down.

Competition is now likely to be more intense and as such any collusion may well begin to break down. Pricing policy may become more aggressive as businesses attempt to hold on to their market share. Price wars may break out, only to be followed later by a 'truce' and a degree of price collusion returning.

It is in this stage particularly that firms may invest considerably in product innovation in order to 'breathe new life' into old products, especially if there is competition from new types of product. Thus the upgrading of hi-fi cassette recorders, with additional features such as Dolby S, was one way in which producers hoped to beat off competition from digital cassette recorders and later minidisc recorders and CD burners.

The decline stage

Eventually, as the market becomes saturated, or as new superior alternative products are launched, sales will start to fall. Competition will therefore be intense, as firms aim to maintain market share. Various extension strategies will be used, such as price promotions, offers, extended guarantees, better after-sales-service, added features, etc., as firms look for other uses of the product or other markets in which it can sell. Some firms may be driven out of the market.

What happens next depends on whether or not the product becomes obsolete. If it does, sales will eventually dry up, firms will leave the market as there is no longer any point in competing. This is shown by line (a) in the figure. However, if the product is not obsolete, although not many new customers may buy it, some existing users will need replacements. This is illustrated by line (b) in the figure. In this case, sales will stop falling and the market may return to a stable oligopoly, possibly with a greater chance of tacit price collusion, as firms know that sales growth is very unlikely.

As we saw in Box 3.5, advertising has increasingly moved online and the newspaper industry has suffered from this, moving from maturity to decline, as sales have fallen with so much free information online. However, in reaction to this, newspapers have used a variety of extension strategies, developing their online content and making many of this content free to view. By adapting to changing times and tastes, the newspaper sector has found a way into a seemingly new market. However, with declining revenues from their newspaper sales, some do now charge for access to online content. *The Times, The Washington Post, The Wall Street Journal* and the *Financial Times* are just some of the publications that have implemented a paywall requiring consumers to take out a subscription to access all of their online content (see the blog on the Sloman Economics News site, *The decline of the newspaper*).

RECAP

1. Traditional economic theory assumes that businesses will set prices corresponding to the output where the marginal costs of production are equal to marginal revenue. They will do so in pursuit of maximum profits. The difficulties that a business faces in deriving its marginal cost and revenue curves suggest that this is unlikely to be a widely practised pricing strategy.

2. Cost-based pricing involves the business adding a profit mark-up to its average costs of production. The profit mark-up set by the business is likely to alter depending upon market conditions.

3. Many businesses practise price discrimination in an attempt to maximise profits from the sale of a product.

Third-degree price discrimination is the most common form and to do this, firms must be able to set prices, separate markets so as to prevent resale from the cheap to the expensive market and identify distinct demand elasticities in each market.

4. Products will be priced differently depending upon where they are in the product's life cycle. New products can be priced cheaply so as to gain market share, or priced expensively to recoup cost. Later on in the product's life cycle, prices will have to reflect the degree of competition, which may become intense as the market stabilises or even declines.

QUESTIONS

1. As an illustration of the difficulty in identifying monopolies, try to decide which of the following are monopolies: a train operating company; your local evening newspaper; the village hairdresser; the Royal Mail; Microsoft Office suite of programs; Interflora; the London Underground; ice creams in the cinema; Guinness; food on trains; the board game 'Monopoly'.

2. For what reasons would you expect a monopoly to charge (a) a higher price, and (b) a lower price than if the industry were operating under perfect competition?

3. Will competition between oligopolists always reduce total industry profits?

4. In which of the following industries is collusion likely to occur: bricks, beer, margarine, cement, crisps, washing powder or carpets? Explain why.

5. Draw a diagram like that in Figure 5.5, only this time assume that there are three firms, each considering the two strategies of keeping price the same or reducing it by a set amount. Identify the best response for each firm. Is the game still a 'dominant strategy game'?

6. Having watched the clip from the film A Beautiful Mind, can you work out why the situation that Russell Crowe described as being a 'Nash equilibrium' is actually not a Nash equilibrium? Specifically, in the example used, would all of the males be best responding if they behave as John Nash suggests they should?

7. Consider the following sequential game. Mr New-Entrant is about to enter a market, where there is an established firm run by Mrs Incumbent. Mr New-Entrant has to decide whether to enter the market aggressively (with deals and lots of advertising) or enter more passively. Once Mr New-Entrant has made his decision and entered the market, Mrs Incumbent has to decide between acquiescing (accepting that there is a new competitor) and fighting (trying to drive Mr New-Entrant out of the market). If Mr New-Entrant decides to use aggressive tactics, he will make £2m profit if Mrs Incumbent acquiesces and £0.75m profit if she fights, while Mrs Incumbent would make £1m profit if she acquiesces and £0.75m if she fights. On the other hand, if Mr New-Entrant enters the market passively and Mrs Incumbent acquiesces, both will make £0.5m. If Mrs Incumbent chooses to fight despite the passive entrance, she will make £2m profit, while Mr New-Entrant will make £1m.

(a) Draw the game tree, clearly identifying who is the first mover, what each player's actions are and what their payoffs are.

▶

(b) What is the Nash equilibrium? (Hint: there is more than one.) Which Nash equilibrium do you think is the most likely to occur and why?

(c) If Mrs Incumbent threatens that she will fight irrespective of the tactics Mr New-Entrant uses, should Mr New-Entrant believe that this threat is credible? Should this influence his decision?

8. Make a list of six aims that a manager of a high street department store might have. Identify some conflicts that might arise between these aims.

9. When are increased profits in a manager's personal interest?

10. Since advertising increases a firm's costs, will prices necessarily be lower with sales revenue maximisation than with profit maximisation?

11. Are customers' interests best served by profit-maximising firms, answerable primarily to shareholders, or by firms where various stakeholder groups are represented in decision making?

12. A frequent complaint of junior and some senior managers is that they are frequently faced with new targets from above, and that this makes their life difficult. If their complaint is true, does this conflict with the hypothesis that managers will try to build in slack?

13. Outline the main factors that might influence the size of the profit mark-up set by a business.

14. If a cinema could sell all its seats to adults in the evenings at the end of the week, but only a few on Mondays and Tuesdays, what price discrimination policy would you recommend to the cinema in order for it to maximise its weekly revenue?

15. How will a business's pricing strategy differ at each stage of its product's life cycle? First assume that the business has a monopoly position at the launch stage; then assume that it faces a high degree of competition right from the outset.

Business growth and strategy

Business issues covered in this chapter

- ■ What are the objectives of strategic management?
- ■ What are the key competitive forces affecting a business?
- ■ What choices of strategy towards competitors are open to a business?
- ■ What internal strategic choices are open to a business and how can it make best use of its core competences when deciding on its internal organisation?
- ■ By what means can a business grow and how can growth be financed?
- ■ Should businesses seek to raise finance through the stock market?
- ■ Under what circumstances might a business want to merge with another and what are the options?
- ■ What are the advantages and problems of remaining a small business?
- ■ What issues arise in starting up a business?

6.1 STRATEGIC ANALYSIS

For much of the time most managers are concerned with routine day-to-day activities of the business, such as dealing with personnel issues, checking budgets and looking for ways to enhance efficiency. In other words, they are involved in the detailed operational activities of the business.

Some managers, however, especially those high up in the business, such as the managing director, will be thinking about big, potentially complex issues which affect the whole company. For example, they might be analysing the behaviour of competitors, or evaluating the company's share price or considering ways to expand the business. In other words, these managers are involved in the *strategic* long-term activities of the business. This is known as *strategic management*.

It involves *analysing* the alternative long-term courses of action for the firm and then *making choices* of what strategy to pursue.

The strategic choices that are made depend on the firm's aims. Most firms have a 'mission statement' which sets out the broad aims. However, with multiple stakeholders, the aims in practice might be difficult to establish. It is thus in the *actual* decisions that

Definition

Strategic management The management of the strategic long-term decisions and activities of the business.

are taken that the firm's aims can best be judged. In practice, these aims are often complex, with economic objectives, such as profit, market share, product development and growth being mixed with broader social, ethical and environmental objectives.

We look at strategic analysis in this section and strategic choices in section 6.2.

Strategic analysis of the external business environment

In Chapter 1 we considered STEEPLE analysis: the various dimensions of the business environment and how they shape and influence business activity. In this section we will take our analysis of the business environment forward and consider more closely those factors that are likely to influence the *competitive advantage* of the organisation.

The greater the competitive advantage of a firm, whether through lower costs or through less elastic demand for its products, the greater the rate of supernormal profit it will be able to make. In developing their strategy, firms seek to address these two dimensions: costs and demand.

Competitive advantage. The various factors that enable a firm to compete more effectively with its rivals. These can be supply-side factors, such as superior technology, better organisation, or greater power or efficiency in sourcing its supplies – resulting in lower costs; or they could be demand-side ones, such as producing a superior or better-value product in the eyes of consumers, or being more conveniently located – resulting in higher and/or less elastic demand.

Five forces of competition

In 1980, Professor Michael Porter of Harvard Business School identified five factors which are likely to affect an organisation's competitiveness and success (see Figure 6.1).[1] Examining the relevance of each of these factors to its own environment helps a firm choose an appropriate strategy to enhance its competitive opportunities and to protect itself from competitive threats. The five 'forces' that Porter identified are:

- the bargaining power of suppliers;
- the bargaining power of buyers;
- the threat of potential new entrants;
- the threat of substitute products;
- the extent of competitive rivalry.

The bargaining power of suppliers. Most business organisations depend upon suppliers, whether to provide raw materials or simply stationery. Indeed,

---

[1] Michael E. Porter, *Competitive Strategy: Techniques for Analyzing Industries and Competitors* (The Free Press, 1980).

Definition

Competitive advantage The various factors, such as lower costs or a better product, that give a firm an advantage over its rivals.

Figure 6.1   Five forces of competition

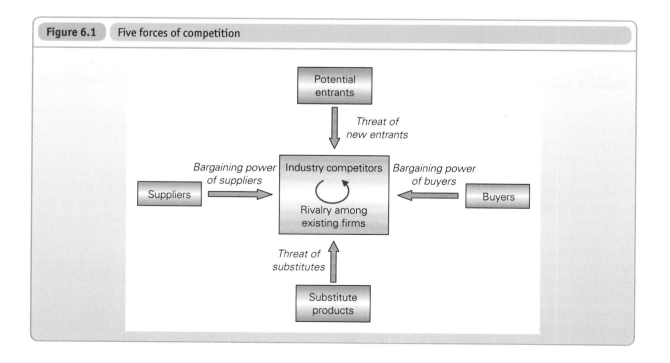

many businesses have extensive supply or 'value chain' networks (as we shall discuss below). Such suppliers can have a significant and powerful effect on a business when:

- there are relatively few suppliers in the market, reducing the ability of the business to switch from one supply source to another;
- there are no alternative supplies that can be used;
- the cost of the supplies forms a large part of the firm's total costs;
- a supplier's customers are small and fragmented and as such have little power over the supplying business.

Car dealers often find that car manufacturers can exert considerable pressure over them in terms of pricing, display and after-sales service.

The bargaining power of buyers. The bargaining power of companies that purchase a firm's products will be greater when:

- these purchasing companies are large and there are relatively few of them;
- there are many other firms competing for the purchasing companies' custom, and hence a firm that produces an undifferentiated product (such as vegetables) is likely to be more prone to 'buyer power' than one that produces a unique or differentiated product;
- the costs for the purchasing companies of switching to other suppliers are low;
- purchasing companies could relatively easily produce the good themselves and thereby displace the supplying firm.

Some large firms, such as supermarkets, have significant buyer power over suppliers – for example, farmers and food processors in the case of supermarkets. They often have many alternative supply sources, both domestic and international, and can easily move from one to another with relatively little switching cost. This puts pressure on suppliers to reduce their prices and this has only grown with globalisation. As communication and transport have become easier and cheaper, this has allowed companies to develop lower-cost supply chains in developing countries. This may, however, raise some ethical issues, as we consider in section 9.2.

The threat of potential new entrants. The ability of new firms to enter the market depends largely on the existence and effectiveness of various barriers to entry. These barriers to entry were described in section 5.2 (pages 116–7).

Barriers to entry tend to be very industry, product and market specific. Nevertheless, two useful generalisations can be made. First, companies with products that have a strong brand identity will often attempt to use this form of product differentiation to restrict competition; second, manufacturers will tend to rely on economies of scale and low costs gained from experience as means of retaining a cost advantage over potential rivals.

The threat of substitutes. The availability of substitute products can be a major threat to a business and its profitability, as many close substitutes implies a relatively price elastic demand. Issues that businesses need to consider in relation to the availability of substitute products are:

- the ability and cost to customers of switching to the substitute;
- the threat of competitors bringing out a more advanced or up-to-date product;
- the impact that substitute products are likely to have on pricing policy.

The makers of games consoles such as Sony, Nintendo and Microsoft have faced the arrival of substitutes, as people can now play games such as *Minecraft* and *Candy Crush* on their Smartphones and tablets instead of using a PlayStation 4 or Xbox One. The Steam download service owned by Valve also means that games such as *Call of Duty* can be downloaded and played on a personal computer as a substitute to using a console. Hence the sale of handheld consoles has fallen. With rapid technological change, it is highly likely that another new substitute will enter this market. So firms operating in the games console market will need to reconsider their strategies as the market continues to change.

The extent of competitive rivalry. As we saw in the previous two chapters, the degree of competition a firm faces is a crucial element in shaping its strategic analysis. Competitive rivalry will be enhanced when there is the potential for new firms to enter the market, when there is a real threat from substitute products and when buyers and suppliers have some element of influence over the firm's performance. In addition to this, competitive rivalry is likely to be enhanced in the following circumstances:

- There are many competitors, each of a similar size. This is a particular issue when firms are competing in a global market.
- Markets are growing slowly. This makes it difficult to acquire additional sales without taking market share from rivals.
- Product differentiation is difficult to achieve; hence switching by consumers to competitors' products is a real threat.
- There are high exit costs. When a business invests in non-transferable fixed assets, such as highly specialist

capital equipment, it may be reluctant to leave a market and will compete fiercely to maintain its market position. On the other hand, high exit costs may deter firms from entering a market in the first place and thus reduce the threat of competition.

- There exists the possibility for merger and acquisition. This competition for corporate control may have considerable influence on the firm's strategy.

Porter's model is designed to identify and analyse the competitive factors influencing the firm. Often, however, success might be achievable not via competition but rather through co-operation and collaboration. For example, a business might set up close links with one of its major buyers; or businesses in an industry might collaborate over research and development, thereby saving on costs. As we saw in sections 5.3 and 5.4, firms have a considerable incentive to collude with their rivals so as to increase their combined profits and avoid damaging competition.

Ideally, in order to plan its strategy, a firm should be able to identify and quantify each of the five forces affecting it. In practice, however, firms often face considerable uncertainty about the market in which they operate. Just how will rivals, suppliers and buyers behave? How will consumer tastes change? What new firms and new products will enter the market?

The actions of complementors. Some economists add a sixth force – that of 'complementors' (a term coined by Andrew Grove of Intel). *Complementors* are firms producing complements. For example, Intel, with its *Celeron, Xeon* and *Core i3, i5, i7* and *i9* processors is a complementor to both Microsoft, with its *Windows*, and various computer manufacturers, such as Dell, Asus and HP. Where firms are complementors, there is an incentive to form strategic alliances (see pages 163–4) so as to benefit from co-operation and a reduction in uncertainty.

Porter himself added an alternative sixth force: government. Clearly there are many ways in which government policies impact on business and hence on the strategies that should be adopted, such as tax policy, price controls and regulation, as we discussed in Box 2.5. We examine government policies at a micro level in Chapter 9. Chapter 11 looks at macroeconomic policies.

Internal strategic analysis: analysing the value chain

To develop an advantage over its rivals, a business also needs to be organised effectively. Strategic analysis, therefore, also involves managers assessing the internal workings of the business, right from the purchase and delivery of inputs, to the production process, to delivering and marketing the product, to providing after-sales service.

Value-chain analysis, also developed by Michael Porter, is concerned with how each of these various operations adds value to the product and contributes to the competitive position of the business. Ultimately it is these value-creating activities that shape a firm's strategic capabilities. A firm's value chain can be split into two separate sets of activities: primary and support (see Figure 6.2).

Primary activities
Primary activities cover those that involve the product's physical creation or delivery, its sale and distribution and its after-sales service. Such primary activities can be grouped into five categories:

- *Inbound logistics.* Here we are concerned with the handling of inputs, and the storage and distribution of such inputs throughout the business.

Definitions

Complementors Firms producing complementary goods (products that are used together).

Value chain The stages or activities that help to create product value.

Figure 6.2	The value chain

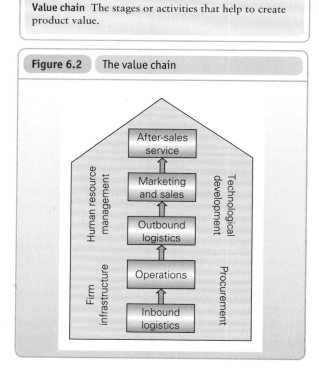

Pause for thought

1. *Given that the stronger the competitive forces the lower the profit potential for firms, describe what five-force characteristics an attractive and unattractive industry might have.*
2. *Go through each of the five forces and identify to what extent they influence (a) costs and (b) demand elasticity.*

- *Operations*. These activities involve the conversion of inputs into the final product or service. Operations might include manufacturing, packaging and assembly.
- *Outbound logistics*. These are concerned with transferring the final product to the consumer. Such activities would include warehousing and transport.
- *Marketing and sales*. This section of the value chain is concerned with bringing the product to the consumer's attention and would involve product advertising and promotion.
- *Service*. This can include activities such as installation and repair, as well as customer requirements such as training.

A business might attempt to add value to its activities by improving its performance in one or more of the above categories. For example, it might attempt to lower production costs or be more efficient in outbound logistics.

Support activities

Such primary activities are underpinned by support activities. These are activities that do not add value directly to any particular stage within the value chain. They do, however, provide support to such a chain and ensure that its various stages are undertaken effectively. Support activities include:

- *Procurement*. This involves the acquisition of inputs by the firm.
- *Technological development*. This includes activities within the business that support new product and process developments, such as the use of research departments.

- *Human resource management*. Activities in this category include things such as recruitment, training and wage negotiation and determination.
- *Firm infrastructure*. This category includes activities such as financial planning and control systems, quality control and information management.

As well as creating value directly themselves, most firms benefit from outsourcing certain value-chain activities, such as employing an expert firm to do its advertising or using an external delivery firm for distribution. The companies a firm uses are likely to have economies of scale in their specialist activity (see pages 90–1) and can therefore offer the service at a lower cost than the firm could provide in-house.

Outsourcing, however, involves transaction costs (see pages 93–4) and these must be weighed against the other cost savings. Value-chain analysis, therefore, concerns any business that the firm deals with and hence a value chain can be highly complex.

With the background to strategic analysis defined, we can now shift our focus to consider strategic choice and implementation. What strategies are potentially open to businesses and how do they choose the right ones and set about implementing them?

Pause for thought

Is it possible to add value to the firm by improving any or all of these support activities?

RECAP

1. Strategic management differs from operational management (the day-to-day running of the business) as it focuses on issues which affect the whole business, usually over the long term.

2. In conducting strategic analysis the business should assess its external and internal environment.

3. The Five Forces Model of the external environment identifies those factors that are most likely to influence the competition faced by a business. The five forces are: the bargaining power of suppliers, the bargaining power of buyers, the threat of potential new entrants, the threat of substitutes, and the extent of competitive rivalry.

4. To these five, some economists add a sixth – the actions of complementors. Porter added an alternative sixth factor – the government.

5. The internal environment can be assessed by value-chain analysis. The value chain can be split into primary and support activities. Primary activities are those that directly create value, such as operations, marketing and sales. Support activities are those that underpin value creation in other areas, such as procurement and human resource management.

6.2 STRATEGIC CHOICE

As with strategic analysis, strategic choices fall into two main categories. The first concerns choices to do with the external business environment, e.g. choices of how to compete and what markets to target. The second concerns choices about the internal organisation of the firm and how to use its resources.

Environment- or market-based strategic choices

As with many other areas in this field, our analysis of market-based choices starts with the observations of Michael Porter. As an extension of his Five Forces Model of competition, Porter argued that there are three fundamental (or 'generic') strategies that a business might adopt:

- cost leadership – competing through lower costs;
- differentiation – competing by producing a product different from rivals' products;
- focus – producing a specialised product for a market niche.

In order to identify which of these was the most appropriate strategy, a business would need to establish two things: (a) the basis of its competitive advantage – whether it lies in lower costs or product differentiation; (b) the nature of the target market – is it broad or a distinct market niche?

Cost leadership

A business that is a 'low-cost leader' is able to manufacture and deliver its product more cheaply than its rivals, thereby gaining competitive advantage. The strategic emphasis here is on driving out inefficiency at every stage of the value chain. 'No-frills' budget airlines, such as easyJet and Ryanair, are classic examples of companies that pursue a cost-leadership strategy.

A strategy based upon cost leadership may require a fundamentally different use of resources or organisational structure if the firm is to stay ahead of its

---

| BOX 6.1 | BUSINESS STRATEGY THE SAMSUNG WAY |

Staying ahead of the game

The Samsung Group is a major South Korean conglomerate involved in a number of industries, including machinery and heavy engineering, construction, financial services and consumer electronics. It has over 480 000 employees across its global operations and is a major international investor and exporter.

This box outlines some of the strategic initiatives taken by one of its most successful divisions, Samsung Electronics, which has become the world's largest mobile phone producer. By 2018, it had 18.9 per cent of the global mobile phone market, above Apple's approximately 15 per cent share, but lower than its 21.4 per cent share in 2017. It is also the world's largest producer of TVs with a 20.1 per cent market share. Although it is facing growing competition from Chinese companies, such as Huawei, its success in this highly competitive market is impressive, especially given the serious financial concerns, high debts and poor profitability it had following the Asian financial crisis in the late 1990s.

But, how has Samsung become so successful in this highly competitive market?

Strong leadership. This had formerly come from Mr Yoon-Woo Lee, who was the vice-chairman and CEO of Samsung Electronics and credited with much of its initial success. A clear vision of the future of the sector and Samsung's place within it was developed and a younger management team was introduced. Samsung's vision of 'Inspire the World, Create the Future', reflected its three key strengths: 'New Technology', 'Innovative Products' and 'Creative Solutions'.[1]

The aim was for Samsung to become the leading electronics company in the world, measured by the quantity and quality of the goods it produces. Although it has made significant improvements in its revenue, it still remains second behind Apple, but ahead of American giants, Microsoft, Google and IBM.[2]

Reorganisation. There was a dramatic streamlining of the business and the decision-making structure in the late 1990s. Aggressive measures were taken to improve the division's finances by cutting jobs, closing unprofitable factories, reducing inventory levels and selling corporate assets. The company was then 'de-layered', ensuring that managers had to go through fewer layers of bureaucracy, thereby speeding up the approval of new products, budgets and marketing plans.

New products. Samsung Electronics invested heavily in research and development (R&D) to increase its product portfolio and reduce the lead time from product conception to product launch, which is crucial in such a fast-paced sector.[3] This means it can charge premium prices for state-of-the-art products. In 2018, Samsung was the world's top R&D investor, with €13.44 billion invested, followed by Alphabet (Google) and Volkswagen. Indeed, significant investment in R&D for many years has been one of the key factors behind its continued success.[4]

It has engaged in a number of strategic alliances with major players such as Red Hat, Sony, IBM and Qualcomm to share R&D costs and this constant innovation has helped Samsung to maintain its competitiveness in the market. Since 2006, Samsung has been in second place behind IBM every year in terms of the number of patents successfully registered with the United States Patent Office, filing 5850 in 2018.[5] In the EU, Samsung was ranked in fourth place in 2017, having filed 2016 cases with the European Patent Office.[6] In December 2017, it launched Samsung Research, which is a result of a reorganisation of the company's Software R&D Centre and Digital Media & Communications.

Driving down costs. Samsung invests heavily in modern factories that can cope with large production runs and gain

---

[1] http://www.samsung.com/us/aboutsamsung/samsung_group/values_and_philosophy/

[2] 'The World's Largest Public Companies' (Forbes, 2018).

[3] Carrie Marshall, 'Samsung's strategy: No niche too small, no combination too weird', *TechRadar* (21 June 2013).

[4] *EU Industrial R&D Scoreboard,* European Commission (17 December 2018).

[5] Douglas A McIntyre 'IBM Tops 2018 US Patents with 9100', *247 Wall St* (8 January 2019).

[6] *2017 European Patent Office Annual Report* (European Patent Office, 2018).

rivals. Walmart's hub and spoke distribution system is an example; the company distributes its products to shops from regional depots in order to minimise transport costs.

In addition, firms that base their operations on low costs in order to achieve low prices (although that may not necessarily be the aim of low costs) are unlikely to have a high level of brand loyalty. In other words, if customer choice is going to be driven largely by price, demand is likely to be relatively price elastic. Other virtues of the product that might tie in buyers, such as quality or after-sales service, are largely absent from such firms' strategic goals.

Differentiation

A differentiation strategy aims to emphasise and promote the uniqueness of the firm's product; to make demand less elastic. Therefore, high rather than low prices are often attached to such products. Product characteristics such as quality, design and reliability are the basis of the firm's competitive advantage. Hence a strategy that adds to such differences and creates value for the customer needs to be identified.

Such a strategy might result in higher costs, especially in the short term, as the firm pursues constant product development through innovation, design and research. However, with the ability to charge premium prices, revenues may increase more than costs, i.e. the firm may achieve higher profits. Mobile phone handset producers such as Apple and Samsung provide a good example. Even though they are in fierce competition with each other, both firms focus their strategy on product differentiation in

---

maximum economies of scale. To this end Samsung also supplies components to its competitors as well as making them for its own product range. For example, it sells OLED display panels for Apple's *iPhone X*. Further, production systems are flexible enough to allow customisation for individual buyers, ensuring that selling prices are above the industry average. Alongside longer production runs, Samsung is concerned with ensuring that production costs are minimised by making its own business units compete with external rivals.

Developing its brand image. Rather than just investing in the products where it makes the most profits, Samsung invests in and develops a variety of products, as part of raising its brand identity. It has focused particularly on sports marketing as part of this, including sponsoring the Rugby World Cup in 2015, the 2016 Summer Olympics in Rio de Janeiro and the 2018 Winter Olympics in Pyeongchang. As a result of these strategies, Samsung rose from 42nd in BusinessWeek/Interbrand's list of the top 100 global brands in 2001 to 6th in 2018, with a brand value of just under $60 billion.[7]

Recent developments and challenges

Samsung's commitment to product innovation has helped it to maintain its position of strength in the market, but the company is facing intense competition and has experienced some challenges in recent years.

Between 2010 and 2013, its Galaxy brand of smartphones helped its growth, but competition from Apple at the high-end, and from companies such as Huawei in China at the lower-end, have created issues. Samsung has continued to launch its Galaxy brands, with successful developments in March 2015 and 2016, which gave it a total operating profit of $13.2 billion in the first six months of 2016, almost half of which was accounted for by the mobile division. However, the new handset launched in August 2016 created issues for the company. Charging the phone could cause batteries to overheat and catch fire and hence the phones were recalled

and then withdrawn from the market, costing the company $5.3 billion of forgone operating profits.

Other issues have also harmed the company's reputation, particularly when, in 2017, the vice-chairman of Samsung Electronics, Lee Jae-Yong (also the grandson of the founder Lee Byung-Chul) was found guilty of bribing the then South Korean President and was jailed for two-and-a-half years. He was freed in February 2018, when the sentence was suspended, but this did lead to questions about the Lee family's future role in the management of Samsung Electronics and its governance structures. Despite the issues, the business made record operating profits of $14.1 billion in the 4th quarter of 2017, with its full year profits up by 83 per cent on the previous year.

However, 4th quarter performance in 2018 showed a 10 per cent fall in revenue from the same time the previous year ($53.4 billion) and a 29 per cent fall in quarterly operating profit ($9.7 billion). Samsung had previously warned about its results, noting the sluggish demand for smartphones and tablets that had also affected Apple. It expected that demand would drop further in the 1st quarter of 2019. Despite the weaker performance in the final quarter of 2018, operating profit for the fiscal year was $53 billion, which makes it the second year in a row when record financial results were set.

Samsung continues to diversify into new products, such as components for driverless cars and connected car technologies. But in a rapidly changing environment, the market is likely to become increasingly competitive for this tech giant.

1. *What dangers do you see with Samsung's recent business strategy?*

2. *What makes Samsung's policies that we have examined in this box 'strategic' as opposed to merely 'operational'?*

Examine the ways in which Samsung is marketing one of its latest products. How is this influenced by the competition it faces? Is it playing 'catch-up' with competitors, or is it innovating to try to get ahead of its competitors?

---

[7] *Best Global Brands 2018 Ranking* (InterBrand, 2018).

terms of features and performance, not price. Screen size and resolution, camera quality, speakers, apps, battery life and overall design are all characteristics used in the competitive battle.

Differentiation in this way, and in fast changing sectors, can be costly and risky. However, the rewards are potentially large. Differentiated products attract customers, but they tend to be more expensive, which could deter buyers. Firms must weigh up the costs and benefits from such a strategy.

Focus strategy

Rather than considering a whole market as a potential for sales, a focus strategy involves identifying market niches and designing and promoting products for them. In doing so a business may be able to exploit some advantage over its rivals, whether in terms of costs, or product difference. An example is Häagen-Dazs ice cream (a division of General Mills). The mass low-cost ice cream market is served by other large multinational food manufacturers and processors (such as Unilever, with its Wall's brand), and by supermarkets' own brands, but the existence of niche high-quality ice cream markets offers opportunities for companies like Häagen-Dazs and Ben & Jerry's. By focusing on such consumers, they are able to sell and market their product at premium prices.

Niche markets, however profitable, are by their nature small and as such limited in their growth potential. There is also the possibility that niches might shift over time or even disappear. This would require a business to be flexible in setting out its strategic position.

Internal resource-based strategic choices

Resource-based strategy focuses on exploiting a firm's internal organisation and production processes in order to develop its competitive advantage. What the firm will seek to exploit or to develop is one or more 'core competencies'.

Core competencies

Core competencies are those skills, knowledge, technologies and product specifications that underpin the organisation's competitive advantage over its rivals. These competencies are likely to differ from one business to another, reflecting the uniqueness of each individual organisation, and ultimately determining its potential for success. The business should seek to create and exploit these competencies, whether in the design of the product or in its methods of production.

> **KEY IDEA 21**
>
> *Core competencies.* The areas of specialised expertise within a business that underpin its competitive advantage over its rivals. These competencies could be in production technologies or organisation, in relationships with suppliers, in the nature and specifications of the product, or in the firm's ability to innovate and develop its products and brand image.

Thus Coca-Cola has a core competence in developing an image of a product; Tesco has a core competence in sourcing cheap but reliable supplies; Intel has a core competence in technological research and development that can yield significant continuing advances in the speed and efficiency of memory chips and processor cores; Ikea has a core competence in sourcing low-cost furniture and accessories and selling them at a highly competitive price in low-cost suburban sites where a wide choice is on view and instantly available.

In many cases, however, firms do not have any competencies that give them a distinctive competitive advantage, even though they may still be profitable. In such instances, strategy often focuses either on *developing* such competencies or simply on more effectively using the resources the firm already has.

Can a core competence be sustained?

To sustain a competitive advantage into the *long run*, the competence must satisfy the following four criteria. It must be:

- *Valuable*: a competence that helps the firm deal with threats or contributes to business opportunities;
- *Rare*: a competence or resource that is not possessed by competitors;
- *Costly to imitate*: a competence or resource that other firms find difficult to develop and copy;
- *Non-substitutable*: a competence or resource for which there is no alternative.

> **Definition**
>
> **Core competencies** The key skills of a business that underpin its competitive advantage.

> **Pause for thought**
>
> *Referring back to Box 6.1, what core competencies does Samsung have? Remember, you must justify a core competence in terms of all four listed criteria.*

Reactions of competitors

The success of a firm's strategic choices depends crucially on the reactions of rival firms. As we saw in the section on game theory (section 5.4), a firm has to be careful that strategic choices, such as developing new product lines or breaking into new markets, do not result in a 'war' with rivals that will end up with all 'players' worse off. The technology to produce a virtually everlasting light bulb has been available for many years, but it has not been in the interests of manufacturers to produce one, as it would force rivals to do the same with a resulting loss of future sales. To avoid this classic prisoners' dilemma (see pages 129–30) there has been tacit collusion between manufacturers not to launch such a product.

Sometimes, it is worth firms taking the risk of stimulating retaliatory action from rivals. If it estimates that its market position or core competencies give it a competitive advantage, then it will take the risk of launching a new product, embarking on a marketing campaign, using a new technology or restructuring its organisation. If rivals do retaliate, its core competencies may enable it to do well in any competitive battle.

RECAP

1. Strategic choice often involves a consideration of both external and internal factors.

2. External environment- or market-based strategies are of three types: cost leadership strategy, where competitiveness is achieved by lower costs; differentiation strategy, where the business promotes the uniqueness of its product; focus strategy, where competitiveness is achieved by identifying market niches and tailoring products for different groups of consumers.

3. Internal strategy normally involves identifying core competencies as the key to a business's competitive advantage. To give a business a sustained competitive advantage, core competencies must be valuable, rare, costly to imitate and non-substitutable.

4. When making strategic choices, firms should take into account the likely reactions of competitors and they can use game theory to help.

BOX 6.2   THE RATIOS TO MEASURE SUCCESS

Using numbers to decide

Whenever a firm makes a decision, numerous factors will be considered. Market opportunities will be analysed, the actions of competitors predicted and the economic environment studied. However, crucial to any decision will be the health of the business itself. Owners and managers will need to look at all the firm's numbers before taking any action and there are some ratios that will give a business some key information.

We typically classify ratios into groups based on the information that they show. In this box, we split the ratios into three categories: profitability, financial efficiency and liquidity, and outline the main ratios within each category.

Profitability ratios

These ratios do exactly what they suggest: they provide information about a business's profitability. By measuring a firm's ability to generate earnings and profits, they indicate the success of a firm over time and provide a means of comparison with its competitors. The three main profitability ratios are:

■ *Gross Profit Margin*: this measures the ratio of gross profit to sales revenue. Gross profit is calculated by subtracting the variable costs of goods sold from gross revenue and so measures the profitability of a company before fixed costs (overheads) are taken into account. It is expressed as a percentage and is calculated as:

$$\text{Gross Profit Margin} = \frac{\text{Gross profit}}{\text{Sales turnover}} \times 100$$

■ *Net Profit Margin*: this measures the ratio of net profit to sales revenue. Net profit is revenue minus *all* costs: that is, not only the variable costs of production (to give gross profit), but also fixed costs, such as rent, insurance, heating and lighting, salaries (unrelated to output) and also taxes. It gives us information about how effective a firm is at turning sales into profits and thus whether or not a business adds value during the production process. Net profit margin is is also expressed as a percentage and is calculated as:

$$\text{Net Profit Margin} = \frac{\text{Net profit}}{\text{Sales turnover}} \times 100$$

■ *Return on Capital Employed (ROCE)*: this measures the efficiency with which a business uses its funds to generate returns. Capital employed refers to the company's total assets minus its current liabilities and the ROCE is calculated as:

$$\text{ROCE} = \frac{\text{Earnings (before interest and taxes)}}{\text{Capital employed}} \times 100$$

While all three ratios are important and high gross and net profit margins are good indicators that a firm is performing effectively, it is particularly important for a firm to compare these two profitability ratios, as looking at them separately can often lead to misleading conclusions. For example, if a firm's gross profit margin is rising, but its net profit margin is falling, then it means that the firm is generating more profit from its

▶

sales, but that its costs are increasing at an even faster rate. That is, the company may be becoming less efficient.

Just as it is important to examine the trends in profit margins, analysing a firm's ROCE over time is also essential and an upward trend suggests that the firm is earning more in revenue for every £1 of capital employed in the business. Profit margins and ROCE should always be compared between firms within an industry and it is always worth remembering that what is seen as a high profit margin or ROCE in one industry may be a low one in another industry.

1. What steps might a firm take to improve a) gross profit margin; b) net profit margin; and c) ROCE?

Financial efficiency ratios

These are ratios that analyse the efficiency with which a business manages its resources and assets. Once again, there are three key ratios:

- *Asset Turnover ratio*: this ratio looks at the assets (or resources) that a firm has and analyses the amount of sales that are generated from this asset base. Consider a pizza kitchen that has a given level of assets (e.g. work-space, ovens). This ratio will measure the level of sales generated relative to this asset base. The higher the sales, the more efficiently is this firm using its assets; so a higher asset turnover figure is a good indicator of financial efficiency. It is calculated as:

$$\text{Asset Turnover} = \frac{\text{Sales}}{\text{Net assets}} \times 100$$

- *Stock Turnover*: this measures the frequency with which a firm orders in new stock. Holding stock can be extremely costly, as it means that money has already been spent on purchasing or producing the items, but no income has been received from their sale. Thus, a higher figure for stock turnover implies that less money is tied up in stock. This particular ratio will vary significantly from one industry to another and you would expect some industries to have a very high level of stock turnover, due to the nature of the products they are selling. For example, firms whose sales are subject to fluctuation (due, say, to the weather) may need to hold higher stocks. Therefore, although it is suggested that a higher figure for stock turnover is better, this is not always the case. Stock turnover is calculated as:

$$\text{Stock Turnover} = \frac{\text{Cost of sales}}{\text{Average stock held}}$$

- *Debtor and Creditor Days*: these two ratios measure the effectiveness of a firm in collecting payments from and making payments to other traders. Many businesses offer trade credit, where you can buy something today, but pay for it later. Such incentives can be crucial, but it can cause problems when you are the firm offering the trade credit. Debtor days show how long a firm's customers on average take to pay their bill and creditor days show how long a firm takes to pay the bills that it owes. As you will probably realise, comparing these two figures is essential. Ideally, debtor days should be lower than creditor days, as this implies that firm A receives the money it is owed

before it has to make payments to those to whom it owes money. They are calculated as follows:

$$\text{Debtor Days} = \frac{\text{Trade debtors}}{\text{Revenue}} \times 365$$

and

$$\text{Creditor Days} = \frac{\text{Trade payables}}{\text{Cost of sales}} \times 365$$

With the business environment under continuous financial pressure, it is vital to use resources efficiently. Businesses in all sectors will want to analyse trends in these financial efficiency ratios, as a means of identifying areas where improvements can be made.

2. What type of figure would you expect a green grocer to have for its stock turnover? How might this compare with a furniture store?
3. What are the advantages and disadvantages of offering trade credit?

Liquidity ratios

Many businesses have debts, but the key question is whether they have the ability to repay these debts. Liquidity ratios provide this information and we consider three key ratios:

- *Current Ratio*: this is a basic measure of how a firm's current assets compare with its current liabilities. If a firm's assets are higher than its liabilities, this suggests that the firm has sufficient funds for the day-to-day running of the business. It is calculated as:

$$\text{Current Ratio} = \frac{\text{Current assets}}{\text{Current liabilities}}$$

- *Acid Test Ratio* (or *Quick Ratio*): this is very similar to the current ratio. However, instead of comparing all current assets with liabilities, the acid test ratio excludes stocks, sometimes called 'inventories' (e.g. raw materials), as these cannot readily be turned into cash and hence are termed 'illiquid'. They would first have to be made into the finished product before any cash could be earned. The calculation is therefore very similar to the current ratio:

$$\text{Acid Test Ratio} = \frac{\text{Current assets} - \text{Stock}}{\text{Current liabilities}}$$

Some businesses will need to carry much higher levels of stocks (or 'inventories') than others and will therefore have a low acid test ratio relative to their current ratio. For example, most manufacturers will need to have a much higher proportion of stocks than most service-sector firms, such as solicitors or accountants. This does not make their businesses necessarily more risky. Ratios need to be judged, therefore, according to what would be expected in a particular industry.

- *Gearing Ratio* (or *Leverage Ratio*): this is a key ratio for any firm, but also for any individual thinking about investing in it. It shows how much of a firm's finance is through debt (e.g. long-term borrowing, mortgages or bonds), on which the firm has to pay interest, as opposed to equity (ordinary shares), on which the firm does not pay interest but rather a share of profit. How much profit the firm distributes to shareholders can be adjusted according to what the firm feels it can afford. The higher the gearing ratio the more the business is funded through debt. Gearing is calculated as the percentage of debt to total capital employed (debt and equity capital):

$$\text{Gearing Ratio} = \frac{\text{Debt}}{\text{Capital employed}} \times 100$$

A similar ratio to the gearing ratio is the *Debt-to-Equity* Ratio. In this ratio the numerator is the same, but the denominator is equity capital (i.e. ordinary share capital).

$$\text{Debt/Equity Ratio} = \frac{\text{Debt}}{\text{Equity capital}} \times 100$$

A firm's gearing and debt-to-equity ratios are measures of its financial stability. The higher the ratios, the greater the commitment of the firm to paying interest, and the greater the risk, therefore, if the firm is in financial difficulty, as these commitments have to be met.

Since the financial crisis of 2007/8, firms have become more focused on having sufficient liquidity, as all firms need cash to survive. A current ratio of between 1.5 and 2 suggests that a firm has sufficient cash, without having excessive working capital. Again, comparing this ratio over time and with other firms in the same sector is important to give an indication of relative performance.

For many people, gearing is the most informative ratio, especially as it provides information about the long-term prospects of the business. As the gearing ratio gets higher (perhaps above 50 per cent), it is a signal that the firm may begin to run into problems when repaying debts. Although sometimes debt can be cheaper than equity finance!

4. *Would you expect the current ratio or the acid test to have a higher figure for any given firm?*
5. *If you were looking to invest in a business, how might you interpret a company that has a gearing ratio of 80 per cent?*

The ratios discussed in this box should never be analysed independently, but should always be compared with firms in the same industry. Failing to do so and interpreting them incorrectly can give misleading results, but they remain a good numerical measure of business performance, as discussed in an article about Fonterra, a New Zealand multinational dairy co-operative.[1] Before undertaking any changes relating to market penetration, scale of operation, diversification etc., a firm will consider the above ratios (and many more) to ensure that it is making the best use of its existing resources and that it has sufficient funds to carry out its plans.

---

[1] Keith Woodford , 'Keith Woodford gets under the hood of Fonterra's half year profit announcement and looks at what some of the figures tell us', *interest.co.nz* (23 March 2016).

6.3 GROWTH STRATEGY

The global marketplace has become so competitive and dynamic that simply to remain in the market, many businesses are forced to grow. If a business fails to grow, this could benefit its more aggressive rivals, who may secure a greater share of the market. This could leave the first firm with reduced profits, making it a potential target for acquisition by another firm. Thus business growth is often vital if a firm is to survive.

In this section we consider the various growth strategies open to firms and assess their respective advantages and disadvantages. Growth may be achieved by either *internal* or *external expansion.*

Internal expansion. This is where a business looks to expand its productive capacity by adding to an existing plant or by building a new plant.

External expansion. This is where a business grows by engaging with another. It may do so in one of two ways:

■ The first is to join with another firm to form a single legal identity, through merger or takeover. A *merger* is a situation in which, as a result of mutual agreement, two firms decide to bring together their business operations as one firm. A merger is distinct from a *takeover* in so far as a takeover involves one firm bidding for another's

shares – often against the will of the directors of the target firm. One firm thereby acquires another. For simplicity, we will use the term 'merger' to refer to *both* mergers ('mutual agreements') and takeovers ('acquisitions').

■ The second is to form a *strategic alliance* with one or more firms. This is where firms agree to work together but retain their separate identities.

Definitions

Internal expansion Where a business adds to its productive capacity by adding to existing or by building new plants.

External expansion Where business growth is achieved by merging with or taking over businesses within a market or industry.

Merger The outcome of a mutual agreement made by two firms to combine their business activities.

Takeover (or acquisition) Where one business acquires another. A takeover may not necessarily involve mutual agreement between the two parties. In such cases, the takeover might be viewed as 'hostile'.

Strategic alliance Where two or more firms work together, formally or informally, to achieve a mutually desirable goal.

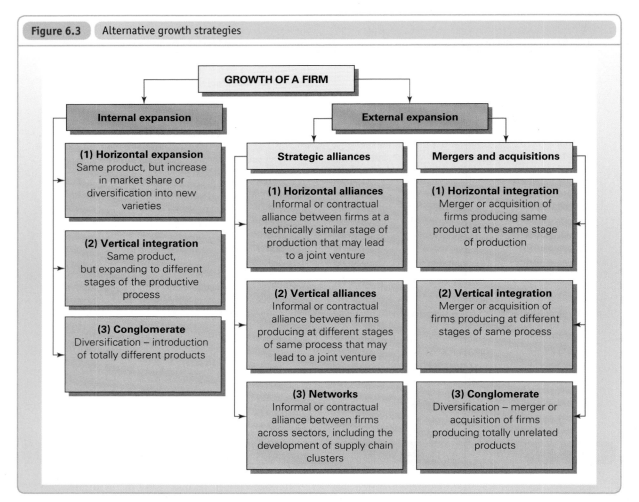

Figure 6.3 Alternative growth strategies

Whether the business embarks upon internal or external expansion, a number of alternative growth paths are open to it. Figure 6.3 shows these various routes, which are considered in the following pages.

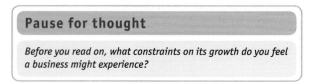

Pause for thought

Before you read on, what constraints on its growth do you feel a business might experience?

Growth by internal expansion

Financing internal growth

Internal growth requires an increase in sales, which in turn requires an increase in the firm's productive capacity. In order to increase its *sales*, the firm is likely to engage in extensive product promotion and may try to launch new products. In order to increase *productive capacity*, the firm will require new investment. Both product promotion and investment require finance and the inability of a firm to access finance may constrain its growth potential.

In the short run, the firm can finance growth by borrowing, by retaining profits or by a new issue of shares. However, there are some constraints.

If a firm borrows money it will have to repay interest and the more it borrows, the more difficult it is to maintain the level of dividends to shareholders. The largest source of finance for investment in the UK is *retained profits,* but if too much of this internal source of finance is used, there will be less available to pay out in dividends. Another option is for a firm to raise capital by a *new issue of shares,* but the problem here is that the distributed profits have to be divided between a larger number of shares, so dividends fall once more. Therefore, whichever way a business finances investment, the more it invests, the more the dividends on shares in the short run will probably fall.

These lower dividends could cause shareholders to sell their shares, unless they are confident that *long-run* profits and hence dividends will rise again, thus causing the share price to remain high in the long run. If shareholders do sell their shares, this will cause share prices to fall, as the supply curve of shares will shift to the right. Firms must therefore weigh up the benefits of growth with the potential costs of a falling share price. The problem is that if they fall too far, firms may become susceptible to being taken over and of certain managers losing their jobs. This is known as the *takeover constraint* and to avoid it, growth-maximising firms need to ensure that they have sufficient profits to distribute in the short run. This is the idea of profit 'satisficing': making sufficient profits to keep shareholders happy.

Hence the rate of business growth is influenced by shareholder demands, expectations, market conditions and by the fear of takeover.

In the long run, a rapidly growing firm may find its profits increasing, especially if it can achieve economies of scale and a bigger share of the market. These profits can then be used to finance further growth.

Clearly there is a crucial link between growth and profitability and it works in two ways. First, growth *depends* on profitability, as the more profitable the firm is, the more likely it is to be able to raise finance for investment. Second, as we have just seen, growth *affects* profitability. In the short run, growth may reduce profits, because of the necessary expenditure on advertising and investment. However, in the long run growth may lead to expansion and hence can increase profits.

Forms of internal expansion

There are three main ways in which a business can grow through internal expansion (see Figure 6.3):

- It can expand or *differentiate its product* within existing markets, by, for example, updating or restyling its product, or improving its technical characteristics. We examined such strategies in Chapter 3.
- Alternatively, the business might seek to expand via *vertical integration*. This involves the firm expanding within the same product market, but at a different stage of production. For example, a car manufacturer might wish to produce its own components ('backward vertical integration') or distribute and sell its own car models ('forward vertical integration').
- As a third option, the business might seek to expand outside of its current product range, and move into new markets. This is known as a process of *diversification*.

Growth through vertical integration

If market conditions make growth through increased sales difficult, then a firm may choose to grow through vertical integration. This has a number of advantages:

Economies of scale. These can occur by the business performing complementary stages of production within a single business unit. The classic example of this is the steel manufacturer combining the furnacing and milling stages of production, saving the costs that would have been required to reheat the iron had such operations been undertaken by independent businesses. Clearly, for most firms, performing more than one stage on a single site is likely to reduce transport costs, as semi-finished products no longer have to be moved from one plant to another.

Other benefits to the vertically integrated firm may include more favourable borrowing rates from financial institutions, due to its size; the ability to negotiate better deals with suppliers and the need for less managerial supervision.

Reduced uncertainty. A business that is not vertically integrated may find itself subject to various uncertainties in the marketplace. Examples include uncertainty over future price movements, supply reliability or access to markets.

Backward vertical integration will enable the business to control its supply chain. Without such integration the firm may feel very vulnerable, especially if there are only a few suppliers within the market. In such cases the suppliers would be able to exert considerable control over price. Alternatively, suppliers may be unreliable.

Forward vertical integration creates greater certainty in so far as it gives the business guaranteed access to distribution and retailing on its own terms. As with supply, forward markets might be dominated by large buyers, which are able not only to dictate price, but also to threaten market foreclosure (being shut out from a market). Forward vertical integration can remove the possibility of such events occurring.

Definitions

Takeover constraint The effect that the fear of being taken over has on a firm's willingness to undertake projects that reduce distributed profits.

Product differentiation In the context of growth strategies, this is where a business upgrades existing products or services so as to make them different from those of rival firms.

Vertical integration A business growth strategy that involves expanding within an existing market, but at a different stage of production. Vertical integration can be 'forward', such as moving into distribution or retail, or 'backward', such as expanding into extracting raw materials or producing components.

Diversification A business growth strategy in which a business expands into new markets outside of its current interests

Barriers to entry. Vertical integration may give the firm greater power in the market by enabling it to erect entry barriers to potential competitors. For example, a firm that undertakes backward vertical integration and acquires a key input resource can effectively close the market to potential new entrants, either by simply refusing to supply a competitor, or by charging a very high price for the input such that new firms face an absolute cost disadvantage. The economies of scale discussed earlier may also act as a barrier to entry, as new entrants will find it difficult to compete with established firms that are benefiting from lower average costs.

Pause for thought

See if you can identify two companies that are vertically integrated and what advantages they have from such integration.

Reduced transactions costs. Vertical integration allows the firm to avoid the buying, selling and other costs associated with dealing with other firms, whether as suppliers or purchasers.

Consider two firms that are involved in frequent transactions with each other: one a car manufacturer, the other a supplier of car exhausts. In an uncertain and changing economic environment, one or both of the firms could exploit the situation to their own advantage because they have different sets of information about the markets in which they operate. The exhaust manufacturer could claim that rising steel prices forces it to put up prices. The car manufacturer could argue that poorer than expected sales forces it to reduce the price it can pay for the exhausts. Only if the contract between them is very tightly specified (is 'complete') can situations such as this be avoided. This is another example of a principal–agent problem (see pages 9–10).

To avoid these transactions costs, firms may prefer to integrate vertically through internal expansion or merger. However, is vertical integration costless?

While vertical integration sounds like a good idea and a business will save on transactions costs, it is likely to incur other costs. A large vertically integrated organisation could be more bureaucratic, with the greater difficulties that come with managing more complex tasks. Although the firm is saving on the costs of monitoring contracts with other firms, managers still have to monitor the behaviour of their own internal divisions and employees and so there is a potential for diseconomies of scale.

Managers may set targets for the various divisions, but unless these are both carefully specified and comprehensive, the problem of moral hazard is likely to occur. Employees may meet the targets but may underperform in areas which are not specifically targeted. One response to this problem is to create more and more specific targets. This, however, is likely to remove flexibility and the opportunity for junior managers to take initiative.

Another problem is that by producing components in-house, the firm will not then be able to source them from elsewhere if cheaper suppliers become available. Thus it may reduce the firm's ability to respond to changing market demands.

Similarly, if a manufacturer buys its components from outside, it could possibly change supplier if the first supplier becomes unreliable. If it produces the components itself, however, switching to an outside supplier may prove more difficult if internal hold-ups occur.

In other words, outsourcing, rather than in-house production, while less secure, can *save* costs by allowing the firm to buy from the cheapest and/or best suppliers. Such suppliers are likely to be in competition with each other and this helps to keep their prices down and quality up. Equally, the ability to shift between retail outlets would allow the firm's products to be sold in the best locations. This may not be possible if it is tied to its own retail network.

Finally, production costs may be higher. Despite the fact that a vertically integrated firm may be large, the *individual* parts of the company may be too small to gain full economies of scale. For example, if a car company produces its own carpets, this carpet production will be on a much smaller scale than if a specialist car carpet manufacturer were to supply *several* car companies.

In deciding its optimum degree of vertical integration, therefore, a firm must weigh up the transactions costs of not integrating against the internal costs of integrating. Many firms are finding that it is better *not* to be vertically integrated but to focus on their core competencies and to outsource their supplies, their marketing and many other functions. That way they put alternative suppliers and distributors in competition with each other.

An alternative is to be *partially* vertically integrated, through a process known as ***tapered vertical integration***. To some extent, this enables the firm to

---

Definition

Tapered vertical integration Where a firm is partially integrated with an earlier stage of production; where it produces some of an input itself and buys some from another firm.

receive the benefits of vertical integration without incurring the costs.

Tapered vertical integration. This involves firms making part of a given input themselves and subcontracting the production of the remainder to one or more other firms. For example, Coca-Cola and Pepsi are large vertically integrated enterprises. They have, as part of their operations, wholly-owned bottling subsidiaries. However, in certain markets they subcontract to independent bottlers both to produce and to market their products.

By making a certain amount of an input itself, the firm is less reliant on suppliers and saves on transactions costs, but does not require as much capital equipment as if it produced all the input itself. A policy of tapered vertical integration suits many multinational companies. In certain countries, they produce the inputs themselves; in others, they rely on local suppliers, drawing on the supplier's competitive advantage in that local market.

Of course, tapered vertical integration may not allow the firm to gain such substantial economies of scale and production may thus be less efficient than under vertical integration. It is, therefore, important to realise that for much of the time firms will face a trade-off.

Growth through diversification

An alternative internal growth strategy to vertical integration is that of diversification, where a firm expands to produce a range of products in different markets. A good example of a highly diversified company is Virgin. The brand began as the name of a small record shop in London, but now includes an airline, trains, a cruise line, banking and finance, gift 'experiences', holidays, hotels, mobile phones, radio, Internet provision, cosmetics and even space travel, to name a few.

If the current market is saturated, stagnant or in decline, diversification might be the only avenue open to the business if it wishes to maintain a high growth performance. In other words, it is not only the level of profits that may be limited in the current market, but also the growth of sales.

Diversification also has the advantage of spreading risks. So long as a business produces a single product in a single market, it is vulnerable to changes in that market's conditions. If a farmer produces nothing but potatoes, and the potato harvest fails, the farmer is ruined. If, however, the farmer produces a whole range of vegetable products, or even diversifies into livestock, then he or she is less subject to the forces of nature and the unpredictability of the market.

In some cases, however, diversification may actually be a risky strategy, as a firm might be developing both a new product and entering a new market. But in most cases, diversification should allow the business to use and adapt existing technology and knowledge to its advantage. The experience, skills and market knowledge of the managers of the business will be crucial to ensure that such a strategy is successful.

Growth through merger

Similar growth paths can be pursued via external expansion. However, in this case the business does not create the productive facilities itself, but purchases existing production. As Figure 6.3 identified, we can distinguish three types of merger: horizontal, vertical and conglomerate.

■ A *horizontal merger* is where two firms at the same stage of production within an industry merge. In February 2015, Facebook completed the acquisition of WhatsApp Messenger, another social media business for $19 billion.[2] There is a potential £12 billion merger between Sainsbury's and Asda,[3] two UK supermarkets, though this has been thrown in doubt by the Competition and Markets Authority's findings that the merger could push up prices and reduce consumer choice (see the blog, *Will the Big 4 become the Big 3?* on the Sloman Economics News site).

■ A *vertical merger* is where businesses at different stages of production within the same industry merge. As such we might identify backward and forward vertical mergers for any firm involved.

One example is the $85 billion takeover of Time Warner by AT&T in June 2018. AT&T was the biggest telecommunication business in the world and the largest provider of fixed-line telephone services and second largest provider of mobile phones in the USA. Time Warner was the third biggest entertainment company in the world, offering a range of TV content. The merger went ahead in June 2018, though the Justice Department

> ### Definitions
>
> **Horizontal merger** Where two firms in the same industry at the same stage of the production process merge.
>
> **Vertical merger** Where two firms in the same industry at different stages in the production process merge.

[2] 'Facebook buys WhatsApp: Mark Zuckerberg explains why', *Telegraph* (19 February 2014).

[3] Ben Chapman, 'Sainsbury's and Asda criticise competition watchdog after £12 billion merger dealt "hammer blow"', *Independent* (20 February 2018).

appealed the decision and, at the time of writing (February 2019), a decision is expected as to whether the merger can remain or if the companies will have to be 'de-merged'.[4]

A second example is the €48 billion merger between the Italian business Luxottica, the largest producer of eyewear frames and the French firm Essilor, the largest manufacturer of lenses, which was approved by the European Commission in March 2018.[5]

■ A *conglomerate merger* is where firms in totally unrelated industries merge. Many of the big multinational corporations, such as Google and Amazon, operate in a number of sectors and regularly buy other firms. For example, in 2014, Amazon purchased Twitch (a video games business), while Google purchased Nest (a thermostats producer). In 2017, Amazon acquired Whole Foods in a $13.7 billion deal and in 2018, Amazon bought Ring, the smart doorbell maker.[6]

A further dimension of business growth that we should note at this point is that all of the above-mentioned growth paths can be achieved by the business looking beyond its national markets. In other words, the business might decide to become multinational and invest in expansion overseas. This raises a further set of issues, problems and advantages that a business might face. These will be discussed in Chapter 7 when we consider multinational business.

Why merge?

Why do firms want to merge with or take over others? Is it purely that they want to grow; are mergers simply evidence of the hypothesis that firms are growth maximisers? Or are there other motives that influence the predatory drive?

Merger for growth. Mergers provide a much quicker means to growth than internal expansion. Not only does the firm acquire new capacity, experience and skills, but also it acquires additional consumer demand. Building up this level of consumer demand by internal expansion might have taken a considerable length of time.

Merger for economies of scale. Once the merger has taken place, the constituent parts can be reorganised through a process of 'rationalisation'. The result can be a reduction in costs. For example, only one head office will now be needed. On the marketing side, the two parts of the newly merged company may now share distribution and retail channels, benefiting from each other's knowledge and operation in distinct market segments or geographical locations.

Evidence is mixed on whether cost savings occur. Some companies do successfully cut costs through mergers, such as Anheuser-Busch Inbev, but others fail to exploit economies of scale or experience disruptions due to the reorganisation, which can sometimes affect morale.

Merger for monopoly power. Here the motive is to reduce competition and thereby gain greater market power and larger profits. This applies mainly to horizontal mergers. With less competition, the firm will face a less elastic demand and be able to charge a higher percentage above marginal cost. What is more, the new more powerful company will be in a stronger position to regulate entry into the market by erecting effective entry barriers, thereby enhancing its monopoly position yet further.

Merger for increased market valuation. A merger can benefit shareholders of *both* firms if it leads to an increase in the stock market valuation of the merged firm. If both sets of shareholders believe that they will make a capital gain on their shares, then they are more likely to give the go-ahead for the merger.

Merger to reduce uncertainty. Firms face uncertainty at two levels. The first is in their own markets. The behaviour of rivals may be highly unpredictable. Mergers, by reducing the number of rivals, can correspondingly reduce uncertainty. At the same time, they can reduce the *costs* of competition (e.g. reducing the need to advertise).

> **Pause for thought**
>
> *Which of the three types of merger (horizontal, vertical and conglomerate) are most likely to lead to (a) reductions in average costs; (b) increased market power?*

The second source of uncertainty is the economic environment. In a period of rapid change, such as often accompanies a boom, firms may seek to protect themselves by merging with others.

Other motives. Other motives for mergers include:

■ Getting bigger so as to become less likely to be taken over oneself.

> **Definition**
>
> **Conglomerate merger** Where two firms in different industries merge.

[4] Claire Atkinson, 'AT&T and Justice Department continue battle over $85.4 billion Time Warner acquisition', *NBC News* (6 December 2018).

[5] Ben Knight, 'The spectacular power of Big Lens', *The Guardian* (10 May 2018).

[6] Dennis Green, 'Amazon's $1 billion acquisition of the doorbell-camera startup Ring is the company doing what it does best – and it should terrify every other retailer', *Business Insider* (3 March 2018).

- Opportunistic. Firms are presented with an unforeseen opportunity. As you can imagine, mergers based on such a motive are virtually impossible to predict, but firms will always be on the look-out for such opportunities.
- Merging with another firm so as to defend it from an unwanted predator (the 'White Knight' strategy).
- Asset stripping. This is where a firm takes over another and then breaks it up, selling off the profitable bits and probably closing down the remainder.
- Empire building. This is where owners or managers favour takeovers because of the power or prestige of owning or controlling several (preferably well-known) companies.
- Geographical expansion. The motive here is to broaden the geographical base of the company by merging with a firm in a different part of the country or the world.

Mergers, especially horizontal ones, will generally have the effect of increasing the market power of those firms involved. This could lead to less choice and higher prices for the consumer. For this reason, mergers have become the target for government competition policy. Such policy is the subject of section 9.5.

BOX 6.3   STRATEGIES IN UNCERTAIN TIMES

Reacting to Brexit and other uncertainties

A testing time for any business is when conditions become uncertain. In deciding whether to invest and grow, firms like to have certainty, both in terms of where they can sell their product and from where they can obtain the inputs.

Many firms sell in both domestic and global markets and uncertainty over the ease with which they can sell abroad can have a significant effect on their behaviour. The same applies to inputs, whether raw materials, capital or labour, and the overall supply chain. Any successful firm needs easy and fast access to inputs and a reliable supply chain and if circumstances in an economy change such that this supply chain is affected, firms may have to react in order to remain competitive.

During a recession, demand for products falls and will then often remain low, as we saw in and after the financial crisis of 2007–8. Global trading conditions were weak and there was a lot of uncertainty about when and how things would improve. Firms were struggling to access finance and many saw costs rising and revenues falling, and hence profits falling.

Geopolitical uncertainty also affects businesses, even those that are not based in the affected countries. Many firms have supply chains that involve companies based in countries across the world and so are indirectly affected by political issues that may arise thousands of miles away. Even things like oil supplies being disrupted in other countries can have serious implications for firms and this uncertainty will affect business behaviour. Economic tensions over trade relations, such as those between China and the USA, also create an uncertain business and economic environment and firms must factor these things into decision making.

One of the biggest causes of uncertainty in recent times has been the run-up to the scheduled date of 29 March 2019 for the UK to leave the EU. There was no agreement in the UK Parliament about the Withdrawal Deal and many firms had spent over two years in a situation of uncertainty, planning for various scenarios, including what appeared to be an increasingly likely 'No Deal' Brexit. HSBC's Chief Executive, John Flint, said 'The longer we have the uncertainty, the worse it's going to be for the customers . . . Customers are absolutely postponing investment decisions . . . and that's been the part of this slowdown that we have seen in the UK'.[1]

So how does uncertainty affect business strategy?

Staff
The labour force is a key component for any firm, but also represents a significant cost. During the financial crisis, demand was falling and many firms found that they had surplus staff, which led to massive job losses across countries and/or staff agreeing to temporary cuts in their hours to avoid redundancies. In the UK, unemployment rose from 5.2 per cent (1.6m) to 8.4 per cent (2.7m) between 2008 and 2012.

With the uncertainty over Brexit, many firms in the UK announced job losses, despite unemployment being at the lowest level since the mid-1970s. Mark Boleat, former political leader of the City of London, believes that Brexit will lead to a loss of 75 000 jobs. An article from the *Independent*[2] considers some of the big companies that had already begun to plan their strategy post-Brexit.

One sector that has been particularly affected is the UK car industry, with more than 10 000 jobs put in jeopardy. Honda will be closing its Swindon plant, leading to 3500 jobs going, while Jaguar Land Rover will cut 4500 jobs, mainly in the UK, and Ford will axe thousands of jobs. These job losses are not entirely related to Brexit. For example, Jaguar Land Rover has also been affected by the falling demand for diesel cars and a slowdown in China, but an uncertain climate in the UK has certainly had an impact on these firms' strategies.

Bank of America Merrill Lynch has transferred 125 jobs to Dublin, while Barclays has said it expects that around 150–200 of its staff will move, mainly to Dublin, in light of

---

[1] See, for example: John-Paul Ford Rojas, 'HSBC sees UK business weaken amid Brexit uncertainty', *MSN Money* (19 February 2019).

[2] Joe Sommerlad and Ben Chapman, 'Which companies are leaving UK, downsizing or cutting jobs ahead of Brexit?', *Independent* (26 February 2019).

▶

Brexit. JPMorgan Chase said its Brexit plans were 'past the point of no return' and that as many as 25 per cent of its 16 000 UK staff could be relocated if there was a 'No deal' Brexit. Philips only has one UK factory, but all operations and 430 jobs will move to the Netherlands and, while this strategy is argued to be unrelated to Brexit, the company did warn that it would have to cut 500 jobs if a favourable deal were not secured.

Plant closure

Businesses benefit from stability and whatever the cause of the uncertainty, firms will react to it and one strategy is to close plants or facilities. This is what many companies warned would happen when the UK leaves the EU, especially if it was without a deal. Pre-Brexit, trade between the UK and EU is not subject to tariffs, but if there was no deal, tariffs might be imposed on goods traded across borders. This would mean higher costs for firms and potentially higher prices for customers. Thus, consumers outside of the UK might turn to products that are not subject to tariffs and hence demand for goods produced in the UK might fall. This, together with the uncertainty of what will happen, has contributed to firms' decisions to close plants in the UK.

For example, the EU and Japan will soon have tariff-free trade. Outside the EU, the UK would not benefit from this tariff-free trade unless an equivalent deal could be reached between the UK and Japan. In light of this, the Japanese car manufacturer, Nissan, will be relocating manufacturing of its X-Trail SUV from Sunderland to Japan, with the European Senior Vice President noting: 'We have taken this decision for the business reasons I've explained but clearly the uncertainty around the UK's future relationship with the EU is not helping companies like ours to plan for the future.'[3]

The Chief Executive of Airbus, Tom Enders, warned in January 2019 that it may have to shut down UK plants, noting: 'It is a disgrace that, more than two years after the result of the 2016 referendum, businesses are still unable to plan properly for the future'.[4]

Aviva has announced it will move £7.8 billion worth of assets to Dublin in preparation for Brexit at 11.59pm on 29 March. Mr Justice Snowden, who approved the transfer of assets said: 'The evidence of [the transferor] is that the uncertainty over the Brexit negotiations means that if it delayed further and did nothing, there is a real risk that substantial numbers of policyholders would be materially prejudiced in event of a "hard" [no-deal] Brexit by the loss of [the transferor's] EU passporting rights.'[5]

Headquarters relocation

As well as closing down plants, companies have also begun the process of relocating their Headquarters. Dyson has relocated its company's headquarters from Wiltshire to Singapore, despite James Dyson's vocal support for Brexit and his assurances that he remains 'enormously optimistic' about Britain's future outside of the EU. Bank of America Merrill Lynch has spent $400 million on moving staff and in moving to its new Paris headquarters. Lloyds of London will be opening up an EU base and is transferring all of its European Economic Area business to a subsidiary in Brussels. In a statement the company said: 'This milestone [regulatory approval from the National Bank of Belgium] moves us closer to our objective of being fully operational in Brussels by 1 January 2019 to ensure we can continue to work closely with our EU27 partners post-Brexit.'[6]

Panasonic and Sony will both be relocating their European headquarters to Amsterdam and the Dutch government said that around 25 companies were talking to it about relocating to Amsterdam.

In addition to many larger businesses considering cutting plants, jobs or relocating to other countries, many SMEs also expressed their intentions to relocate. Many were concerned about the bureaucracy and red tape that Brexit might cause, while others cited reasons such as stock delays being a cause for concern due to delays at borders. Many SMEs pride themselves on being responsive to customer demands and operate in niche markets, so delays in receiving stock and items could prove to be disastrous.

Brexit has created an environment of uncertainty and the impact was already being felt in a range of industries before the scheduled withdrawal date. In January 2019, EY (Ernst & Young, through monitoring companies via its Financial Services Brexit Tracker, said: 'Since the EU Referendum, 36 per cent (80/222) of UK financial services companies tracked have said they are considering or have confirmed relocating operations and/or staff to Europe. This rises to 56 per cent (27 out of 48) amongst universal banks, investment banks and brokerages.'[7] EY found that 20 companies had announced that assets will be moved out of London and into various cities across Europe and that, between September and November 2018, nine financial services companies stated they would be 'implementing product adjustments in light of Brexit'.

? If the uncertainty is caused by a recession, what things could a business focus on and why are they important?

Q Select a business. How has it responded to Brexit or other changes that have created an uncertain business environment? (Hint: use the Internet to help you research its strategy.)

---

[3] See, for example: Angus Walker, 'Nissan hits out at Brexit 'uncertainty' as it confirms new X-Trail to be made in Japan not Sunderland', *ITV News* (2 February 2019).
[4] See, for example: Benjamin D. Katz and Joe Mayes, 'Airbus Threat to Quit U.K. Over Brexit Adds to Risk of Exodus', *Bloomberg* (24 January 2019).
[5] See, for example: Pedro Gonçalves, 'Aviva to move £9bn in assets to Dublin as Brexit looms', *International Investment* (22 February 2019).

[6] 'Lloyd's Brussels: Our base in the heart of Europe', *Lloyd's Press Release* (June 2018).
[7] 'EY Financial Services Brexit Tracker: Heightened uncertainty drives financial services companies to move almost £800 billion of assets to Europe; EY (7 January 2019).

Growth through strategic alliances

One means of achieving growth is through the formation of strategic alliances with other firms: either horizontally or vertically within an industry or as a network of firms across different industries. They are a means of expanding business operations relatively quickly and at relatively low cost, and are a common way in which firms can deepen their involvement in global markets.

A well-known example of strategic alliances is in the airline industry (see Figure 6.4). Members co-operate over frequent flyer programmes, share business-class airport lounges and code share on various flights.

What forms can strategic alliances takes?
Joint ventures. A ***joint venture*** is where two or more firms decide to create, and jointly own, a new inde-

pendent organisation. Joint ventures can be either horizontal or vertical. For example, in 2018, Amazon, JPMorgan Chase and Berkshire Hathaway announced that they were creating a not-for-profit healthcare company. Qualcomm and Samsung formed a strategic alliance in January 2018 to develop processors for the transition to 5G. FilmFlex was an example of a vertical strategic alliance, bringing film and TV makers into the retail sector, but Sony and Disney sold FilmFlex to the US-based company Vubiquity in May 2014.

Definition

Joint venture Where two or more firms set up and jointly own a new independent firm.

Figure 6.4 Airline strategic alliances, 2017

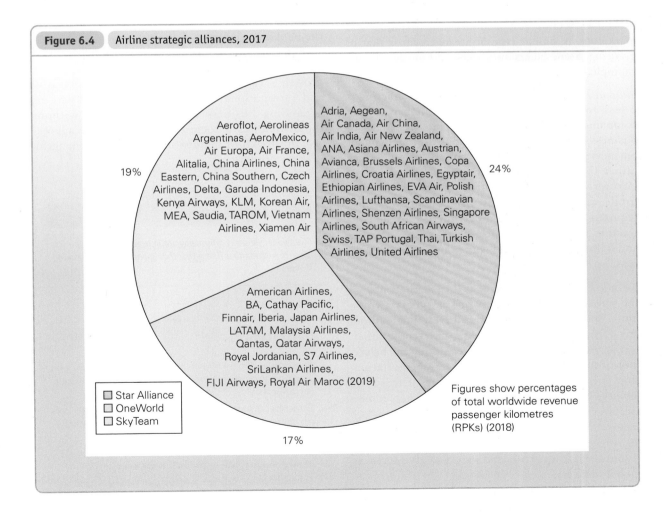

□ Star Alliance
□ OneWorld
□ SkyTeam

Figures show percentages of total worldwide revenue passenger kilometres (RPKs) (2018)

Consortia. A *consortium* is usually created for very specific projects, such as a large civil engineering work. As such, it has a very focused objective and once the project is completed the consortium is sometimes dissolved. TransManche Link, the Anglo-French company that built the Channel Tunnel, is an example of a defunct consortium. Camelot, by contrast, the company that runs the UK National Lottery was owned in equal shares by Cadbury Holdings, De La Rue Holdings, Fujitsu Services, Royal Mail Enterprises and Thales Electronics, each of which had particular expertise to bring to the consortium. It was sold to Ontario Teachers' Pension Plan in March 2010.

Franchising and licensing. A less formal strategic alliance is where a business agrees to franchise its operations to third parties. McDonald's and Coca-Cola are good examples of businesses that use a franchise network. In such a relationship the franchisee is responsible for manufacturing and/or selling, and the franchiser retains responsibility for branding and marketing. A similar type of arrangement is that of *licensing.* Some lagers and beers sold in the UK, for example, are brewed under licence.

Subcontracting. Like franchising, *subcontracting* is a less formal source of strategic alliance, where companies maintain their independence. When a business sub-contracts, it employs an independent business to manufacture or supply some service rather than conduct the activity itself. Car manufacturers are major subcontractors. Given the multitude and complexity of components that are required to manufacture a car, the use of subcontractors to supply specialist items, such as brakes and lights, seems a logical way to organise the business, as Nissan has found.[7]

Networks. *Networks* are less formal than any of the above alliances. A network is where two or more businesses work collaboratively but without any formal relationship binding one to the other. Rather than a formal contract regulating the behaviour of the partners to the agreement, their relationship is based upon an understanding of trust and loyalty. Networks are common in the motor vehicle, electronics, pharmaceutical and other high-tech sectors. Networks can be at both the national and local level and give firms access to technology and resources at lower costs and may also give access to global markets.

Why form strategic alliances?

As a business expands, possibly internationally, it may well be advantageous to join with an existing player in the market. Such a business would have local knowledge and an established network of suppliers and distributors.

In addition, strategic alliances allow firms to share risk. The Channel Tunnel and the consortium of firms that built it is one such example. The construction of the Channel Tunnel was a massive undertaking and far too risky for any single firm to embark upon. With the creation of a consortium, risk was spread, and the various consortium members were able to specialise in their areas of expertise.

They also allow firms to pool capital. Projects that might have prohibitively high start-up costs, or running costs, may become feasible if firms co-operate and pool their capital. In addition, an alliance of firms, with their combined assets and credibility, may find it easier to generate finance, whether from investors in the stock market or from the banking sector.

The past 30 years have seen a flourishing of strategic alliances. They have become a key growth strategy for business both domestically and internationally. They are seen as a way of expanding business operations quickly without the difficulties associated with the more aggressive approach of acquisition or the more lengthy process of merger.

Pause for thought

Give two reasons why a firm may prefer to form a strategic alliance with another firm rather than merging with it or taking it over.

Definitions

Consortium Where two or more firms work together on a specific project and create a separate company to run the project.

Franchise A formal agreement whereby a company uses another company to produce or sell some or all of its product.

Licensing Where the owner of a patented product allows another firm to produce it for a fee.

Subcontracting Where a firm employs another firm to produce part of its output or some of its input(s).

Network An informal arrangement between businesses to work together towards some common goal.

---

[7] Adrian Pearson, '5200 jobs predicted as Sunderland gets Nissan business park', *The Journal* (14 March 2014).

RECAP

1. A business can expand either internally or externally by merging with other firms or by forming strategic alliances. In each case, there are three potential growth strategies open to business: product differentiation, vertical integration and diversification.

2. Growth by internal expansion may be financed by ploughing back profits, by share issue or by borrowing. Whichever method a firm uses, it will require sufficient profits if it is to avoid becoming vulnerable to a takeover.

3. Vertical integration involves remaining in the same market, but expanding into a different stage of production. Vertical integration can reduce a firm's costs through various economies of scale. It can eliminate the various transactions costs associated with dealing with other firms. It can also help to reduce uncertainty, as the vertically integrated business can hopefully secure

supply routes and/or retail outlets. This strategy can also enhance the business's market power by enabling it to erect various barriers to entry.

4. Diversification offers the business a growth strategy that not only frees it from the limitations of a particular market, but also enables it to spread its risks and seek profit in potentially fast-growing markets.

5. There are three types of merger: horizontal, vertical and conglomerate. There are various possible advantages of mergers, including growth, economies of scale, market power, increased share values or reduction in uncertainty.

6. One means of achieving growth is through the formation of strategic alliances with other firms. They have the advantage of allowing easier access to new markets, risk sharing and capital pooling.

6.4 FINANCING GROWTH AND INVESTMENT

If businesses are to grow, they will need to invest. In this section we consider the sources of finance for investment, and the roles played by various financial institutions.

Sources of business finance

As mentioned in section 6.3 above, the firm can finance growth by borrowing, by retaining profits or by a new issue of shares.

Many companies rely on their own resources to finance investment and growth. Indeed, the largest source of finance for investment in the UK is firms' own internal funds (i.e. ploughed-back profit).

Given, however, that business profitability depends in large part on the general state of the economy, internal funds as a source of business finance are likely to show considerable cyclical variation. When profits are squeezed in an economic downturn, as we saw after 2008, this source of investment will decline (but so also will the *demand* for investment; after all, what is the point in investing if your market is declining?).

Other sources of finance, which include borrowing and the issue of shares and debentures, are known as 'external funds'. These are then categorised as short-term, medium-term or long-term sources of finance.

■ Short-term finance is usually in the form of a short-term bank loan or overdraft facility, and is used by firms as a form of working capital to aid them in their day-to-day business operations.

■ Medium-term finance, again provided largely by banks, is usually in the form of a loan with set repayment targets. It is common for such loans to be made at a fixed rate of interest, with repayments designed to fit in with the business's expected cash flow. Bank lending tends to be the most volatile source of business finance and is particularly sensitive to the state of the economy, especially over the past ten years. While part of the reason is the lower demand for loans during a recession, another aspect is the caution of banks in granting loans if prospects for the economy are poor. This caution was also exacerbated by the banking crisis.

■ Long-term finance, especially in the UK, tends to be acquired through the stock and bond markets. The proportion of business financing from this source clearly depends on the state of the stock market and, in turn, on the economy. In the late 1990s, from 2004 to 2007 and eventually after the world began to recover from the financial crisis, stock markets were buoyant and the proportion of funds obtained through share issue increased. Stock market prices, however, declined from 2000 to early 2003 and again between 2007 and 2009 and so the proportion of investment funding through new issues also fell. Given the volatility of stock markets as worries about the global economy persist, the scope for funding from new issues is likely to remain variable.

Despite the traditional reliance on the stock market for long-term sources of finance, there has been a growing involvement of banks in recent years, although banks have been criticised for continuing to be too cautious. This can result in a problem of *short-termism*, with bankers often demanding a quick return on their money or charging high interest rates, and being less concerned to finance long-term investment. This has been a particular problem faced by small and medium-sized enterprises (SMEs).

In many other European countries, such as Germany and France, banks provide a significant amount of *long-term*, fixed interest rate finance. While this tends to increase companies' gearing ratios and thus increases the risk of bankruptcy, it does provide a much more stable source of finance and creates an environment where banks are much more committed to the long-run health of companies. For this reason the net effect may be to *reduce* the risks associated with financing investment. Nevertheless, with many European banks since the financial crisis facing problems of inadequate finance, many have become more cautious about lending to business in recent years. This has hampered recovery from recession.

Another source of finance is that from outside the country. This might be direct investment by externally based companies in the domestic economy or from foreign financial institutions. In either case, a major determinant of the amount of finance from this source is the current state of the economy and predictions of its future state. With the uncertainty over the future of the UK's economy post-Brexit, this source of finance was particularly affected and was one of the reasons why some companies moved or are considering moving their operations to other countries, where the future is more certain. One of the major considerations with obtaining finance from abroad is anticipated changes in the exchange rate (see Chapter 13). If the exchange rate is expected to rise, this will increase the value of any given profit in terms of foreign currency. As we shall see, the exchange rate is susceptible to uncertainty and to expectations of the future state of an economy and so, again, Brexit has added to the volatility of this source of finance.

The stock market

In this section, we will look at the role of the stock market and consider the advantages and limitations of raising capital through it. We will also consider whether the stock market is efficient.

The role of the Stock Exchange

The London Stock Exchange operates as both a primary and secondary market in capital.

As a *primary market* it is where public limited companies (see page 7) can raise finance by issuing new shares, whether to new shareholders or to existing ones. To raise finance on the Stock Exchange a business must be 'listed'. The Listing Agreement involves directors agreeing to abide by a strict set of rules governing behaviour and levels of reporting to shareholders. A company must have at least three years' trading experience and make at least 25 per cent of its shares available to the public. In June 2019, there were 938 UK and 220 international companies on the Official List. These companies in total had an equity market value of £3861.5 billion. During 2018, companies on this list raised £17.7 billion of equity capital, which is significantly lower than the figures for 2008 and 2009, when £66.7 billion and £77.4 billion were raised respectively.

As well as those on the Official List, there are some 900 companies on the Alternative Investment Market (AIM). Companies listed here tend to be young but with growth potential, and do not have to meet the strict criteria or pay such high costs as companies on the Official List. The market value of these companies as of June 2019 was £100 236.5.

As a *secondary market*, the Stock Exchange enables investors to sell existing shares to one another. In 2018, approximately £5.5 billion of trade in UK equities and debt securities took place on an average day.

The advantages and disadvantages of using the stock market to raise capital

As a market for raising capital the stock market has a number of advantages:

- It brings together those that wish to invest and those that seek investment. It thus represents a way that savings can be mobilised to create output, and does so in a relatively low-cost way.
- Firms that are listed on the Stock Exchange are subject to strict regulations. This is likely to stimulate investor confidence, making it easier for businesses to raise finance.

Definitions

Short-termism Where firms and investors take decisions based on the likely short-term performance of a company, rather than on its long-term prospects. Firms may thus sacrifice long-term profits and growth for the sake of quick return.

Primary market in capital Where shares are sold by the issuer of the shares (i.e. the firm) and where, therefore, finance is channelled directly from the purchasers (i.e. the shareholders) to the firm.

Secondary market in capital Where shareholders sell shares to others. This is thus a market in 'second-hand' shares.

- The process of merger and acquisition is facilitated by having a share system. It enables a business more effectively to pursue this as a growth strategy.

The main weaknesses of the stock market for raising capital are:

- The cost to a business of getting listed can be immense, not only in a financial sense, but also in being open to public scrutiny. Directors' and senior managers' decisions will often be driven by how the market is likely to react, rather than by what they perceive to be in the business's best interests. They always have to think about the reactions of those large shareholders in the City that control a large proportion of their shares.
- It is often claimed that the stock market suffers from short-termism. Investors on the Stock Exchange are more concerned with a company's short-term performance and its share value. In responding to this, the business might neglect its long-term performance and potential.

Is the stock market efficient?

One of the arguments made in favour of the stock market is that it acts as an arena within which share values can be accurately or efficiently priced. If new information comes on to the market concerning a business and its performance, this will be quickly and rationally transferred into the business's share value. This is known as the *efficient market hypothesis*. So, for example, if an investment analyst found that, in terms of its actual and expected dividends, a particular share was under-priced and thus represented a 'bargain', the analyst would advise investors to buy. As people then bought the shares, their price would rise, pushing their value up to their full worth. So by attempting to gain from inefficiently priced securities, investors will encourage the market to become more efficient.

 KEY IDEA 22

Efficient capital markets. Capital markets are efficient when the prices of shares accurately reflect information about companies' current and expected future performance.

If the market were perfectly efficient in this sense, then no gain could be made from studying a company's performance and prospects, as any such information would *already* be included in the current share price. In selecting shares, you would do just as well by pinning the financial pages of a newspaper on the wall, throwing darts at them, and buying the shares the darts hit!

If the stock market were perfectly efficient, it would only be unanticipated information that would cause share prices to deviate from that which reflected expected average yields. Such information must, by its nature, be random, and as such would cause share prices to deviate randomly from their expected price, or follow what we call a *random walk*. Evidence suggests that share prices do tend to follow random patterns.

Pause for thought

1. *For what reasons is the stock market not perfectly efficient?*
2. *How might some people gain from the lack of efficiency?*

Definitions

Efficient (capital) market hypothesis The hypothesis that new information about a company's current or future performance will be quickly and accurately reflected in its share price.

Random walk Where fluctuations in the value of a share away from its 'correct' value are random. When charted over time, these share price movements would appear like a 'random walk' – like the path of someone staggering along drunk!

RECAP

1. Business finance can come from internal and external sources. Sources external to the firm include borrowing and the issue of shares, both of which can be very volatile and fluctuate with the state of, and level of uncertainty in, the economy.

2. The stock market operates as both a primary and secondary market in capital. As a primary market it channels finance to companies as people purchase new shares. It is also a market for existing shares.

3. It helps to stimulate growth and investment by bringing together companies and people who want to invest in

them. By regulating firms and by keeping transaction costs of investment low, it helps to ensure that investment is efficient.

4. It does impose costs on firms, however. It is expensive for firms to be listed and the public exposure may make them too keen to 'please' the market. It can also foster short-termism.

5. The stock market is relatively efficient. It achieves efficiency by allowing share prices to respond quickly and fully to publicly available information.

6.5 STARTING SMALL

How often do you hear of a small business making it big? Not very often, and yet many of the world's major corporations began life as small businesses. From acorns have grown oak trees! But small and large businesses are usually organised and run quite differently and face very different problems.

Unfortunately, there is no single agreed definition of a 'small' firm. In fact, a firm considered to be small in one sector of business, such as manufacturing, may be considerably different in size from one in, say, the road haulage business. Nevertheless, the most widely used definition is that adopted by the EU[8] for its statistical data. Three categories of small and medium-sized enterprise (SME) are distinguished. These are shown in Table 6.1.

Of the whole UK economy in 2018, data from the Department for Business, Energy & Industrial Strategy show that micro businesses (between 0 and 9 employees) accounted for 95.6 per cent of all firms, 21.0 per cent of turnover and provided 32.5 per cent of all employment. All SMEs together (less than 250 employees) accounted for 99.9 per cent of all firms, 51.6 per cent of turn-over and 60.3 per cent of employment.[9]

Evidence suggests that a small business stands a significantly higher chance of failure than a large business, and yet many small businesses survive and some grow. What characteristics distinguish a successful small business from one that is likely to fail?

Pause for thought

Before you read on, try to identify what competitive advantages a small business might have over larger rivals.

---

[8] *What is an SME?*, Internal Market, Industry, Entrepreneurship and SMEs, European Commission.

[9] *Business Population Estimates 2018*, Department of Business Energy & Industrial Strategy (17 October 2018).

Competitive advantage and the small-firm sector

The following have been found to be the key competitive advantages that small firms might hold:

Flexibility. Small firms are better able to respond to changes in market conditions and to meet customer requirements effectively. For example, they may be able to develop or adapt products for specific needs. Small firms may also be able to make decisions quickly, avoiding the bureaucratic and formal decision-making processes that typify many larger companies.

Quality of service. Small firms are more able to deal with customers in a personal manner and offer a more effective after-sales service.

Production efficiency and low overhead costs. Small firms can avoid some of the diseconomies of scale that beset large companies. A small firm can benefit from: management that avoids waste; good labour relations; the employment of a skilled and motivated workforce; lower accommodation costs. In a 2017 survey of SME managers by the UK Department for Business, Energy & Industrial Strategy (BEIS), 80 per cent ranked themselves as having strong people management skills.[10]

Product development. Many small businesses operate in niche markets, offering specialist goods or services. The distinctiveness of such products gives the small firm a crucial advantage over its larger rivals. A successful small business strategy, therefore, would be to produce products that are clearly differentiated from those of large firms in the market, thereby avoiding head-on competition – competition which the small firm would probably not be able to survive.

---

[10] *Longitudinal Small Business Survey Year 2 (2016): Panel Report*, Department for Business, Energy & Industrial Strategy (July 2017), p. 32.

Table 6.1	EU SME definitions			
Criterion		**Micro**	**Small**	**Medium**
1.	Maximum number of employees	9	49	249
2a.	Maximum annual turnover	€2m	€10m	€50m
2b.	Maximum annual balance sheet total	€2m	€10m	€43m
3.	Maximum % owned by other firms which are large enterprise(s)	25%	25%	25%

Note: to qualify as an SME criteria 1 and 3 must be met and either 2a or 2b

Innovation. Small businesses, especially those located in high-technology markets, are frequently product or process innovators. Such businesses, usually through entrepreneurial vision, manage successfully to match such innovations to changing market needs. Many small businesses are, in this respect, path breakers or market leaders.

Problems facing small businesses

Despite some competitive advantages, there are a number of factors that hinder the success of small firms.

Selling and marketing. Small firms face many problems in selling and marketing their products, especially overseas. Small firms are perceived by their customers to be less stable and reliable than their larger rivals. This lack of credibility is likely to hinder their ability to trade. This is a particular problem for 'new' small firms which have not had long enough to establish a sound reputation. In the BEIS survey cited above, only 54 per cent of SME managers ranked themselves as 'strong' at developing and introducing new products or services.[11]

Funding R&D. Given the specialist nature of many small firms, their long-run survival may depend upon developing new products and processes in order to keep pace with changing market needs. Such developments may require significant investment in research and development. However, the ability of small firms to attract finance is limited, as many of them have virtually no collateral and they are frequently perceived by banks as a highly risky investment. In the same survey, only 29 per cent of SME managers ranked themselves as 'strong' at accessing external finance.[12] As we saw in Chapter 1, this can limit their scope for expansion.

Management skills. A crucial element in ensuring that small businesses not only survive but grow is the quality of management. If key management skills, such as being able to market a product effectively, are limited, then this will limit the success of the business.

Economies of scale. Small firms will have fewer opportunities and scope to gain economies of scale, and hence their costs may be somewhat higher than their larger rivals. This will obviously limit their ability to compete on price.

The role of entrepreneurs

Crucial to the success and growth of small businesses are the personality, skills and flair of the owner(s). Fostering their entrepreneurial talents has become a key element in government economic strategy around the world. Indeed, the creation of an entrepreneurial culture within society is often considered a prerequisite for economic prosperity.

But what exactly is an entrepreneur? Entrepreneurs are sources of new ideas and new ways of doing things. That is, they are at the forefront of invention and innovation, providing new products and developing markets.

International comparisons of entrepreneurship

The *Global Entrepreneurship Monitor* (GEM) provides a framework for analysing entrepreneurship. It suggests that entrepreneurship is a complex phenomenon that can exist at various stages of the development of a business. So someone who is just starting a venture and trying to make it in a highly competitive environment is entrepreneurial. And so too, but in a different way, are established business owners if they are innovative, competitive and growth-minded.

GEM's Global Report measures entrepreneurial activity in a country by the percentage of those aged 18 to 64 who are business owners, whether early stage or established. The 2018/19 report[13] was based on a survey of individuals across 49 different countries.

Total early-stage Entrepreneurial Activity (TEA) measures those who are involved in setting up a business or are a new business owner within the last 42 months. The report finds that TEA tends to be lower in developed economies, such as in North America and Europe, where alternative job opportunities exist. Similar trends exist in other regions of the world, with the higher income countries in Latin America and East and South Asia also exhibiting lower TEA levels relative to lower income countries in each region. The highest TEA rate of the countries studied was found in Angola (41 per cent), with many developed economies, including the UK, Switzerland, France and Germany with rates below 10 per cent.

Figure 6.5 shows data on nascent, new and established business owners and shows a range of countries to give a comparison of entrepreneurial activity. The report shows that the UK had a combined total of just under 15 per cent of entrepreneurial activity, which compares favourably with a variety of countries in Europe, but is some way behind the USA and Canada and various countries in Africa. It is somewhat difficult to look at how countries have developed over time, as consistent time-series data are not available, as not all countries report every year and the concept of 'established entrepreneurs' was only introduced in 2005.

---

[11] Ibid., p. 32.

[12] Ibid., p. 32.

[13] Niels Bosma and Donna Kelley, *Global Entrepreneurship Monitor: 2018/19 Global Report*, GEM (21 January 2019).

| Figure 6.5 | Entrepreneurial activity as a percentage of the adult population (2018) |

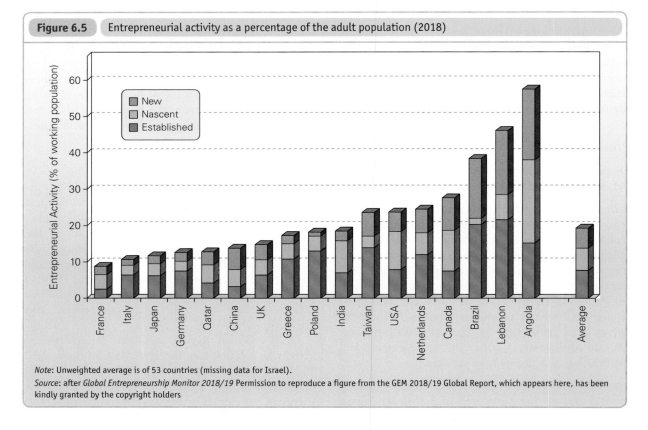

Note: Unweighted average is of 53 countries (missing data for Israel).

Source: after *Global Entrepreneurship Monitor 2018/19* Permission to reproduce a figure from the GEM 2018/19 Global Report, which appears here, has been kindly granted by the copyright holders

The Global Report also introduced the National Entrepreneurship Context Index (NECI) which provides an overall assessment of the environment for entrepreneurship in the 54 economies considered. Qatar, Indonesia and The Netherlands are the top three nations, with the USA ranked in 6th place, China in 11th, Germany in 19th, Chile in 26th, the UK in 30th, Lebanon in 35th, Saudi Arabia in 41st and Angola ranked in 50th place. Across the board, NECI scores are higher in East and South East Asia, while Latin American and Caribbean countries are consistently much lower.

Attitudes towards entrepreneurship

Despite challenging economic times in many countries, there is still a generally positive feeling about the opportunities for starting a business. However, in some countries, few people appear to take these opportunities, perhaps deterred by a belief that they lack the capability to do so or by the fear of failure. For example, the GEM Report found that over 80 per cent of people in Sweden perceive there to be opportunities to start a venture. This was the highest of all countries, followed by Saudi Arabia, Angola, Sudan and the USA. Yet in Sweden, less than 40 per cent of respondents felt that they had the abilities to pursue the abundant opportunities and this may explain Sweden's relatively low TEA rate, at approximately 7 per cent.

In India and Thailand, approximately 50 per cent of the working age population believe both that there are good opportunities and that they have the capabilities to start a business. However, of these people, over half indicate that they would be prevented from starting a business due to the fear of failure. A similar pattern can be observed in Europe and North America, though there are exceptions, such as Canada, where there is a high fear of failure (over 25 per cent), but a high TEA rate.

Another factor which affects entrepreneurial activity is the way people regard entrepreneurs. Throughout Europe and North America, between 66 and 75 per cent of people believe successful entrepreneurs have a high status, but few view it as a good career choice for themselves or others. The reverse is true in most economies in Latin America and the Caribbean, perhaps because being an entrepreneur is seen as more of an ordinary job, while in the Middle East and Africa, entrepreneurs are highly regarded and becoming one is seen as a good career choice. Furthermore, there appears to be some link between whether people think becoming an entrepreneur is a good career choice and how easy they think it is to start a business. For example, approximately 66 per cent of adults in Thailand and Indonesia believe starting a business is easy and, across the two countries, an average of 75 per cent of adults think it is also a good career choice.

Policies towards entrepreneurship

SMEs are an important part of any economy, contributing to employment, innovation and growth and so various forms of support do exist.

UK policy. The UK's 2010 Coalition government developed a strategy for the encouragement and promotion of entrepreneurial talent and over the years, various grants, tax concessions and advisory services have been established to encourage the establishment of new SMEs and to help them grow.

Pause for thought

Why might the government wish to distinguish SME start-up policies from SME growth and performance policies?

A new Department for Business, Energy & Industrial Strategy (BEIS) was created in July 2016, aiming to review the most effective methods for improving productivity of SMEs and to support businesses to start and grow. The UK government and the EU also offer grants and other forms of assistance through regional, urban, social and industrial policy that small firms may be able to tap into.

The British Business Bank, opened in 2014, aims to increase the supply of lending to SMEs. Start Up Loans are available, which are government-backed unsecured loans of up to £25 000, available to those who have set up a business within the past two years and cannot find another source of finance. The Enterprise Finance Guarantee scheme also facilitates lending to more established SMEs that are still unable to obtain a loan, by providing a government-backed guarantee covering 75 per cent of the value of an individual loan.

The UK government has also funded various mentoring schemes to help SMEs, as some evidence suggests that this improves their survival rates, though funding was withdrawn for some schemes in 2016, as part of budget cuts. Examples include the Get Mentoring project and the GrowthAccelerator initiative. The government expects large businesses

increasingly to provide the finance for these types of national schemes. For example, Mentorsme is operated by the British Bankers' Association. The government has also established 39 regional Growth Hubs across the country to provide business support at the local level.

EU policy. In the EU, the Small Business Act was adopted in June 2008 and revised in 2011 to strengthen loan guarantee schemes and improve access to venture capital markets. One of the more recent and important schemes run by the EU to support SMEs was the Competition and Innovation Framework Programme (CIP) which had a budget of €3.62 billion and operated from 2007 to 2013. CIP was replaced by the programme for the Competitiveness of Enterprises and Small and Medium-sized Enterprises (COSME) which has a planned budget of €2.3 billion and runs from 2014–20.

A new Executive Agency for Small and Medium-sized Enterprises (EASME) was created in January 2014 to manage most parts of COSME on behalf of the EU, but all the action and policies that were carried out under CIP are now part of the Horizon 2020 (H2020) programme, which has a budget of €80 billion.

Policies implemented under the COSME programme include *The Loan Guarantee Facility (LGF),* which is similar to the UK's EFG scheme; *Equity Facility for Growth (EFG),* which provides financial support for venture capital funds that invest in SMEs and the *Enterprise Europe Network (EEN)* which provides support for businesses to grow internationally.

The commitment to SMEs in countries across the world has grown in recent years, in recognition of the valuable role that they play within an economy, not only as employers and contributors to output, but in respect of their ability to innovate and initiate technological change. The GEM Report notes the changing nature of entrepreneurship and that in order for an economy to have high rates of entrepreneurial activity, a stable and dynamic economy is needed, with opportunities for very different types of entrepreneurs, such as early-stage, opportunity-motivated, family business and social entrepreneurship.

Pause for thought

Is business failure necessarily a 'bad thing' for a country?

BOX 6.4	HOTEL CHOCOLAT

A small, fast-growing ethical business

Hotel Chocolat is a UK-based luxury chocolate manufacturer founded in 1993 by Angus Thirwell and Peter Harris. They had previous experience of the confectionery sector, having established the Mint Marketing Company in 1988, which sold packaged mints to the corporate market. A number of their customers asked them if they sold confectionery other than mints, which led them to move into the chocolate business with the creation of Choc Express in 2003.

Their initial sales were primarily from mail-order catalogues. The company then developed an on-line store, which helped it to collect much better marketing data than most of its rivals that sold their products through supermarkets.

In 2003, Choc Express was rebranded as Hotel Chocolat, and in 2004, it opened its first retail store in Watford. The business now operates in 168 location across the UK, including shops, cafés, schools of chocolate and its *Rabot 1745* restaurant in London. Chocolate boutiques have been opened in Denmark, while a franchise agreement led to its launch in the Sogo department store in Hong Kong.

The business is still heavily reliant on the domestic market with 96 per cent of its sales in 2017 taking place in the UK, but its overall performance is strong. In 2018, the firm showed that year-on-year revenue was up by 13 per cent to £80.7 million and profits before tax were up by 7 per cent to £13.8 million. Its operational highlights from February 2019 note that its growth strategy is on track, with a further 14 stores opened in the UK and Republic of Ireland; efficiencies being captured from the vertically integrated supply chain and a growth in the digital customer case. The company has also engaged in forward vertical integration. It originally outsourced the production of its chocolates, but they are all now produced at its own factory in Cambridgeshire.[1]

As well as through its own website, the chocolates it makes can also be purchased on-line through Amazon and Ocado. They are also available in John Lewis and Fenwick department stores.

A tasting club was created in 1998, where, for a fee, customers receive a monthly box of new chocolates, which they have to rate on a 'taste scorecard'. This tasting club has over 55 000 members and provides valuable market research data on the public's tastes. In 2018, the company launched its M-Box, which is a weekly subscription service that provides customers with four recipes each week in easy-to-carry wraps. Therefore its strategy is very responsive to consumer tastes and moves with the times.

The rapid growth in the business has been helped by its use of 'chocolate bond' crowdfunding. These bonds pay investors' interest, not in money, but in chocolate and have helped to raise over £5 million. In May 2016, the company raised £55.5m through its public sale of shares and listing on the Alternative Investment Market (AIM) of the London Stock Exchange. The two founding partners each made £20 million, while £12 million was used to finance the opening of new stores and improve the company's website.

The company's growth has been based on premium chocolates with authentic, wholesome ingredients: i.e. without artificial flavourings or hydrogenated fats. The product range covers chocolate slabs, boxed chocolates, gift boxes and chocolate fancies, such as chocolate-covered 'Amaretto and Almond Sultanas' and 'Dark with Chilli and Cocoa Nibs'. They also offer products for the corporate sector, vegetarians, vegans and diabetics and in 2017, launched the first no-added-sugar milk chocolate. A range of beauty products was launched in November 2012 as well as a cookbook entitled *A New Way of Cooking with Chocolate*. The business introduced a cocoa-infused gin advent calendar for Christmas 2017.

Fair trading

In 2004, Hotel Chocolat engaged in backward vertical integration and purchased a 140-acre cocoa plantation on the Caribbean island of St Lucia. The company refurbished the estate, began to plant new seedlings and worked towards gaining full organic accreditation. In 2011, it opened the Boucan luxury hotel and restaurant on the plantation.

The company realised early on in St Lucia that developing a sustainable industry for the long term, offering a high-quality and consistent supply of cocoa, required that it support local cocoa growers. For over 20 years prior to the purchase of the plantation, cocoa in St Lucia had been in decline. Local growers had no guarantee that harvested crops would be bought and, when crops were sold, payment could take up to six months to arrive. Under these circumstances cocoa production was loss making.

The company has developed a programme of 'engaged ethics' to develop sustainable production and fair standards. Hotel Chocolat now guarantees that farmers who embrace the programme will be able to sell all the cocoa they produce at 30 to 40 per cent above the market price and will be paid within one week. The company buys all of the cocoa 'wet' (unfermented), to ensure consistent quality, allowing farmers to concentrate on growing and replanting. All of this is supported by advice and technical expertise. By 2011 the company had 120 cocoa growing partners including both new and established farmers.

As it develops the chocolate factory, Hotel Chocolat plans to bring other St Lucians into the supply chain, including chocolate workers, drivers, tour guides, engineers and support staff, all of whom will be trained and developed.

Performing well in a difficult market

Hotel Chocolat chose a good country to establish its business as people in the UK are some of the largest consumers of chocolate in the world. In 2017 they consumed 8.61 kg of chocolate per capita.[2]

However, the market environment was very difficult for chocolate producers during 2014–17. Increasingly

---

[1] https://www.hotelchocolat.com/uk/engaged-ethics/our-people/Our-Story.html

[2] 'A feast of innovation: Global Easter chocolate launches up 23% on 2017' *Mintel Press Office* (27 March 2018).

health-conscious consumers started to switch away from chocolate to healthier snacks containing less sugar. Mintel reported that the quantity of chocolate purchased in the UK fell by 1 per cent in 2015.[3] The downward trend continued with Euromonitor reporting a 1 per cent fall in the value of sales in 2017.[4] IRI research also found that in 2017 the sales of famous chocolate brands in the UK such as Cadbury's Dairy Milk, Galaxy and Aero fell by 4.2, 5.2 and 12.5 per cent, respectively.

The costs of cocoa also increased sharply in commodity markets. The average price of cocoa increased from around $2 per kilogram in February 2013 to over $3 per kilogram for much of the 2014–16 period. Since then, however, the price has fallen and from mid-2017 to mid-2018, it was around $2 again.

Despite these tough trading conditions, Hotel Chocolat has continued to perform strongly. In March 2015 it made greater profits than Thorntons, its main high street rival. In 2017 the company's revenue increased by 12 per cent and its pre-tax profits doubled to £11.2m.

Hotel Chocolat's approach to excellence in chocolate products has clearly helped it to succeed in difficult market conditions. According to the Department for

Environment, Food and Rural Affairs and the Department for International Trade, global demand for British chocolate is increasing and it is worth £1.1 billion to the UK economy. The data indicate that £680 million of chocolate was bought by foreign consumers in 2017 and exports of chocolate have increased by 84 per cent since 2010. Furthermore, Hotel Chocolat appears to have gained, as many consumers appear to have become more focused on quality rather than the quantity of chocolate they purchase. The business's strong sense of corporate and social responsibility has also helped it to appeal to an increasing number of ethical consumers.

Unsurprisingly, the firm has received a number of awards. In 2007, *Retail Week* judged Hotel Chocolat the 'Emerging Retailer of the Year', while in 2016 it won Lloyds Bank 'Mid-Market Business of the Year' and won 18 Academy of Chocolate Awards in 2018. The future for this company looks positive.

1. **What conditions existed to enable Hotel Chocolat's small business to do so well in such a short period of time?**
2. **What dangers do you see in the growth strategy adopted by Hotel Chocolat?**

Choose another 'fair trading' company and consider whether its strategy has been in its long-term busines interests.

---

[3] 'Mintel in the media', Mintel blog (13 July 2015).
[4] 'Chocolate Confectionery in the UK', Country Report, Euromonitor International (July 2018).

RECAP

1. Small firms survive because they provide or hold distinct advantages over their larger rivals. Such advantages include: greater flexibility, greater quality of service, production efficiency, low overhead costs and product innovation.

2. Small businesses are prone to high rates of failure, however. This is due to problems of credibility, finance and limited management skills.

3. Entrepreneurial activity varies from country to country, but most recognise that it is an important ingredient in the health of the economy. Generally, the difficulties and risks of setting up a new business are less than people expect.

QUESTIONS

1. What do you understand by the term 'business strategy'? Explain why different types of business will see strategic management in different ways. Give examples.

2. Outline the five forces of competition referred to in section 6.1. Identify the strengths and weaknesses of analysing industry in this manner.

3. Investigate a particular industry and assess its competitive environment in terms of the five forces of competition.

4. Distinguish between a business's primary and support activities in its value chain. Why might a business be inclined to outsource its support activities? Can you see any weaknesses in doing this?

5. What do you understand by the term 'core competence' when applied to a business? What are the arguments for and against a firm narrowly focusing on its core competencies?

6. Explain the two-way relationship between a business's rate of growth and its profitability.

7. Distinguish between an internal and external growth strategy. Identify a range of factors which might determine whether a firm chooses to pursue an internal or external strategy.

8. What is meant by the term 'vertical integration'? Why might a business wish to pursue such a growth strategy?

▶

9. A firm can grow by merging with or taking over another firm. Such mergers or takeovers can be of three types: horizontal, vertical or conglomerate. Which of the following is an example of which type of merger (takeover)?

   (a) A soft drinks manufacturer merges with a pharmaceutical company.
   (b) A car manufacturer merges with a car distribution company.
   (c) A large supermarket chain takes over a number of independent grocers.

10. To what extent will consumers gain or lose from the three different types of merger identified above?

11. Assume that an independent film company, which has always specialised in producing documentaries for a particular television broadcasting company, now wishes to expand. Identify some possible horizontal, vertical and other closely related fields into which it may choose to expand.

12. What are the advantages and disadvantages for a company in using the stock market to raise finance for expansion?

13. In what sense can the stock market be said to be efficient? Why is it unlikely to be perfectly efficient?

14. Compare and contrast the competitive advantages held by both small and big business.

15. Has the weak economic climate since 2008 affected small businesses? Do you think it is easier or more difficult to set up a business during a recession? Explain your answer.

7 Chapter

Multinational corporations and business strategy in a global economy

Business issues covered in this chapter

- What is meant by globalisation and what are the costs and benefits of it?
- What is the magnitude and pattern of global foreign direct investment and how has it changed?
- What are the key factors that make a nation attractive to foreign investors?
- What forms do multinational corporations take?
- Why do companies become multinational?
- In what ways do multinationals have a cost advantage over companies based in a single country?
- What competitive advantages do multinationals have over companies based in a single country?
- What disadvantages are companies likely to face from having their operations spread over a number of countries?
- What are the advantages and disadvantages of multinational investment for the host state?
- How can the multinational use its position to gain the best deal from the host state?

The world economy has become increasingly interdependent over the past few decades, with improved communications and an increasingly global financial system. This has meant that in many respects a firm's global strategy is simply an extension of its strategy within its own domestic market. However, opening up to global markets can provide an obvious means for a business to expand its markets and spread its risks, especially with the process of globalisation. It also is a means of reducing costs, whether through economies of scale or from accessing cheap sources of supply or low-wage production facilities.

A firm's global growth strategy may involve simply exporting or opening up factories or outlets abroad, or it may involve merging with businesses in other countries or forming strategic alliances. As barriers to trade and the international flow of capital have come down, so more and more businesses have sought to become multinational. The result is that the global business environment has tended to become more and more competitive.

For developing economies, such as India and China, the benefits of this new wave of globalisation are substantial. Foreign companies invest in high value-added, knowledge-rich production, most of which is subsequently exported. Economic growth is stimulated and wages rise. Increased consumption then spreads the benefits more widely throughout the economy, as we will discuss in more detail in Chapter 10. There are, however, costs. Many are left behind by the growth, and inequalities deepen both between and within countries. There are also often significant environmental costs as rapid growth leads to increased pollution, environmental degradation and the depletion of resources.

7.1 THE GLOBALISATION DEBATE

The world economy is becoming much more integrated and interdependent and this means that more and more businesses are operating in an increasingly global environment, sourcing from and selling to any country in the world. Until recently, international trade has grown much faster than countries' output and companies now invest more abroad than within their domestic markets.

This process of *globalisation* has been driven by many factors, such as technological advances and the changing social, cultural and political landscape. Globalisation is therefore a multi-dimensional concept.

The OECD defines *economic globalisation* as 'a process of closer economic integration of global markets: financial, product and labour'.[1] Similarly, the IMF refers to economic globalisation as 'the increasing integration of economies around the world, particularly through the movement of goods, services, and capital across borders'. It argues that this definition can be broadened further to include 'the movement of people (labour) and knowledge (technology) across international borders'.[2]

Benefits of globalisation

There are many aspects of globalisation that bring significant benefits, to both consumers and companies.

Historically, globalisation meant multinational companies locating many manufacturing jobs in developing countries, where they could take advantage of cheaper labour and hence keep their costs down and/or profits up. This in turn meant that consumers could benefit from lower prices, even though it inevitably resulted in an exodus of jobs from developed to developing countries.

Increasingly, firms are now also locating 'knowledge-based' jobs in developing countries, taking advantage of the improvements in the education and training that has taken place in countries such as China and India. Therefore, firms can now benefit from a massive number of well-trained and well-educated workers, who are still much cheaper to employ than their American or European counterparts.

Freer trade and more competition mean that countries and businesses within them are encouraged to think, plan and act globally, and this helps the spread of technology. This, in turn, means that more countries are able to specialise in particular products and processes and hence competitive advantages can be exploited. All of this contributes to faster economic growth and these benefits are felt by developing and developed countries alike.

Many developing nations have seen significant benefits from foreign investment, even though much of the output is exported to developed nations. Jobs are created, which helps to stimulate economic growth and wage rises, all of which help to generate increased consumption across the economy. Supporters of globalisation point to the decrease in the number of people living in extreme poverty. According to World Bank estimates, 10 per cent of the world's population lived on less than US$1.90 a day in 2015 compared to 35 per cent in 1990 (in 2011 prices).

Furthermore, supporters argue that globalisation has fostered closer political ties between the nations of the world, bringing us closer together and stabilising relationships. Globalisation has brought people many more experiences and opportunities, such as eating new food, new holiday destinations, greater access to a wide variety of entertainment and a better understanding of different cultures.

Costs of globalisation

However, for all the benefits of globalisation, critics claim that there are many losers and that the benefits are not equally spread between those who do gain. It may thus deepen inequalities.

While some countries benefit from investment, others are unable to attract it. Furthermore, once multinational companies are based in a developing nation, they can exploit cheaper labour and use this to increase their dominant position in a market. Increased competition does have many benefits, but it also increases the pressure on companies to cut costs and hence can lead to downward pressure on wages, often affecting those people who are already in the most vulnerable positions.

Critics also argue that by accelerating the pace of industrial change, globalisation has meant an often painful adjustment process for some nations, as they

---

Definitions

Globalisation The process whereby the world is becoming increasingly interconnected, economically, technologically, socially, politically, culturally and environmentally.

Economic globalisation The process whereby the economies of the world are becoming increasingly integrated.

---

[1] Angel Gurría, *Managing Globalisation and The Role of The OECD*, OECD (20 September 2006).
[2] IMF staff, *Globalization: A Brief Overview*, IMF (May 2008).

try to adapt to an international supply chain, and those working in or relying on traditional industries have suffered the consequences. Finance has also become more internationalised and there has been significant growth in loans to businesses and individuals. While this does bring benefits, we have seen the effects of unsustainable loans and the repercussions of volatile financial markets.

Furthermore, globalisation can also lead to significant environmental damage through pollution and the excessive use of natural resources. It can create an environment that is dominated by big brands in food, drink, TV, music, etc. Thus it is argued by critics that, rather than globalisation opening up the world to different cultures, Western culture is becoming the dominant one.

> **Pause for thought**
>
> *Using the STEEPLE categories, in what ways has the USA influenced the business environment in countries outside the USA?*

There are both benefits and costs to globalisation and supporters and critics both agree that the impact of it on different groups will never be equal. For many years, globalisation has been a seemingly unstoppable force, but more recently we have seen a rise in protectionist policy. Is the era of hyper-globalisation coming to an end? Clearly if it is, there will be important implications for businesses in terms of their markets, employees, costs and their overall strategy.

7.2 MULTINATIONAL CORPORATIONS

One of the outcomes and drivers of globalisation has been the development and growth of *multinational corporations* (MNCs), sometimes called *transnational corporations* (TNCs). The name itself points to the size and importance that such companies have in the global economy, but what exactly is an MNC? At the most basic level, it is a business that either owns or controls subsidiaries in more than one country. It is this ownership or control of productive assets in other countries that makes the MNC distinct from an enterprise that does business overseas by simply exporting goods or services.

In 1990, foreign subsidiaries of all MNCs had assets of $6.2 trillion and employed 28.6 million people, with sales of $7.1 trillion, equivalent to 30.4 per cent of global GDP. According to the 2019 World Investment Report (WIR),[3] by 2018 the foreign affiliates of all MNCs had assets of $110.5 trillion, employed 76 million people and had sales of $27.2 trillion, equivalent to 32.2 per cent of global GDP. Globalisation has had a huge role in increasing the presence and importance of MNCs. However, with the globalisation debate continuing and uncertainty prevalent across the world, concern by policymakers, especially in developing countries, is growing.

Diversity among MNCs

While all MNCs have overseas subsidiaries, this fails to reflect the immense diversity of them.

Size. Many, if not most, of the world's largest firms are multinationals. Indeed, the turnover of some of them exceeds the national income of many countries (see Table 7.1).

And yet there are also thousands of very small, often specialist multinationals, which are a mere fraction of the size of the giants. What is more, since the mid-1980s many large multinational businesses have been downsizing.

Organisational structure. As part of this downsizing, many MNCs have been shrinking the size of their headquarters, removing layers of bureaucracy to speed up decision making, and reorganising their global operations into smaller autonomous profit centres. Gone is the philosophy that big companies will inevitably do better than small ones.

In fact, it now appears that multinationals are seeking to create a hybrid form of business organisation, which combines the advantages of size (i.e. economies of scale) with the responsiveness and market knowledge of smaller firms. The key for the modern multinational is flexibility, and to be at one and the same time both global and local.

The nature of business. MNCs cover the entire spectrum of business activity, from manufacturing to extraction, agricultural production, chemicals, processing, service provision and finance. There is no 'typical' line of activity of a multinational.

> **Definition**
>
> **Multinational (or transnational) corporations** Businesses that either own or control foreign subsidiaries in more than one country.

---

[3] *World Investment Report 2018*, UNCTAD (June 2018).

Table 7.1	Comparison of the largest MNCs (by gross revenue) and selected countries (GDP), 2017	
MNC rank	Country or company (headquarters)	GDP ($bn) or gross revenue ($bn)
	USA	*19 485*
	China	*12 015*
	Japan	*4873*
	UK	*2628*
	Poland	*525*
1	Walmart, USA	500
	Thailand	*484*
	Austria	*417*
2	State Grid, China	349
3	Sinopec Group, China	327
4	China National Petroleum	326
5	Royal Dutch Shell, Netherlands	311
6	Toyota Motors, Japan	265
	Bangladesh	*262*
7	Volkswagen, Germany	260
	Finland	*253*
8	BP, UK	245
9	Exxon Mobil, USA	244
10	Berkshire Hathaway, USA	242
	Vietnam	*241*
11	Apple, USA	229
12	Samsung, South Korea	212
	New Zealand	*201*
	Greece	*201*
	Qatar	*167*
	Luxembourg	*63*
	Slovenia	*49*
	Iceland	*24*
	Jamaica	*15*
	Sierra Leone	*4*

Sources: Companies: Fortune Global 500 (http://fortune.com/global500/) 2018; Countries: World Economic Outlook database, IMF

Production locations. Some MNCs are truly 'global', with production located in a wide variety of countries and regions. Other MNCs, by contrast, locate in only one other region, or in a very narrow range of countries.

There are, however, several potentially constraining factors on the location of multinational businesses. For example, businesses concerned with the extraction of raw materials will locate as nature dictates! Businesses that provide luxury services will tend to locate in advanced or emerging countries, where the demand for such services is high or has high growth prospects. Others locate according to the resource intensity of the stage of production. Thus a labour-intensive stage might be located in a developing country where wage rates are relatively low. Another stage, which requires a high level of automation, might be located in an industrially advanced country that has the necessary technology and workforce skills.

Ownership patterns. As businesses expand overseas, they are faced with a number of options. They can decide to go it alone and create wholly owned subsidiaries. Alternatively, they might share ownership, and hence some of the risk, by establishing a joint venture with a foreign company. In such cases, the MNC might have a majority or minority stake in the overseas enterprise.

In certain countries, where MNC investment is regulated, many governments insist on owning or controlling a share in the new enterprise. Much of the time, it will depend on the type of business and how important it is to the host country. Although it still applies to only a small percentage of total MNCs, there has been a rise in state involvement in MNCs, where the government is a part owner of the company. It mainly occurs in capital-intensive industries, such as oil and gas.

Overseas business relative to total business. MNCs differ in respect of how extensive their overseas operations are relative to their total business. Just 24 per cent of Walmart's sales in 2017 came from overseas subsidiaries, while 87 per cent of Samsung's sales came from its foreign affiliates.

The above characteristics of MNCs reveal that they represent a wide and very diverse group of enterprises. Beyond sharing the common link of having production activities in more than one country, MNCs differ widely in the nature and forms of their overseas business, and in the relationship between the parent and its subsidiaries.

> **Pause for thought**
>
> *Given the diverse nature of multinational business, how useful is the definition given on page 177 for describing a multinational corporation?*

Trends in multinational investment

We can estimate the size of multinational investment by looking at figures for foreign direct investment (FDI). FDI represents the finance used either to purchase the assets for setting up a new subsidiary (or expanding an existing one), or to acquire an existing business operation through merger or acquisition.

In 1990, global FDI inflows were the equivalent of just 0.9 per cent of global GDP at $205 billion. In the decade that followed, but particularly between 1998 and 2000, FDI inflows increased significantly, such that by 2000, they were the equivalent of 4 per cent of global GDP. There was then another period of growth in FDI inflows between 2004 and 2007 and in both periods of growth, there was a surge in cross-border mergers and acquisitions (M&As). Between 1990 and 2000, there was a three-fold increase in the number and a ten-fold increase in the value of global M&As, with the value reaching $960 billion (2.8% of GDP) and by 2007, a new peak of over $1.03 trillion (1.8% of global GDP) was reached. Total FDI reached a peak of $1.89 trillion in 2007.

The period following the financial crisis saw a 20 per cent fall in global FDI inflows in both 2008 and 2009, with the value of cross-border M&As falling by 72 per cent to just $288 billion. The post-crisis period was marked by significant volatility in FDI flows. They had recovered somewhat by 2011, reaching $1.56 trillion, but then declined in 2013 and again in 2014 to reach $1.36. The value of global FDI flows then increased by 49.8 per cent in 2015 to reach a new peak of $2.03 trillion, but then fell in the following three years to reach $1.30 trillion in 2018. Consequently, by 2018, global inward FDI flows were 31 per cent below their 2007 level. You can see the trend in FDI flows in Figure 7.1.

FDI has historically been highly concentrated, with most flows going to developed countries, but the

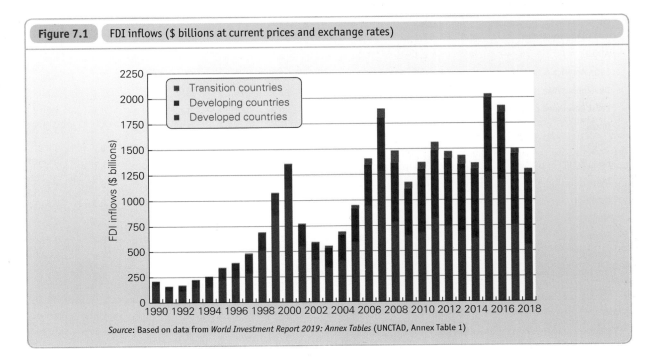

| Figure 7.1 | FDI inflows ($ billions at current prices and exchange rates) |

Source: Based on data from *World Investment Report 2019: Annex Tables* (UNCTAD, Annex Table 1)

proportion going to developing countries has been generally rising, as you can see in Figure 7.1 and in Table 7.2. In 2000, 82.5 per cent of world FDI flows went to developed countries, with only 17.1 per cent going to developing countries. Despite a fall in share between 1998 and 2000, developing and transitional (i.e. former communist) economies have seen rises in their share of global FDI in most years. By 2018, 57.0 per cent of global FDI went to developing and transitional economies.

As you can see from the table, the percentage of FDI going to individual nations has varied considerably and so has the value of FDI flows. The UK is one country where its value and share of global FDI flows has been particularly volatile since 2000. For example, between 2004 and 2009, the UK was the largest recipient in Europe of global FDI flows. At its peak in 2005, it received 19.3 per cent of global FDI flows at $182.9 billion. After 2009, the UK was overtaken by Germany, as its value of FDI flows fell to a low of

2.7 per cent ($42.2 billion) in 2011, with a further decline to 1.9 per cent in 2015. It then recovered in 2016, reaching 10.5 per cent of global FDI flows, only to fall to 6.8 per cent in 2017 and 5.0 per cent in 2018 with fears over the effects of Brexit.

Meanwhile, in Germany, FDI flows have been somewhat less volatile than in the UK since 2000, between −1.5 per cent and 9.1 per cent of global FDI. In France, they have fluctuated between −0.6 and 6.7 per cent; in the Netherlands, between −0.5 and 8.8 per cent and in Belgium, between −0.9 and 6.3 per cent. The percentage of global FDI flows that countries receive is largely driven by the prospects of the economy itself, while the size of the flows also depends on the state of the global economy. This is true of all countries, though the relative prospects of various regions, including economic uncertainty, political stability and access to/availability of resources do have an effect.

The USA has been the largest recipient of FDI and remained so in 2018 (the latest data currently

Table 7.2	Distribution of world FDI inflows, 1990–2018 (percentage of world FDI inflows)								
Region	1990–92	1993–97	1998–2000	2001–3	2004–7	2008–9	2010–11	2012–14	2015	2016–18
Developed counltries	**74.5**	**61.6**	**78.5**	**67.5**	**63.7**	**54.4**	**51.1**	**48.4**	**62.4**	**53.3**
Europe	49.6	35.3	48.1	47.3	42.6	30.0	30.3	24.9	35.2	24.8
Australia	3.3	2.0	0.7	1.5	1.7	2.9	3.3	4.1	1.4	3.1
France	10.0	6.2	3.6	2.4	2.1	2.6	1.6	1.2	2.2	1.9
Germany	1.1	2.1	7.8	6.1	2.9	1.3	4.6	1.1	2.0	1.8
Ireland	0.7	0.5	1.6	3.5	−1.0	0.5	2.3	3.5	10.7	−0.6
Japan	1.1	0.2	0.8	1.2	0.5	1.3	−0.1	0.4	0.1	0.8
UK	11.3	5.9	9.1	3.7	12.0	6.9	3.4	3.1	1.9	7.7
USA	16.7	20.2	24.9	14.3	14.7	16.4	14.6	14.1	23.0	21.2
Developing countries	**25.1**	**37.1**	**20.8**	**30.5**	**32.3**	**39.0**	**44.0**	**46.8**	**35.8**	**43.6**
Africa	2.0	2.1	1.1	2.8	2.7	4.4	3.2	3.8	2.8	2.8
Latin America & Caribbean	7.1	10.2	8.1	9.1	7.3	8.3	12.4	12.7	7.7	9.3
Developing Asia	15.8	24.8	11.6	18.6	22.2	26.2	28.4	30.1	25.3	31.4
Least developed countries	0.7	0.6	0.5	1.3	0.8	1.3	1.5	1.8	1.9	1.5
Brazil	0.8	1.9	3.1	2.5	1.8	2.6	6.0	4.8	2.4	3.9
China	3.8	11.4	4.4	8.2	6.5	7.7	8.2	8.8	6.7	8.6
Hong Kong	1.5	2.6	2.8	2.5	3.5	4.3	5.7	6.0	8.6	7.3
India	0.1	0.5	0.3	0.8	1.1	3.1	2.2	2.0	2.2	2.7
Malaysia	2.4	1.9	0.3	0.4	0.5	0.3	0.7	0.8	0.5	0.6
Singapore[1]	2.4	3.0	1.2	2.0	2.5	1.2	3.3	4.5	2.9	4.8
South Korea[1]	0.7	0.6	0.9	1.0	1.1	0.8	0.7	0.7	0.2	0.9
Mexico	2.4	2.8	1.5	3.8	2.4	1.8	1.8	2.3	1.8	2.0
Transition economies	**0.4**	**1.3**	**0.7**	**2.0**	**4.1**	**6.6**	**4.9**	**4.8**	**1.8**	**3.1**
Russia	0.2	0.6	0.3	0.8	2.3	3.7	2.3	2.6	0.6	1.6

Note: Shaded areas represent years of declining or weak global FDI; classifications based on UNCTAD country classifications
[1] In some datasets these countries are classified as developed countries.
Source: Based on data from *World Investment Report 2019: Annex Table 1* (UNCTAD)

available from UNCTAD), accounting for 19.4 per cent of global FDI inflows. Mainland China was second (10.7%) and Hong Kong the third (8.9%). The EU received 21.4 per cent of global FDI flows in 2018 (larger than the USA). Although FDI is now less concentrated than it has been, Sub-Saharan Africa still accounts for only 2.4 per cent of global FDI and much of this was to the resource-rich countries of Nigeria, Angola and South Africa.

Pause for thought

With the emergence of China, India and the CEECs, the position of some countries (such as the UK, Germany and other countries in Europe) as an attractive place for FDI has been under threat. What do you think the governments of such nations might do either to minimise FDI outflows or to attract a greater volume of FDI inflows?

RECAP

1. There is great diversity among multinationals in respect to size, nature of business, size of overseas operations, location, ownership and organisational structure.

2. Foreign direct investment (FDI) tends to fluctuate with the ups and downs of the world economy. Over the years, however, FDI has accounted for a larger and larger proportion of total investment.

3. Inflows of FDI were traditionally highly concentrated in the developed world, but the share received by developing economies has been increasing and overtook that of developed countries in 2014.

4. The share and value of FDI flows depends on the prospects of individual economies and the state of the global economy. The USA has remained the largest individual recipient of FDI, followed by China.

BOX 7.1 — CROSS-BORDER MERGER ACTIVITY

An international perspective

With increased globalisation, cross-border M&As are becoming more common and data indicate that in some countries these deals are now more frequent than deals where one domestic company merges with another one.

Cross-border M&As can be crucial for a firm looking to gain rapid entry into an overseas market and there has been increased activity both within and between developed and developing economies. But, what have been the trends, patterns and driving factors in mergers and acquisitions (M&As) around the world in recent years, especially as the process of globalisation has accelerated?

The 1990s

The early years of the 1990s saw relatively low M&A activity as the world was in recession, but as world economic growth picked up, so worldwide M&A activity increased. Economic growth was particularly rapid in the USA, which became the major target for acquisitions.

With the dismantling of trade barriers and increased financial deregulation, globalisation accelerated and with this came increased competition. Companies felt the need to become bigger in order to compete more effectively.

In Europe, M&A activity was boosted by the development of the Single Market, which came into being in January 1993. Companies took advantage of the abolition of trade barriers in the EU, which made it cheaper and easier for them to operate on an EU-wide basis. As 1999 approached, and with it the arrival of the euro, so European merger activity reached fever pitch, stimulated also by the strong economic growth experienced throughout the EU.

By 2000, annual worldwide M&A activity was some three times the level of the beginning of the 1990s. There were some very large mergers, including a $67 billion merger of

pharmaceutical companies Zeneca of the UK and Astra of Sweden in 1998, a $183 billion takeover of telecoms giant Mannesmann of Germany by Vodafone of the UK in 1999 and a $40.3 billion takeover of Orange of the UK by France Telecom in 2000.

Other sectors in which merger activity was rife included financial services and the privatised utilities sector. In the UK in particular, most of the privatised water and electricity companies were taken over, with buyers attracted by the sector's monopoly profits. French and US buyers were prominent.

The 2000s

The decade from 2000 saw fluctuations in the value and number of mergers and acquisitions as the state of the economy changed and the period in particular saw a change in the worldwide pattern of M&A activity. Whilst this predominantly involved a company in a neighbouring country, or a country that is a traditional trading partner, increasingly both European and US companies looked to other parts of the world to expand their activities.

The number of net cross-border deals[1] peaked at 6497 in 2000 and had a combined total value of $960 billion. However, a worldwide economic slowdown after 2000 led to a fall in both the number and value of mergers throughout most of the world. The value of cross-border M&As in 2003 was $165 billion – a fall of 82.8 per cent from the peak of three years earlier. Activity began to increase again after

---

[1] Net cross-border mergers and acquisitions are calculated considering sales of companies in a host economy to foreign MNCs. It excludes sales of foreign affiliates (already owned by foreign MNCs) to other foreign MNCs. Divestments (sales of foreign affiliates to domestic firms) are subtracted from the value (number).

▶

2003 as economic growth in the world economy began to accelerate. Two major target regions were (a) the 10 countries that joined the EU in 2004 plus Russia and (b) Asian countries, especially India and China.

In 2007 the number of cross-border mergers reached a new peak of 7582 with a combined total value of over $1.03 trillion. However, the recession of 2008–9 led to both the number and value of cross-border deals falling dramatically. Recession is a difficult time for deal making and the number of withdrawn mergers – that is, where two firms agree in principle to merge but later pull out of a deal – increased. As chart (a) shows, the value of cross-border M&As in 2009 was just $288 billion – a fall of 72 per cent from the record high in 2007. With the USA economy performing well, the value of M&A activity grew in 2018, despite worries about a trade war between the USA and China and continuing concerns over Brexit. The value rose 17.6 per cent to $816 billion, but the number fell slightly from 6967 to 6821.

The 2010s

With the faltering recovery of 2010 there was a small increase in global M&As. However, the eurozone crisis and fears about the state of the public finances of the USA had a negative impact on M&A activity in 2012 and 2013.

Economic growth and growing business confidence saw M&A activity grow quickly again in 2015 and 2016. The combined market value of cross-border deals in these two years was $735 billion and $887 billion respectively – the highest values since the financial crisis. The ability of firms to borrow money cheaply, because of historically low interest rates, slow rates of internal growth and large cash reserves were seen as important drivers behind this increase. A large number of mergers also appear to be defensive moves by firms facing the threat of new competition from Amazon, Facebook and Netflix.

Given the uncertainty generated by the Brexit vote in the UK and the election of President Trump in the USA, many observers were surprised to see relatively strong performance in merger activity in 2016. However, despite a small rise in the number of deals in 2017, the value of them fell by 22 per cent to $694 billion.

A changing pattern of M&As

We have a seen a big change in the pattern of cross-border M&A activity since the 1990s and in chart (b), you can see three interesting trends in regional M&A activity when comparing the period from 1993 to 1997 with that from 2013 to 2018:

- North America's global share of cross-border M&As rose from 20.7 per cent in the mid-1990s to 25.5 per cent in the mid-2010s. Its share measured by value also increased, from 19.8 per cent to 34.9 per cent. However, this was caused by it having an unusually high share of cross-border M&A activity by value of 43.4 per cent in 2015, 42.3 per cent in 2016 and 43.1 per cent in 2017. In 2013 and 2014, its average share by value was just 18.6 per cent.
- Asian countries (excluding Japan) saw a dramatic increase in their share of the number of cross-border M&As from 8.3 per cent in the mid-1990s to 12.8 per cent in the mid-2010s. Their share by value increased from 3.2 per cent to 10.6 per cent. China and India have been particularly attractive places because of their fast-growing economies and lower costs, including cheaper labour and tax rates. Also, these countries have become more receptive to all forms of FDI, including M&As. However, M&A investment in both countries fell significantly in 2015. It fell from $56.8 billion to $12.4 billion in China and $7.9 billion to $1.3 billion in India. The downward trend continued in China, falling to $11.1 billion in 2016, $8.3 billion in 2017 and $7.6 billion in 2018, whereas in India it rebounded back up to $8.0 billion in 2016, $22.8 billion in 2017 and $33.2 billion in 2018.
- EU countries have seen a reduction in their share of the number of cross-border M&As from 50.9 per cent in the mid-1990s to 42.1 per cent in the mid-2010s; and a fall in their share of the value from 42.1 to 37.6 per cent over the same period.

Looking ahead

The 2019 World Investment Report[2] forecast that global investment was expected to increase in 2019 as expectations rebounded from the low levels of the previous year. Nevertheless, the growth in FDI would be a modest 10 per cent (to around $1.5 trillion). This was because of a weak long-term

[2] *World Investment Report 2019* (June 2019).

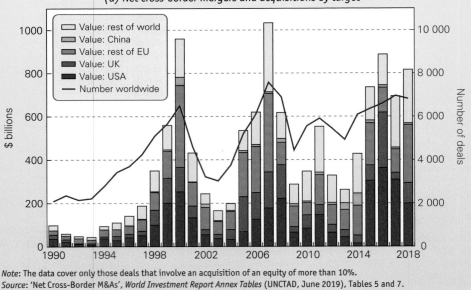

(a) Net cross-border mergers and acquisitions by target

Note: The data cover only those deals that involve an acquisition of an equity of more than 10%.

Source: 'Net Cross-Border M&As', *World Investment Report Annex Tables* (UNCTAD, June 2019), Tables 5 and 7.

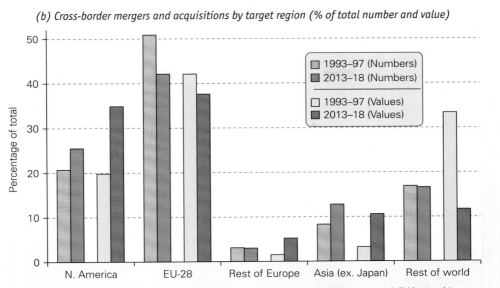

(b) Cross-border mergers and acquisitions by target region (% of total number and value)

Source: 'Cross Border Mergers & Acquisitions' *World Investment Report Annex Tables* (UNCTAD, June 2019), Tables 5 and 7.

underlying FDI trend and because of various risks. These include trade tensions between the USA and other countries, such as China and the EU, and a growth in protectionist sentiments in the USA and elsewhere. In addition long-term projections for global economic growth remained subdued.

Over the longer term, FDI growth is expected to be subdued. There are several reasons for this, including growing restrictions on foreign ownership in various developing countries, a decline in the global average rate of return on FDI (down from 8 per cent in 2010 to 6.8 per cent in 2018 and set to decline further) and structural changes in industry that involve the 'adoption of digital technologies in global supply chains across many industries, causing a shift towards intangibles and increasingly asset-light forms of international production, as reaching global markets and exploiting efficiencies from cross-border operations no longer requires heavy asset footprints'.[3]

The emergence of developing and transition economies has had an impact in many areas and their growing importance in the share of cross-border M&As cannot be understated. The host economy for the majority of cross-border M&As is a developed economy, but the size of that majority has been declining. In the early 1990s, developed countries were the destination of between 85 and 95 per cent (by value) of

cross-border M&As. By 2014, this had fallen to 68.5 per cent, though it has since risen to lie at 84.4 per cent in 2018.

The origin of M&A activity has also been changing and this trend is expected to continue. Following the financial crisis, investors from developing and transition economies became an increasingly important source of global M&A activity. From 2000 to 2008, around 14 per cent of M&As (by value) typically originated from these economies. In the period from 2009 to 2014 this rose to 33 per cent and was as high as 49 per cent in 2013. It then fell back to stand at 12 per cent in 2018 as FDI from developed countries increased once more. Looking ahead, the role of developing and transition economies will continue to evolve and their importance as both the host and origin economy is likely to grow.

1. *Are the motives for merger likely to be different in a recession from in a period of rapid economic growth?*
2. *What factors might explain the significance of developing and transition economies, not only as a destination for FDI, but also increasingly as a source of FDI?*

Use newspaper and other resources to identify the costs and benefits of a recent cross-border merger or acquisition.

[3] *Ibid.* p.15

7.3 BUSINESS STRATEGY IN A GLOBAL ECONOMY

The global marketplace can provide massive opportunities for firms to expand: access to new markets, new customers, new supply sources, new ideas and skills. At the same time, the growth of multinationals presents major competitive threats to domestic firms, as new market entrants from abroad arrive with lower costs, innovative products and marketing, or some other core competence which the domestic firm finds difficult to match. In this section we explore the

strategic implications for business in facing up to the global economic system.

Types of multinational expansion

As we saw in section 6.3, businesses can look to expand in one of two ways: through either internal or external expansion. MNCs are no exception to this rule. They can expand overseas, either by creating a new production facility from scratch (such as Nissan in the north-east of England), or by merging with or taking over existing foreign producers (such as the acquisition of Asda by Wal-Mart or of Jaguar by Ford). They can also engage in an international strategic alliance. Examples include the joint venture in 2006 between Finland's Nokia and Japan's Sanyo to produce mobile phones for the North American market, the 2014 alliance between Spotify and Uber to allow people to access their Spotify accounts from Uber cars via the Uber app, and the 2009 alliance between Fiat and Chrysler to share distribution channels and technology.

We need also to distinguish between horizontal, vertical or conglomerate expansion.

- *Horizontally integrated multinational.* This type of multinational seeks to produce essentially the same product in different countries (but perhaps with some variations in product specification to suit the needs and tastes of the local market). The primary objective of this strategy is to achieve growth by expanding into new markets, as shown by cell C in the growth vector matrix in Figure 3.4 on page 75.
- *Vertically integrated multinational.* In this case, the multinational undertakes the various stages of production in different countries. Thus in some countries it will go backwards into the business's supply chain to the components or raw materials stages, and in others it will go forwards into the product's assembly or distribution. Oil companies such as Shell and Exxon Mobil (Esso) are good examples of vertically integrated multinationals, undertaking in a global operation the extraction of crude oil, controlling its transportation, refining it and producing by-products, and controlling the retail sale of petrol and other oil products. The principal motive behind such a growth strategy is to be able to exert greater control over costs and reduce the uncertainty of the business environment.
- *Conglomerate multinational.* Such multinationals produce a range of different products in different countries. By this process of diversification, conglomerate multinationals look to spread risks, and maximise returns through the careful buying of overseas assets. Unilever is a good example of a conglomerate multinational. It employs over 165 000 people in over 190 countries, producing various food, home care and personal care products, which are sold in more than 170 countries. It has around 400 brands, 14 of which generate sales in excess of €1 billion a year. These brands include Wall's, Carte D'Or and Ben & Jerry's ice cream; Knorr soups; Bovril and Marmite; Colmans' mustard; Hellman's mayonnaise; Lipton and PG Tips tea; Domestos, Cif, Persil and Comfort; Timotei and TRESemmé shampoos; VO5, Toni and Guy and Brylcreem hair products; Vaseline, Dove and Simple soaps; Pond's skin care products; Impulse, Lynx, Sure and Brut fragrances and antiperspirants.

We do also see joint ventures being formed by multinationals for projects where risks and development costs are high. This is particularly true for large MNCs. A good example is the decision by Sony and Panasonic in 2014 to join forces with Innovation Network Corporation of Japan (INCJ) and Japan Display Inc. (JDI) to set up a new company, JOLED Inc. to develop and produce OLED displays for tablets and laptops.

As noted at the beginning of section 7.2, MNCs are a diverse group of enterprises and we can distinguish between their different motives for going abroad. Some MNCs use their multinational base primarily as a means of reducing costs (vertically integrated multinationals), whereas others use it primarily to achieve growth (horizontal and conglomerate multinationals). Let us now consider how, by going multinational, such goals might be achieved.

Going global to reduce costs

The costs and availability of labour and other resources. Nations, like individuals, are not equally endowed with resources. Some nations are rich in labour, some in capital and some in raw materials. In general, the more plentiful a resource, the lower will be its cost. Multinationals take advantage of this. For example, they might locate labour-intensive activities, such as an assembly plant, in low-wage developing countries, but complex R&D operations in countries with the necessary technology and skilled labour. It is factors such as this which give MNCs a competitive advantage over purely national firms.

Cost differences between countries are ruthlessly exploited by Nike, the American sportswear manufacturer. An example is given in a *Portland Business Journal* article, which looks at the cost of making a

---

Definitions

Horizontally integrated multinational A multinational that produces the same product in many different countries.

Vertically integrated multinational A multinational that undertakes the various stages of production for a given product in different countries.

Conglomerate multinational A multinational that produces different products in different countries.

pair of sneakers (trainers!).[4] Nike has organised itself globally such that it can respond rapidly to changing cost conditions in its international subsidiaries. Its product development operations are carried out in the USA, but all of its production operations are sub-contracted out to over 40 overseas locations, mostly in South and South-East Asia. If wage rates, and hence costs rise in one host country, then production is simply transferred to a lower-cost subsidiary. Another example is Gap Inc., which is examined in Case Study A.1 on the book's website.

Pause for thought

1. *Before reading on, try to identify ways in which locating production overseas might help to reduce costs.*
2. *Identify some of the potential strengths and weaknesses of businesses having their value chains located in a variety of different countries.*

As businesses relocate many dimensions of their value chain, the structure and organisation of the business takes on a web-like appearance, with its various operations being spread throughout the world. The key thing for a company's headquarters is having the information about their costs and the costs of its subsidiaries, so that production can simply follow the movements in market forces.

The quality of inputs. The location of multinational operations does not depend simply on factor *prices*; it also depends on the *quality* of resources. For example, a country might have a highly skilled or highly industrious workforce, and it is this, rather than simple wage rates, that attracts multinational investment. The issue here is still largely one of costs. Highly skilled workers might cost more to employ *per hour,* but if their productivity is higher, they might well cost less to employ *per unit of output.* Take the case of Nike again. Product innovation and research, along with marketing and promotion, are all undertaken in the USA, which has a cost advantage in these areas, not through lower wage rates, but through experience and skills.

If a country has both lower-priced resources and high-quality resources, it will be very attractive to multinational investors. In recent years, the UK government has sought to attract multinational investment through its lower labour costs and more flexible employment conditions than those of its European rivals, while still having a relatively highly trained labour force compared with those in developing countries. However, as the relocation of many call-centre and IT jobs to developing countries shows, such advantages are disappearing fast in many sectors. Though here it is worth noting that, due to many customer complaints, a number of large companies have brought their call centres back to the UK, including BT, Santander and EE.

Entrepreneurial and managerial skills. Managers in MNCs are often more innovative in the way they do business and organise the value chain than managers of domestic firms. In some cases, this is essential. With the arrival of Japanese multinationals in the UK, it became instantly apparent that Japanese managers conducted business in a very different way from their British counterparts. The most fundamental difference concerned working practices, such as the use of quality circles. Japanese MNCs quickly established themselves as among the most efficient and productive businesses in the UK (see section 8.5 on the flexible firm) and this made it necessary for UK firms to respond.

Cost reductions through 'learning by doing'. This is where skills and productivity improve with experience. Such learning effects apply not only to workers in production, sales, distribution, etc., but also to managers, who learn to develop more efficient forms of organisation. When a firm expands globally, there may be more scope for learning by doing. For example, if a firm employs low-cost labour in developing countries, initially the lower cost per worker will, to some extent, be offset by lower productivity. As learning by doing takes place and productivity increases, these initial small cost advantages may become much more substantial.

Economies of scale. By increasing the scale of its operation, and by each plant in each country specialising in a particular part of the value chain, the multinational may be able to gain substantial economies of scale.

MNCs are likely to invest heavily in R&D in an attempt to maintain their global competitiveness. The global scale of their operations allows them to spread the costs of this R&D over a large output (i.e. the R&D has a low average fixed cost). MNCs, therefore, are often world leaders in process innovation and product development.

Reducing transactions costs. By setting up an overseas subsidiary (as opposed merely to exporting to that country), the MNC can save on the transactions costs of arranging a contract with an overseas import agent or with a firm in the host country to make the product under licence. Many firms go through a sequence from exporting to overseas investment. Nissan, for example, exported its cars to the UK using local motor vehicle retailers to distribute them

---

[4] Matthew Kish, 'The cost breakdown of a $100 pair of sneakers', *Portland Business Journal* (19 December 2014).

prior to establishing a greenfield manufacturing site in the North East of England in 1984. Toyota and Honda entered the UK in the same way.

Transport costs. A business locating production overseas would be able to reduce transport costs if those overseas plants served local or regional markets, or used local raw materials.

Government policies. One of the biggest cost advantages concerns the avoidance of tariffs (customs duties). If a country imposes tariffs on imports, then, by locating within that country (i.e. behind the 'tariff wall'), the MNC gains a competitive advantage over its rivals which are attempting to import their products from outside the country, and which are thus having to pay the tariff. MNCs may, therefore, be able to pass their cost savings on to consumers in the form of lower prices, or maintain prices and increase their profit margins. These, in turn, could be used for R&D. Following the UK vote to exit the EU, the tariff negotiations for trade with EU countries are of paramount importance for businesses located in the UK. As we have already seen, the outcome of these negotiations will be a key factor influencing firms' decisions about their location.

Costs might also be reduced as a result of various government incentives to attract inward investment. Examples include: favourable tax rates, substantial depreciation allowances and the provision of subsidised premises. Such cost-cutting incentives may help to reduce the fixed costs of the investment and hence reduce its risk.

In highly competitive global markets, even small cost savings might mean the difference between success and failure. Thus MNCs will be constantly searching for ways of minimising costs and locating production where the greatest advantage might be gained.

Going global to access new markets

International markets can offer businesses massive new opportunities for growth and expansion. Such markets would be particularly attractive to a business where domestic growth opportunities are limited as a result of either the maturity of the market or shifting consumer tastes. The global financial crisis affected many developed countries particularly harshly and, as a consequence, developing countries saw an increase in the FDI from investors in both developed and developing countries. The more buoyant economic conditions in many of these nations presented investors with an opportunity to access new markets and take advantage of more stable economic circumstances. In addition to the possibility of extra sales, expanding into new markets offers other advantages:

Spreading risks. One of the main advantages of a larger and more diverse market is to spread risks. The firm is no longer tied to the specific market conditions of one particular country or region. As such, falling sales in one region of the global economy might be effectively offset by increased sales elsewhere. We have seen this in the brewery industry and particularly in a range of German and Japanese businesses, including Toyota and Honda. This strategy was successful as companies were able to sustain their profitability despite slumps in key markets.

Exploiting competitive advantages in new markets. The multinational's superior technology, superior-quality products and more effective marketing may allow it to compete particularly effectively in markets that, up until now, have been dominated by domestic producers.

Learning from experience in diverse markets. Successful businesses will learn from their global operations, copying or amending production techniques, organisation, marketing, etc. from one country to another as appropriate. In other words, they can draw lessons from experiences in one country for use in another.

Increasingly it seems that the globalisation of business is like a game of competitive leapfrog, with businesses having to look overseas in order to maintain their competitive position in respect to their rivals. A fiercely competitive global environment, in which small cost differences or design improvements can mean the difference between business success and failure, ensures that strategic thinking within a global context is high on the business agenda.

The product life cycle and the multinational

By shifting production overseas at a particular point in the product's life cycle, the business is able to reduce costs and maintain competitiveness. The product life cycle hypothesis was discussed in section 5.6 (pages 141–3). However, it is worth reviewing its elements here in order to identify how an MNC, by altering the geographical production of a good, might extend its profitability.

A product's life cycle can be split into four phases: launch, growth, maturity and decline. These were shown in Figure 5.11 (page 142).

The launch phase. This will tend to see the new product developed and produced in the same economy and then exported to the rest of the world. At this stage of the product's life cycle, the novelty of the product and the monopoly position of the producer enable the business to charge high prices and make high profits.

| BOX 7.2 | ATTRACTING FOREIGN INVESTORS |

The Global Opportunity Index

In the past, UNCTAD has published both an FDI Attraction Index and an FDI Potential Index, which gave different measures of the relative attractiveness of different countries for FDI. Today, there is a Country Attractiveness Index, authored by Ben Jelili Riadh, which ranks 109 countries.

Since 2013, the Milken Institute has published a Global Opportunity Index (GOI), which ranks nations according to their attractiveness to foreign multinationals. The index provides some interesting insights into the changing pattern of FDI flows and provides useful information to both companies and countries. For companies it provides information on which countries are the most attractive in terms of low costs, including low taxes, good protection for business, strong economic performance and good returns. For countries it provides guidance as to how they can implement government policy in the most effective way to attract more investment.

The January 2019 report presented the GOI of 147 countries.[1] The methodology tracked their performance based on 51 variables aggregated under five categories. Each variable is measured on a scale of 0 to 10, with 10 being the best scenario. Within each category, each variable is given equal weight and then aggregated. The categories are:

- *Business Perception*: this measures the explicit and implicit costs associated with business operations, such as tax burden and transparency.
- *Financial Services*: this measures the size of and access to financial services in a country by considering the country's infrastructure and access to credit.

[1] See the Milken Institute's IFM website at http://globalopportunityindex.org/opportunity.taf?page=rankings and the report: Claude Lopez and Jonathon Adams-Kane, Global Opportunity Index 2018: Emerging G20 Countries and Capital Flow Reversal, Milken Institute (January 2019).

Global opportunity index ranking 2018

GOI Ranking	Country	Business Perception	Financial Services	Institutional Framework	Economic Fundamentals	International Standards and Policy
1	Hong Kong*	1	3	3	3	16
2	Singapore*	4	7	5	8	17
3	Netherlands*	12	13	18	6	10
4	Australia	8	1	14	34	3
5	UK	10	5	4	40	7
9	Canada	22	2	2	43	12
12	Belgium*	13	18	20	41	1
15	South Korea	3	11	24	20	38
17	USA	11	17	7	46	22
18	Germany	18	39	21	31	4
19	Japan	7	4	23	59	23
23	Estonia*	29	54	19	9	19
26	France	15	30	25	64	26
34	Chile*	64	37	36	58	14
40	China	33	14	73	28	83
48	Saudi Arabia	89	43	43	53	43
55	Russia	54	32	80	47	88
61	Mexico	58	53	72	68	66
63	India	112	65	33	72	44
67	South Africa	61	9	28	124	120
74	Turkey	71	66	92	62	96
95	Brazil	137	29	88	145	69
111	Nigeria*	57	125	83	141	115
123	Uganda*	100	124	111	144	102
133	Chad*	146	147	139	138	40
141	Zimbabwe*	144	116	121	131	134
147	Sudan*	132	140	147	142	141

Source: Based on *Global Opportunity Index* (IFM Milken Institute, 2019)
Note: * denotes a non-G20 country

▶

- *Institutional Framework*: this measures the extent to which an individual country's institutions provide a supportive framework to businesses.
- *Economic Fundamentals*: this indicates the current economic strength of a country vis-à-vis the global economic outlook. It focuses on the country's macroeconomic performance, trade openness, quality and structure of the labour force and modern infrastructure.
- *International Standards and Policy*: this reflects the extent to which a country's institutions, policies and legal system facilitate international integration by following international standards.

The rankings

The table shows the *overall* GOI ranking for a selection of G20 and non-G20 countries in 2018.

The Netherlands is now the top country in Europe, having overtaken the UK, while the top nation from Latin America is Chile, placed 34th and from Africa is Botswana, placed 51st. Nations from the Asia–Pacific region continue to feature towards the top of the rankings, with six nations in the top 20 (Hong Kong placed 1st, Singapore 2nd, Australia 4th, New Zealand 8th, South Korea 15th and Japan 19th).

Despite the growth in the share of FDI going to developing economies, many lag behind developed economies in two key

areas: Business Perception and the Institutional Framework. This especially applies to the least developed countries.

Key issues seem to be the perception of the cost of doing business, issues of corruption and those surrounding the labour market and the legal system. There also appear to be concerns about access to financial data, inadequate financial accounting and auditing, the efficacy of the legal system and the protection available to investors, such as property rights and corporate governance.

Therefore, while developing and transition economies have made progress in attracting FDI, the top spots are still dominated by the developed world and the bottom is comprised of developing nations, largely those in Africa. There is clearly a long way to go for this region to become as attractive as the developed world.

? *What measures might a country adopt to improve its attractiveness to foreign investors?*

🔍 *Undertake a literature search based around the determinants of Foreign Direct Investment. Write a short literature review summarising your findings.*

The growth phase. As the market begins to grow, other producers will seek to copy or imitate the new product. Hence supply increases and prices begin to fall. In order to maintain competitiveness, the business will look to reduce costs, and at this stage might consider shifting production overseas to lower cost production centres.

Maturity. At the early stage of maturity, the business is still looking to sell its product in the markets of the developed economies. Thus it may still be happy to locate some of its plants in such economies. As the original market becomes increasingly saturated, however, the MNC will seek to expand into markets abroad which are at an earlier stage of development. Part of this expansion will be by the MNC simply exporting to more of these economies, but increasingly it will involve relocating its production there too.

Maturity and decline. By the time the original markets are fully mature and moving into decline, the only way to extend the product's life may be to cut costs and sell the product in the markets of developing countries. The location of production may shift once again, this time to even lower cost countries. By this stage, the country in which the product was developed will almost certainly be a net importer (if there is a market left for the product), but it may well be importing the product from a subsidiary of the same company that produced it within that country in the first place!

Thus the product life cycle model explains how firms might first export and then engage in FDI. It explains how firms transfer production to different locations to reduce costs and enable profits to be made from a product that could have become unprofitable if its production had continued from its original production base.

RECAP

1. Why businesses go multinational depends largely on the nature of their business and their corporate strategy. Two of the major reasons are (a) reducing costs by locating production where inputs are cheaper and/or more productive; (b) accessing markets in other countries in order to achieve growth in sales.

2. MNC investment is often governed by the product life cycle. In this theory, a business will shift production around the world seeking to reduce costs and extend a given product's life. The phases of a product's life will be conducted in different countries. As the product nears maturity and competition grows, reducing costs to maintain competitiveness will force business to locate production in low-cost markets, such as developing economies.

BOX 7.3   GROCERS GO GLOBAL

International expertise plus local knowledge – a winning combination?

In Carrefour's Chinese stores, you will see a fresh snake counter alongside the fish department! Walmart boasts that in its Chinese stores you can find local delicacies such as whole roasted pigs and live frogs. Are fresh snakes and live frogs what's needed to succeed in China? It would seem so. Global companies thinking local, customising themselves to each market, is increasingly seen as the key to success in Asia and elsewhere around the world.

The expansion of European and American supermarkets into countries around the world has been underway for a number of years. Driven by stagnant markets at home with limited growth opportunities, the major players, such as Walmart from the USA, Carrefour and Casino from France, Tesco in the UK, Ahold from Holland and Metro from Germany, have been looking to expand their overseas operations – but with mixed success.

Eastern expansion

In recent times, Asia has been the market's growth sector, with China a particular attraction. In the five years to 2013, the Chinese supermarket sector grew at an average annual rate of 12.3 per cent, although the rate has slowed slightly since.

Other countries have also seen foreign retailers moving in. Tesco entered the Thai market in 1998. Tesco Lotus, the company's regional subsidiary, is now the country's number one retailer. In 2019 it had over 1700 stores across Thailand, employing more than 50 000 people. Carrefour and Walmart have also opened hundreds of new outlets within the region over the past few years. Walmart also owns Seiyu, the major Japanese group of supermarkets, shopping centres and department stores.

The advantages that international retailers have over their domestic competitors are expertise in systems, distribution, the range of products and merchandising. However, given the distinctive nature of markets within Asia, businesses must learn to adapt to local conditions. Joint ventures and local knowledge are seen as the key ingredients to success.

The changing market in Asia

With the rapid expansion of hypermarkets throughout Asia, the retail landscape is undergoing revolutionary change. With a wide range of products all under one roof, from groceries to pharmaceuticals to white goods, and at cut-rate prices, local neighbourhood stores stand little chance in the competitive battle. 'Mom and pop operations have no economies of scale.' As well as local retailers, local suppliers are also facing a squeeze on profits, as hypermarkets demand lower prices and use their buying power as leverage.

Such has been the dramatic impact these stores have had upon the retail and grocery sector that a number of Asian economies, such as Malaysia and Thailand, have introduced restrictions on the building of new outlets.

China, one of the toughest markets to enter, had restricted foreign companies to joint venture arrangements until 2004. Tesco's answer to these restrictions was to go into a 50:50 partnership with Taiwanese food supplier Ting Hsin. Initially, the stores were not the Tesco supermarkets with which customers in the UK are familiar. Instead, they had an orange colour scheme and few brands that the average British shopper would recognise. In 2006 Tesco increased its stake to 90 per cent and with this came the familiar Tesco branding.

Since 2004, there has been considerable expansion by global retailers in China. By mid-2015, Carrefour, the biggest international retailer in the Chinese market had over 230 hypermarkets, having had just 24 in 2000. By 2018, it had 466 stores in Asia, including 370 hypermarkets.

Eastern challenges

However, the expansion into China and other Asian markets has not been without difficulties for global retailers. Tesco entered the traditionally closed market of Japan in 2003 and by 2010, it had opened 128 stores, employing 3604 people. However, Tesco decided to leave Japan in 2012, after nine years in the market.[1] In 2014, Carrefour announced that it was leaving India, less than four years after having opened its first store in the country, blaming underperformance, due, in part, to being required to make infrastructure investment and source many of its products locally.[2]

Even in markets like China the pace of expansion is tending to slow. In May 2014, Tesco completed the establishment of a joint venture with state-run China Resources Enterprise (CRE).[3] This left Tesco owning 20 per cent of the business and CRE 80 per cent. The venture brought together Tesco's 131 stores in China with CRE's nearly 3000 outlets.

With relatively slower economic growth in China and complex local market conditions, Tesco, Carrefour and Walmart did begin to pull back on their global expansions and although they are continuing, it is at a slower rate. Philip Clarke, Tesco's CEO said about China:

> It's more of a marathon than a sprint. Many retailers putting down more space in the market; few seeing that translate into profitable growth.[4]

A Bloomberg industry analyst added:

> The rate of same-store sales increases is not what they [chains] were expecting it to be. The rate of addition of capacity has probably exceeded the growth of the market.[5]

? *What are the advantages and disadvantages to developing countries of the expansion of global supermarket chains?*

🔍 *Undertake desktop research on developments in the supermarket sector in a country of your choice. Prepare a short PowerPoint presentation to summarise these developments and the reasons for them.*

---

[1] 'Tesco to leave Japanese market after nine years', *BBC News* (18 June 2012).

[2] 'Carrefour to exit India Business', *BBC News* (8 July 2014).

[3] 'Tesco completes the establishment of Joint Venture with CRE', *Tesco News Release* (29 May 2014).

[4] 'Tesco stumbles with Wal-Mart as China shoppers buy local', *Bloomberg* (19 October 2012).

[5] Ibid.

7.4 PROBLEMS FACING MULTINATIONALS

In the vast majority of cases, businesses go multinational for sound business and economic reasons, which we have outlined above. However, multinational corporations may face a number of problems resulting from their geographical expansion:

- *Language barriers.* The problem of working in different languages is a barrier that the MNC must overcome. English is widely spoken throughout the business world, especially in developed countries, thus the extent of the language barrier may depend on the characteristics of the host country and how common a language English actually is. Further, if an MNC tends to employ expatriates, communication will be more difficult with local staff, who may feel alienated and thus be less productive.

- *Selling and marketing in foreign markets.* Strategies that work at home might fail overseas, given wide social and cultural differences. Many US multinationals, such as McDonald's and Coca-Cola, are frequently accused of imposing American values in the design and promotion of their products, irrespective of the country and its culture. This can lead to resentment and hostility in the host country, which may ultimately backfire on the MNC.

- *Attitudes of host governments.* Governments will often try to get the best possible deal for their country from multinationals. This could result in governments insisting on part ownership in the subsidiary (either by themselves or by domestic firms), or tight rules and regulations governing the MNC's behaviour, or harsh tax regimes. In response, the MNC can always threaten to locate elsewhere.

- *Communication and coordination between subsidiaries.* Diseconomies of scale may result from an expanding global business. Lines of communication become longer and more complex, especially when language is an issue. These problems are likely to be greater, the greater is the attempted level of control exerted by the parent company, i.e. the more the parent company attempts to conduct business as though the subsidiaries were regional branches. Multinational organisational structures where international subsidiaries operate largely independently of the parent company will tend to minimise such problems.

Within any global strategy there will be a degree of economic and political risk. However, as MNCs look to invest more in developing economies or emerging markets such as China, this risk will increase, as there are more and more uncertainties. However, it is often within emerging markets that the greatest returns are achieved. It is essentially this trade-off between potential returns and risk that a firm needs to consider in its strategic decisions (see Box 7.4).

A global business will need a strategy for effectively embracing foreign cultures and traditions in its working practices, and for devising an efficient global supply chain. Some businesses may be more suited to deal with such global issues than others.

The global strategy trade-off

A firm's drive to reduce costs and enhance profitability by embracing a global strategy is tempered by one critical consideration – the need to meet the very different demands of customers in foreign markets. To minimise costs, a firm may seek to standardise its product and its operations throughout the world. However, to meet foreign buyers' needs and respond to local market conditions, a firm may be required to differentiate both its product and its operations, such as marketing. In such cases, customisation will *add* to costs and generate a degree of duplication within the business. If a business is required to respond to local market conditions in many different markets, it might be faced with significantly higher costs. But if it fails to take into account the uniqueness of the market in which it wishes to sell, it may lose market share.

The trade-off between the cost reduction and local responsiveness can be a key strategic consideration for a firm to take into account when selling or producing overseas. As a general rule we will tend to find that cost pressures will be greatest in those markets where price is the principal competitive weapon. Where product differentiation is high, and attributes such as quality or some other non-price factor predominates within the competitive process, local responsiveness will tend to shape business thinking. In other words, cost considerations will tend to be secondary.

RECAP

1. Although becoming an MNC is largely advantageous to the business, it can experience problems with language barriers, selling and marketing in foreign markets, attitudes of the host state and the communication and coordination of global business activities.

2. An MNC will often find a trade-off between producing a standardised product in order to cut costs and producing a customised product in order to take account of local demand conditions.

FDI is more likely to occur if a nation has buoyant economic growth, large market size, high disposable income, an appropriate demographic mix, low inflation, low taxation, few restrictive regulations on business, a good transport network, an excellent education system, a significant research culture, etc. In highly competitive global markets, such factors may make the difference between success and failure.

Advantages

Host governments are always on the look-out to attract foreign direct investment. They are often prepared to put up considerable finance and make significant concessions, such as tax breaks, to attract overseas business. So, what benefits do MNCs bring to the economy?

Employment
If MNC investment is in new plants (as opposed to taking over an existing company) this will generate employment. Most countries attempt to entice MNCs to depressed regions where investment is low and unemployment is high. Often these will be regions where a major industry has closed (e.g. the coal mining regions of South Wales). The employment that MNCs create is both direct, in the form of people employed in the new production facility, and indirect, through the impact that the MNC has on the local economy. This might be the consequence of establishing a new supply network, or simply the result of the increase in local incomes and expenditure, and hence the stimulus to local business.

It is possible, however, that jobs created in one region of a country by a new MNC venture, with its superior technology and working practices, might cause a business to fold elsewhere, thus leading to increased unemployment in that region.

Pause for thought

Why might the size of these regional 'knock-on effects' of inward investment be difficult to estimate?

The balance of payments
A country's balance of payments (see section 13.1) is likely to improve on a number of counts as a result of inward MNC investment.

First, the investment represents a direct flow of capital into the country.

Second, and perhaps more importantly (especially in the long term), MNC investment is likely to result

in both *import substitution* and export promotion. Import substitution will occur as products, previously purchased as imports, are now produced domestically. Export promotion will be enhanced as many multinationals use their new production facilities as export platforms. For example, many Japanese MNCs invest in the UK in order to gain access to the European Union. Concerns about whether leaving the EU would discourage such inward investment was one of issues raised during the referendum campaign on whether the UK should remain in or leave the EU.

The beneficial effect on the balance of payments, however, will be offset to the extent that profits earned from the investment are repatriated to the parent country, and to the extent that the exports of the MNC displace the exports of domestic producers.

Technology transfer
Technology transfer refers to the benefits gained by domestic producers from the technology imported by the MNC. Such benefits can occur in a number of ways.

The most common is where domestic producers copy the production technology and working practices of the MNC. This is referred to as the 'demonstration effect' and has occurred widely in the UK, as British businesses have attempted to emulate many of the practices brought into the country by Japanese multinationals.

In addition to copying best practice, technology might also be transferred through the training of workers. When workers move jobs from the MNC to other firms in the industry, or to other industrial sectors, they take their newly acquired technical knowledge and skills with them.

Taxation
MNCs, like domestic producers, are required to pay tax and therefore contribute to public finances. Given the highly profitable nature of many MNCs, the level of tax revenue raised from this source could be highly significant.

Definitions

Import substitution The replacement of imports by domestically produced goods or services.

Technology transfer Where a host state benefits from the new technology that an MNC brings with its investment.

Disadvantages

Thus far we have focused on the positive effects resulting from multinational investment. However, multinational investment may not always be beneficial in either the short or the long term.

Uncertainty. MNCs are often 'footloose', meaning that they can simply close down their operations in foreign countries and move if opportunities present themselves elsewhere, as we saw with Tesco and Carrefour (see Box 7.3). This is especially likely with older plants which would need updating if the MNC were to remain, or with plants that can be easily sold without too much loss. Also, during the maturity and decline stage of the product life cycle, cost-cutting may be essential and the MNC may move production to even lower cost countries.

The ability to close down its business operations and shift production, while being a distinct economic advantage to the MNC, is a prime concern facing the host nation. If a country has a large foreign multinational sector within the economy, it will become very vulnerable to such footloose activity, and face great uncertainty in the long term. It may thus be forced to offer the multinational 'perks' (e.g. grants, special tax relief or specific facilities) in order to persuade it to remain. These perks are clearly costly to the taxpayer.

Control. The fact that an MNC can shift production locations not only gives it economic flexibility, but enables it to exert various controls over the host country. This is particularly so in many developing countries, where MNCs are not only major employers but in many cases the principal wealth creators. Thus attempts by the host state, for example, to improve worker safety or impose pollution controls may be against what the MNC sees as its own best interests. It might thus oppose such measures or even threaten to withdraw from the country if such measures are not modified or dropped. The host nation is in a very weak position.

Transfer pricing. MNCs, like domestic producers, are always attempting to reduce their tax liabilities. One unique way that an MNC can do this is through a process known as *transfer pricing*, which refers to the price a business charges itself for transferring partly finished products from one division of the company to another. By manipulating this internal pricing system, the MNC can reduce its profits in countries with high rates of profit tax, and increase them in countries with low rates of profit tax.

For example, take a vertically integrated MNC where subsidiary A in one country supplies components to subsidiary B in another. The price at which the components are transferred between the two subsidiaries (the 'transfer price') will ultimately determine the costs and hence the levels of profit made in each country. Assume that in the country where subsidiary A is located, the level of corporation tax (the tax on company profits) is half that of the country where subsidiary B is located. If components are transferred from A to B at very high prices, then B's costs will rise and its profitability will fall. Conversely, A's profitability will rise. The MNC clearly benefits as more profit is taxed at the lower rather than the higher rate. Had it been the other way around, with subsidiary B facing the lower rate of tax, then the components would be transferred at a low price. This would increase subsidiary B's profits and reduce A's.

The practice of transfer pricing was starkly revealed in the *Guardian* newspaper in February 2009. Citing a paper that examined the flows of goods priced from US subsidiaries in Africa back to the USA, it stated that 'the public may be horrified to learn that companies have priced flash bulbs at $321.90 each, pillow cases at $909.29 each and a ton of sand at $1993.67, when the average world trade price was 66 cents, 62 cents and $11.20 respectively'.[5]

The environment. Many MNCs are accused of simply investing in countries to gain access to natural resources, which are subsequently extracted or used in a way that is not sensitive to the environment. Host nations, especially developing countries that are keen for investment, are frequently prepared to allow MNCs to do this. They often put more store on the short-run gains from the MNC's presence than on the long-run depletion of precious natural resources or damage to the environment. (We consider the environment in Chapter 9.) Governments, like many businesses, often have a very short-run focus; they are concerned more with their political survival (whether through the ballot box or through military force) than with the long-term interests of their people.

Definition

Transfer pricing The pricing system used within a business to transfer intermediate products between its various divisions, often in different countries.

Pause for thought

1. *What problems is a developing country likely to experience if it adopts a policy of restricting, or even preventing, access to its markets by multinational business?*
2. *To what extent is the relationship between host state and multinational a principal–agent one? What problems arise specifically from this relationship?*

---

[5] Prem Sikka, 'Shifting profits across borders', *The Guardian* (12 February 2009).

BOX 7.4   INVESTING IN AFRICA

Why not Africa?

Africa accounts for approximately 17 per cent of the world's population and, despite its land-mass and some extremely large countries, the region accounts for only 3 per cent of global GDP.

According to UNCTAD, Africa received just 2.9 per cent of inward FDI flows in 2017, up from 0.7 per cent in 2000, but lower than its peak of 4.8 per cent in 2009. Africa also experienced a decline in its average return on foreign investment from 12.3 per cent in 2012 to 6.3 per cent in 2017. This was greater than the global decline from 8.1 per cent to 6.7 per cent over the same period and could discourage future FDI in Africa.[1]

One key thing that does affect Africa's FDI inflows and makes the region particularly vulnerable, is its dependence on commodities and hence on commodity prices. As a result of this, FDI flows do seem to show a cyclical effect, moving with commodity prices.

For example, between 2016 and 2018, FDI flows to Africa have fallen by 20 per cent and although structural factors can explain part of this, a significant factor was the fall in oil prices and the 'lingering effects from the commodity bust', resulting in a sharp drop in the flows to commodity-exporting countries, including Egypt, Nigeria and Angola. With commodity prices now recovering and general improvements in macroeconomic indicators, the World Investment Report for 2018 expects FDI inflows into the continent to increase by 20 per cent in 2018 to £50 billion.[2]

The barriers to trade and inward investment
With 20 per cent of the world's land mass, the African continent should be a key target for multinational investment, but as we know, this has not yet been the case. What are the barriers that still remain within this continent that prevent it from receiving a greater share of investment from multinational companies?

Geography: There are 54 countries, but few cities within Africa have populations beyond 4 million. Any company will need access to skilled labour and sufficient customer demand and so, despite the continent's size, there are only a few locations where a company might consider investing. A related issue that also reflects Africa's sheer size, is the time it takes to travel between these cities that are spread across the continent. According to the Boston Consulting Group: 'From any city in Europe, you can reach the countries aggregating 70 per cent of Europe's GDP in 3 hours or less. In Southeast Asia or Latin America, a comparable trip takes 8 hours. In Africa, a similar journey requires 15 hours.'[3] This simply means that trade across the region is more difficult, more time consuming and hence more costly, thereby deterring investment in the region.

Geopolitical tensions: There are still many conflicts within Africa. Geopolitical tensions create uncertainty in supply chains and finance and also about the general macroeconomic stability of a country. New economic alliances are emerging, with over 50 per cent of countries having seen a change in political leadership. While this is positive in many ways, it is also changing the 'spheres of influence' and such changes may be a deterrent to foreign investment.

Economic fragmentation: There are 16 trade zones in Africa, which immediately presents complexity for any company investing in one of the 54 African countries. There are visa issues with travel to many countries and this impacts the ease of doing business if the right people cannot get access to live, work or do business in the region. In order to reach $1 trillion in GDP, we have to sum the GDP from 24 African countries. This is more than any other region. The economic indicators in Africa are such that vast numbers of the population do not have sufficient income to provide a feasible market for many goods and services and, in some countries, the lack of stability in the macroeconomy or in the whole region means that businesses would face too high a degree of uncertainty.[4]

Infrastructure and institutions: All businesses require infrastructure, whether it is good transport links, including road, rail and air; good communication systems, such as access to the Internet and mobile phone coverage; or good health care and education facilities. Well-developed and stable institutions are also required, such as a sound legal framework; policy to address corruption, accountability and transparency.

Given the land-mass of Africa, transport infrastructure is vital, but the region lacks major road and rail networks and has few direct flights between big cities. This makes it more difficult to connect businesses and people and thus increases the cost of doing business for African companies. The Boston Consulting Group found that the average cost of shipping and distributing goods to market in Africa is equal to 320 per cent of the value of these goods. In South America, the figure is 200 per cent and in East Asia and North America, it is 140 per cent.

The implications of these barriers are that companies based in Africa will face difficulties in accessing skilled labour and have a much smaller and less wealthy market in which they can sell. If they are looking to export products, they have to compete on a global scale, but their costs of production are higher, due to poor transport and communication infrastructure. The lack of developed and stable institutions also means greater uncertainty for businesses and in many cases, a lack of data and information, which are crucial to any business to ensure it fully understands its local market.

The competitive advantages of African companies
Despite the barriers that businesses face, many commentators see Africa as a region that is prime for investment. The USA, the UK, France and China are the biggest investors in Africa and have been for over a decade. However, it is from African companies where significant increases in inward FDI can be observed. Between 2006/7

---

[1] UNCTADstat data center.

[2] *World Investment Report 2018,* UNCTAD (6 June 2018).

[3] Patrick Dupoux, Lisa Ivers, Stefano Niavas and Abdeljabbar Chraïti, *Pioneering one Africa,* Boston Consulting Group (4 April 2018).

[4] Ibid.

▶

and 2015/16, the average annual amount of African inward FDI by African companies nearly tripled from $3.7 billion to $10 billion: but still only from 0.26 to 0.52 per cent of total inward FDI in Africa.

In the same period, there was also a significant increase in the average number of yearly intra-African M&A deals, rising from 238 to 418. Africa has also seen significant growth in its exports. But at an annual average of 2.7 per cent between 2010 and 2019 for sub-Saharan Africa, this is still below the global average of 4.8 per cent

In its report, 'Dueling with Lions',[5] the Boston Consulting Group identified four competitive advantages that African companies have, which may be the key to the future development of the region.

- Focus: a commitment to Africa
- Field: on-the-ground experience and proximity to decision makers
- Facts: a good understanding of the data and information that are relevant to local markets
- Flexibility: an ability to make quick decisions and navigate informal business environments

These factors have enabled many African companies to grow at home and abroad and, on average, the top 30 African companies are now operating in 16 African countries, which has increased from just eight in 2008.

In addition to these advantages, there have also been changes in other areas.

- Improvements in many African airlines, with more countries being served and new routes established, often ahead of passenger demand, has meant that travel is easier and cheaper. For example, Ethiopian Airways flew to 36 nations in 2016, up from just 24 in 2006.
- African financial institutions have also expanded their businesses, as have telecommunication companies.
- Internet penetration was above 30 per cent in 2016, indicating significant improvements in infrastructure.
- International logistic companies are also helping to drive an increase in intra-African trade, which has increased by 120 per cent to $64 billion between 2005 and 2016.

The implication is that the region is increasingly offering better connectivity for people and businesses, both in terms of transport and communications.

As investment in the continent's infrastructure continues, the opportunities for business will improve. The International Monetary Fund has found that almost 50 per cent of the 40 fastest growing emerging and developing countries are in Africa.[6] With more intra-African trade and the launch of the African Continental Free Trade Area (AfCFTA) in March 2018, the region's macroeconomic indicators may improve and this will help to attract larger FDI inflows from more nations. The AfCFTA is expected to generate a total GDP of $3.4 trillion and this may be a key pull for foreign investment.

1. *In what ways might a growing African continent benefit the rest of the world?*
2. *Should multinational companies be cautious about investing in Africa?*

Do a data search on a range of macroeconomic indicators for Africa over the past 20 years. Plot the figures along with similar data for the world and for China, India, the USA and the UK. Write a brief report on your findings.

---

[5] Patrick Dupoux, Lisa Ivers, Adham Abouzied, Abdeljabbar Chraïti, Fatymatou Dia, Hamid Maher and Stefano Niavas, *Dueling with Lions: Playing the new game of business success in Africa*, Boston Consulting Group (10 November 2015).

[6] *World Economic Forum on Africa* (World Economic Forum, 2019).

RECAP

1. Host states find multinational investment advantageous in respect to employment creation, contributions to the balance of payments, the transfer of technology and the contribution to taxation.

2. They find it disadvantageous, however, in so far as it creates uncertainty; foreign business can control or manipulate the country or regions within it; tax payments can be avoided by transfer pricing; and MNCs might misuse the environment.

QUESTIONS

1. What do you understand by the term 'economic globalisation'? Is it a good thing?

2. Using the FDI database in the statistics section of the UNCTAD website (UNCTADStat) at (http://unctadstat. unctad.org/EN/), find out what has happened to FDI flows over the past five years (a) worldwide; (b) to and from developed countries; (c) to and from developing countries; (d) to and from the UK. Explain any patterns that emerge.

3. What are the advantages and disadvantages to a developed economy of having a large multinational sector?

4. How might the structure of a multinational differ depending on whether its objective of being multinational is to reduce costs or to grow?

5. Choose a multinational company and then, by using its website, assess its global strategy.

6. How might a business's strategy in the domestic and global economy be affected by the onset of recession?

7. If reducing costs is so important for many multinationals, why is it that they tend to locate production not in low-cost developing economies, but in economies within the developed world?

8. 'Going global, thinking local.' Explain this phrase, and identify the potential conflicts for a business in behaving in this way.

9. Explain the link between the life cycle of a product and multinational business.

10. Assess the advantages and disadvantages facing a host state when receiving MNC investment.

11. Debate the following statement: 'Multinational investment can be nothing but good for developing economies seeking to grow and prosper.'

Labour and employment

Business issues covered in this chapter

- How are wage rates determined in a perfect labour market?
- What are the determinants of the demand and supply of labour and their respective elasticities?
- What forms of market power exist in the labour market and what determines the power of employers and labour?
- What effects do powerful employers and trade unions have on wages and employment?
- How has the minimum wage affected business and employment?
- What is meant by a 'flexible' labour market and how has increased flexibility affected working practices, employment and wages?
- How will various incentives affect the motivation and productivity of workers?
- Should senior executives be given large bonuses and stock options?
- What is the impact on the labour market and productivity of higher education?

In this chapter we consider how labour markets affect business. In particular, we will focus on the determination of wage rates in different types of market: ones where employers are wage takers, ones where they can choose the wage rate, and ones where wage rates are determined by a process of collective bargaining. We will also consider some of the problems that emerge in labour markets, such as discrimination and low pay, and some labour market policies, such as tax credits and the minimum wage.

8.1 MARKET-DETERMINED WAGE RATES AND EMPLOYMENT

The labour market has undergone substantial changes in recent years. Advances in technology leading to greater automation, changes in the pattern of output, a growing need to be competitive in international markets and various social changes have all contributed to changes in work practices and in the structure and composition of the workforce. Major changes in the UK are discussed in Case Study C.15 on the student website.

When we consider wage rates, an obvious question is why do some people earn very high wages, whereas others, who perhaps work just as hard, if not harder, earn much less? Why, for example, do top sportsmen and sportswomen get paid so much, but, perhaps more interestingly, why do only *some* of them get paid so much? Luis Suárez, Eden Hazard and Sergio Agüero are great footballers and earn very high wages. But have you ever wondered why they earned so much more than Lin Dan and Domagoj Duvnjak? Probably not. They are Chinese and Croatian and were seen as world greats in badminton and handball, respectively.

Economics allows us to develop a theory that explains why the greatest ever sportsperson in one discipline can be paid so little relative to merely great sportspeople in other disciplines. You can read about the salaries of footballers and the revenues and costs of their clubs on the Sloman Economics News site in the blog, *Why is it so difficult to make a profit? The problem of players' pay in the English Premier League* and also in an article in *Goal*[1] that looks at the clubs who pay the most

Perfect labour markets

Before we can answer such questions, we first need to consider how wages are determined and to do this we must make a similar distinction to that made in the theory of the firm: the distinction between perfect and imperfect markets. Although in practice few labour markets are totally perfect, many do at least approximate to it.

The key assumption of a perfect labour market is that everyone is a *wage taker*. In other words, neither employers nor employees have any economic power to affect wage rates. This situation is not uncommon. Small employers are likely to have to pay the 'going wage rate' to their employees, especially where the employee is of a clear category, such as an electrician, a bar worker, a secretary or a porter. As far as employees are concerned, being a wage taker means not being a member of a union and therefore not being able to use collective bargaining to push up the wage rate.

We assume also that there is perfect knowledge on the part of workers and employers and that there are no barriers that prevent the movement of labour. Therefore, workers are aware of available jobs and can move to new jobs and different parts of the country in response to higher wages, better working conditions, better promotion opportunities, etc. Likewise, employers know the type of workers that are available, how productive they are and how motivated. Finally, it is normally assumed that

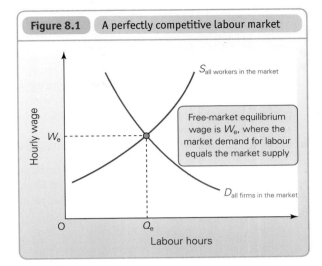

Figure 8.1 A perfectly competitive labour market

Free-market equilibrium wage is W_e, where the market demand for labour equals the market supply

workers of a given category are identical in terms of productivity.

Wage rates and employment under perfect competition are determined by the interaction of the market demand and supply of labour. This is illustrated in Figure 8.1. The curves show the total number of hours workers would supply and the number of hours of labour firms would demand for each wage rate in a particular labour market. The equilibrium market wage rate is W_e, where demand equals supply. Equilibrium employment in terms of the total number of hours people are employed in the market is Q_e.

Generally, it would be expected that the supply and demand curves slope the same way as in goods markets. The higher the wage paid for a certain type of job, the more workers will want to do that job. This gives an upward-sloping supply curve of labour. On the other hand, the higher the wage that employers have to pay, the less labour they will want to employ. Either they will simply produce less output, or they will substitute other factors of production, like machinery, for labour. Thus the demand curve for labour slopes downwards.

We now turn to look at the supply and demand for labour in more detail.

The supply of labour

As we have seen, the supply of labour curve will typically be upward sloping. The *position* of the market supply curve of labour will depend on the number

Pause for thought

Which of these assumptions do you think would be correct in each of the following cases: (a) supermarket checkout operators, (b) agricultural workers, (c) crane operators, (d) business studies teachers, (e) call centre workers?

Definition

Wage taker The wage rate is determined by market forces.

[1] Stephen Crawford, 'Football salaries: Premier League clubs dominate wages list as Barcelona lead the way', *Goal* (29 November 2017).

of people willing and able to do the job at each given wage rate. This depends on three things:

- the number of qualified people;
- the non-wage benefits or costs of the job, such as the pleasantness or otherwise of the working environment, job satisfaction or dissatisfaction, status, power, the degree of job security, holidays, perks and other fringe benefits;
- the wages and non-wage benefits in alternative jobs.

The wage rate is measured on the vertical axis, so a change in this variable will cause a movement along the supply curve. A change in any of these other three determinants will shift the whole curve.

Pause for thought

Which way will the supply curve shift if the wage rates in alternative jobs rise?

The elasticity of the market supply of labour

How *responsive* will the supply of labour be to a change in the wage rate? If the market wage rate goes up, will a lot more labour become available or only a

little? It's not just a question of workers being *willing* to work, but also about them actually being *able* to increase the supply of labour at the higher wage. This responsiveness (elasticity) depends on (a) the difficulties and costs of changing jobs and (b) the time period.

Another way of looking at the elasticity of supply of labour is in terms of the *mobility of labour*: the willingness and ability of labour to move to another job, whether in a different location (geographical mobility) or in a different industry (occupational mobility). The mobility of labour (and hence the elasticity of supply of labour) will be higher when there are alternative jobs in the same location, when alternative jobs require similar skills and when people have good information about these jobs. It is also much higher in the long run, when people have the time to acquire new skills and when the education system has had time to adapt to the changing demands of industry.

Definition

Mobility of labour The ease with which labour can either shift between jobs (occupational mobility) or move to other parts of the country in search of work (geographical mobility).

BOX 8.1   NEW WAYS OF WORKING

Changes in the labour market

The labour market has changed beyond recognition, with new jobs being created, new ways of working and much of this is due to technology. One key effect has been to increase labour market flexibility, as people can now work from home almost as effectively as they can in an office.

Telecommuting

Mobile phones, the Internet, Skype, conference calls, etc. all mean that more people are now '*telecommuting*' and it has been found that where 'telecommuting networks' have been established, gains in productivity have arisen, when compared with office workers. Most studies indicate rises in productivity of over 35 per cent and at the same time a reduction in staff absenteeism. With fewer interruptions and less chatting with fellow workers, less working time is lost, and the stress-free environment leads to individual workers' performance being enhanced with workers being more attentive.

Less commuting means time is saved and workers avoid the stress of commuting. There are also environmental gains from less congestion and pollution, and also savings from lower maintenance, heating and lighting costs. A report found that if the 50 million potential teleworkers in the USA worked from home 50 per cent of the time, the reduction in greenhouse gases would be comparable to all workers in New York State no longer using the roads.[1]

Telecommuting also opens up the labour market to a wider group of workers, who either live further afield or may find it more difficult to leave the home, e.g. single parents and the disabled. This not only improves efficiency, as a better use is made of the full labour force, but enhances equity as well.

In the 2017 State of Telecommuting in the U.S. Employee Workforce report,[2] it was found that, in the previous 10 years, the number of people telecommuting in the USA had increased by 115 per cent. Gallup's report on the State of the American Workplace found that, in 2016, 43 per cent of US workers reported working remotely.[3] According to the ONS, in the UK, in 2017, there were 4.3 million workers who worked from home or with home as a base. This represented 13.6 per cent of the 31.9 million people in work, up from 11.1 per cent in 1998.[4]

Technology has therefore permitted a rise in home working and this has increased labour mobility. Work can be taken to the workers rather than the workers coming to the work. Increasingly, we are seeing international telecommuting, with workers basing themselves in different counties. With the creation of transoceanic fibre optical cable networks, international data transmission has become both faster and

---

[1] Kate Lister and Tom Harnish, *The State of Telework in the U.S.*, Telework Research Network (June 2011).

[2] *2017 State of Telecommuting in the U.S. Employee Workforce*, Global Workplace Analytics and FlexJobs (June 2017).

[3] Greg Kratz, 'Report Summary: "State of the American Workplace," Gallup', *1 Million for Work Flexibility* (13 April 2017).

[4] Data showing employment and home workers, for the period, *Labour Force Survey: January to March 2015 to 2017 and Annual Population Survey October 2016 to September 2017'*, ONS (18 January 2018).

cheaper. Some familiar examples include international teleworkers in call centres, especially those employed by multinational companies. Also, increasingly workers are able to purchase property in cheaper countries and continue to do their jobs remotely, taking advantage of cheap budget airlines if they need to go into the office.

However, despite the benefits from home working, some firms across Europe and the USA are cutting back on telecommuting, requiring employees to be in the office during working hours. Many companies are claiming that this is due to a change in the type of work, with technological innovations requiring teams to be in the office.

1. *What effect is telecommuting likely to have on (a) trade union membership; (b) trade union power?*
2. *How are the developments referred to in this box likely to affect relative house prices between capital cities and the regions?*

Online recruitment

The labour market's flexibility has also been enhanced by increasing use of online recruitment technologies. Firms have their own online vacancy boards and use social networking sites to target different audiences. Those searching for jobs use a range of online sites, such as Monster and Fish4jobs to register for job alerts by e-mail or mobile phone and to register their CV.

This new recruitment process has improved the efficiency with which information is relayed to the employers and suppliers of labour and increases their search horizons. As well as reaching a wider and more targeted audience, recruitment costs are lowered and the recruitment cycle is shortened and made more efficient by the use of Internet technologies. On the downside, it does appear that e-recruitment is leading to more unsuitable candidates applying for vacancies, which does cost money.

According to the Chartered Institute of Personnel and Development:

> Technology plays an increasingly important role in recruitment, ranging from attracting candidates through to the selection process. Electronic techniques are also being used to slim down the number of potential candidates. In particular, using online recruitment can mean employers receive large numbers of applications from unsuitable candidates, so it can be helpful also to use technology to help manage the application forms.[5]

3. *Explain how a firm's flexibility would be enhanced by online recruitment.*
4. *If a firm is trying to achieve flexibility in its use of labour, do you think this would be harder or easier in a period of recession? Explain why.*

The gig economy

Workers in the gig economy are self-employed, but are often contracted to an employer. They are paid by the job (or 'gig': like musicians), rather than being paid a wage. Much of the work is temporary, although many in the gig economy, such as taxi drivers and delivery people stick with the same job. The gig economy is just one further manifestation of the growing flexibility of labour markets, which have also seen a rise in temporary employment, part-time employment and zero-hour contracts. A report by the Resolution Foundation[6] found that the numbers of self-employed workers has risen to almost 5 million since the financial crisis. This is a growth of 22 per cent. Data from the ONS indicate that between 2001 and 2017, the number of self-employed has increased by 45 per cent.

The gig economy provides a number of benefits for workers, as they have greater flexibility in their choice of hours and many work wholly or partly from home. Many do several 'gigs' simultaneously, which gives variety and interest. This flexible working also provides a greater opportunity for people to work the optimum number of hours, such that they work up to the point where the marginal benefit from work, in terms of pay and enjoyment, equals the marginal cost, in terms of effort and sacrificed leisure. However, there is less job security and fewer benefits, and pay tends to be much lower, as they have much less bargaining power than the traditional worker.

From the firm's point of view, many of these disadvantages to the workers are advantages for them. Gig workers have previously been cheaper to employ, as they did not need to be paid sick pay, holiday pay or redundancy.

However, various court cases in the UK challenged the classification of those working in this way, requiring that they be classed as 'workers' and not 'independent contractors' and consequently that, as workers, they were entitled to the national minimum wage, rest breaks and holiday pay. The Conservative government in 2019 was pushing ahead with plans to boost the rights of such workers, as part of the overhaul of various aspects of employment law.

Labour markets have therefore becoming increasingly flexible and more efficient over the past few decades. We explore this further in section 8.4. What is more, with technology continuing to improve, it is likely that we will move towards newer and faster ways of working, even if in some cases, it might mean a return to more traditional types of working.

5. *Give some examples of work which is generally or frequently done in the gig economy.*

Choose a particular company that employs people on a flexible basis. What benefits does it gain from so doing? What are the advantages and disadvantages for people working for the company on flexible terms?

---

[5] 'Selection methods', *CIPD Factsheet* (Chartered Institute of Personnel and Development, 2013).

[6] Dan Tomlinson and Adam Corlett, *A Tough Gig? The Nature of Self-employment in 21st Century Britain and Policy Implications*, Resolution Foundation (February 2017).

The demand for labour: the marginal productivity theory

The market demand curve for labour will typically be downward sloping. To see why, let us examine the behaviour of a profit-maximising firm.

The profit-maximising approach

How many workers will a profit-maximising firm want to employ? The firm will answer this question by weighing up the costs of employing extra labour against the benefits. It will use exactly the same principles as in deciding how much output to produce.

Pause for thought

During the 2000s, the Central and Eastern European countries (CEECs) began to join the EU. What effect do you think the expansion of the EU has had on the position and elasticity of the supply curve of various types of labour?

In the goods market, the firm will maximise profits where the marginal cost of an extra unit of *goods* produced equals the marginal revenue from selling it: $MC = MR$.

In the labour market, the firm will maximise profits where the marginal cost of employing an extra *worker* equals the marginal revenue that the worker's output earns for the firm: MC of labour = MR of labour. To understand this, consider what would happen if they were not equal. If an extra worker adds more to a firm's revenue than to its costs, the firm's profits will increase if that extra worker is employed. But as more workers are employed, diminishing returns to labour will set in (see pages 82–3). Each extra worker will produce less than the previous one, and thus earn less revenue for the firm. Eventually the marginal revenue from extra workers will fall to the level of their marginal cost. At that point the firm will stop employing extra workers. There are no additional profits to be gained. Profits are at a maximum.

Measuring the marginal cost and revenue of labour

Marginal cost of labour (MC_L). This is the extra cost of employing one more worker. Under perfect competition the firm is too small to affect the market wage. It faces a horizontal supply curve. In other words, it can employ as many workers as it chooses at the market wage rate. Thus the additional cost of employing one more person will simply be the wage rate: $MC_L = W$.

Marginal revenue of labour (MRP_L). The marginal revenue that the firm gains from employing one more worker is called the *marginal revenue product of labour* (MRP_L). The MRP_L is found by multiplying two elements – the *marginal physical product* of labour (MPP_L) and the marginal revenue gained by selling one more unit of output (MR):

$$MRP_L = MPP_L \times MR$$

The MPP_L is the extra output produced by the last worker. Thus if the last worker produces 100 tonnes of output per week (MPP_L), and if the firm can sell each unit for £2 (MR), then the worker's MRP is £200. This extra worker is adding £200 to the firm's revenue.

The profit-maximising level of employment for a firm

The MRP_L curve is illustrated in Figure 8.2. As more workers are employed, there will come a point when diminishing returns set in (point x). Thereafter the MRP_L curve slopes downwards. The figure also shows the MC_L 'curve' at the current market wage W_e. Every worker is paid an identical wage and so the curve is horizontal, showing that the cost of employing each extra worker (MC_L) is the same, whether it is the 50th or the 500th worker.

Profits are maximised at an employment level of Q_e, where MC_L (i.e. W) = MRP_L. Why? At levels of employment below Q_e, MRP_L exceeds MC_L. The firm will increase profits by employing more labour. At levels of employment above Q_e, MC_L exceeds MRP_L. In this case the firm will increase profits by reducing employment.

Definition

Marginal revenue product of labour The extra revenue a firm earns from employing one more unit of labour.

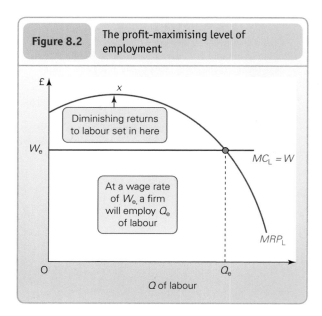

Figure 8.2	The profit-maximising level of employment

Derivation of the firm's demand curve for labour

No matter what the wage rate is, if a firm is a profit-maximising employer of labour, the quantity of labour demanded will be found from the intersection of W (MC_L) and MRP_L (see Figure 8.3). At a wage rate of W_1, Q_1 labour is demanded (point a); at W_2, Q_2 is demanded (point b); at W_3, Q_3 is demanded (point c).

Thus the MRP_L curve shows the quantity of labour employed at each wage rate. But this is just what the demand curve for labour shows. Thus, the MRP_L curve is the demand curve for labour.

There are three determinants of the demand for labour:

- *The wage rate.* This determines the position *on* the demand curve. (Strictly speaking, we would refer here to the wage determining the 'quantity demanded' rather than the 'demand'.)
- *The productivity of labour* (MPP_L). This determines the position *of* the demand curve.
- *The demand for the good.* The higher the market demand for the good, the higher will be its market price, and hence the higher will be the MR, and thus the MRP_L. This too determines the position *of* the demand curve. It shows how the demand for labour (and other inputs) is a *derived demand*, i.e. one derived from the demand for the good. For example, the higher the demand for houses, and hence the higher their price, the higher will be the demand for bricklayers.

A change in the wage rate is represented by a movement *along* the demand curve for labour. A change in the productivity of labour or in the demand for the good *shifts* the curve.

Market demand and its elasticity

For the same reason that the firm's demand for labour is downward sloping, so the whole market demand for labour will be downward sloping. At higher wage rates, firms in total will employ less labour. The *elasticity* of this market demand for labour (with respect to changes in the wage rate) depends on various factors. Elasticity will be greater:

The greater the price elasticity of demand for the good. If costs of production rise (e.g. a rise in wage rates), this will drive up the price of the good. If the market demand for the good is elastic, this rise in price will lead to a significant fall in sales and hence a bigger drop in the number of people employed.

> ### Pause for thought
>
> *If the productivity of a group of workers rises by 10 per cent, will the wage rate they are paid also rise by 10 per cent? Explain why or why not.*

The easier it is to substitute labour for other inputs and vice versa. If labour can be readily replaced by other inputs (e.g. machinery), then a rise in the wage rate will lead to a large reduction in labour as workers are replaced by these other inputs.

The greater the wage cost as a proportion of total costs. If wages are a large proportion of total costs and the wage rate rises, total costs will rise significantly; therefore production and sales will fall significantly, and so will the demand for labour.

The longer the time period. Given sufficient time, firms can respond to a rise in wage rates by reorganising their production processes. For example, they could move towards greater automation on production lines or introduce new technologies.

Wages and profits under perfect competition

The wage rate (W) is determined by the interaction of demand and supply in the labour market. This will be equal to the value of the output that the last person produces (MRP_L).

Profits to the individual firm will arise from the fact that the MRP_L curve slopes downward (diminishing returns). Thus the last worker adds less to the

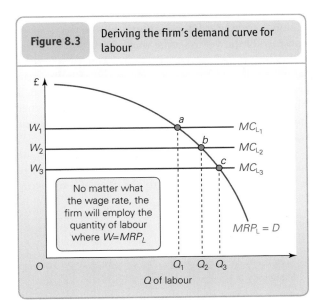

Figure 8.3	Deriving the firm's demand curve for labour

No matter what the wage rate, the firm will employ the quantity of labour where $W = MRP_L$

> ### Definition
>
> **Derived demand** The demand for an input depends on the demand for the good that uses it.

revenue of firms than previous workers already employed.

If *all* workers in the firm receive a wage equal to the *MRP* of the *last* worker, everyone but the last worker will receive a wage *less* than their *MRP*. This excess of MRP_L over W of previous workers provides a surplus to the firm over its wages bill (see Figure 8.4). Part of this will be required for paying non-wage costs; part will be the profits for the firm.

Perfect competition between firms will ensure that profits are kept down to *normal* profits. If the surplus over wages is such that *supernormal* profits are made, new firms will enter the industry. As supply rises, the price of the good (and hence MRP_L) will fall, and as these new firms demand more labour, wages rates will be bid up, until only normal profits remain.

Figure 8.4 Wages and a firm's surplus over wages

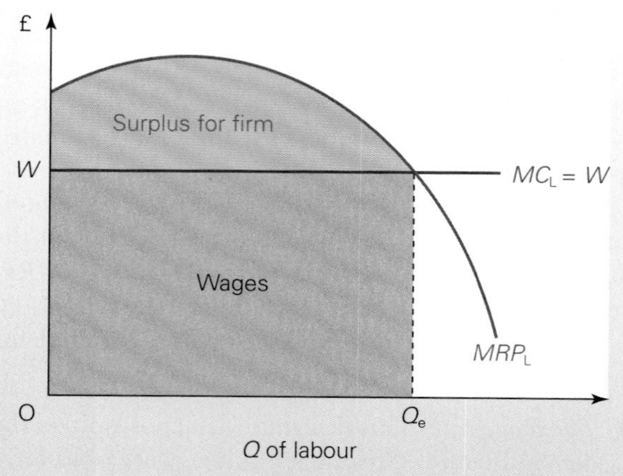

RECAP

1. Wages in a competitive labour market are determined by the interaction of demand and supply. The market supply of labour in any labour market is likely to be upward sloping.
2. The elasticity of labour supply will depend largely upon the geographical and occupational mobility of labour. The more readily labour can transfer between jobs and regions, the more elastic the supply of labour.
3. The demand for labour is traditionally assumed to be based upon labour's productivity. Marginal productivity

theory assumes that the employer will demand labour up to the point where the cost of employing one additional worker (MC_L) is equal to the revenue earned from the output of that worker (MRP_L). The firm's demand curve for labour is its MRP_L curve.

4. The elasticity of demand for labour is determined by: the price elasticity of demand for the good that labour produces; the substitutability of labour for other factors; the proportion of wages to total costs; and time.

8.2 POWER IN THE LABOUR MARKET

Firms with power

In the real world, many firms have the power to influence wage rates: they are not wage takers. This is one of the major types of labour market 'imperfection'.

When a firm is the only employer of a particular type of labour, this situation is called a *monopsony*. Royal Mail used to be a monopsony employer of postal workers.[2] Another example is when a factory is the only employer of certain types of labour in that district. It therefore has local monopsony power.

When there are just a few employers, this is called *oligopsony*. We saw an example in Box 5.3, where we briefly looked at the big supermarkets, not as the only employers of a particular type of labour, but as the main buyers of certain products. Thus, they have significant power over farmers and other suppliers and can use that power to force down the prices they pay, thus cutting their costs.[3]

Monopsonists (and oligopsonists too) are 'wage setters', not 'wage takers'. Thus a large employer in a small town may have considerable power to resist wage increases or even to force wage rates down. On a national scale, the UK's National Health Service has considerable power in setting wages for health workers.

Such firms face an upward-sloping supply curve of labour. This is illustrated in Figure 8.5. If the firm wants to take on more labour, it will have to pay a higher wage rate to attract workers away from other industries. But conversely, by employing less labour it can get away with paying a lower wage rate.

The supply curve shows the wage that must be paid to attract a given quantity of labour. The wage it pays is the *average cost* to the firm of employing

Definitions

Monopsony A market with a single buyer or employer.
Oligopsony A market with just a few buyers or employers.

[2] 'Royal Mail loses postal monopoly', *BBC News* (18 February 2005).
[3] Sarah Butler and Miles Brignall, 'Dairy farmers call for supermarket boycott as milk prices fall', *The Guardian* (6 August 2015).

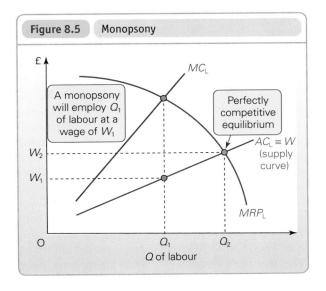

Figure 8.5 Monopsony

A monopsony will employ Q_1 of labour at a wage of W_1

Perfectly competitive equilibrium

$AC_L \equiv W$ (supply curve)

MRP_L

MC_L

Q of labour

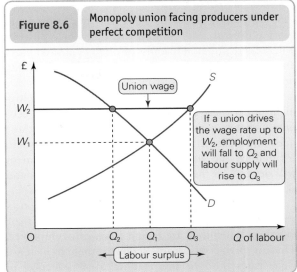

Figure 8.6 Monopoly union facing producers under perfect competition

Union wage

If a union drives the wage rate up to Q_2, employment will fall to Q_2 and labour supply will rise to Q_3

Labour surplus

Q of labour

labour (AC_L): i.e. the cost per worker. The supply curve is also therefore the AC_L curve.

The *marginal* cost of employing one more worker (MC_L) will be above the wage (AC_L) (see Figure 8.5). The reason is that the wage rate has to be raised to attract extra workers. The MC_L will thus be the new higher wage paid to the new employee *plus* the small rise in the total wages bill for existing employees: after all, they will be paid the higher wage too.

The profit-maximising employment of labour would be at Q_1, where $MC_L = MRP_L$. The wage (found from the AC_L curve) would thus be W_1.

If this had been a perfectly competitive labour market, employment would have been at the higher level Q_2, with the wage rate at the higher level W_2, where $W = MRP_L$. What in effect the monopsonist is doing, therefore, is forcing the wage rate down by restricting the number of workers employed.

The role of trade unions

How can unions influence the determination of wages, and what might be the consequences of their actions?

The extent to which unions will succeed in pushing up wage rates depends on their power and militancy. It also depends on the power of firms to resist and on their ability to pay higher wages. In particular, the scope for unions to gain a better deal for their members depends on the sort of market in which the employers are producing.

Unions facing competitive employers
If the employers are producing in a highly competitive goods market, unions can raise wages only at the expense of employment. Firms are likely to be earning little more than normal profit. Thus if unions force up wages, the marginal firms may make losses,

leading to their eventual exit from the industry. Fewer workers will be employed. The fall in output will lead to higher prices. This will enable the remaining firms to pay a higher wage rate.

Figure 8.6 illustrates these effects. If unions force the wage rate up from W_1 to W_2, employment will fall from Q_1 to Q_2. There will be a surplus of people ($Q_3 - Q_2$) wishing to work in this industry for whom no jobs are available.

The union is in a doubly weak position. Not only will jobs be lost as a result of forcing up the wage rate, but also there is a danger that these unemployed people could undercut the union wage, unless the union can prevent firms employing non-unionised labour.

In a competitive market, then, the union is faced with the choice between wages and jobs. Its actions will depend on its objectives.

Wages can be increased without a reduction in the level of employment only if, as part of the bargain, the productivity of labour is increased. This is called a *productivity deal*. The MRP curve, and hence the demand curve in Figure 8.6, shifts to the right.

Pause for thought

At what wage rate in Figure 8.6 would employment be maximised: (a) W_1; (b) a wage rate above W_1; (c) a wage rate below W_1?

Definition

Productivity deal Where, in return for a wage increase, a union agrees to changes in working practices that will increase output per worker.

Bilateral monopoly

One interesting observation is that the largest and most powerful trade unions are often in industries where there are monopsonist or oligopsonist employers. In such cases, trade unions act as a countervailing power to the large employer.

What will be the wage rate and level of employment under these circumstances? Unfortunately, economic theory cannot give a precise answer to these questions. There is no 'equilibrium' level as such. Ultimately, the wage rate and level of employment will depend on the relative bargaining strengths and skills of unions and management.

Strange as it may seem, unions may be in a stronger position to make substantial gains for their members when they are facing a powerful employer. There is often considerable scope for them to increase wage rates *without* this leading to a reduction in employment, or even for them to increase both the wage rate *and* employment. The reason is that if firms have power in the *goods* market too, and are making supernormal profit, then there is scope for a powerful union to redistribute some of these profits as wages.

The actual wage rate under bilateral monopoly is usually determined through a process of negotiation or 'collective bargaining'. The outcome of this bargaining will depend on a wide range of factors, which vary substantially from one industry or firm to another.

Collective bargaining

Sometimes when unions and management negotiate, *both* sides can gain from the resulting agreement. For example, the introduction of new technology may allow higher wages, improved working conditions and higher profits. Usually, however, one side's gain is the other's loss. Higher wages mean lower profits. Either way, both sides will want to gain the maximum for themselves.

The outcome of the negotiations will depend on the relative bargaining strengths of both sides. In bargaining there are various threats or promises that either side can make. For these to be effective, of course, the other side must believe that they will be carried out.

Union *threats* might include strike action, *picketing, working to rule* or refusing to co-operate with management, for example in the introduction of new technology. Alternatively, in return for higher wages or better working conditions, unions might *offer* no-strike agreements (or an informal promise not to take industrial action), increased productivity, reductions in the workforce or long-term deals over pay.

In response to, or in an attempt to prevent, industrial action, employers might *threaten* employees with plant closure, *lock-outs*, redundancies or the employment of non-union labour. Or they might *offer*, in return for lower wage increases, various 'perks' such as productivity bonuses, profit-sharing schemes, better working conditions, more overtime, better holidays or security of employment.

Industrial action imposes costs on both unions and firms. Unions lose pay; firms lose revenue. It is usually in both sides' interests to settle by negotiation. Nevertheless, to gain the maximum advantage at the negotiations, each side must persuade the other that it will carry out its threats if pushed. It can be useful to employ game theory here to consider how the actions of each side in the negotiation may be affected by how it thinks the other side will behave. In addition, the credibility of the threats and promises issued by both the employer and the trade union can affect the behaviour of both sides and hence the outcome of the negotiation.

In 1978–9, the UK experienced a period known as 'The Winter of Discontent',[4] when strikes took place simultaneously across a number of sectors. A blog on the Sloman Economics News site, *The Winter of Discontent: the sequel?* considers a similar period of industrial unrest that could have occurred in 2009. This is also discussed in Box 8.2, together with the recent strikes in the UK Higher Education System. Although the rationale for strike action varies in each case, costs are nearly always imposed on the wider economy and on society.

In some cases, governments may become involved and can influence the outcome of collective bargaining, as we saw in the Winter of Discontent and also more recently in the junior doctors' strikes. There are also arbitration and conciliation services, which can be used to try to resolve conflicts. In the UK, the Advisory Conciliation and Arbitration Service (ACAS) conciliates in around one thousand disputes each year, roughly half of these involving pay-related issues. It also provides, on request by both sides, an arbitration service, where its findings will be binding.

The approach described so far has essentially been one of confrontation. The alternative is for both sides to concentrate on increasing the total net income of the firm by co-operating on ways to increase efficiency or the quality of the product. This approach is more likely when unions and management have built up an atmosphere of trust over time.

Definitions

Picketing Where people on strike gather at the entrance to the firm and attempt to dissuade workers or delivery vehicles from entering.

Working to rule Workers do no more than they are supposed to, as set out in their job descriptions.

Lock-outs Union members are temporarily laid off until they are prepared to agree to the firm's conditions.

---

[4] 'Winter of Discontent: 30 years on'; *BBC News* (6 September 2008).

BOX 8.2 | **WHAT DO POST, AIRLINES, BINS, BUSES AND UNIVERSITIES HAVE IN COMMON?**

The winter of discontent: parts 1–3

In the winter of 1978/9 (dubbed the 'Winter of Discontent'), the UK economy almost ground to a halt when workers across the country went on strike. Miners, postal workers, bin-men, grave diggers, healthcare ancillaries, train and bus drivers, gas and electricity workers, lorry drivers for companies such as BP and Esso and workers at Ford all went on strike; there were even unofficial strikes by ambulance drivers. The chart shows the number of days lost per year on a rolling 12-month basis.

Industrial action continued in 1980 and 1981, as the UK economy fell into recession and unemployment rose. In 1984–5, further large-scale disruption occurred as the National Union of Miners went on strike.

Although this occurred nearly 40 years ago, it looked as though lightning was about to strike for the second time in 2009 as the world economy plunged into a deep recession in the aftermath of the credit crunch. There were fears that Britain was entering months of industrial unrest, as bus drivers, bin-men, airline and underground staff and firefighters followed the postal workers' lead and protested at changes to their pay, shift patterns and working conditions.

In the latter half of 2009 and early 2010, industrial action spread rapidly in the UK (and in other countries across the world). From bins to buses, and trains to planes, there was massive disruption, affecting everyone and reducing output at a vulnerable time for the country.

Some 1.5 million customers were affected by Underground strikes and businesses suffered from fewer shoppers and lost working hours, as staff struggled to get to work. Bin strikes imposed 'external costs' on customers, who had to pass piles of rubbish in some areas, such as Leeds, and again this impacted sales. Research by the London Chamber of Commerce suggested that the postal strikes alone cost London more than £500 million in lost business.[1]

[1] Tom Sands, 'Postal strike costs London £500m', *Parcel2Go.com* (26 October 2009).

In 2010, the Coalition government was elected and began its 'austerity policies' and this led to trade unions mobilising. Public-sector unions were particularly vocal in response to curbs in their pay and pensions and further industrial action ensued. In mid-2010, the Public and Commercial Services Union threatened to re-launch strikes which had begun in March involving 200 000 civil servants, but which had been suspended for the election. In March 2013, the Public and Commercial Services Union (PCS) voted to strike in response to job losses, changes in pensions and public-sector pay being frozen for two years for those earning above £21 000.

Further postal strikes took place over the 2013 Easter weekend and again in the run-up to Christmas in 2014. Baggage handlers at Stansted airport threatened to walk out following shift changes which could adversely affect their pay. This followed a four-day strike over the Jubilee weekend in June 2012.

Civil servants were called in to cover UK border control posts, which was the first time that the government recruited other members of the civil service to break a strike by immigration officials.

But fewer days are lost to strike action

However, despite industrial action continuing to be a cause of concern, the number of days lost through strike action has been considerably less in recent years than in the 1970s and 1980s (see the chart).

Partly this is because the proportion of workers in unions has fallen. In 1980, 53.2 per cent of employees were members of a trade union; by 2017, just 22.9 per cent were. As the labour market becomes more flexible, a growing proportion of workers are employed on zero-hour contracts, on a part-time or casual basis, or on a self-employed basis in the 'gig economy' (see section 8.4). Most of these workers are not union members.

Annual working days lost through industrial disputes in the UK (millions) (cumulative 12-month totals adjusted monthly)

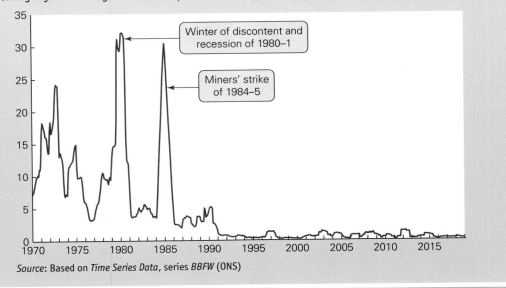

Source: Based on *Time Series Data*, series *BBFW* (ONS)

Part of the reason for fewer days lost through strike action, however, is that industrial action has become 'smarter'. Strikes can be for a very short time, such as a day or even a couple of hours, but at crucial times. Or unions can take action short of striking. For example, their members can refuse to do certain duties that are not specified in their contracts; or they can work more slowly by making sure that everything is done 'thoroughly' and that everything is fully checked.

Let us now examine two sectors which have been subject to industrial action in recent times.

Airlines

We have considered the airline industry in a number of chapters so far and now we look at some of the labour market issues it experiences.

Strikes in the airline industry occurred, alongside many others mentioned, from 2009, particularly over the Christmas period. BA cabin crew went on strike after talks broke down regarding pay freezes, working practices and redundancies. In 2010, strikes continued, with those in March estimated to have cost BA approximately £45 million.[2]

The Spanish airline, Iberia, also experienced strikes over the renewal of contracts in 2009, which led to 400 flights cancelled in two days, leaving thousands of passengers stranded. Pilots from India's Jet Airways held a five-day strike during September 2009, and Germany's Lufthansa had to cancel thousands of flights in early 2010, when 4000 pilots went on strike, with fears of foreign pilots being used to maintain the airline's profitability. Estimates suggest this cost the company some £21.9 million per day.

Airlines were severely hit by the recession, as holidays abroad became a luxury for cash-strapped consumers. While many airlines had other problems as well, lower revenues and profits meant that cost savings were needed, and so staff had to be cut. BA lost over £400 million in 2008, due to lower passenger numbers, and the resulting strike action imposed further costs, such as lost revenue, hiring in planes and crew, and buying seats on rival carriers.

In 2016, Lufthansa again faced serious problems when it had to cancel 4500 flights, which affected 350 000 passengers. In 2017, BA was in the news again after it cancelled thousands of flights, when 1400 workers went on strike over pay concerns.

In 2018, strikes in the airline industry continued. Ryanair suffered from a 24-hour walk-out from cabin crew and pilots across Europe, which required the company to cancel 8 per cent of its 2400 daily flights. Ryanair said that air traffic control staff shortages would be the main reason for flight cancellations in 2019, which would be higher than in 2018. According to a French parliamentary report, air traffic control-related delays account for around 15 per cent of all flight delays across Europe and cost airlines around £263 million each year.[3]

According to SkyCop, strikes by pilots and cabin crew are likely to become more of a problem, due to the vulnerability of airline finances and pilot shortages.[4] We have already seen the departure of Airberlin, Alitalia, Monarch and Flybmi within Europe and these companies may only be the first victims of this market.

UK higher education

In February and March 2018, academics from 61 UK universities began a prolonged period of strike action. There was significant disruption in many universities and departments. Lectures were cancelled and there were changes to assessments due to content not being taught. This had a negative impact on the experience of many students.

While many strikes occur because of pay or working conditions, the strikes in the higher education sector related to changes to the pensions received by academics, who would have seen a significant fall in their pension pot. The University and College Union indicated that the planned changes would cost academics £10 000 per year. Academics argued that they had chosen to work in a relatively low-paid sector, expecting a more generous pension on retirement and that these changes would markedly affect their standard of living, the recruitment of top researchers, the quality of teaching and the overall student experience.

The strike certainly gained media attention, not least because of the negative impact on students. Picket lines were set up; yet, despite the freezing temperatures and snow on the ground, striking academics were not deterred.

The strike received support from a wide range of people, including non-striking academics, the public and many students. However, there were many others who were critical, including some students, who understandably argued that their education, and even their future, was being affected. With tuition fees capped at £9000 and most universities charging this fee, there were calls from students to receive refunds or compensation, as they felt like they were now 'customers'. The impact of the strikes was felt not just in the UK, but concern was also expressed in other countries, particularly China, which has 170 000 nationals studying at UK universities.

The strike did have an impact and by the middle of week 2, employers had agreed to meet the union through the Advisory, Conciliation and Arbitration Service (ACAS), leading to initial talks. However, no agreement was reached and further strikes were planned. Both sides did eventually come to an agreement, however, with both parties contributing more to the pension pot.[5]

Despite the volume of industrial action we continue to observe, there has been growing recognition that employers and employees can learn from each other and with co-operation everyone can be made better off. However, negotiations often fail to resolve issues and industrial action, with its associated costs, results.

1. *Are strikes the best course of action for workers? In the cases outlined above, would you have advised any other responses by either side?*

[2] 'BA strike: talks between airline and union resume', *BBC News* (7 April 2010).
[3] Kim Willsher, 'French air traffic control 'causes third of Europe's air traffic delays' *The Guardian* (18 June 2018).
[4] 'Airline strikes: how much longer should passengers suffer?' *SkyCop* (February 2018).
[5] Richard Adams, 'UK university strike action to end after staff vote to accept offer'; *The Guardian* (13 April 2018).

2. Which strike do you think was the most costly to (a) consumers, (b) businesses and (c) the economy? Explain.
3. Why do strains on public finances lead to continued industrial unrest?

Choose a recent industrial dispute and examine (a) the arguments used by both sides to justify their position; (b) the courses of action taken by both sides; (c) the sequence of events; and (d) how it was resolved (if it has been).

RECAP

1. In an imperfect labour market, where a business has monopoly power in employing labour, it is known as a monopsonist. Such a firm will employ workers to the point where $MRP_L = MC_L$. Since the wage is below the MC_L, the monopsonist, other things being equal, will employ fewer workers at a lower wage than would be employed in a perfectly competitive labour market.

2. If a union has monopoly power, its power to raise wages will be limited if the employer operates in a highly competitive goods market. A rise in wage rates will force the employer to cut back on employment, unless there is a corresponding rise in productivity.

3. In a situation of bilateral monopoly (where a monopoly union faces a monopsony employer), the union may have considerable scope to raise wages above the monopsony level, without the employer wishing to reduce the level of employment. There is no unique equilibrium wage. The wage will depend on the outcome of a process of collective bargaining between union and management.

8.3 MINIMUM WAGES

Minimum wages are used widely in developed countries. Figure 8.7 shows the minimum wage rates in a number of countries in 2017. These are adjusted for inflation and given in 2017 prices. They are also converted to US dollars at 'purchasing-power parity' exchange rates, which adjust the market exchange rate to reflect purchasing power: i.e. the exchange rates at which one dollar would be worth the same in purchasing power in each country. This allows more meaningful comparisons between countries.

As of February 2019, 22 of the 28 EU member countries had a national minimum wage.[5] These rates varied considerably. But, three broad groupings can be identified: one where minimum wages were lower than €600 a month, which comprised only Eastern European EU member states (Bulgaria, Latvia, Romania, Hungary, Croatia, the Czech Republic, Slovakia, Poland, Estonia and Lithuania); an intermediate set, largely made up of Southern European countries, where minimum wages range from €750 to less than

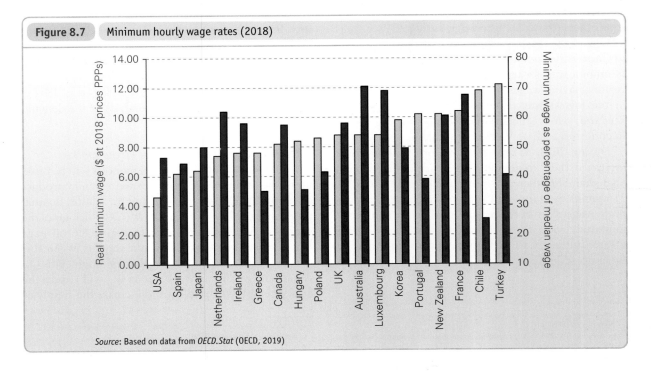

Figure 8.7 Minimum hourly wage rates (2018)

Source: Based on data from *OECD.Stat* (OECD, 2019)

€1100 a month (Portugal, Greece, Malta, Slovenia and Spain) and a final set of the most affluent nations, where the national minimum wage was €1450 or above per month (the UK, France, Germany, Belgium, the Netherlands, Ireland and Luxembourg).[6]

There is a significant spread of minimum wages across Europe, with Luxembourg having the highest hourly wage at €12.08 in 2019, which is over seven times as high as Bulgaria's, which was just €1.72 per hour. However, in the year to February 2019, Bulgaria's wage has increased by over 10 per cent, compared to just a 3.6 per cent increase in Luxembourg, so the gap has been closing. Spain and Lithuania have increased their minimum wages by the most over that same period, with increases of 22.4 per cent and 38.4 per cent, respectively.

In assessing minimum wages across countries, it is also important to take into account the price level that consumers face in each country. Although significant gaps do still remain, adjusting the minimum wages into purchasing power parity standards means Luxembourg's minimum wage is now around 3 times higher than Bulgaria's. Other countries also have minimum wages in place, including Japan, where the minimum wage was ¥874 ($7.90) per hour in 2018.

Regional minimum wages. In the USA, there is a federal minimum wage of $7.25 per hour, which has remained unchanged since 2009. However, in March 2019, The House Committee on Education and Labor voted to raise the minimum wage to $15 per hour, which now means that it will be voted on in the House of Representatives.[7] However, there are additional minimum wages by state, with 18 US states increasing their wage at the start of 2019 and four others to increase the wage during 2019.

One of the reasons why wage costs have increased in China is rises in minimum wages. As with the USA, minimum wages vary across the country, with some regions having wages that are now higher than those in the lowest wage countries in the EU, including Bulgaria, while others remain similar to wage levels in countries such as Vietnam and India.

During 2018, 15 provinces/regions within China increased their minimum wages, including Beijing, Shanghai, Shenzhen and Tibet and in 2017, 20 of the 31 regions in mainland China pushed up their minimum wage. Part of the reason for the vast number of minimum wage rates is the fact that regions have greater authority to make adjustments and most of them do set different wage levels for different areas,

depending on factors such as the stage of development, a rural or urban location, prices and the cost of living.[8]

A living wage. Despite past increases in the minimum wage in the UK (and elsewhere), critics still argue that it is insufficient and is not a 'real living wage'. The Living Wage Foundation publishes a Real Living Wage,[9] which in 2018/19 was £9.00 per hour and £10.55 in London for all workers aged 18 and over. It is based on the cost of living and is designed to lift those working full time out of poverty. It is voluntarily paid by around 4700 UK employers, including one third of FTSE 100 companies.

In response to the Foundation's living wage campaign, a higher minimum wage was introduced in the UK in April 2016 for people aged 25 and over and is called the 'National Living Wage'. It has since increased each year and for 2019/20 was £8.21 per hour. The government aims to increase it to 60 per cent of median income by 2020/21. There are also other minimum wages for different groups in the economy, including £7.70 for those between 21 and 24, £6.15 per hour for those aged 18–20 and £4.35 for under-18s.

Although the National Living Wage has helped to raise living standards, variations in the cost of living in different parts of the UK have led people to argue that minimum wages should vary depending on where you live, as we see in the USA and China, particularly including a London weighting. Furthermore, there are continuing demands that the National Living Wage should equal the Real Living Wage.

Critics of a national minimum wage argue that it can cause unemployment and, with it, a *rise* in poverty. Supporters argue that it not only helps to reduce poverty among the low paid, but also has little or no adverse effects on employment and may even *increase* employment.

In order to assess the background to this debate, we need to revisit our earlier analysis of the demand and supply of labour.

Minimum wages in a competitive labour market

In a competitive labour market, workers will be hired up to the point where the marginal revenue product of labour (MRP_L), i.e. the demand for labour, is equal to the marginal cost of labour (MC_L), which gives the supply curve. Referring back to Figure 8.6 on page 203, the free-market equilibrium wage is W_1 in this particular industry and the level of employment is Q_1. A national minimum wage, set at W_2, will reduce the level of employment to Q_2 and increase the supply of

[5] See: Karel Fric, *Statutory Minimum Wages 2018*, Eurofound (6 February 2018).

[6] In each case, the countries are given in order with the country providing the lowest minimum wage listed first.

[7] See: Alina Selyukh, 'Bill raising Federal minimum wage to $15 heads to U.S. House floor', *NPR News* (6 March 2019).

[8] See: Alexander Chipman Koty and Qian Zhou, 'Minimum wages in China 2018–19'; *China Briefing* (14 December 2018).

[9] *What is the Real Living Wage?* Living Wage Foundation.

labour to Q_3, thereby creating unemployment of the amount Q_3-Q_2.

The level of unemployment created as a result of the national minimum wage will be determined not only by the level of the minimum wage, but also by the elasticity of labour demand and supply. The more elastic the demand and supply of labour, the bigger the unemployment effect will be. Evidence suggests that the demand for low-skilled workers by any given employer is likely to be relatively wage sensitive. The most likely reason for this is that many of the goods or services produced by low-paid workers are very price sensitive, the firms frequently operating in very competitive markets, where there are many substitutes. If one firm alone raised its prices, to compensate for higher wage rates, it might well lose a considerable number of sales and hence reduce employment.

However, minimum wage legislation applies to *all* firms. If all the firms in an industry or sector put up their prices in response to higher wages, demand for any one firm would fall much less. Here the problem of consumers switching away from a firm's products, and hence of that firm being forced to reduce its workforce, would mainly only occur (a) if there were cheaper competitor products from abroad or (b) if other firms produced the products with more capital-intensive techniques, involving fewer workers to whom the minimum wage legislation applied.

Minimum wages and monopsony employers
In an imperfect labour market where the employer has some influence over rates of pay, the impact of the national minimum wage on levels of employment is even less clear-cut.

The situation is illustrated in Figure 8.8 (which is similar to Figure 8.5 on page 203). With no minimum wage a monopsonistic employer will employ Q_1 workers: where the MC_L is equal to MRP_L. At this point the firm is maximising its return from the labour it employs. Remember that the MC_L curve lies above the supply of labour curve (AC_L), since the additional cost of employing one more unit of labour involves paying all existing employees the new wage. The wage rate paid by the monopsonist will be W_1.

If the minimum wage is set at W_2, the level of employment within the firm is likely to grow! Why should this be so? The reason is that the minimum wage cannot be bid down by the monopsonist cutting back on its workforce. The minimum wage rate is thus both the new AC_L and also the new MC_L; employers will thus choose to employ Q_2 workers, where MRP_L = (the new) MC_L. Thus the imposition of a minimum wage rate has *increased* the level of employment.

Clearly, if the minimum wage rate were very high then, other things being equal, the level of employment would fall. This would occur in Figure 8.8 if the

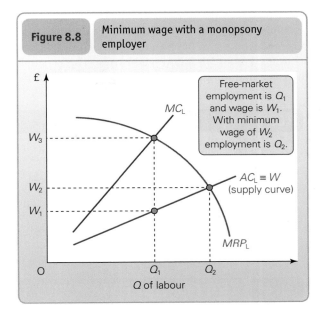

Figure 8.8 Minimum wage with a monopsony employer

minimum wage rate were above W_3. Employment would be below Q_1. But even this argument is not clear-cut, given that (a) a higher wage rate may increase labour productivity by improving worker motivation and (b) other firms, with which the firm might compete in the product market, will also be faced with paying the higher minimum wage rate. The resulting rise in prices is likely to shift the MRP_L curve to the right.

Pause for thought

If a rise in the minimum wage causes employers to substitute machines for workers, will this necessarily lead to higher unemployment?

On the other hand, to the extent that the imposition of a minimum wage rate reduces a firm's profits, this may lead it to cut down on investment, which may threaten long-term employment prospects.

Evidence on the effect of minimum wages
Evidence from various countries suggests that modest increases in the minimum wage have had little effect upon employment. While some employers might reduce the quantity of labour they employ, others might respond to their higher wage bill, and hence higher costs, by improving productive efficiency.

Since the introduction of minimum wages in many countries, there is little evidence to suggest that employers have responded by employing fewer workers. Costs have certainly risen, most recently in China, but despite minimum wages rising in many countries and regions relative to both median and mean hourly wage rates, unemployment rates have remained fairly stable. Part of this is due to fairly buoyant economies, but also to the difficulties in substituting labour in many industries. Fairly small increases in minimum wages have therefore had little effect on unemployment, though in the UK firms did express their concern about costs and prices if they were forced to pay the higher Real Living Wage. The issue then, seems to be how *high* can the minimum wage be set before unemployment begins to rise?

RECAP

1. Statutory minimum wage rates have been adopted in many countries.

2. In a perfect labour market, where employers are forced to accept the wage as determined by the market, any attempt to impose a minimum wage above this level will create unemployment. Amounts of additional unemployment are likely to be low, however, because the demand and supply of labour are relatively inelastic to changes in wage rates that apply to *all* firms.

3. In an imperfect labour market, where an employer has some monopsonistic power, the impact of a minimum wage is uncertain. The impact will depend largely upon how much workers are currently paid below their *MRP* and whether a higher wage encourages them to work more productively.

8.4 THE FLEXIBLE FIRM AND THE MARKET FOR LABOUR

The past 30 years have seen sweeping changes in the ways that firms organise their workforce. Three world recessions combined with rapid changes in technology have led many firms to question the wisdom of appointing workers on a permanent basis to specific jobs. Instead, they want to have the greatest flexibility possible to respond to new situations. If demand falls, they want to be able to 'shed' labour without facing large redundancy costs. If demand rises, they want rapid access to additional labour supplies. If technology changes, say with the introduction of new computerised processes, they want to have the flexibility to move workers around, or to take on new workers in some areas and lose workers in others.

What many firms seek, therefore, is flexibility in employing and allocating labour. What countries are experiencing is an increasingly flexible labour market, as workers and employment agencies respond to the new 'flexible firm'. More than half of all firms today are using flexible forms of work.

There are three main types of flexibility in the use of labour:

■ *Functional flexibility.* This is where an employer is able to transfer labour between different tasks within the production process. It contrasts with traditional forms of organisation where people were employed to do a specific job, and then stuck to it. A functionally flexible labour force will tend to be multi-skilled and relatively highly trained to enable them to move effectively between jobs, as needed.

■ *Numerical flexibility.* This is where the firm is able to adjust the size and composition of its workforce according to changing market conditions. To achieve this, the firm is likely to employ a large proportion of its labour on a part-time or casual basis, or even subcontract out specialist requirements, rather than employing such labour skills itself. Also, the changing nature of the family structure has increased the availability of part-time and casual workers, as women's participation in the workforce continues to grow.

■ *Financial flexibility.* This is where the firm has flexibility in its wage costs. In large part it is a result of functional and numerical flexibility. Financial flexibility can be achieved by rewarding individual effort and productivity rather than paying a given rate for a particular job. Such rates of pay are increasingly negotiated at the local level rather than being nationally set. The result is not only a widening of pay differentials between skilled and unskilled workers, but also growing differentials in pay between workers within the same industry but in different parts of the country.

Figure 8.9 shows how these three forms of flexibility are reflected in the organisation of a *flexible firm*,

---

Definitions

Functional flexibility Where employers can switch workers from job to job as requirements change.

Numerical flexibility Where employers can change the size of their workforce as their labour requirements change.

Financial flexibility Where employers can vary their wage costs by changing the composition of their workforce or the terms on which workers are employed.

Flexible firm A firm that has the flexibility to respond to changing market conditions by changing the composition of its workforce.

Figure 8.9   The flexible firm

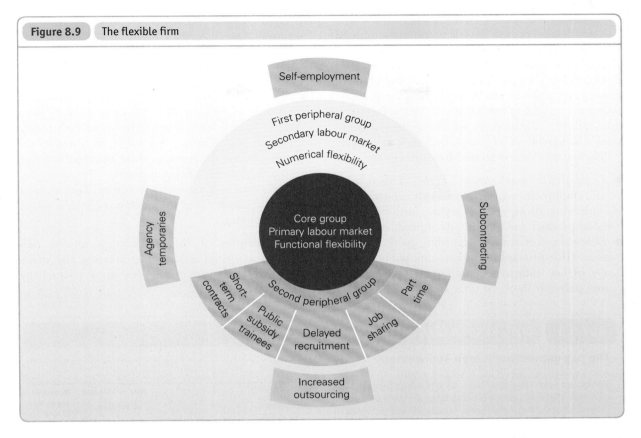

an organisation quite different from that of the traditional firm. The most significant difference is that the labour force is segmented. The core group, drawn from the *primary labour market*, will be composed of *functionally* flexible workers, who have relatively secure employment and are generally on full-time permanent contracts. Such workers will be relatively well paid and receive wages reflecting their scarce skills.

The periphery, drawn from the *secondary labour market*, is more fragmented than the core, and can be subdivided into a first and a second peripheral group. The first peripheral group is composed of workers with a lower level of skill than those in the core, skills that tend to be general rather than firm specific. Thus workers in the first peripheral group can usually be drawn from the external labour market. Such workers may be employed on full-time contracts, but they will generally face less secure employment than those workers in the core.

The business gains a greater level of numerical flexibility by drawing labour from the second peripheral group. Here workers are employed on a variety of short-term, part-time contracts, often through a recruitment agency. Some of these workers may be working from home, or online from another country, such as India, where wage rates are much lower. Workers in the second peripheral group have little job security.

As well as supplementing the level of labour in the first peripheral group, the second periphery can also provide high-level specialist skills that supplement the core. In this instance the business can subcontract or hire self-employed labour, minimising its commitment to such workers. The business thereby gains both functional and numerical flexibility simultaneously. An example is workers in the hotel industry, many of whom have little job security and who are on short-term or zero-hour contracts.[10]

Pause for thought

How is the advent of flexible firms likely to alter the gender balance of employment and unemployment?

Definitions

Primary labour market The market for permanent full-time core workers.

Secondary labour market The market for peripheral workers, usually employed on a temporary or part-time basis, or a less secure 'permanent' basis.

[10] Margaret Deery and Leo K. Jago, *The Core and the Periphery: An Examination of the Flexible Workforce Model in the Hotel Industry*) (Centre for Hospitality and Tourism Research, Victoria University, Melbourne, 2002).

The Japanese model

The application of new flexible working patterns has become more prevalent in businesses in the UK and elsewhere in Europe and North America. In Japan, flexibility has been part of the business way of life for many years and was crucial in shaping the country's economic success in the 1970s and 1980s. In fact we now talk of a Japanese model of business organisation, which many of its competitors seek to emulate.

The model is based around four principles:

- *Total quality management (TQM).* This involves all employees working towards continuously improving all aspects of quality, both of the finished product and of methods of production.
- *Elimination of waste.* According to the 'just-in-time' (JIT) principle, businesses should take delivery of just sufficient quantities of raw materials and parts, at the right time and place. Stocks are kept to a minimum and hence the whole system of production runs with little, if any, slack. For example, supermarkets today have smaller storerooms relative to the total shopping area than they did in the past, and take more frequent deliveries.
- *A belief in the superiority of teamwork.* Collective effort is a vital element in Japanese working practices. Teamwork is seen not only to enhance individual performance, but also to involve the individual in the running of the business and thus to create a sense of commitment.
- *Functional and numerical flexibility.* Both are seen as vital components in maintaining high levels of productivity.

The principles of this model are now widely accepted as being important in creating and maintaining a competitive business in a competitive marketplace.

BOX 8.3 DOES GENDER INEQUALITY STILL EXIST?

The pay gap between men and women

Women earn less than men in the UK and most other countries. Although action is being taken across the world, via measures such as government regulation and increased transparency through the publication of gender pay gaps, the gap still persists.

According to the Annual Survey of Hours and Earnings (ASHE) released by the ONS, the UK gender pay gap for median hourly pay of full-time employees in the UK fell to 8.6 per cent in 2018.[1] In other words, the median earnings for women was 8.6 per cent less than that for men. The gap has closed only slightly in recent years (e.g. it was 9.4 per cent in 2014), but it still reflects a long-term downward trend: in 1970, women typically earned 37 per cent less than men and by 2000 it had fallen to 20 per cent.

In terms of *mean* hourly earnings, the gap is bigger. In 2018, full-time female workers earned 13.7 per cent less than full-time male workers. The table shows mean hourly earnings (excluding overtime) for a range of occupations. As you can see, the gender pay gap varies from occupation to occupation.

Average (mean) gross hourly pay, excluding overtime, for selected occupations, full-time UK employees on adult rates, 2018

Occupation	Men £ per hour	Women £ per hour	Women's pay as % of men's
Librarians	20.18	14.03	69.5
Chief executives and senior officials	60.03	42.36	70.6
Legal Professionals	36.05	27.31	75.8
Architects	24.02	18.98	79.0
Medical practitioners	37.36	30.24	80.9

Occupation	Men £ per hour	Women £ per hour	Women's pay as % of men's
Accountants	24.96	20.44	81.9
HE Lecturers	30.84	25.58	82.9
Hairdressers and barbers	9.56	8.20	85.8
Sales assistants and retail cashiers	10.62	9.22	86.8
Management consultants and business analysts	24.09	21.09	87.5
Senior Police Officers	28.91	25.38	87.8
Bus and coach drivers	12.05	11.02	91.5
Chefs	10.54	9.86	93.5
Secondary school teachers	23.59	22.37	94.8
Laboratory technicians	12.47	11.96	95.9
Nurses	18.10	17.48	96.6
Bar staff	8.39	8.22	98.0
Social workers	18.62	18.63	100.1
All occupations	**18.48**	**15.95**	**86.3**
Average gross weekly pay (incl. overtime)	742.20	599.30	80.7
Average weekly hours worked (incl. overtime)	40.3	37.8	
Average weekly overtime	1.4	0.5	

Source: Annual Survey of Hours and Earnings: 2018 Provisional Results, Tables 1.1a, 1.10a, 1.11a, and 14.6a ONS (25 October 2018)

The gender pay gap continues to persist in nations across the world and you can compare a range of countries in the following figure, which looks at the difference between the median earnings of women relative to the median earnings of men.

Why does the gender pay gap persist?

There are several reasons why the gender pay gap, although declining, still persists.

[1] 'Employee earnings in the UK: 2018' *Annual Survey of Hours and Earnings,* ONS (25 October 2018).

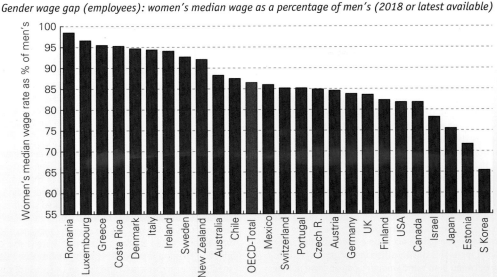

Gender wage gap (employees): women's median wage as a percentage of men's (2018 or latest available)

Source: Based on data from *StatExtracts* (OECD, 2019)

Marginal product of labour. The marginal product of labour plays an important role in determining wages, as it is a key component of the *MRP*. It may be that the marginal productivity of labour in typically female occupations is lower than that in typically male occupations. This may be due to questions of physical strength or that women tend to work in more labour-intensive occupations. If there is less capital equipment per female than there is per male worker, then the marginal product of a woman is likely to be less than that of a man.

The existence of this *occupational* segregation means that women are more likely to be employed in more poorly paid occupations and thus the gender pay gap is somewhat expected. Evidence from the EU as a whole suggests that occupational segregation is a significant factor in explaining pay differences.

Historically, women have had fewer educational opportunities than men and while this is no longer the case in the UK or in many other nations, it is still a highly relevant factor in many other countries, which reduces a woman's marginal product relative to a man's.

Unionisation. Data suggest that women in many countries are less likely to join trade unions and tend to be in occupations with weaker unions. This means that men typically have greater bargaining power than women. For example, in the USA in 2018, male union membership was 11.1 per cent, while female union membership stood at 9.9 per cent. Both figures have declined since 2017, but prior to that, female membership was falling, while male membership had been rising.

In the UK, the picture is different: in 2017, 25.6 per cent of female workers were in unions, while the figure for male workers was 20.9 per cent.[2] By contrast, in 1995, the figures for female and male workers were 29.7 per cent and 35.0 per cent respectively. Part of the reason for this changing picture is the decline in manufacturing industry, where there was a higher proportion of male workers but where unionisation was higher. Today, the higher figure for female workers is partly due to the

higher proportion of women in health and education employment, where unionisation rates are high.

Social perceptions. A man's job was traditionally seen as more 'important' than a woman's job and so women have tended to be less geographically mobile, with more limited outside options and this has acted to reduce women's bargaining power.

Career breaks. Women are more likely to take breaks to have a family and to be part-time workers. Training is very costly and thus firms are often more willing to invest money in training men (who are more likely to be around for longer) than women and this pushes up men's marginal product.

A study by the Institute for Fiscal Studies (IFS)[3] estimated that for every year a woman takes away from work her earnings fall by 2 per cent below those who remain in work. It also noted the longer-term detrimental effect on women's earnings when switching from full-time to part-time employment. When this happens, while their wage does not fall immediately over time, their growth in earnings falls behind those of people working full time.

Historical legacy. Women's pay in the past tended to be lower than men's and often it had little to do with differences in productivity. Equal pay legislation has had an effect, but past practices of gender discrimination in the labour market still persist in many workplaces.

Many of the above reasons for unequal pay might be viewed as rational, especially if they result from differences in marginal productivity. But, what about the last point: the historical legacy of discrimination? Pure discrimination based on gender still exists. But what are the effects?

Economic effects of gender discrimination

Consider the wage rates set for men and women by a firm that has monopsony power and discriminates against women, despite the fact that both men and women have the same

[2] See: *Trade Union Membership Statistics 2017*, Table 1.6, Department of Business, Energy & Industrial Strategy (31 May 2018).

[3] William Elming, Robert Joyce and Monica Costa Dias, 'The gender wage gap', *IFS Briefing Note BN186*, Institute for Fiscal Studies (23 August 2016).

marginal productivity. By discriminating against women, the demand for women is lower than it otherwise would be. That is, the firm applies a negative discriminatory factor to the women's *MRP*, which acts to shift this curve to the left and thus pushes down their relative wage. It also reduces the number of women employed in equilibrium. This is a form of negative discrimination.

But, what will happen to men's wages and the number of males employed by this firm? It might be that men's wages and the equilibrium number employed are left to be determined by their actual *MRP* and thus there is no positive discrimination. On the other hand, firms could apply economic discrimination in favour of men, thus adding a positive discriminatory factor to men's *MRP* curve (shifting it to the right), thereby pushing their wage up and employing more of them. This might have to be done if the firm requires a specific number of workers and by reducing the proportion of women (due to negative discrimination), the excess demand for workers must be made up by a relatively larger proportion of men. This positive discrimination makes the inequality between men's and women's pay and the number of workers employed even larger.

The glass ceiling

Although legislation has been passed to enforce equal pay, discrimination and prejudice still remain a concern. In 2010, a review in the UK looked at the number of women employed at the very top of the biggest companies (FTSE 100 and 250). This led to the Davies Report, which set a target of 25 per cent of Board members of FTSE 100 companies being occupied by women by 2015, from a starting point of 12.5 per cent in 2011.[4] The target set by Lord Davies was met, with a figure of 26.1 per cent. Subsequently, a new target of 33 per cent was set for 2020. By July 2018, 29.0 per cent of Board members of FTSE 100 companies were occupied by women.[5]

Cranfield University continues to publish its Female FTSE Board report and this indicates the progress made in the UK.[6]

---

[4] *Women on Boards: The Davies Report*, GOV.UK (February 2011).

[5] Ruth Sealy, *Board Diversity Reporting*, Financial Reporting Council and University of Exeter Business School, Professor (September 2018).

[6] Susan Vinnicombe, Elena Doldor and Ruth Sealy, *The Female FTSE Board Report 2018*, Cranfield University (1 June 2018).

Various measures were suggested in the Davies Report to increase female board members, such as discussion with company Chairs on the issue, pressure from investors and a requirement for companies to report on their diversity policies. Other things that may have helped to boost female representation include data that indicate the benefits of female board membership. In 2018, a report from McKinsey found that those companies in the upper quartile for gender diversity in their executive teams were 21 per cent more likely to have above-average profitability than companies in the bottom quartile.[7]

Across the EU, work is ongoing to improve female board membership. However, in October 2017, women accounted for just 25.3 per cent of board members in the largest publicly listed companies in EU members, according to a European Commission report.[8] There is also significant variation in the percentage of female board members, ranging from a high of 43.3 per cent in France to a low of less than 10 per cent in Malta and Estonia. There is still clearly a long way to go, but progress is being made, albeit at a 'snail's pace' according to The European Institute for Gender Equality (EIGE).[9]

1. *Drawing a diagram similar to Figure 8.5 on page 203, illustrate the effect of negative economic discrimination and positive economic discrimination.*
2. *What measures could governments introduce to increase the number of women getting the highest paid jobs?*

Download data on the Gender Pay Gap from the labour market earnings database on Eurostat. Using the latest available data, create a chart showing the variation in the size of the gender pay gap across a selection of EU member countries along with the gap for the UK.

---

[7] Vivian Hunt, Sara Prince, Sundiatu Dixon-Fyle and Lareina Yee, *Delivering through Diversity*, McKinsey & Company (January 2018).

[8] Christina Boll and Andreas Lagemann, *Gender Pay Gap in EU Countries Based on SES (2014)* (European Commission, 2018).

[9] *2018 Report on Equality between Men And women in the EU* (European Commission, 2018).

RECAP

1. Changes in technology have had a massive impact upon the process of production and the experience of work. Labour markets and business organisations have become more flexible as a consequence.

2. There are three major forms of flexibility: functional, numerical and financial. The flexible firm incorporates these different forms of flexibility into its business operations.

3. It organises production around a core workforce, which it supplements with workers and skills drawn from a periphery. Peripheral workers tend to hold general skills rather than firm-specific skills and are employed on part-time and temporary contracts.

4. The application of the flexible firm model is closely mirrored in the practices of Japanese business. Commitments to improve quality, reduce waste, build teamwork and introduce flexible labour markets are seen as key components in the success of Japanese business organisation.

Wages are a reward for labour. They are also, from a business perspective, a means of motivating the labour force. For example, the possibility of promotion to a post paying a higher wage can be a key incentive for employees to improve their performance. Another example is piece rates. This is where workers are paid according to the amount they produce. The more they produce, the higher their pay. Similarly, a firm may pay commission to its sales force – as an incentive to sell more. Sometimes the firm will pay its senior executives bonuses related to company performance.

Because of the use of pay as a means of encouraging better performance by workers or management, firms will sometimes pay above the market rate. They pay what is known as an *efficiency wage rate*.

Efficiency wages

The *efficiency wage hypothesis* states that the productivity of workers rises as the wage rate rises. As a result, employers are frequently prepared to offer wage rates above the market-clearing level, attempting to balance increased wage costs against gains in productivity. But why may higher wage rates lead to higher productivity? There are three main explanations.

Less 'shirking'. In many jobs it is difficult to monitor the effort that individuals put into their work. In such cases piece rates or commission may be impracticable. Workers may thus get away with shirking or careless behaviour, especially in a large company, where this becomes a good example of the principal–agent problem (see pages 9–10).

The business could attempt to reduce shirking by imposing a series of sanctions, the most serious of which would be dismissal. The greater the wage rate currently received, the greater will be the cost to the individual of dismissal (the opportunity cost in terms of the salary forgone), and the less likely it is that workers will shirk. The business will benefit not only from the additional output, but also from a reduction in the costs of having to monitor workers' performance. As a consequence, the efficiency wage rate for the business will lie above the market-determined wage rate.

Reduced labour turnover. If workers receive on-the-job training or retraining, then to lose a worker once the training has been completed is a significant cost to the business, as it does not receive any of the benefits, yet incurs all of the costs. A few decades ago, workers tended to remain in the same job for much of their lives, but the labour market has changed, and it is now not unusual for workers to change jobs several times throughout their working life. As such, this issue of training has become more problematic. However, labour turnover, and hence its associated costs, can be reduced by paying a wage above the market-clearing rate. By paying such a wage, the business is seeking a degree of loyalty from its employees.

Improved morale. A simple reason for offering wage rates above the market-clearing level is to motivate the workforce – to create the feeling that the firm is a 'good' employer that cares about its employees. As a consequence, workers might be more industrious and more willing to accept the introduction of new technology (with the reorganisation that it involves).

> ### Pause for thought
>
> *Give some examples of things an employer could do to increase the morale of the workforce other than raising wages. How would you assess whether they were in the interests of the employer?*

The paying of efficiency wages above the market-clearing wage will depend upon the type of work involved. Workers who occupy skilled positions are likely to receive efficiency wages considerably above the market wage. This is especially true where the business has invested time in their training, which makes them costly to replace. By contrast, workers in unskilled positions, where shirking can be easily monitored, little training takes place and workers can be easily replaced, are unlikely to command an 'efficiency wage premium'. In such situations, rather than keeping wage rates high, the business will probably try to pay as little as possible and so the minimum wage legislation is likely to be important for such workers.

> ### Definitions
>
> **Efficiency wage rate** The profit-maximising wage rate for the firm after taking into account the effects of wage rates on worker motivation, turnover and recruitment.
>
> **Efficiency wage hypothesis** A hypothesis that states that a worker's productivity is linked to the wage he or she receives.

Principal–agent relationships in the labour market

The need to pay efficiency wages above the market rate is an example of the principal–agent problem (see pages 9–10). The worker, as an agent of the employer (the principal), is not necessarily going to act in the principal's interest.

At the time when people are interviewed for a job, they will clearly be keen to make a good impression on their potential employer and may promise all sorts of things. Once employed, however, a 'moral hazard' occurs (see pages 59–60 and 62) – workers will be tempted to take it easy. The principal (the firm) will therefore attempt to prevent this occurring. One solution, as we have seen, is to pay an efficiency wage. Another is to tighten up on job monitoring by managers. For example, regular performance appraisal could be instituted, with sanctions imposed on workers who underperform. Such sanctions could range from support in the form of additional training to penalties in the form of closer monitoring, lost pay, lost bonuses or even dismissal. Another solution is to offer rewards for good performance in the form of bonuses or promotion.

In general, however, the poorer the information on the part of the principal (the greater the 'information asymmetry'), the more the employee will be able to get away with.

Pause for thought

Does a moral hazard apply to employers as well as workers? If so, how might it affect employers' behaviour?

There is also an 'adverse selection' problem for the employer (see pages 59 and 62). The most able workers are those most likely to leave for a better job elsewhere. The workers who elect to stay are likely to be the least able. To counter this problem, the employer might need to be willing to promote people to more senior posts to encourage them to stay.

Executive pay

By Friday 4 January 2019, the earnings of the top bosses in the UK had already exceeded the annual salary for that year of a typical full-time worker, according to calculations from the High Pay Centre[11] and the Chartered Institute of Personnel and Development (CIPD). The August 2018 Report by the CIPD found that in 2017, average FTSE 100 CEO pay increased by 23 per cent to £5.7 million (having fallen by 17 per cent in 2016 to £4.6 million).[12] The ONS finds that the average UK salary in 2017 increased by just 2.5 per cent to £29 009. The High Pay Centre also finds that pay levels for FTSE 100 CEOs are now 150 times the median UK salary – an increase from 60 times the average in 2000. The implication of this is 'that FTSE 100 CEOs, working an average 12-hour day, will only need to work for 29 hours in 2019 to earn the average worker's annual salary, two hours fewer than 2018.'[13]

In the USA, even bigger pay differentials are evident. In 2016, the average earnings of the CEOs of the top 350 companies was $15.6 million and a report from the Economic Policy Institute,[14] found that their pay was 271 times the average annual pay of an American worker ($58 000). This ratio has increased from just 30 times the average American worker's salary in 1978, though is lower than the figure for 2014, when CEOs pay packets were 299 times the average American salary.

There continues to be much resentment over the pay differential between the top bosses and typical workers, especially as top executives continued to receive pay rises and bonus packages in the years following the financial crisis, while many other workers saw their pay frozen.

Performance-related pay

One of the key things that has increased the resentment is that, in many cases, all components of executive pay have increased, even those related to company performance – and this has happened even when company performance has declined. For the top earners, salaries typically account for a relatively small percentage of their overall income. Incentives and bonuses often considerably outstrip basic salaries and it is increases in these aspects that has led to such significant increases in executive pay.

Incentives and bonuses account for around 80 per cent of executive pay in the USA. In the UK, the CIPD's 2018 report found that the base salary of CEOs increased from £885 000 to £918 000 between 2016 and 2017 (3.7 per cent). At the same time, total remuneration increased from £4.5 million to £5.7 million (26.7 per cent), such that in 2017, base salary accounted for just 16.2 per cent of total pay, with other incentives making up the rest. They

---

[11] 'It's "Fatcat Friday" – CEO pay for 2019 surpasses the amount the average UK worker earns all year', *HPC blog*, High Pay Centre (3 January 2019).

[12] *Executive Pay: Review of FTSE 100 Executive Pay*, CIPD (August 2018).

[13] 'It's "Fatcat Friday" . . . ', op. cit.

[14] Lawrence Mishel and Jessica Schieder, *CEO Pay Remains High Relative to the Pay of Typical Workers and High-wage Earners*, Economic Policy Institute (20 July 2017).

include things such as annual bonuses, *long-term incentive plans (LTIPs)*, restricted stock awards, *stock (or share) options* and *stock appreciation rights (SARs)*. The idea is that CEOs and top executives have an incentive to improve their company's performance, and hence the dividends of shareholders, and, if this occurs, they are rewarded with bonuses.

The 2018 review of FTSE 100 pay found that payments from long-term incentive plans increased from £213 million in 2016 to £313 million in 2017. This increase was in part related to the strong stock market performance over the period, but was this driven entirely or even mostly by the performance of the CEO? Think back to Chapter 6 and Box 2.1 where we considered the stock market. While some companies may be performing well, the general state of the economy and the attractiveness of investing in the stock market also determines overall performance and this typically has little to do with the actions of the CEO. Therefore, in many cases, CEOs receive increases in bonuses that typically do not reflect the performance of the company.

The January 2019 Report from the CIPD and High Pay Centre quotes the Investment Association in noting that 'Rising levels of executive pay over the last 15 years have not been in line with the performance of the FTSE over the same period.'[15] The same applies for the top 350 companies, where the report notes: 'Increases to each of the different components of typical FTSE 350 executive pay awards have been found to be much greater than any improvements in company performance, as measured by the metrics commonly used in most executive pay packages.'

Assessing incentive schemes

So why do CEOs receive such high pay packets, such as the £47 million salary paid to Persimmon's CEO, Jeff Fairburn?

Incentive schemes are there to reward talented individuals, who are working in a very tough job. They are leading extremely large companies and hence are leading industrial growth within an economy. They are required to take significant risks, set strategy and steer the company through uncertain times, while dealing with the challenges and opportunities that a more globalised economy presents. Some commentators indicate that being a CEO requires a standard 100-hour working week. Therefore, genuine incentives may well encourage risk-taking and good performance.

They also be required to attract the right talent in the first place. The number of individuals who have the skills and ambition required to be a successful CEO is limited and so attracting the right person does come at a cost. FTSE companies are competing with each other, not just in the market place for the goods and services they are supplying, but also in the labour market. Therefore high remuneration packages may be essential in attracting and in retaining staff at the top of the company. Losing an effective CEO to a rival company could be very costly to the long-run performance of the business.

However, it is not just successful CEOs that receive big payments. CEOs of poorly performing companies also receive high remuneration packages and one issue with this is that it can create resentment and harm industrial relations if senior managers feel that such pay is unjustified.

As Andrew Hill from the *Financial Times* states, 'Ultimately, businesses function with the blessing of workers, shareholders, customers and voters. If business leaders are universally seen as immoral and grasping, cynicism and mistrust will flourish and choke enterprise.'[16]

Market imperfections. One reason why CEOs' performance may sometimes have little to do with pay is that there may exist a degree of market imperfection and poor governance, such that CEOs are able to persuade boards of directors to give them the pay that they want. The evidence suggests that in many cases this is true, with remuneration committees failing to exercise discretion in determining pay policy. There have been recommendations that firms should 'adopt a more flexible, individualised approach to executive pay, rather than automatically deferring to the prevailing LTIP model'. This was echoed by the

---

Definitions

Long-term incentive plan (LTIP) A reward system aimed at improving long-term performance, whereby shares or cash bonuses are paid out if performance meets certain targets/criteria over a longer period of time, typically three years.

Stock (or share) options The right to buy shares in the future at a fixed price set today. When granted to senior executives as a reward they do not involve any outlay by the company. They act as an incentive, however, since the better the company performs, the more the market value of its shares is likely to rise above the option price and the more the executive stands to gain by exercising the option to buy shares at the fixed price and then selling them at the market price.

Stock appreciation rights (SARs) Automatic bonuses linked to rises in the company's stock market price.

---

[15] *RemCo Reform: Governing Successful Organisations that Benefit Everyone*, High Pay Centre and CIPD (January 2019) http://highpaycentre.org/files/report_for_website.pdf

[16] Andrew Hill, 'Bonuses are bad for bankers and even worse for banks', *Financial Times* (25 January 2016).

Government's 2017 response to the Green Paper on Corporate Governance.[17]

The problem of benchmarking. Furthermore, CEO pay also gets benchmarked. Companies compare themselves with others and have an incentive to place their company in the higher percentiles, as if a company places itself say below the 50th percentile, is it indicating that it is a poor company? In benchmarking themselves in this way, CEOs' pay for one company is therefore compared with that of others and when one CEO in a particular peer groups receives their pay packet, the size of it filters through to other CEOs, who ask for higher pay and this then feeds

back to the original CEO's pay packet in the next round. The benchmark continues to rise and hence so do the pay packets of all CEOs.

Addressing concerns. We have seen various attempts to address these problems. Caps on executive pay have been introduced across the EU. There is more transparency in terms of the payments that CEOs receive and what they comprise. At the start of 2019, new regulations in the UK will mean that companies must publish details of the pay differential between the CEO and the workers at each quartile of the pay distribution for UK employees. Therefore in 2020 Annual Reports, we should start to see a clearer picture of inequality within companies and this may add pressure to company governance to reconsider pay policy.

---

[17] *Corporate Governance Reform: The Government response to the green paper consultation,* Department for Business, Energy & Industrial Strategy (August 2017).

| BOX 8.4 | EDUCATION, EARNINGS, PRODUCTIVITY AND TALENT |

Developing human capital

Every year of education adds to an individual's human capital, but does an increase in that human capital actually cause an increase in productivity and, in turn, contribute towards the growth of the economy? There are two conflicting theories.

The *human capital model* suggests that education is causally related to higher productivity and hence to economic growth. Education is therefore an investment, which will not only boost individual earnings, but also create economic growth.

The *signalling or screening hypothesis,* however, sees education beyond a certain level, not as a means of boosting productivity and growth, but as a filter – a means of signalling to employers who is the best person for the job.

While there is a consensus that a basic level of education is essential for productivity and growth within a nation, there is less agreement about the role of higher education. So, why go to university?

According to the human capital model, a university degree boosts productivity and hence *MPP* and *MRP,* and by shifting the *MRP* curve to the right, with an upward-sloping supply of labour curve, it will push up the equilibrium wage rate.

Returns from a university degree

There is significant evidence to support the higher lifetime earnings for individuals from obtaining a university degree.

UK data

In 2018, the Institute for Fiscal Studies found that an average 29 year-old man who has graduated from university will earn 28 per cent more than the average man who only obtained five GCSEs A*– C.[1] The figure is 50 per cent for an average 29-year-old woman. Once the data are adjusted for pre-university characteristics, such as those attending university being from richer families and having higher pre-university attainment, the figures change to 8 and 28 per cent, respectively. Once an

individual is aged 30 or over, returns on average increase further, meaning there is an even bigger return on lifetime earnings for those attending higher education.

An earlier report by the Department for Business Innovation and Skills[2] in August 2013 found that additional lifetime earnings from a degree, over not having a degree, were 28 per cent for men (or £168 000) and 53 per cent for women (or £252 000). Moreover a 'good' degree was found to have further returns relative to a lower-class degree of £76 000 and £85 000 for men and women, respectively.

In the UK, the number of students going into higher education has increased over the past 20 years, but the average return of a university education has remained fairly stable.

The returns by degree subject and institution vary significantly. For example, those students studying economics and medicine earn 60 per cent more than history and English graduates.[3]

US data

Similarly large returns are also evident in the USA. A report from Payscale in 2016 looked at US data. It showed that back in 1972 graduates typically earned 20 per cent more than non-graduates. Since then this figure has increased to 70 per cent.[4]

Another research paper[5] in 2015 found that men with a high school diploma earn around $1.54 million over their lifetime, compared to $2.43 million and $3.05 million for those with a bachelor's degree and a postgraduate degree, respectively. The figures for women are $811 000, $1.44 million and $1.87 million respectively, illustrating the extent of gender inequality.

---

[2] 'The impact of university degrees on the lifecycle of earnings: some further analysis', *BIS Research Paper no. 112,* Department for Business, Innovation & Skills (August 2013).

[3] Chris Belfield et al., *op. cit.*

[4] Arwen Armbrecht, *Which Degrees Give the Best Financial Return?,* World Economic Forum (11 January 2016).

[5] Christopher R. Tamborini et al. 'Education and Lifetime Earnings in the United States', *Demography* vol. 52,4 (2015): 1383–407.

---

[1] Chris Belfield et al., *The Impact of Undergraduate Degrees on Early-career Earnings,* Department for Education and Institute for Fiscal Studies (November 2018).

As in the UK, once demographic and socioeconomic factors are accounted for, the lifetime returns decrease, with the additional lifetime earnings from having a bachelor's degree standing at $655 000 for men and $445 000 for women.

Productivity and talent gaps

Despite UK higher education participation rates being above 40 per cent for well over a decade, and in 2016/17 standing at 49.8 per cent, there is still a persistent productivity gap with other nations, particularly in the G7. According to the ONS,[6] in 2016 the average productivity in the G7 countries (excluding the UK) was 19.5 per cent higher than in the UK in terms of output per hour worked and 19.9 per cent higher in terms of output per worker. The gap was even wider with the USA, France, Germany, where output per worker was 29.2, 29.6 and 35.5 per cent higher than in the UK. What is more, the gap has widened in recent years. In 2008 average G7 (excluding the UK) output per hour was just 13.3 per cent higher than in the UK.

There are many explanations for the productivity gap, including a lack of vocational education, too many low-skilled and low-paid jobs, poor management, under-investment and a lack of finance for investment, a lack of innovation and inflexibility in working practices. The 2019 CEO survey and report from PwC highlighted the information and skills gap, noting the 'shortage of skilled talent to clean, integrate, and extract value from big data and move beyond baby steps toward artificial intelligence (AI).' It also noted that 'despite billions of dollars of investment . . . the gap between the information CEOs need and what they get has not closed in the past ten years.'[7] When asked, 54 per cent of CEOs noted that there was a 'lack of analytical talent' and 55 per cent said that the lack of skills was impeding innovation.

These findings were echoed by the Manpower Group's Talent Shortage Survey,[8] which surveyed 39 195 employers in 43 countries and territories. The survey found that

---

[6] *International Comparisons of Productivity*, Tables 1 and 2, ONS (April 2018).
[7] *CEOs' Curbed Confidence Spells Caution: 22nd Annual Global CEO Survey*, pwc (2019).
[8] *Solving the Talent Shortage: 2018 Talent Shortage Survey* (Manpower Group, 2018).

45 per cent of employers could not fill jobs due to a lack of skills, and that for organisations with more than 250 employees, this figure increases to 67 per cent. In the UK, 50 per cent of large businesses reported problems with recruitment but, relative to the rest of the world, UK employers had one of the lowest numbers in terms of reporting difficulty in accessing talent. In 2018, only 19 per cent of UK employers reported difficulty in accessing talent, compared to 89 per cent in Japan, 76 per cent in Hong Kong, 51 per cent in Germany, 46 per cent in the USA and 24 per cent in the Netherlands. The country that had the least reported difficulty was China at 13 per cent.

There has been a global response to the talent and skills issue, with governments taking action to increase investment in education, with new apprenticeship schemes and vocational courses, schemes to make finance more accessible for new companies and incentives for firms to invest in new learning platforms. Employers are looking to recruit outside of traditional pools of labour, offering higher salaries and better benefits, changing the educational and experience requirements of their jobs and investing more in training and development.

As the world continues to move towards an increasingly technological society, with AI and big data growing in importance, it is paramount that the education and skills of the workforce move forwards as well.

1. *Draw a diagram showing the possible impact of a university education on an individual's earnings.*
2. *Do you think there is a problem of allocative efficiency with regards to the UK's productivity gap? Could online recruitment agencies help?*
3. *How would you attempt to measure the marginal productivity of a person hired for a specific talent?*
4. *Do you think it would be a good idea for companies to pay talented people more than the value of their marginal product?*

Choose a country and investigate policy measures that have been introduced to increase labour productivity. What lessons could be learned by other countries from this experience.

RECAP

1. The efficiency wage hypothesis states that a business is likely to pay a wage above the market-clearing rate in order to reduce shirking, reduce labour turnover and stimulate worker morale.

2. Employment is an example of a principal–agent relationship. Workers (the agents) may underperform as a result of lack of information on their performance by their employer (the principal). To combat this problem, employers may link pay more closely with output or monitor the performance of workers more closely.

3. Executive pay has risen much more rapidly than average pay. In addition to high salaries, many senior managers receive considerable bonuses, shares, share options and other perks. High pay may be necessary to act as an incentive for risk taking and to attract high calibre people. It is also often, however, a reflection of poor governance at the top of industry and in many cases is unrelated to performance.

QUESTIONS

1. If a firm faces a shortage of workers with very specific skills, it may decide to undertake the necessary training itself. If on the other hand it faces a shortage of unskilled workers it may well offer a small wage increase in order to obtain the extra labour. In the first case it is responding to an increase in demand for labour by attempting to shift the supply curve. In the second case it is merely allowing a movement along the supply curve. Use a demand and supply diagram to illustrate each case. Given that elasticity of supply is different in each case, do you think that these are the best policies for the firm to follow?

2. The wage rate a firm has to pay and the output it can produce varies with the number of workers as follows (all figures are hourly):

Number of workers	1	2	3	4	5	6	7	8
Wage rate (AC_L) (£)	3	4	5	6	7	8	9	10
Total output (TPR_L)	10	22	32	40	46	50	52	52

Assume that output sells at £2 per unit.

(a) Copy the table and add additional rows for TC_L, MC_L, TRP_L and MRP_L. Put the figures for MC_L and MRP_L in the spaces between the columns.

(b) How many workers will the firm employ in order to maximise profits?

(c) What will be its hourly wage bill at this level of employment?

(d) How much hourly revenue will it earn at this level of employment?

(e) Assuming that the firm faces other (fixed) costs of £30 per hour, how much hourly profit will it make?

(f) Assume that the workers now form a union and that the firm agrees to pay the negotiated wage rate to all employees. What is the maximum to which the hourly wage rate could rise without causing the firm to try to reduce employment below that in (b) above? (See Figures 8.5 and 8.8.)

(g) What would be the firm's hourly profit now?

3. How do you think the supply of labour curve has been affected by the UK's vote to leave the EU?

4. For what types of reason does the marginal revenue product differ between workers in different jobs?

5. If, unlike a perfectly competitive employer, a monopsonist has to pay a higher wage to attract more workers, why, other things being equal, will a monopsonist pay a lower wage than a perfectly competitive employer?

6. The following are figures for a monopsonist employer:

Number of workers (1)	Wage rate (£) (2)	Total cost of labour (£) (3)	Marginal cost of labour (£) (4)	Marginal revenue product (£) (5)
1	100	100		
			110	230
2	105	210		
			120	240
3	110	230		
				240
4	115			
				230
5	120			
				210
6	125			
				190
7	130			
				170
8	135			
				150
9	140			
				130
10	145			

Fill in the missing figures for columns (3) and (4). How many workers should the firm employ if it wishes to maximise profits?

7. To what extent could a trade union succeed in gaining a pay increase from an employer with no loss in employment?

8. Drawing on recent examples, consider the extent to which strike action is likely to help trade union members achieve their various aims.

9. Do any of the following contradict the theory that the demand for labour equals the marginal revenue product: wage scales related to length of service (incremental scales), nationally negotiated wage rates, discrimination, firms taking the lead from other firms in determining this year's pay increase?

10. 'Statutory minimum wages will cause unemployment.' Is this so? Explain.

11. What is the efficiency wage hypothesis? Explain what employers might gain from paying wages above the market-clearing level.

12. Identify the potential costs and benefits of the flexible firm to (a) employers and (b) employees.

13. How have changes in society, laws and technology affected the UK labour market?

14. Provide a case for and against high bonuses.

9 Chapter

Government, the firm and the market

Business issues covered in this chapter

■ To what extent does business meet the interests of consumers and society in general?
■ In what sense are perfect markets 'socially efficient' and why do most markets fail to achieve social efficiency?
■ How do business ethics influence business behaviour?
■ What is corporate responsibility and is it in a business's interest to operate in a socially responsible manner?
■ In what ways do governments intervene in markets and attempt to influence business behaviour?
■ What forms do government environmental policies take, and how do they affect business?
■ How does the government attempt to prevent both the abuse of monopoly power and collusion by oligopolists?
■ How are privatised industries regulated and how has competition been increased in these industries?

Even though most countries today can be classified as 'market economies', governments nevertheless intervene substantially in the activities of business in order to protect the interests of consumers, workers or the environment.

Firms might collude to fix prices, use misleading advertising, create pollution, produce unsafe products, or use unacceptable employment practices. In such cases, government is expected to intervene to correct for the failings of the market system, e.g. by outlawing collusion, by establishing advertising standards, by taxing or otherwise penalising polluting firms, by imposing safety standards on firms' behaviour and products, or by protecting employment rights.

In this chapter we examine the ways in which markets might fail to protect people's interests, whether as consumers or simply as members of society. We also look at the different types of policy the government can adopt to correct these 'market failures'.

9.1 MARKET FAILURES

Markets and social objectives

One of the key arguments for government intervention in the behaviour of business is that, if left to its own devices, the private enterprise system will fail to achieve 'social efficiency'.

So what is meant by social efficiency? If the extra benefits to society – or *marginal social benefit* (MSB) – of producing more of any given good or service exceed the extra costs to society – or *marginal social cost* (MSC) – then it is said to be socially efficient to produce more. For example, if people's gains from having additional motorways exceed *all* the additional costs to society (both financial and non-financial) then it is socially efficient to construct more motorways.

If, however, the marginal social cost of producing more of any good or service exceeds the marginal social benefit, then it is socially efficient to produce less.

It follows that if the marginal social benefit of any activity is equal to the marginal social cost, then the current level is the optimum. To summarise, for *social efficiency* in the production of any good or service:

$MSB > MSC \rightarrow$ produce more

$MSB < MSC \rightarrow$ produce less

$MSB = MSC \rightarrow$ keep production at its current level

Similar rules apply to consumption. For example, if the marginal social benefit of consuming more of any good or service exceeds the marginal social cost, then society would benefit from more of the good being consumed.

 KEY IDEA 23 *Social efficiency.* This is achieved where no further net social gain can be made by producing more or less of a good. This will occur where marginal social benefit equals marginal social cost.

In the real world, the market rarely leads to social efficiency: the marginal social benefits from the production of most goods and services do not equal the marginal social costs. It is this failure of the market to allocate resources efficiently, which gives governments the justification to intervene. In this section we examine why the free market fails to lead to social efficiency and what the government can do to rectify the situation.

Types of market failure

Externalities

Sometimes when businesses make production decisions, it is not just the firm and its consumers which are affected. For example, there may be impacts on the environment. Similarly, when we make consumption decisions, we can affect people other than ourselves.

These effects on other people, whether by firms or individuals are called *externalities*; they are the side-effects or 'third-party' effects of production or consumption and can be either desirable or undesirable. Whenever other people are affected beneficially, there are said to be *external benefits*. Whenever other people are affected adversely, there are said to be *external costs*. If such externalities exist, the free market will not lead to social efficiency. (See, for example, the article 'Deforestation, soil erosion and chemical runoff sometimes the result of farming' from AG Week,[1] which looks at some of the externalities that arise from farming.)

In our analysis so far in this book, we have assumed there are no externalities and hence the costs and benefits to society are the same as the costs and benefits to the individual consumer or producer. However, when we introduce externalities, we now have to consider:

- The *social cost*: comprised of the private cost faced by the firm(s) from the production of any good or service plus any externalities of production (positive or negative).

Definitions

Marginal social benefit (*MSB*) The additional benefit gained by society of producing or consuming one more unit of a good.

Marginal social cost (*MSC*) The additional cost incurred by society of producing or consuming one more unit of a good.

Social efficiency Production and consumption at the point where *MSB* = *MSC*.

Externalities Costs or benefits of production or consumption experienced by society but not by the producers or consumers themselves. Sometimes referred to as 'spillover' or 'third-party' costs or benefits.

External benefits Benefits from production (or consumption) experienced by people other than the producer (or consumer).

External costs Costs of production (or consumption) borne by people other than the producer (or consumer).

Social cost Private cost plus externalities in production.

---

[1] Harwood D. Schafer and Daryll E. Ray, 'Deforestation, soil erosion and chemical runoff sometimes the result of farming', *Agweek* (21 March 2016).

- The *social benefit*: comprised of the private benefits enjoyed by consumers from the consumption of any good or service, plus any externalities of consumption (positive or negative).

 Externalities are spillover costs or benefits. Where these exist, even an otherwise perfect market will fail to achieve social efficiency.

KEY IDEA 24

There are four different types of externality: (i) negative externalities in production; (ii) positive externalities in production; (iii) negative externalities in consumption and (iv) positive externalities in consumption.

When we think about externalities in production, we are considering a producer which imposes either costs or benefits on other parties and so in these cases, there is a difference between the *marginal private cost to the producer* and the *marginal social cost* of production. If we have externalities in consumption, then a consumer imposes either costs or benefits on other parties and here we see a difference between the *marginal private benefit to the consumer* and the *marginal social benefit*.

Let's consider the first case above where a firm imposes an *external cost* during the production process. For simplicity, we assume that there are no externalities in consumption and that the firm is perfectly competitive and so it faces a horizontal demand curve (see section 4.4 on page 101).

External costs produced by business. Consider a chemical firm that dumps waste in a river or pollutes the air. Assuming this firm wants to maximise profits, it will produce where its marginal costs equals its marginal revenue (or price) at Q_1 in Figure 9.1. The market price (P) is what people

buying the good are prepared to pay for one more unit of it (this is the marginal utility as we saw on pages 57–8) and it therefore reflects their *marginal private benefit* (MB). As we have assumed no externalities from consumption, the marginal *private* benefit to consumers is the same as the marginal *social* benefit (MSB).

However, when the firm decides how much to produce, it considers the costs *it* incurs from producing an extra unit (e.g. raw materials, labour, etc.) and hence only considers its *marginal private costs* (MC). But, in this case, when the firm produces each additional unit of output, the community bears additional costs, such as noise or air pollution and these are the *external costs* (i.e. the *negative externality*). To find the marginal *social* cost we need to add together the marginal private and external costs. In this case, the marginal social cost (MSC) of chemical production exceeds the marginal private cost (MC): the difference is the *marginal external cost*. Diagrammatically, the MSC curve is above the MC curve. This is shown in Figure 9.1.

The socially optimum output would be Q_2, where P (i.e. MSB) = MSC. The firm, however, produces Q_1, as it is only concerned with the costs *it* incurs by producing. This output, however, is more than the optimum. Thus external costs lead to *overproduction* from society's point of view.

The problem of external costs arises in a free market economy because no one has legal ownership of the air or rivers and no one, therefore, can prevent or charge for their use as a dump for waste. Such a 'market' is missing. Control must, therefore, be left to the government or local authorities.

Other examples of firms producing external costs include extensive farming that destroys hedgerows and wildlife, nuclear waste from nuclear power stations, global warming from carbon emissions and the noise caused by aircraft. In all of these cases, society bears some of the costs of production, but profit-maximising firms only consider their *private costs* and hence too much is produced. This means that the free market fails to lead to a socially efficient allocation of resources.

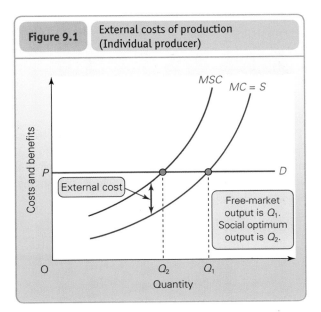

Figure 9.1   External costs of production (Individual producer)

Free-market output is Q_1.
Social optimum output is Q_2.

Pause for thought

In Figure 9.1, the impact of a negative externality in production is illustrated on one profit-maximising firm under perfect competition. Illustrate the impact of a negative externality in production on the market as a whole. (Note: the demand curve will be downward sloping.)

Definition

Social benefit Private benefit plus externalities in consumption.

External benefits produced by business. Sometimes firms' actions *benefit* people other than consumers. An example is research and development. If other firms have access to the results of the research, then clearly the benefits extend beyond the firm that finances it. However, since the firm only receives the private benefits, it will conduct less than the optimal amount of research. What is the point in a firm conducting further research if many of the benefits simply go to other firms? Similarly, a forestry company planting new woodlands will not take into account the beneficial effect on the atmosphere, and hence it will plant less than the socially optimal number of trees.

In such cases, the *MSC* curve is now *below* the *MC* curve and hence the output produced by the firm (private optimum) will be lower than the social optimum.

External costs in consumption. Consider when you or a family member uses a car. Other people suffer from the exhaust fumes, the added congestion, the noise, etc. These 'negative externalities' make the marginal social benefit of using cars less than the marginal private benefit (i.e. marginal utility to the car user). Other examples of negative externalities of consumption include littering, noisy radios in public places, the smoke from cigarettes and the policing and health costs from consuming alcohol. The individuals doing these things have little incentive to consider the negative effects on others.

External costs in consumption are illustrated in Figure 9.2. Being a perfectly competitive market, consumers are individually price takers. They face a given market price (P); the supply curve to them is effectively horizontal: i.e. they can buy as much as they like at the market price. The marginal private benefit (i.e. the marginal utility) is given by MB ($= D$). This is shown

as a downward sloping demand curve, where higher levels of consumption are associated with a lower level of marginal utility (i.e. lower marginal private benefit). The negative externalities have the effect of reducing the marginal benefit to society as a whole (*MSB*). The *MSB* curve thus lies below the *MB* curve.

The actual level of consumption by the 'rational' self-interested consumer is Q_1, where $MB = P$. The *socially optimal* level of consumption is Q_2, where $MSB = P$. The free market therefore leads to a level of consumption by each consumer *above* the socially optimal level.

External benefits in consumption. Rather than using a car to travel to a football match or to go shopping, perhaps you go by train. In this case, other people benefit from less congestion and exhaust fumes and fewer accidents on the roads. Thus the marginal social benefit of rail travel is greater than the marginal private benefit (i.e. the marginal utility to the rail passenger) and the *MSB* curve now lies *above* the *MB* curve. Other examples of positive externalities of consumption include deodorants, vaccinations and attractive gardens in front of people's houses. For example, if one person is vaccinated against a disease, it not only benefits them, but also benefits others, who can no longer catch the disease from that person. In such cases, by not taking into account the effect on others, too little will be consumed.

To summarise, whenever there are external costs, there will be too much produced or consumed. Whenever there are external benefits, there will be too little produced or consumed. The market will not equate *MSB* and *MSC* and so it fails to provide the socially optimal level of output.

> **Pause for thought**
>
> *Give other examples of each of the four types of externality (external costs and benefits in both production and consumption). In each case, draw a diagram showing the difference between the marginal social and private cost and benefit curves and the actual and socially optimal level of output.*

Public goods

There is a category of goods where the positive externalities are so great that the free market, whether perfect or imperfect, may not produce at all. They are called *public goods*. Examples include pavements,

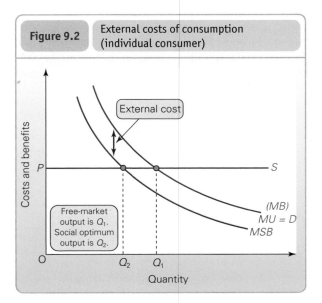

Figure 9.2	External costs of consumption (individual consumer)

> **Definition**
>
> **Public good** A good or service which has the features of non-rivalry and non-excludability and as a result would not be provided by the free market.

flood control dams, public drainage, public services such as the police and even government itself.

Public goods have two important characteristics: *non-rivalry* and *non-excludability*.

Non-rivalry. Rivalry occurs when one person's consumption of a good reduces the amount of it available for others. For example, if I consume a bar of chocolate, every chunk I eat reduces the amount of the chocolate bar left for you.

If, however, a good is perfectly *non-rivalrous*, then as I increase my consumption of the product, it has no impact on the ability of you or a 'rival' consumer to 'consume' the good. For example, imagine that you go outside and find that your neighbour is letting off fireworks. Your decision to watch (and enjoy) the fireworks does not reduce the number of fireworks left for them to watch. The firework display is non-rivalrous – at least up to the point where people start getting in each other's way (as we shall see below).

> ### Pause for thought
>
> *Given our definition of public goods, can you now define a private good?*

In reality, many goods and services will be neither perfectly rival nor non-rival. In particular, a good may be non-rivalrous to begin with, but as additional people consume it (or the size of the population (N) gets bigger), rivalry may become a problem, due to the 'crowding effect'. You and a friend may be able to watch a video on your mobile phone, but if more and more people try to watch it with you, eventually crowding will become a problem, with some people prevented from seeing the video. There is now rivalry in consumption. The level of N at which crowding occurs will vary depending on the good or service in question. It may only take three or four people watching a mobile phone video on the same phone for this 'good' to become rival, but there may have to be thousands or even millions of people watching a firework display before that 'good' becomes rivalrous in consumption.

It is therefore helpful to think about goods as having different degrees of rivalry depending on their particular characteristics.

Non-excludability. Excludability occurs when the supplier of a good can restrict who consumes it, usually by charging a price. Only those consumers who are prepared to pay that price will be able to have the good. For those goods already in the hands of consumers, excludability occurs when they can prevent other people benefiting too. In some cases, it is very easy to prevent people who have not purchased the good from benefiting from it – for example, goods consumed in your own home.

However, there are some goods and services for which it is either too costly or simply not feasible to prevent people who have not paid for the good from enjoying the benefits of it. Such goods have the property of being *non-excludable*.

As is the case with rivalry, it is helpful to think about goods exhibiting differing degrees of excludability.

In some circumstances, it may be theoretically possible to exclude non-payers but, in reality, the transactions costs involved are too great. For example, it may be very difficult to prevent anyone from fishing in the open ocean or enjoying the benefits of walking in a country park. If a good is non-excludable, consumers can get the benefits free and thus have no incentive to pay themselves. This is known as the *free-rider problem* and it is considered in more detail in Box 9.1.

> **KEY IDEA 25**
>
> *The free-rider problem.* People are often unwilling to pay for things if they can make use of things other people have bought. This problem can lead to people not purchasing things which it would be to their benefit and that of other members of society to have.

When goods have these two features of non-rivalry and non-excludability, the free market will simply not provide them, as private firms would be unable to charge a price.

However, these goods often have large social benefits relative to private benefits: that is large positive externalities. This makes them socially desirable, but privately unprofitable. No one person would pay to have a pavement built along their street. The private benefit would be too small relative to the cost. And yet the social benefit to all the other people using the pavement will far outweigh the cost. But they have no incentive to pay for it, as they can simply *free ride* and use it for nothing.

> ### Definitions
>
> **Non-rivalry** Where the consumption of a good or service by one person will not prevent others from enjoying it.
>
> **Non-excludability** Where it is not possible to provide a good or service to one person without it thereby being available for others to enjoy.
>
> **Free-rider problem** When it is not possible to exclude other people from consuming a good that someone has bought.

BOX 9.1   THE PROBLEM OF FREE-RIDERS

A charitable solution?

Public goods present society with a problem, because of their inherent characteristics. Consider two individuals, Daniel and Emily, who are deciding whether or not to put on a firework display in their respective gardens and let's assume that these fireworks give them both utility. The nature of the firework display means that all those in the vicinity can enjoy it.

Now think about the decision of buying fireworks from Daniel's point of view. If he assumes that Emily will buy fireworks and put on a display, then Daniel has no incentive to buy fireworks as well. Instead, he can benefit from Emily's display without having to pay for it. The same applies to Emily. This is the free-rider problem: no-one has an incentive to contribute to the provision of a public good, because everyone assumes that others will contribute, meaning they can freely benefit.

This situation provides a useful application of game theory. The Nash equilibrium (see pages 128–9) for both Daniel and Emily (under certain assumptions) is to free-ride. But, if everyone free-rides then in equilibrium, no-one contributes and the public good (the firework display) would not be provided.

This is an example of the prisoners' dilemma: given that society benefits from the public good, everyone would actually be better off contributing (and there would be an explosive firework display!) But of course, without collaboration, no individuals have any incentive to change their behaviour!

1. Construct a pay-off matrix similar to that in Figure 5.5 (on page 128) showing a Nash equilibrium where neither player contributes. Explain why this situation could be improved.

Encouraging provision

So, given that no firm or individual has a monetary incentive to provide a public good, how is it that they are still provided?

If the public were left to make voluntary contributions, we already know that there might be cases of free-riding. But, even if everyone agrees to contribute, there is another problem. All the contributors must agree on how much of the public good they want to be provided and how much they are willing to pay. Sometimes negotiation might have to take place between the contributors to determine the optimal amount of the public good and their willingness to contribute. Here there may be a role for government

provision, subsidisation and/or government intervention to enforce compulsory contributions, such as through taxation.

Encouraging donations to charities

But, is there another option that will encourage individuals to contribute to a public good without being forced into it? Charities have created an innovative way of doing this.

The motivations behind charitable donations vary, but often it is because of the 'warm glow'[1] we get from knowing that we have donated and that our donation will help someone else.

However, charitable donations suffer from free-riding. Many people are not concerned with how much they give individually, but more with how much society gives as a whole. If we see others donating, we know that they are contributing towards the objective of reducing poverty, helping fight diseases, or some other worthy cause, and thus we benefit from knowing that others are helping, without having to contribute ourselves. In other words, we can free-ride off other people's donations. The good cause is thus a public good. If this was how everyone thought, then charitable donations would be zero – we would end up in the prisoners' dilemma game where no-one contributes.

To counter this, charities often frame their adverts in such a way that we see our donations as if they are going to a particular child/family or animal. By introducing the idea of 'sponsor a child', a private good emerges. Even though our contributions go to the wider public good of cutting poverty or saving rainforests, we have less of an incentive to free-ride, believing that we are helping a particular person, animal or even tree. By doing this, charities can avoid the prisoner's dilemma, which certainly does exist in society.

2. If you see your donations to charity as a private good, explain whether there is any externality to giving to charity.
3. How does charitable giving become a public good?

Devise and conduct a small survey to establish examples of the extent to which individuals free-ride in particular situations and what incentives could be devised to prevent the free-riding.

---

[1] James Andreoni, 'Impure altruism and donations to public goods: A theory of warm-glow giving', *The Economic Journal*, Volume 100, Issue 401 (June 1990), pp. 464–77.

As a result of this problem, we often see public goods provided by the government, or by a private firm subsidised by the government. Their provision will be financed through taxation and will significantly increase the utility of society. (Note that not all goods and services produced by the public sector come into the category of public goods and services; thus education and health are publicly provided, but they *can* be, and indeed are, privately provided too.)

Pause for thought

1. Which of the following have the property of non-rivalry: (a) a can of drink; (b) public transport; (c) a radio show; (d) the sight of flowers in a public park?
2. How easy is it for a broadcaster of a TV show, such as Game of Thrones, or a sporting event, such as a live football match, to prevent non-payers from watching the transmission?

Market power

When there are no externalities, a perfect market will result in social efficiency. This can be seen from Figures 9.1 and 9.2. If there are no externalities, then the MSC and MC curves will be one and the same, as will the MSB and MB (MU) curves. Firms will produce where MC (= MSC) = P. Consumers will consume where MU (= MSB) = P. Thus the perfect free market with no externalities will result in the socially optimal level of production and consumption: where $MSC = MSB$.

However, whenever markets are imperfect, whether as pure monopoly or monopsony or as some form of imperfect competition, the market will fail to equate MSB and MSC, even if there are no externalities.

Take the case of monopoly. A monopoly will produce less than the socially efficient output. This is illustrated in Figure 9.3. A monopoly faces a downward-sloping demand curve, and therefore marginal revenue is below average revenue (= P = MSB). Profits are maximised at an output of Q_1, where marginal revenue equals marginal cost (see Figure 5.2 on page 119). Assuming no externalities, the socially efficient output would be at the higher level of Q_2, where $MSB = MSC$.

To summarise, firms with market power, if they are trying to maximise (or even increase) profit, will tend to set prices above the perfectly competitive level and thus reduce output below the socially efficient level.

Imperfect information

Markets can only operate efficiently if people have good knowledge of costs and benefits as they affect them. In the real world there is often a great deal of ignorance and uncertainty. Consumers are often ignorant of the properties of goods until they have bought them – by which time it is too late. This is especially relevant for larger consumer 'durables' that are purchased infrequently, such as washing machines or cars. Advertising may contribute to people's ignorance by misleading them as to the benefits of a good.

Firms are often ignorant of market opportunities, prices, costs, the productivity of labour (especially white-collar workers), the activity of rivals, etc.

Many economic decisions are based on expected future conditions. Since the future can never be known for certain, many decisions will be taken that later turn out to be wrong.

One particular type of imperfect information is when the different sides in an economic relationship have different amounts of information. This is known as 'asymmetric information' and as we saw on pages 9–10, it is at the heart of the principal–agent problem.

Protecting people's interests

The government may feel that people need protecting from poor economic decisions that they make on their own behalf. It may feel that in a free market people will consume too many harmful things. Often such goods bring immediate benefits, whereas the costs happen in the future (e.g. eating unhealthy but tasty food or smoking). Thus if the government wants to discourage smoking, drinking and eating sugary products, it can put taxes on tobacco, alcohol and high-sugar products. In more extreme cases it could make various activities illegal, such as prostitution, certain types of gambling, and the sale and consumption of drugs.

Alternatively, the government may feel that people consume too little of things that are good for them, such as education, health care and sports facilities. Such goods are known as *merit goods*. The government could either provide them free or subsidise their production.

Government may also need to protect people from poor economic decisions that are made on their behalf by other people. For example, parents make decisions on behalf of their young children. This can be reversed years later when children make decisions on behalf of their elderly parents. Even if the people making the decision are doing so with the best intentions, they may lack the information to make the best choices. On other occasions, they may not really care. Government may thus feel it necessary to intervene to protect the interests of those whose welfare depends on choices made by others.

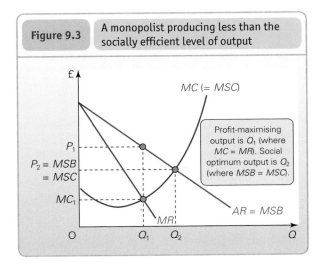

| Figure 9.3 | A monopolist producing less than the socially efficient level of output |

Profit-maximising output is Q_1 (where $MC = MR$). Social optimum output is Q_2 (where $MSB = MSC$).

Definition

Merit goods Goods which the government feels that people will under-consume and which therefore ought to be subsidised or provided free.

RECAP

1. Social efficiency is achieved at the output where $MSC = MSB$ for each good and service. In practice, however, markets will fail to achieve social efficiency. This provides a justification for government intervention in the market.

2. Externalities are spillover costs or benefits. Whenever there are external costs, the market will (other things being equal) lead to a level of production and consumption above the socially efficient level. Whenever there are external benefits, the market will (other things being equal) lead to a level of production and consumption below the socially efficient level.

3. Public goods will not be provided by the market. The problem is that they have large social benefits relative to private benefits, and without government intervention it would not be possible to prevent people having a 'free ride', thereby making it unprofitable to supply.

4. Monopoly power will (other things being equal) lead to a level of output below the socially efficient level.

5. Ignorance and uncertainty may prevent people and firms from consuming or producing at the levels they would otherwise choose.

6. In a free market there may be inadequate provision for dependants and an inadequate output of merit goods.

9.2 FIRMS AND CORPORATE RESPONSIBILITY

Gone are the days when companies could get away with showing no concern for the broader issues of society and focus solely on maximising their own profits. While it is still the case that many firms are focused on shareholders and profits, many of the world's most famous companies have placed greater importance on achieving other societal objectives.

An open letter from Blackrock Chairman and CEO Larry Fink to CEOs said, in reference to long-term corporate growth advice, that: 'Society is demanding that companies, both public and private, serve a social purpose. To prosper over time, every company must not only deliver financial performance, but also show it makes a positive contribution to society.'[2]

Changing expectations and attitudes

The term '*corporate social responsibility (CSR)*' (or simply '*corporate responsibility (CR)*') encompasses many of the aims set out in such reports and forms a key component in many companies' *business ethics*. Society now expects firms to adhere to certain moral and social principles and, in response, business attitudes have changed. For example, in a 2016 global survey of CEOs carried out by PwC (PriceWaterhouse Coopers),[3] 64 per cent of respondents stated that they planned to increase expenditure on CSR in the future and that it was increasingly becoming a core part of their business. Firms increasingly see themselves as more than just economic institutions, with responsibilities to all of their stakeholders, including workers, suppliers, the community and broader society.

Activities that fall within CSR can typically be categorised into four areas:

■ *Environmental activities,* such as using energy more efficiently, reducing wastage, increasing recycling and using more renewable sources of energy.

In many top corporations, *environmental scanning* is an integral part of the planning process. This involves the business surveying social and political trends in order to remain in tune with consumer concerns. Examples include Google's 2017 announcement that all its energy usage would come from renewable sources and Lego's target of producing all core products and packaging with sustainable materials by 2030.

■ *Donating money/equipment/employees' time to charities, good causes and local community projects.* Research by the Charities Aid Foundation[4] found that FTSE 100 companies donated £1.9 billion to charities in 2016, though the figure had fallen by over 25 per cent since 2013. In 2017, a division of Microsoft donated $1.2 billion worth of software and services to non-profit organisations.

Definitions

Corporate (social) responsibility Where a business considers the interests and concerns of a community rather than just its shareholders.

Business ethics The values and principles that shape business behaviour.

Stakeholder An individual affected by the operations of a business.

Environmental scanning Where a business surveys social and political trends in order to take account of changes in its decision-making process.

---

[2] *Larry Fink's 2019 letter to CEOs* BlackRock.

[3] 'Redefining business success in a changing world', *19th Annual Global CEO Survey* (PwC, January 2016).

[4] *Corporate Giving by the FTSE 100*, Charities Aid Foundation (2019).

- *Fair and ethical treatment of employees.* This might include paying fair wages, reducing gender inequality, increasing female representation on boards and greater support for physical/mental wellbeing. For example, Virgin Group, Netflix, Amazon and Google have all extended the period of maternity and paternity leave.
- *Fair/ethical treatment of suppliers.* This might include providing fair contracts and prices to suppliers and only using suppliers that meet certain CSR benchmarks. An example is Toyota GB's procurement policy,[5] which requires all suppliers to comply with laws, regulations and social norms and give proper consideration to environmental issues.

Pause for thought

Green taxes (e.g. on carbon emission) are designed to 'internalise' environmental externalities and thereby force firms to take such externalities into account in their decision making. Should such taxes be reduced for firms that adopt a more environmentally responsible approach?

For many years we have seen increasing importance being placed on CSR by both customers and businesses. This has had a knock-on effect: as more and more companies have focused on various aspects of social responsibility, so this has increased the pressure on those companies that were more reluctant to engage.

Some companies make a big play of their focus on tackling various issues, such as food wastage, environmental damage, working conditions and fair pay. Indeed, some of the world's most famous companies now publish annual reports outlining their progress towards achieving various societal goals. For example,

each year Google issues an Environmental Report, BMW produces a Sustainable Value Report, Lego publishes a Responsibility Report and The Walt Disney Company produces a Corporate Citizenship Report.

However, the late 2010s have been problematic for countless companies, including Apple, Volkswagen, Samsung, 21st Century Fox and Facebook, with scandals hitting them in a range of areas, including sexual harassment, bribery, fraud and emissions, to name a few. One of the giants that has escaped or effectively dealt with scandal is Google, which, according to the Chief Reputation Officer of the Reputation Institute is 'still viewed as an employer of choice. It's an aspirational, 'do no evil' kind of company.'[6] However, as you will see in Box 9.5, it has faced issues elsewhere.

Ranking companies by CSR

The Reputation Institute has been publishing the Global CSR 100 RepTrack annually since 2011. This examines and measures the CSR reputations of global companies. It surveys more than 230 000 individuals across a number of countries and then ranks global companies based on their performance in corporate responsibility. In 2018, Google took the top spot in terms of its reputation, but overall, it noted an average 1.4 point decline in the reputation of the companies. Table 9.1 shows the top ten companies based on the Reputation Institute's ranking.

The Reputation Institute's 2018 report highlighted that it was redefining the idea of corporate social responsibility, noting that the 'social' part can often mean other elements (such as labour, environmental and fiscal responsibilities) are overlooked by

---

[5] *Procurement Policy*, Toyota (GB) plc.

[6] *The World's Most Reputable Companies for Corporate Responsibility 2018*, Forbes and the Reputation Institute (11 October 2018).

Table 9.1	2018 Global CR 100 RepTrack ranking		
Rank 2018	**Company**	**Score 2018**	**Rank 2017 (Score 2017)**
1	Google	71.9	3 (73.9)
2	The Walt Disney Company	69.5	4 (73.5)
3	Lego	69.4	1 (74.4)
4	Natura	69.4	–
5	Novo Nordisk	68.7	–
6	Microsoft	68.1	2 (74.1)
7	Bosch	68.1	5 (71.0)
8	Canon	67.6	23 (69.2)
9	Michelin	67.6	15 (69.7)
10	Ikea	67.2	13 (69.7)

Source: 2018 and 2017 Global CSR 100 RepTrack Data Reputation Institute

companies. This has led to the Institute renaming corporate social responsibility as just corporate responsibility (CR).

One good example identified by the RepTrak data is Lego. Not only does this company rank more highly than any other company in the CR RepTrak when it comes to product transparency, but it is also focused on environmental sustainability. In March 2018, it announced that it would be starting production on pieces made from plant-based plastic sourced from sugarcane and these became available later in 2018. It has a broader objective of using sustainable materials in all core products and packaging by 2030. Stephen Hahn-Griffiths, the Chief Reputation Officer of the Reputation Institute said:

> Lego is a very solid corporate entity, a very purposeful company that drives learning through play while respecting the environment. It's literally putting its sense of purpose and sense of corporate responsibility into its products.[7]

Corporate responsibility undoubtedly has an increasingly important role to play in business, but even for firms that retain a focus on profits, can improvements in their corporate responsibility help to improve their financial performance?

Pause for thought

Why do you think there have been such big increases in spending on CSR over the past few years?

Why corporate responsibility?

Media coverage about firms that are committed to corporate responsibility and those that are not has grown in recent years and this has led to growing awareness and concern among consumers about the companies they support and the products that they buy. Consumers are increasingly favouring companies which are openly committed to sustainability and ethical practices. Firms hope that adopting such policies will enhance brand image and so strengthen loyalty, improve profitability and even help the firm in raising finance and attracting trading partners.

Many studies have attempted to identify and evaluate the economic returns from social responsibility, including business growth rates, stock prices, sales and revenue. A survey by van Beurden

and Gössling[8] evaluated the findings of 34 studies that considered the link between business ethics and enhanced profits. They concluded that 23 studies showed a positive link, nine suggested neutral effects or were inconclusive, and the remaining two suggested that there was a negative relationship. Other more recent studies have shown a similar mixture of results, including some finding a positive impact,[9] a negative impact[10] and no relationship.[11]

There are many issues in looking at this relationship, including difficulties in defining and measuring CSR or CR, difficulties in measuring a firm's performance and problems in linking improvements with particular changes. However, it is certainly the case that there are growing benefits to a company of being seen as a responsible company.

Consumer trends

In the Ethical Consumer Markets Report 2018,[12] it was found that UK consumers are turning towards more sustainable options. The report commissioned a YouGov survey which found that over 25 per cent of respondents had avoided buying a product or using a service in 2017 because of its negative environmental impact. This was an increase of 65 per cent from 2016. So, while this may not represent a positive figure for companies that exhibit corporate responsibility, it gives an indication of the cost of not being responsible. The report also found that, on average, households were spending £1238 per year on ethical products, compared to just £542 a decade previously, and that the ethical market in the UK in 2017 was worth £83.33 billion, having increased from £13.5 billion in 2000. Younger consumers, in particular, are showing greater awareness about the products they buy and this, therefore, has a positive impact on company sales and profits.

Similar trends are evident in the EU, with 71 per cent of European consumers seeing the importance of sustainable and ethical living, which was 7 percentage points higher than in 2011. A study by

---

[7] Vicky Valet, 'The World's most reputable companies for Corporate Responsibility 2018', *Forbes* (11 October 2018).

[8] Peter van Beurden and Tobias Gössling, 'The Worth of Values – A literature review on the relation between Corporate Social and Financial Performance', *Journal of Business Ethics*, vol. 82, no. 2, October 2008, pp. 407–24.

[9] W. Rodgers, H. L. Choy and A. Guiral, 'Do investors value a firm's commitment to social activities?' *Journal of Business Ethics*, vol. 114, pp. 607–23 (2013).

[10] C. W. Peng and M. L. Yang, 'The effect of corporate social performance on financial performance: The moderating effect of ownership concentration', *Journal of Business Ethics*, vol. 123, pp. 171–82 (2014).

[11] M. G. Soana, 'The relationship between corporate social performance and corporate financial performance in the banking sector', *Journal of Business Ethics*, vol. 104, pp. 133–48 (2011).

[12] *Ethical Consumer Markets Report 2018*, Ethical Consumer Research Association (1 June 2018).

Cone Communications in 2017[13] found that 87 per cent of US consumers bought a product because the company stood for an issue they cared about. Furthermore, 75 per cent would not buy an item if the company acted in a way that was contrary to their beliefs and in the 12 months before the survey, over 50 per cent of respondents stated that they had boycotted a company for irresponsible business actions.

Awards and recognition

There are many more awards available to recognise and promote corporate social responsibility and a growing number of national and international reports focus on or include CSR as a key component, such as PwC's CEO survey, the Reputation Institute's RepTrack and Ethical Consumer Markets Report, to name a few. The 'Most admired companies' lists, such as those presented by *Management Today* in the UK and *Fortune* in America are published annually and winning such awards has huge public-relations and marketing potential. This can significantly contribute to a firm's socially responsible image.

The publicity that companies get from such awards and reports appears to be having an increasingly large impact on consumers and, with growing awareness amongst the public, any companies that fall foul of society's standards for responsible business receive vast media coverage. As noted, there have been a number of recent scandals, whereby the company's financial performance has been affected. One good example is Volkswagen's diesel emissions scandal.

In September 2015, the United States Environmental Protection Agency found that VW had deliberately programmed its diesel engines such that, when tested, the car's emissions would meet US standards, despite emitting up to 40 times more when being driven in practice. Following this, regulators around the world began to investigate VW and the stock price of the company fell by a third. Looking at the company's subsequent financial performance, it has continued to be affected. In the USA, VW was fined $2.8 billion in April 2017 and, as of August 2018, its total cost in terms of fines and compensation for customers reached $32 billion. Third-quarter operating profit, taking into account the costs related to the scandal, were down by 48 per cent in 2017 compared to the same time in 2016. Perhaps there will also be a long-run cost in terms of the damage done to Volkswagen's brand, though only time will tell. However, this is something that is very difficult to measure.

Effect on recruitment

Another benefit to firms of being socially responsible is that such companies may find it easier to recruit and hold on to their employees.

In a number of surveys of graduate employment intentions, students have claimed that they would be prepared to take a lower salary in order to work for a business with high ethical standards and a commitment to socially responsible business practices.

- An international survey in 2005 showed that 28 per cent of job seekers considered the ethical conduct and values of an employer to be an important factor in deciding whether to apply for work there.[14]
- In the 2017 Cone Communications CSR Study (see above), consumers said that being a good employer was the most important responsible business practice a firm could have.
- A UN initiative 'Principals for Responsible Management Education' surveyed the attitudes of business students on CSR. In the 2016 report, over 90 per cent of business students said they would be willing to sacrifice some percentage of their future salary to work for a responsible employer. In the 2018 report,[15] 23.1 per cent of surveyed students reported that it was 'absolutely essential' to work for a responsible employer, with a further 47 per cent and 23.9 per cent reporting that it was 'very important' and 'fairly important'.

All the data clearly indicate that ethical consumption and employment is growing, with individuals valuing environmental responsibility and active participation in the community when making decisions. Box 9.2 gives an example of a company that has built its reputation on being socially and environmentally responsible – The Body Shop.

Despite the growing awareness among consumers and companies of the benefits and costs of corporate responsibility, there are still many firms and consumers that care little about the social or natural environment. There is thus a strong case for government intervention to correct market failures. This is the subject of section 9.3.

---

[13] *The 2017 Cone Communications CSR Study*, Cone Communications (21 May 2017).

[14] 'What Makes a Great Employer?', *MORI survey* for Manpower (11 October 2005).

[15] Debbie Haski-Leventhal and Stephanie Manefield, 'The State of CSR and RME in Business Schools: The Students' Voice', *Fourth Biennial Survey, 2018*, UN Principles of Responsible Management Education (PRME) and Macquarie University (2018).

BOX 9.2	THE BODY SHOP

Is it 'worth it'?

The Body Shop was founded in 1976 and shot to fame in the 1980s. It stood for environmental awareness and an ethical approach to business. But its success had as much to do with what it sold as what it stood for. It sold natural cosmetics, Raspberry Ripple Bathing Bubbles and Camomile Shampoo, products that were immensely popular with consumers.

Its profits increased from a little over £1 million in 1985 (€1.7 million) to approximately €54.8 million in 2015 (though falling from €77.5 million in 2012). Over the same period, sales increased even more dramatically, from £4.9 million to €967.2 million in 2015 and in that year, Body Shop International had over 3100 stores, operating in 61 countries, with its latest planned expansion into China.

What makes this success so remarkable is that The Body Shop did virtually no advertising. Its promotion stemmed largely from the activities and environmental campaigning of its founder Anita Roddick, and the company's uncompromising claims that it sold only 'green' products and conducted its business operations with high ethical standards. It actively supported green causes such as saving whales and protecting rainforests, and it refused to allow animal testing for its products. Perhaps most surprising in the world of big business was its high-profile initiative 'trade not aid', whereby it claimed to pay 'fair' prices for its ingredients, especially those supplied from people in developing countries, who were open to exploitation by large companies.

The growth strategy of The Body Shop focused on developing a distinctive and highly innovative product range, and at the same time identifying such products with major social issues of the day, such as the environment and animal rights.

Its initial expansion was based on a process of franchising:

> . . . franchising. We didn't know what it was, but all these women came to us and said, if you can do this and you can't even read a balance sheet, then we can do it. I had a cabal of female friends all around Brighton, Hove and Chichester, and they started opening little units, all called The Body Shop. I just supplied them with gallons of products – we only had 19 different products, but we made it look like more as we sold them in five different sizes![1]

In 1984 the company went public. In the 1990s, however, sales growth was less rapid and in 1998 Anita Roddick stepped down as Chief Executive, but for a while she and her husband remained as co-chairs. In 2003 she was awarded a knighthood and became Dame Anita Roddick. Sales then grew rapidly from 2004 to 2006 from €553 million to €709 million.

Acquisition of The Body Shop by L'Oréal

A dramatic strategic event occurred in 2006 when The Body Shop was sold to the French cosmetics giant L'Oréal, which was 26 per cent owned by Nestlé. This resulted in the magazine, *Ethical Consumer,* downgrading The Body Shop's ethical rating from 11 out of 20 to a mere 2.5 and calling for

a boycott of the company. Three weeks after the sale, the daily BrandIndex recorded an 11 point drop in The Body Shop's consumer satisfaction rating from 25 to 14.

There were several reasons for this. L'Oréal's animal-testing policies conflicted with those of The Body Shop and L'Oréal had been accused of being involved in price fixing with other French perfume houses. L'Oréal's part-owner, Nestlé, had also been subject to various criticisms for ethical misconduct, including promoting formula milk to mothers with babies in poor countries rather than breast milk and using slave labour in cocoa farms in West Africa.

Anita Roddick, however, believed that, by taking over The Body Shop, L'Oréal would develop a more ethical approach to business, and it did publicly recognise that it needed to develop its ethical and environmental policies. It adopted a new Code of Business Ethics in 2007 and gained some external accreditation for its approach to sustainability and ethics. L'Oréal was ranked as one of the world's 100 most ethical companies by Ethisphere in 2007 and in 2016, it was again part of this list for the seventh time.

L'Oréal set itself three targets as part of its environmental strategy (2005–15), including a 50 per cent reduction in greenhouse gas emissions, water consumption and waste per finished product unit. It donated $1.2 million to the US Environment Protection Agency to help bring an end to animal testing and in March 2013, it announced a 'total ban on the sale in Europe of any cosmetic product that was tested on animals or containing an ingredient that was tested on animals after this date.' It also promised that 'By 2020, we will innovate so that 100% of products have an environmental or social benefit.' Sadly, Anita Roddick died in 2007 and so has not been able to witness these changes.

L'Oréal also looked to inject greater finance into the company aimed at improving the marketing of products. In autumn 2006 a transactional website was launched and there were greater press marketing campaigns. L'Oréal made a public commitment to focus on enriching rather than exploiting people and the planet. This commitment extended its emphasis never to test on animals and was also focused on biodiversity and resources and the fair treatment of its farmers and suppliers.[2]

Recent performance

The Body Shop's performance has been less good in recent years. It suffered during the financial crisis, with profits and sales falling, though they then recovered up to 2014. Since then The Body Shop's financial performance has deteriorated, with its profits falling by 38 per cent and sales by 5 per cent in 2016.

In June 2017, L'Oréal announced that it had agreed to sell The Body Shop for €1bn (£877m) to Natura Cosmeticos, the largest Brazilian cosmetics business. Natura was awarded 'B corp' status[3] in 2014 as it met certain standards for environmental performance, accountability and

---

[1] 'Q & A with The Body Shop's Dame Anita Roddick', *Success Stories,* Startups (4 September 2007).

[2] See: https://www.thebodyshop.com/en-gb/commitment

[3] Companies awarded B Corps status are certified by the non-profit B Lab as meeting rigorous standards of social and environmental performance, accountability, and transparency.

transparency. Commenting on the purchase of the Body Shop, the co-chair of Natura's board said:

> The complementarity of our international footprints, the sustainable use of biodiversity in our products, a belief in ethics in management and fair relations with communities and a high degree of innovation constitutes the pillars of the journey on which we are now embarking.[4]

It will be interesting to see if The Body Shop's performance significantly improves under new ownership as part of the

group Natura &Co. Initial indications seemed good, with net revenue rising by 36 per cent and profits by 62 per cent in the 2018 financial year.

What assumptions has The Body Shop made about the 'rational consumer'?

Find out how The Body Shop's economic performance has been affected by its attitudes towards ethical issues. (You could do an Internet search to find further evidence about its performance and the effects of its sale to L'Oréal and then to Natura Cosmeticos.)

---

[4] See: Sarah Butler, 'L'Oréal to sell Body Shop to Brazil's Natura in €1bn deal', *The Guardian* (9 June 2017).

RECAP

1. Sometimes firms are not aggressive profit maximisers but, instead, take a more socially responsible approach to business, focusing on issues such as environmental impact, ethical factors, working conditions and fair contracts/prices for suppliers.

2. Evidence suggests that as the corporate responsibility of firms grows, economic performance is often enhanced through strengthened brand loyalty, higher sales and turnover, rising share prices, access to capital and higher employee retention.

3. Various reports and rankings are produced annually that assess companies' corporate responsibility and these can have a significant effect on consumer awareness as to which companies are particularly reputable. This, in turn, can affect business performance.

4. Although there are growing numbers of consumers and businesses that are concerned with ethical and environmental issues, these still represent a niche market.

9.3 GOVERNMENT INTERVENTION IN THE MARKET

Given the various failures of the free market, what forms can government intervention take? There are several policy instruments that the government can use. At one extreme, it can totally replace the market by providing goods and services itself. At the other extreme, it can merely seek to persuade producers, consumers or workers to act differently. Between the two extremes the government has a number of instruments it can use to change the way markets operate. The major ones are taxes, subsidies, laws and regulatory bodies.

Taxes and subsidies

When there are market imperfections, social efficiency will not be achieved. Marginal social benefit (*MSB*) will not equal marginal social cost (*MSC*). A different level of output would be more desirable.

Taxes and subsidies can be used to correct these imperfections. Essentially the approach is to tax those goods or activities where the market produces too much and subsidise those where the market produces too little.

Taxes to internalise negative externalities. Let's return to the chemical firm polluting the air as

depicted in Figure 9.1 on page 223. The pollution is costly to society, but the firm does not directly incur any of these costs, hence more than the social optimum is produced. However, by taxing the firm, the government increases the firm's marginal private cost (*MC*), moving this curve closer to the *MSC* curve and so makes the firm pay towards the cost of the pollution it causes. It internalises the externality, moving the profit-maximising output closer to the socially optimum output.

If the tax is equal to the full amount of the marginal external cost, then the firm's private marginal cost becomes equal to the marginal social cost. In Figure 9.1, the firm will now maximise profits at Q_2, the socially optimal output.

Subsidies to internalise positive externalities. If we consider the forestry company planting new trees and providing external benefits to society, the government may want to subsidise the firm so that it reduces the firm's costs and encourages it to plant more trees. The subsidy will shift the firm's *MC* curve closer to the *MSC* curve and so by contributing towards the costs of planting trees, the profit-maximising output moves closer to the socially optimum output.

> ### Pause for thought
>
> *Draw two diagrams to illustrate (a) the effect of a tax on the consumption of a good with a negative externality in consumption; (b) the effect of a subsidy on the consumption of a good with a positive externality in consumption. Base your diagrams on Figure 9.2.*

Assessing the use of taxes and subsidies

Many economists favour the tax/subsidy solution to market imperfections, especially externalities, but what are their advantages and disadvantages?

Advantages. Although they are a form of government intervention, taxes and subsidies still allow the market to operate, which promotes the efficient allocation of resources. It forces firms to bear the full social costs and benefits of their actions and has the flexibility of being adjustable according to the magnitude of the problem. For example, the bigger the external costs of a firm's actions, the bigger the tax can be.

What is more, by taxing firms for imposing negative externalities, such as polluting, they are encouraged to find cleaner ways of producing. The tax thus acts as an incentive over the longer run to reduce pollution: the more a firm can reduce its pollution, the more taxes it can save. Likewise, when *good* practices are subsidised, firms have the incentive to adopt more good practices, as it reduces their costs and may thus improve profitability.

Limitations. Despite the advantages, there are some issues, which mean that sometimes taxes and subsidies are not feasible or practical. All firms produce different levels and types of externality and operate under different degrees of imperfect competition. It would be expensive and administratively very difficult, if not impossible, to charge every offending firm its own particular tax rate (or grant every relevant firm its own particular rate of subsidy).

Even if a government did vary the tax/subsidy on each firm based on the size of the externality, how would it actually measure the externality? This is especially problematic if the costs and benefits are in the long run.

Furthermore, in many cases, it can be difficult to determine which firm should bear the cost or receive the benefit. Which firms have caused the pollution and how much? Without this information, it is impossible to fix the 'correct' tax or subsidy on a firm.

This doesn't mean it is impossible to internalise the externality, but it can be difficult and potentially costly to 'fine-tune' such a system.

In section 9.4, we examine specifically how taxes and subsidies can be used to achieve various environmental and social goals.

Legislation and regulation

The use of legislation

Laws are frequently used to correct market imperfections. Laws can be of three main types: those that prohibit or regulate behaviour that imposes external costs, those that prevent firms providing false or misleading information, and those that prevent or regulate monopolies and oligopolies.

The advantage of legal restrictions is that they are usually easy to understand and administer. Furthermore, it is often safer to make products illegal rather than merely imposing taxes. In cases where consumer information is very poor, legal intervention can also help to protect consumers from purchasing unsafe products. However, legal restrictions tend to be a rather blunt weapon. For example, imposing a legal limit on pollution levels leaves little incentive for firms to continue reducing their emissions once the target has been met.

The use of regulation

Thus, rather than using legislation to ban or restrict various activities, a more 'subtle' approach can be adopted. This involves the use of various regulatory bodies. Having identified possible cases where action might be required (e.g. potential cases of pollution, misleading information or the abuse of monopoly power), the regulatory body may conduct an investigation; prepare a report containing its findings and recommendations and it might also have the power to enforce its decisions.

Regulatory bodies exist in many countries. In the UK, there are regulatory bodies for each of the major privatised utilities (see section 9.6). The Competition and Markets Authority provides the framework for UK competition policy and investigates and reports on suspected cases of anti-competitive practices and can order such firms to cease or modify these practices (see section 9.5).

In the USA, there is extensive financial regulation, such as through the Financial Industry Regulator and a regulator for Commodity Futures Trading, though less regulation in other areas. Each member of the EU has a regulatory body responsible for rail and there is a regulatory body overseeing the airlines. China has a number of regulatory bodies, such as the China Securities Regulatory Commission and the China Banking Regulatory Commission, while Japan has the Financial Services Agency. Although the specific aims and remit of each regulatory body differ, the broad objective typically concerns the promotion of competition and protection of consumers.

Government provision

As we saw with public goods, such as street lights, private firms do not have an incentive to provide them, thus government may provide them itself and finance this through compulsory contributions, such as taxes, or pay private firms to provide them.

Government provision may also occur with merit goods: neither education nor healthcare are public goods, yet in most countries, they are provided by the government. In this way, the government ensures that individuals consume the 'right' amount of the good or service. This is especially important if consumers are unaware of how beneficial the good might be.

Another way in which governments may intervene to correct market failures is through the provision of information, either directly or through one of its agencies, such as a job centre. By providing information about the negative effects of smoking or of eating certain foods, the government is trying to reduce the consumption of these goods to their social optimum. Information is also provided about schools, employment and prices to help consumers make more informed decisions and to provide a greater degree of certainty for firms.

Price controls

As we saw in Box 2.5, price controls can be used either to raise prices above or reduce prices below the free-market level. The government or another body could set prices below the market equilibrium price to prevent a monopoly or oligopoly from raising prices above the socially efficient level. For example, in the UK the energy regulator, *Ofgem*, introduced a price cap in April 2017 on the energy bills of customers who used pre-payment meters.

Alternatively, the government could set prices *above* the competitive market equilibrium to reduce the level of social inefficiency caused by a negative externality and/or poor economic decision making by individuals. An efficient outcome would be reached if a minimum price was set at a level where the marginal social benefit was equal to the marginal social cost.

Although our discussion has focused on government intervention with the aim of changing the optimum quantity, intervention can also be used on equity grounds. Most people would argue that the free market fails to lead to a *fair* distribution of resources, if it results in some people living in great affluence while others live in extreme poverty. Clearly what constitutes 'fairness' is a highly contentious issue.

Some forms of government intervention, such as direct provision of a good or service or the introduction of a price control may therefore also have the objective of equity, in particular of redistributing incomes. Thus, minimum prices on farm products can be used to protect the incomes of farmers, and minimum wage legislation can help those on low incomes. On the consumption side, low maximum rents might be put in place with the intention of helping those on low incomes afford housing. However, as we mentioned in Box 2.5, price controls can cause shortages and surpluses and hence further government intervention may be required to address the inefficiencies caused by the intervention.

RECAP

1. Governments intervene in markets in a number of ways. One is the use of taxes to curb production or subsidies to increase it. Taxes and subsidies have the advantages of 'internalising' externalities and of providing incentives to reduce external costs. The problem with using taxes and subsidies is in identifying the appropriate rates, since these will vary according to the impact of the externality.

2. Another is to use legislation or regulation to encourage or force businesses to behave in a more socially desirable way. They can be easy to understand and administer but are often a very blunt form of intervention.

3. In some cases, the government or an agency may provide information to correct a market failure. However, if the market failure is substantial, then the government may choose to intervene and provide the good itself.

4. Price controls can be used to help achieve the socially desirable outcome. The objectives of such intervention may also be based on grounds of equity, including the protection of certain groups.

9.4 ENVIRONMENTAL POLICY

Growing concerns over global warming, acid rain, the depletion of the ozone layer, industrial and domestic waste, traffic fumes and other forms of pollution have made the protection of the environment a major political and economic issue. As you can see from successive blogs on the Sloman Economics

News site, worldwide action has been taken in the recent past to try to tackle global warming and climate change.[16] So what policy instruments are open to government?

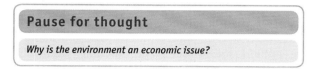

Pause for thought

Why is the environment an economic issue?

Green taxes and subsidies

Increasingly countries are introducing 'green' taxes in order to discourage pollution as goods are produced, consumed or disposed of. To achieve the socially efficient output level, the tax should be equal to the marginal external cost and, in such cases, the price with the tax would then better reflect the full costs to society. An alternative is to subsidise activities that reduce pollution, with the subsidy being equal to the marginal external benefit. Both methods create continuous pressure to reduce (increase) production or consumption of goods that cause negative (positive) externalities.

Although countries do modify existing taxes, especially as new information becomes available about the environmental damage caused by certain products, countries have also been introducing new environmental taxes. Table 9.2 shows the range of such taxes used around the world.

OECD data show that in 2016 (the latest available date) as a percentage of GDP, environmental tax revenues are highest in Serbia at 4.48 per cent, followed by Denmark at 4.0 per cent and 3.95 per cent in Slovenia. The OECD weighted average was 1.63 per cent, with the European average sitting above that at 2.47 per cent, both of which are significantly above the USA (0.66%), Japan (1.35%) and China[17] (0.7%).

Energy continues to be the sector generating the biggest tax revenues as a percentage of GDP across the OECD countries at 1.17 per cent, followed by Motor Vehicles and Transport at 0.4 per cent. Significant variations are still apparent across countries, particularly concerning fuel taxes, which are particularly high in countries such as the UK, though the amount of tax revenue generated from this has fallen with the freezing of fuel duties and a growth in more energy-efficient vehicles and electric cars. Despite the use of energy taxes, many countries set the rates for such taxes below levels that fully reflect the environmental damage associated with energy consumption. This, it is argued, amounts to a form of energy subsidy (see the blog *Fossil fuel externalities only partially reflected in energy taxes* on the Sloman Economics News site).

In 2015, the UK introduced a 5p charge on plastic carrier bags, following similar charges in other countries.[18] Although this is not a tax and the revenue generated does not go to the government, it is a method being used to try to tackle over-use of plastic bags. You can find further details on the government website.[19]

---

[16] See the blogs: '20:20 climate vision?'; 'Wrong Climate at talks'; 'A changing climate at the White House'; 'The run-up to Copenhagen'; 'An Accord from discord - reflections on Copenhagen'; 'An historic agreement at the Paris Climate Change Conference'; 'Laying down the rules to address climate change: the outcome of COP24'.

[17] Data from China are for 2015 and are noted as both an estimate and incomplete.

[18] See: *List by Country*; *'Bag Charges, Taxes and Bans'*, The Grocery Box Company Limited.

[19] 'Carrier bags: why there's a charge', *Policy Paper*, Department for Environment Food & Rural Affairs (11 January 2018).

Table 9.2	Types of environmental taxes and charges

Motor fuels	Other goods	Air transport
Leaded/unleaded	Batteries	Noise charges
Diesel (quality differential)	Plastic carrier bags	Aviation fuels
Carbon/energy taxation	Glass containers	
Sulphur tax	Drink cans	**Water**
	Tyres	Water charges
Other energy products	CFCs/halons	Sewage charges
Carbon/energy tax	Disposable razors/	Water effluent charges
Sulphur tax or charge	cameras	Manure charges
NO_2 charge	Lubricant oil charge	
Methane charge	Oil pollutant charge	**Direct tax provisions**
	Solvents	Tax relief on green investment
Agricultural inputs		Taxation on free company cars
Fertilisers	**Waste disposal**	Employer-paid commuting expenses
Pesticides	Municipal waste charges	taxable
Manure	Waste-disposal charges	Employer-paid parking expenses
	Hazardous waste charges	taxable
Vehicle-related taxation	Landfill tax or charges	Commuter use of public transport tax
Sales tax depends on car size	Duties on waste water	deductible
Road tax depends on car size		

BOX 9.3 **A STERN REBUKE**

It's much cheaper to act now on global warming than to wait

The analysis of global warming is not just for climate scientists. Economists have a major part to play in examining its causes and consequences and the possible solutions. And these solutions are likely to have a major impact on business.

Perhaps the most influential study of climate change in recent times was the Stern Review. This was an independent review, commissioned by the UK Chancellor of the Exchequer, and headed by Sir Nicholas Stern, the then head of the Government Economic Service and former chief economist of the World Bank. Here was an economist using the methods of economics to analyse perhaps the most serious problem facing the world.

> Climate change presents a unique challenge for economics: it is the greatest and widest-ranging market failure ever seen. The economic analysis must therefore be global, deal with long time horizons, have the economics of risk and uncertainty at centre stage, and examine the possibility of major, non-marginal change.[1]

First the bad news . . .

According to the Stern Report, if no action was taken, global temperatures would rise by some 2–3°C within 50 years. As a result, the world economy would shrink by up to 20 per cent – and that would be just the average. The countries most seriously affected by floods, drought and crop failure could shrink by considerably more. These tend to be the poorest countries, least able to bear the costs of these changes.

Rising sea levels could displace some 200 million people; droughts could create tens or even hundreds of millions of 'climate refugees' and 15–40 per cent of species could face extinction.

. . . Then the good

The report concluded that if action is taken now, these consequences could be averted – and at relatively low cost: a sacrifice of just 1 per cent of global GDP (global income) could, if correctly targeted, be enough to stabilise greenhouse gases to a sustainable level. To achieve this, action would need to be taken to cut emissions from their various sources. This would involve a mixture of four things:

- Reducing consumer demand for emissions-intensive goods and services.
- Increased efficiency, which can save both money and emissions.
- Action on non-energy emissions, such as avoiding deforestation.
- Switching to lower-carbon technologies for power, heat and transport.

The report recommended a range of policies focused on altering incentives. This could involve taxing polluting activities; subsidising green alternatives, including the development of green technology; establishing a price for

carbon through trading carbon (see the section on tradable permits on page 239) and regulating its production; and encouraging behavioural change through education, better labelling of products, imposing minimum standards for building and encouraging public debate.

We consider some of these alternatives in this section of the chapter.

Did we heed the warnings?

The Stern Report was produced over ten years ago, but has progress been made? Steps have been taken around the world, but there is growing concern by various institutions, such as the OECD, that a global response is still required. Are national governments acting with the urgency that is needed?

In 2014, the Intergovernmental Panel on Climate Change (IPCC) issued its Fifth Assessment Report (AR5),[2] which consisted of three working group reports looking at the physical science; the impacts, adaptation and vulnerability and the mitigation of climate change, with economists playing a key role in the second and third reports.

Echoes of the Stern Report were evident in the impact report.[3] It explained the current effects of climate change across the world, the world's lack of preparedness for the risks associated with climate change, and that opportunities do exist for us to take action now. Although adaptation is occurring, it is largely focused on reacting to past events rather than preparing for future changes. According to Chris Field, the Co-Chair of the second Impact Working Group:

> Climate-change adaptation is not an exotic agenda that has never been tried. Governments, firms, and communities around the world are building experience with adaptation. This experience forms a starting point for bolder, more ambitious adaptations that will be important, as climate and society continue to change.

The opportunities for action were reiterated by the Mitigation Working Group, which published its own report,[4] including a summary for policy makers. Although it noted progress in policy development within countries at the sectoral level, it identified a substantial time lag between the implementation of policies and the impact on the environment, noting that since 2008 emission growth has not yet deviated from the previous trend. Further, it reported that to make the necessary reductions in emissions, investment patterns would need to change significantly.

Currently, the IPPC is working on its sixth Assessment Report, which will be published in 2022.

Political developments

In the meantime, there have been developments on the political front. In 2015, at the COP21 climate change conference in Paris, an agreement was reached between the

---

[1] *Stern Review in the Economics of Climate Change: Executive Summary,* HM Treasury (30 October 2006).

[2] *The Fifth Assessment Report (AR5)* (IPCC, 2014).
[3] *Climate Change 2014: Impacts, Adaptation, and Vulnerability, from Working Group II of the IPCC* (IPCC, 2014).
[4] *Climate Change 2014: Mitigation from Climate Change, from Working Group III of the IPCC* (IPCC, 2014).

▶

195 countries present. The Paris Agreement committed countries to limiting global warming to 'well below' 2°C and preferably to no more than 1.5°C. above pre-industrial levels.

However, with the election of Donald Trump, the US administration has become much more sceptical about climate change. The president said the USA would exit the 2015 Paris Agreement and has taken measures to slow the switch from coal. US carbon dioxide emissions increased 3.4 per cent in 2018.

Brazil too, under its new president, Jair Bolsanaro, elected in 2018, is much more sceptical about climate change and is reluctant to take measures to reduce greenhouse gas emissions, such as curbing the destruction of the Amazonian rain forest. The Australian government is similarly sceptical and rejects the IPCC's call to phase out coal power by 2050, saying that Australia will continue to exploit its coal reserves.

But despite these developments, in December 2018, at the UN climate change conference in Poland (COP24), 196

countries agreed to a rulebook for targeting, measuring and verifying emissions. However, the measures already agreed which would be covered by the rulebook will be insufficient to meet the 2°C, let alone the 1.5°C, target agreed in 2015 in Paris (see the blog on the Sloman news site, *Laying down the rules to address climate change: the outcome of COP24*).

1. *Would it be in the interests of a business to reduce its carbon emissions if this involved an increase in its costs?*
2. *How is the concept of 'opportunity cost' relevant in analysing the impact of business decisions on the environment?*
3. *The Stern Report was produced in 2006, but there has been a lack of progress. Why do you think progress has been so slow? Does this reflect a lack of political will or scepticism about the extent of climate change?*

Search for and assess recent political developments in addressing climate change.

Choosing the tax rate

The rule here is simple: to achieve the socially efficient output of a polluting activity, the government should impose a tax equal to the marginal external cost (or grant a subsidy equal to the marginal external benefit).

Consider again a chemical works that emits smoke from a chimney, imposing an external cost on others ($MSC > MC$) and polluting the atmosphere.

This is illustrated in Figure 9.4. For simplicity, it is assumed that the firm is a price taker. It produces Q_1 where $P = MC$ (its profit-maximising output), but takes no account of the external pollution costs it imposes on society. If the government imposes a tax on production equal to the marginal pollution cost, it will effectively 'internalise' the externality. The firm will have to pay an amount equal to the external cost it creates. The firm's MC curve thus shifts upwards to become the same as the MSC curve. It will therefore now maximise profits at Q_2, which is the socially optimum output where $MSB = MSC$.

As we have already seen, identifying the socially efficient tax rate is difficult and even if two firms produce the same amount of pollution, it is difficult to determine the environmental damage caused, as the ability of the environment to cope with the pollution may vary from one place to another. Furthermore, over time the harmful effects are likely to build up and so estimating the future cost is practically impossible.

One other factor to consider when using environmental taxes and subsidies is the elasticity of demand. The less elastic the demand for the product at its current price, the less effective will a tax be in cutting production and hence in cutting pollution. Thus, taxes on petrol have to be very high to make significant reductions in the consumption of petrol and hence the exhaust gases that contribute towards global warming and acid rain. But those on lower incomes spend a higher proportion of their income on such taxes and hence the tax will also have a significant redistributive effect, which must be considered within broader government policy.

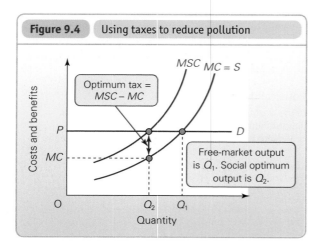

Figure 9.4   Using taxes to reduce pollution

Optimum tax = $MSC - MC$

Free-market output is Q_1. Social optimum output is Q_2.

Pause for thought

Why is it easier to use taxes and subsidies to tackle the problem of car exhaust pollution than to tackle the problem of peak-time traffic congestion in cities?

Laws and regulations

The traditional way of tackling pollution has been to set maximum permitted levels of emission or resource use, or minimum acceptable levels of environmental quality, and then to fine firms contravening these limits. Measures of this type are known as ***command-and-control (CAC) systems***. Clearly, there have to be inspectors to monitor the amount of pollution, and the fines have to be large enough to deter firms from exceeding the limit.

Virtually all countries have environmental regulations of one sort or another. For example, the EU has over 200 items of legislation covering areas such as air and water pollution, noise, the marketing and use of dangerous chemicals, waste management, the environmental impacts of new projects (such as power stations, roads and quarries), recycling, depletion of the ozone layer and global warming.

Assessing CAC systems. Given the uncertainty over the environmental impacts of pollutants, especially over the longer term, it is often better to play safe and set tough emissions standards. These could always be relaxed at a later stage if the effects turn out to be less damaging, but it might be too late to reverse damage if the effects turn out to be more serious. Taxes may be a more sophisticated means of reaching a socially efficient output, but CAC methods are usually more straightforward to devise, easier to understand by firms and easier to implement.

The weakness of command-and-control systems is that they fail to offer business any incentive to do better than the legally specified level. By contrast, with a pollution tax, the lower the pollution level, the less tax there will be to pay. There is thus a continuing incentive for businesses progressively to cut pollution levels and introduce cleaner technology.

Tradable permits

A policy measure that has grown in popularity in recent years is that of ***tradable permits***. This is a combination of command-and-control and market-based systems. A maximum permitted level of emission is set for a given pollutant for a given factory, and the firm is given a permit to emit up to this amount. If it emits less than this amount, it is given a credit for the difference, which it can then use in another of its factories. Another option is to sell the credits to another firm. This firm can then pollute over its permitted level, by an amount equal to the credits. Thus the overall level of emissions is set by CAC methods, whereas their distribution is determined by the market.

Take the example of firms A and B, which are currently each producing 12 units of a pollutant. Now assume that a standard is set permitting them to produce only 10 units each. If firm A managed to reduce the pollutant to 8 units, it would be given a credit for 2 units. It could then sell this to firm B, enabling B to continue emitting 12 units. The effect would still be a total reduction of 4 units between the two firms.

However, by allowing them to trade in pollution permits, pollution reduction can be concentrated in the firms where it can be achieved at lowest cost. In our example, if it cost firm B more to reduce its pollution than firm A, then the permits could be sold from A to B at a price that was profitable to both (i.e. at a price above the cost of emission reduction to A, but below the cost of emission reduction to B).

Pause for thought

To what extent will the introduction of tradable permits lead to a lower level of total pollution (as opposed to its redistribution)?

A similar principle can be used for using natural resources. Thus fish quotas could be assigned to fishing boats or fleets or countries. Any parts of these quotas not used could then be sold.

The EU carbon trading system

As part of its objective to reduce greenhouse gas emissions as set out in the Kyoto Protocol (see Case Study C.24 on the book's website), the EU launched a carbon Emissions Trading System (ETS).

Phases I and II. From January 2005 until December 2007, governments across the EU27 allocated credits, called Emission Unit Allowances (EUAs) to approximately 12 000 industrial plants. These credits represented a limit for each company in terms of its emissions. Under the scheme, any company exceeding its allowance could purchase permits from other companies that managed to cut their emissions below their allowance. These 'greener' companies could therefore make a profit by selling their surplus credits and thus a trading system across Europe was created. In January 2008, phase II of the ETS began, whereby all existing allowances from phase I became invalid. The same basic principles were in place, but now companies were able to use emission reductions in countries outside of the EU to offset their emissions within the EU.

Definitions

Command-and-control (CAC) systems The use of laws or regulations backed up by inspections and penalties (such as fines) for non-compliance.

Tradable permits Each firm is given a permit to produce a given level of pollution. If less than the permitted amount is produced, the firm is given a credit. This can then be sold to another firm, allowing it to exceed its original limit. This is known as a 'cap and trade' scheme.

Phase III. As phase II was beginning, the European Commission published proposals for phase III, commencing in January 2013 and with such a long lead-in time, companies had sufficient time to adapt their strategies and production techniques.

Lessons were learned from phases I and II, with an initial move to an *EU-wide cap* on the volume of emissions and the total quantity of EUAs that would be issued, rather than the more decentralised, country-based allocation. Furthermore, while a proportion of EUAs *could* be auctioned in phases I and II, very few actually were.

From 2013, the size of the EU-wide cap was reduced by 38 million tonnes of NO_2 per year. By 2020 this would result in emissions being 21 per cent lower than in 2005. The EU also proposed that they will be 43 per cent lower by 2030. This will require a larger annual reduction of 2.2 per cent from 2021, as discussed in the EU's 2030 framework for climate and energy policy.

Phase III also moved towards the auctioning of EUAs. The average number of EUAs auctioned during phase III is just under 50 per cent. Only firms in manufacturing and the power industry in certain member states continue to be allocated the majority of their allowances at no charge.

A Market Stability Reserve (MSR) was introduced in 2019, aiming to deal with the imbalance between demand and supply. This controls the volume of allowances auctioned relative to the total number in circulation. Any EUAs that are not auctioned are placed into the MSR and can be released if required.

Phase IV. In November 2017, proposals were agreed for phase IV of the scheme, which operates from 2021 to 2030.

- The cap on the total number of EUAs will remain, but will now decrease at a faster rate of 48 million tonnes per year, compared to the 38 million in phase III.
- A revised Market Stability Reserve (MSR) will operate in phase IV, with the volume of EUAs being auctioned falling at a faster rate if there is a surplus of EUAs in circulation.
- Finally, if the number of allowances in the MSR is greater than the total number auctioned the previous year, then they will be permanently removed from the market.

The hope is that these changes will help to stabilize prices and allow the market system to operate more effectively.

Assessing the system of tradable permits

The main advantage of tradable permits is that they combine the simplicity of CAC methods with the benefits of achieving pollution reduction in the most efficient way. There is also the advantage that firms have a financial incentive to cut pollution. This might then make it easier for governments to impose tougher standards (i.e. impose lower permitted levels of emission).

There are, however, various problems with tradable permits. One is the possibility that trade will lead to pollution being concentrated in certain geographical areas. The equity of the allocation of allowances was a big concern in phases I and II, especially when some countries were set tougher targets than others. Some countries had a strong incentive to game the system by setting an aggregate cap that was greater than the volume of emissions actually being produced. This kept costs down for firms in that country, which helped to maintain its national economic competitiveness. However, this problem was addressed in phase III with the EU-wide cap.

Finally, the effectiveness of the system will depend on the demand for EUAs relative to the total number of EUAs issued by authorities. If the supply of allowances significantly exceeds demand in this secondary market, then the price will fall to a relatively low level and firms will lack the necessary incentives to invest in new energy-efficient technology. This was a major criticism of phase I, as the price of EUAs fell from a peak of €30 to just €0.02 per tonne.

The situation did improve with allowances tightened in phase II, but from 2011 until 2017, the price remained below €10 per tonne, significantly under the level the Stern Report had indicated was required to stabilise levels of CO_2 and to incentivise a change in behaviour. The recession was partly to blame, as weak trading conditions kept the price low, as firms cut back on production, but we were also seeing a boom in renewable and energy-efficient technology.

While the system is far from perfect, progress has been made in refining the carbon trading system and there is general agreement that the system has the potential to be effective, especially with the new changes introduced in phase IV. Whether the UK will remain in the EU ETS or leave after Brexit is still to be determined. Non-EU members, such as Norway and Iceland do participate in the scheme, while Switzerland does not, but has aligned its scheme so that allowances can be traded.

Pause for thought

Should all emitters of carbon, including aircraft and agriculture, be included in carbon trading schemes?

BOX 9.4   THE PROBLEM OF URBAN TRAFFIC CONGESTION

The most congested cities

Since the 1950s, there has been almost continuous growth in vehicle miles driven in most countries. According to the Department for Transport, in 1951 in Great Britain, 37 billion vehicle miles were travelled; in 2017 this had risen to 237.1 billion. Over the past 20 years, the only form of road transport that has declined in terms of vehicle miles is buses, falling by 24.7 per cent since 1997.[1]

There are many reasons for the increase in vehicle miles, including population growth and density, easier access to cars, income growth, changes in employment patterns and location. The National Travel Survey finds that in 2016, 77 per cent of British households had access to a car, compared to just 14 per cent in 1951.[2] Although the rate of traffic growth has been slowing since the 1990s and the length of the road network has increased from 184 837 miles in 1951 to 246 709 in 2017, the obvious conclusion of such large increases in vehicle usage and miles driven is traffic congestion.[3]

A report by the INRIX[4] considers traffic congestion globally. The table shows some of the cities most impacted in terms of hours lost and travel time per person travelling and speed for the marginal mile.

When looking at the full rankings, it is interesting to note that, when ranking by hours lost in congestion, eight of the top 10 cities are European and it is the age of these cities that is a key contributing factor.

---

[1] *Road Traffic Estimates: Great Britain 2017,* Department for Transport (5 July 2018)
[2] *National Travel Survey: 2017,* Department for Transport (26 July 2018)
[3] *Road Length Statistics: Road length (miles) by road type in Great Britain,* Department for Transport (5 July 2018)
[4] Trevor Reed and Joshua Kidd, *2018 Global Traffic Scorecard,* INRIX Research (February 2019)

The 2018 INRIX report uses London as a case study and finds that in Great Britain, seven cities have annual delays that are greater than 140 hours, with London reaching 227 hours. The report estimates that the congestion delays in London alone cost the country £7.9 billion. Although significant improvements have been made to public transport and there has been significant growth in cycle rates, the road network in London has not changed, with many roads dating back before the Romans. So, with massive population growth in the city, congestion has worsened.

The externalities of congestion

Traffic congestion is a classic example of the problem of externalities. When people use their cars, not only do they incur private costs (petrol, wear and tear on the vehicle, tolls, the time taken to travel, etc.), but also, they impose costs on other people. These external costs include the following:

Congestion costs: time. When a person uses a car, it adds to the congestion, slowing the traffic and increasing the journey time of other car users, as we saw in the table above.

Congestion costs: monetary. Congestion increases fuel consumption and the costs of wear and tear. When a motorist adds to congestion, therefore, there are additional monetary costs imposed on other motorists. The INRIX estimates that the congestion delays imposed on London drivers are £1680 per person annually.

Environmental costs. Cars emit fumes and create noise, reducing the quality of the environment for pedestrians, other road users and especially those living along the road. Driving can cause accidents, a problem that increases as

Most congested cities in the world

2018 Impact Rank (2017)	Urban area	Hours lost in congestion (Rank 2018)	Inner city last mile travel time (minutes)	Inner city last mile speed (mph)
1 (1)	Moscow	210 (10)	5	11
2 (3)	Istanbul	157 (32)	6	10
3 (2)	Bogota	272 (1)	8	7
4 (4)	Mexico City	218 (9)	7	9
5 (5)	São Paulo	154 (39)	6	10
6 (6)	London	227 (6)	8	7
7 (8)	Rio de Janeiro	199 (13)	5	13
8 (7)	Boston, MA	164 (25)	6	11
9 (9)	Saint Petersburg	200 (12)	6	11
10 (13)	Rome	254 (2)	8	8
14 (14)	Singapore	105 (106)	4	15
15 (16)	Berlin	154 (40)	5	11
16 (18)	Paris	237 (5)	7	8

Source: Trevor Reed and Joshua Kidd, *Global Traffic Scorecard*, INRIX Research (February 2019)

drivers become more impatient as a result of delays. However, the Department for Transport finds that the risk of injury or death in a road accident has fallen almost every year since 1949, due to safer vehicles, technological progress, various road safety policies and better education and training.

Exhaust gases cause long-term environmental damage and are one of the main causes of the greenhouse effect and of the increased acidity of lakes and rivers and the poisoning of forests. They can also cause long-term health problems (e.g. for asthma sufferers). In Great Britain, road transport accounted for 23 per cent of the UK's CO_2 emissions in 2015. There has, however, been an increase in the number of newly registered ultra-low emission vehicles, rising from 4314 in 2013 to 53 195 in 2017.[5]

The socially efficient level of road usage

These externalities mean that road usage will be above the social optimum. This is illustrated in the diagram. Costs and benefits are shown on the vertical axis and are measured in money terms. Thus any non-monetary costs or benefits (such as time costs) must be given a monetary value. The horizontal axis measures road usage in terms of cars per minute passing a specified point on the road.

For simplicity it is assumed that there are no external benefits from car use and that therefore marginal private and marginal social benefits are the same. The *MSB* curve is shown as downward sloping. The reason for this is that different road users put a different value on any given journey. If the marginal (private) cost of making the journey were high, only those for whom the journey had a high marginal benefit would travel. If the marginal cost of making the journey fell, more people would make it, assuming the marginal cost was less than the marginal benefit. Thus the greater the number of cars, the lower the marginal benefit.

The marginal (private) cost curve (*MC*) is likely to be constant up to the level of traffic flow at which congestion begins to occur. This is shown as point *a* in the diagram. Beyond this point, marginal cost is likely to rise as time costs increase (i.e. journey times lengthen) and as fuel consumption rises.

The marginal *social* cost curve (*MSC*) is drawn above the marginal private cost curve. The vertical difference between the two represents the external costs. Up to point *b*, external

costs are simply the environmental costs. Beyond point *b*, there are also external congestion costs, since additional road users slow down the journey of *other* road users. These external costs get progressively greater as traffic grinds to a halt.

The actual level of traffic flow will be at Q_1, where marginal private costs and benefits are equal (point *e*). The socially efficient level of traffic flow, however, will be at the lower level of Q_2 where marginal social costs and benefits are equal (point *d*). In other words, there will be an excessive level of road usage.

So what can governments do to 'internalise' these externalities? To achieve a reduction in traffic to Q_2 the motorist should be charged an amount equal to *d–c* in the diagram. In practice this is difficult, as the external cost is hard to measure and congestion and its costs vary with location and the time of day.

Solutions to congestion

Even if motorists cannot be charged an amount equal to *d–c*, there are various things that can be done to reduce congestion and get closer to the socially efficient level of road usage.

Direct provision. One solution is to build more roads, but this may encourage more people to use the roads, expecting congestion to have fallen. This is what happened in London, when the M25 was built. Another issue is where will these roads lie? Some cities simply do not have the capacity for this. If new roads are built, this could adversely affect people living nearby and some people's homes may have to be demolished. There are also environmental concerns if new roads mean destruction of natural habitat, more noise and air pollution.

Another option would be to increase or improve public transport, such as more buses, new park-and-ride schemes, better underground/metro systems and rail networks. A key aspect here is to make public transport an attractive alternative. Thus flexibility, cost, comfort and reliability are important considerations.

Regulation and legislation. Car use and access could be restricted to cut the demand. For example, more bus and cycle lanes could be introduced; vehicles could be banned from city centres; certain streets could be designated as pedestrian-only; parking could be restricted and various side streets could be made no-entry from main roads.

In 2015, Oslo announced plans to ban all private vehicles from the city centre by 2019. Although this was subsequently pushed back to 2020, a variety of measures were introduced, including increasing congestion tolls, pedestrianising a number of streets and eliminating parking spaces. Many other cities have introduced measures to curb cars. For example, in Paris, the first Sunday of every month is now car-free from 10am to 6pm. Several cities, including London, Madrid and Brussels, have introduced low-emission zones to reduce exhaust pollution.

However, one issue with these policies is that they may simply divert the congestion to areas beyond the zones and many businesses in the zones complain that it is harder for customers and workers to access them. In the case of parking restrictions, these may cause people to 'park in orbit' and simply drive around looking for a space, thus adding to

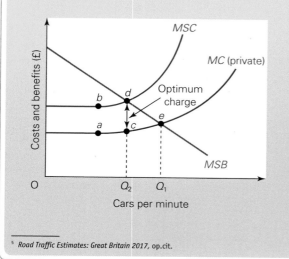

congestion. People may also park illegally or down side streets, causing different negative externalities to be imposed. Nevertheless, many cities are hailing their restrictions as successful in reducing congestion and pollution.

Market solutions

The solution favoured by many economists is to use the price mechanism to encourage car users to change their behaviour. Various taxes are already imposed on road users and so one option would be to increase those taxes, thereby increasing the private costs of using cars and internalising the externality. However, some taxes on car owners are fixed costs (such as annual vehicle tax) and so may reduce car ownership but will do little to reduce car use.

Furthermore, if higher taxes are imposed on car *use,* such as fuel taxes, every car user pays them, even if they are driving on uncongested roads. Furthermore, the demand for fuel is price inelastic and so higher fuel costs may have little effect on fuel consumption. Similarly, subsidies could be used on public transport to reduce the cost and internalise the positive externality.

Road Pricing. These schemes are in place in many cities around the world, such as toll roads in France, a congestion charging zone in London and sophisticated variable road pricing schemes in Barcelona, Orlando, Lisbon, Singapore and Oslo. Such schemes may vary with the time of day or with the actual level of congestion (measured, say, by traffic speed or the volume of cars).

Successful developments

The INRIX report found that, while European cities experience the highest hours lost from congestion, they are also 'the most progressive in reallocating road space to other transportation modes and for the public use.' It highlights the aggressive policy in Paris of eliminating traffic from the lower quays on the Seine River (though a Court has ruled for a second time that this ban will be revoked); Barcelona's 'superblock' schemes, where certain blocks are pedestrianised; Germany's consistent investment in rail and road networks and its infrastructure growth for cyclists and pedestrians; and London's re-allocation of road space towards bicycles, pedestrians and public transport.

The report also notes the London congestion zone introduced in 2003, when London became the second city behind Singapore to take significant measures to reduce congestion in targeted areas. From 2004/5 to 2016/17, the number of trips taken on public transport increased by 41 per cent or by 402 million trips. However, data indicate that average speeds on roads in the congestion zone are actually lower than they were prior to its adoption in 2003.

Singapore is the city where the most aggressive road management systems are in place and, although congestion is still a major issue here, this is largely driven by the sheer population. Despite this, it ranks in an impressive 106th place in terms of hours wasted.

Much more work is needed across the globe to tackle traffic congestion, especially given the environmental impact and cost to the economy. However, changes are occurring, with technological progress helping with the growth of low-emission and electric vehicles, as well as more sophisticated road charging schemes.

> The radical shift away from the personal automobile, predominately in European cities, constitutes a new frontier in mobility and an opportunity for data driven solutions.[6]

One message is clear: no single solution is enough. Multiple policies will be needed to tackle both the demand- and the supply-side issues of road transport.

Explain how, by varying the charge to motorists according to the time of day or level of congestion, a socially optimal level of road use can be achieved.

Referring to a town or city with which you are familiar, consider what would be the most appropriate mix of policies to deal with its traffic congestion problems.

---

[6] *Road Traffic Estimates: Great Britain 2017*, op.cit. (p. 6).

RECAP

1. There are three main types of environmental policy instrument: taxes and subsidies; command-and-control systems; tradable permits.

2. Taxes and subsidies have the advantages of 'internalising' externalities and of providing incentives to reduce external costs. The problem with using taxes and subsidies is in identifying the appropriate rates, since these will vary according to the environmental impact.

3. Command-and-control systems, such as making certain practices illegal or putting limits on discharges, are a less sophisticated alternative to taxes or subsidies. However, they may be preferable when the environmental costs of certain actions are unknown and it is wise to play safe.

4. Tradable permits are where firms are given permits to emit a certain level of pollution and then these can be traded. A firm that can relatively cheaply reduce its pollution below its permitted level can sell this credit to another firm which finds it more costly to do so. The ETS is the world's largest carbon trading scheme.

9.5 COMPETITION POLICY AND BUSINESS BEHAVIOUR

Competition, monopoly and the public interest

Most markets in the real world are imperfect, with firms having varying degrees of market power. But will this power be against the public interest? This question has been addressed by successive governments in framing legislation to deal with monopolies and oligopolies.

Market power enables firms to push up prices and make supernormal profit, thereby 'exploiting' the consumer. The less substitute products there are, the greater the firm's power and the higher prices will be relative to the costs of production. This is illustrated in Figure 9.5 (which is similar to Figure 5.2 on page 119).

The firm maximises profits at Q_1, where $MC = MR$. Profits are shown by the shaded area. The greater the firm's market power, the steeper will be the firm's AR and MR curves. The bigger will be the gap between price (point a) and marginal cost (point b). Remember that under perfect competition, price equals marginal cost (see Figure 4.4 on page 101). This is shown by point c, which is at a lower price and a higher output.

Although a lack of competition can result in higher prices and removes the incentive to become more efficient, market power is not necessarily a bad thing, as we saw in section 5.2. Economies of scale may allow a monopolist to charge a lower price than a more competitive firm; the threat of new competitors overcoming entry barriers may prevent firms from exploiting their position; and supernormal profits can provide funds for research and development or capital investment, potentially leading to new or innovative products.

The three broad areas of competition policy

There are three broad areas of competition policy.

Monopoly policy. This seeks to prevent firms from abusing a dominant market position. Therefore, it is not saying that a monopoly (or even an oligopoly) is bad, but that if a firm has dominance in a market, the competition authorities will want to weigh up the gains and losses to the public of the firm's behaviour. For example, will the firm's dominance lead to lower costs, but higher prices and higher profits or will the firm use these higher profits to innovate and improve quality?

Merger policy. Competition authorities typically have powers to control mergers and acquisitions (M&As). In many cases, M&As are good for consumers and the economy, but sometimes they can lead to significant reductions in competition and can lead to a firm being in a dominant position. Mergers can also create a greater chance for collusion from the remaining firms in the market.

Restrictive practice policy. This tends to focus on situations where firms have made agreements to restrict, limit or prevent competition and is nearly always against the interests of society. It is mostly observed in oligopolies, where firms can collude to generate higher joint profits, which in turn will often mean higher prices for customers.

Competition policy could seek to *ban* various structures or activities. For example, it could ban mergers leading to a market share of more than a certain amount, or it could ban price-fixing arrangements between oligopolists. However, most countries prefer to adopt a more flexible approach and examine each case on its merits. Such an approach does not presume that the mere possession of power is against the public interest, but rather that certain uses of that power may be.

EU and UK competition policy

Relevant EU legislation is contained in Articles 101 and 102 of the 2009 Treaty of the Functioning of the European Union (TFEU). Additional regulations covering mergers came into force in 1990 and were amended in 2004. Further minor amendments have since been introduced, and many of these focus on specific market regulations.

Article 101 is concerned with restrictive practices and Article 102 with the abuse of market power. The Articles focus on firms trading between EU members and so do not cover monopolies or oligopolies operating solely within a member country. They are implemented by the European Commission (EC), which monitors compliance, investigates behaviour and imposes fines where unlawful conduct is identified.

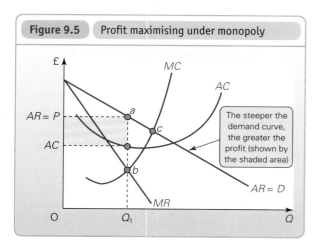

| Figure 9.5 | Profit maximising under monopoly |

The steeper the demand curve, the greater the profit (shown by the shaded area)

In the UK, there have been substantial changes to competition policy since legislation was introduced in 1948. The current approach is based on the 1998 Competition Act and the 2002 Enterprise Act, which brought UK policy in line with EU policy. Chapter I prohibits various restrictive practices, and mirrors EU Article 101. Chapter II prohibits various abuses of monopoly power, and mirrors Article 102. The 2013 Enterprise and Regulatory Reform Act strengthened the Competition Act and introduced new measures for the control of mergers. It also introduced a new body, the Competition and Markets Authority (CMA), to carry out investigations into particular firms or markets suspected of not working in the best interests of consumers and being in breach of one or more of the Acts.

Restrictive practices policy

This covers *agreements* between firms, *joint decisions* and concerted *practices* which prevent, restrict or distort competition. In other words, it covers all types of oligopolistic collusion that are judged to be against the interests of consumers, such as: price fixing; limiting supply, perhaps by each firm agreeing to an output quota; sharing out markets by geographical area, type or size of customer or nature of outlet (e.g. bus companies agreeing not to run services in each other's areas); or agreements between purchasers (e.g. supermarkets) to keep down prices paid to suppliers (e.g. farmers). Other restrictive practices, where authorities have the discretion to decide, on a case-by-case basis, whether or not competition is appreciably restricted include:

- *Collusive tendering or bid rigging.* This is when, in response to a call for tenders for a contract, two or more firms discuss their bids with each other beforehand, rather than submitting them independently. One firm may submit a bid at an artificially high price or may not bid, thus limiting the amount of effective competition.
- *Vertical price-fixing agreements.* These are price agreements between purchasing firms and their suppliers. An example of this is resale price maintenance. This is where a manufacturer or distributor sets the price for retailers to charge. It may well distribute a price list to retailers (e.g. a car manufacturer may distribute a price list to car showrooms).
- *Resale price maintenance* is where a manufacturer agrees with retailers not to sell its product below a specific price. It is thus a way of preventing competition between retailers from driving down retail prices and ultimately the price they pay to the manufacturer. Both manufacturers and retailers, therefore, are likely to gain from resale price maintenance.

- *Agreements to exchange information that could have the effect of reducing competition.* For example, if producers exchange information on their price intentions, it is a way of allowing price leadership (see page 123), a form of tacit collusion, to continue.

Legislation is designed to prevent collusive *behaviour* not oligopolistic *structures* (i.e. the simple existence of co-operation between firms). For example, under the EU's Article 101(3), agreements between oligopolists are allowed to continue if they meet all of the following conditions: (a) they directly enhance the quality of the good/service for the customer; (b) they are the only way to do so; (c) they do not eliminate competition; (d) consumers receive a fair share of the resulting benefits.

If companies are found guilty of undertaking any anti-competitive practices that are in contravention of Article 101, they are ordered to cease the activity with immediate effect and are subject to financial penalties, as you can see in Box 9.5.

Pause for thought

Are all such agreements necessarily against the interests of consumers?

The biggest difference between UK and EU policy was created with the passing of the 2002 Enterprise Act. This made it a *criminal* offence for individuals to implement arrangements that enabled price fixing, market sharing, restrictions in production and bid-rigging irrespective of whether there are appreciable effects on competition. Convicted offenders can receive a prison sentence of up to five years and/or an unlimited fine. Prosecutions can be brought by the Serious Fraud Office or the CMA.

In both the UK and EU, fines are calculated in the same way, taking into account the size of the firm's annual sales affected by the anti-competitive activities; its market share; the length of time the firm has been engaged in anti-competitive practices; past convictions and whether it was the instigator of the cartel. Fines are also capped and cannot be greater than

---

Definitions

Collusive tendering or bid rigging Where two or more firms secretly agree on the prices they will tender for a contract. These prices will be above those which would have been submitted under a genuinely competitive tendering process.

Resale price maintenance Where the manufacturer of a product (legally) insists that the product should be sold at a specified retail price.

10 per cent of a firm's annual total turnover. Both the EU and UK have similar approaches for leniency if, for example, one of the members of a cartel co-operates with the investigating authorities.

However, a problem with any policy to deal with collusion is the difficulty in rooting it out. When firms do all their deals 'behind closed doors' and are careful not to keep records or give clues, then collusion can be very hard to spot.

Monopoly policy

Monopoly policy in the EU and UK relates to the abuse of market power and has also been extended to cover mergers. Policy in both regions follows a two-stage process, whereby the relevant market first has to be identified (i.e. which products and suppliers are close substitutes for one another). Having done this, the authorities must decide if the firm has a dominant position in this market. To do so it looks at factors such as market shares, the position of competitors, the bargaining strength of customers, measures of profitability and the existence of any significant barriers to entry.

If the evidence confirms that the firm does have a dominant position, the authorities then assess whether the firm is using its market power to restrict competition. The authorities will be looking to see if the firm is using its dominant position to carry out either 'exploitative' or 'exclusionary' abuses.

Exploitative abuses are types of business practice that directly harm the consumer (e.g. raising prices other than when costs rise), whereas *exclusionary abuses* are business practices that limit or prevent effective competition from either actual or potential arrivals. Examples of exploitative abuses include:

- A monopolist that charges a higher price, produces a lower output and makes a larger profit than a comparable firm under perfect competition.
- A firm that reduces product quality, limits product ranges, provides poor levels of customer service or offers customers special deals if they make 'all or most' of their purchases of the product from the dominant firm.

However, exploitative abuses can be challenging to identify and correct. Thus most of the focus of competition authorities is on exclusionary abuses. Three specific examples of exclusionary abuses are:

- *Price discrimination.* This is regarded as an abuse only to the extent that the higher prices are excessive, or the lower prices are used to exclude competitors.
- *Predatory pricing.* This is where the price of a product is set at loss-making levels, so as to undercut competitors and drive them out of business. The firm uses profitable parts of its business to subsidise this loss making.
- *Vertical restraints.* This is where a supplying firm imposes conditions on a purchasing firm (or vice versa). For example, a manufacturer may impose rules on retailers about displaying the product or the provision of after-sales service, or it may refuse to supply certain outlets (e.g. perfume manufacturers refusing to supply discount chains, such as Superdrug).

If a business is found guilty of engaging in exclusionary abuses that contravene Article 102 of the TFEU or the Chapter II prohibition of the UK Competition Act, they are ordered to cease the activities with immediate effect and if they fail to do so are subject to financial penalties, which follow a very similar process to those for restrictive practices.

Pause for thought

If a firm was accused of abusing its dominant position in a market, how might it defend its behaviour on efficiency grounds?

Merger policy

The objectives of merger policy in the UK and EU are similar, with M&As being prohibited or at least investigated if they significantly impede effective competition. While the investigation follows a similar process in both regions, there are differences in terms of criteria.

The EU. Mergers that are judged as being large or having an 'EU dimension' are investigated under EU merger policy. A merger is judged as having an 'EU dimension' when no more than two-thirds of each firm's EU-wide business is conducted in a single member state. If a firm does conduct more than two-thirds of its business in one country, then investigation of the merger would be the responsibility of that member state's competition authority.

Mergers are deemed to be 'large' if one of two thresholds are exceeded. The first threshold is

Definitions

Exploitative abuses Business practices that directly harm the customer. Examples include high prices and poor quality.

Exclusionary abuses Business practices that limit or prevent effective competition from either actual or potential rivals.

BOX 9.5	GOOGLE 'GOOGLE'

Has the company abused a dominant position?

There are many companies that have a significant market share in their respective markets and in some cases, this gives the firm dominance. However, simply having a dominant position does not breach EU, UK or US competition laws – it is the *abuse* of that position that leads to investigations and sometimes fines.

The word 'Google' is no longer just the name of a company. It has become a verb, which means 'search for information about (someone or something) on the Internet'. 'Google it' is a common expression and that alone is evidence of the company's market dominance. But has Google abused this dominant position?

Tying you into Google

In July 2018, the European Commission[1] fined Google €4.34 billion, having found the company to have breached EU antitrust rules. The Competition Commissioner, Margrethe Vestager, identified three infringements:

- Google had required Android phone and tablet manufacturers to pre-install its search engine 'Google' and its browser 'Google Chrome' in order to licence Google Play Store on their devices.
- Payments were made to large manufacturers and mobile network operators which had agreed to pre-install only the Google Search app on their devices.
- Other manufacturers were prevented from selling smart devices powered by alternative 'forked' versions of Android, as they were threatened with being denied the ability to pre-install Google's apps.

The first finding relates to an exclusionary abuse, known as 'tying', which firms can use to strengthen a dominant position in a market. It occurs when a firm controlling the supply of a first product (the tying product), insists that its customers buy a second product (the tied product) from it rather than from its rivals.

Google owns the Android OS and this accounts for over 80 per cent of the market share of mobile operating systems in Europe. This means that mobile phone manufacturers mainly have to rely on Android. The Commission found that Google had strengthened its dominant position in search engine and browser markets (the tied products) by placing restrictions on the use of its Android OS (the tying product).

In announcing the ruling, Margrethe Vestager said: 'Google has used Android as a vehicle to cement the dominance of its search engine.' While she acknowledged that consumers are not actually prevented from downloading other browsers or search engines with Google's Android devices, she noted that only 1 per cent of customers use another search engine and only 10 per cent use another browser. She said, 'Once you have it, it is working, very few are curious enough to look for another search app or browser'.

The size of the fine is a record for the EU, reflecting the ongoing nature of Google's business practice, though it could have fined Google up to 10 per cent of its annual revenue (€11.1 billion). Although Google would have no problem in paying the fine, given its cash reserves were over £103 billion, the company is appealing the ruling. In the meantime, it is required to stop the above practices.

The reaction

Following the ruling, the EU was criticised by President Trump. Indeed, the US competition authorities have not imposed any fine on the company. Both the EU and the USA want to promote competition and yet there is clear disagreement about the EU's ruling.

Since Margrethe Vestager has been in charge of competition policy in the EU, there has been a tighter approach to competition, but the USA has always had a more minimalist approach. It prefers to allow markets to function and correct themselves, rather than intervening with 'anti-trust law' (law against oligopolistic or monopolistic practices), suggesting that in many cases, it is a business's efficiency that gives it market dominance. However, it is also the case that Google's control of the search engine market is much higher in the EU than it is in the USA and so Google's dominance is lower in the US market.

The ruling has been welcomed in many areas, including from the trade body, GSMA, that represents mobile operators and the trade group, Fairsearch, which originally made the complaint. The Spokesperson for Fairsearch, Thomas Vinje said:

> This is an important step in disciplining Google's abusive behaviour in relation to Android. . . It means that Google should cease its anti-competitive practices regarding smartphones, but also in other areas – smart TVs in particular – where it is foreclosing competition by using the same practices.[2]

In other areas, reaction has been more mixed, as discussed in the *New York Times*.[3] The USA accused the EU of penalising Google, because it is an American firm, adding to the tensions between the EU and USA regarding tariffs on steel and aluminium.

Others have connected this decision with past EU decisions on similar tying arrangements, particularly two cases with Microsoft and its Internet Explorer browser and its Windows operating system. However, specialists in anti-trust have said that Google's case is very different from Microsoft. When Microsoft was fined for tying customers into its Windows Media Player, the process of adding a rival media player was very time consuming, whereas the process for adding different apps is now very easy. Thus the substitutes available and the degree of competition is very different in these two cases.

Furthermore, the Director of the Center for Business law and Practice at the University of Leeds said: 'The commission put a lot of emphasis on the value of preinstallation. But just because an app is preinstalled doesn't mean consumers are going to use it. It's very easy to download a rival app.'

---

[1] 'Statement by Commissioner Vestager on Commission decision to find Google €4.34 billion for illegal practices regarding Android mobile devices to strengthen dominance of Google's search engine', *European Commission Press Release* (18 July 2018).

[2] 'FairSearch: European Commission Android decision will foster competition', *FairSearch: Google Android Decision press pack* (18 July 2018).

[3] James Stewart, 'Why Trump is right about the EU's penalty against Google', *The New York Times* (26 July 2018).

▶

Other arguments against the ruling include the fact that it is penalising companies which are efficient and lead the market with the best products. The Commissioner did concede that customers could download other apps, but that very few chose to do so. Perhaps the reason is the quality of the product being offered by Google. This is the opinion of antitrust Professor Christopher Sagers, from Cleveland-Marshall College of Law, who said: 'It would make for a pretty solid argument that whatever dominance Google has retained in mobile search has nothing to do with anticompetitive conduct, and rather just reflects its superiority as a product.'[4]

Bing or DuckDuckGo 'Google'

Following the ruling, Google has phased out many of its contractual terms, thereby addressing many of the European Commission's concerns, but Google is still appealing the ruling. However, it appears as though the EU is not finished. In 2017, Google was fined $2.7 billion for 'disadvantaging comparison-shopping rivals in its search results'. In 2018, Google was fined $5 billion for the issues discussed in this Box.

Reports indicate that a further fine is to be expected relating to a warning issued by the EU in 2016 and, once more, it relates to its dominant position. In issuing the warning, Margrethe Vestager said:

We have also raised concerns that Google has hindered competition by limiting the ability of its competitors to place search adverts on third party websites, which stifles consumer choice and innovation. Google now has the opportunity to respond to our concerns. . . . The Commission has a duty . . . to protect European consumers and fair competition on European markets.[5]

It will be interesting to see how both the EU and USA respond to the expected ruling and it is worth continuing to search for Google (using any search engine) to see how its dominant position continues to evolve.

1. Why does Google have a dominant position in the market?
2. What are the arguments for and against penalising Google for breach of anti-trust laws?
3. Has Google received any further fines from other competition authorities and what have they been for?

Devise and conduct a survey with fellow students to establish the extent to which they use Google products and why. Do your findings suggest the abuse of a dominant position?

[5] 'Antitrust: Commission takes further steps in investigations alleging Google's comparison shopping advertised-related practices breach EU rules', *European Commission Press Release* (14 July 2016).

[4] Ibid.

---

exceeded if (a) the firms involved have combined worldwide sales greater than €5 billion and (b) at least two of the firms individually have sales of more than €250 million within the EU. The second threshold is exceeded if (a) the firms involved have combined worldwide sales of more than €2.5 billion; (b) in each of at least three Member States, combined sales of all firms involved are greater than €100 million; (c) in each of the three Member States, at least two of the firms each have domestic sales greater than €25 million; and (d) EU-wide sales of each of at least two firms is greater than €100 million.

If either of these thresholds is exceeded and the merger or acquisition is judged to have an EU dimension, then formal notification of the intention has to be made by the firms to the European Commission. There were 414 notifications in 2018, which is the highest number recorded, with all previous years having consistently been around 300 per year.

The UK. A merger or acquisition can be investigated by the CMA if the resulting company meets one of two conditions: (a) it has a UK turnover that exceeds £70 million or (b) it has a market share of 25 per cent or above. Unlike the EU, merger policy in the UK does not require the participating firms to pre-notify the authorities about a merger that meets either of the

two conditions. A voluntary notice can be made, or the CMA can initiate an investigation following information received from third parties. Around 30 to 40 per cent of merger investigations are typically instigated by the CMA, with no notifications by the firms involved.

A merger can also be completed before it has been officially cleared by the CMA. If the CMA then decides to prevent it, the firms face the costs of having to split the business back into two separate entities. The 2013 Act increased the CMA's power to force companies to reverse integration activities undertaken prior to an investigation.

The investigation. Once an investigation has been initiated, UK and EU policy is similar. A phase 1 or preliminary investigation will take place by the relevant authority and in most cases, the merger is permitted to proceed unconditionally or subject to certain conditions being met. In the EU, over 90 per cent of cases are settled in this phase. For example, in 2018, only ten of the 414 notifications made in the EU went onto the next phase. In the UK in 2017/18, only nine out of the 62 phase I cases were referred for a phase 2 investigation.

In both the EU and the UK, a proposed merger will be referred to a formal, in-depth investigation if the preliminary investigation indicates that there may be a significant impact on competition. Although the firms may offer to undertake certain actions to help address any competitive concerns, at this point there are three possibilities: (a) the merger is allowed to proceed with no conditions attached; (b) the merger is allowed to proceed subject to certain conditions being met; (c) the merger is prohibited.

In November 2017, the merger of Just Eat and Hungryhouse was cleared after a phase 2 investigation.[20] These two businesses are web-based food ordering platforms and the CMA concluded that there would still be plenty of competition in the market after the merger from businesses such as Deliveroo, Uber Eats and Amazon.

In March 2017, the CMA published its final conclusions following its phase 2 investigation into the acquisition of Wincor by Diebold Nixdorf.[21] These businesses supply customer-operated ATMs (cash machines) and the CMA concluded that the deal would lead to a substantial lessening of competition in this market – there were only three major suppliers before the merger. To remedy these competition concerns, the CMA ordered Diebold Nixdorf to sell either Diebold's or Wincor's UK customer-operated ATM business to a new approved owner. In June 2017, Diebold Nixdorf sold Diebold's ATM business in the UK to Cennox. The CMA accepted this remedy.

In the UK, the final judgment on any investigation is left to the CMA, apart from in a few exceptional circumstances when a minister can intervene. This is where the proposed merger or acquisition would have an impact on either national security, media plurality or the stability of the financial system. For example, in September 2017 the Secretary of State for Digital, Culture, Media and Sport referred the proposed acquisition of Sky Plc by 21st Century Fox to the CMA because of concerns over the impact of the deal on media plurality. In January 2018, the CMA[22] published it provisional finding that the takeover should be prohibited. However, the final decision would rest with the government. As it turned out, 21st Century Fox was outbid by US media giant, Comcast, which acquired Sky in September 2018.

In the EU, the only merger or acquisition prohibited in 2016 was the proposed acquisition of mobile network operator, O2, by Hutchinson (owner of Three). Two M&As were prohibited in 2017. These were (a) the proposed takeover of the cement business Cemex Croatia by the two German companies, HeidelbergCement and Schwenk; and (b) the proposed merger between the London Stock Exchange Group and Deutsche Börse AG.

The EU's current measures were put in place in 1990 and up until February 2019, only 29 mergers have been prohibited, out of a total of 7289 notifications. In the UK, between 2004/5 and 2017/18, ten mergers out of the 143 phase 2 investigations have been prohibited.

The EU has been criticised for being too easily influenced by firms, allowing M&As to go ahead with few, if any restrictions. This highlights a trade-off that policy makers face, as they want to encourage competition within the EU and thus prevent mergers, but they also want companies to be sufficiently large that they can become world leaders and compete in a global marketplace.

The UK has also received criticism for the relatively few cases investigated. For example, a review by the National Audit Office found that during the period 2012–14, the UK authorities issued enforcement fines of £65 million (in 2015 prices).[23] Over the same period, the German competition authorities issued fines of £1.4 billion. One explanation for this smaller number of cases may be fear of failure by the CMA. Many firms believe that they have a far greater chance of getting infringement decisions overturned in the UK than in other countries. This fear of successful appeals may deter the CMA from beginning the cases in the first place.

At the time of writing, there is some uncertainty about the impact on competition policy of the UK's exit from the European Union. The current system is referred to as a 'One Stop Shop'. Cases are investigated by either the CMA or the EC but not by both of them. If the UK leaves the Single Market, then both the CMA and EC may have to investigate the same cases. This could result in a big increase in the workload of the CMA. Firms may also face a situation where two different agencies produce contradictory conclusions: i.e. one prohibits while the other clears the same merger.

[20] 'CMA clears Just Eat / Hungryhouse merger', *Press Release*, Competition and Markets Authority (16 November 2017).

[21] *Diebold / Wincor Nixdorf Merger Inquiry*, Competition and Markets Authority (29 June 2017).

[22] 'CMA provisionally finds Fox/Sky deal not in the public interest', *Press Release*, Competition and Markets Authority (23 January 2018).

[23] *The UK Competition Regime*, National Audit Office (5 February 2016).

RECAP

1. Competition policy in most countries recognises that monopolies, mergers and restrictive practices can bring both costs and benefits to the consumer. Generally, though, restrictive practices tend to be more damaging to consumers' interests than simple monopoly power or mergers.

2. Legislation in the UK and the EU follows similar processes for restrictive practices, monopoly and merger policy. In the UK, legislation is covered by the 1998 Competition Act and 2002 Enterprise Act, and the Competition and Markets Authority is the unified body charged with ensuring that firms abide by the legislation. In the EU, Articles 101 and 102 of the 2009 Treaty of the Functioning of the European Union (TFEU) govern competition policy.

3. Cartel agreements are a criminal offence and certain other types of collusive behaviour can be curtailed by the competition authorities in the UK and EU if they are against the public interest.

4. The abuse of monopoly power by a dominant firm can also be prevented by the CMA and the EU. Such abuses include charging excessively high prices, vertical restraints and predatory pricing.

5. Mergers over a certain size are investigated by the competition authorities for a ruling as to whether they should be permitted. Most mergers in the EU and UK are approved either unconditionally or with conditions attached. Few are prohibited.

9.6 THE REGULATION OF BUSINESS

Regulation and the privatised industries

In the late 1940s and early 1950s the Labour government *nationalised* many of the key transport, communications and power industries, such as the railways, freight transport, airlines, coal, gas, electricity and steel. The Thatcher and Major governments in the 1980s and early 1990s sold these industries to the private sector in a programme of *privatisation*. However, many of these privatised industries had considerable market power and so it was felt necessary to regulate their behaviour.

Many other countries have followed similar programmes of privatisation and, in many cases, it has helped to revitalise ailing industries, as well as being seen as an opportunity for governments to raise revenues and thus ease budgetary problems.

Regulation in practice

To some extent the behaviour of privatised industries may be governed by general monopoly and restrictive practice legislation. For example, following a two-year investigation into the energy industry, in 2016 the CMA published a report with various recommendations.[24]

In addition to the CMA, there is a separate regulatory office to oversee the structure and behaviour of each of the privatised utilities. These regulators are as follows: the Office of Gas and Electricity Markets (Ofgem), the Office of Communications (Ofcom), the Office of Rail and Road (ORR) and the Water Services Regulation Authority (Ofwat). The regulators set terms under which the industries have to operate and they supervise the competitive behaviour of the firms. For example, ORR sets the terms under which

rail companies have access to the track and stations. The terms set by the regulator can be reviewed by negotiation between the regulator and the industry. If agreement cannot be reached, the CMA acts as an appeal court and its decision is binding.

Price regulation. The regulator for each industry also sets limits to the prices that certain parts of the industry can charge. These parts are those where there is little or no competition, e.g. the charges made to electricity and gas retailers by National Grid, the owner of the electricity grid and major gas pipelines.

The price-setting formulae are essentially of the 'RPI minus X' variety. What this means is that the industries can raise their prices by the rate of increase in the retail price index (i.e. by the rate of inflation) *minus* a certain percentage (X) to take account of expected increases in efficiency. Thus, if the rate of inflation were 3 per cent, and if the regulator considered that the industry (or firm) could be expected to reduce its costs by 2 per cent ($X = 2\%$), then price rises would be capped at 1 per cent. The $RPI - X$ system is thus an example of *price-cap regulation*. The idea of this system of regulation is

Definitions

Nationalised industries State-owned industries that produce goods or services that are sold in the market.

Privatisation Selling nationalised industries to the private sector. This may be through the public issue of shares, by a management buyout or by selling it to a private company.

Price-cap regulation Where the regulator puts a ceiling on the amount by which a firm can raise its price.

[24] *Modernising the Energy Market*, Competition and Markets Authority (24 June 2016)

that it forces the industry to pass cost savings on to the consumer.

In March 2008, Ofgem began a two-year review of regulation in the energy industry called $RPI - X@20$. In 2010 it announced plans for a new system of price regulation called $RIIO$ (Revenue = Incentives + Innovation + Outputs) to be introduced in 2013. Under the system, firms' prices and hence permitted revenue (R) should not only depend on costs but should also have an element for incentives (I), innovation (I) and the quality of output (O).

The $RIIO$ approach is similar to $RPI-X$ but places much greater weight on the quality of the output supplied and allows the climate change agenda to be addressed as part of the price control process.

Pause for thought

If an industry regulator adopts an RPI – X formula for price regulation, is it desirable that the value of X should be adjusted as soon as cost conditions change?

Assessing the system of regulation in the UK

The system that has evolved in the UK has various advantages over other systems that tend to focus on the level of *profits*:

- It is a discretionary system, with the regulator able to judge individual examples of the behaviour of the industry on their own merits. The regulator has a detailed knowledge of the industry which would not be available to government ministers or other bodies such as the CMA. The regulator could thus be argued to be in the best position to decide on whether the industry is acting in the public interest.
- The system is flexible, since it allows for the licence and price formula to be changed as circumstances change.
- Both RPI minus X and the $RIIO$ formulae provide an incentive for the privatised firms to be as efficient as possible. If they can lower their costs (by more than X in the case of the RPI minus X formula) they will, in theory, be able to make and retain larger profits. If, on the other hand, they do not succeed in reducing costs sufficiently, they will make a loss. There is thus a continuing pressure on them to cut costs. In the traditional US system, where *profits* rather than *prices* are regulated, there is little incentive to increase efficiency, since any cost reductions must be passed on to the consumer in lower prices, and do not, therefore, result in higher profits.

There were, however, some inherent problems with the 'RPI minus X' formula, which were identified in the $RPI - X@20$ review:

- It motivated organisations to cut their costs, but did not provide strong enough incentives for them to deliver a high-quality service to their customers.
- Where some aspects of the quality of service were taken into account, they were different from those most highly valued by the network's customers.
- There was a tendency to focus on reforming certain parts of the regulatory structure rather than thinking about the impact on the framework as a whole.
- The five-year duration of each price regulation was too short and deterred long-run investment. Indeed, not enough attention was given to longer-run and more dynamic elements of competition such as innovation.
- If price regulation *underestimates* the scope for cost reductions, then firms may be able to make excessive profits. For example, Ofgem reported that during the final period of $RPI - X$ regulation, all the gas distribution and network companies made greater than expected profits. Also, the House of Commons Public Accounts Committee criticised Ofwat for regularly underestimating the water companies' scope for cost reduction, enabling them to make excess profits of £1.2 billion between 2010 and 2015.
- If price regulation *overestimates* the scope for cost reductions, the reduction in firms' profits might lead to reduced investment and innovation.

In response to these limitations, Ofgem decided that the terms of the new $RIIO$ system would apply for eight (not five years) and firms' ability to raise prices would be conditional on key performance indicators, such as customer satisfaction, reliability, the environmental impact, social obligations and safety. It is, however, difficult for the regulator to find effective performance measures for these attributes of the network companies' output.

Although the price controls under $RIIO$ were meant to be tougher, in 2017, Citizens Advice claimed that the transmission and network operators made excess profits of £7.5 billion over an eight-year period because the $RIIO$ price controls were not demanding enough.[25] In particular, it accused Ofgem of (a) overestimating the risk for investors, (b) assuming interest rates would be much higher than they actually were and (c) giving incentives for firms to inflate their project cost projections by allowing them to keep a share of any underspend. It called for the £7.5 billion of 'unjustified' profit to be paid back to consumers.

---

[25] 'Energy networks making £7.5bn in unjustified profit over 8 years, Citizens Advice finds', *Citizens Advice Press Release* (12 July 2017).

Despite the changes that have been made, other problems do still remain with the system of regulation.

- Regulation has become increasingly complex. This makes it difficult for the industries to plan and may lead to a growth of 'short-termism'. One of the claimed advantages of privatisation was to give greater independence to the industries from short-term government interference and allow them to plan for the longer term. In practice, one type of interference may have been replaced by another.
- As regulation becomes more detailed and complex and as the regulator becomes more and more involved in the detailed running of the industry, so managers and regulators will become increasingly involved in a game of strategy, each trying to outwit the other. Information will become distorted and time and energy will be wasted in playing this game of cat and mouse. This is an example of the principal–agent problem (see pages 9–10), where the agent (the company) is trying to avoid carrying out the wishes of the principal (the regulator).
- As the regulator becomes more involved in the industry, they may be persuaded to see the managers' point of view and hence they could become less strict. This idea is known as *regulatory capture*. While it certainly remains a potential problem, commentators do not believe this has become an issue.

One way in which the dangers of ineffective or over-intrusive regulation can be avoided is to replace regulation with competition wherever this is possible. Indeed, one of the major concerns of the regulators has been to do just this. (See Case Studies C.36 and C.37 on the book's website for ways in which competition has been increased in the gas and electricity industries.)

Regulation versus competition

Where natural monopoly exists (see page 116), competition is impossible in a free market. Of course, the industry *could* be broken up by the government, with firms prohibited from owning more than a certain percentage of the industry. But this would lead to higher costs of production. Firms would be operating further back up a downward-sloping long-run average cost curve. Regulation is therefore an effective means of curbing excessive profits.

However, many parts of the privatised industries are not natural monopolies. In the case of electricity, it is really only the *grid* and local powerlines that are natural monopolies. In the case of gas and water, it is the pipelines and for the railways, it is the tracks. It would be wasteful to duplicate these.

Other parts of these industries, however, have generally been opened up to competition (with the exception of water). In 2018 there were over 40 different suppliers of energy including the so-called 'Big Six' (SSE, Npower, E.ON, British Gas, Scottish Power and EDF Energy). Thus there are now many producers and sellers of electricity and gas. This is possible because they are given access, by law, to the national and local electricity grids and gas pipelines. The telecommunications market too has become more competitive with the growth of mobile phones and lines supplied by cable operators.

As competition has been introduced into these industries, so price-cap regulation has been progressively abandoned. For example, in 2006 Ofcom abandoned price control of BT and other phone companies over line rentals and phone charges. This was in response to the growth in competition from cable operators, mobile phones and free Internet calls from companies such as Skype.

Despite attempts to introduce competition into the privatised industries, they are still dominated by giant companies. Even if they are no longer strictly monopolies, they still have considerable market power and the scope for price leadership or other forms of oligopolistic collusion is great. The CMA report on the energy industry concluded that customers were paying £1.4 billion a year more than they would have, if the retail market had been fully competitive. Therefore, the role of regulators remains important in monitoring the behaviour of firms and outcomes in the market.

Although regulation through the price formula had been abandoned as elements of competition were introduced, the energy sector is one market where we have seen price caps being used once more. In April 2017, a temporary price for some energy customers was introduced and this was extended to include more customers in February 2018. The impact of these price controls will need to be carefully monitored.

> ### Definition
>
> **Regulatory capture** Where the regulator is persuaded to operate in the industry's interests rather than those of the consumer.

RECAP

1. Regulation in the UK has involved setting up regulatory offices for the major privatised utilities. These generally operate informally, using negotiation and bargaining to persuade the industries to behave in the public interest.

2. As far as prices are concerned, parts of the industries are required to abide by an 'RPI minus X' formula. This forces them to pass potential cost reductions on to the consumer. At the same time, they are allowed to retain any additional profits gained from cost reductions

greater than X. This provides them with an incentive to achieve even greater increases in efficiency.

3. Many parts of the privatised industries are not natural monopolies. In these parts, competition may be a more effective means of pursuing the public interest.

4. Various attempts have been made to make the privatised industries more competitive, often at the instigation of the regulator. Nevertheless, considerable market power remains in the hands of many privatised firms, and thus the need for regulation will continue.

QUESTIONS

1. Assume that a firm discharges waste into a river. As a result, the marginal social costs (MSC) are greater than the firm's marginal (private) costs (MC). The following table shows how MC, MSC, AR and MR vary with output.

Output	1	2	3	4	5	6	7	8
MC (£)	23	21	23	25	27	30	35	42
MSC (£)	35	34	38	42	46	52	60	72
TR (£)	60	102	138	168	195	219	238	252
AR (£)	60	51	46	42	39	36.5	34	31.5
MR (£)	60	42	36	30	27	24	19	14

(a) How much will the firm produce if it seeks to maximise profits?
(b) What is the socially efficient level of output (assuming no externalities on the demand side)?
(c) How much is the marginal external cost at this level of output?
(d) What size tax would be necessary for the firm to reduce its output to the socially efficient level?
(e) Why is the tax less than the marginal externality?
(f) Why might it be equitable to impose a lump-sum tax on this firm?
(g) Why will a lump-sum tax not affect the firm's output (assuming that in the long run the firm can still make at least normal profit)?

2. Distinguish between publicly provided goods, public goods and merit goods.

3. Some roads could be regarded as a public good, but some could be provided by the market. Which types of road could be provided by the market? Why? Would it be a good idea?

4. Make a list of pieces of information a firm might want to know and consider whether it could buy the information and how reliable that information might be.

5. Why might it be better to ban certain activities that cause environmental damage rather than to tax them?

6. How suitable are legal restrictions in the following cases?

(a) Ensuring adequate vehicle safety (e.g. tyres with sufficient tread or roadworthy vehicles).
(b) Reducing traffic congestion.
(c) Preventing the use of monopoly power.
(d) Ensuring that mergers are in the public interest.
(e) Ensuring that firms charge a price equal to marginal cost.

7. In what ways might business be socially responsible?

8. What economic costs and benefits might a business experience if it decided to adopt a more socially responsible position? How might such costs and benefits change over the longer term?

9. Using a demand and supply diagram, explain why carbon prices fell at the beginning of the Emissions Trading System (ETS), due to emissions allowances being too generous.

10. What problems are likely to arise in identifying which firms' practices are anti-competitive? Should the CMA take firms' assurances into account when deciding whether to grant an exemption?

11. If anti-monopoly legislation is effective enough, is there ever any need to prevent mergers from going ahead?

12. If two or more firms were charging similar prices, what types of evidence would you look for to prove that this was collusion rather than mere coincidence?

13. Should governments or regulators always attempt to eliminate the supernormal profits of monopolists/oligopolists?

14. Should regulators of utilities that have been privatised into several separate companies permit (a) horizontal mergers (within the industry); (b) vertical mergers; (c) mergers with firms in other related industries (e.g. gas and electricity suppliers)?

15. Assess some of the arguments for and against the imposition of price controls in the retail energy market.

ADDITIONAL PART C CASE STUDIES ON THE *ECONOMICS AND THE BUSINESS ENVIRONMENT* **WEBSITE (www.pearsoned.co.uk/sloman)**

C.1 **B2B electronic marketplaces.** This case study examines the growth of firms trading with each other over the Internet (business to business or 'B2B') and considers the effects on competition.

C.2 **Measuring monopoly power.** This analyses how the degree of monopoly power possessed by a firm can be measured.

C.3 **X-inefficiency.** A type of inefficiency suffered by many large firms, resulting in a wasteful use of resources.

C.4 **Airline deregulation in the USA and Europe.** Whether the deregulation of various routes has led to more competition and lower prices.

C.5 **Bakeries: oligopoly or monopolistic competition.** A case study on the bread industry, showing that small-scale local bakeries can exist alongside giant national bakeries.

C.6 **Oligopoly in the brewing industry.** A case study showing how the UK brewing industry is becoming more concentrated.

C.7 **Cut throat competition.** An examination of the barriers to entry to the UK razor market.

C.8 **OPEC.** A case study examining OPEC's influence over oil prices from the early 1970s to the present day.

C.9 **Hybrid strategy.** Is it good for companies to use a mix of strategies?

C.10 **Stakeholder power.** An examination of the various stakeholders of a business and their influence on business behaviour.

C.11 **Hypergrowth companies.** Why do some companies grow quickly and are they likely to be a long-term success?

C.12 **Price discrimination in the cinema.** An illustration of why it may be in a cinema's interests to offer concessionary prices at off-peak times, but not at peak times.

C.13 **Peak-load pricing.** An example of price discrimination: charging more when it costs more to produce.

C.14 **How do companies set prices?** The findings of Bank of England and ECB surveys.

C.15 **Labour market trends.** This case study describes the changing patterns of employment in the UK, from the rise in service-sector employment and fall in manufacturing employment, to the rise in part-time working and a rise in female participation rates.

C.16 **The rise and decline of the labour movement.** A brief history of trade unions in the UK.

C.17 **How useful is marginal productivity theory?** How accurately does the theory describe employment decisions by firms?

C.18 **Profit sharing.** An examination of the case for and against profit sharing as a means of rewarding workers.

C.19 **Should health care provision be left to the market?** This identifies the market failures that would occur if health care provision were left to the free market.

C.20 **Corporate social responsibility.** An examination of social responsibility as a goal of firms and its effect on business performance.

C.21 **Technology and economic change.** How to get the benefits from technological advance.

C.22 **Can the market provide adequate protection for the environment?** This explains why markets generally fail to take into account environmental externalities.

C.23 **Green taxes.** Are they the perfect answer to the problem of pollution?

C.24 **Selling the environment.** The market-led solution of the Kyoto Protocol.

C.25 **Evaluating new road schemes.** The system used in the UK of assessing the costs and benefits of proposed new roads.

C.26 **Road pricing in Singapore.** A case study showing the methods Singapore has used to cut traffic congestion.

C.27 **Restricting car access to Athens.** A case study that examines how the Greeks have attempted to reduce local atmospheric pollution from road traffic.

C.28 **Environmental auditing.** Are businesses becoming greener? A growing number of firms are subjecting themselves to an 'environmental audit' to judge just how 'green' they are.

C.29 **A lift to profits.** The EC imposes a record fine on four companies operating a lift and escalator cartel.

C.30 **Taking your vitamins at a price.** A case study showing how vitamin-producing companies were fined for price fixing.

C.31 **What price for peace of mind?** Exploiting monopoly power in the sale of extended warranties on electrical goods.

C.32 **Fixing prices of envelopes at mini-golf meetings.** The European Commission's investigation into the market for both standardised and customised paper envelopes in the EU.

C.33 **Fixing the price of car parts.** Investigations of global cartels in the car parts industry by competition authorities around the world.

C.34 **The right track to reform.** Reorganising the railways in the UK.

C.35 **Competition in the pipeline.** An examination of attempts to introduce competition into the gas industry in the UK.

C.36 **Selling power to the people.** Attempts to introduce competition into the UK electricity industry.

WEBSITES RELEVANT TO PART C

Numbers and sections refer to websites listed in the Web Appendix and hotlinked from this book's website at **www.pearsoned. co.uk/sloman/**

- For news articles relevant to Part C, Google the Sloman Economics News site.

- For general news on the microeconomic environment of business see websites in section A of the Web Appendix, and particularly A1–5, 7–9, 11, 12, 20–26, 35, 36. See also links to newspapers worldwide in A38, 39, 42, 43 and 44 and the news search feature in Google at A41.

- For student resources relevant to Part C, see section C, see sites C1–10, 14, 19.

- For games and simulations relevant to Part C, see section D, and particularly sites D3, 6–9, 12–14, 16–20.

- For sites that look at competition and market power, including competition policy, see section E, sites E4 and 10; and section G, sites G7 and 8. See also links in I7, 11, 14 and 15. UK regulatory bodies can be found at sites E11, 15, 16, 19, 22.

- For information on stock markets, see sites F18 and A1, 3, 22–25; B27.

- For data on SMEs, see the SME database in B3 or E10.

- For information on pricing in the UK, see section E, and particularly site E10 and the sites of the regulators of the privatised industries: E15, 16, 19, 22.

- For UK data on labour markets, see site B3 > *Employment and Labour Market*. For international labour market data see site H3 > *Statistics and databases*.

- Links to the TUC and Confederation of British Industry sites can be found in section E at E32 and 33.

- For information on taxes and subsidies, see E30, 36; G13. For use of green taxes, see H5; G11; E2, 14.

- For information on health and the economics of health care (Case Study C.19 on the website), see E8; H8.

- For sites favouring the free market, see C17; E34. See also C18 for the development of ideas on the market and government intervention.

- For policy on the environment and transport, see section E for UK sites: E2, 7, 11, 14, 29 and 39; and section G for EU sites: G10, 11 and 19. See also H11.

The macroeconomic environment of business

The success of an individual business depends not only on its own particular market and its own particular decisions. It also depends on the whole macroeconomic environment in which it operates, including the international environment.

If the economy is booming, then individual businesses are likely to be more profitable than if the economy is in recession. It is thus important for businesses to understand the forces that affect the whole business climate.

One of these forces is the level of confidence, both of consumers and business. If business confidence is high, then firms are more likely to invest. Similarly, if consumer confidence is high, spending in the shops is likely to be high and this will increase business profitability. The result will be economic growth. If, however, people are predicting a recession, firms will hold off investing and consumer spending may well decline. This could tip the economy into recession.

In Chapter 10 we look at the various national forces affecting the performance of the economy.

Another key ingredient of the macroeconomic environment is government policy and the actions of the central bank (the Bank of England in the UK or the European Central Bank (ECB) in the eurozone). If the government raises taxes or the central bank raises interest rates this could impact directly on business profitability and on business confidence. We examine domestic macroeconomic policies in Chapter 11.

In the final two chapters we turn to the international macroeconomic environment. In Chapter 12 we look at the role of international trade. We see how countries and firms can gain from trade and why, despite this, governments sometimes choose to restrict trade.

Then in Chapter 13 we examine the flows of finance across international exchanges. We see how exchange rates are determined and how changes in exchange rates affect business. We study the euro and whether having a single currency for many EU countries benefits business. Finally, we look at attempts by governments worldwide to co-ordinate their macroeconomic policies.

The economy and business activity

Chapter

10

Business issues covered in this chapter

- What are the main macroeconomic objectives and how do they conflict with each other?
- What determines the level of activity in the economy and hence the overall business climate?
- What are aggregate demand and aggregate supply and how do they determine equilibrium national income and the price level?
- If a stimulus is given to the economy, what will be the effect on business output?
- Why do economies experience periods of boom followed by periods of recession? What determines the length and magnitude of these 'phases' of the business cycle?
- How are interest rates determined?
- What determines the supply of money in the economy and how does this affect interest rates?
- What are the causes of unemployment and how does unemployment relate to the level of business activity?
- What are the causes of inflation and how does inflation relate to the level of business activity?
- What are the costs of inflation and unemployment and to whom do they apply?

10.1 THE KEY MACROECONOMIC OBJECTIVES

There are several macroeconomic variables that governments seek to control. The macroeconomic environment will influence all aspects of businesses, including their markets, their costs and their potential profitability. We can group these macroeconomic elements into six key areas.

Economic growth. This is defined as the percentage change in the level of an economy's output from one period to the next – normally over 12 months. Governments aim to achieve economic growth over the long term. They will aim for a stable *rate of economic growth*, which avoids both short-term rapid growth that cannot be sustained and periods of recession. However, economies are unstable and growth

rates will fluctuate, as is evident by recent history in both developed and developing nations.

Unemployment. The number of unemployed people are those of working age who are without work, but who are available for work at the current wage rate. We normally refer to the *rate of unemployment*. This is

Definitions

Rate of economic growth The percentage increase in output over a twelve-month period.

Rate of unemployment The number unemployed expressed as a percentage of the total workforce (i.e. those employed and those unemployed).

the number unemployed as a percentage of the total workforce. Reducing unemployment is a key macroeconomic objective for government, as unemployment poses many costs for different groups across society. These costs are considered in more detail in Box 10.4. In many developed economies, including the UK, there has been a move towards more flexible contracts and the issue of *underemployment* has become more of a problem. This is where people work fewer hours than they would like.

Inflation. This refers to a general rise in prices throughout the economy. The *rate of inflation* is the percentage increase in the level of prices over a 12-month period.

Government policy aims to keep inflation low and stable, as this will aid economic decision making by creating a more certain economic environment. In fact, this has led many governments to adopt a policy of inflation targeting and to delegate responsibility for this to its central bank, which controls interest rates to achieve the inflation target (we consider this in section 11.2). A low and stable rate of inflation, in turn, affects the business climate and confidence and can help to encourage investment.

In recent years we have become used to low inflation rates, with some countries, particularly Japan, even experiencing falling prices, or deflation, as discussed in the blog on the Sloman Economics News site, *Japan's deflation fears grow*. Despite, slightly higher inflation rates in many countries in 2008 and again in 2010–11, they have still remained low relative to the past, particularly the 1970s, when inflation rates in many developed countries rose into the double figures (see Figure 10.12 on page 285). (It had been as high as 24 per cent in the UK in 1975.)[1] We consider inflation in more detail in section 10.7 and analyse the costs in Box 10.4.

The balance of payments. This records all transactions between the residents of a country and the rest of the world. Credit items include all receipts *from* other countries (which therefore earn foreign currency), for example through the sale of exports, from inward investment expenditure and from interest/dividends earned from abroad. Debit items include all payments *to* other countries (which therefore represent our demand for foreign currency), for example through the purchase of imports, investment spending abroad and interest/dividends paid to foreign investors.

Governments aim to provide an environment in which exports can grow without an excessive growth in imports. They also aim to make the economy attractive to inward investment. In other words, they seek to create a climate in which the country's earnings of foreign currency at least match, or preferably exceed, the country's demand for foreign currency: they seek to achieve a favourable *balance of payments*.

If we start to spend more foreign currency than we earn, one of two things must happen. Both are likely to be a problem:

■ *The balance of payments will go into deficit.* In other words, there will be a shortfall of foreign currencies. The government will therefore have to borrow money from abroad, or draw on its foreign currency reserves to make up the shortfall. This is a problem because, if it goes on for too long, overseas debts will mount, along with the interest that must be paid; and/or reserves will begin to run low.

■ *The exchange rate will fall.* The *exchange rate* is the rate at which one currency exchanges for another. For example, the exchange rate of the pound into the dollar might be £1 = $1.50. If the government does nothing to correct the balance of payments deficit, then the exchange rate must fall. A lower exchange rate (i.e. fewer dollars, yen, euros, etc. to the pound) will make UK goods cheaper to overseas buyers, and thus help to boost UK exports. A falling exchange rate is a problem, however, because it pushes up the price of imports and may fuel inflation. Also, if the exchange rate fluctuates, this can cause great uncertainty for traders and can damage international trade and economic growth.

We consider the balance of payments and exchange rates in more detail in Chapter 13.

Financial well-being. It is increasingly recognised that the behaviour of individuals, businesses, governments and nations is affected by their financial well-being. If consumers and firms are worried

---

[1] 'Inflation Great Britain 1975', *Inflation.EU: Worldwide Inflation Data*, Triami Media BV in co-operation with HomeFinance.

Definitions

Underemployment Those working fewer hours than they would like to work.

Rate of inflation The percentage increase in prices over a 12-month period.

Balance of payments account A record of the country's transactions with the rest of the world. It shows the country's payments to or deposits in other countries (debits) and its receipts (credits) from other countries. It also shows the balance between these debits and credits under various headings.

Exchange rate The rate at which one national currency exchanges for another. The rate is expressed as the amount of one currency that is necessary to purchase *one unit* of another currency (e.g. $1.25 = £1).

about their financial well-being, they are likely to become more cautious: consumers may hold back on spending and try to reduce their debts; businesses may be more cautious about investing. If governments are concerned about government debt, they are likely to try to reduce spending and/or increase taxation.

Financial stability. A core aim of the government and the central bank is to ensure the stability of the financial system. After all, financial markets and institutions are an integral part of economies. Their well-being is crucial to the well-being of an economy.

Because of the global interconnectedness of financial institutions and markets, problems can spread globally like a contagion. The financial crisis of the late 2000s showed how financially distressed financial institutions, businesses and households can cause serious economic upheaval on a global scale and it re-emphasised the importance of financial stability in creating macroeconomic stability. As we shall see in section 11.2, a major part of the global response to the financial crisis has been to try to ensure that financial institutions are more financially resilient. In particular, financial institutions should have more loss-absorbing capacity and therefore be better able to withstand 'shocks' and deteriorating macroeconomic conditions.

Government macroeconomic policy

From the above issues we can identify six macroeconomic policy objectives that governments typically pursue:

- High and stable economic growth;
- Low unemployment;
- Low and stable inflation;
- The avoidance of balance of payments deficits and excessive exchange rate fluctuations;
- The avoidance of excessively financially-distressed sectors of the economy, including government;
- A stable financial system.

Unfortunately, these policy objectives may conflict. For example, a policy designed to accelerate the rate of economic growth may result in a higher rate of inflation; a balance of payments deficit and excessive borrowing. Governments are thus often faced with awkward policy choices. All the choices they make will impact on business. In understanding these choices and their implications, it is important to analyse the determinants of the key issues that shape the macroeconomic environment.

> ### Pause for thought
>
> *What are some of the other conflicts that might exist between the macroeconomic objectives and other societal objectives?*

RECAP

1. The macroeconomic environment of business is characterised by a series of interrelated macroeconomic variables. These include: economic growth, unemployment, inflation, the balance of payments, exchange rates, the financial well-being of households, businesses and governments, and the stability of the financial system.

2. Government macroeconomic policy seeks to influence these variables: e.g. to increase the rate of economic growth and reduce unemployment. However, the macroeconomic objectives of governments will often conflict with each other and so, to some extent, governments will have to prioritise.

10.2 BUSINESS ACTIVITY AND THE CIRCULAR FLOW OF INCOME

We now turn to the question of what determines the overall level of business activity. One of the most important determinants, at least in the short run, is the level of spending on firms' output. The more consumers spend, the more firms will want to produce in order to meet that consumer demand. We use the term 'aggregate demand' (*AD*) to represent the total level of spending on the goods and services produced within the country over a given time period (normally a year). This spending consists of four elements: consumer spending on domestically produced goods and services (C_d), investment expenditure within the

country by firms, whether on plant and equipment or on building up stocks (*I*), government spending on goods and services (such as health, education and transport) (*G*) and the expenditure by residents abroad on this country's exports (*X*). Thus:

$$AD = C_d + I + G + X$$

A small change you may sometimes see to the above equation is imports (*M*) being subtracted from exports. In the above equation, note that 'C' has a subscript of 'd' showing that only domestic consumption is being taken into account. That is consumption of imports is already excluded. If C_d becomes just C (i.e. total consumption), then we must also subtract imports from the four components to ensure we are only considering the total spending in the domestic economy. The equation then becomes:

$$AD = C + I + G + X - M$$

The total annual output of goods and services on which aggregate demand is spent is called GDP, or 'gross domestic product'. As long as there is spare capacity in the economy, a rise in aggregate demand will stimulate firms to produce more. GDP will rise.

A simple way of understanding this process is to use a 'circular flow of income diagram'. This is shown in Figure 10.1.

In the diagram, the economy is divided into two major groups: *firms* and *households*. Each group has two roles. Firms are producers of goods and services; they are also the employers of labour. Households (which include all individuals) are the consumers of goods and services; they are also the suppliers of labour. In the diagram there is an inner flow and various outer flows of income between these two groups.

Before we look at the various parts of the diagram, a word of warning. Do not confuse *money* and *income*. Money is a stock concept. At any given time, there is a certain quantity of money in the economy (e.g. £1 trillion). But that does not tell us the level of national *income*. Income is a flow concept, measured as so much *per period of time*.

The relationship between money and income depends on how rapidly the money *circulates*: its 'velocity of circulation'. (We will examine this concept in detail later on.) If there is £1 trillion of money in the economy and each £1 on average is paid out as income twice each year, then annual national income will be £2 trillion.

The inner flow, withdrawals and injections

The inner flow

Firms pay incomes to households in the form of wages and salaries. Some households also receive incomes from firms in the form of dividends on shares, or interest on loans or rent on property. Thus on the left-hand side of the diagram the money that flows *directly* from firms to households is simply household incomes.

Households, in turn, pay money to domestic firms when they *consume domestically produced goods and services* (C_d). This is shown on the right-hand side of the inner flow. There is thus a circular flow of payments from firms to households to firms and so on.

Definition

Consumption of domestically produced goods and services (C_d) The direct flow of money payments from households to firms.

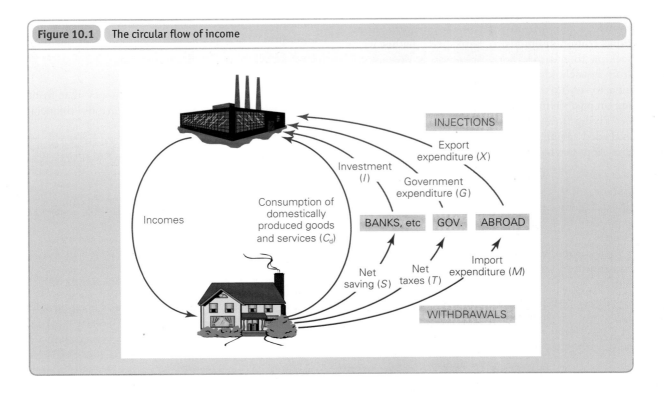

Figure 10.1 The circular flow of income

If households spend *all* their incomes on buying domestic goods and services, and if firms pay out *all* the income they receive from selling the goods and services back to domestic households in the form of wages, dividends, etc., and if the speed at which money flows around the system (the velocity of circulation) does not change, the flow will continue at the same level indefinitely. The money just goes round and round at the same speed and incomes remain unchanged.

Pause for thought

Would this argument still hold if prices rose?

In the real world, of course, it is not as simple as this. Not all income gets passed on round the inner flow; some is *withdrawn*. At the same time, incomes are *injected* into the flow from outside. Let us examine these withdrawals and injections.

Withdrawals

When households receive income, not all of it will be spent on domestic goods and services and hence there will be withdrawals from the inner flow. There are three forms of *withdrawals* (W) (or *leakages*, as they are sometimes called):

Net saving (S). Saving is income that households choose not to spend but to put aside for the future. Savings are normally deposited in financial institutions such as banks and building societies. This is shown in the bottom right of the diagram. Money flows from households to 'banks, etc.'. What we are seeking to measure here, however, is the net flow from households to the banking sector. We therefore have to subtract from saving any borrowing or drawing on past savings by households in order to get the *net* saving flow. Of course, if household borrowing exceeded saving, the net flow would be in the other direction; it would be negative.

Net taxes (T). When people pay taxes (to either central or local government), this represents a withdrawal of money from the inner flow in much the same way as saving; only in this case people have no choice!

Some taxes, such as income tax and social security contributions (employees' national insurance contributions in the UK), are paid out of household incomes. Others, such as VAT and excise duties, are paid out of consumer expenditure. Yet others, such as corporation tax, are paid out of firms' incomes before being received by households as dividends on

shares. For simplicity, however, taxes are shown in Figure 10.1 as being withdrawn at just one point. It does not affect the argument.

When, however, people receive *benefits* from the government, such as working tax credit, child benefit and pensions, the money flows the other way. Benefits are thus equivalent to a 'negative tax'. These benefits are known as *transfer payments*. They transfer money from one group of people (taxpayers) to others (the recipients).

In the model, 'net taxes' (T) represents the *net* flow to the government from households and firms. It consists of total taxes minus benefits.

Import expenditure (M). Not all consumption is of home-produced goods. Households spend some of their incomes on imported goods and services, or on goods and services that use imported components. Although the money that consumers spend on such goods initially flows to domestic retailers, most of it will eventually find its way abroad when the retailers or wholesalers themselves import the products. This expenditure on imports constitutes the third withdrawal from the inner flow, as the money flows abroad.

Total withdrawals are simply the sum of net saving, net taxes and the expenditure on imports:

$$W = S + T + M$$

Injections

Only part of the demand for firms' output (aggregate demand) arises from consumers' expenditure. The remainder comes from other sources outside the inner flow. These additional components of spending are known as *injections* (J). There are three types of injections:

Investment (I). This is the flow of money that firms spend which they obtain from various financial

---

Definitions

Withdrawals (*W*) (or leakages) Incomes of households or firms that are not passed on round the inner flow. Withdrawals equal net saving (*S*) plus net taxes (*T*) plus import expenditure (*M*): $W = S + T + M$.

Transfer payments Moneys transferred from one person or group to another (e.g. from the government to individuals) without production taking place.

Injections (*J*) Expenditure on the production of domestic firms coming from outside the inner flow of the circular flow of income. Injections equal investment (*I*) plus government expenditure (*G*) plus expenditure on exports (*X*).

institutions – either past savings or loans, or through a new issue of shares. They may invest in plant and equipment or may simply spend the money on building up stocks of inputs, semi-finished or finished goods. Note that we exclude from investment any money that is spent on imported components, equipment, etc. As this money flows abroad it is counted as an import (M).

Government expenditure (G). When the government spends money on goods and services produced by domestic firms, this counts as an injection. Examples of such government expenditure are spending on roads, hospitals and schools. Note that government expenditure in this model does not include state benefits. These transfer payments, as we saw above, are the equivalent of negative taxes and have the effect of reducing the T component of withdrawals. It also excludes any money spent on imported components. This is counted as imports.

Export expenditure (X). Money flows into the circular flow from abroad when residents abroad buy our exports of goods and services. Note that, as with the other two injections, only those parts of exports made in the country should be counted. Any imported materials or components into the exports should be deducted.

Total injections are thus the sum of investment, government expenditure and exports:

$$J = I + G + X$$

Aggregate demand, which is the total spending on output, is thus $C_d + J$.

The relationship between withdrawals and injections

There are indirect links between saving and investment via financial institutions, between taxation and government expenditure via the government (central and local), and between imports and exports via foreign countries. These links, however, do not guarantee that $S = I$ or $G = T$ or $M = X$.

Take investment and saving. The point here is that the decisions to save and invest are made by *different* people, and thus they plan to save and invest different amounts. Likewise the demand for imports may not equal the demand for exports.

As far as the government is concerned, it may choose not to make $T = G$. It may choose not to spend all its tax revenues and thus run a 'budget surplus' ($T > G$); or it may choose to spend more than it receives in taxes and run a 'budget deficit' ($G > T$), by borrowing or printing money to make up the difference.

Since the financial crisis, many countries have been dealing with large budget deficits, having bailed out banks and injected money to stabilise the macroeconomy. As a means of reducing government borrowing and cutting budget deficits, countries such as the UK adopted a range of austerity measures. They had some success in reducing the UK's public-sector net borrowing (PSNB). It fell from £153.1 billion (9.9 per cent of GDP) in 2009/10 to £23.5 billion (1.1 per cent of GDP) in 2018/19. It is forecast to fall to £12.0 billion (0.5 per cent of GDP) in 2023/24, according to data from the Office for Budget Responsibility (OBR) in March 2019.[2]

Thus planned injections (J) may not equal planned withdrawals (W). But if they are not equal, what will be the consequences?

If injections exceed withdrawals, for example because of increased confidence leading to more investment, the level of expenditure will rise (the increase in spending from injections is greater than the reduction in spending from withdrawals). The extra spending will generate extra incomes. In other words, GDP will rise; there will be economic growth. This, as we shall see later in the chapter, will tend to reduce unemployment as firms take on more labour to meet the extra demand. It may, however, lead to a rise in inflation as the extra demand drives up the price of goods and services more rapidly than would have been the case. There will also tend to be a deterioration in the balance of payments, as import demand rises due to the higher domestic incomes, and higher inflation makes imports relatively cheaper and exports more expensive.

If planned injections are *less* than planned withdrawals then the opposite of each of the above will occur. GDP will fall (there will be negative economic growth); unemployment will rise; inflation will fall; and the balance of payments will improve.

> ### Pause for thought
>
> 1. If injections exceed withdrawals, will GDP go on rising indefinitely, or will a new equilibrium be reached? If so, explain how. (We answer this in the next section.)
> 2. What will be the effect on each of the key macroeconomic variables if planned injections are less than planned withdrawals?

Changes in injections and withdrawals thus have a crucial effect on the whole macroeconomic environment in which businesses operate.

---

[2] *Public Finances Databank*, OBR (13 March 2019).

RECAP

1. Business activity is affected by the level of aggregate demand. Aggregate demand equals $C_d + I + G + X$ or $C + I + G + X - M$.

2. The circular flow of income model depicts the flows of money income and expenditure round the economy. The inner flow shows the direct flows between firms and households. Money flows from firms to households in the form of wages and other incomes, and back again as consumer expenditure on domestically produced goods and services.

3. Not all incomes get passed on directly round the inner flow. Some is withdrawn in the form of saving; some is paid in taxes; and some goes abroad as expenditure on imports.

4. Likewise not all expenditure on domestic firms' products is by domestic consumers. Some is injected from outside the inner flow in the form of investment expenditure, government expenditure and expenditure on the country's exports.

5. Planned injections and withdrawals are unlikely to be the same.

6. If injections exceed withdrawals, GDP will rise. As a result, unemployment will tend to fall and inflation will tend to rise. The reverse will happen if withdrawals exceed injections.

10.3 THE DETERMINATION OF BUSINESS ACTIVITY

We have seen that the relationship between planned injections and planned withdrawals determines whether GDP will rise or fall. But *by how much*?

Assume there is a rise in injections – say firms decide to invest more. Aggregate demand $(C_d + J)$ will be higher. Firms will use more labour and other resources and thus pay out more incomes to households. Households will respond to this by consuming more and so firms will sell more.

Firms will respond to this by producing more, and thus using still more labour and other resources. Household incomes will rise again. Consumption and hence production will rise again, and so on. There will thus be a *multiplied* rise in GDP and employment. This is known as the *multiplier effect*.

The process, however, does not go on forever. While households will spend more on domestic consumption as incomes rise, they will also save more (S), pay more taxes (T) and buy more imports (M). In other words, withdrawals (W) rise. When withdrawals have risen to match the increase in injections, *equilibrium* will be achieved and GDP and employment will stop rising. The process can be summarised as follows:

$$J > W \rightarrow GDP\uparrow \rightarrow W\uparrow \text{ until } J = W$$

Similarly, an initial fall in injections (or rise in withdrawals) will lead to a multiplied fall in GDP and employment:

$$J < W \rightarrow GDP\downarrow \rightarrow W\downarrow \text{ until } J = W$$

Thus equilibrium in the circular flow of income can be at *any* level of GDP and employment.

Identifying the equilibrium level of GDP

Equilibrium can be shown on a 'Keynesian 45° line diagram'. This is named after the great economist, John Maynard Keynes (1883–1946) (see Case Study D.4 on the book's website). Keynes argued that GDP (i.e. national income) is determined by aggregate demand. A rise in aggregate demand will cause national income to rise; a fall in aggregate demand will cause national income to fall.

Equilibrium national income can be at any level of capacity. If aggregate demand is buoyant, equilibrium national income could be where businesses are operating at full capacity with full employment. If aggregate demand is low, however, equilibrium national income could be at well below full capacity with high unemployment (i.e. a recession). Keynes argued that it is important, therefore, for governments to manage the level of aggregate demand to avoid recessions.

Figure 10.2 plots various elements of the circular flow of income, such as consumption, withdrawals, injections and aggregate demand, against national income (Y). Two continuous lines are shown.

Definitions

Multiplier effect An initial increase in aggregate demand of £xm leads to an eventual rise in GDP that is greater than £xm.

Equilibrium GDP The level of GDP where injections equal withdrawals and where, therefore, there is no tendency for GDP to rise or fall.

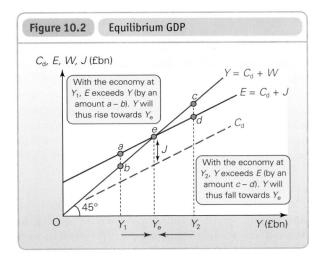

Figure 10.2 Equilibrium GDP

C_d, E, W, J (£bn)

> With the economy at Y_1, E exceeds Y (by an amount $a - b$). Y will thus rise towards Y_e

$Y = C_d + W$

$E = C_d + J$

C_d

> With the economy at Y_2, Y exceeds E (by an amount $c - d$). Y will thus fall towards Y_e

45°

O Y_1 Y_e Y_2 Y (£bn)

The 45° line out from the origin plots $C_d + W$ against national income. It is a 45° line because by definition $Y = C_d + W$. To understand this, consider what can happen to the income earned from GDP: either it must be spent on domestically produced goods (C_d) or it must be withdrawn from the circular flow – there is nothing else that can happen to it. Thus if GDP were £100 billion, then $C_d + W$ must also be £100 billion. If you draw a line such that whatever value is plotted on the horizontal axis (national income) is also plotted on the vertical axis ($C_d + W$), the line will be at 45° (assuming that the axes are drawn to the same scale).

The other continuous line plots the 'aggregate expenditure line' (E). It consists of $C_d + J$, i.e. the total spending on domestic firms and hence also reflects AD.

To show how this line is constructed, consider the dashed line. This shows C_d. It is flatter than the 45° line, as for any given rise in GDP and hence people's incomes, only *part* will be spent on domestic products, while the remainder will be withdrawn: i.e. C_d rises less quickly than income. The E line consists of $C_d + J$. But we have assumed that J is constant with respect to changes in GDP. Thus the E line is simply the C_d line shifted upward by the amount of J.

If aggregate expenditure exceeded GDP, at say Y_1, there would be excess demand in the economy (of $a - b$). In other words, people would be buying more than was currently being produced. Firms would thus find their stocks dwindling and would therefore increase their level of production. In doing so, they would employ more labour and other inputs. National income (GDP) would thus rise. As it did so, C_d and hence E would rise. There would be a movement up along the E line.

But because not all the extra incomes earned from the rise in national income would be consumed (i.e. some would be withdrawn), expenditure would rise

less quickly than income: the E line is flatter than the Y line. As income rises towards Y_e, the gap between the Y and E lines gets smaller. Once point e is reached, $Y = E$. There is then no further tendency for national income to rise.

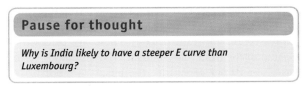

Pause for thought

Why is India likely to have a steeper E curve than Luxembourg?

If GDP exceeded aggregate expenditure, at say Y_2, there would be insufficient demand for the goods and services currently being produced ($c - d$). Firms would find their stocks of unsold goods building up. They would thus respond by producing less and employing fewer factors of production. GDP would thus fall and go on falling until Y_e was reached.

Aggregate demand and aggregate supply

Another model we can use to find the equilibrium level of national income is aggregate demand and aggregate supply and you will notice many similarities between this model and the demand and supply model we developed in Chapter 2. This model, unlike the Keynesian model of Figure 10.2, also takes account of overall price changes in the economy. The model is illustrated in Figure 10.3. It plots the overall price level in the economy on the vertical axis and national output on the horizontal axis.

Note that the price level can be represented by a price index, which is an average of the prices of all goods and services weighted by the quantity

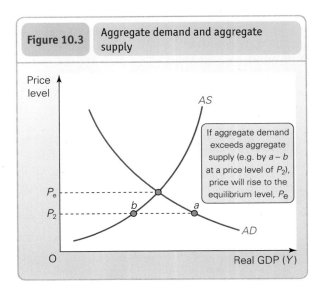

Figure 10.3 Aggregate demand and aggregate supply

Price level

AS

> If aggregate demand exceeds aggregate supply (e.g. by $a - b$ at a price level of P_2), price will rise to the equilibrium level, P_e

P_e

P_2 b a

AD

O Real GDP (Y)

purchased, with the price index set at 100 in some base year set by the statistical authorities (e.g. 2015). Thus if the index rises from 100 in 2015 to 104 in 2016, this shows that prices have on average risen by 4 per cent.[3]

Note also that national output is the same as real national income or real GDP. This is national income or GDP after taking account of inflation. It is expressed in 'constant prices'. These are prices that existed in the base year. Thus if GDP in money terms has risen 10 per cent since the base year, but prices have risen by 8 per cent, then *real* GDP (i.e. national output) has risen by only 2 per cent.

Aggregate demand

As we have seen, 'aggregate demand' (*AD*) represents the total level of spending on the goods and services produced within the country and it is typically written as:

$$AD = C + I + G + X - M$$

The aggregate demand curve shows how much national output (real GDP) will be demanded at each level of prices. It is a downward sloping curve, showing that as prices rise, people demand fewer products. There are three main reasons for this:

- If prices rise, people will be encouraged to buy fewer of their own country's products and more imports instead (which are now relatively cheaper); also the country will sell fewer exports. Thus aggregate demand will be lower.
- As prices rise, people will need more money in their accounts to pay for their purchases. With a given supply of money in the economy, this will drive up interest rates (as we will see in Figure 10.8 on page 279). Higher interest rates will discourage borrowing and encourage saving. Both will have the effect of reducing spending and hence reducing aggregate demand.
- If prices rise, the value of people's savings will be eroded. They may thus save more (and spend less) to compensate.

Pause for thought

Why are the three effects described above all substitution effects? Is there an income effect which can help to explain the shape of the aggregate demand curve?

---

[3] The rate of inflation is calculated using the formula

$$\frac{P_t - P_{t-1}}{P_{t-1}} \times 100$$

where P_t is the price index in the current year and P_{t-1} is the price index the previous year.

Aggregate supply

Aggregate supply is the total amount of goods and services supplied by firms within the country. The aggregate supply curve slopes upwards – at least in the short run. In other words, the higher the level of prices, the more will be produced. The reason is simple: provided that input prices (and, in particular, wage rates) do not rise as rapidly as product prices, firms' profitability will rise as prices rise. This will encourage them to produce more.

Equilibrium

The equilibrium level of national income and the equilibrium price level occurs where aggregate demand equals aggregate supply. To demonstrate this, consider what would happen if aggregate demand exceeded aggregate supply: e.g. at P_2 in Figure 10.3. The resulting shortages throughout the economy would drive up prices. This would cause a movement up along both the *AD* and *AS* curves until $AD = AS$ (at P_e and Y_e).

If something changes such that the aggregate demand and/or aggregate supply curves shift, we will move to a new equilibrium level of national output (real GDP) and a new equilibrium price level.

Shifts in the AD or AS curves

As we saw in Chapter 2, when there was a change in the price of the good we were modelling, there was a movement *along* the demand and supply curves. Other determinants of demand and supply caused the curves to shift. The same applies to aggregate demand and aggregate supply. If there is a change in the price level there will be a movement *along* the *AD* and *AS* curves. If any other determinant of *AD* or *AS* changes, the respective curve will shift.

The aggregate demand curve will shift if there is a change in any of its components – consumption of domestic products, investment, government expenditure or exports. Thus if the government decides to spend more, or if consumers spend more as a result of lower taxes, or if business confidence increases so that firms decide to invest more, the *AD* curve will shift to the right.

This is illustrated in Figure 10.4. The rise in aggregate demand is illustrated by a shift in the *AD* curve from AD_1 to AD_2. Real GDP (real national income) rises from Y_1 to Y_2. But the price level also rises – from P_1 to P_2. The steeper the aggregate supply curve, the larger the price rise and the smaller the rise in real GDP. In other words, the less responsive firms are to a rise in demand, the more will prices rise. The *AS* curve is likely to be steeper the less spare capacity there is in the economy – in other words, the closer the economy is to full employment. This suggests that as you move up the *AS* curve it will get progressively steeper.

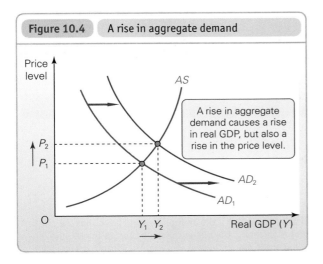

Figure 10.4 A rise in aggregate demand

A rise in aggregate demand causes a rise in real GDP, but also a rise in the price level.

This model provides a useful means of analysing how various changes in policy and broader macroeconomic conditions will affect the government's macroeconomic objectives. For example, if government expenditure increases, the aggregate demand curve will shift to the right and this will lead to a new higher equilibrium level of national income (as in Figure 10.4). Once again, we can see how there will be a multiplied rise in GDP, as firms take on more workers, households receive more income and so spend more money. This, in turn, encourages firms to produce more, use even more labour and so on.

The size of the multiplier

As we have seen, when aggregate expenditure rises, this will cause a multiplied rise in national income (GDP). The size of the *multiplier* is given by the letter k, where:

$$k = \Delta Y / \Delta E$$

Thus, if aggregate expenditure rose by £10 million (ΔE) and as a result GDP rose by £30 million (ΔY), the multiplier would be 3. Figure 10.5 is drawn on the assumption that the multiplier is 3.

Assume in Figure 10.5 that aggregate expenditure rises by £20 billion, from E_1 to E_2. This could be

The aggregate supply curve will shift if there is a change in any of the variables that are held constant when we plot the curve. Several of these variables, notably technology, the labour force and the stock of capital, change only slowly – normally shifting the curve gradually to the right. This typically represents an increase in potential output.

By contrast, wage rates and other input prices can change significantly in the short run and are thus the major causes of shifts in the short-run supply curve. For example, a general rise in wage rates throughout the economy reduces the amount that firms wish to produce at any level of prices. The aggregate supply curve shifts upwards to the left. A similar effect will occur if other costs, such as oil prices or indirect taxes, increase.

Definition

The multiplier The number of times a rise in GDP (ΔY) is bigger than the initial rise in aggregate expenditure (ΔE) that caused it. Using the letter k to stand for the multiplier, the multiplier is defined as $k = \Delta Y / \Delta E$.

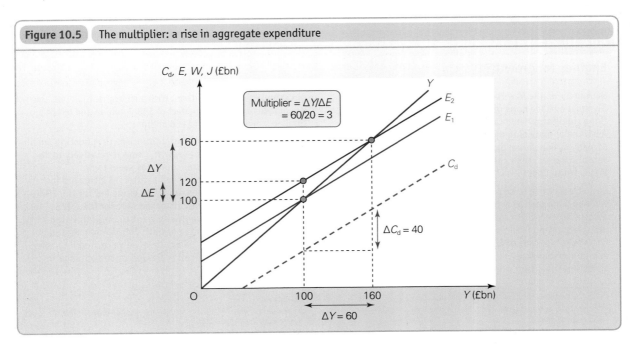

Figure 10.5 The multiplier: a rise in aggregate expenditure

Multiplier = $\Delta Y / \Delta E$
= 60/20 = 3

$\Delta C_d = 40$

$\Delta Y = 60$

caused by a rise in injections, or by a fall in withdrawals (and hence a rise in consumption of domestically produced goods) or by some combination of the two. Equilibrium GDP rises by £60 billion, from £100 billion to £160 billion (where the E_2 line crosses the Y line).

Box 10.1 shows how the size of the multiplier can be calculated in advance.

BOX 10.1 DOING THE SUMS

Calculating the size of the multiplier

What determines the size of the multiplier? The answer is that it depends on the 'marginal propensity to consume domestically produced goods' (mpc_d). The mpc_d is the proportion of any rise in national income/GDP that is spent on domestically produced goods (i.e. the proportion that is not withdrawn):

$$mpc_d = \Delta C_d / \Delta Y$$

So, if you are given £100, but choose to spend only £70 on home-produced products, then only 70 per cent of the income you were given was spent on domestically produced goods. Some of the remaining £30 may be taken as taxation; you may choose to save part of it; or you might decide to spend it on imports. Either way, £30 is withdrawn from the circular flow of income. The proportion of the rise in income that is spent on domestically produced goods is:

$$mpc_d = \Delta C_d / \Delta Y = £70/£100 = 7/10 = 0.7$$

In Figure 10.5, $mpc_d = \Delta C_d / \Delta Y = £40\text{bn}/£60\text{bn} = {}^2/_3$ (i.e. the slope of the C_d line). The higher the mpc_d the greater the proportion of income generated from GDP that recirculates around the circular flow of income and thus generates extra output.

The **multiplier formula** is given by:

$$k = \frac{1}{1 - mpc_d}$$

In our example, with $mpc_d = {}^2/_3$

$$k = \frac{1}{1 - {}^2/_3} = \frac{1}{{}^1/_3} = 3$$

If the mpc_d were ${}^3/_4$, the multiplier would be 4. Thus the higher the mpc_d, the higher the multiplier. In the UK, the value of the mpc_d is between ${}^1/_3$ and ${}^1/_2$. This gives a value for the multiplier of between 1.5 and 2.

1. *Think of two reasons why a country might have a steep E line, and hence a high value for the multiplier.*
2. *Assume that 0.1 of any rise in income is saved, 0.2 goes in taxes and 0.1 is spent on imports. What is the mpc_d? What is the value of the multiplier?*
3. *The formula for the multiplier can also be written as $k = 1/mpw$ (where mpw is the marginal propensity to withdraw). Why is this?*

Definition

Multiplier formula The formula for the multiplier is $k = 1/(1 - mpc_d)$.

BOX 10.2 THE ECONOMICS OF PLAYING HOST

Engines for growth?

Back in 1956, the *New York Times* reported on the Australian Olympics and the hope of its officials that the event might bring significant benefits, either with people settling in Australia or just doing more business. This has been the hope of many nations when bidding to host any number of big sporting events, such as the Olympics or the Football and Rugby World Cups.

Such events came to be regarded as 'economic engines', with winning a bid seen as a great victory, despite the huge costs associated with it. For example, American Football is a massive sporting event in the USA and in the 1994 Championship Game of Super Bowl XXVIII, an economic impact analysis by Humphrey,[1] estimated there would be 306 680 visitors per day. Each would spend $252 per day, leading to a

direct impact of $77.3 million. With a multiplier of 2.148, this would lead to an indirect effect of $88.7 million and hence a total economic benefit of $166 million.

Despite the assertions of many countries that hosting such an event is an engine for growth, there is relatively little evidence to support it and countries seem to be recognising this. Whereas twelve different cities bid for the 2004 Olympics Games, only five cities bid for the 2020 Games and only two were left in the race for the 2022 Winter Games, which eventually went to Beijing. Philip Porter from the University of South Florida commented that 'The bottom line is, every time we've looked – dozens of scholars, dozens of times – we find no real change in economic activity.'[2]

[1] See: V. A. Matheson , 'Economic multipliers and mega-event analysis', *Faculty Research Series Working Paper No. 04-02*, Department of Economics, College of The Holy Cross (June 2004).

[2] Binyamin Appelbaum, 'Does hosting the Olympics actually pay off', *The New York Times Magazine* (5 August 2014).

However, for developing nations, it can be a signal to the rest of the world. Many believe that emerging nations, such as Brazil, are keen to host such big sporting events as a means of showcasing their growing economic power and often pushing infrastructure projects through much more quickly, to the benefit of the nation. Such visibility is hoped to make them more attractive to foreign investors, who see significant investment going into infrastructure and expect the nation's prosperity to improve, creating greater incomes and demand. This is the evidence found by a 2009 study by Andrew Rose, who noted that emerging economies hosting the Olympics benefit from an increase in trade.

Yet, it is not only the hosts that benefit. The research found that emerging nations which simply bid for the Olympics also experienced an increase in trade as a result of this signal – not because of any additional spending.[3] Perhaps here we have a method that delivers big benefits, without such big costs.

The macroeconomic impact

An obvious starting point in terms of estimating the macroeconomic effect of hosting a big sporting event is to look at the construction industry. Before the event, significant investment in stadiums, hotels, transport and general infrastructure is needed and this creates jobs for those involved in their construction, but also means that these workers use their incomes to buy other goods and services. This, in turn, increases aggregate demand, which creates further demand and so on. The multiplier begins to work, and not just in the regions where such investment took place.

The multiplier will create knock-on effects throughout the national economy. The workers involved in the pre-event activities may also develop new skills during their training, which will be of long-term benefit. The investment in infrastructure will last for years and the regeneration of particular areas may bring in new businesses and home-owners, adding to the local multiplier effects.

During the event, there is also significant expenditure, including spending by visitors, spectators and the participants on everything from hotels and transport, to food and souvenirs, together with the inevitable expenditure on security. This then adds to the multiplier effect: higher expenditure generating higher incomes, generating higher consumption, generating higher incomes, and so on.

Estimating benefits and costs

It is, however, difficult to estimate the overall *benefits* of any sporting event, in particular because, although many do occur before and during the event, there are likely to be other benefits that occur in the long term. Many of these benefits may well be non-monetary and hence estimating their value is problematic.

The *costs* of hosting any event are easier to estimate. But there are also opportunity costs to consider, with investment in infrastructure, such as stadiums, meaning less money available for other services. Most of the costs occur before or during the event – before most of the benefits. Hence, it can be a case of weighing up short-term costs against long-term benefits. These large upfront costs are perhaps causing fewer countries to bid for the honour of hosting key sporting events. Indeed, data and reports reviewing numerous such events indicate that the costs are nearly always underestimated and rise quickly during the construction process.

London, Brazil and Russia

The London Olympics

A study commissioned by Lloyds Banking Group[4] provided a broad assessment of the impact of the London 2012 Olympic Games, before, during and after. The study found that, over a twelve-year period, the London 2012 Olympics would generate a £16.5 billion contribution to GDP, with the construction industry benefiting from 78 000 additional jobs between 2005 and 2017 and generating a multiplier effect of over £5 billion. Additional tourist visits would also occur, creating an additional 61 000 years of employment and contributing £2 billion to UK GDP.

There were, however, concerns that London would take most of the benefits, with other regions in the UK contributing to the cost, but receiving few benefits. In a 2005 study[5] it was estimated that although there would be a direct gain to London's GDP of £5900 million over the period 2005–16, UK GDP as a whole would rise by only £1936 million. In other words, some of the gain to London would be at the expense of the rest of the UK as resources were diverted to London.

A post-games analysis[6] was conducted, finding that the Games would generate £28 billion to £41 billion in gross value added (GVA) and would create 618 000 to 893 000 years of employment by 2020. Further, the report found that there had been a spending boost from domestic and international visitors and the Brand of Britain was positively affected with 63 per cent of people who saw the coverage saying they were more interested in holidaying in the UK. The Legacy of the Games has also led to greater participation in sport.

The football World Cup

The football World Cup is another major sporting event and the net economic benefit, after adjusting for inflation, has been estimated at $11.9 billion for Japan and South Korea in 2002 and $14.1 billion for Germany in 2006, $5.6 billion for South Africa in 2010.[7]

The Brazilian World Cup. A report by the Economic Research Institute Foundation[8] determined that the Brazilian World Cup would inject $13 billion into the economy, with a boost to tourism alone of $3 billion and the creation of 1 million jobs. However, the estimated cost of hosting the tournament was around $11.5 billion, with the cost of stadiums tripling to $3.68 billion. Furthermore, there were serious social costs, with estimates suggesting that every month, at least one construction worker died. This is similar to the data for Qatar, due to host the 2022 World Cup, where figures show that on average one worker dies per day.

[4] *The Economic Impact of the London 2012 Olympic and Paralympic Games,* Oxford Economics, commissioned by Lloyds Banking Group (July 2012).

[5] *Olympic Games Impact Study: Final Report,* PricewaterhouseCoopers (December 2005).

[6] *Post-Games Evaluation; Meta-Evaluation of the Impacts and Legacy of the London 2012 Olympic Games and Paralympic Games',* Department for Culture, Media & Sport (July 2013).

[7] Simon Chadwick, 'Hard evidence: what is the world cup worth?', *The Conversation* (4 June 2014).

[8] See: Mirele Matsuoka De Aragao, 'Economic Impacts of the FIFA World Cup in Developing Countries', *ScholarWorks at WMU,* Western Michigan University (17 April 2015).

[3] Ibid.

Looking back at the 2014 World Cup, it appears that it did little to help the Brazilian economy, possibly making poverty and inequality worse, increasing debt and delivering a lower than expected increase in the number of tourists. Brazil then hosted the 2016 Olympics and similar issues emerged, with the original budget of $2.93 billion increasing to $13.2 billion and thousands being evicted from their homes to free-up land.

The Russian World Cup. In 2018, Russia hosted the football World Cup and, once again, expectations were high for the long-term benefits, albeit many of them intangible. Data indicate that Russia spent over $14 billion to host the tournament and it did generate thousands of additional jobs during the construction phase, with personal incomes estimated to have increased by $6.6 billion. However, Moody's Investor Service published a report that stated:

> Russia will only experience a short-lived economic benefit from hosting the 2018 FIFA World Cup tournament . . . Much of the economic impact has already been felt through infrastructure spending, and even there the impact has been limited. World Cup-related investments in 2013–17 accounted for only 1 percent of total investments.[9]

The Russian government estimated that the impact of the 2018 World Cup would be equal to approximately 1 per cent of its GDP and that between 2013 and 2023, there would be a boost to GDP of between $26 billion and $30.8 billion. There was certainly a positive impact for the country during the games with 570 000 foreigners and 700 000 Russians attending events related to the World Cup, thus giving tourism a significant boost. Visitors to the country are expected to remain high for a few years, with an annual growth rate in visitors of 4 per cent expected up to 2022.

Many analysts think that the longer-term monetary benefits will be minimal, however, but the Russian government sees the main benefits as being more intangible, generating a legacy for future generations.

Happiness

The overall impact of any sporting event is always going to be difficult to estimate and it is likely that a final answer will only be known decades after the event, once the full multiplier and legacy benefits have materialised. By then, of course, it is too late if the positive economic impact is less than expected. However, one final benefit should be considered: something that is not always given the attention it deserves – happiness.

Research routinely indicates that sporting events create happiness and a 'feel-good' factor and that monetary benefits do arise from this boost in happiness. Business can benefit from better morale, especially if areas are available for its employees to watch events, though the impact on productivity and absenteeism is less certain!

Euro 96 (UEFA European Football Championship), hosted by England, is estimated to have resulted in an average benefit to UK residents of £165 per head in terms of happiness. Referring to these non-monetary benefits, Victor Matheson, from the College of the Holy Cross in Massachusetts said:

> It's [hosting the Olympics or World Cup] like a wedding . . . It won't make you rich, but it may make you happy.[10]

The big questions are then 'just how happy?' and 'how much does a nation value that happiness?'

1. One issue that arose in London was whether the benefits of hosting the Olympic Games would be confined to London. Give some examples of industries in the rest of the UK which could have benefited from increased expenditure in London.
2. When a nation hosts a big sporting event, there will be a multiplier effect. Why would the magnitude of the full multiplier effect on the whole economy be difficult to estimate?
3. Deciding whether hosting a big sporting event is worthwhile requires a full analysis of costs and benefits, including externalities. Identify some external costs and benefits from hosting the Olympics or the World Cup.

Investigate a recent international sporting event and find out estimates of the costs and benefits of that event to the host nation.

---

[9] See: Holly Ellyatt, 'The World Cup will give Russia's economy a boost – just don't expect it to last', *CNBC* (14 June 2018).

[10] Binyamin Applebaum, *op.cit.*

RECAP

1. In the simple circular flow of income model, equilibrium national income (GDP) is where withdrawals equal injections: where $W = J$.

2. Equilibrium can be shown on a Keynesian 45° line diagram. Equilibrium is where national income (Y) or GDP (shown by the 45° line) is equal to aggregate expenditure (E).

3. The aggregate demand (AD)/aggregate supply (AS) model can also be used to determine equilibrium national income. In addition, it shows the equilibrium price level. Any factor that shifts AD or AS will cause a change in the equilibrium level of national income and the equilibrium price level.

4. If there is an initial increase in aggregate expenditure (ΔE), which could result from an increase in injections or a reduction in withdrawals, there will be a multiplied rise in GDP. The multiplier is defined as $\Delta Y/\Delta E$.

5. The size of the multiplier depends on the marginal propensity to consume domestically produced goods (mpc_d). The larger the mpc_d, the more will be spent each time incomes are generated round the circular flow, and thus the more will go around again as *additional* demand for domestic product. The multiplier formula is $1/(1 - mpc_d)$.

10.4 THE BUSINESS CYCLE

Economic growth tends to fluctuate. In some years there is a high rate of economic growth; the country experiences a boom. In other years, economic growth is low or even negative; the country experiences a *recession*. This cycle of booms and recessions is known as the *business cycle* or *trade cycle*.

 KEY IDEA 26 *Economies suffer from inherent instability.* As a result, economic growth and other macroeconomic indicators tend to fluctuate.

The business cycle is illustrated in Figure 10.6. The first thing to note in the diagram is the ceiling to output. This is where all resources, including labour, are fully employed and so it represents the maximum output the economy can produce. This full-capacity output grows over time for two reasons:

■ *Resources may increase.* This could be the result of an increase in the working population or as a result of investment in new plant and equipment, thus increasing the stock of capital.
■ *Resources may become more productive.* The most likely reasons for this are technical progress and more efficient working practices. Both will lead to an increase in either the marginal product of labour or of capital, or both.

The diagram shows the cyclical fluctuations in actual output (GDP). Four 'phases' of the business cycle can be identified.

1. *The upturn.* In this phase, a stagnant economy begins to recover and growth in GDP resumes. Business confidence begins to grow.

2. *The expansion.* During this phase, there is rapid economic growth; the economy is booming. Rapid growth in consumer demand creates a climate of business confidence and firms respond by producing more, investing more and employing more people. The economy moves closer to full-capacity output.

3. *The peaking-out.* During this phase, growth slows down or even ceases. Business confidence wanes.

4. *The slowdown, recession or slump.* During this phase, there is little or no growth or even a decline in output. Increasing slack develops in the economy as many businesses produce less and hold off from investing.

The third (dashed) line shows the trend of GDP over time (i.e. ignoring the cyclical fluctuations around the trend). If the average level of capacity that is unutilised stays constant from one cycle to another, then the trend line will have the same slope as the full-capacity output line. If, however, the average level of capacity that is unutilised falls from one peak to the next, then the gap between the trend line and the output ceiling (full-capacity) line will become narrower. The trend line will have a steeper slope than the output ceiling line.

Pause for thought

Will the ceiling to output be in any way affected by the short-run rate of growth of GDP? If so, how?

The business cycle in practice

The business cycle illustrated in Figure 10.6 is a 'stylised' cycle. It is nice and smooth and regular. Drawing it this way allows us to make a clear distinction between each of the four phases. In practice, however, business cycles are highly irregular. They are irregular in two ways:

The length of the phases. Some booms and recessions are short-lived, lasting only a few months or so.

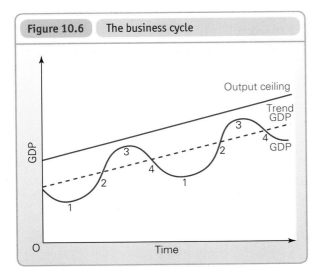

Figure 10.6 The business cycle

Definitions

Recession A period of falling GDP: i.e. of negative economic growth. Officially, a recession is where this occurs for two quarters or more.

Business cycle or **trade cycle** The periodic fluctuations of national output around its long-term trend.

Others are much longer, lasting perhaps three or four years. The 2008–9 recession was closely followed by another one (2011–12) in several countries, including the eurozone, with the intermediate economic upturn only short-lived. This is known as a double-dip recession and at the beginning of 2013, there were concerns in some countries that this would become a triple-dip recession, although this was narrowly avoided.

The magnitude of the phases. Sometimes in phase 2 there is a very high rate of economic growth – much higher than the longer-term average. On other occasions in phase 2, growth is much gentler. Sometimes in phase 4 there is a recession, with an actual decline in output (e.g. in the early 1980s, the early 1990s and late 2000s). On other occasions, phase 4 is merely a 'pause', with growth simply slowing down (e.g. in the early 2000s and late 2010s).

Nevertheless, despite the irregularity of the fluctuations, cycles are still clearly discernible, especially if we plot *growth* on the vertical axis rather than the *level* of output. This is done in Figure 10.7, which shows the business cycles in selected industrial economies from 1970 to 2022.

Causes of cyclical fluctuations

Why does the business cycle occur and what determines the length and magnitude of the phases of the cycle? To understand this, we can turn to aggregate demand, as it is changes in aggregate demand that determine short-run economic growth. There are three questions we need to answer.

■ What causes aggregate demand to change in the first place?
■ Why do the effects of changes in aggregate demand persist? In other words, why do booms and recessions last for a period of time?
■ Why do booms and recessions come to an end? What determines the turning points?

What causes aggregate demand to change in the first place?

As we have seen, anything that affects one or more of the four components of aggregate demand (C_d, I, G or X) could be the reason for a change in national income (real GDP). For example, an increase in business confidence could increase investment; an increase in consumer confidence could increase consumption. A cut in interest rates may encourage increased business and consumer borrowing, and hence an increase in investment and consumption. A cut in taxes will increase consumption, as consumers have more 'disposable' income. A rise in government expenditure will directly increase aggregate demand. A change in conditions abroad, or a change in the exchange rate, will affect imports and exports. (We examine these external factors in Chapter 13.)

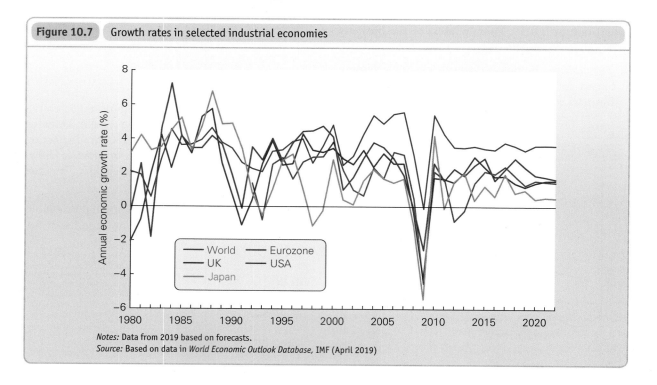

Figure 10.7   Growth rates in selected industrial economies

Notes: Data from 2019 based on forecasts.
Source: Based on data in *World Economic Outlook Database,* IMF (April 2019)

Some of these factors, such as taxes and government expenditure, can be directly controlled by the government. In other words, government policy can be directed at controlling aggregate demand and hence the course of the business cycle. We call this 'demand management policy' – again we will look at this in the next chapter.

Why do booms and recessions persist for a period of time?

Time lags. It takes time for changes in aggregate demand to be fully reflected in changes in GDP and employment. The multiplier process takes time. Moreover, consumers, firms and government may not all respond immediately to new situations. Their responses are spread out over a period of time.

'Bandwagon' effects. Once the economy starts expanding, expectations become buoyant. People think ahead and adjust their expenditure behaviour; they consume and invest more *now*. Likewise, in a recession a mood of pessimism may set in. The effect is cumulative.

One crucial effect here is called the *accelerator*. A rise in injections will cause a multiplied rise in GDP. But this rise in GDP will, in turn, cause a rise in investment, as firms seek to expand capacity to meet the extra demand. This compounds the increase in demand, as investment is itself an injection into the circular flow. This is the accelerator. The increased investment then causes a further multiplied rise in income. This then causes a further accelerator effect, a further multiplier effect, and so on.

Pause for thought

Under what circumstances would you expect a rise in national income to cause a large accelerator effect?

Why do booms and recessions come to an end? What determines the turning points?

Ceilings and floors. Actual output can go on growing more rapidly as long as there is slack in the economy. As full employment is approached, however, and as more and more firms reach full capacity, so a ceiling to output is reached.

At the other extreme, there is a basic minimum level of consumption that people tend to maintain. During a recession, people may not buy much in the way of luxury and durable goods, but they will continue to buy food and other basic goods. There is thus a floor to consumption.

The industries supplying these basic goods will need to maintain their level of replacement investment. Also, there will always be some minimum investment demand as firms, in order to survive competition, need to install the latest equipment (such as computer hardware). There is thus a floor to investment too.

Echo effects. Durable consumer goods and capital equipment may last several years, but eventually they will need replacing. The necessary replacement of goods and capital purchased in a previous boom may help to bring a recession to an end.

The accelerator. For investment to continue rising, consumer demand must rise at a *faster and faster* rate. After all, firms invest to meet *extra* demand. They will therefore only invest more than the last period if the extra demand is more than in the last period: i.e. if the growth rate is *increasing*. If this does not happen, investment will fall back and the boom will break.

Random shocks. National or international political, social or natural events can affect the mood and attitudes of firms, governments and consumers, and thus affect aggregate demand.

Changes in government policy. In a boom, a government may become most worried by unsustainably high growth and inflation and thus pursue contractionary policies. In a recession, it may become most worried by unemployment and lack of growth and thus pursue expansionary policies, as many governments did during the global recession of the late 2000s. These government policies, if successful, will bring about a turning point in the cycle.

Pause for thought

Why is it difficult to predict precisely when a recession will come to an end and the economy will start growing rapidly?

Definition

Accelerator The level of investment depends on the rate of increase in consumer demand, and as a result is subject to substantial fluctuations. Increases in investment via the accelerator can compound the multiplier effect.

BOX 10.3 **SENTIMENT AND SPENDING**

Do people have the confidence to spend and invest?

Keynesian economists have frequently pointed to the importance of confidence or sentiment in influencing expenditure decisions. 'Confidence shocks' are often identified as a source of economic volatility. But what is confidence? Is it something tangible and can it be measured?

Measures of confidence

Each month, consumers and firms across the European Union are asked a series of questions, the answers to which are used to compile indicators of consumer and business confidence. For instance, consumers are asked about how they expect their financial position to change. They are offered various options such as 'get a lot better', 'get a lot worse' and balances are then calculated on the basis of positive and negative replies.[1]

The chart plots economic sentiment in the EU for consumers and different sectors of business since the

---

[1] Search: *Business and consumer surveys*, European Commission.

mid-1990s. It captures the volatility of economic sentiment. This volatility is generally greater amongst businesses than consumers, and especially so in the construction sector. However, confidence fell dramatically across all groups during the financial crisis of the late 2000s.

Confidence and expenditure

Now compare the volatility of economic sentiment in Chart (a) with the annual rates of growth in household consumption and gross capital formation (investment) in Chart (b). You can see that volatility in economic sentiment is reflected in patterns of both consumer and investment expenditure. However, capital formation is significantly more volatile than household spending.

What is less clear is the extent to which changes in sentiment *lead* to changes in spending. In fact, a likely scenario is that spending and sentiment interact. High rates of spending growth may result in high confidence through

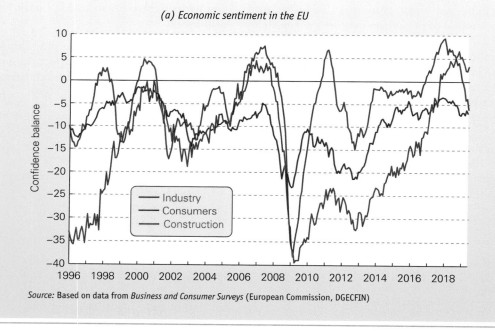

(a) Economic sentiment in the EU

Source: Based on data from Business and Consumer Surveys (European Commission, DGECFIN)

RECAP

1. Economic growth fluctuates with the course of the business cycle.

2. The cycle can be broken down into four phases: the upturn, the expansion, the peaking-out, and the slowdown or recession.

3. In practice, the length and magnitude of these phases varies; the cycle is thus irregular.

4. A major part of this explanation of the business cycle is the instability of investment. The accelerator theory explains this instability. It relates the *level* of investment to *rises* in GDP and consumer demand.

5. Other reasons for fluctuations in aggregate demand include time lags, 'bandwagon' effects, ceilings and floors to output, echo effects, swings in government policy and random shocks.

economic growth, which in turn leads to more spending. The reverse is the case when economic growth is subdued: low spending growth leads to a lack of confidence, which results in low spending growth and so low rates of economic growth.

Therefore, while confidence may be a source of volatility it may also be part of the process by which shocks are transmitted through the economy. Consequently, it may be contributing to amplifying the peaks and troughs of the business cycle.

What makes measures of confidence particularly useful is that they are published monthly. By contrast, measures of GDP and spending are published annually or quarterly and with a considerable time delay. Therefore, measures of confidence are extremely timely for policy makers and provide them with

very useful information about the likely path of spending and output growth.

1. *What factors are likely to influence the economic sentiment of (i) consumers; and (ii) businesses?*
2. *Can consumers become more optimistic while businesses become more pessimistic, and vice versa?*

Using time series data from the European Commission based on business and consumer survey data, plot a line chart to show the path of consumer confidence for any two countries of your choice. Describe the patterns you observe noting any similarities or differences between the consumer confidence profile of the two countries.

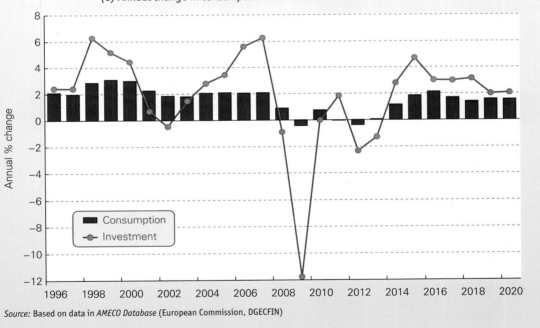

(b) Annual change in consumption and investment in the EU

Source: Based on data in *AMECO Database* (European Commission, DGECFIN)

10.5 MONEY, INTEREST RATES AND BUSINESS ACTIVITY

Business and interest rates

The financial sector was badly affected by the 'credit crunch' and many consumers and businesses struggled to obtain finance. This illustrated just how important financial institutions are in affecting businesses and the wider macroeconomy. It also presented many important questions for governments, central banks and regulators across the world.

One important determinant of business activity is the rate of interest. If interest rates rise, it will be more expensive for businesses to borrow and the rate of return on their investments will need to be higher to cover these borrowing costs; this will curtail investment. Higher interest rates are a particular problem for businesses that have a high ratio of borrowing at variable interest rates to their total turnover. In such cases, not only will a rise in interest rates discourage investment, it may also make it difficult for the business to find the money to pay the interest – to 'service' its debt.

Higher interest rates make saving more profitable, but it will also make it more expensive for the general public to borrow. If interest rates rise, whether on personal loans, on credit cards or on mortgages, consumers may well cut back on their borrowing and spending. Aggregate demand will fall.

Interest rates are also seen as a 'barometer' of the future course of the economy. If the central bank (the Bank of England in the UK) raises interest rates, this may be taken as a sign that the economy will slow down, especially if it is expected that rates are likely to be raised again in the near future. Business confidence may fall and so too, therefore, may investment. However, it all depends on how the rise in interest rates is interpreted. If it is seen as a means of preventing excessive expansion of the economy and therefore allowing expansion to be sustained, albeit at a more moderate rate, this may actually encourage investment. Thus expectations and how people interpret various changes in the instruments of government policy are likely to have a crucial effect on the course of the economy.

But what determines interest rates? In a free market, interest rates are determined by the demand for and supply of money. In practice, free-market interest rates may be seen as too high or too low by the central bank, in which case it will seek to alter them. This process of altering interest rates by the country's central bank is known as 'monetary policy'. We examine monetary policy in the next chapter. Here we look at the determination of interest rates in a free market.

The meaning of money

Before going any further we must define precisely what we mean by 'money'. An easy task, surely! However, money is more than just notes and coins. In fact, the main component of a country's money supply is not cash, but deposits in banks and other financial institutions.

The bulk of bank deposits appear merely as book-keeping entries in the banks' accounts. Banks therefore keep only a very small proportion of deposits in their safes or tills in the form of cash, but most of the time, they will still have enough cash to meet customer demands. This is because, normally, only a small fraction of a bank's total deposits will be withdrawn at any one time. Furthermore, only a very small proportion of transactions are conducted in cash. Most use debit or credit cards, tap-and-pay-enabled mobile phones or direct transfers from one account to another.

However, in September 2007, we did see a 'run on a bank', when people lost confidence in Northern Rock and many customers started to withdraw cash from their accounts, such that the demand for withdrawals was higher than the deposits kept within the banks. In cases such as this, central banks or governments have to intervene to protect people's deposits by making more cash available to the bank or, in the last resort, by nationalising the bank. This is what happened with Northern Rock in February 2008.

> ### Pause for thought
>
> *Why are debit and credit cards not counted as money?*

We typically use two measures of money: a narrow measure, which consists of *cash in circulation* (i.e. outside the central bank) and a *broad money* measure, which includes cash in circulation with the public (but not in banks) plus all deposits in banks and building societies. In the UK this measure of broad money is known as *M4*. In most other European countries and the USA, it is known as *M3*. There are, however, minor differences between countries in what is included.

In 1970, the stock of M4 in the UK was around £25 billion, equivalent to 48 per cent of annual GDP. By 2018 this had grown to £2.4 trillion, equivalent to about 115 per cent of annual GDP.

The supply of money

Banks and the creation of credit

By far the largest element of broad money supply is bank deposits. It is not surprising then that banks play an absolutely crucial role in the monetary system. This was clearly evident between 2007 and 2009, when we saw the collapse of parts of the banking sector in many countries, including the UK, directly contributing to the global recession.

Banks are able to create additional money by increasing the amount of bank deposits. They do this

> ### Definitions
>
> **Cash in circulation** The measure of narrow money in the UK. This is all cash outside the Bank of England: in banks, in people's purses and wallets, in businesses' safes and tills, in government departments, etc.
>
> **M4 (in UK)** Cash outside the banks plus all bank and building society deposits (including cash).
>
> **M3 (in eurozone and elsewhere)** Cash outside the banks, bank deposits and various other assets that can be relatively easily turned into cash without loss.

by lending to people: granting people overdrafts or loans. When these loans are spent, the shops deposit the money in their bank accounts, or have it directly transferred when debit cards are swiped across their tills. Thus the additional loans granted by the banks have become deposits in the shops' bank accounts. These deposits can be used by banks as the basis for further loans. These in turn create further deposits and so on. The process is known as the 'creation of credit'.

Can this process go on indefinitely? The answer is no. Banks must keep a certain proportion of their deposits in the form of cash to meet the demands of their customers for cash. That is, your demands to make withdrawals from your bank account.

Let us say that 10 per cent of a bank's deposits have to be in the form of cash, then non-cash deposits would account for the remaining 90 per cent. So if additional cash of £10 million were deposited in the banking system, banks would need to hold 10 per cent (£1 million) as cash, but could lend out the remaining £9 million.

When this £9 million is spent in shops or businesses, they will deposit it into their bank accounts, such that bank deposits increase by an extra £9 million. Of this extra £9 million, only 10 per cent needs to be held in the form of cash (£0.9 million), while the remainder (£8.1 million) can be lent out. And so the process continues; money supply expands.

In this example, banks could create non-cash deposits of an additional £90 million – but no more. Of the total new deposits of £100 million, cash would be 10 per cent (the original £10 million extra) and non-cash deposits would be 90 per cent, thus adhering to the 10 per cent cash ratio.

This effect is known as the *bank (or deposits) multiplier*. In this simple example with a cash ratio of 1/10 (i.e. 10 per cent), the deposits multiplier is 10. An initial increase in deposits of £10 million allowed total deposits to rise by £100 million. In this simple world, therefore, the deposits multiplier is the inverse of the cash ratio (L).

Deposits multiplier $= 1/L$

The creation of credit: the real world
In practice, the creation of credit is not as simple as this.

First, while banks must have access to cash if their customers want it, banks can keep some of the money deposited in them in a form that can be readily converted into cash rather than holding it as cash itself. There are various short-term securities that banks hold for this purpose. These securities can be sold for cash at very short notice. Securities held for these purposes are known as 'near money' and, together with cash, form banks' 'liquid assets'. What banks have to look at, therefore, is the *liquidity ratio*, the ratio of liquid assets to total deposits.

Second, at certain times banks may decide that it is prudent to hold a bigger proportion of liquid assets. If Christmas or the summer holidays are approaching and people are likely to make bigger cash withdrawals, banks may decide to hold more liquid assets. In the wake of the banking crisis of 2008, where many of banks' assets fell in value, banks chose to hold more liquid assets in an attempt to increase confidence. Alternatively, banks may *want* to make loans, but customers may not want to borrow, if they are concerned about the future and the repayments. In these circumstance banks may find themselves with a higher liquidity ratio than normal.

On the other hand, there may be an upsurge in consumer demand for credit. Banks may be very keen to grant additional loans and thus make more profits, even though they have acquired no additional cash or other liquid assets. In such circumstances they may be prepared to operate with a lower liquidity ratio than normal.

What causes the money supply to rise?
The money supply might rise as a result of banks responding to an increased demand for credit. They may be prepared to operate with a lower liquidity ratio to meet this demand. Indeed, with the increased use of credit and debit cards, we have seen a trend of banks increasingly choosing a lower liquidity ratio – at least until the banking crisis of 2008/9.

Another source of extra money is from abroad. Sometimes central banks will choose to build up the foreign currency reserves. For example, the Bank of England will buy foreign currencies on the foreign exchange market using sterling. When the recipients

---

Pause for thought

If banks choose to operate with a 5 per cent liquidity ratio and receive an extra £100 million of cash deposits: (a) What is the size of the deposits multiplier? (b) How much will total deposits have expanded after the multiplier has worked through? (c) By how much will total credit have expanded?

Definitions

Bank (or deposits) multiplier The number of times greater the expansion of bank deposits is than the additional liquidity in banks that caused it: $1/L$ (the inverse of the liquidity ratio).

Liquidity ratio The ratio of liquid assets (cash and assets that can be readily converted to cash) to total deposits.

of this extra sterling deposit it in UK banks, or spend it on UK exports and the exporters deposit the money in UK banks, credit will be created on the basis of it, leading to a multiplied increase in money supply.

One of the main reasons for an increase in money supply is government borrowing. If the government spends more than it receives in tax revenues, it will have to borrow to make up the difference. This difference is known as *public-sector net borrowing (PSNB)*. The government borrows by selling interest-bearing securities. These are of two main types: (a) short-term securities in the form of Treasury bills – these have a three-month period to maturity (i.e. the date on which the government pays back the loan); (b) longer-term securities in the form of bonds, also known as 'gilts' – these often have several years to maturity.

Such securities could be sold to the central bank. The money paid to the government is in effect being *created* by the country's central bank and when it finds its way to the banks, the banks can use it as the basis for credit creation. Similarly, if the government borrows through additional Treasury bills, and if these are purchased by the banking sector, there will be a multiplied expansion of credit. The banks will now have additional liquid assets (bills), which can be used as the basis for credit creation.

Since 2009/10, many central banks have taken emergency measures to increase the supply of money, known as 'quantitative easing'. This has involved central banks buying existing bonds from banks and other financial institutions and thereby releasing new money into the banking system. It was hoped that this extra liquidity in the banking system would encourage banks to lend.[4] However, although it provided extra money to the banks, bank lending grew more slowly than was hoped. Also much of the extra money was used for buying assets, such and shares and existing property, rather than for extra production (GDP) and consumption.

As a result, quantitative easing was continued for much longer and the amount of additional money released was much greater than originally anticipated. Indeed, the ECB only halted its quantitative easing programme, worth €30 billion per month, in December 2018. It has pumped a total of nearly €2.5 trillion into the eurozone economy through its bond-buying programme.

The credit crunch is considered in more detail in Box 11.3.

The demand for money

The demand for money refers to the desire to *hold* money; to keep your wealth in the form of money, rather than spending it on goods and services or using

it to purchase financial assets such as bonds or shares. But why should people want to hold on to money, rather than spending it or buying some sort of security such as bonds or shares? There are two main reasons.

The first is that people receive money only at intervals (e.g. weekly or monthly) and not continuously. They thus require to hold balances of money in cash or in current accounts ready for spending later in the week or month.

The second is as a form of saving and thus of storing wealth. Money in a bank account earns a relatively small, but safe rate of return and so has the advantage of carrying no risk. Some assets, such as company shares or bonds, may earn you more on average, but there is a chance that their price will fall. In other words, they are risky.

What determines the size of the demand for money?
What would cause the demand for money to rise? This would occur if people's incomes rose. The more you earn, the more money you are likely to hold in the bank or in cash. A rise in money ('nominal') incomes in a country can be caused either by a rise in real GDP (i.e. real output) or by a rise in prices, or some combination of the two.

The demand for money would also rise if people thought that share prices or the prices of other securities were likely to fall. In such circumstances, owning shares or other forms of securities may be seen as too risky. To avoid this risk, people will want to hold money instead. Some clever (or lucky) individuals anticipated the 2008 stock market decline (see Box 2.1). They sold shares and 'went liquid'.

Financial innovations have also had an effect on the size of the demand for money. The increased use of credit and debit cards has reduced the demand for money, especially with the advent of contactless payments, while changes to current accounts, such that you can now earn interest on them, have encouraged people to hold more money in bank accounts.

The rate of interest. In terms of the operation of money markets, this is the most important determinant. It is related to the opportunity cost of holding money. The opportunity cost is the interest forgone by not holding higher interest-bearing assets, such as bonds or shares. Generally, if rates of interest rise, they will rise more on bonds and other securities than on bank accounts. The demand for money will thus

> ### Definition
>
> **Public-sector net cash borrowing (PSNB)** The (annual) deficit of the public sector (central government, local government and public corporations), and thus the amount that the public sector must borrow.

4 See also: 'What is quantitative easing?', *BBC News* (3 December 2015).

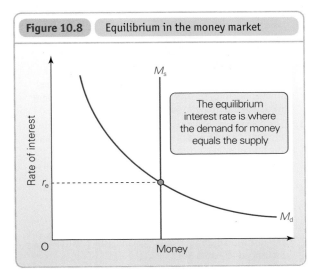

Figure 10.8 Equilibrium in the money market

The equilibrium interest rate is where the demand for money equals the supply

fall as people switch to these alternative securities. The demand for money is thus inversely related to the rate of interest. This is illustrated in Figure 10.8.

Pause for thought

Which way is the demand-for-money curve likely to shift in each of the following cases? (a) Prices rise, but real incomes stay the same; (b) Interest rates abroad rise relative to domestic interest rates; (c) People anticipate that share prices are likely to fall in the near future.

The equilibrium rate of interest

Equilibrium in the money market occurs when the demand for money (M_d) is equal to the supply of money (M_s). Figure 10.8 shows the demand for and supply of money plotted against the rate of interest. For simplicity, it is assumed that the supply of money is independent of interest rates, and is therefore drawn as a vertical straight line.[5]

The equilibrium rate of interest is r_e. But why? If the rate of interest were above r_e, people would have money balances surplus to their needs. They would use these to buy shares, bonds and other assets. This would drive up the price of these assets. But the price of assets is inversely related to interest rates. The higher the price of an asset (such as a government bond), the less will any given interest payment be as a percentage of its price (e.g. £10 as a percentage of £100 is 10 per cent, but as a percentage of £200, it is only 5 per cent). Thus a higher price of assets will correspond to lower interest rates.

As the rate of interest fell, so there would be a movement down along the M_s and M_d curves. The interest rate would go on falling until it reached r_e. Equilibrium would then be achieved.

Similarly, if the rate of interest were below r_e, people would have insufficient money balances. They would sell securities, thus lowering their prices and raising the rate of interest until it reached r_e.

Causes of changes in interest rates

We saw above what would cause an increase in the supply of money. If money supply does increase, the M_s line will shift to the right in Figure 10.8. This will cause a fall in the rate of interest to the point where the new M_s line intersects with the M_d curve.

A change in interest rates will also occur if the demand for money changes (i.e. the M_d curve shifts). For example, a rise in incomes would lead to people wanting to hold larger money balances. This would shift the M_d curve to the right and drive up the rate of interest.

In practice, most central banks seek to *control* the rate of interest. We see how it achieves this in the next chapter.

Effects of changes in interest rates

As we will see in Chapter 11, interest rates are a powerful tool and can affect many of the components of aggregate demand. A reduction in interest rates (e.g. from a rise in money supply) will lead to a rise in investment and consumer spending as firms and consumers borrow more.

There will also be an effect on the exchange rate, as lower interest rates discourage people, both at home and abroad, from holding the country's currency. As we shall see in Chapter 13, this will tend to drive down the exchange rate. This, in turn, will make exports cheaper and imports more expensive. Exports (an injection) will rise and imports (a withdrawal) will fall.

The overall effect of a fall in interest rates will be to boost aggregate demand and this will then lead to a multiplied rise in GDP. How much aggregate demand increases depends on (a) the elasticity of the demand-for-money curve – the steeper the M_d curve, the more interest rates will fall for any given rise in money supply; (b) the responsiveness of businesses and consumers to a change in interest rates – the more responsive they are, the bigger will be the rise in aggregate demand and hence the bigger the multiplied rise in GDP.

Pause for thought

Assume that interest rates fall. Under what circumstances will this lead to (a) a large rise in business investment; (b) little or no change in business investment?

---

[5] In practice, the supply-of-money curve is likely to be upward sloping. The reason is that a rise in aggregate demand will lead to an increased demand for money and hence a rise in interest rates. At the same time, banks are likely to respond to the rise in demand for money by creating more credit, thereby increasing the money supply. In other words, the higher interest rates correspond to an increased supply of money.

RECAP

1. Interest rates are an important determinant of business activity. They are determined by the interaction of the demand and supply of money.

2. Money in its narrow sense includes just cash in circulation. Money is normally defined more broadly, however, to include all bank deposits, not just those in the form of cash. M4 is the name given in the UK to this broader measure of the money supply, while M3 is used in the EU and the USA.

3. Bank deposits expand through a process of credit creation. If banks' liquid assets increase, they can be used as a base for increasing loans. When the loans are redeposited in banks, they form the base for yet more loans, and thus a process of multiple credit expansion takes place. The ratio of the increase of deposits to an expansion of banks' liquidity base is called the 'bank multiplier'. It is the inverse of the liquidity ratio.

4. Money supply will rise if (a) banks respond to an increased demand for money by increasing credit without an increase in liquidity; (b) there is an inflow of money from abroad; (c) the government finances its borrowing by borrowing from the banking sector.

5. The demand for money is determined mainly by people's incomes, the risk attached to alternatives to money and the rate of interest (the opportunity cost of holding money). The higher the rate of interest, the lower the demand for money.

6. The equilibrium rate of interest is where the supply of money is equal to the demand. A rise in the rate of interest can be caused by an increased demand for money or a reduced supply. Changes in the rate of interest will affect aggregate demand, which will have a multiplied effect on GDP.

10.6 UNEMPLOYMENT

We saw in Chapter 8 how employment is determined in individual labour markets. In this section we look at the overall level of employment and unemployment in the economy. This depends in part on the level of business activity. When the economy is booming, employment will be high and unemployment low as businesses take on more labour to meet the extra demand.

Measuring unemployment

The unemployed are not simply those who do not have a job – we would not count a child as being unemployed! The usual definition that economists use for the *number unemployed* is: *those of working age who are without work, but who are available for work at current wage rates.*

Unemployment can be expressed either as a number (e.g. 1.5 million) or as a percentage (e.g. 4 per cent). If the figure is to be expressed as a percentage, then it is a percentage of the total *labour force*. The labour force is defined as: *those in employment plus those unemployed*. Thus if 32.7 million people were employed and 1.3 million people were unemployed, the *unemployment rate* would be:

$$\frac{1.3}{32.7 + 1.3} = 0.382 = 3.82 \text{ per cent}$$

Two common measures of unemployment are used in official statistics. The first is *claimant unemployment*. This is simply a measure of all those in receipt of unemployment-related benefits. In the UK, claimants receive the 'job-seeker's allowance'.

The second measure is the *standardised unemployment rate*. Since 1998, this has been the main measure used by the UK government. It is the measure used by the International Labour Organization (ILO) and the Organisation for Economic Co-operation and Development (OECD), two international organisations that publish unemployment statistics for many countries.

In this measure, the unemployed are defined as people of working age who are without work, available to start work within two weeks and *actively seeking employment* or waiting to take up an appointment. The figures are compiled from the results of national labour force surveys. In the UK the labour force survey is conducted quarterly.

Definitions

Number unemployed (economist's definition) Those of working age, who are without work, but who are available for work at current wage rates.

Labour force The number employed plus the number unemployed.

Unemployment rate The number unemployed expressed as a percentage of the labour force.

Claimant unemployment Those in receipt of unemployment-related benefits.

Standardised unemployment rate The measure of the unemployment rate used by the ILO and OECD. The unemployed are defined as people of working age who are without work, available for work and actively seeking employment.

But is the standardised unemployment rate likely to be higher or lower than the claimant unemployment rate? The standardised rate is likely to be higher to the extent that it includes people seeking work who are nevertheless not entitled to claim benefits, but lower to the extent that it excludes those who are claiming benefits and yet who are not actively seeking work. Clearly, the tougher the benefit regulations, the lower the claimant rate will be relative to the standardised rate.

While claimant unemployment statistics are very easy to collect, the figure is affected by changes to benefit eligibility. Thus historical or country comparisons can be very difficult, as benefit regulations do change over time and different countries adopt different approaches to unemployment benefits. Given these difficulties, the standardised unemployment rate has become the accepted measure of unemployment.

Unemployment and the labour market

We now turn to the causes of unemployment. These causes fall into two broad categories: *equilibrium* unemployment and *disequilibrium* unemployment. To make clear the distinction between the two, it is necessary to look at how the labour market works.

Figure 10.9 shows the aggregate demand for labour and the aggregate supply of labour: that is, the total demand and supply of labour in the whole economy. The *real* average wage rate is plotted on the vertical axis. This is the average wage rate expressed in terms of its purchasing power: in other words, after taking inflation into account.

The *aggregate supply of labour curve* (AS_L) shows the number of workers *willing to accept jobs* at each wage rate. This curve is relatively inelastic, since the size of the workforce at any one time cannot change significantly. Nevertheless, it is not totally inelastic because (a) a higher wage rate will encourage some people to enter the labour market (e.g. parents raising children) and (b) the unemployed will be more willing to accept job offers rather than continuing to search for a better-paid job.

The *aggregate demand for labour curve* (AD_L) slopes downward. The higher the wage rate, the fewer workers firms will want to employ. They may decide to cut back on production, thereby reducing the number of workers they need, or the higher wage rate may encourage firms to economise on labour and to substitute other inputs for it.

The labour market is in equilibrium at a wage of W_e, where the demand for labour equals the supply. If the wage were above W_e, the labour market would be in a state of disequilibrium. At a wage rate of W_2, there is an excess supply of labour of $a - b$. This is called *disequilibrium unemployment*.

For disequilibrium unemployment to occur, two conditions must hold:

- The aggregate supply of labour must exceed the aggregate demand.
- There must be a 'stickiness' in wages. In other words, the wage rate must not immediately fall to W_e.

Even when the labour market *is* in equilibrium, however, not everyone looking for work will be employed. Some people will hold out, hoping to find a better job. The curve N in Figure 10.10 shows the total number in the labour force. The horizontal difference between it and the aggregate supply of labour curve (AS_L) represents the excess of people looking for work over those actually willing to accept jobs. Q_e represents the equilibrium level of employment and the distance $d - e$ represents the *equilibrium level of unemployment*. This is sometimes known as

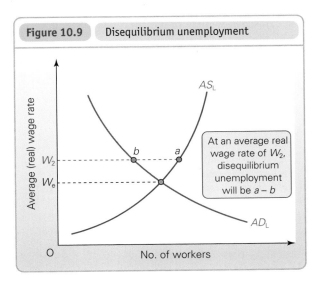

| **Figure 10.9** | Disequilibrium unemployment |

At an average real wage rate of W_2, disequilibrium unemployment will be $a - b$

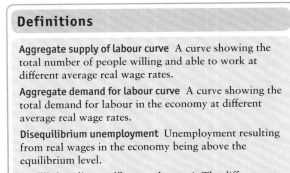

Definitions

Aggregate supply of labour curve A curve showing the total number of people willing and able to work at different average real wage rates.

Aggregate demand for labour curve A curve showing the total demand for labour in the economy at different average real wage rates.

Disequilibrium unemployment Unemployment resulting from real wages in the economy being above the equilibrium level.

Equilibrium ('natural') unemployment The difference between those who would like employment at the current wage rate and those willing and able to take a job.

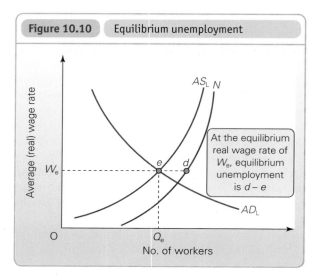

Figure 10.10 Equilibrium unemployment

At the equilibrium real wage rate of W_e, equilibrium unemployment is $d - e$

Pause for thought

If this analysis is correct, namely that a reduction in wages will reduce the aggregate demand for goods, what assumption must we make about the relative proportions of wages and profits that are spent (given that a reduction in real wage rates will lead to a corresponding increase in rates of profit)? Is this a realistic assumption?

the *natural level of unemployment*. There are some interesting articles about this level of unemployment in the Sloman Economics News site blog, *A full employment target*.

It is also important to note that, even if unemployment data show a low rate of unemployment, there may still be quite high **underemployment**. This is when workers would like to work more hours than they currently do. This is discussed in the blog, *The State of the Labour Market in the UK* on the Sloman Economics News site and in a *Guardian* article.[6] This has become a particular problem in the UK, where there has been a move towards more flexible contracts (see Box 8.1 and section 8.4).

Types of disequilibrium unemployment

There are two main causes of disequilibrium unemployment.

Real-wage unemployment

Real-wage unemployment is where wages are set above the market-clearing level, for example at W_2 in Figure 10.9. This could be the result of either minimum wage legislation or the activities of trade unions.

Although trade unions do have the power to drive up wages in some industries, their power has been reduced, not only through government intervention, but also through more flexibility in labour markets and globalisation. This means that firms are facing intense competition from rivals in emerging economies, such as China and India, and hence they sometimes cannot afford to match the pay demands of the trade unions. Furthermore, they can use labour from other countries if domestic labour is too expensive.

Although minimum wages push the wage rate above the equilibrium, evidence from the UK suggests that the rate has not been high enough to have a significant adverse effect on employment.

Demand-deficient unemployment

Demand-deficient unemployment is associated with economic recessions or slowdowns. Many countries experienced a rise in unemployment in the recession of 2008/9 and the recession/slowdown of 2011/12.

As the economy moves into recession, consumer demand falls. Firms find that they are unable to sell their current level of output. For a time they may be prepared to build up stocks of unsold goods, but sooner or later they will start to cut back on production and cut back on the amount of labour they employ. In Figure 10.9 the AD_L curve shifts to the left. With real wages being 'sticky' downwards, the aggregate demand for labour is now less than the aggregate supply. Disequilibrium unemployment occurs. The deeper the recession becomes and the longer it lasts, the higher will demand-deficient unemployment become.

As the economy recovers and begins to grow again, so demand-deficient unemployment will start to fall. As this type of unemployment varies across the business cycle, it is frequently referred to as 'cyclical unemployment'. Figure 10.11 shows the fluctuations in unemployment in various industrial economies. If you compare this figure with Figure 10.7 on page 272, you can see how unemployment tends to rise in recessions/slowdowns and fall in booms.

Definitions

Underemployment Where people would like to work more hours than they currently do – e.g. where part-time workers would like to work full time or more part-time hours.

Real-wage unemployment Disequilibrium unemployment caused by real wages being driven up above the market-clearing level.

Demand-deficient (or cyclical) unemployment Disequilibrium unemployment caused by a fall in aggregate demand with no corresponding fall in the real wage rate.

---

[6] Greg Jericho, 'Underemployment is growing and there is no easy policy fix', *The Guardian* (13 August 2018).

| Figure 10.11 | Standardised unemployment rates in selected industrial economies |

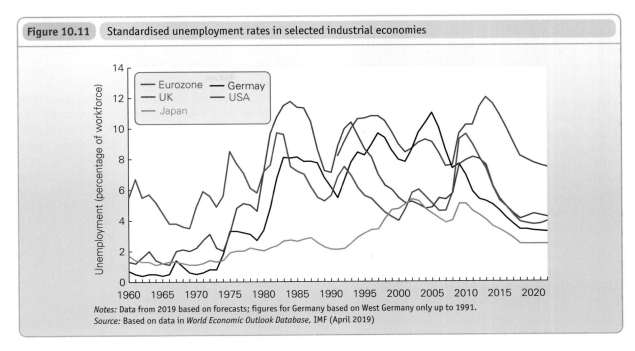

Notes: Data from 2019 based on forecasts; figures for Germany based on West Germany only up to 1991.
Source: Based on data in *World Economic Outlook Database,* IMF (April 2019)

Equilibrium unemployment

Looking at Figure 10.11, you can see how unemployment was higher in the 1980s and 1990s than in the 1970s. Much of the reason for this was the growth in equilibrium unemployment. Similarly, the lower unemployment in the early and mid-2000s across many developed nations (with the exception of Japan) was largely the result of a fall in equilibrium unemployment. This has been partly caused by greater labour mobility associated with more flexible labour markets, as we discussed in Chapter 8.

Although there may be overall *macro*economic equilibrium, with the *aggregate* demand for labour equal to the *aggregate* supply, and thus no disequilibrium unemployment, at a *micro*economic level supply and demand may not match. In other words, there may be vacancies in some parts of the economy, but an excess of labour (unemployment) in others. This is equilibrium unemployment. There are various types of equilibrium unemployment.

Frictional (search) unemployment
Frictional unemployment occurs when people leave their jobs, either voluntarily or because they are sacked or made redundant, and are then unemployed for a period of time while they are looking for a new job. They may not get the first job they apply for, despite a vacancy existing. The employer may continue searching, hoping to find a better qualified person. Likewise, unemployed people may choose not to take the first job they are offered. Instead they may continue searching, hoping that a better one will turn up.

The problem is that information is imperfect. Employers are not fully informed about what labour is available; workers are not fully informed about what jobs are available and what they entail. Both employers and workers, therefore, have to search: employers search for the right labour and workers search for the right jobs. The search process has been aided by the development of the Internet and online recruitment agencies, as discussed in Chapter 8, particularly in Box 8.1.

Structural unemployment
Structural unemployment occurs when the structure of the economy changes. Employment in some industries may expand while in others it contracts. There are two main reasons for this:

A change in the pattern of demand. Some industries experience declining demand. This may be due to a change in consumer tastes. Certain goods may go out of fashion. Or it may be due to competition from other industries. For example, consumer demand may shift away from coal and to other fuels. This will lead to structural unemployment in mining areas.

A change in the methods of production (technological unemployment). New techniques of production often allow the same level of output to be produced with fewer workers. This is known as 'labour-saving technical progress'. Unless output expands sufficiently to absorb the surplus labour, people will be made redundant. This creates *technological unemployment*. An example is the job losses in the banking industry caused by the increase in the number of cash machines and by the development of telephone and Internet banking. This is discussed in the blog, *Job losses and labour mobility*, on the Sloman Economics News site. There have also been job losses within the Royal Mail, due to the new modern and efficient technologies being used in sorting offices. You can read about concerns of technological unemployment in the blog, *The rise of the machines*.

Pause for thought

Why is structural unemployment sometimes referred to as 'mismatch unemployment'?

Structural unemployment often occurs in particular regions of the country. When it does, it is referred to as *regional unemployment*. This is most likely to occur when particular industries are concentrated in particular areas. For example, the decline in the South Wales coal mining industry led to high unemployment in the Welsh valleys and more recently, the decline in the steel industry in the UK brought substantial unemployment to former 'steel towns', such Redcar in Teesside.

Seasonal unemployment

Seasonal unemployment occurs when the demand for certain types of labour fluctuates with the seasons of the year. This problem is particularly severe in holiday areas such as Cornwall, where unemployment can reach very high levels in the winter months.

Definitions

Technological unemployment Structural unemployment that occurs as a result of the introduction of labour-saving technology.

Regional unemployment Structural unemployment occurring in specific regions of the country.

Seasonal unemployment Unemployment associated with industries or regions where the demand for labour is lower at certain times of the year.

RECAP

1. The two most common measures of unemployment are claimant unemployment (those claiming unemployment-related benefits) and ILO/OECD standardised unemployment (those available for work and actively seeking work or waiting to take up an appointment).

2. Unemployment can be divided into disequilibrium and equilibrium unemployment.

3. Disequilibrium unemployment occurs when the average real wage rate is above the level that will equate the aggregate demand and supply of labour. It can be caused by unions or government pushing up wages (real-wage unemployment) or by a fall in aggregate

demand but a downward 'stickiness' in real wages (demand-deficient or cyclical unemployment).

4. Equilibrium unemployment occurs when there are people unable or unwilling to fill job vacancies. This may be due to poor information in the labour market and hence a time lag before people find suitable jobs (frictional unemployment), to a changing pattern of demand or supply in the economy and hence a mismatching of labour with jobs (structural unemployment – specific types being technological and regional unemployment), or to seasonal fluctuations in the demand for labour.

10.7 INFLATION

Inflation refers to rising price levels, while deflation[7] refers to falling price levels. The rate of inflation measures the annual percentage increase in prices. If

the rate of inflation is negative, then prices are falling and we are measuring the rate of deflation.

The most commonly used measure of inflation is that of *consumer* prices. The UK government publishes a consumer prices index (CPI) each month, and the rate of inflation is the percentage increase in that index over the previous 12 months. Figure 10.12

---

[7] Sometimes a situation of falling prices is referred to as 'negative inflation'. Deflation can also refer to a policy of contracting aggregate demand so as to slow down an economy that is expanding at an unsustainably fast rate and/or with inflation above the target rate.

shows the rates of inflation for various industrial economies from 1970 to 2020. As you can see, inflation was particularly severe between 1973 and 1983, and relatively low in the mid-1980s. In the case of Japan, it experienced a prolonged period of deflation in the 2000s and the early 2010s.

The distinction between real and nominal values. Nominal figures are those using current prices, interest rates, etc. Real figures are figures corrected for inflation.

> **Pause for thought**
>
> *What long-term economic benefits might deflation generate for business and the economy in general?*

Before we proceed, a word of caution: be careful not to confuse a rise or fall in *inflation* with a rise or fall in *prices*. A rise in inflation means a *faster* increase in prices. A fall in inflation means a *slower* increase in prices (but still an increase so long as inflation is positive).

Rates of inflation are also given for the prices of other goods and services. For example, indices are published for commodity prices, food prices, house prices, import prices, prices after taking taxes into account, wages and so on. Their respective rates of inflation are simply their annual percentage increase. Countries also publish a 'GDP deflator'. This is the price index for GDP as a whole, set at 100 in a selected base year. Inflation is sometimes measured as the annual percentage increase in the GDP deflator.

When there is inflation, we have to be careful in assessing how much national output, consumption, wages, etc. are increasing. Take the case of GDP. GDP in year 2 may seem higher than in year 1, but this may be partly (or even wholly) the result of higher prices. Thus GDP in money terms may have risen by 5 per cent, but if inflation is 3 per cent (i.e. the GDP deflator has risen by 3 per cent), *real growth in GDP* will be only 2 per cent. In other words, the volume of output will be only 2 per cent higher.

Causes of inflation

We can use our model of aggregate demand (*AD*) and aggregate supply (*AS*) (see Figure 10.3 on page 265) to consider the causes of inflation and the side effects that can occur.

Demand-pull inflation
When the *AD* curve shifts to the right, output will rise and unemployment may fall as a result. However, at the same time, prices will rise. *Demand-pull inflation*

> **Definitions**
>
> **Real growth values** Values of the rate of growth in GDP or any other variable after taking inflation into account. The real value of the growth in a variable equals its growth in money (or 'nominal') value minus the rate of inflation.
>
> **Demand-pull inflation** Inflation caused by persistent rises in aggregate demand.

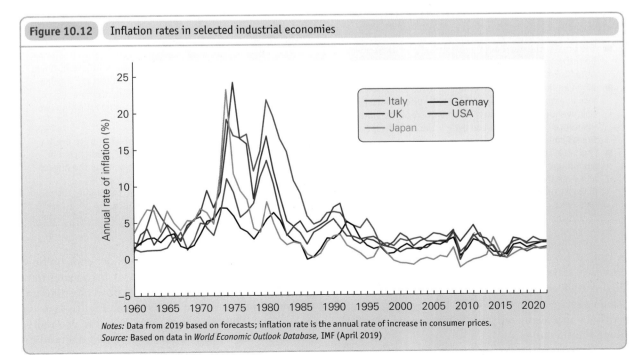

Figure 10.12 Inflation rates in selected industrial economies

Notes: Data from 2019 based on forecasts; inflation rate is the annual rate of increase in consumer prices.
Source: Based on data in *World Economic Outlook Database,* IMF (April 2019)

BOX 10.4 INFLATION AND UNEMPLOYMENT: HOW COSTLY?

Do they really matter?

Unemployment and inflation are two key macroeconomic objectives and governments across the world place great importance on managing them. Indeed, the primary objective of many central banks is to keep inflation at a target rate: 2 per cent in the USA and the UK (± 1 percentage point for the UK) and 'below 2 per cent but close to it over the medium term' in the eurozone.

When inflation rises (or falls) outside of its target or upper/lower bounds or when unemployment begins to creep up, newspaper headlines feed off these unfavourable trends; the opposition party questions the government's policies and business confidence and expectations begin to decline. So, why are rising rates of unemployment and inflation so costly and who suffers?

Unemployment

The most obvious cost of unemployment is to the individual. Anyone who is unemployed will suffer a financial cost through lost earnings, which is measured as the difference between their previous wages and the unemployment benefits they receive. For many, there is an additional cost of unemployment that is non-monetary. If people become unemployed and find it difficult to get another job, they may lose confidence in their abilities; their self-esteem is likely to fall; and they are much more likely to succumb to stress-related illness.

In addition, unemployment will also impose costs on friends and family. If the unemployed individual was the only bread-winner in the household then an entire family could be pushed into poverty. Unemployment may also put a strain on personal relationships and evidence suggests that it can also lead to an increase in domestic violence and the separation of families.

While many aspects of the above two effects are non-monetary, there are numerous financial costs to the wider economy.

- The greater the number of unemployed, the greater will be the government's expenditure on unemployment and other out-of-work benefits.
- When an individual becomes unemployed and suffers a loss in earnings, the government will suffer from a loss in tax revenue, through lower income tax receipts, national insurance contributions and even lower VAT receipts, due to less consumer expenditure.
- High rates of unemployment will require extra public spending on benefit offices, social services, health care and even the police. These first three effects therefore place a greater burden on the government and the taxpayer.

- Unemployment represents a loss of output, as the economy is operating below its maximum potential. Resources are wasted and thus the economy is inefficient.
- The individual's loss in income will also affect other people. As an individual's income falls, their demand for goods and services will also tend to decline. Thus, they spend less money, so firms sell fewer goods. Profits may then decline and so could tax receipts. If the decline in sales is severe, workers may face a cut in pay (or smaller wage increases) or even lose their jobs. We described this type of unemployment as demand-deficient unemployment. The knock-on effects of operating below full employment can therefore be severe.
- The costs of long-term unemployment can be extremely high to both the individual and the economy. A lack of self-esteem and confidence in your ability is likely to become worse the longer you are unemployed. In severe cases, it can lead to health problems, which pose an additional cost to the government, through expenditure on healthcare. The longer an individual is without work, the more likely it is that they will lose their skills and thus become less suitable for new jobs. Alternatively, if they re-enter employment they are likely to require retraining and this could be a costly expenditure for a firm, which may deter the firm from hiring that worker.

Long-term involuntary unemployment is a big economic and social problem, as demotivated and unskilled workers are a drain on a country's resources. Keeping unemployment down and helping people back to work is therefore a key government policy. And it is not just to relieve the strain on the economy, but to provide help to the affected families, motivate the individuals and ensure that when a job does become available, the individual's skills are still there.

Inflation

The costs of inflation vary and depend crucially on whether or not people can correctly anticipate the rate of inflation. If we can correctly anticipate it and fully adjust prices and incomes to take it into account, then the costs of inflation are relatively small and are largely confined to the following two costs:

- Consumers have to adjust their idea of a fair price every time the inflation rate changes. The opportunity cost in terms of the time and energy taken to counter the effects of inflation are known as *shoe leather costs*.
- Firms need to adjust their price labels, catalogues, menus, etc. These costs are known as *menu costs*.

is caused by continuing rightward shifts of the *AD* curve, as shown in Figure 10.13 (which is similar to Figure 10.4 on page 267). Firms will respond to the rise in aggregate demand partly by raising prices and partly by increasing output (there is a move upwards along the *AS* curve).

Just how much they raise prices depends on how much their costs rise as a result of increasing output. This in turn depends upon how close actual output is to the output ceiling (see Figure 10.6 on page 271). The less slack there is in the economy, the more will firms respond to a rise in demand by

However, people frequently make mistakes when predicting the rate of inflation and do not fully take it into account. The higher the rate of inflation, the more of a problem this becomes, as higher rates of inflation tend to be more volatile. This then leads to further problems.

- With high rates of inflation, domestically produced goods become relatively more expensive compared with those from abroad. Thus the country's exports become less competitive and we would expect to see a fall in their demand. At the same time, foreign goods become relatively cheaper and thus more imports are demanded. These two forces together will worsen the country's balance of payments. In response, the exchange rate must fall or interest rates must rise, which can lead to further problems, as discussed in Chapter 13.
- Inflation can adversely affect the distribution of income by redistributing income away from those in the weakest bargaining positions and on fixed incomes towards those with the economic power to demand higher pay rates.
- Some assets, such as property, rise in value with inflation and so high rates of inflation will also redistribute wealth to those with these assets and away from those with money in savings accounts that pay an interest rate below the rate of inflation.
- As inflation rises, it typically fluctuates more and this creates uncertainty, which can be particularly costly for businesses. Firms find it more difficult to predict their own costs and revenues and those of their competitors. This may act to reduce their incentive to invest. If investment falls, then this might reduce aggregate demand and hence the rate of economic growth.
- More resources will typically be needed, such as accountants and financial experts to help firms deal with the uncertainties created by high inflation.

If the increases in the price level enter the hundreds or thousands of per cent per year, this is known as *hyperinflation*. In such circumstances, the costs of inflation will increase significantly. As prices rise, workers will demand higher wage rates and as these push up costs of production, and so workers will demand even higher wages to maintain their standard of living. A 'wage-price spiral' can develop.

In extreme cases, people stop saving and instead spend money as fast as possible or even stop using money as a means of exchange. Hyperinflation has occurred in various countries, including Germany in the early 1920s, Hungary in 1946, Serbia and Montenegro in 1992–4 and in Zimbabwe between 2005 and 2008, where inflation peaked at an estimated 6.5 quindecillion novemdecillion percent – 65 followed by 107 zeros! (See Case Study D12 on the student website and the blogs on the Sloman Economic News site, *A remnant of hyperinflation in Zimbabwe* and *Who wants to be a millionaire?*) More recently, Venezuela has been suffering from hyperinflation and a collapse in the economy. In January 2019, the rate of inflation reached nearly 2.7 million per cent.

Everything in moderation

Some unemployment, especially equilibrium unemployment, is generally considered to be a good thing. It means that if demand rises, there are spare resources to meet this demand. Furthermore, if workers voluntarily leave their job to find a new one, then it is reasonable to assume that the benefits of the new job will compensate for this temporary loss of income. Such a workforce is likely to lead to greater allocative efficiency and a more flexible labour market that will be more responsive to changing economic circumstances. This therefore benefits the wider economy.

It is a similar story with inflation. The target rate is 2 per cent, but when inflation falls below 1 per cent, there is just as much as concern as there is when it rises above 3 per cent. Thus, 0 per cent inflation is not necessarily a good thing. The reason is that modest inflation allows relative wages and prices to change more easily to reflect changes in demand and supply. For example, given that many employers would find it difficult to cut nominal wage rates, by leaving them unchanged, *real* wages will fall by the rate of inflation. In other words, the purchasing power of a given wage rate will be eroded by the rate of inflation.

Deflation can be catastrophic for an economy. People will be reluctant to spend, believing that, if they wait, goods will become cheaper. The result can be declining sales and profits, and rising unemployment and bankruptcy rates. Indeed, the Japanese economy was paralysed for over a decade by deflation, as discussed in the Sloman Economics News site blogs, *Japan's interesting monetary stance as deflation fears grow* and *Japan's deflation fears grow (update)*.

Therefore, inflation and unemployment are not necessarily bad, as long as they are kept at manageable levels. With both of these objectives, as with many things, moderation is the key.

1. *If you were in government, would you ever advocate zero unemployment?*
2. *Who are likely to be the winners and losers from inflation?*

Draw up a list of those who are most likely to gain and those who are most likely to lose from inflation.

raising their prices (the steeper will be the *AS* curve).

Demand-pull inflation is typically associated with a booming economy. Many economists therefore argue that it is the counterpart of demand-deficient (cyclical) unemployment. When the economy is in recession, demand-deficient unemployment will be high, but demand-pull inflation will be low. When, on the other hand, the economy is near the peak of the business cycle, demand-pull inflation will be high, but demand-deficient unemployment will be low.

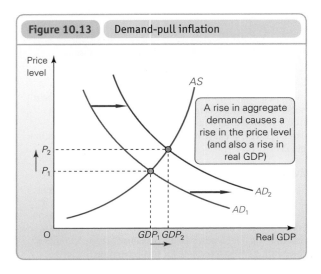

Figure 10.13 Demand-pull inflation

A rise in aggregate demand causes a rise in the price level (and also a rise in real GDP)

Cost-push inflation

Cost-push inflation is associated with continuing rises in costs and hence continuing upward (leftward) shifts in the *AS* curve (see Figure 10.14). If firms face a rise in costs, they will respond partly by raising prices and passing the costs on to the consumer, and partly by cutting back on production (there is a movement back along the *AD* curve).

Just how much firms raise prices and cut back on production depends on the shape of the aggregate demand curve. The less elastic the *AD* curve – in other words, the less consumers, firms and the government are prepared to cut back on real expenditure – the less sales will fall as a result of any price rise, and hence the more will firms be able to pass on the rise in their costs to consumers as higher prices.

The rise in costs may originate from a number of different sources, such as higher wages as a result of trade unions pushing up wages independently of the

demand for labour, firms using their monopoly power to make bigger profits by pushing up prices independently of consumer demand, or import prices rising independently of the level of aggregate demand (e.g. OPEC putting up oil prices).

In all these cases, inflation occurs because one or more groups are exercising economic power. The problem is likely to get worse, therefore, if there is an increasing concentration of economic power over time (e.g. if firms or unions get bigger and bigger, and more monopolistic) or if groups become more militant.

Another cause of cost-push inflation is rising prices of various commodities – not just oil, but copper, aluminium, iron ore and other minerals – and also agricultural prices. The process of globalisation has helped to keep these cost-push pressures down, but with the growth in demand for raw materials and food from China and other rapidly developing economies, such as India and Brazil, the price of various commodities, especially oil, has become a problem. For example, the near tripling of oil prices from $51 per barrel in January 2007 to over $140 per barrel in July 2008 and then again from $41 a barrel in January 2009 to $126 per barrel in May 2011 (see Box 2.4) put upward pressure on costs and prices globally. (For more recent examples of oil price movements and their effects on the economy see the blogs, *OPEC deal pushes up oil prices, Rising oil prices – winners and losers* and *Oil prices: the ups and the downs,* on the Sloman Economics News site.)

Thus, what starts with a rise in aggregate demand in these countries (demand-pull inflation), becomes cost-push inflation for other countries having to pay higher prices for the commodities they import.

Demand-pull and cost-push inflation together

Demand-pull and cost-push inflation can occur together, since wage and price rises can be caused both by increases in aggregate demand and by independent causes pushing up costs. Even when an inflationary process *starts* as either demand-pull or cost-push, it is often difficult to separate the two.

An initial cost-push inflation may encourage the government to expand aggregate demand to offset rises in unemployment. Alternatively, an initial demand-pull inflation may strengthen the power of

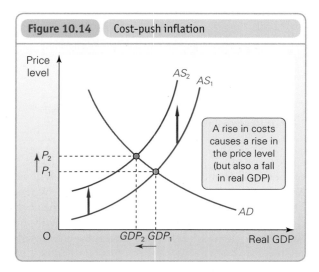

Figure 10.14 Cost-push inflation

A rise in costs causes a rise in the price level (but also a fall in real GDP)

Definition

Cost-push inflation Inflation caused by persistent rises in costs of production (independently of demand).

certain groups, who then use this power to drive up costs. Either way, the result is likely to be continuing rightward shifts in the *AD* curve and upward shifts in the *AS* curve. Prices will carry on rising.

Expectations and inflation

Workers and firms take account of the *expected* rate of inflation when making decisions.

Imagine that a union and an employer are negotiating a wage increase. Let us assume that both sides expect a rate of inflation of 5 per cent. The union will be happy to receive a wage rise somewhat above 5 per cent. That way the members would be getting a *real* rise in incomes. The employers will be happy to pay a wage rise somewhat below 5 per cent. After all, they can put their price up by 5 per cent, knowing that their rivals will do approximately the same. The actual wage rise that the two sides agree on will thus be somewhere around 5 per cent.

Now let us assume that the expected rate of inflation is 10 per cent. Both sides will now negotiate around this benchmark, with the outcome being somewhere round about 10 per cent.

Thus the higher the expected rate of inflation, the higher will be the level of pay settlements and price rises, and hence the higher will be the resulting actual rate of inflation.

In recent years the importance of expectations in explaining the actual rate of inflation has been increasingly recognised by economists, and it has prompted them to discover just what determines people's expectations.

Pause for thought

How might the announcements of policy makers affect people's expectations of inflation?

BOX 10.5 AIRLINES AND THE MACROECONOMY

We have already considered the airline industry from a microeconomic perspective and we now consider how it will be affected by macroeconomic changes. But before we consider the airline industry, it is important to understand how the macroeconomic issues change as we move through the different phases of the business cycle.

The business cycle and macroeconomic issues

Fluctuations in aggregate demand will not only result in fluctuations in output, but also in other key macroeconomic variables. This is because in the short term (up to about two years) they are likely to be dependent on aggregate demand and so vary with the course of the business cycle.

In the expansionary phase of the business cycle (phase 2), aggregate demand grows rapidly. There will be relatively rapid growth in output and (demand-deficient) unemployment will fall. It is likely that household incomes will be rising. However, the growing shortages lead to higher (demand-pull) inflation and a deteriorating balance of payments as the extra demand 'sucks in' more imports and as higher prices make domestic goods less competitive internationally.

At the peak of the cycle (phase 3), unemployment is probably at its lowest and output at its highest (for the time being). However, growth has already ceased or at least slowed down. Inflation and balance of payments problems are probably acute and so, despite household incomes probably being at their highest in real terms, inflation is likely to result in continued increases in household expenditure in nominal (money) terms.

As the economy moves into phase 4 (let us assume that this is an actual recession with falling output), the reverse will happen to that of phase 2. Falling aggregate demand will make growth negative and unemployment higher, and household incomes are likely to fall. But inflation is likely to slow down and the balance of payments will improve. These two improvements may take some time to occur, however.

1. *Using an AD/AS diagram, show what happens when the economy moves into recession. How can you use the diagram to explain the impact on the macroeconomic issues of growth, unemployment and inflation, as the economy moves through the phases of the business cycle?*

The macroeconomic impact on airlines

There is a huge variety of holidays available to households, varying in terms of cost, location and mode of transport, but for many people a holiday means air travel. Add to that the large number of business flights, both domestic and international, and it is hardly surprising that International Air Transport Association (IATA) expected that 1 per cent of world GDP (or $919 billion) would be spent on air travel in 2019.

During periods of growth, household incomes tend to rise, perhaps due to wages rising, or more people being employed. With higher incomes, we are likely to see a higher demand for air travel, as more families go on holiday or choose to go to more exotic locations, and as business activity increases. Passenger numbers are therefore likely to rise during times of economic expansion or booms.

This means that an airline's revenues are likely to increase, though there will be differences for airlines depending on the flights they offer: e.g. short-haul versus long-haul. However, during periods of growth and expansion, inflationary pressures can emerge and we often see oil prices rising during times of boom. As oil is a key input for airlines, this can mean that there is a significant impact on costs. Therefore, despite growth in revenues, higher costs mean there is an uncertain impact on airline profits.

▶

During times of a recession or downturn, household incomes fall. People are likely cut back on some things, particularly the more luxury items such as foreign holidays, which have a high income elasticity of demand. Business travel too is likely to fall. The decline in passenger numbers is likely to reduce airlines' revenue and profit. However, it may also be the case that inflationary pressures are lower and hence falling fuel costs might give airlines some breathing space.

Data on passenger numbers, revenue and profit

The chart shows the number of passengers using air transport from 1996 to 2017. It looks at the percentage change from one year to the next for a range of countries and the eurozone.

While the different specific macroeconomic circumstances in each country mean that the demand for air travel from national airlines varies, we can identify some global patterns. These include a large fall in passenger demand during the financial crisis, when household incomes globally were squeezed particularly badly. IATA data finds that in 2009, airline revenues fell by 14 per cent (or $82 billion). The financial crisis was particularly interesting as, despite the recession, oil prices were actually rising. This combination of factors pushed US airlines into losses of $26.4 billion in 2008–9. But then, as the global economy recovered, so did demand for air travel worldwide.

According to IATA, stronger global growth in 2018 meant that passenger demand grew faster than the growth in airline capacity. But fuel costs have also been growing, with airlines' annual fuel bill expected to have risen to $200 billion by 2019, representing 24.2 per cent of average operating costs (up from 21.4 per cent in 2017).[1]

The higher fuel costs have also led to more airlines retiring older aircraft and hence orders for new aircraft are up. With stronger growth and unemployment at record low levels, unit labour costs have also risen significantly. When unemployment is low and the economy is growing, firms want to take on more workers to meet the higher demand. However, the lack of unemployed workers means that, in order to attract workers, firms have to offer higher wages and may sometimes use that tactic to poach workers from other firms. In 2019, unit labour costs were expected to have increased by an average of 2.1 per cent. Therefore, despite higher economic growth leading to increased passenger numbers, the wage and price effects of inflation are likely to squeeze airline profits.[2]

The effects of macroeconomic policy changes

Another key factor that affects airlines is macroeconomic policy, whether it be through taxes, interest rates or investment in infrastructure (we consider this in Chapter 11).

Airlines are a cause of both air and noise pollution and so governments impose taxes on airlines to internalise the externalities that are created (see page 233). As interest rates change, borrowing costs for households and firms are affected and so not only does this affect the saving and consumption decisions of households, it also affects the costs to airlines in terms of borrowing on financial markets and servicing any debts.

Another key macroeconomics factor to consider is the exchange rate, which we cover in more detail in Chapter 13. For many airlines, the currency in which their revenues are earned will be different from the currency in which their costs are incurred. Fuel is priced in dollars and so airlines based outside the USA must purchase dollars on the foreign exchange market in order to buy a given quantity of fuel. This means that as the exchange rate between the domestic currency and dollars changes, so does the cost of buying the fuel. Any significant change in the exchange rate can therefore have a positive or negative effect on profits.

One interesting example here is UK-based airlines and the impact on them of Brexit. When the UK voted to leave the EU in June 2016, the pound began to depreciate in value. This meant that British airlines had to spend more pounds to get

---

[1] *Economic Performance of Airline Industry,* IATA (12 December 2018).

[2] Ibid.

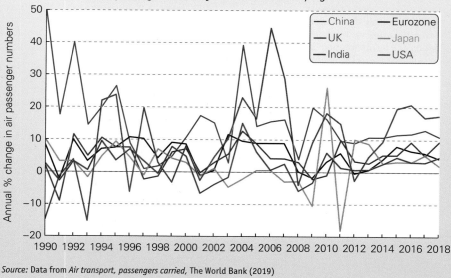

Air passenger numbers for selected countries/regions

Legend: China, Eurozone, UK, Japan, India, USA

(Y-axis: Annual % change in air passenger numbers, ranging from −20 to 50. X-axis: years 1990 to 2018)

Source: Data from *Air transport, passengers carried,* The World Bank (2019)

the necessary dollars to buy a given quantity of fuel. The higher cost of fuel, together with various other costs that are also priced in dollars, such as aircraft leases, pushed up these airlines' costs and meant profits were hit. Monarch's costs rose by £50 million, while easyJet saw the fall in the pound push up its costs by £90 million. This was one of the key factors that led to the demise of Monarch and later of Flybmi.

The World Trade Center

Airlines are also affected by random shocks, such as health epidemics and particularly terrorist attacks. In the aftermath of the September 11th 2001 terrorist attack on the World Trade Center, airlines took a significant hit, with a $22 billion (or 6 per cent) fall in annual revenue, from which they took three years to recover. Understandably, the US market saw the biggest impact, with the number of flights being handled by US airports falling from 38 047 commercial on September 10th 2001 to just 252 on September 12th 2001. Passenger traffic declined by 5.9 per cent for the remainder of 2001 and a further 1.4 per cent in 2002, relative to 2000. It was not until 2004 that the airline industry in the USA really began to recover. However, Barclays Capital, noted that: 'The events of 9.11. . . marked a permanent decline in [US] domestic airline demand.'

An IATA report notes that:

Total domestic operating revenue per $100 of nominal US GDP declined from around $0.823 in 2000 to $0.687 in 2010, representing a shortfall of $18 billion for 2010 and $142 billion for the 2001–10 period. US airline revenues fell from $130.2 billion in 2000 to $107.1 billion in 2002.

Losses of $19.6 billion were reported in 2001–2. Losses for 2001–5 totalled $57.7 billion.'[3]

Airlines operate in a global world and hence they are affected by a huge range of macroeconomic factors. Not only does the stability of the domestic economy affect their performance, but they are also impacted by the state of the economy in the countries to which they fly. They are very susceptible to changes in national income and to the rate of economic growth and their profits tend to exhibit a cyclical pattern that mirrors the business cycle. There is therefore a great deal of macroeconomic uncertainty, which airlines must factor into their business planning.

2. *When the economy is growing, why might airlines experience both positive and negative effects on their profits?*
3. *Research a country of your choice and look at the general trends in its macroeconomic data, particularly looking at economic growth, unemployment and inflation since 2000. What has happened to passenger numbers and the profits of the airline industry in that country? Do these data correspond with the macroeconomic trends? Explain your answer.*

Research current passenger numbers for various airlines over the past three years. Explain any changes over these three years. To what extent were the causes of these changes macroeconomic?

[3] *The Impact of September 11 2001 on Aviation'* (IATA, 2010).

RECAP

1. Inflation is the annual percentage increase in prices.
2. Demand-pull inflation occurs as a result of increases in aggregate demand. It is typically associated with a booming economy.
3. Cost-push inflation occurs when there are increases in

the costs of production independent of rises in aggregate demand.
4. Expectations play a crucial role in determining the rate of inflation. The higher people expect inflation to be, the higher it will be.

QUESTIONS

1. What are the key macroeconomic objectives of government? Are there likely to be any conflicts between them?
2. The following table shows index numbers for real GDP (national output) for various countries ($2010 = 100$).

Using the formula $G = (GDP_t - GDP_{t-1})/GDP_{t-1} \times 100$ (where G is the rate of growth, GDP is the index number of output, t is any given year and $t - 1$ is the previous year):

	2010	2011	2012	2013	2014	2015	2016	2017	2018
USA	100.0	101.6	103.9	105.6	108.3	111.4	113.1	115.6	119.0
Japan	100.0	99.9	101.4	1032.4	103.8	105.2	106.2	108.0	109.4
Eurozone	100.0	101.6	100.7	100.5	101.8	103.9	105.8	108.3	110.8
UK	100.0	101.5	103.0	105.1	108.3	110.8	113.0	115.0	116.8

Source: AMECO database (European Commission, DGECFIN)

(a) Work out the growth rate (*G*), for each country for each year from 2011 to 2018.

(b) Plot the figures on a graph. Describe the pattern that emerges.

3. In terms of the UK circular flow of income, are the following net injections, net withdrawals or neither? If there is uncertainty, explain your assumptions.

(a) Firms are forced to take a cut in profits in order to give a pay rise.

(b) Firms spend money on research.

(c) The government increases personal tax allowances.

(d) The general public invests more money in building societies.

(e) UK investors earn higher dividends on overseas investments.

(f) The government purchases US military aircraft.

(g) People draw on their savings to finance holidays abroad.

(h) People draw on their savings to finance holidays in the UK.

(i) The government runs a budget deficit (spends more than it receives in tax revenues).

4. Give some examples of events that could shift (a) the *AD* curve to the left; (b) the *AS* curve to the left.

5. Assume that the multiplier has a value of 3. Now assume that the government decides to increase aggregate demand in an attempt to reduce unemployment. It raises government expenditure by £100 million with no increase in taxes. Firms, anticipating a rise in their sales, increase investment by £200 million, of which £50 million consists of purchases of foreign machinery. By how much will GDP rise? (Assume that nothing else changes.)

6. What factors could explain why some countries have a higher multiplier than others?

7. At what point of the business cycle is the country now? What do you predict will happen to growth over the next two years? On what basis do you make your prediction?

8. Why does a booming economy not carry on booming indefinitely? Why does an economy in recession pull out of that recession?

9. For what possible reasons may one country experience a persistently faster rate of economic growth than another?

10. Imagine that the banking system receives additional deposits of £100 million and that all the individual banks wish to retain their current liquidity ratio of 20 per cent.

(a) How much will banks choose to lend out initially?

(b) What will happen to banks' deposits when the money that is lent out is spent and the recipients of it deposit it in their bank accounts?

(c) How much of these latest deposits will be lent out by the banks?

(d) By how much will total deposits (liabilities) eventually have risen, assuming that none of the additional liquidity is held outside the banking sector?

(e) What is the size of the deposits multiplier?

11. What effects will the following have on the equilibrium rate of interest? (You should consider which way the demand and/or supply curves of money shift.)

(a) Banks find that they have a higher liquidity ratio than they need.

(b) A rise in incomes.

(c) A growing belief that interest rates will rise from their current level.

12. Would it be desirable to have zero unemployment?

13. Consider the most appropriate policy for tackling each of the different types of unemployment.

14. Under what circumstances will a reduction in unemployment be accompanied by (a) an increase in inflation; (b) a decrease in inflation? Explain your answer.

15. Do you personally gain or lose from inflation? Explain.

16. Imagine that you had to determine whether a particular period of inflation was demand-pull, or cost-push, or a combination of the two. What information would you require in order to conduct your analysis?

Chapter 11

National macroeconomic policy

Business issues covered in this chapter

- What sorts of government macroeconomic policy are available to government and how will they affect business activity?
- What will be the impact on the economy and business of various fiscal policy measures?
- What determines the effectiveness of fiscal policy in smoothing out fluctuations in the economy?
- What fiscal rules are adopted by different governments and is following them always a good idea?
- What is the impact on the economy of monetary policy?
- How does monetary policy work and what are the roles of central banks, such as the Bank of England, the Federal Reserve and European Central Bank (ECB)?
- How does targeting inflation influence interest rates and hence business activity?
- Are there better rules for determining interest rates other than sticking to a simple inflation target?
- How can supply-side policy influence business and the economy?
- What types of supply-side policies can be pursued and what is their effectiveness?

A key influence on the macroeconomic environment of business is the government. Governments aim to achieve macroeconomic stability, which involves sustained and stable economic growth, low unemployment, low and stable inflation and stable financial institutions. Governments also seek to achieve faster but sustainable growth rates over the longer term. To achieve these objectives, various types of policy are used. This chapter looks at the three main categories of macroeconomic policy.

The first is *fiscal policy*. This is where the government uses the balance of taxation (a withdrawal from the circular flow of income) and government expenditure (an injection) to influence the level of aggregate demand. If the economy is in recession, the government could increase government expenditure and/or cut taxes. This is called expansionary fiscal policy and the effect would be a higher level of aggregate demand and hence a multiplied rise in GDP and lower unemployment. If the economy was expanding too rapidly in a way that was unsustainable and hence with rising inflation, the government could do the reverse by using deflationary (or contractionary) fiscal policy: it could cut government expenditure and/or raise taxes. This would help to slow down the economy and dampen inflation.

Definition

Fiscal policy Policy to affect aggregate demand by altering government expenditure and/or taxation.

The second type of policy is *monetary policy*. Here the government sets the framework of policy, which in many countries, including the UK, means setting a target for the rate of inflation. In the UK the rate is 2 per cent, as it is in the USA, and below 2 per cent but close to it over the medium term in the eurozone. The central bank is then charged with adjusting interest rates to keep inflation on target.

These first two types of policy are referred to as *demand-side* or *demand management policies* as they seek to control the level of aggregate demand.

The third category of policy is *supply-side policy*. This seeks to control aggregate supply directly. For example, the government might seek ways of encouraging greater productivity through increased research and development or better training programmes. Or it might seek to improve the country's transport and communications infrastructure, for example by investing in the railways or building more roads. By increasing aggregate supply, the economy's capacity to produce expands.

The difference between demand-side and supply-side policies is illustrated in Figures 11.1(a) and (b). Both diagrams show an aggregate demand and an aggregate supply curve.

Demand-side policy seeks to shift the *AD* curve. This is illustrated in Figure 11.1(a). An expansionary fiscal or monetary policy would shift the *AD* curve to the right, say from AD_1 to AD_2. This will increase GDP (to Y_2), thereby helping to reduce unemployment. On the other hand, it will result in higher prices: the price level will rise to P_2.

A contractionary fiscal or monetary policy would help to curb rightward shifts in the *AD* curve or even cause the curve to shift to the left. The policy could be used to tackle inflation, but it would run the risk of a reduction in the rate of growth of GDP, or even a recession, and higher unemployment.

Supply-side policy seeks to shift the *AS* curve to the right. If successful, it will lead to both higher GDP and employment and lower prices (or at least lower inflation). This is illustrated in Figure 11.1(b). A rightward shift in the aggregate supply curve from AS_1 to AS_2 results in a rise in GDP to Y_2 and a fall in the price level to P_2.

Definitions

Monetary policy Policy to affect aggregate demand by central bank action to alter interest rates or money supply.

Demand-side or demand management policy Policy to affect aggregate demand (i.e. fiscal or monetary policy).

Supply-side policy Policy to affect aggregate supply directly.

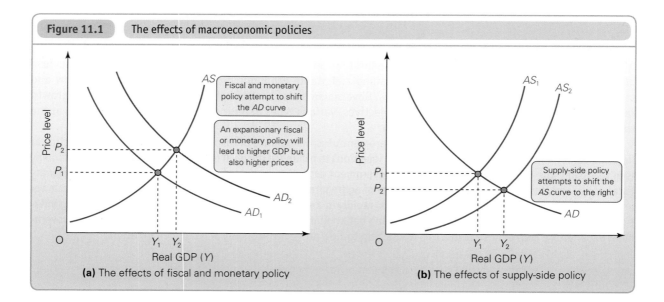

Figure 11.1   The effects of macroeconomic policies

Fiscal and monetary policy attempt to shift the *AD* curve

An expansionary fiscal or monetary policy will lead to higher GDP but also higher prices

Supply-side policy attempts to shift the *AS* curve to the right

(a) The effects of fiscal and monetary policy

(b) The effects of supply-side policy

11.1 FISCAL POLICY

Fiscal policy is a type of demand-management policy and involves the government changing the level of government expenditure and/or tax rates to achieve its broader macroeconomic objectives. We can therefore think about fiscal policy as performing two main functions:

- *To prevent the occurrence of fundamental disequilibrium in the economy.* In other words, expansionary fiscal policy could be used to prevent a severe recession. Such a situation occurred in the 1930s with the Great Depression and in 2008–9 as governments around the world adopted 'stimulus packages' by increasing government expenditure and cutting taxes to prevent an even deeper recession, as discussed in the blog *The World Economy* on the Sloman Economics News site. Likewise deflationary fiscal policy could be used to prevent excessive inflation, such as that experienced in many countries in the early 1970s.
- *To smooth out the fluctuations in the economy associated with the business cycle.* This would involve reducing government expenditure or raising taxes during a boom. This would dampen down the expansion and prevent 'overheating' of the economy, with its attendant rising inflation. Conversely, with a slowing economy, the government should cut taxes or raise government expenditure in order to boost economic growth and prevent a rise in unemployment. However, it is not always possible for expansionary policies to be used, especially if it is felt that the government has insufficient funds to finance them.
- If these stabilisation policies are successful, they will amount merely to *fine-tuning*. Problems of excess or deficient demand will never be allowed to get severe. Any movement of aggregate demand away from a steady growth path will be immediately 'nipped in the bud'.

One final use of fiscal policy is to influence the capacity of the economy. While fiscal policy is a demand-side policy, it can be used to influence aggregate supply. Government spending could be directed towards infrastructure, or tax incentives could be given to businesses to encourage investment or to promote research and development. In so doing, the government can positively affect an economy's potential output and thus shift aggregate supply to the right.

Public finances

Central government deficits and surpluses

Since an expansionary fiscal policy involves raising government expenditure and/or lowering taxes, this has the effect of either increasing the *budget deficit* or reducing the *budget surplus*. A budget deficit in any one year is where central government's expenditure exceeds its revenue from taxation. A budget surplus is where tax revenues exceed central government expenditure.

With the exception of short periods in 1969–70, 1987–90 and 1998–2001, governments in the UK, like most governments around the world, have run budget deficits. These deficits soared in the recession of 2008–9, with lower tax revenues, higher benefit payments and increased government expenditure. This is clearly evident for the USA in the blog, *Backing to the edge of the fiscal cliff* and from the series of blogs regarding eurozone debt: *Saving the eurozone? Saving the world? Parts A, B, C* and *D* all on the Sloman Economics News site.

Public-sector deficits and surpluses

To get a better view of the overall *stance of fiscal policy* – just how expansionary or contractionary it is – we need to look at the deficit or surplus of the entire public sector: namely, central government, local government and public corporations.

If the public sector spends more than it earns, it will have to finance the deficit through borrowing: known as *public-sector net borrowing (PSNB)*. For example, if the public sector runs a deficit in the current year of, say, £1 billion, then it will have to

Definitions

Fine-tuning The use of demand management policy (fiscal or monetary) to smooth out cyclical fluctuations in the economy.

Budget deficit The excess of central government's spending over its tax receipts.

Budget surplus The excess of central government's tax receipts over its spending.

Fiscal stance How expansionary or contractionary fiscal policy is.

Public-sector net borrowing The difference between the expenditures of the public sector and its receipts from taxation, the surpluses of public corporations and the sale of assets.

borrow £1 billion this year in order to finance it. The principal form of borrowing is through the sale of government bonds (sometimes known as gilt-edged securities or 'gilts').

Deficits are shown as positive figures (the government must borrow). They add to the accumulated debts from the past. The accumulated debts of central and local government are known as the *general government debt*. If the public sector runs a *surplus* (a negative PSNB), then this will be used to *reduce* the general government debt.

Table 11.1 shows general government deficits/surpluses and debt for selected countries, expressed as a proportion of GDP.

> ## Pause for thought
>
> *Why are historical and international comparisons of deficit and debt measures best presented as proportions of GDP?*

As you can see, in the period from 1995 to 2007, all the countries, with the exception of Ireland and Sweden, ran an average deficit. In the period from 2008 to 2020, the average deficits increased for most countries. And the bigger the deficit, the faster debt increased.

The business cycle and public finances. While government policy does affect public finances, they are also affected by the business cycle. If the economy is booming with people earning high incomes, the amount paid in taxes will be high. Also, in a booming economy the level of unemployment will be low and thus so too will be unemployment benefits. The combined effect of this is to reduce the public-sector deficit (or increase the surplus).

By contrast, if the economy is depressed, tax revenues will be low and the amount paid in benefits will be high. This will increase the public-sector deficit (or reduce the surplus).

In order to show just the direct effects of government policy on the deficit or surplus, we can remove the cyclical component. This gives with the cyclically adjusted public-sector net borrowing figure.

Attempts to cut public-sector deficits
In recent years, there has been a concerted effort by many governments to cut government borrowing and reduce the size of their budget deficits. Figure 11.2 shows the UK's PSNB as a percentage

> ## Definition
>
> **General government debt** The accumulated central and local government deficits (less surpluses) over the years, i.e. the total amount owed by central and local government, both to domestic and overseas creditors.

Table 11.1	General government deficits/surpluses and debt as a percentage of GDP			
	General government deficits (−) or surpluses (+)		General government debt	
	Average 1995–2007	Average 2008–2020	Average 1996–2007	Average 2008–2020
Belgium	−1.3	−2.6	106.1	102.1
France	−3.0	−4.0	61.8	91.6
Germany	−3.0	−0.1	60.9	69.4
Greece	−6.7	−5.8	102.4	163.5
Ireland	+1.2	−6.6	41.5	80.3
Italy	−3.6	−3.1	106.5	124.5
Japan	−5.7	−5.6	142.9	224.7
Netherlands	−1.5	−1.6	55.1	59.0
Portugal	−4.3	−4.7	58.6	114.5
Spain	−1.4	−6.0	52.9	83.7
Sweden	0.0	+0.2	55.3	39.5
UK	−2.0	−4.9	39.7	80.1
USA	−2.8	−7.1	62.0	100.6
Eurozone	−2.7	−2.7	69.1	86.7

Note: Data from 2018 are forecasts.
Source: Based on data from *AMECO database*, Tables 16.3 and 18.1 (European Commission, DG ECFIN)

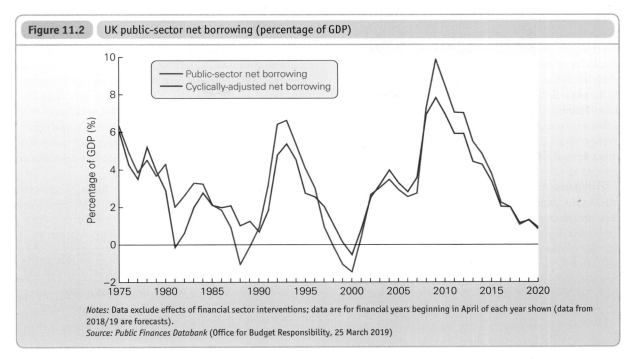

Figure 11.2 UK public-sector net borrowing (percentage of GDP)

Notes: Data exclude effects of financial sector interventions; data are for financial years beginning in April of each year shown (data from 2018/19 are forecasts).
Source: Public Finances Databank (Office for Budget Responsibility, 25 March 2019)

of GDP from 1960 to 2020, as well as the cyclically adjusted data. Note the huge increase in the PSNB in 2009 as tax revenues fell in the recession and as the government attempted to reduce the depth of the recession by increasing expenditure. By 2009/10 the PSNB had reached £155 billion or 10.3 per cent of GDP.

In subsequent years, the PSNB fell significantly, as tackling the UK's deficit was the number one economic priority of the Coalition government (2010–15) and the Conservative government (2015–). The government embarked on a series of spending cuts and tax rises, but with economic growth significantly lower than hoped for, total public-sector spending initially fell by much less than planned. Through continued cuts, it had fallen to 1.1 per cent of GDP by 2018/19, though whether or not it begins to increase once more with the uncertainty surrounding Brexit, remains to be seen.

Many other countries also made headway in cutting their deficits, but for some countries, the state of their finances was such that international support was needed. For example, Greece required a bailout from the eurozone countries and three loans totalling €298 billion from the IMF to help reduce its budget deficit, which was 15.1 per cent of GDP in 2009 and after falling somewhat, rose to 13.2 per cent in 2013. Its national debt rose dramatically from 103 per cent of GDP in 2007 to a peak of 183 per cent in 2018. (See the following blogs on the Sloman Economics News site: *On the edge: can Greece avoid debt restructuring?; Rescuing Greece? Rescuing the euro?; Greece lightening?; Wanted: a Deus ex Machina for Greece* and

When the light at the end of the tunnel is yet another oncoming train: Greece's woes set to continue.)

Other countries that have required bailouts include Ireland, Portugal, Spain, Argentina and Cyprus, to name a few. However, there is debate about the effectiveness of bailouts and loans and whether they actually cause more problems in the long run than they solve, as discussed in a *DW* article.[1] Whatever the case for or against them, the past decade has been painful for many countries and while the pain may be lessening, it is likely to remain for some years.

Pause for thought

If government is running a budget deficit, does this necessarily mean that GDP will increase?

The use of fiscal policy

Automatic fiscal stabilisers

To some extent, government expenditure and taxation will have the effect of *automatically* stabilising the economy. For example, as GDP rises, the amount of tax people pay automatically rises. This rise in withdrawals from the circular flow of income will help to dampen down the rise in GDP. This effect will be bigger if taxes are *progressive* (i.e. rise by a bigger percentage than GDP) as is the case with income tax in the UK.

---

[1] Uwe Hessler, 'IMF bailouts – roads to stability or recipes for disaster?' *DW* (4 September 2018).

Some government expenditure will have a similar effect. For example, total government expenditure on unemployment benefits will fall if rises in GDP cause a fall in unemployment. This again will have the effect of dampening the rise in GDP.

Taxes whose revenues rise as national income rises and benefits that fall as national income rises are known as *automatic fiscal stabilisers*. The more they change as income changes, the bigger the stabilising effect on national income.

Discretionary fiscal policy

Automatic stabilisers cannot *prevent* fluctuations, they merely reduce their magnitude. If there is a fundamental disequilibrium in the economy or substantial fluctuations in GDP, these automatic stabilisers will not be enough. The government may thus choose to *alter* the level of government expenditure or the rates of taxation. This is known as *discretionary fiscal policy*.

If government expenditure on goods and services (roads, health care, education, etc.) is raised, this will create a full multiplied rise in GDP. The reason is that all the money gets spent and thus all of it goes to boosting aggregate demand.

Pause for thought

Why will the multiplier effect of government transfer payments, such as child benefit, pensions and social security benefits be less than the full multiplier effect from government expenditure on goods and services?

Cutting taxes (or increasing benefits), however, will have a smaller effect on GDP than raising government expenditure on goods and services by the same amount. The reason is that cutting taxes increases people's *disposable* incomes, of which only part will be spent. Part will be withdrawn into extra saving, imports and other taxes. In other words, not all the tax cuts will be passed on round the circular flow of income as extra expenditure. Thus if one-fifth of a cut in taxes is withdrawn and only four-fifths is spent, the tax multiplier will only be four-fifths as big as the government expenditure multiplier.

Expansionary fiscal policy will have indirect effects on virtually all firms, as aggregate demand will rise, which will increase GDP and this in turn means higher consumer demand. Those firms whose products have high income elasticity of demand may see a significant increase in sales. We may also see higher investment, via the accelerator (see page 273), benefiting businesses in construction and the production of capital equipment.

There will also be direct effects from higher government expenditure. For example, more money may be spent on new roads or hospitals or the refurbishment of premises, which will create additional work, income and spending for those in the construction and building industries.

Similar effects would also occur from tax cuts. For example, lower corporation taxes will increase after-tax profits and cuts in national insurance contributions will increase disposable income and hence consumer demand.

Many of these effects were the aims of governments in the aftermath of the financial crisis and recession.

Pause for thought

Apart from the industries mentioned above, what other industries are likely to benefit directly from an expansionary fiscal policy?

The effectiveness of fiscal policy

How successful will fiscal policy be? Will it be able to 'fine-tune' aggregate demand? Will it be able to achieve the level of GDP that the government would like it to achieve? Before changing government expenditure or taxation, the government will need to calculate the effect of any such change on GDP, employment and inflation. Predicting these effects, however, is often very unreliable.

Difficulty in predicting effects of changes in government expenditure. A rise in government expenditure of £x may lead to a rise in total injections (relative to withdrawals) that is smaller than £x. A major reason for this is a phenomenon known as *crowding out*. If the government relies on *pure fiscal policy* – that is, if it does not finance an increase in the budget deficit by

Definitions

Automatic stabilisers Tax revenues that automatically rise and government expenditure that automatically falls as national income rises. The more they change as income changes, the bigger the stabilising effect on national income.

Discretionary fiscal policy Deliberate changes in tax rates or the level of government expenditure in order to influence the level of aggregate demand.

Crowding out Where increased public expenditure diverts money or resources away from the private sector.

Pure fiscal policy Fiscal policy which does not involve any change in money supply.

increasing the money supply – it will have to borrow the money from individuals and firms. It will thus be competing with the private sector for finance and will have to offer higher interest rates. This will force the private sector also to offer higher interest rates, which may discourage firms from investing and individuals from buying on credit. Thus government borrowing *crowds out* private borrowing. In the extreme case, the fall in consumption and investment may completely offset the rise in government expenditure, with the result that aggregate demand does not rise at all.

Difficulty in predicting effects of changes in taxes. A cut in taxes, by increasing people's disposable income, increases not only the amount they spend, but also the amount they save. The problem is that it is not easy to predict the relative size of these two increases. In part it will depend on whether people feel that the cut in tax is only temporary, in which case they may simply save the extra disposable income, or permanent, in which case they may adjust their consumption upwards.

Difficulty in predicting the resulting multiplied effect on GDP. The sizes of the multiplier and accelerator (see pages 264 and 273) are difficult to predict, mainly because the effects depend largely on confidence. For example, if the business community believes that a cut in taxes will be successful in pulling the economy out of recession, firms will invest. This will help to bring about the very recovery that firms predicted. There will be a big multiplier effect. If, however, businesses are pessimistic about the likely success of the policy, they are unlikely to invest. The economy may not recover. The credibility of the government and its policies may have a large influence here.

Another effect of confidence is on consumer spending and this directly affects the size of the multiplier. If people are confident about their future employment and that their incomes will grow, they are likely to spend more from any rise in income (and save less). The multiplier effect will be relatively large. If they are pessimistic, they will be likely to save more of any rise in income; the multiplier will be smaller. But it is difficult to predict these effects and thus how large the final multiplied rise in GDP will be.

If the individual sizes of the multiplier and accelerator are difficult to predict, then the effect of their interactions will be impossible to estimate. If the change in investment is even slightly different from what was initially predicted, the effect of this will become magnified as time progresses.

Random shocks. Forecasts cannot take into account unpredictable events, such as major industrial disputes, wars or terrorist attacks. Furthermore, even events that, with hindsight, should have been predicted, such

as the financial crisis, are not. Unpredictable and unpredicted events do occur and may seriously undermine the government's fiscal policy. This risk has perhaps grown in recent decades with globalisation, as countries are now so interdependent that an individual nation is no longer insulated from the effects of events that occur in another country.

> **Pause for thought**
>
> *Give some other examples of 'random shocks' that could undermine the government's fiscal policy.*

Problems of timing. Fiscal policy can involve considerable time lags. It may take time to recognise the nature of the problem before the government is willing or able to take action; tax or government expenditure changes take time to plan and implement – changes will have to wait until the next Budget to be announced and may come into effect some time later; the effects of such changes take time to work their way through the economy via the multiplier and accelerator.

If these time lags are long enough, fiscal policy could even be *de*stabilising. Expansionary policies taken to cure a recession may not take effect until the economy has *already* recovered and is experiencing a boom. Under these circumstances, expansionary policies are quite inappropriate; they simply worsen the problems of overheating. Similarly, deflationary (contractionary) policies taken to prevent excessive expansion may not take effect until the economy has already peaked and is plunging into recession. The deflationary policies only deepen the recession.

This problem is illustrated in Figure 11.3. Path (a) shows the course of the business cycle without government intervention. Ideally, with no time lags, the economy should be dampened in stage 2 and stimulated in stage 4. This would make the resulting course of the business cycle more like path (b), or

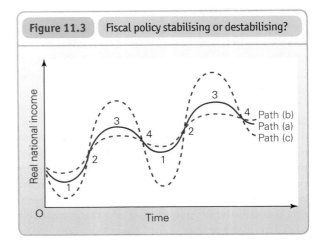

Figure 11.3 Fiscal policy stabilising or destabilising?

even, if the policy were perfectly stabilising, a straight line. With the presence of time lags, however, deflationary policies taken in stage 2 may not come into effect until stage 4, and expansionary policies taken in stage 4 may not come into effect until stage 2. In this case the resulting course of the business cycle will be more like path (c). Quite obviously, in these circumstances 'stabilising' fiscal policy actually makes the economy *less* stable.

Imperfect information. Although we have some idea about where the economy is in the business cycle, we can never be certain. The government may believe that the economy is at the very bottom; however, the economy could actually still be moving towards the bottom or even have entered the recovery phase. Government policy may, therefore, be based on inaccurate information about the economy's current position and again, we could see fiscal policy that has a *destabilising* effect. If the fluctuations in aggregate demand can be forecast, and if the lengths of the time lags are known, then all is not lost. At least the fiscal measures can be taken early, and their delayed effects can be taken into account.

Fiscal rules

Given the problems of pursuing active fiscal policy, many governments had, until the recession of 2008–9, taken a much more passive approach. Instead of changing the policy as the economy changed, a rule was set for the level of public finances. This rule was then applied year after year, with taxes and government expenditure being planned to meet that rule. For example, a target could be set for the PSNB, with government expenditure and taxes being adjusted to keep the PSNB at or within its target level. Box 11.1 looks at some examples of fiscal targets.

The UK's approach to fiscal policy
Fiscal rules of the labour government (1997–2010). With Labour's election in 1997, two fiscal rules were introduced. This approach was very similar to that adopted within the eurozone, as set out in the Stability and Growth Pact (see Box 11.1). By following rules, fiscal policy as a means of adjusting aggregate demand had been largely abandoned.

The first of the Labour government's rules was called the 'golden rule'. This committed the government to borrowing only to invest (e.g. in roads, hospitals and schools) over the economic cycle and not to fund current spending (e.g. on wages, administration and benefits). Investment was exempted from the zero-borrowing rule, because of its direct contribution towards the growth of GDP. As the golden rule used an average rule over the cycle, automatic

stabilisers were able to work, with deficits of receipts over current spending occurring when the economy was in recession or had sluggish growth as a means of stimulating the economy.

The second fiscal rule was its 'sustainable investment rule', whereby a target was set to maintain a public-sector net debt of no more than 40 per cent of GDP averaged over the economic cycle.

The crisis of 2008–9. Things changed dramatically in 2008 and 2009. With the economy sliding into recession, the government argued that more discretionary fiscal policy would be needed than was allowed by the fiscal rules and so they were abandoned. VAT was cut from 17.5 per cent to 15 per cent for 13 months and £3 billion of capital spending on projects such as motorways, schools and new social housing was brought forward from 2010/11 to help the process. This led to a big increase in public-sector gross investment to over 5 per cent of GDP, having averaged at around 3 per cent of GDP for the previous ten years and government spending continued to rise.

As we saw in Figure 11.2, public-sector net borrowing continued to grow, reaching 10.3 per cent of GDP in 2009/10, up from 2.6 per cent in 2007/8. Consequently, public-sector net debt grew from £557 billion (35.5 per cent of GDP) in 2007/8 to £1.0 trillion (64.8 per cent of GDP) in 2009/10.

Rules of the coalition government (2010–15). In May 2010, the Coalition government took office and this meant a change in the direction of fiscal policy. The aim was now to bring down public-sector borrowing. The government embarked on a series of spending cuts and tax rises (dubbed 'austerity policies') and the framework for this was called the 'fiscal mandate'. It included achieving a cyclically-adjusted current balance by 2015/16 – a balance of tax revenues and current (as opposed to investment) expenditure at the sustainable level of national income. This was essentially a return to Labour's golden rule and was supplemented by a target for the ratio of public-sector debt to GDP to be falling by 2015/16.

The 'consolidation package' was implemented with £99 billion of spending cuts by 2015/16 and tax increases of £23 billion. Spending cuts therefore accounted for 81 per cent of this consolidation package. As it turned out, however, in real terms total public-sector spending fell by just 1.5 per cent between 2010/11 and 2014/15. Part of the cause was the adverse effect on aggregate demand of the contractionary fiscal policy, which led to a lack of economic growth. Benefits fell less rapidly, therefore, than the government hoped.

Problems were also exacerbated by the crisis in the eurozone from 2011, with concerns over debt levels and the possibility of default. Growth and

| BOX 11.1 | THE FISCAL FRAMEWORK IN THE EUROZONE |

Constraining the discretion over fiscal policy

If the government persistently runs a budget deficit, government debt will rise. If this debt rises faster than GDP, then it will account for a growing proportion of GDP. There is then likely to be an increasing problem of 'servicing' this debt, i.e. paying the interest on it. The government could find itself having to borrow more and more to meet the interest payments, and so government debt could rise faster still. As the government borrows more, it will have to pay higher interest rates to attract finance (unless this is offset by quantitative easing by the central bank: see pages 312–3). These higher interest rates may crowd out borrowing and hence investment by the private sector (see page 298).

The possibility of financial crowding out contributed towards many governments embarking on a strategy of fiscal consolidation during early 2010. But the recognition of this problem and the need for a fiscal framework had been shaping fiscal policy across Europe (and the USA) for some time. However, the financial crisis called into question how rigid any framework should be and hence how much discretion over fiscal policy national governments should have.

The EU stability and growth pact

In June 1997, at the European Council in Amsterdam, the EU countries agreed on a Stability and Growth Pact (SGP) for those countries adopting the euro. It stated that governments should seek to balance their budgets (or even aim for a surplus) averaged over the course of the business cycle. In addition, general government deficits should not exceed 3 per cent of GDP in any one year. A country's deficit was only permitted to exceed 3 per cent if its GDP had declined by at least 2 per cent (or 0.75 per cent with special permission from the Council of Ministers). Otherwise, countries with deficits exceeding 3 per cent were required to make deposits of money with the European Central Bank (ECB). These would then become fines if the excessive budget deficits were not eliminated within two years. The UK, however, was not legally bound by this procedure.

There were two main aims of targeting a zero budget deficit over the business cycle. The first was to allow automatic stabilisers to work without 'bumping into' the 3 per cent deficit ceiling in years when economies were slowing. The second was to allow a reduction in government debts as a proportion of GDP (assuming that GDP grew on average at around 2–3 per cent per year).

From 2002, with slowing growth, Germany, France and Italy breached the 3 per cent ceiling. By 2007, however, after two years of relatively strong growth, deficits had been reduced well below the ceiling.

But then the credit crunch hit. As the EU economies slowed, so deficits rose. To combat the recession, in November 2008 the European Commission announced a €200 billion fiscal stimulus plan, mainly in the form of increased public expenditure. €170 billion of the money would come from member governments and €30 billion from the EU, amounting to a total of 1.2 per cent of EU GDP. The money was for a range of projects, such as job training, help to small businesses, developing green energy technologies and energy efficiency. Most member governments quickly followed, by announcing how their specific plans would accord with the overall plan.

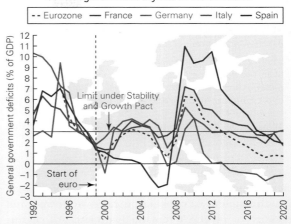

General government deficits in the eurozone

Note: data from 2019 based on forecasts.
Source: Based on data in *Statistical Annex to the European Economy* (European Commission).

The combination of the recession and the fiscal measures pushed most eurozone countries' budget deficits well above the 3 per cent ceiling (see the chart). The recession in EU countries deepened markedly in 2009, with GDP declining by 4.5 per cent in the eurozone as a whole, and by 5.6 per cent in Germany, 5.5 per cent in Italy, 3.6 per cent in Spain and 2.9 per cent in France. Consequently, the deficits were not seen to breach SGP rules.

In light of the deterioration of public finances, which in some cases required bailouts and loans from both the EU and the IMF, the EU established the European Stability Mechanism (ESM). This was a funding mechanism that became operational in October 2012 and could provide loans to countries or purchase the countries' bonds in the primary market, as part of a financial assistance package.

The fiscal compact

With many countries experiencing burgeoning deficits (Greece, Spain and Ireland had deficits of 11.0, 9.6 and 29.3 per cent, respectively) and some countries requiring financial assistance, the SGP was no longer seen as a credible vehicle for constraining deficits: it needed reform.

The treaty, known as the 'Fiscal Compact', required that from January 2013 national governments not only abided by the excessive deficit procedure of the SGP but also kept structural deficits at no higher than 0.5 per cent of GDP. Structural deficits are that part of a deficit not directly related to the economic cycle and so would exist even if the economy were operating at its normal level of output.

In the cases of countries with a debt-to-GDP ratio significantly below 60 per cent, the structural deficit is permitted to reach 1 per cent of GDP. Finally, where the debt-to-GDP ratio exceeds 60 per cent, countries should, on average, reduce it by one-twentieth per year.

The average structural deficit across the eurozone fell from 4.2 per cent of GDP in 2010 to 0.7 per cent in 2018, but rose slightly to 1.0 per cent in 2019. This improvement since 2010

▶

was mirrored in most individual eurozone countries, with particularly large improvements in Greece (−9.4 to +4.6 per cent) and Ireland (−9.1 to −0.2 per cent), both of which had received financial assistance with conditions attached that they cut spending and raise taxes. Nonetheless, most countries still had structural deficits in excess of the 0.5 per cent deficit limit of the Fiscal Compact, with some countries, such as France, Spain and Italy, having a structural deficit over 2 per cent of GDP.

Where a national government is found by the European Court of Justice not to comply with the Fiscal Compact, it has the power to fine that country up to 0.1 per cent of GDP payable to the European Stability Mechanism (ESM). One might question the logic of fining countries already in financial difficulty, but if countries receive no punishment for breaking

rules or receive bailouts, a moral hazard problem may emerge (see pages 59–60 and 62).

1. *What effects will increased government investment expenditure have on general government deficits (a) in the short run; (b) in the long run?*
2. *If there is a danger of global recession, should governments loosen the strait-jacket of fiscal policy targets?*

From the AMECO database download data on the actual and cyclically-adjusted budget balance, as a percentage of GDP, for general government debt (net lending). Then, for Germany and the UK, plot a time-series chart showing both balances across time. Finally, compose a short briefing note summarising the patterns in your chart.

unemployment became worse across much of Europe, growth rates in key emerging nations slowed and recovery in the USA remained modest. All of this negatively impacted UK exports and with such low confidence and uncertainty, household and business spending was low. The principal fiscal objectives were thus not met during the 2010–15 parliamentary period, although the government claimed that 'significant progress' had been made on its fiscal consolidation, especially in light of these 'external' events.

Rules of the conservative government (2015–). Although the new Conservative administration elected in 2015 still had the aim of reducing the

budget deficit, it did loosen the fiscal mandate. There were new targets (a) to reduce cyclically adjusted public-sector net borrowing to below 2 per cent of GDP by 2020/21 and (b) for public-sector net debt as a percentage of GDP to be falling in 2020/21. The government believed that these rules struck a balance between ensuring the long-term sustainability of the public finances and providing government with sufficient discretion to provide further support for the economy, particularly given the UK's decision to leave the European Union.

Table 11.2 shows the OBR's data on cyclically adjusted public-sector net borrowing from 2010 to

Table 11.2	Public-sector net borrowing forecasts								
Percentile	10	20	30	40	50 (median)	60	70	80	90
2010–11					7.0				
2011–12					5.9				
2012–13					5.9				
2013–14					4.4				
2014–15					4.3				
2015–16					3.4				
2016–17					2.0				
2017–18					2.0				
2018–19	0.1	0.5	0.7	1.0	1.2	1.4	1.6	1.9	2.3
2019–20	−0.2	0.3	0.7	1.0	1.3	1.6	1.9	2.2	2.7
2020–21	−1.3	−0.6	0.0	0.4	0.8	1.3	1.7	2.3	3.0
2021–22	−1.6	−0.9	−0.3	0.3	0.7	1.2	1.8	2.5	3.4
2022–23	−1.6	−1.0	−0.5	0.0	0.6	1.1	1.8	2.6	3.7
2023–24	−1.9	−1.2	−0.7	−0.1	0.5	1.2	1.9	2.9	4.2

Source: Economic and Fiscal Outlook, Charts and tables, Chart 5.4, OBR (March 2016)

| Figure 11.4 | Cyclically adjusted public-sector net borrowing fan chart |

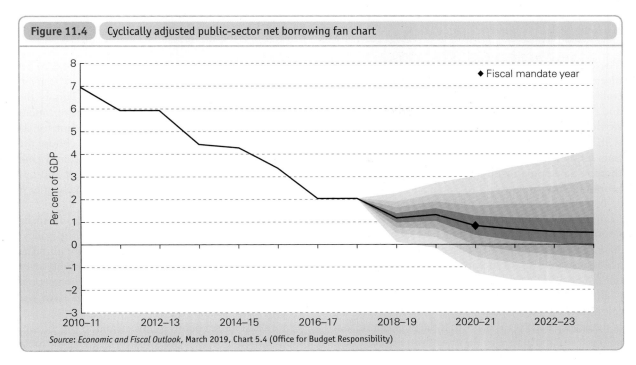

Source: *Economic and Fiscal Outlook*, March 2019, Chart 5.4 (Office for Budget Responsibility)

2018 and then includes the forecasts until 2024, with different probabilities, shown in 20 per cent probability bands, based on official forecast errors from past data. As you can see, the forecasts are subject to significant uncertainty, which only grows as we look further into the future, as so many factors do affect the public-sector borrowing requirement.

The data from Table 11.2 are then replicated in Figure 11.4, which shows a fan chart, with different shaded bands reflecting the probability of different outcomes occurring. The solid black line illustrates the OBR's median forecast and each successive pair of the lighter shaded areas around this median forecast shows 20 per cent probability bands. Thus public-sector net borrowing has a 90 per cent probability of being within the bands of the fan chart in each year.

Although the forecast suggests a falling PSNB, economic uncertainty continues to affect the global economy and meeting the new fiscal mandate will be dependent on both global demand and consumer and business confidence in the coming years.

RECAP

1. The government's fiscal policy will determine the size of the budget deficit or surplus and the size of the PSNB.

2. Automatic fiscal stabilisers are tax revenues that rise and benefits that fall as GDP rises. They have the effect of reducing the size of the multiplier and thus reducing cyclical upswings and downswings.

3. Discretionary fiscal policy is where the government deliberately changes taxes or government expenditure in order to alter the level of aggregate demand.

4. There are problems in predicting the magnitude of the effects of discretionary fiscal policy. Expansionary fiscal policy can crowd out private expenditure, but the extent of crowding out is hard to predict and depends on business confidence. Also it is difficult to predict how people's spending will respond to changes in taxes. Various random shocks can knock fiscal policy off course.

5. There are various time lags involved with fiscal policy. If these are very long, the policy could be destabilising rather than stabilising.

6. Today many governments prefer a more passive approach towards fiscal policy. Targets are set for one or more measures of the public-sector finances, and then taxes and government expenditure are adjusted so as to keep to the target.

7. Nevertheless, in extreme circumstances, as occurred in 2008–9, governments have been prepared to abandon rules and give a fiscal stimulus to their economies.

11.2 MONETARY POLICY

The Bank of England's Monetary Policy Committee meets regularly to set Bank Rate Similarly, other central banks, such as the European Central Bank (ECB) and the Federal Reserve in the USA, meet regularly to set their rates, and in particular the rate at which they will lend to other banks. These central bank rates thus influence many other rates in the economy and thereby have a major influence on a range of macroeconomic indicators.

Before the onset of recession in 2009, central banks changed their interest rates fairly frequently as economic conditions changed. For several years from 2009, however, central banks kept their interest rates at historic lows in an attempt to revive their economies. This is illustrated in Figure 11.5.

But is monetary policy simply the setting of interest rates? In reality, it involves the central bank intervening in the money market to ensure that the interest rate that has been announced is also the *equilibrium* interest rate.

The policy setting

In framing its monetary policy, the government must decide on the goals of the policy. Is the aim simply to control inflation, or does the government wish also to affect output and employment, or does it want to control the exchange rate?

A decision also has to be made about who is to carry out the policy. There are three possible approaches here.

In the first, the government both sets the policy and decides the measures necessary to achieve it. Here the government would set the interest rate, with the central bank simply influencing money markets to achieve this rate. This occurred in the UK before 1997.

The second approach is for the government to set the policy *targets,* but for the central bank to be given independence in deciding interest rates. This is the approach adopted in the UK today. The government has set a target rate of inflation of 2 per cent for 24 months hence, but then the MPC is free to choose the rate of interest. It is supposed to keep inflation within ±1 percentage point of the 2 per cent target and has to write a letter to the Chancellor of the Exchequer if it fails to do so.

The third approach is for the central bank to be given independence not only in carrying out policy, but in setting the policy targets. The ECB, within the statutory objective of maintaining price stability over the medium term, decided on the target of keeping inflation below, but close to, 2 per cent over the medium term (see Box 11.3).

More and more countries have begun to use the second or third approach, with inflation targeting the most common policy objective. Part of the reasoning behind this is the apparent failure of discretionary macroeconomic policies, as they suffer from time lags and therefore can fail to straighten out the business cycle. But, why is inflation and not the money supply targeted?

Money supply targets were adopted by many countries in the 1980s, including the UK, but money supply targets proved very difficult to achieve. The money supply depends on the amount of credit banks create and this is difficult for the authorities to control. Furthermore, even if money supply is controlled, this does not necessarily mean that aggregate demand will be controlled; people may simply adjust the amount they hold in their bank accounts. The money supply is still targeted in some countries, although typically it is not the main target. Inflation, on the

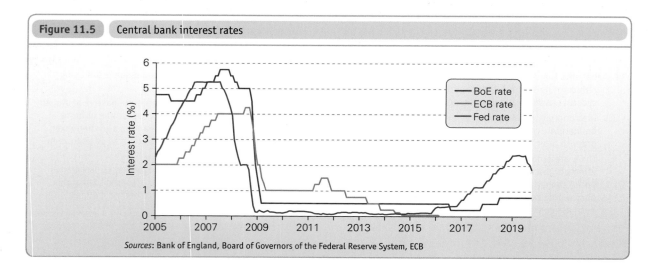

Figure 11.5   Central bank interest rates

Sources: Bank of England, Board of Governors of the Federal Reserve System, ECB

other hand, is the main target for macroeconomic policy, although some countries, such as the USA, in the light of the recession and slow recovery of recent years, began targeting other indicators, such as a maximum rate of unemployment.

Inflation targets have proved relatively easy to achieve – at least once they have been in place for a while. Initially there can be problems, especially if the actual rate of inflation is way above the target level. The high rates of interest necessary to bring inflation down can cause a recession. However, once inflation has been brought close to its target level, the objective is then to maintain it at that level and most countries have had success in doing this. Furthermore, success at meeting an inflation target seems to breed more success, as the policy and the government gain credibility. If inflation is on target, people expect inflation to remain on target and these expectations then help to keep inflation at the desired level.

With the persistent slow growth in many countries in the years following the financial crisis, inflation had tended to be somewhat below target. But with interest rates close to zero, there was little scope for further cuts in interest rates to bring inflation back up to target. Generally, however, inflation targeting has been moderately successful in keeping inflation close to target or a little below.

But this has created another potential problem. With worldwide inflation having fallen, and with global trade and competition helping to keep prices down, there is now less of a link between inflation and the business cycle. Booms no longer seem to generate the inflation they once did. Gearing interest rate policy to maintaining low inflation could still see economies experiencing unsustainable booms, followed by recession. Inflation may be controlled, but the business cycle may not be.

Implementing monetary policy

Assume that inflation is too high relative to its target or that the government (or central bank) wants to alter its monetary policy (e.g. choose a new target). What can it do? There are two main approaches. The first is to alter the money supply; the second is to alter interest rates. These are illustrated in Figure 11.6, which shows the demand for and supply of money (this is similar to Figure 10.8 on page 279). With an initial supply of money of M_S, the equilibrium interest rate is r_1.

Assume that the central bank wants to tighten monetary policy in order to reduce inflation. It could (a) seek to shift the supply of money curve to the left, from M_S to M_S' (resulting in the equilibrium rate of interest rising from r_1 to r_2), (b) raise the interest rate directly from r_1 to r_2, and then manipulate the money supply to reduce it to M_S'.

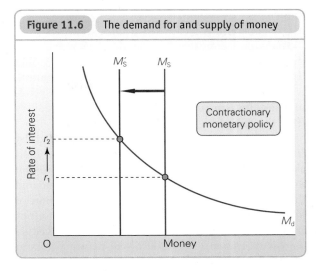

Figure 11.6 The demand for and supply of money

Techniques to control the money supply

The main way that the central bank seeks to control the money supply is through *open-market operations*. This involves the sale or purchase by the central bank of government securities (bonds or bills; see page 278) in the open market. These sales (or purchases) are *not* in response to changes in the public-sector deficit and are best understood, therefore, in the context of an unchanged deficit.

Pause for thought

Explain how open-market operations could be used to increase the money supply.

If the central bank wishes to *reduce* the money supply, it takes money from the banking system by selling more securities. When people buy these securities, they pay for them by drawing on their accounts in banks. Thus banks' balances with the central bank are reduced. If this brings bank reserves below their prudent liquidity ratio, banks will reduce advances. There will be a multiplied contraction of credit and hence of money supply.

In response to the financial crisis and the recession that followed, central banks, including the Bank of England, the ECB and the Federal Reserve, actively *increased* the money supply, through the process

Definition

Open-market operations The sale (or purchase) by the authorities of government securities in the open market in order to reduce (or increase) money supply.

known as 'quantitative easing'. Aggressive open-market operations were used to *buy* securities from the banking sector, thereby releasing new money into the banking system. The hope was that banks would use the new money as the basis for credit creation, with the extra lending stimulating consumer spending and investment and thereby helping recovery from the recession.

The money supply can also be controlled by requiring banks to hold a certain proportion of their assets in liquid form. This is known as the '*minimum reserve ratio*'. If the central bank raises this ratio and thus requires banks to hold a higher proportion of liquid assets, then banks must reduce the amount of credit they grant; the money supply will fall. Reducing the minimum reserve ratio will permit banks to increase credit.

Techniques to control interest rates

The approach to monetary control today in most countries is to focus directly on interest rates. Normally an interest rate change will be announced, and then open-market operations will be conducted by the central bank to ensure that the money supply is adjusted so as to make the announced interest rate the *equilibrium* one. Let us assume that the central bank decides to raise interest rates. What does it do?

In general, it will seek to keep banks short of liquidity. This will happen automatically on any day when tax payments by banks' customers exceed the money they receive from government expenditure. This excess is effectively withdrawn from banks and ends up in the government's account at the central bank. Even when this does not occur, sales of government debt by the central bank (see above) will effectively keep the banking system short of liquidity.

How do banks acquire the necessary liquidity? The Bank of England (like other central banks) is willing to lend money to the banks on a short-term basis. It does this by entering into a *sale and repurchase ('repo') agreement* with the banks. This is an agreement whereby the banks sell some of their government bonds ('gilts') to the Bank of England on a temporary basis, agreeing to buy them back again at the end of a set period of time. The Bank of England is in effect giving a short-term loan to the banks and is thus tiding them over the period of liquidity shortage. In this role, the Bank of England is acting as *lender of last resort*, and ensures that the banks never run short of money.

Because banks frequently have to borrow from their central bank, it can use this to force through interest rate changes. The point is that the central bank can *choose the rate of interest to charge* (i.e. the repo rate). This will then have a knock-on effect on other interest rates throughout the banking system.

The impact of monetary policy on business and the economy

Although interest rates are set by the central bank, they remain a key tool of macroeconomic policy, in particular because a change in interest rates can affect so many of the key components of aggregate demand and hence the government's objectives. An increase in interest rates will have the following effects:

- It increases the return on saving and hence may discourage consumption, thus reducing aggregate demand.
- It may discourage business investment, thereby reducing aggregate demand and also long-term economic growth.
- It adds to the costs of production, to the costs of house purchase and generally to the cost of living, for example through higher mortgage repayments. Higher interest rates are thus cost inflationary.
- It is politically unpopular, since the general public does not like paying higher interest rates on overdrafts, credit cards and mortgages.
- As we shall see in the next chapter, high interest rates encourage inflows of money from abroad. This drives up the exchange rate, making domestically produced goods expensive relative to goods made abroad. This can be very damaging for export industries and industries competing with imports. Many firms in the UK suffered badly between 1997 and 2007 from a high exchange rate, caused partly by higher interest rates in the UK than in both the eurozone and, until 2006, in the USA.

A change in interest rates will therefore impact businesses, but by how much will the level of business activity and/or inflation be affected? This depends on the nature of the demand for loans. If this demand is

---

Definitions

Quantitative easing A deliberate attempt by the central bank to increase the money supply by buying large quantities of securities through open-market operations.

Minimum reserve ratio A minimum ratio of cash (or other specified liquid assets) to deposits (either total or selected) that the central bank requires banks to hold.

Sale and repurchase agreement (repo) An agreement between two financial institutions whereby one in effect borrows from another by selling some of its assets, agreeing to buy them back (repurchase them) at a fixed price and on a fixed date.

Lender of last resort The role of the Bank of England as the guarantor of sufficient liquidity in the monetary system.

(a) unresponsive to interest rate changes or (b) unstable because it is significantly affected by other determinants (such as anticipated income or foreign interest rates), then it will be very difficult to control by controlling the rate of interest.

Problem of an inelastic demand for loans

If the demand for loans is inelastic (i.e. a relatively steep M_d curve in Figure 11.6), any attempt to reduce demand will involve large rises in interest rates. The problem will be compounded if the demand curve shifts to the right, due, say, to a consumer spending boom. The effects described above will therefore be larger, such as a bigger decrease in business investment and hence a potentially larger dampening effect on long-term growth.

Evidence suggests that the demand for loans may indeed be quite inelastic. Especially in the short run, many firms and individuals simply cannot reduce their borrowing commitments. In fact, higher interest rates may force some people and firms to borrow *more* in order to finance the higher interest rate payments.

Problem of an unstable demand

Accurate monetary control requires the central bank to be able to predict the demand curve for money (in Figure 11.6). Only then can it set the appropriate level of interest rates. Unfortunately, the demand curve may shift unpredictably, making control very difficult. The major reason is *speculation*.

For example, if people think interest rates will rise and bond prices fall, in the meantime they will demand to hold their assets in liquid form. The demand for money will rise. Similarly, if people think exchange rates will rise, they will demand sterling while it is still relatively cheap. The demand for money will rise.

It is very difficult for the central bank to predict what people's expectations will be. Speculation depends so much on world political events, rumour and 'random shocks'.

If the demand curve shifts very much, and if it is inelastic, then monetary control will be very difficult. Furthermore, the central bank will have to make frequent and sizeable adjustments to interest rates. These fluctuations can be very damaging to business confidence and may discourage long-term investment.

The net result of an inelastic and unstable demand for money is that substantial interest rate changes may be necessary to bring about the required change in aggregate demand. An example occurred in 2008, when interest rates were cut drastically, first in the USA and then in the UK, the eurozone and most other countries. But, while this helped to reduce the decline in GDP, it was not enough to prevent recession.

Difficulties with choice of target

Assume that the government or central bank sets an inflation target. Should it then stick to that rate, come what may? Might not an extended period of relatively low inflation warrant a lower inflation target? The government must at least have the discretion to change the rules, even if only occasionally.

Then there is the question of whether success in achieving the target will bring success in achieving other macroeconomic objectives, such as low unemployment and stable economic growth. The problem is that something called *Goodhart's Law* is likely to apply. The law, named after Charles Goodhart, formerly of the Bank of England, states that attempts to control an indicator of a problem may, as a result, make it cease to be a good indicator of the problem.

Targeting inflation may make it become a poor indicator of the state of the economy. If people believe that the central bank will be successful in achieving its inflation target, then those expectations will feed into their inflationary expectations, and not surprisingly the target will be met. But that target rate of inflation may now be consistent with both a buoyant and a depressed economy.

An example occurred in 2008, when there was a rapid slowdown in the economy and yet cost-push pressures from higher commodity prices pushed up the inflation rate. Simply targeting the current rate of inflation would have involved higher interest rates, which would have deepened the recession. A similar argument applied to the UK after the Brexit vote. The fall in the pound threatened to push up inflation and yet the Bank of England decided to cut Bank Rate. The aim was to ward off a downswing in the economy.

Thus achieving the inflation target may not tackle the much more serious problem of creating stable economic growth and an environment which will therefore encourage long-term investment.

> ## Definition
>
> **Goodhart's Law** Controlling a symptom or indicator of a problem is unlikely to cure the problem; it will simply mean that what is being controlled now becomes a poor indicator of the problem.

Use of a Taylor rule

Given the potential problems in adhering to simple inflation rate targets, many economists have advocated the use of a *Taylor rule*.[2] A Taylor rule takes two objectives into account – (1) inflation and (2) either economic growth or the rate of unemployment – and seeks to get the optimum degree of stability of the two. The degree of importance attached to each of the two objectives can be decided by the government or central bank. The central bank adjusts interest rates when either the rate of inflation diverges from its target or the rate of economic growth (or unemployment) diverges from its sustainable (or equilibrium) level.

Take the case where inflation is above its target rate but economic growth is at its target rate. The central bank following a Taylor rule will raise the rate of interest. It knows, however, that this will reduce economic growth. This, therefore, limits the amount that the central bank is prepared to raise the rate of interest. The more weight it attaches to stabilising inflation, the more it will raise the rate of interest. The more weight it attaches to maintaining stable economic growth, the less it will raise the rate of interest.

Thus the central bank has to trade off inflation stability against stable economic growth. This trade-off can be large when there are significant cost-push factors affecting the rate of inflation. In such circumstances, the weights attached to these two objectives become especially important.

The Bank of England's approach

The Bank of England uses a rule that is apparently simpler than the Taylor rule, but in reality is more

sophisticated. The Bank of England targets inflation alone; in this sense the rule is simpler. But the inflation figure on which it bases its interest rate decisions is the *forecast* rate of inflation, not the current rate; in this sense it is more sophisticated.

The Bank of England publishes a quarterly *Inflation Report,* which contains the MPC's projections for inflation and real GDP growth for the next three years, assuming that interest rates follow market expectations. These projections are known as 'fan charts' and are shown in Figure 11.7.

In each case, the darkest central band represents 10 per cent likelihood, as do each of the eight subsequent pairs of lighter areas out from the central band. Thus inflation and GDP growth are considered to have 90 per cent probability of being within their respective fan. The bands get wider as the time horizon is extended, indicating increasing uncertainty about the outcome. Also, the less reliable are considered to be the forecasts by the MPC, the wider will be the fan. The dashed line indicates the two-year target point. Thus in quarter 1 of 2019, the 2 per cent inflation target was for quarter 1 of 2021.

These projections form the basis for the Monetary Policy Committee's monthly deliberations. If the projected inflation in 24 months' time is off

---

[2] Named after John Taylor, from Stanford University, who proposed that for every 1 per cent that GDP rises above sustainable GDP, real interest rates should be raised by 0.5 percentage point and for every 1 per cent that inflation rises above its target level, real interest rates should be raised by 0.5 percentage point (i.e. nominal rates should be raised by 1.5 percentage points).

Definition

Taylor rule A rule adopted by a central bank for setting the rate of interest. It will raise the interest rate if (a) inflation is above target or (b) economic growth is above the sustainable level (or unemployment below the equilibrium rate). The rule states how much interest rates will be changed in each case. In other words, a relative weighting is attached to each of these two objectives.

Figure 11.7	Fan chart of CPI inflation and GDP growth projections

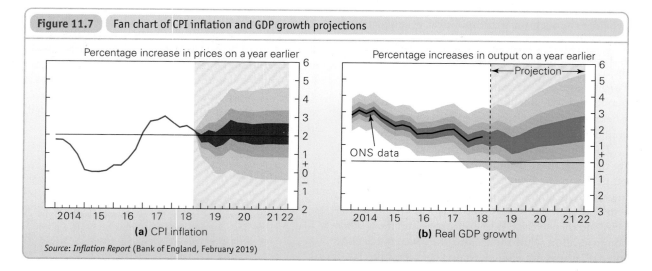

(a) CPI inflation

(b) Real GDP growth

Source: Inflation Report (Bank of England, February 2019)

target, the MPC will change interest rates accordingly. The advantage of this is that it sends a very clear message to people that inflation *will* be kept under control. People will therefore be more likely to adjust their expectations accordingly and keep their borrowing in check.

Pause for thought

If people believe that the central bank will be successful in keeping inflation on target, does it matter whether a simple inflation rule or a Taylor rule is used? Explain.

Although projections are made for GDP growth, these are to help inform the forecast for inflation. GDP growth is not itself an explicit target.

Inflation targeting was introduced in the UK in 1992. For virtually all of the period from 1993 to 2007 inflation diverged by no more than 1 percentage point from the target. Since then, with the turmoil of international commodity price fluctuations and recession, there has been a little more variation, but still small by historical standards. Inflation has ranged from 5.2 per cent in the year to September 2011, to −0.1 per cent in the years to April, September and October 2015, to 3.1 per cent in the year to November 2017.

Despite the relatively high rate of inflation in 2011 and again in late 2017 (when the 3 per cent upper band was breached), interest rates were not increased as this would have dampened aggregate demand and economic growth even further. The Bank of England argued that this was still consistent with targeting a 2 per cent inflation in 24 months' time as the low level of aggregate demand would have caused inflation to fall below 2 per cent if interest rates had been raised.

BOX 11.2   THE CENTRAL BANKS OF THE USA AND THE EUROZONE

Managing the monetary system

The Federal Reserve

The Federal Reserve (or 'Fed') is the central bank in the USA, set up in 1913. Although it consists of 12 regional Federal Reserve Banks, it is the Federal Reserve Board in Washington that sets monetary policy and the Federal Open Market Committee (FOMC) that decides how to carry it out.

As is the case with many other central banks across the world, the Fed has independence from government. Its objectives include low inflation (2 per cent over the medium term), sustainable growth, low unemployment and moderate long-term interest rates. In these objectives, it is therefore different from the European Central Bank (ECB) and the Bank of England, which primarily target price stability. The problem in the Federal Reserve is that the various objectives often conflict with each other and when this happens, an assessment must be made as to which presents the most pressing problem.

If inflation is low, then monetary policy can be used to pursue other objectives, such as stimulating the economy. For example, if a recession is expected, the Fed may cut interest rates. Any increase in aggregate demand will push up prices, but if inflation is low, then this is unlikely to cause a problem. The higher inflation is, the more problematic an expansionary monetary policy becomes, as any boost to aggregate demand will worsen inflationary pressures. However, this is not to say that high inflation precludes a loose monetary policy.

With the onset of the financial crisis in 2007–8, the Federal Reserve faced two problems. Not only was the economy slowing, but inflation was rising. Any reduction in interest rates to boost the economy would therefore push up inflation, but any increase in interest rates to bring inflation under control would slow the economy even further.

Prioritising was therefore crucial and, in this instance, the Fed focused on the slow-down in the economy and so cut interest rates several times. In August 2007, the rate was 5.25 per cent, but one year later, it had fallen to 2 per cent, despite rising inflation.

Inflation did then begin to fall and, with the recession deepening, further rate cuts occurred, leaving interest rates between 0 and 0.25 per cent by December 2008 (see Figure 11.5 on page 304). They remained in this range, lower than both the Bank of England and, for most of the time, the ECB, until the Federal Reserve took the first step to return 'to normal' by raising rates by one quarter of 1 per cent in December 2015. It then raised rates several more times, so that by April 2019 they stood at between 2.25 and 2.5 per cent.

The instruments used by the FOMC to carry out the monetary policy as set out by the Federal Reserve include:

- Open-market operations, whereby Treasury bills and government bonds are bought and sold. These enable the FOMC to change the money supply.
- A discount rate, known as the 'federal funds rate', which is the rate of interest at which the Fed is willing to lend to banks, thereby providing them with liquidity on which they can create credit.
- Variable minimum reserves, which determine the percentage of various assets which banks are legally required to hold in the form of non-interest-bearing reserves.

1. *In what ways is the Fed's operation of monetary policy (a) similar to and (b) different from the Bank of England's?*

►

The European Central Bank

The European Central Bank (ECB) is based in Frankfurt and has the responsibility for operating monetary policy across the eurozone. In a similar way to the Federal Reserve, the ECB has overall control of monetary policy, but it is the role of the central banks of individual countries to issue currency and carry out the monetary policy set in Frankfurt. The target of monetary policy for the ECB is much more focused than that of the Federal Reserve, as its primary objective is a responsibility for achieving price stability across the eurozone. The medium-term target is for the weighted average inflation rate across all members of the eurozone to be below but close to 2 per cent.

Alongside this primary target, the ECB's monetary policy strategy also follows 'a two-pillar approach to the analysis of the risks to price stability.' These involve an analysis of (a) monetary developments and (b) economic developments. The former involves analysing monetary aggregates, such as M3, while the latter analyses economic activity, the labour market, cost indicators, fiscal policy and the balance of payments. The ECB then attempts to 'steer' short-term interest rates to influence economic activity to maintain price stability in the euro area in the medium term.

The main tools used by the ECB in implementing its monetary policy include:

- Open-market operations in government bonds and other recognised assets, mainly in the form of repos to keep the ECB's desired interest rate at the equilibrium rate.
- Setting a minimum reserve ratio for eurozone banks of 2 per cent, primarily to prevent excessive lending. This was reduced to 1 per cent in January 2012 to help stimulate bank lending and was the first time that this tool has been used as part of an active monetary policy.

Between 2005 and 2009, interest rates in the eurozone had been lower than those set in both the UK and USA (see Figure 11.5). With the financial crisis and subsequent recession, both the Fed and the Bank of England began cutting their interest rates, but in July 2008, the ECB increased its rate to 4.25 per cent (the first increase in a year). The move was in response to higher inflation, which had reached 4 per cent in the eurozone. Although evidence showed growth in the eurozone was decelerating, the primary objective of price stability was the focus.

The increase, however, was short-lived, as by early 2009, with the eurozone entering a deep recession, the main interest rate had been cut to just 1 per cent. After a brief rise in 2011, it was then cut again. With growth continuing to be low, the rate was eventually cut to 0 per cent in March 2016 and then remained at that level, contrary to the actions of the Fed.

Other ECB rates have also remained low, including a 'deposit rate' of −0.4 per cent from March 2016. This means that banks are charged for depositing money with the ECB. The hope was that this would encourage banks to lend to each other or to households and businesses, and consequently, stimulate the economy.

The operation of the Fed, ECB and Bank of England are similar in many ways, given their independence and use of interest rates to steer the economy. Central banks across the world also responded in similar ways to the financial crisis with a mixture of interest rate cuts and quantitative easing, as we will discuss in Box 11.3.

2. *How does the ECB's operation of monetary policy differ from that in the UK?*
3. *Interest rates have been cut in the eurozone on several occasions since 2011 and eventually stood at 0 per cent in March 2016. The aim has been to stimulate economic growth (and to return inflation to the target). However, the growth rate has fallen since 2017 and was forecast to be just 1.3 per cent for 2019. Why might low interest rates not create economic growth?*

Research the justifications used by the ECB for some of its recent interest-rate decisions. Do they suggest that monetary policy is successful in meeting its objectives?

Using monetary policy

It is impossible to use monetary policy as a precise means of controlling aggregate demand. It is especially weak when it is pulling against the expectations of firms and consumers and when it is implemented too late. However, if the authorities operate a tight monetary policy firmly enough and long enough, they should eventually be able to reduce lending and aggregate demand. But there will inevitably be time lags and imprecision in the process.

An expansionary monetary policy is even less reliable. If the economy is in recession, no matter how low interest rates are driven, or however much the money supply is expanded, people cannot be forced to borrow if they do not wish to. Firms will not borrow to invest if they predict a continuing recession. This was a serious problem in 2008–9. Despite substantial increases in the money supply by central banks throughout 2009 as a means of encouraging banks to lend to each other and to customers, both firms and consumers were reluctant to borrow. There was too much uncertainty and confidence was low. As such, monetary policy struggled to stimulate aggregate demand.

A particular difficulty in using interest rate reductions to expand the economy arises if the repo rate is nearly zero but this is still not enough to stimulate the economy. The problem is that (nominal) interest rates cannot be negative, for clearly nobody would be willing to lend in these circumstances. Japan was in such a situation in the early 2000s. It was caught in what is known as the *liquidity trap*. The UK and many euro-zone countries were in this position in the early 2010s. Despite record low interest rates and high levels of liquidity, borrowing and lending remained low, given worries about fiscal austerity and its dampening effects on economic growth. Paul Krugman discusses the liquidity trap in his *New York Times* blog.[3]

Despite these problems, changing interest rates can often be quite effective in the medium term. After all, they can be changed very rapidly. There are not the time lags of implementation that there are with fiscal policy. Indeed, since the early 1990s most governments or central banks in OECD countries have

used interest rate changes as the major means of keeping aggregate demand and inflation under control. Up until 2008, this policy had been successful. The question remains as to whether they can be successful again in managing the economy, now that we are gradually seeing some very small increases in rates in some countries.

---

[3] Paul Krugman, 'Monetary policy in a liquidity trap', *The New York Times* (11 April 2013).

Definition

Liquidity trap When interest rates are at their floor and thus any further increases in money supply will not be spent but merely be held in bank accounts as people wait for the economy to recover and/or interest rates to rise.

BOX 11.3 THE CREDIT CRUNCH AND ITS AFTERMATH

Causes of the crisis and responses to its longer-term effects

Banks and other financial institutions want to make profits but, at the same time as pursuing this objective, they must also have sufficient funds to meet the day-to-day demands of their customers to withdraw money from their accounts. These two objectives often conflict, as the more liquid an asset, the less profitable it is likely to be and *vice versa*. For example, personal and business loans to customers are profitable to banks, but highly illiquid, as they are difficult to convert into cash without loss. On the other hand, keeping cash reserves in the bank will generate no profits, but they are completely liquid.

Banks must therefore hold a range of assets, with varying degrees of profitability and liquidity. It is this conflict which may have sown the seeds for the credit crunch that affected economies across the world.

Bank loans across the world had increased rapidly. Many of these loans were secured against property and were thus illiquid. However, there is a process by which banks can increase the liquidity of their balance sheets, and therefore expand the size of their illiquid assets, and many used this strategy prior to the credit crunch. The process is known as *securitisation*.

Securitisation is a form of financial engineering, where a financial institution pools some of its assets, such as residential mortgages, and sells them to an intermediary, known as a special purpose vehicle (SPV). The SPV, in purchasing these assets, gives the financial institution cash today, allowing them to make further advances. To finance their purchase, the SPV will issue bonds to investors (noteholders).

Securitisation grew rapidly in the UK and USA, especially among banks. In the UK, the flows of securitised loans increased from under £3 billion in 1999 to over £100 billion by 2008.

Risks and the sub-prime market

The increase in securitisation up to 2008 highlights the strong demand among investors for these securities. The

attraction of these fixed-income products for the noteholders was the potential for higher returns than on (what were) similarly-rated products.

However, investors have no recourse should people with mortgages fall into arrears or, worse still, default on their mortgages. The securitisation of assets can therefore be highly risky for all those in the securitisation chain and consequently for the financial system as a whole.

The pooling of advances in itself *reduces* the cash-flow risk facing investors. However, there is a *moral hazard* problem here (see pages 59–60 and 62). The pooling of the risks may encourage lenders to lower their credit criteria by offering house purchasers higher income multiples (advances relative to annual household incomes) or higher loan-to-value ratios (advances relative to the price of housing).

Towards the end of 2006 the USA witnessed an increase in the number of defaults by households on residential mortgages. This was a particular problem in the *sub-prime market* – higher-risk households with poor credit ratings. Similarly, the number falling behind with their payments rose. This was on the back of rising interest rates. As long as house prices

Definitions

Moral hazard The temptation to take more risks when you know that someone else will cover the risks if you get into difficulties. In the case of banks taking risks, the 'someone else' may be another bank, the central bank or the government.

Sub-prime debt Debt where there is a high risk of default by the borrower (e.g. mortgage holders who are on low incomes facing higher interest rates and falling house prices).

▶

were rising, people could always sell their house to pay off their loan. But in 2006/7 US house prices were falling, forcing many people to default.

These problems in the US sub-prime market were the catalyst for the liquidity problem that beset financial systems in 2007 and 2008. Where these assets were securitised, investors (largely other financial institutions) suffered from the contagion arising from arrears and defaults.

Securitisation also internationalised the contagion. Investors are global so that advances, such as a US family's residential mortgage, can cross national borders as part of a securitised asset. As the contagion spread globally, financial institutions across the world ended up having to write off debts. They thus saw their balance sheets deteriorate and this eventually led to the collapse in the demand for securitised assets.

Perhaps more important than this, was the lack of trust between banks. Banks did not want to lend to each other, in case they were lending to a bank with worthless assets, meaning they were unlikely to repay any loan. Inter-bank lending therefore virtually dried up, as did liquidity. And so began the credit crunch, spreading rapidly from one nation to the next.

 1. *Does securitisation necessarily involve a moral hazard problem?*

How did the world respond?

With banks failing and confidence lacking, measures were introduced in many countries to provide stability for the financial system and to support ailing financial institutions. From summer 2007, central banks, including the US Federal Reserve and the Bank of England, became increasingly proactive in injecting liquidity into the financial system.

Then from late 2008, central banks cut interest rates so that by early 2009 they were virtually zero (see Figure 11.5 on page 304). Programmes of quantitative easing were adopted, first by the Fed, then by the Bank of England, then the Bank of Japan[1] and eventually in 2015 by the ECB.

US measures

In October 2008, just one month after the collapse of Lehman Brothers in the USA, a $700 billion rescue package was adopted for the USA's struggling financial system, known as the *Troubled Asset Relief Program (TARP)*. The aim was to provide liquidity to the banking system. In addition, the Federal Reserve announced a planned purchase of $100 billion of corporate debt issued by government-sponsored financial enterprises and $500 billion of mortgage-backed securities.

With growth not increasing fast enough, a second round of quantitative easing ('QE2') was announced in November

2010, with the Fed buying $600 billion of Treasury securities by the end of quarter 2 of 2011. Then in September 2012 it launched QE3, saying that it would spend an additional $40 billion per month, which was then increased to $85 billion per month in December 2012. The Fed also announced that it would keep the federal funds rate near zero 'at least through 2015'.

Quantitative easing finally ended in October 2014, with the Fed having purchased a total of $3.5 trillion in assets.[2] With the US economy on a seemingly more stable footing, interest rates were finally increased in December 2015, after much speculation as to when the first rate rise would come. Since then, they have steadily risen, moving above 1 per cent in June 2017 and rising above 2 per cent in October 2018.

 2. *How significant was the decision by Janet Yellen, the then Chair of the Federal Reserve, to begin raising interest rates? What did the interest rate rises mean for other economies?*

ECB measures

Various measures were taken in the eurozone, although these were not initially designed to increase money supply. A *Securities Market Programme (SMP)* began in May 2010 with the objective of supplying liquidity to the banking system. Under the programme, the ECB used existing funds to purchase various assets, including government bonds, from banks. Under SMP, the plan was for banks to buy them back at some point in the future (a form of repo).

Between December 2011 and February 2012, the ECB lent over €1 trillion to banks in the form of three-year loans at a mere 1 per cent rate of interest in return for a range of collateral. The hope was that the loans would help banks pay off maturing debt and allow banks to increase their lending. Also it was hoped that the banks would use the loans to buy government bonds, thereby easing the debt crisis in countries such as Greece, Portugal, Spain, Ireland and Italy. The reserve ratio (see Box 11.2) was also reduced in January 2012 from 2 per cent to 1 per cent, again with the objective of helping to alleviate some of the constraints on the volume of bank lending by financial institutions.

As concerns developed throughout 2012 about the future of the euro and the ability of countries, such as Greece, Spain and Italy to remain in the monetary union and be able to borrow at affordable interest rates, a replacement for the SMP was announced. It would involve a more extensive programme of purchasing existing government bonds of countries in difficulty and so the scheme was designed to help troubled banks and troubled countries, rather than boosting the eurozone economy as a whole. The purchases of bonds were not time limited and the aim was to drive down these countries' interest rates and thereby make it cheaper to issue new bonds when old ones matured. These Outright Monetary Transactions (OMTs) were part of the ECB's strategy to do 'whatever it takes' to hold the single currency together

---

[1] As we shall see in Box 11.4 on page 315, the Bank of Japan had previously used quantitative easing in the early 2000s in an attempt to stimulate a stagnant economy.

[2] See: Jeff Kearns, 'The Fed eases off', *Bloomberg* (15 September 2015).

(see the blog *How can the ECB ease monetary policy?* on the Sloman Economics News site).

With the eurozone still failing to achieve economic growth, the ECB announced that it was adopting a negative deposit rate (the rate paid to banks for overnight deposits in the ECB) and that it was embarking on a further series of targeted long-term refinancing operations to provide long-term loans to commercial banks at cheap rates until September 2018.

Eventually, in 2015, the ECB announced that it was introducing quantitative easing. This would be a large-scale programme whereby it would create new money to buy €60 billion of existing assets every month, mainly bonds of governments in the eurozone held largely by banks. This programme of asset purchases began in March 2015 and was set to continue until at least September 2016, bringing the total of assets purchased by that time to over €1.1 trillion (see the blog *The ECB takes the plunge – at last* on the Sloman Economics News site).

However, the end of 2015 saw a divergence of monetary policy between the ECB and the Fed.[3] As the Fed raised rates and held off on any further quantitative easing, the ECB cut its deposit rate from −0.2 to −0.3 and announced a further extension of the quantitative easing programme from September 2016 to March 2017, by which time the total would be €1.5 trillion. The deposit rate was further reduced to −0.4 per cent in March 2016, while the quantitative easing programme was increased to €80 billion per month. With economic growth picking up, monthly purchases fell back to €60 billion per month from April 2017 and then to €30 billion per month from January 2018 until the end of September 2018 and finally €15 billion per month for the final three months of 2018, at which point the programme was brought to a close. This took the ECB's total asset purchases to around €2.6 trillion.

UK measures

With the onset of the credit crunch, various packages for generating liquidity were introduced, including a *Credit Guarantee Scheme* in late 2008, which made £250 billion available. This meant that if bank A lent to bank B and bank B then defaulted, the government would repay bank A. The guarantees were provided by HM Treasury for a fee payable each quarter and were designed to assist with the refinancing of maturing wholesale funding. This lending was crucial to kick-start the economy, build confidence and stimulate consumer spending. The Credit Guarantee Scheme came to an end in November 2012, suggesting that the financial system was returning to normality.

Northern Rock, Bradford and Bingley, the Royal Bank of Scotland and Lloyds Banking Group were just some of the UK financial institutions that were exposed during the financial crisis. In the case of RBS and Lloyds Banking Group, the government responded by making billions of pounds worth of

extra capital available, in the form of new shares owned by the government (and thus the taxpayer). In the case of Northern Rock, it was taken into full government ownership in February 2008 and so represented complete nationalisation.

Perhaps the most radical measure was a programme of *quantitative easing* under the *Asset Purchase Facility (APF)*. This involved the Bank of England buying high quality assets, mainly government bonds, from private institutions, such as pension funds, insurance companies and banks. These assets are purchased with newly created electronic money. The money, once deposited in banks, not only eases the liquidity position of banks but also becomes the basis for credit creation. The hope was that this would increase aggregate demand.

By 2013, four rounds of quantitative easing had taken place, beginning in March 2009 (£200 billion), October 2011 (£75 billion), February 2012 (£50 billion) and July 2012 (£50 billion), bringing the total to £375 billion, or 24 per cent of annual GDP.

The major problem with quantitative easing, however, was that banks did not increase lending as much as had been hoped, preferring to retain a higher proportion of reserves in the Bank of England. The reason was partly a lack of willingness of banks to lend in an uncertain economic climate, and partly a lack of demand for loans from consumers and businesses, who have also lacked confidence in the economy and have sought to reduce their debts.

There was much speculation that soon after the Fed took the leap to raise interest rates, the Bank of England would follow suit. However, in April 2016, all members of the MPC voted to keep interest rates fixed at 0.5 per cent (where they had been for over seven years). So, despite growth returning and quantitative easing seemingly at an end, there was not yet a complete return to 'normality'.

Then in August 2016, with concerns about the prospects for the UK economy following the vote to leave the European Union, the Bank of England increased its purchases of government bonds by a further £60 billion to £435 billion. Additionally, it agreed to purchase up to £10 billion of UK corporate bonds. Interest rates were also cut to 0.25 per cent and remained there until November 2017, when they were increased back to 0.5 per cent, before rising to 0.75 per cent in August 2018.

3. *Why may supplying extra liquidity to banks not necessarily be successful in averting a slow-down in borrowing and spending?*

4. *Why is there a potential moral hazard in supporting failing banks? How could the terms of a bailout help to reduce this moral hazard?*

Find out what use has been made of quantitative easing in Japan. How successful has it been in stimulating the Japanese economy?

---

[3] See: Mohamed El Erian, 'The Fed and the ECB: when monetary policy diverges', *The Guardian* (2 December 2015).

RECAP

1. The government or central bank can use monetary policy to restrict (or increase) the growth in aggregate demand by reducing (or increasing) money supply directly or by reducing (or increasing) the demand for money by raising (or lowering) interest rates.

2. The money supply can be reduced (increased) directly by using open-market operations. This involves the central bank selling (purchasing) more government securities and thereby reducing (increasing) banks' reserves when their customers pay for them from their bank accounts.

3. The current method of control in the UK involves the Bank of England's Monetary Policy Committee announcing the interest rate and then the Bank of England bringing this rate about by its operations in the repo market. It keeps banks short of liquidity, and then supplies them with liquidity through gilt repos at the chosen interest rate (gilt repo rate or 'Bank Rate'). This then has a knock-on effect on interest rates throughout the economy.

4. Higher interest rates, by reducing the demand for money, effectively also reduce the supply. However, with an inelastic demand for loans, interest rates may have to rise to very high levels in order to bring the required reduction in monetary growth.

5. Lower interest rates should stimulate the economy. However, if confidence by consumers and business is low, even interest rates approaching zero may be insufficient to achieve the required stimulus, as was seen in the years following the financial crisis of 2007–8.

6. Controlling aggregate demand through interest rates is made even more difficult by *fluctuations* in the demand for money. These fluctuations are made more severe by speculation against changes in interest rates, exchange rates, the rate of inflation, etc.

7. Nevertheless, controlling interest rates is a way of responding rapidly to changing forecasts, and can be an important signal to markets that inflation will be kept under control, especially when, as in the UK and the eurozone, there is a firm target for the rate of inflation.

8. Achieving inflation targets became increasingly easy in the 1990s and 2000s, but in the process, inflation became increasingly less related to other key objectives, such as economic growth or unemployment.

9. Some economists advocate using a Taylor rule, which involves targeting a weighted average of inflation and economic growth.

10. The Bank of England bases its decisions on the forecast inflation rate in two years' time. It adjusts interest rates if this forecast rate of inflation diverges from 2 per cent.

11.3 SUPPLY-SIDE POLICY

In considering economic policy up to this point we have focused our attention upon the demand side, where slow growth and unemployment are due to a lack of aggregate demand, and inflation is due to excessive aggregate demand. Many of the causes of these problems lie on the supply side, however, and as such require an alternative policy approach.

If successful, 'supply-side policies' will shift the aggregate supply curve to the right (see Figure 11.1(b) on page 294), thus increasing output for any given level of prices (or reducing the price level for any given level of output). Supply-side policies effectively increase an economy's capacity to produce; they may also raise the rate at which this potential output grows over time. These are policies, therefore, that can improve long-term economic growth.

Supply-side policies can take various forms. They can be 'market orientated' and focus on ways of 'freeing up' the market, such as encouraging private enterprise, risk taking and competition: policies that provide incentives and reward initiative, hard work and productivity. Alternatively, they can be interventionist in nature and focus on means of counteracting the deficiencies of the free market.

Either way, business leaders will be keen to have a supply-side policy that is favourable to them. This could be lower business taxes, improved education and training, a better transport and communications infrastructure or making regulation more 'light touch'. The Confederation of British Industry (and similar organisations in other countries), business pressure groups and also individual companies will seek to influence politicians in formulating supply-side policies. Frequently the argument is that 'business-friendly' policies will make the country more competitive.

Market-orientated supply-side policies

Radical market-orientated supply-side policies were first adopted in the early 1980s by the Thatcher government in the UK and the Reagan administration in the USA, but were subsequently copied by other right and centre-right governments around the world. The essence of this type of supply-side policy is to encourage and reward individual enterprise and initiative, and to reduce the role of government; to put more reliance on market forces and competition, and less on government intervention and regulation.

BOX 11.4   JAPAN'S VOLATILE PAST AND PRESENT

The lost decades

When Shinzo Abe came to power in December 2012, Japan's growth had averaged just 0.8 per cent for the previous two decades, compared with 1.3 per cent for Germany, 2.3 per cent for the UK, 2.6 per cent for the USA, 4.9 per cent for South Korea and 10.4 per cent for China.

By contrast, before the 1990s the Japanese economy had been booming with an average annual growth rate of over 4 per cent from 1980 to 1990 and the highest GNP per capita growth rate in the world by the late 1980s. However, speculation in the housing and stock markets during this booming period led to interest rate increases and in 1992, annual growth fell to just 0.8 per cent, before contracting by 0.5 per cent in 1993, as shown in the chart. And so began two decades of stagnation, pessimism, deflation and some might say, bad luck for Japan.

Struggling to combat recession in the 1990s

To combat Japan's initial downturn, numerous stimulus packages were implemented, with tax cuts and spending rises, leading to a general government deficit of over 5 per cent of GDP by 1996 and an increase in general government debt from 67.9 per cent of GDP in 1992 to 94.0 per cent of GDP by 1996.

Japan briefly returned to growth in 1996, but by then the Asian economies as a whole were performing poorly, and Japan fell back into recession. Despite the poor state of its public finances (an average budget deficit of 5.2 per cent of GDP and general government debt of 117.2 per cent of GDP in the late 1990s), expansionary fiscal policy was used once more. An initial ¥16 trillion (£80 billion) was injected into the economy in April 1998, followed by a further ¥18 trillion (£90 billion) 6 months later. Free shopping vouchers were also distributed to 35 million citizens worth ¥700 billion (£3.5 billion).[1]

However, the impact was muted. Uncertainty over jobs and future growth, together with a collapsing financial sector meant that businesses did not respond to the cuts in business taxes. Investment fell and individuals chose to save rather than spend, as shown in the figure above (a high marginal propensity to save has been a future of the Japanese economy). With a lack of demand, prices remained low and deflation continued to plague the economy.

?

1. *If government spending was rising and taxes were falling, why would aggregate demand not increase?*

By 2000, the government's stimulus was having an effect, but bad luck hit once more, when the USA and the EU moved into recession in 2001. As demand for Japan's exports fell, a pessimistic mood returned, but this time expansionary fiscal policy was not feasible, with a general government deficit of over 6 per cent of GDP and national debt that now stood above 140 per cent of GDP.

Interest rates had already been cut to near 0 per cent and so the Bank of Japan was the first to turn to quantitative easing, injecting some ¥35 trillion (£178 billion) into banks between 2001 and 2004. Finally, the economy was recovering, with economic growth averaging 1.9 per cent between 2002 and 2007. Despite inflation becoming positive in 2006 and the hope that this would deter people from saving, demand remained low and by 2008, general government debt was almost 192 per cent of GDP.

---

[1] 'The economy rescue plan for Japan's economy', *BBC News* (12 November 1998).

Output, consumption and investment growth in Japan

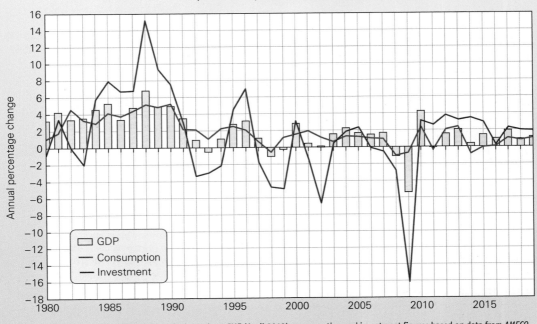

Sources: GDP figures from *World Economic Outlook Database*, IMF (April 2019); consumption and investment figures based on data from *AMECO database*, European Commission

▶

More bad luck

Having been hit firstly with the Asian economies slowing in 1996 and then with the EU and USA slowing in 2001, 2008 saw Japan's third dose of bad luck, as the financial crisis hit and the world plunged into recession. This led to Japan's deepest recession, with the economy shrinking by 9.2 per cent between Q2 2008 to Q1 2009 (see chart).

Despite the abysmal public finances, two stimulus packages of ¥11.7 trillion (£56.8 billion) and then of further ¥27 trillion (£170 billion) were introduced in August 2008 and early 2009, together with cash hand-outs to households.[2]

However, the crisis continued and Japan's GDP was now falling at an annual rate of 12.7 per cent. A powerful earthquake and devastating tsunami hit the east coast of Japan on 11 March 2011, further damaging the weak economy and taking the lives of more than 15 000 people.

In August 2011, the Bank of Japan provided ¥15 trillion of support to the banking system to provide stability and intervention occurred in the foreign exchange market[3] to combat the strength of the Japanese yen, which had appreciated by 10 per cent between June 2009 and August 2011, further weakening export demand. In the same month, the Central Bank of Japan announced its intention to increase the size of its quantitative easing programme[4] to ¥50 trillion and this was expanded further to ¥80 trillion by September 2012. In addition, the Ministry of Finance set up a fund worth over £60 billion to enable Japanese firms to expand operations overseas.[5] The combination of these measures meant that 2012 saw the return of growth.

However, as the world outlook deteriorated, the economic woes returned and the government was once again facing a dilemma over stimulating the economy or further increasing its already phenomenal general government debt, which, at 236.6 per cent of GDP, was the highest in the developed world.

Abenomics: the three arrows

When Shinzo Abe came to office in December 2012, he developed a three-pronged approach to save the Japanese economy, known as the 'three arrows' (see the blogs, *Japan's three arrows* and *Japan's arrows missing their target* on the Sloman Economics News site).

One 'arrow' was a fiscal policy package estimated to be worth over $100 billion. This focused on large-scale infrastructure and investment projects. At the same time, a long-term plan was set out for fiscal consolidation (i.e. reducing the deficit), once economic growth returned. In the short term, Japan was not expected to have any difficulty in financing the higher deficit, given that most of the borrowing was internal and denominated in yen.

Another arrow was monetary policy, with the Bank of Japan introducing an inflation target of 2 per cent[6] and

expanding its quantitative easing programme[7] in 2013. The central bank was hoping to address the issue of stagnant or falling prices, which had led to deflation and such low demand for so many years. Japanese consumers and businesses had become used to waiting to spend in the hopes of being able to buy at lower prices and 'Abenomics' aimed to address this.

The third arrow was supply-side policy. Various policies were adopted to boost capacity and productivity. In addition to the new infrastructure expenditure, policies focused on increased domestic and inward private-sector investment, encouraging more women into work and the deregulation of goods, capital and labour markets.

The three-pronged approach had some success, with inflation finally rising, reaching 3.7 per cent in May 2014, but growth remained fragile at only 0.4 per cent in 2014. This was driven largely by a fall in the volume of consumption after the country's sales tax rose in April 2014, as part of the long-term plan to reduce the deficit and debt.

Despite small glimmers of hope, the fragility of economic growth persisted, with both consumption and investment growth remaining poor. Planned increases in the sales tax were delayed until 2017 and then until October 2019, as pessimism once again beset the Japanese people. The planned fiscal consolidation package and subsequent objectives for public finances were pushed back to 2025 and even now, forecasts indicate that it will be unlikely if these targets are met.

The Bank of Japan introduced a negative interest rate on some deposits placed with it in January 2016, hoping to avoid a return to deflation. Then, in July 2018 it adopted for the first time a policy of *forward guidance* for policy rates designed to influence people's expectations.[8] This guidance pointed to interest rates remaining at their 'extremely low levels' for 'an extended period of time'. The Bank of Japan also acknowledged that wage- and price-setting behaviour meant that it would take longer than expected for it to meet its inflation target of 2 per cent.

The Bank of Japan has indicated that 'continuous powerful monetary easing' will continue for some time. Fiscal stimulus packages have been somewhat ineffective at stimulating aggregate demand and general government debt still remains at over 235 per cent of GDP, with the IMF forecasting that by 2023, it will still be 235.4 per cent of GDP. Despite concerted policy in all three areas, economic fragility persists.

2. *If tax cuts are largely saved, should an expansionary fiscal policy be confined to increases in government spending?*

3. *What are Japans' three arrows and have they been successful?*

Write a brief report updating the story in this box to the current day. Imagine that the report has to be presented as a briefing paper for a minister of your country who wishes to be informed of the economic policies being pursued by the Japanese government and what their likely impacts will be on (a) the Japanese economy and (b) your own country. Your report should highlight any specific changes that have been made to policy and should consider their likely effects. Produce charts to back-up your analysis.

2. Justin McCurry, 'Japan helps small firms and families with bumper stimulus package', *The Guardian* (30 October 2008).
3. 'Japan government and central bank intervene to cut yen', *BBC News* (4 August 2011).
4. *Enhancement of Monetary Easing,* Bank of Japan (4 August 2011).
5. 'Japan opens $100bn fund to help firms beat yen strength', *BBC News* (24 August 2011).
6. *The "Price Stability Target" under the Framework for the Conduct of Monetary Policy,* Bank of Japan (22 January 2013).
7. *Introduction of the "Quantitative and Qualitative Monetary Easing"*, Bank of Japan (4 April 2013).

8. *Strengthening the Framework for Continuous Powerful Monetary Easing,* Bank of Japan (31 July 2018).

Reducing government expenditure

The desire of many governments to cut government expenditure is not just to reduce the size of the public-sector deficit; it is also an essential ingredient of their supply-side strategy.

In most countries the size of the public sector, relative to GDP, grew substantially between the 1950s and 1970s. A major aim of conservative-led governments throughout the world has been to reverse this trend. The public sector is portrayed as more bureaucratic and less efficient than the private sector. What is more, it is claimed that a growing proportion of public money has been spent on administration and other 'non-productive' activities, rather than on the direct provision of goods and services.

Two things are needed, it is argued: (a) a more efficient use of resources within the public sector and (b) a reduction in the size of the public sector. This would allow private investment to increase with no overall rise in aggregate demand. Thus the supply-side benefits of higher investment could be achieved without the demand-side costs of higher inflation.

In practice, governments have found it very difficult to cut their expenditure relative to GDP. However, as we saw in section 11.1, many countries were faced with trying to do this after the financial crisis and global economic slowdown of the late 2000s. Governments had to make difficult choices, particularly concerning the levels of services and the provision of infrastructure.

> **Pause for thought**
>
> *Why might a recovering economy (and hence a fall in government expenditure on social security benefits) make the government feel even more concerned to make discretionary cuts in government expenditure?*

Tax cuts

Taxes can affect a variety of choices that individuals make, often leading them to substitute one activity for another. There are three common examples of taxes that affect aggregate supply. These are (a) taxing labour income, (b) taxing interest earned on savings and (c) taxing firms' profits. Over time, many counties have reduced the marginal rates of taxation in each of these three areas and one of the aims has been to affect the supply side of the economy.

Income tax cuts. The UK's basic rate of income tax in 1979 was 33 per cent, with the top rate of tax at 83 per cent. By 2008, the standard and top rates were 20 per cent and 40 per cent respectively. But in 2010, a higher top rate of tax was imposed of 50 per cent (for those earning above £150 000). One of the reasons for this rise in the top rate was to reduce the deficit in public finances. Later, in 2013, the top rate was reduced to 45 per cent, the argument being that if the top rate is too high, it acts as a disincentive to work and promotion. You can read about the debate over the economic justification for this top rate of income tax in the blog, *A 50p top tax rate: more or less money for the government?* on the Sloman Economics News site.

Cuts in the marginal rate of income tax are claimed to have many beneficial effects, e.g. people work longer hours; more people wish to work; people work more enthusiastically; unemployment falls; employment rises. The evidence regarding the truth of these claims, however, is less than certain.

For example, will people be prepared to work longer hours? On the one hand, each hour worked will be more valuable in terms of take-home pay, and thus people may be encouraged to work more and have less leisure time. This is a substitution effect (see page 28); people substitute work for leisure. On the other hand, a cut in income tax will make people better off, and therefore they may feel that they can cut down on the number of hours they work, assuming they have a choice. This is an income effect (see page 28); they can afford to work less. The evidence on these two effects suggests that they just about cancel each other out. Anyway, for many people there is no such choice in the short run. There is no chance of doing extra or fewer hours or working a shorter week. In the long run, there may be some flexibility in that people can change jobs.

> **Pause for thought**
>
> *If the basic rate of income tax is cut, which will be the larger effect – the income effect or the substitution effect – for people (a) on low incomes just above the tax threshold and (b) on very high incomes? What will be the effect on hours worked in each case (assuming that the person has a choice)?*

Tax cuts for business and other investment incentives. A number of financial incentives can be given to encourage investment. Market-orientated policies seek to reduce the general level of taxation on profits, or to give greater tax relief to investment.

A cut in corporation tax (the tax on business profits) will increase after-tax profits. This will create more money for ploughing back into investment, and the higher after-tax return on investment will encourage more investment to take place. In 1983 the main rate of corporation tax in the UK stood at 52 per cent. A series of reductions have taken place since then, with the main rate having fallen to 19 per cent by 2017 and due to fall to 17 per cent by 2020. The government hoped that such low rates would make the UK an attractive destination for business investment. Governments have also looked to give firms R&D expenditure credits and investment allowances, which reduce a firm's tax liability, increase net profit and encourage firms to invest more, thus increasing the capacity of the economy.

The danger of countries cutting taxes to make them more internationally competitive, however, is that it is a prisoners' dilemma game (see pages 129–30). Countries cannot all have lower taxes than each other! You may simply end up with global taxes being lower and governments receiving less tax revenue. Governments thus have to make a judgement as to whether or not cutting taxes will stimulate other countries to do the same.

However, there has been more global co-operation[4] over tax policy as countries seek to tackle large firms which have been able to avoid paying high tax bills, through both illegal means and various legal loopholes. Problems of tax evasion (illegal) and tax avoidance (legal) are not new, but we have seen some significant cases of both by some high-profile firms, including Amazon,[5] Starbucks,[6] Google[7] and Apple.[8]

Reducing the power of labour

The argument here is that if labour costs to employers are reduced, their profits will probably rise. This could encourage and enable more investment and hence economic growth. If the monopoly power of labour is reduced, then cost-push inflation will also be reduced.

The Thatcher government took a number of measures to curtail the power of unions. These included the right of employees not to join unions, preventing workers taking action other than against their direct employers, and enforcing secret ballots on strike proposals. It set a lead in resisting strikes in the public sector.

As labour markets have become more flexible, with increased part-time working, zero-hour

contracts and short-term contracts, and as the process of globalisation has exposed more companies to international competition, so this has further eroded the power of labour in many sectors of the economy (see section 8.4). In the aftermath of the recession of 2008–9, however, there was an increase in industrial action and protests in many countries. This continued with the extensive government spending cuts designed to bring down budget deficits and with the resulting rise in unemployment (see Box 8.2 for the case of the UK).

Policies to encourage competition

If the government can encourage more competition, this should have the effect of increasing national output and reducing inflation. Four major types of policy have been pursued under this heading.

Privatisation. If privatisation simply involves the transfer of a natural monopoly into private hands (e.g. the water companies), the scope for increased competition is limited. However, where there is genuine scope for increased competition (e.g. in the supply of gas and electricity), privatisation can lead to increased efficiency, more consumer choice and lower prices.

Alternatively, privatisation can involve the introduction of private services into the public sector (e.g. private contractors providing cleaning services in hospitals, or refuse collection for local authorities). Private contractors may compete against each other for the franchise, thus driving down costs, but the quality of the service may then need monitoring.

Introducing market relationships into the public sector. This is where the government tries to get different departments or elements within a particular part of the public sector to 'trade' with each other, so as to encourage competition and efficiency. The most well-known examples are within education and health.

The process often involves 'devolved budgeting'. For example, in the UK, schools either can become 'academies' and then spend a centrally allocated grant as they choose, or, if they are still maintained by the local authority, can also decide how to spend the budget allocated to them. The objective is to encourage them to become more efficient, cutting costs, thereby reducing the burden on either tax payers or council tax payers. However, one result is that schools have tended to appoint inexperienced (and hence cheaper) teachers rather than those who can bring the benefits of their years of teaching. Although

[4] 'Fury at corporate tax avoidance leads to call for a global response', *The Guardian* (18 May 2013).

[5] Mark Bou Mansour, 'Why is Amazon still paying little tax in the UK?', *Tax Justice Network* (10 August 2018).

[6] 'Starbucks "paid just £8.6m UK tax in 14 years"', *BBC News* (16 October 2012).

[7] 'Google to pay UK £130m in back taxes', *The Telegraph* (22 January 2016).

[8] 'Paradise Papers: Apple shifted billions offshore to avoid tax', *DW* (7 November 2017).

this is a cost-saving approach, it could also be viewed as inefficient.

Another UK example is in the National Health Service. In 2003, the government introduced a system whereby hospitals could apply for 'foundation trust' status. If successful, they are given much greater financial autonomy in terms of purchasing, employment and investment decisions. Applications are judged by NHS Improvement, the independent health regulator, which also oversees and supports the operation of foundation trusts. By August 2019, there were 151 foundation trusts. Critics argue that funds have been diverted to foundation hospitals and away from the less well-performing hospitals where greater funding could help that performance. In the 2012 Health and Social Care Act, the government proposed that in due course all NHS hospitals become foundation trusts.

The Private Finance Initiative (PFI). Public–private partnerships (PPS) are a way of funding public expenditure with private capital. In the UK the *Private Finance Initiative* (PFI), as it was known, began in 1992. Under PFI, a private company, after a competitive tender, is contracted by a government department or local authority to finance and build a project, such as a new road or a prison. The government then pays the company to maintain and/or run it, or simply rents the assets from the company. The public sector thus becomes a purchaser of services rather than a direct provider itself. More details of PFI can be found in Case Study D.24 on the student website.

Critics claim that PFI projects have resulted in low quality of provision and that cost control has often been poor, resulting in a higher burden for the taxpayer in the long term. What is more, many of the projects have turned out to be highly profitable for the private provider, suggesting that the terms of the original contracts were too lax. In 2012 the UK government published reforms to the PFI process following concerns about the quality of provision and the costs being incurred. More recently, they have been described as 'inflexible and overly complex' and the OBR described them as a 'source of significant fiscal risk to government'. The government decided that, while that existing PFIs will be honoured, no further ones will be awarded.

Free trade and capital movements. The opening up of international trade and investment is central to a market-orientated supply-side policy. One of the first measures of the Thatcher government (in October 1979) was to remove all controls on the purchase and sale of foreign currencies, thereby permitting the free inflow and out-flow of capital, both long term and short term. Most other industrialised countries also removed or relaxed exchange controls during the 1980s and early 1990s.

The Single European Act of 1987, which came into force in 1993, was another example of international liberalisation (we examine this in section 12.4). It was designed to create a 'single market' in the EU: a market without barriers to the movement of goods, services, capital and labour. This has been largely achieved, although some restrictions on trade between members do still apply. In the UK, the free movement of labour was one of the major factors that led to the EU referendum and the country's decision to leave the EU.

Critics have claimed that, in the short term, industries may be forced to close by the competition from cheaper imported products, which can have a major impact on employment in the areas affected. A major election promise of the Trump campaign was that 'putting America first' would involve a move away from free trade and giving specific protection to US industries, such as vehicles and steel. We examine such arguments in section 12.2.

Interventionist supply-side policy

As we have seen, supply-side policy is designed to increase potential output – the capacity of the economy to produce. Potential output depends on the quantity and quality (productivity) of inputs. This in turn depends to a large extent on investment – in education and training to increase labour productivity, in research and development, and in new capital.

But can investment be left to the market? Investment often involves risks. Firms may be unwilling to take those risks, since the costs of possible failure may be too high. When looked at nationally, however, the benefits of investment might well have substantially outweighed the costs, and thus it would have been socially desirable for firms to have taken the risk. Successes would have outweighed failures. This might therefore be a case of market failure that justifies government intervention.

> **Pause for thought**
>
> *What specific market failures could explain under investment?*

Table 11.3	Gross fixed capital formation as a percentage of GDP, 1960–2020					
Year (average)	UK	Germany[a]	Japan	EU–15[b]	USA	Eurozone
1960–70	19.3	24.9	33.4	24.1	22.1	–
1971–80	21.0	22.5	34.2	24.0	22.3	–
1981–90	20.7	20.3	30.5	21.8	22.8	–
1991–2000	18.6	23.5	29.8	21.4	21.2	20.5
2001–10	17.0	19.8	24.1	21.1	21.5	22.0
2011–20	16.5	20.4	23.7	19.9	20.3	20.5

[a] West Germany prior to 1991
[b] The 15 members of the EU prior to the accession of ten new members in May 2004
Note: Figures from 2018 are based on forecasts.
Source: Based on data in *European Economy Statistical Annex* (European Commission, 2019). Reproduced with permission

Even when firms do wish to make such investments, they may find difficulties in raising finance. This can be a serious problem for small firms or start-up companies with no previous track record of investment.

Most developed countries have seen a decline in investment as a percentage of GDP, as Table 11.3 shows. The table also shows that the UK has had a lower level of investment relative to GDP than other industrialised countries.

Pause for thought

How can the UK's low level of investment relative to GDP be explained?

If the free market provides too little investment, there is a case for government intervention to boost investment. There are various approaches a government can take.

Funding research and development. There are potentially large externalities (benefits) from research and development (see page 244). Firms investing in developing and improving products, and especially firms engaged in more general scientific research, may produce results that provide benefits to many other firms. Thus the *social* rate of return on investment may be much higher than the private rate of return. Investment that is privately unprofitable for a firm may therefore still be economically desirable for the nation.

To increase a country's research and development, the government could fund universities or other research institutes through various grants, perhaps allocated by research councils. Alternatively, it could provide grants or tax relief to private firms to carry out R&D.

According to the OECD, R&D spending (both public and private) as a percentage of GDP for various countries include: Japan 3.2 per cent, Sweden 3.3 per cent, Germany 3.0 per cent; USA 2.8 per cent; France 2.2 per cent; and the UK just 1.7 per cent.[9] Box 11.5 examines research and development in various countries and its effects on productivity.

Direct provision. Improvements in infrastructure – such as a better motorway system – can be of direct benefit to industry. Alternatively, the government could provide factories or equipment to specific firms. The IMF,[10] OECD[11] and other international organisations have been calling for greater international expenditure on infrastructure as a way of increasing not only potential output but also aggregate demand.

Training. There are substantial external benefits from training. In other words, the benefits to the economy of trained labour extend beyond the firms undertaking the training when workers move to new jobs. The problem is that when this happens, the benefits are lost to the firm that provided the training. This, therefore, gives firms little incentive to invest heavily in training; hence the need for the government to step in.

The government may set up training schemes, or encourage educational institutions to make their courses more vocationally relevant, or introduce new

---

[9] 'GERD as a percentage of GDP', *Main Science and Technology Indicators* (OECD, 2019).

[10] Abdul Abiad, David Furceri and Petia Topalova, *IMF Survey: The Time Is Right for an Infrastructure Push*, IMF (30 September 2014).

[11] 'Fostering investment in infrastructure'; *OECD* (January 2015).

BOX 11.5	**PRODUCTIVITY**

A supply-side issue

Supply-side policies are those designed to increase the capacity of the economy. They focus on increasing either the quantity or productivity of inputs into production. In this box, we focus on productivity – of both labour and capital. The faster the growth in productivity, the faster is likely to be the country's rate of economic growth. Any government seeking to raise the long-term growth rate, therefore, must find ways of stimulating productivity growth.

On what does the growth of productivity depend? There are seven main determinants:

■ Private investment in new physical capital (machinery and buildings) and in research and development (R&D).
■ Public investment in education, R&D and infrastructure.
■ Training and the development of labour skills.
■ Innovation and the application of new technology.
■ The organisation and management of inputs into production.
■ The rate of entry of new firms into markets: generally such firms will have higher productivity than existing firms.
■ The business environment in which firms operate. Is there competition over the quality and design of products? Is there competitive pressure to reduce costs?

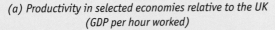

1. *Identify some policies a government could pursue to stimulate productivity growth through each of the above means.*

Productivity expands the economy's potential output and this helps drive prices downwards. This, in turn, stimulates real aggregate demand and actual economic growth. More productive workers are likely to receive higher wages, which in turn generates higher consumption, leading to higher output and investment via the multiplier and accelerator, This, in turn, stimulates further advances in productivity.

Higher productivity of capital will lead to higher returns from investment and so investors may embark upon new projects and enterprises, which may stimulate further productivity growth and higher output. In the long run, this may lead to lower costs, thus boosting their international competitiveness, increasing their market share and encouraging further investment and productivity growth.

It is clear that the prosperity of a nation rests upon its ability to improve its productivity. The more successful it is in doing this, the greater will be its rate of economic growth.

Labour productivity in the UK

Chart (a) shows comparative labour productivity levels of various countries using GDP per hour worked. This measure is a better one than output per worker, which would give low figures for countries with many part-time workers and high figures for full-time workers who work very long hours but are not very efficient. GDP per hour worked is thus a good measure to gauge worker efficiency.

As you can see, GDP per hour worked is lower in the UK than the other countries, with the exception of Japan. For example, in 2016, compared with the UK, output per hour was 35.5 per cent higher in Germany, 30 per cent higher in

(a) Productivity in selected economies relative to the UK (GDP per hour worked)

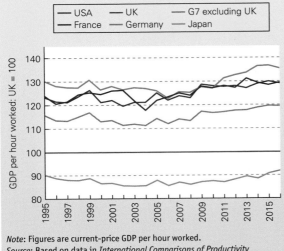

Note: Figures are current-price GDP per hour worked.
Source: Based on data in *International Comparisons of Productivity* (National Statistics, 2019)

(b) Gross expenditure on R&D (% of GDP)

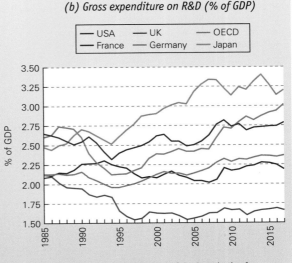

Note: OECD = 36 members (as of April 2019) of the Organisation for Economic Co-operation and Development.
Source: *Gross Domestic Spending on R&D* (OECD, 2019)

►

France and 29 per cent higher in the USA. Compared with the rest of the G7 countries, UK output per hour was 19.5 per cent lower, and hence essentially unchanged from the 19.6 per cent productivity gap recorded in 2015, which was an historic high. A major explanation of lower productivity in the UK is the fact that for decades it has invested a smaller proportion of its national income than most other industrialised nations.

One of the key causes of a lack of labour productivity is a mismatch between the aggregate supply of labour and the aggregate demand for labour. The issue can be traced to problems of immobility, either occupational or geographical. As markets change, labour may be unable to respond, as workers either don't have the right skills or qualifications or live too far away.

Supply-side policies might look to increase labour market flexibility, for example by supporting retraining, enhancing skills, providing better information and extending flexible working. If supply-side policies are successful in increasing the flexibility and skills of the workforce, this will increase the stock of human capital. Although this in itself is a benefit to the economy, it also brings another benefit, which we examine next.

2. *Another way of measuring labour productivity is to use output per worker. Is this a better method of measuring labour productivity than GDP per hour worked? How might we explain differences in productivity between the nations shown in figure (a), especially if we use different means of measurement?*

Capital productivity and R&D

If an economy's human capital increases, it will increase the effectiveness with which the economy's existing stock of physical capital can be employed and this contributes to further accumulation of physical capital. If workers are more skilled, they are able to contribute to the development of new products, processes and techniques and hence this improves the quality of capital.

Some economists argue that competition helps the development of new ideas and leads to technological progress, as firms look to gain a competitive advantage by developing better products and more cost-effective processes than their rivals. However, supply-side policies are also important, such as those that encourage the clustering of businesses, for example via enterprise zones, to make the sharing of ideas easier and those that involve incentives for firms to engage in R&D.

The European Commission's 'EU Industrial R&D Investment Scoreboard' analyses data from the world's top 2500

companies in R&D.[1] The 2018 report showed that R&D spending by these companies rose by 8.3 per cent in 2017/18, bringing the R&D total to €736.4 billion. US companies continue to invest the most at 37 per cent (778 companies), with EU companies accounting for 27 per cent of the total, Japanese and Chinese companies accounting for 14 per cent and 10 per cent, respectively and 12 per cent coming from the rest of the world. Growth in R&D expenditure has occurred in all regions/countries noted, but growth in China and the USA has outstripped that in the EU and Japan.

In the UK, lower R&D is one of the factors that has contributed to the productivity gap between it and other G7 countries and has a negative impact on its long-term economic growth. Although many UK-based companies are some of the world's largest R&D spending companies, it is a lack of R&D expenditure by government that appears to hold the country back.

Successive UK governments have tried to address this by using supply-side policies to encourage R&D. One example is the use of R&D incentives for small and medium-sized enterprises that enable them to offset a multiple of R&D costs against corporation tax. Meanwhile, from April 2016, larger companies were able to claim a taxable credit worth 11 per cent of R&D expenditures. However, only around one-third of UK R&D is financed by the government and despite supply-side policies aimed at encouraging R&D through the tax system, UK gross expenditure on research and development as a percentage of GDP has been lower than that of its main economic rivals for many years.

With a lack of government support for R&D, countries will inevitably face a productivity gap. The cost of R&D can be prohibitive for many firms and this means that while some firms may engage in it, those that receive greater government funding, through supply-side policies, are able to engage at significantly higher levels. It may cost the government in the short term, but supply-side policies are long term in nature. This trade-off can be a difficult one for governments, especially when their position is unstable.

3. *The productivity slowdown in the developed economies began before the financial crisis. What can explain this slowdown?*
4. *Why is R&D an example of a market failure?*

Find out what supply-side policies a country other than the UK has pursued. Compare them with those adopted in the UK.

---

[1] 'The EU Industrial R&D Investment Scoreboard, 2018', *Economics of Industrial Research and Innovation (IRI)* (European Commission, 2018).

vocational qualifications. Alternatively, the government could provide grants or tax relief to firms which themselves provide training schemes. Well-targeted training can lead to substantial improvements in labour productivity. The UK invests little in training programmes compared with most of its industrial competitors.

Advice and persuasion. The government may engage in discussions with private firms in order to find ways to improve efficiency and innovation. It may bring firms together to exchange information, so as to co-ordinate their decisions and create a climate of greater certainty. It may bring firms and unions together to try to create greater industrial harmony.

Assistance to small firms. Various forms of advisory services, grants and tax concessions could be provided to stimulate investment by small companies.

For example, in the UK small companies' financial support for R&D expenditure comes through corporation tax relief. This means they can reduce the profits liable for tax by engaging in R&D. Support to small firms in the UK is examined in Case Study D.25 on the book's website.

Nationalisation. This is essentially the opposite of privatisation, whereby a private industry is taken into public ownership. Privatisation did become commonplace across many industrialised countries. However, with the credit crunch and the subsequent collapse of many financial institutions, some banks were taken into part of full public ownership, such as Northern Rock and RBS. Therefore, nationalisation, perhaps just temporary, may be a suitable solution for rescuing vital industries suffering extreme market turbulence.

RECAP

1. Supply-side policies, if successful, will shift the aggregate supply curve to the right, and help to achieve faster economic growth without higher inflation.

2. Market-orientated supply-side policies aim to increase the rate of growth of aggregate supply and reduce the rate of unemployment by encouraging private enterprise and the freer play of market forces.

3. Reducing government expenditure as a proportion of GDP is a major element of such policies.

4. Tax cuts can be used to encourage more people to take up jobs, and people to work longer hours and more enthusiastically. The effects of tax cuts will depend on how people respond to incentives.

5. Various policies can be introduced to increase competition. These include privatisation, introducing market relationships into the public sector, and freer international trade and capital movements.

6. The UK has had a lower rate of investment than most other industrialised countries. This has contributed to a historically low rate of economic growth and imports of manufacture growing faster than exports. In response many argue for a more interventionist approach to supply-side policy.

7. Intervention can take the form of grants, supporting research and development, advice and persuasion, investing in training and the direct provision of infrastructure.

QUESTIONS

1. 'The existence of a budget deficit or a budget surplus tells us very little about the stance of fiscal policy.' Explain and discuss.

2. Adam Smith, the founder of modern economics, remarked in *The Wealth of Nations* (1776) concerning the balancing of budgets, 'What is prudence in the conduct of every private family can scarce be folly in that of a great kingdom.' What problems might there be if the government decided to follow a balanced budget approach to its spending?

3. Imagine you were called in by the government to advise on whether it should attempt to prevent cyclical fluctuations by the use of fiscal policy. What advice would you give and how would you justify the advice?

4. Why is it difficult to use fiscal policy to 'fine-tune' the economy?

5. When the Bank of England announces that it is putting down interest rates, how will it achieve this, given that interest rates are determined by demand and supply?

6. How does the Bank of England or another central bank attempt to achieve the target rate of inflation of 2 per cent? What determines its likelihood of success in meeting the target?

7. To what extent did central banks face a dilemma in 2008, when faced with rising inflation and the onset of recession?

8. What is meant by a Taylor rule? In what way is it a better rule for central banks to follow than one of adhering to a simple inflation target?

9. Under what circumstances would adherence to an inflation target lead to (a) more stable interest rates, (b) less stable interest rates, than pursuing discretionary demand management policy?

10. Define demand-side and supply-side policies. Are there any ways in which such policies are incompatible?

11. Why might it take time for the benefits of supply-side policies to become evident?

12. What types of tax cuts are likely to create the greatest (a) incentives, (b) disincentives to effort?

13. Imagine that you are asked to advise the government on ways of increasing investment in the economy. What advice would you give and why?

14. How can increasing the effectiveness of labour improve both the productivity of labour and the productivity of capital?

15. In what ways can interventionist supply-side policy work with the market, rather than against it? What are the arguments for and against such policy?

12 Chapter

The global trading environment

Business issues covered in this chapter

■ How has the pattern of trade changed over the years?
■ What are the benefits to countries and firms of international trade?
■ Which goods should a country export and which should it import?
■ What determines the competitiveness of a particular country and any given industry within it?
■ Why do countries sometimes try to restrict trade and protect their domestic industries?
■ What are the consequences of protectionism?
■ What is the role of the World Trade Organization (WTO) in international trade?
■ What are preferential trading arrangements and what are their effects?
■ How has the 'single market' in the EU benefited its members?
■ Has the business environment in the EU become more competitive?
■ What benefits arise from the accession of new member states?
■ Why did the UK consider leaving and eventually vote to leave the EU?
■ What happened in the Brexit negotiations in the two years after Article 50 was triggered?

The macroeconomic environment of business extends beyond the domestic economy that we examined in the previous two chapters. As we saw in Chapter 7, many firms are global in their reach. They are clearly affected not only by the economic situation at home, but also by the various countries in which they are based. For many, this means the global economy.

But even firms that are based solely in one country are still affected by the global macroeconomic situation. They may source some of their supplies from abroad, export some of their output or, as is the case with Tata Steel,[1] face competition from foreign firms. In other words, firms are locked into the global economy through the process of international trade.

Trading affects not only individual firms – it affects whole economies. Countries can become richer as a result of an open trading environment. Indeed, if we did not trade, items such as coffee, bananas and exotic fruits may not be available to us! We examine arguments for free trade in section 12.1.

Totally free trade, however, may bring problems to countries or to groups of people within those countries. Many people argue strongly for restrictions on trade, including America's President Trump.[2] Textile workers see

[1] Sean Farrell, 'How the UK steel crisis unfolded' *The Guardian* (20 April 2016).
[2] Kellie Ell, 'Trump is "dead serious about protectionism and tariffs," says analyst', *CNBC* (11 July 2018).

their jobs threatened by cheap imported cloth and the steel industry in developed countries is under threat from cheap Chinese exports. Car manufacturers worry about falling sales as customers switch to Japanese models or other East Asian ones. But are people justified in fearing international competition, or are they merely trying to protect some vested interest at the expense of everyone else? Section 12.2 examines the arguments for restricting trade and its consequences.

If there are conflicting views as to whether we should have more or less trade, what has been happening on the world stage? Section 12.3 looks at the various moves towards making trade freer and at the obstacles that have been met, especially with greater US protectionist policies and the UK's impending exit from the EU.

A step on the road to freer trade is for countries to enter free-trade agreements with just a limited number of other countries. In section 12.4, we look at probably the world's most famous preferential trading system, the European Union and, in particular, at the development of a 'single European market'. Finally, we consider the growth of the European Union and the developments following the UK's vote to leave it and the uncertainty that has been created.

12.1 INTERNATIONAL TRADE

The patterns of world trade

As we saw in Chapter 7, globalisation has led to greater interdependence between nations and an increase in world trade is just one example of this. Most nations have been committed to freer trade and with the World Trade Organization overseeing the dismantling of trade barriers, international trade has consistently grown faster than world GDP. From 1980 to 2018, the average annual rate of growth of world real GDP was 3.48 per cent, whereas the average rate of growth in the volume of world trade was 5.33 per cent.

This means that trade has grown as a proportion of countries' GDP. The ratio of the sum of world exports and imports of goods and services to world GDP has risen from around 25 per cent in 1960 to around 60 per cent in 2019 and with this, international interdependence has only increased.

A good example of this interdependence was the global recession of the late 2000s. In 2009, world output fell by 2.1 per cent. Worldwide merchandise exports, however, fell by approximately 12 per cent in volume terms and their value declined by 23 per cent. In the years following the financial crisis, world trade grew again, but at a slower pace. However, by 2017 the ratio of trade growth to GDP growth returned to the historical average of 1.5.

While the volume of trade in goods (merchandise trade) dwarfs that in services, there has been growth in the value of both for many decades (see Figure 12.1). In 1980, the value of world merchandise exports was

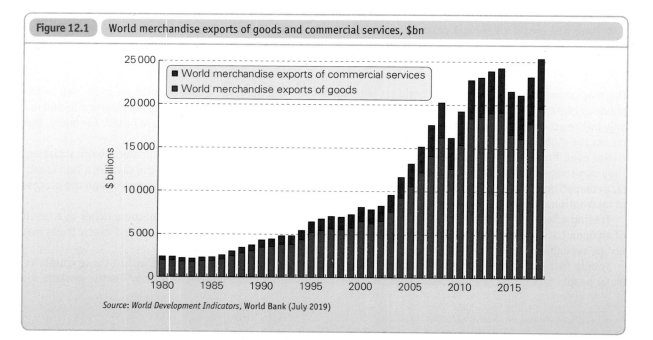

Figure 12.1 World merchandise exports of goods and commercial services, $bn

Source: *World Development Indicators*, World Bank (July 2019)

estimated at just under $2 trillion. By 2018 this had grown to $19.6 trillion. For the service sector, the value of exports stood at $384 billion in 1980, increasing to $5.8 trillion by 2018.[3]

For most countries, exports of goods are larger than exports of services. In 1980, the volume of exports of goods as a percentage of GDP was 18 per cent and that of services was 3.3 per cent. By 2018, the figures had risen to 22.8 per cent and 6.7 per cent, respectively. Although both figures fell between 1980 and 1991 and then again following the financial crisis, they were both significantly higher in 2018 than they were in 1980, with the recovery of services since 2009 outstripping that in goods.

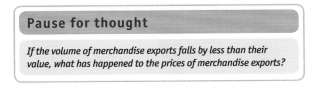

Pause for thought

If the volume of merchandise exports falls by less than their value, what has happened to the prices of merchandise exports?

The growing importance of developing countries in world trade

As we saw in section 7.2, developing and emerging nations are now receiving a greater share of multinational investment and a similar trend is apparent with world trade. Developed countries have, until recently, dominated world trade. In 1980, the percentage of world merchandise exports originating from developed countries was 79.8 per cent; in 2018, it was 66.4 per cent.

The reason for this changing global pattern of trade is that many of the countries with the most rapid *growth* in exports can now be found in the developing world. The growth in merchandise exports from the group of developing nations collectively known as the BRICS[4] (Brazil, Russia, India, China and South Africa) has been especially rapid. Between them they accounted for just 5.5 per cent of the value of world exports in 1992. In 2018 they accounted for 18.3 per cent of world exports.

More recently, other countries, such as Mexico, Turkey, Indonesia, Cambodia and Vietnam, have joined the ranks of rapidly growing 'newly industrialised' developing countries. Many of these newly industrialised countries are in Asia. Indeed, the volume of exports from developing countries in Asia grew by an average of 5.4 per cent per year in the 10 years to 2018.

Figure 12.2 shows the geographical origin of exports in 2018. Despite a more rapid growth in trade values in other regions in recent times, Europe remains an important geographical centre for trade. In 2018 it accounted for 37.6 per cent of world exports by value (and was the destination for 36.9 per cent of imports). While some African countries have experienced significant growth in trade since the early 1990s, many of the poorest African countries have seen negligible growth in trade over the period. Hence, in 2018 Africa accounted for only 2.5 per cent of world exports by value (and was the destination for 3.0 per cent of imports).

China continues to be the largest exporter, with a 13.1 per cent share of global merchandise exports, followed by the USA (8.8 per cent) and Germany (8.2 per cent). Of these three top nations, China has seen the biggest growth in the value of its exports since 2016. These three countries together account for $5.7 trillion of world merchandise exports. They are also the largest *importers* of both goods and services, but in both cases, the USA takes the top spot. It has a 13.5 per cent and 9.8 per cent share of merchandise imports and of commercial services imports, respectively. This is followed by China (11.0 and 9.5 per cent) and Germany (6.6 and 6.4 per cent). It is only in the export of commercial services, where China loses its position at the top of the rankings and instead the top three exporters are the USA (14.0 per cent), the UK (6.5 per cent) and Germany (5.6 per cent). China takes fifth place with a 4.6 per cent share.

Despite the growth in the share of world trade of developing economies, trade is still dominated by a few countries. In 2018, the top ten merchandise exporters accounted for 51.1 per cent of world merchandise exports and the top ten exporters of commercial services accounted for 53.5 per cent of world services exports.[5]

Case Study D.26 on the student website provides further analysis of the geographical patterns in the trade of merchandise goods and commercial services.

The advantages of trade

Specialisation as the basis for trade

Why do countries trade with each other and what do they gain from it? The reasons for international trade are really only an extension of the reasons for trade *within* a nation. Rather than people trying to be self-sufficient and doing everything for themselves, it makes sense to specialise.

Firms specialise in producing certain types of goods. This allows them to gain economies of scale

---

[3] Note that these are nominal values (i.e. the current prices of each year) and do not take account of inflation. In real 'volume' terms, as stated in the text, the average growth in trade in goods and services was 5.33% between 1980 and 2018).

[4] Sometimes the term is used to refer just to the first four countries. When South Africa is excluded, the term is written BRICs rather than BRICS.

[5] The top ten merchandise exporters in order were: China, USA, Germany, Japan, Netherlands, Republic of Korea, Hong Kong, France, Italy and UK. The top ten exporters of commercial services in order were: USA, UK, Germany, France, China, Netherlands, Ireland, India, Japan and Singapore.

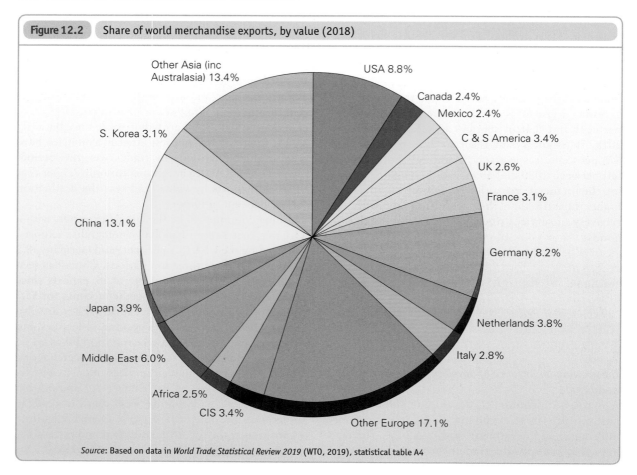

Figure 12.2 Share of world merchandise exports, by value (2018)

Other Asia (inc Australasia) 13.4%
USA 8.8%
Canada 2.4%
Mexico 2.4%
C & S America 3.4%
UK 2.6%
France 3.1%
Germany 8.2%
Netherlands 3.8%
Italy 2.8%
Other Europe 17.1%
CIS 3.4%
Africa 2.5%
Middle East 6.0%
Japan 3.9%
China 13.1%
S. Korea 3.1%

Source: Based on data in *World Trade Statistical Review 2019* (WTO, 2019), statistical table A4

and to exploit their entrepreneurial and management skills and the skills of their labour force.

Countries also specialise. They produce more than they need of certain goods (whether finished goods, raw materials or intermediate goods). What is not consumed domestically is exported. The revenues earned from the exports are used to import goods which are not produced in sufficient amounts at home. The same applies to various services, such as banking and tourism.

But which goods and services should a country specialise in? What should it export and what should it import? The answer is that it should specialise in those goods and services in which it has a *comparative advantage*.

The law of comparative advantage

Countries have different resources. They differ in population density, labour skills, climate, raw materials, capital equipment, etc. Thus the ability to supply goods differs between countries, especially as many of these differences are relatively or even completely immobile, such as a country's climate or geography.

What this means is that the relative costs of producing goods will vary from country to country.

For example, one country may be able to produce 1 fridge for the same cost as 6 tonnes of wheat or 3 MP4 players, whereas another country may be able to produce 1 fridge for the same cost as only 3 tonnes of wheat but 4 MP4 players. It is these differences in relative costs that form the basis of trade.

At this stage we need to distinguish between *absolute advantage* and *comparative advantage*.

Absolute advantage. When one country can produce a good with fewer resources than another country, it is said to have an *absolute advantage* in that good. If France can produce grapes with fewer resources than the UK, and the UK can produce barley with fewer resources than France, then France has an absolute advantage in grapes and the UK an absolute advantage in barley. Production and consumption of both grapes and barley will be maximised by each country specialising and then trading with the other country. Both will gain.

Definition

Absolute advantage A country has an absolute advantage over another in the production of a good if it can produce it with fewer resources than the other country.

Comparative advantage. The above seems obvious, but trade between two countries can still be beneficial even if one country could produce all goods with fewer resources than the other, providing the relative efficiency with which goods can be produced differs between the two countries.

Take the case of a developed country that is absolutely more efficient than a developing country at producing both wheat and cloth. Assume that with a given amount of resources (labour, land and capital) the alternatives shown in Table 12.1 can be produced in each country.

Despite the developed country having an absolute advantage in both wheat and cloth, the developing country has a *comparative advantage* in wheat, and the developed country has a comparative advantage in cloth. This is because wheat is relatively cheaper in the developing country: only 1 metre of cloth must be sacrificed to produce 2 kilos of wheat, whereas 8 metres of cloth would have to be sacrificed in the developed country to produce 4 kilos of wheat. In other words, the opportunity cost of wheat is 4 times higher in the developed country (8/4 compared with 1/2).

KEY IDEA 28

Law of comparative advantage. Trade can benefit all countries if they specialise in the goods in which they have a comparative advantage.

But why do they gain if they specialise according to this law? And just what will that gain be? We consider these questions next.

The gains from trade based on comparative advantage

Before trade, unless markets are very imperfect, the prices of the two goods are likely to reflect their opportunity costs. For example, in Table 12.1, since the developing country can produce 2 kilos of wheat for 1 metre of cloth, the price of 2 kilos of wheat will roughly equal 1 metre of cloth.

Assume, then, that the pre-trade exchange ratios of wheat for cloth are as follows:

Developing country : 2 wheat for 1 cloth
Developed country : 1 wheat for 2 cloth (i.e. 4 for 8)

Both countries will now gain from trade, provided the exchange ratio is somewhere between 2:1 and 1:2. Assume, for the sake of argument, that it is 1:1. In other words, 1 unit of wheat trades internationally for 1 unit of cloth. How will each country gain?

The developing country gains by exporting wheat and importing cloth. At an exchange ratio of 1:1, it now only has to give up 1 kilo of wheat to obtain a metre of cloth, whereas before trade it had to give up 2 kilos of wheat.

The developed country gains by exporting cloth and importing wheat. Again at an exchange ratio of 1:1, it now only has to give up 1 metre of cloth to obtain a kilo of wheat, whereas before it had to give up 2 metres of cloth.

> ### Pause for thought
>
> *Draw up a similar table to Table 12.1, only this time assume that the figures are: developing country: 6 wheat or 2 cloth; developed country: 8 wheat or 20 cloth. What are the opportunity cost ratios now? Which country should produce which good?*

On the other hand, cloth is relatively cheaper in the developed country. Here the opportunity cost of producing 8 metres of cloth is only 4 kilos of wheat, whereas in the developing country 1 metre of cloth costs 2 kilos of wheat. Thus the opportunity cost of cloth is 4 times higher in the developing country (2/1 compared with 4/8).

To summarise, countries have a comparative advantage in those goods that can be produced at a lower opportunity cost than in other countries.

If countries are to gain from trade, they should export those goods in which they have a comparative advantage and import those goods in which they have a comparative disadvantage. Given this, we can state a *law of comparative advantage*.

> ### Pause for thought
>
> *Show how each country could gain from trade if the developing country could produce (before trade) 3 wheat for 1 cloth and the developed country could produce (before trade) 2 wheat for 5 cloth, and if the exchange ratio (with trade) was 1 wheat for 2 cloth. Would they both still gain if the exchange ratio was (a) 1 wheat for 1 cloth; (b) 1 wheat for 3 cloth?*

> ### Definitions
>
> **Comparative advantage** A country has a comparative advantage over another in the production of a good if it can produce it at a lower opportunity cost, i.e. if it has to forego less of other goods in order to produce it.
>
> **The law of comparative advantage** Provided opportunity costs of various goods differ in two countries, both of them can gain from mutual trade if they specialise in producing (and exporting) those goods that have relatively low opportunity costs compared with the other country.

Table 12.1	Production possibilities for two countries				
			Kilos of wheat		Metres of cloth
Developing country	Either		2	or	1
Developed country	Either		4	or	8

Thus both countries have gained from trade.

The actual exchange ratios will depend on the relative prices of wheat and cloth after trade takes place. These prices will depend on total demand for and supply of the two goods. It may be that the trade exchange ratio is nearer to the pre-trade exchange ratio of one country than the other. Thus the gains to the two countries need not be equal.

Other gains from trade

Another major advantage from trade is the extra competition it brings. Competition from imports may stimulate greater efficiency at home, which could decrease a firm's costs. It could also prevent domestic monopolies/oligopolies from charging high prices. It may stimulate greater research and development and the more rapid adoption of new technology, which might enable faster growth, through the expansion of the supply side of the economy (see section 11.3). It may lead to a greater variety of products being made available to consumers. Finally, the extra price competition will help to keep inflation low.

Not all countries will have immediate comparative cost advantages. However, when they begin specialisation, possible cost savings from economies of scale may emerge. These benefits may then generate a comparative advantage. This reason for trading is particularly relevant for smaller nations, where trade can be essential to create a large enough market to support large-scale industries.

In some countries, such as China and Germany, exports can also be a key cause of growth and so trade acts as an 'engine of growth', especially as export demand is likely to grow over time, particularly when

---

| BOX 12.1 | THE CHANGING FACE OF COMPARATIVE ADVANTAGE |

What next for China?

Comparative advantage enables specialisation and trade, and this can be one of the key factors that helps a country to grow and develop. China's emergence as an economic power is due to many things, but its ability to exploit its comparative advantage is certainly one such factor.

A country's comparative advantage often derives from its abundant resources and China used its abundance of cheap labour. With labour costs estimated to be between 60 and 90 per cent lower than in the USA, it was this that attracted many manufacturing companies to China, making a range of products using low- and moderately-skilled jobs.

China is the largest recipient of foreign direct investment (FDI) out of the developing nations, and worldwide it is second only to the USA. According to the 2018 World Investment Report China received $136 billion of FDI in 2017.[1]

However, it is not just the quantity of labour that explained China's dominance in manufacturing. While many of its workers are low-skilled, many are educated. Furthermore, Paul Krugman notes another key factor:

> 'China's dominant role in the export of many labor-intensive manufactured goods surely reflects its combination of relatively abundant labor and relatively high manufacturing competence.'[2]

It is unsurprising that companies, such as Nike and Foxconn, would take advantage of lower costs of production and locate factories in China. But, while China has benefited from this, many developed nations have seen a decline in their manufactured exports. Countries like the UK and USA gradually adjusted and moved to exploit their comparative advantage in the services sector. They saw a comparative disadvantage emerge in manufactured items.

This changing comparative advantage as a country develops is well-documented and could it be that China will soon begin to see its own comparative advantage change? China's low labour costs are crucial, but these have been rising, as workers demand higher wages, shorter hours and larger benefits. Data suggest that labour costs have been growing at some 20 per cent per year.

The first effect of this has been for some labour-intensive businesses to migrate towards inland China, where labour costs are lower.

However, in other cases the move has been more significant. With a comparative advantage in low-cost labour disappearing, some labour-intensive businesses have left China, moving to other nations, which can boast cheaper labour, such as Bangladesh, Cambodia, Indonesia and Vietnam. This is especially the case for companies specialising in the production of clothes and shoes.

But the story will not stop there. These industries require labour and as long as this remains the case, when a country begins to grow this will lead to higher wage demands, which in turn will raise costs. Production will shift once more.

Moving up the value chain

So, what does this mean for China? When the USA and Europe lost their comparative advantage in the production of cheap manufactured products, they had to look elsewhere. They developed a comparative advantage in the production of sophisticated products requiring highly skilled labour. They also increasingly specialised in the services sector. However, with rising costs in emerging economies, more manufacturing, especially of high-value products, is being returned to these developed nations.

Research from 2013 published in the *Harvard Political Review*[3] considers the iPhone and electronics manufacturing in terms

[1] *World Investment Report 2018* (UNCTAD, 2018).

[2] Paul Krugman, 'Increasing returns in a comparative advantage world', p. 45, in Robert M. Stern, *Comparative Advantage, Growth, and the Gains from Trade and Globalization,* Chapter 7 (World Scientific, 2011).

[3] Lauren Dai, 'The comparative advantage of nations: How global supply chains change our understanding of comparative advantage', *Harvard Political Review* (25 June 2013).

the exports have a high-income elasticity of demand. Finally, there are some non-economic advantages from trading, such as closer political ties and cultural and social benefits that emerge when countries have close trading relationships.

The competitive advantage of nations

The theory of comparative advantage shows how countries can gain from trade, but why do countries have a comparative advantage in some goods rather than others?

One explanation is that it depends on the resources that countries have. If a country has plenty of land, then it makes sense to specialise in products that make use of this abundant resource. Thus Canada produces and exports wheat. If a country has a highly skilled workforce and an established research base, then it makes sense to specialise in high-tech products and export these. Thus Germany exports many highly sophisticated manufactured products. Many developing countries, by contrast, with plentiful but relatively low-skilled workers specialise in primary products or simple manufactured products that are labour-intensive.

In other words, countries should specialise in goods which make intensive use of their abundant resources. But this still does not give enough detail as to why countries specialise in the precise range of products that they do. Also, why do countries both export and import the

of comparative advantage and the value chain. While the data on gross trade statistics confirm the decline of US competitiveness in this industry, the 'value-added trade statistics reveal the rising robustness of the United States' comparative advantage in electronics.' The suggestion of the author is that, while China dominates in the sale of many finished exports, the simple sales data actually overstate China's productive capacity. Developed countries, such as the USA, the UK and Japan, often contribute to the value of the final products in terms of intellectual capital, design and technology.

China will need to follow the pattern of the Western economies; its companies and workers will need to move up the value chain to find products that they can specialise in, which are not easily transferable to lower-wage countries. This is no easy task, as moving up the value chain will involve entering into direct competition with countries that have had time to develop their comparative advantage.

> China's reliance on cheap labor has powered the country's economy to unprecedented heights. But China's manufacturing sector is running into problems these days: squeezed from one end by places with even lower labor costs, such as Laos and Vietnam, and yet struggling to move to higher ground making more advanced products because of competition from developed nations such as Germany and the United States.[4]

Despite the difficulties of doing this, China has already begun the move towards the high valued-added industries, such as the petrochemical industry; and some key electronics firms, such as Huawei, are beginning to compete effectively with more established giants, such as Samsung and Apple.

Key to this move has been the progress of the Chinese education system, which has led to more and more students going on to college and university and this means the labour force is becoming increasingly skilled.

Another thing to bear in mind is the changing nature of the Chinese domestic market, which has led to a significant expansion in demand and this, in turn, has continued to make it an attractive place for global investment. More companies are locating their headquarters and R&D centres in China and this is helping China to establish a comparative advantage in a new area. It is already the world's largest e-commerce market and this digitisation is creating many opportunities for Chinese industry, in areas where both old and new comparative advantages were held.

You can read more about China's future in an article from the World Economic Forum[5] and in a report from McKinsey & Company.[6]

The changing nature of comparative advantage can cause problems for workers, businesses and countries, but benefits also emerge through greater competition, choice and innovation. The next few decades are likely to see some significant changes in the structure of industry in all countries.

Why are countries likely to see their comparative advantage change as they develop?

Investigate a particular Chinese company and try to establish in what ways it might be exploiting or developing comparative advantage.

---

[4] Jia Lynn Yang, 'China's manufacturing sector must reinvent itself, if it's to survive', *The Washington Post* (23 November 2012).

[5] Long Guoqiang, *What is the Future of Chinese Trade?*, World Economic Forum (21 January 2015).

[6] 'China's fast climb up the value chain', *McKinsey Quarterly*, McKinsey & Company (May 2018).

same products? Why do many countries produce and export cars, but also import many cars too?

It is widely agreed that there are four key determinants of why nations are highly competitive in certain products but less so in others.[6] This is illustrated in Figure 12.3

Available resources. These include 'given' resources, such as raw materials, population and climate, but also specialised resources that have been developed by humans, such as the skills of the labour force, the amount and type of capital, the transport and communications infrastructure, and the science and technology base. These specialised resources vary in detail from one country to another and give them a competitive advantage in very specific products. Once an industry has started to develop, this may attract further research and development, capital investment and training, all of which are very specific to that industry. This then further builds the country's competitive advantage in that industry. Thus, the highly developed engineering skills and equipment in Germany gives it a competitive advantage in producing well-engineered cars.

Demand conditions in the home market. The more discerning customers are within the country, the more this will drive the development of each firm's products and the more competitive the firm will then become in international markets. The demand for IT solutions within the USA drove the development of the software industry and gave companies such as Microsoft, Intel and Google an international advantage.

Strategy of rival firms. Competition between firms is not just in terms of price. Competitive rivalry extends to all aspects of business strategy, from product design, to marketing, to internal organisation, to production efficiency, to logistics, to after-sales support.

The very particular competitive conditions within each industry can have a profound effect on the development of firms within that industry and determine whether or not they gain an international competitive advantage. Strategic investments and rivalry gave Japanese electronics companies an international competitive advantage.

Supporting industries. Firms are more likely to be successful internationally if there are well-developed supporting industries within the home economy. These may be industries providing specialist equipment or specialist consultancy, or they may simply be other parts of the main value chain, from suppliers of inputs to distributors of the firms' output. The more efficient this value chain, the greater the competitive advantage of firms within the industry. Think back to Box 4.3, where we considered the competitive advantage of Hollywood and the relocation of so many supported and related industries to this area.

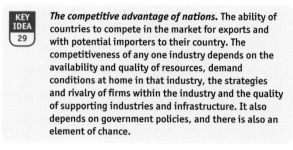

KEY IDEA 29

The competitive advantage of nations. The ability of countries to compete in the market for exports and with potential importers to their country. The competitiveness of any one industry depends on the availability and quality of resources, demand conditions at home in that industry, the strategies and rivalry of firms within the industry and the quality of supporting industries and infrastructure. It also depends on government policies, and there is also an element of chance.

The above four determinants of competitive advantage are interlinked and influence each other, as shown in Figure 12.3. For example, the nature of supporting industries can influence a firm's strategic decision about whether to embark on a process of vertical integration or de-integration. Similarly, the nature of supporting industries depends on demand conditions in these industries and the availability of resources.

With each of the four determinants, competitive advantage can be stimulated by appropriate government supply-side policies, such as a supportive tax regime, investment in transport and communications infrastructure, investment in education and training, competition policy and sound macroeconomic management of the economy. Also chance often has a large part to play. For example, the pharmaceutical company that discovers a cure for AIDS or for various types of cancer will then have a significant competitive advantage.

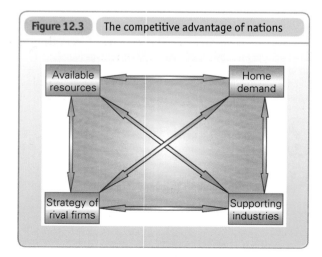

Figure 12.3 The competitive advantage of nations

Pause for thought

Give two other examples of ways in which the determinants of competitive advantage are interlinked.

---

[6] See, for example: Michael E. Porter, *The Competitive Advantage of Nations* (New York: The Free Press, 1998).

The terms of trade

What price will our exports fetch abroad? What will we have to pay for imports? The answer to these questions is given by the *terms of trade*. The terms of trade are defined as:

$$\frac{\text{The average price of exports}}{\text{The average price of imports}}$$

expressed as an index, where prices are measured against a base year in which the terms of trade are assumed to be 100. Thus, if the average price of exports relative to the average price of imports has risen by 20 per cent since the base year, the terms of trade will now be 120. If the terms of trade rise (export prices rising relative to import prices), they are said to have 'improved', since fewer exports now have to be sold to purchase any given quantity of imports. Changes in the terms of trade are caused by changes in the demand and supply of imports and exports and by changes in the exchange rate.

Pause for thought

Assume that a developing country exports primary products whose demand on world markets is inelastic with respect to income. Assume also that it imports manufactured products whose demand in the country is elastic with respect to income. What is likely to happen to its terms of trade over the years as this country and other countries around the world experience economic growth?

RECAP

1. Despite a decline in world trade in the recession following the financial crisis, world trade has grown significantly over the past few decades. Although exports and imports in both goods and services are still dominated by developed countries, developing nations are taking an increasingly large share of world trade. China, in particular, has seen significant growth in both exports and imports of goods and services and is the world's largest exporter of goods.

2. Countries can gain from trade if they specialise in producing those goods in which they have a comparative advantage, i.e. those goods that can be produced at relatively lower opportunity costs.

3. If two countries trade, then, provided that the trade price ratio of exports and imports is between the pre-trade price ratios of these goods in the two countries, both countries can gain.

4. Trade can generate numerous benefits to firms and consumers, including promoting competition, cutting prices, increasing choice and acting as an engine for growth.

5. The terms of trade give the price of exports relative to the price of imports expressed as an index, where the base year is 100.

12.2 TRADE RESTRICTIONS

We have seen how trade can bring benefits to all countries. But when we look around the world, we still observe countries with barriers to trade. Indeed, some countries, such as the USA, have increased their barriers. Politicians know that trade involves costs as well as benefits.

In this section, we examine the arguments for restricting trade. Are people justified in fearing international competition, or are they merely trying to protect some vested interest at the expense of everyone else?

Types of restriction

If a country chooses to restrict trade, there are a number of protectionist measures open to it. Governments may:

- impose customs duties (or *tariffs*) on imports;
- restrict the amount of certain goods that can be imported ('quotas');
- subsidise domestic products to give them a price advantage over imports;
- impose administrative regulations designed to exclude imports, such as customs delays or excessive paperwork;
- favour domestic producers when purchasing equipment (e.g. defence equipment).

Governments may also favour domestic producers by subsidising their exports in a process known

Definitions

Terms of trade The price index of exports divided by the price index of imports and then expressed as a percentage. This means that the terms of trade will be 100 in the base year.

Tariffs Taxes (customs duties) on imports. These could be a percentage of the value of the good (an 'ad valorem' tariff), or a fixed amount per unit (a 'specific' tariff).

as *dumping*. The goods are 'dumped' at artificially low prices in the foreign market.

In looking at the costs and benefits of trade, the choice is not the stark one of whether to have free trade or no trade at all. Although countries may sometimes contemplate having completely free trade, typically they limit their trade. However, they certainly do not ban it altogether.

Arguments for restricting trade

The following are the main arguments that have been used to restrict trade.

The infant industry argument. Some industries in a country may be in their infancy but have a potential comparative advantage. This is particularly likely in developing countries. Such industries are too small yet to have gained economies of scale; their workers are inexperienced; there is a lack of back-up facilities – communications networks, specialist research and development, specialist suppliers, etc. – and they may have only limited access to finance for expansion. Without protection, these *infant industries* will not survive competition from abroad.

Protection from foreign competition, however, will allow them to expand and become more efficient. Once they have achieved a comparative advantage, the protection can then be removed to enable them to compete internationally. A risk here, however, is that the protectionist measure is not removed once the industry has become established and thus the incentive for efficiency may disappear.

The senile industry argument. This is similar to the infant industry argument. It is where industries with a potential comparative advantage have been allowed to run down and can no longer compete effectively. They may have considerable potential but simply be unable to make enough profit to afford the necessary investment without some temporary protection. This is one of the most powerful arguments used to justify the use of special protection for the automobile and steel industries in the USA.

Pause for thought

How would you set about judging whether an industry had a genuine case for infant or senile industry protection?

To prevent 'dumping' and other unfair trade practices. A country may engage in dumping by subsidising its exports. The result is that prices may no longer reflect comparative costs. Thus the world would benefit from tariffs being imposed by importers to counteract the subsidy. An example is Chinese steel, which has been heavily subsidised and dumped on European and other markets. This has been a serious problem for European steel producers, which have found it virtually impossible to compete. A high-profile case was that of Tata Steel, which decided to pull out of the UK. The EU responded by imposing duties on various types of Chinese steel.[7]

Pause for thought

Does the consumer in the importing country gain or lose from dumping?

It can also be argued that there is a case for retaliating against countries which impose restrictions on your exports. In the short run, both countries are likely to be made worse off by a contraction in trade. But if the retaliation persuades the other country to remove its restrictions, it may have a longer-term benefit. In some cases, the mere threat of retaliation may be enough to persuade another country to remove its protection and here game theory can provide some useful insights (see pages 133–4).

To prevent the establishment of a foreign-based monopoly. Competition from abroad could drive domestic producers out of business. The foreign company, now having a monopoly of the market, could charge high prices with a resulting misallocation of resources. The problem could be tackled either by restricting imports or by subsidising the domestic producer(s).

All the above arguments suggest that governments should adopt a 'strategic' approach to trade. *Strategic trade theory* argues that protecting certain industries allows a net gain in the long run from increased competition in the market (see Box 12.2).

Definitions

Dumping Where exports are sold at prices below marginal cost – often as a result of government subsidies.

Infant industry An industry which has a potential comparative advantage, but which is, as yet, too underdeveloped to be able to realise this potential.

Senile industry An industry which has a potential comparative advantage but has become run down and so can no longer compete effectively.

Strategic trade theory The theory that protecting/supporting certain industries can enable them to compete more effectively with large monopolistic rivals abroad. The effect of the protection is to increase long-run competition and may enable the protected firms to exploit a comparative advantage that they could not have done otherwise.

---

[7] See: Alan Tovey, 'Steel wars widen as Europe launches probe into claims China is subsidising producers', *The Telegraph* (13 May 2016).

BOX 12.2   STRATEGIC TRADE THEORY

An argument for protection?

Lester Thurow was Professor of Management and Economics at the Massachusetts Institute of Technology (MIT). He is also one of the USA's best-known advocates of 'managed trade'.

Thurow (and others) have been worried by the growing penetration of US markets by imports and called for a carefully worked-out strategy of protection for US industries. The strategic trade theory that they support argues that the real world is complex.

It is wrong, they claim, to rely on free trade and existing comparative advantage. Some industries will require particular policies or interventions that are tailored to their needs.

■ Some industries will require protection against unfair competition from abroad – not just to protect the industries themselves, but also to protect the consumer from the oligopolistic power that the foreign companies will gain if they succeed in driving the domestic producers out of business.
■ Other industries will need special support in the form of subsidies to enable them to modernise and compete effectively with imports.
■ New industries may require protection to enable them to get established – to achieve economies of scale and build a comparative advantage.
■ If a particular foreign country protects or promotes its *own* industries, it may be desirable to retaliate in order to persuade the country to change its mind.

Supporters of *strategic trade theory* hold that comparative advantage need not be the result of luck or circumstance, but may in fact be created by government. By diverting resources into selective industries, usually high tech and high skilled, a comparative advantage can be created through intervention.

An example of such intervention was the European aircraft industry with the creation of the European Airbus Consortium.

The case of Airbus

The Consortium was established in the late 1960s, its four members being Aérospatiale (France), British Aerospace (now BAE Systems) (UK), CASA (Spain) and DASA (Germany), though in 2000 the French, Spanish and German partners merged to form the European Aeronautic Defence and Space Company (EADS) and in 2006, BAE systems sold its 20 per cent stake to EADS. The Consortium was seen as essential for the European aircraft industry to enable it to share high R&D costs, generate economies of scale and to compete effectively with the USA's major players, particularly Boeing. Despite being privately owned, it did receive state aid, especially in its unprofitable early years and so government intervention was directly helping the European aircraft industry.

By the early 2000s, the Consortium had become successful and in 2003 it delivered more passenger aircraft than Boeing for the first time and that continued until 2011. Since then Boeing has retaken the lead, as you can see in the figure below, though in 2018 the gap did close, as Airbus delivered 800 aircraft, while Boeing delivered 806.

The case of Airbus is a good example of strategic trade theory in practice, whereby government assistance helped an industry to compete with rivals. Without the state aid, Airbus would not have been able to grow as it did and hence the civil aircraft market would have been dominated by a single

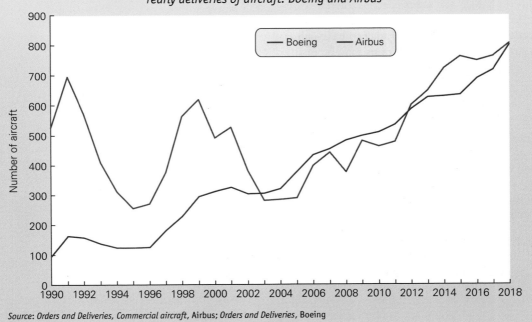

Yearly deliveries of aircraft: Boeing and Airbus

Source: Orders and Deliveries, Commercial aircraft, Airbus; Orders and Deliveries, Boeing

▶

American company. Thus, the presence of Airbus promoted competition and cut prices.

One survey estimated that without Airbus commercial aircraft prices would have been 3.5 per cent higher. Furthermore, there were significant economic spill overs from the Airbus Consortium, such as skills and technology developments that are likely to have benefited other industries. While findings are inconclusive on this, it is clear that, although aggregate R&D in the whole aircraft industry has risen, so has the level of R&D duplication.

Although Boeing is back at the top of the market, the growth of Airbus has been a good thing for competition, with both companies having to become more responsive to customer demand, which in turn benefits passengers. The strategic trade theory that was used to justify state aid, therefore, appears to have been largely vindicated, in creating a more competitive market.

However, one of the consequences of using strategic trade theory in practice to protect an industry (whatever the justification) is the impact on competitors in other countries. The support given to Airbus by the EU created a significant amount of friction between Airbus and Boeing and more broadly between the EU and the USA. The ongoing trade dispute that emerged from the practical application of strategic trade theory is considered in Box 12.3.

1. In what other industries could the setting up of a consortium, backed by government aid, be justified as a means of exploiting a potential comparative advantage?
2. Is it only in industries that could be characterised as world oligopolies that strategic trade theory is relevant?

Examine the complaints made to the World Trade Organization (WTO) by Airbus and Boeing. What were the reasons given by the WTO for upholding or rejecting the complaints?

To spread the risks of fluctuating markets. A highly specialised economy – Zambia with copper, Cuba with sugar – will be highly susceptible to world market fluctuations. Greater diversity and greater self-sufficiency, although maybe leading to less efficiency, can reduce these risks.

To reduce the influence of trade on consumer tastes. The assumption of fixed consumer tastes dictating the pattern of production through trade is false. Multinational companies through their advertising and other forms of sales promotion may influence consumer tastes. Many developing countries object to the insidious influence of western consumerist values expounded by companies such as Coca-Cola and McDonald's. Therefore, while trade can have cultural and social benefits, some restrictions may be justified in order to reduce this 'producer sovereignty'.

To take account of externalities. Free trade will tend to reflect private costs. Both imports and exports, however, can involve externalities. The mining of many minerals for export may adversely affect the health of miners; the production of chemicals for export may involve pollution; the importation of juggernaut lorries may lead to structural damage to houses; shipping involves large amounts of CO_2 emissions (some 3–5 per cent of total world emissions).

The arguments considered so far are of general validity; restricting trade for such reasons could be of net benefit to the world. There are two other arguments, however, that are used by individual governments for restricting trade, where their country will gain, but at the expense of other countries, such that there will be a net loss to the world.

The first argument concerns taking advantage of market power in world trade. If a country, or a group of countries, has monopsony power in the purchase of imports (i.e. they are individually or collectively a very large economy, such as the USA or the EU), then they could gain by restricting imports so as to drive down their price. Similarly, if countries have monopoly power in the sale of some export (e.g. OPEC countries with oil), then they could gain by forcing up the price.

Pause for thought

What other reasons might cause a country (or more specifically its government) to restrict trade with another country?

The second argument concerns giving protection to declining industries. The human costs of sudden industrial closures can be very high. In such circumstances, temporary protection may be justified to allow the industry to decline more slowly, thus avoiding excessive structural unemployment. Such policies will be at the expense of the consumer, however, who will be denied access to cheaper imports. Nevertheless, such arguments have gained huge support from populist movements in the USA and elsewhere and protection for such industries forms part of President Trump's 'America first' policies.

Problems with protection

Tariffs and other forms of protection impose a cost on society. This is illustrated in Figure 12.4, which shows the case of a good that is partly home

Figure 12.4   The cost of protection

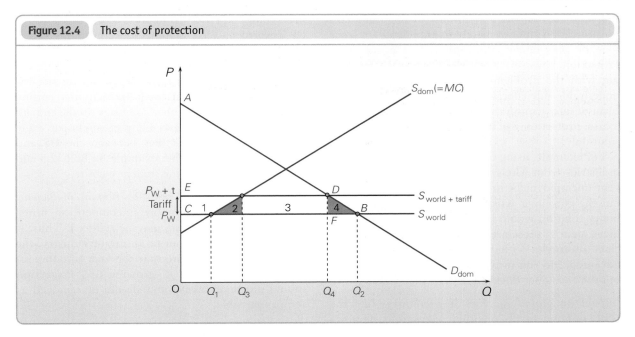

produced and partly imported. Domestic demand and supply are given by D_{dom} and S_{dom}. It is assumed that firms in the country produce under perfect competition. This means that the supply curve is the sum of firms' marginal cost curves. The reason is that a supply curve shows how much will be produced at each price. The marginal cost curve relates quantity to marginal cost. But under perfect competition, given that $P = MR$, and $MR = MC$, P must equal MC. Thus, the supply curve and the MC curve will follow the same line.

Let us assume that the country is too small to affect world prices: it is a price taker. The world price is given at P_w, where Q_2 is demanded, Q_1 is supplied by domestic suppliers and hence $Q_2 - Q_1$ is imported.

Now a tariff is imposed. This increases the price to consumers by the amount of the tariff (similar to a tax being imposed). Price rises to $P_w + t$. Domestic production increases to Q_3, consumption falls to Q_4, and hence imports fall to $Q_4 - Q_3$.

What are the costs of this tariff to the country? Before the tariff, consumer surplus was the whole area under D_{dom} and above the original price, P_w; in other words, area ABC. After the tariff, consumers have to pay a higher price and hence there is a reduction in the difference between their willingness to pay (given by D_{dom}) and the price they now have to pay ($P_w + t$). Thus, consumer surplus falls to area ADE, and hence consumers are worse off (see page 57 for a recap on consumer surplus). The cost to consumers in lost consumer surplus is thus EDBC (i.e. areas 1 + 2 + 3 + 4). But, where does this lost consumer surplus go?

Part will go to firms. The reason is that firms are charging a higher price and hence they will see an increase in their profits (area 1): where profit is given by the area between the price and the MC curve. Thus area 1 is redistributed from consumers to producers.

Part will go to the government. The reason is that the government gets revenue from the tariff payments: i.e. $(Q_4 - Q_3) \times$ tariff (area 3). These revenues can be used, for example, to reduce taxes.

However, some of the consumer surplus is completely lost. It is a net cost to society (areas 2 and 4).

Area 2 represents the extra costs of producing $Q_3 - Q_1$ at home, rather than importing it. If $Q_3 - Q_1$ were still imported, the country would only be paying P_w. By producing it at home, however, the costs are given by the domestic supply curve (= MC). The difference between MC and P_w (area 2) is thus the efficiency loss on the production side.

Area 4 represents the loss of consumer surplus by the reduction in consumption from Q_2 to Q_4. Consumers have saved area FBQ_2Q_4 of expenditure, but have sacrificed area DBQ_2Q_4 of utility in so doing – a net loss of area 4.

Therefore, when a tariff is imposed, there is a net cost to society (areas 2 + 4). Total surplus to society is therefore lower with a tariff than it is without a tariff. Thus, when deciding whether a tariff should be imposed, the government should ideally weigh up the costs to society against any benefits that are gained from protection.

Apart from these direct costs to the consumer, there are several other problems with protection. Some are a direct effect of the protection; others follow from the reactions of other nations.

Protection as 'second-best'. Many of the arguments for protection amount merely to arguments for some type of government intervention in the economy. Protection, however, may not be the best way of dealing with the problem, since protection may have undesirable side effects. There may be a more direct form of intervention that has no side effects. In such a case, protection will be no more than a second-best solution.

For example, using tariffs to protect old inefficient industries from foreign competition may help prevent unemployment in those parts of the economy, but the consumer will suffer from higher prices. A better solution would be to subsidise retraining and investment in those areas of the country in new efficient industries – industries with a comparative advantage. In this way, unemployment is avoided, but the consumer does not suffer.

Impact on global income. If a country, like the USA, imposes tariffs or other restrictions, imports will be reduced. But these imports are other countries' exports. A reduction in their exports will lead to a fall in rest-of-the-world income. This in turn will lead to a reduction in demand for American exports. This, therefore, tends to undo the benefits of the tariffs.

Retaliation. If the USA imposes restrictions on, say, imports from the EU, then the EU may impose restrictions on imports from the USA. Any gain to US firms competing with EU imports is offset by a loss to US exporters. What is more, US consumers suffer, since the benefits from comparative advantage have been lost.

The increased use of tariffs and other restrictions can lead to a trade war, with each country cutting back on imports from other countries. In the end, all countries lose. There are many examples of trade wars. A recent case is that between the US and China.[8] We consider other examples in Box 12.3 and in Case Study D.33 on the student website.

Protection may allow firms to remain inefficient. By removing or reducing foreign competition, firms' incentive to reduce costs may be reduced. Thus, if protection is being given to an infant industry, the government must ensure that the lack of competition does not prevent it 'growing up'. Protection should not be excessive and should be removed as soon as possible.

Bureaucracy. If a government is to avoid giving excessive protection to firms, it should examine each case carefully. This can lead to large administrative costs. It could also lead to corrupt officials accepting bribes from importers to give them favourable treatment.

---

[8] See: 'A quick guide to the US-China trade war', *BBC News* (7 January 2019).

BOX 12.3   BEYOND BANANAS

EU/US trade disputes

Trade relations between the EU and USA have been strained for many years and it has been the role of the WTO to resolve the issues and restore order. The bad blood between the EU and USA started over bananas and although that dispute is resolved, others have emerged over hormone-treated beef, GM foods, steel and aircraft, to name a few.

Bananas

The EU/US 'banana war'[1] began in 1993 when the EU adopted a tariff and quota system that favoured banana producers in African, Caribbean and Pacific (ACP) countries, mostly ex-European colonies. Predictably, Latin American banana producers, owned by large American multinationals like Chiquita and Dole, took exception to this move. Latin American producers, with huge economies of scale, were able to produce bananas at considerably lower cost than producers in the ACP countries. But, faced with significant tariffs on entry into the EU market, their bananas became more expensive. Championed by the USA, the Latin American producers won the case at the WTO for removing the agreement.

The EU, however, failed to comply, arguing that the preferential access to EU markets for ACP producers was part of a general development strategy, known as the 'Lomé Convention', to support developing economies. Without preferential access, it was argued, ACP banana producers simply could not compete on world markets. As a European Commission document highlighted, 'The destruction of the Caribbean banana industry would provoke severe economic hardship and political instability in a region already struggling against deprivation.'[2]

As the EU refused to comply with the WTO ruling, the USA imposed $191 million worth of tariffs on EU exports in March 1999. After a series of battles over the issue at the WTO, the EU finally agreed in 2009 to reform its banana protocol and to cut tariffs on non-ACP bananas from $234 per tonne to $196 per tonne straight away and to $150 by 2016. In return, it would pay compensation to ACP nations.

---

[1] 'European Communities – Regime for the importation, sale and distribution of bananas', *WTO disputes*, WTO (8 November 2012).

[2] 'EC fact sheet on Caribbean bananas and the WTO', *EC Press Release*, memo/97/28 (18 March 1997).

Aircraft

As we saw in Box 12.2, the success of Airbus was in part thanks to government support, and so accusations were made from the USA and in particular, from Boeing, that Airbus was founded upon unfair trading practices and should not be receiving that level of governmental support. For example, the Americans were unhappy with the loans and subsidies, claimed to be $15 billion, which had enabled the Airbus Consortium to develop the aircraft. They claimed that such subsidies were breaking the WTO subsidy code (the SCM agreement) and were thus unfair. Airbus responded that Boeing had received unfair subsidies of $27.3 billion since 1992.

Two panels were set up[3] by the WTO in 2005 to review the two claims and in 2010 Airbus was found guilty of using some illegal subsidies to win contracts through predatory pricing. Nevertheless, the WTO dismissed most of Boeing's claims, as many of the subsidies were reimbursable at commercial rates of interest. However, some of the 'launch aid' for R&D was found to have been given at below market rates and so violated WTO rules. There were appeals against this and in May 2011, as part of a wider ruling on the dispute, the WTO partly overturned the earlier decision that the European government launch aid was an 'unfair subsidy'. The EU accepted the findings in June 2011.

The EU had made ten allegations against Boeing in its initial claim to the WTO and in March 2011, the WTO ruled that Boeing had breached the WTO rules on subsidies in three of the ten allegations. In the May 2011 ruling, the WTO ruled that some of the funding mechanisms used by Boeing were acting as illegal subsidies and must be repaid, totalling some $5.3 billion. The WTO said that Boeing had adversely affected the EU's interests through lost sales and by suppressing the price at which Airbus was able to sell its aircraft, costing Airbus $45 billion.

In April 2012, the USA announced that it would implement the recommendations and rulings made by the Dispute Settlement Body (DSU). However, this was not the end of the story, as in October 2012, the EU alleged that the USA had failed to comply with the recommendations. The EU requested permission from the WTO to impose countermeasures against the subsidy Boeing receives from the US government. The countermeasures would cost Boeing $12 billion, the estimated cost to the EU of the subsidies.

And still the saga continued. In December 2014, the EU made another complaint[4] to the WTO regarding its earlier ruling that state subsidies for Boeing and other aerospace firms set to run until 2024 were illegal, and yet they had been extended until 2040. The EU said that the extension scheme was worth $8.7 billion and represented 'the largest subsidy for the civil aerospace industry in US history'. In response the WTO referred the complaint to a panel in April 2015.

In June 2017, the WTO's compliance panel rejected several EU claims that the USA had failed to withdraw all illegal subsidies to Boeing, but it did find that the USA had not complied with an earlier ruling to abolish illegal tax breaks. Both sides claimed victory! However, at the end of June 2017, the EU challenged the WTO decision and so the case went back to the WTO's appellate body, which was still considering a separate US case over state aid to Airbus. On 15 May 2018, the WTO ruled[5] that Airbus did not use unfair subsidies for narrow-bodied jets, but did for wide-bodied jets and the EU agreed to make changes and comply with the ruling.

At the end of March 2019, the WTO's appeals body ruled[6] that the USA had not complied with the 2012 ruling that it must stop the subsidies to Boeing that it was issuing via tax breaks. As the tax breaks harmed sales of Airbus' A320, the ruling meant that the EU could impose tariffs on US goods to an amount based on the trade losses. Once again, both sides claimed victory in this ongoing battle, with the EU claiming 'a clear victory for the EU and Airbus' and the USA claiming 'a major win for the US'.

Other complaints are still with the WTO and so this trade dispute is far from over.

Steel

Trade disputes involving steel are not unusual and many relate to so-called American 'safeguard measures' on imports of certain steel products. In March 2002, George W. Bush imposed tariffs on steel imports to protect the loss-making US steel industry.

The Americans were accused of putting domestic politics ahead of the country's international legal commitments and the EU, together with other nations, went to the WTO demanding compensation for their resulting lost earnings in the USA.

The EU was also concerned that steel from the rest of the world, otherwise destined for the US market, would be diverted to the EU and this surge in steel imports would drive down steel prices and damage EU producers, making profitability harder to maintain. The EU estimated that the USA's actions could cost it over €2 billion a year in lost sales.

The USA argued that it was often the victim of these practices and that imposing tariffs on steel products was simply a mechanism for tilting the industry back in its favour. However, critics argued that the US steel industry had been in decline for many years and had suffered from prolonged under-investment, making steel expensive and hence inefficient to produce.

In November 2003, the appeals court of the WTO ruled[7] in the EU's favour and declared that the USA's steel tariffs were illegal. This permitted the EU to impose retaliatory tariffs on imports from the USA. To put maximum pressure on the Bush Administration in the run-up to the 2004 Presidential election, the EU threatened to concentrate such tariffs on US goods produced in marginal states, such as North Carolina and Florida: i.e. states that the Republicans needed to win for George Bush to be re-elected.

In December 2003, George Bush announced that the USA was lifting the tariffs.

Although the dispute between the EU and USA cooled for some years, the USA faced ongoing battles with other

---

[3] 'WTO probes EU-US air trade battle', *BBC News* (20 July 2005).

[4] 'United States – Conditional tax incentives for large civil aircraft', *WTO disputes*, WTO (22 September 2017)

[5] Danielle Wiener-Bronner, 'Airbus and Boeing each claim WTO decision as a win', *CNN Business* (15 May 2018).

[6] Sylvia Pfeifer et al., 'WTO rules US failed to stop unfair tax break to Boeing', *Financial Times* (28 March 2019).

[7] 'EU scores steel victory over US', *BBC News* (10 November 2003).

countries, particularly China, accusing it of dumping cheap steel into US markets. This led to the US imposing tariffs on Chinese steel imports in 2009, with further ones in 2015. Other countries also faced accusations of dumping steel into the USA and had tariffs imposed. Brazil responded by notifying the WTO that it was requesting dispute consultations with the USA regarding US tariffs on imports of some Brazilian steel products.

The dispute between the EU and USA was to return with President Trump's executive order that required the US Department of Commerce to investigate steel imports into the USA. In March 2018, President Trump signed an order imposing tariffs of 25 per cent on steel and 10 per cent on aluminium imports from most countries of the world. This did not initially include the EU, Mexico or Canada, but in June of that year, tariffs were also imposed in those areas.

This action sparked retaliation from many countries and complaints were lodged with the WTO. The EU's Commissioner for Trade Cecilia Malmström said:

> . . . the unilateral and unjustified decision of the US to impose steel and aluminium tariffs on the EU means that we are left with no other choice. The rules of international trade . . . cannot be violated without a reaction from our side. Our response is measured, proportionate and fully in line with WTO rules.[8]

The EU's retaliation included the imposition of tariffs on a variety of US imports, as part of a range of rebalancing measures. Tariffs of 10 per cent and 25 per cent were imposed on some products from 22 June 2018, which, as well as steel and aluminium, included various agricultural goods (such as orange and cranberry juice), clothing (such as Levi jeans), Harley-Davidson motorcycles, washing machines and cosmetics – 180 products in all.

Furthermore, the EU set out its intention to impose maximum tariffs of 10, 25, 35 and 50 per cent on a range of products either from 1 June 2021 or after a successful WTO dispute, whichever is sooner. At the start of 2019, the EU also imposed quotas on 26 categories of US steel products, where imports have been on the rise. Any imports above the quota will face a 25 per cent tariff and the measures will remain in place until mid-2021, assuming no change in the US position.

---

[8] 'EU adopts rebalancing measures in reaction to US steel and aluminium tariffs', *European Commission News Archive* (20 June 2018)

Case Study D.33 explores in more detail the issue of trade disputes over steel.

Hormone-treated beef and GM crops

In 1998, the WTO panel ruled against a ban by the EU on imports of hormone-treated beef from the USA (and Canada) and permitted retaliatory sanctions of $116.8 million. The justification for the ban was made on public health grounds and the EU argued that the sanctions should be lifted.

A WTO panel reviewed this and in March 2008, ruled that the USA's and Canada's unilateral sanctions were illegal, but also that the EU hormones directive that banned EU farmers from using certain hormones was not compatible with the WTO agreements on standards to protect the health of humans, plants and animals.

Both sides appealed, but the USA put in place a modified set of duties in January 2009. Then, in April 2009 the USA and EU resolved to work through the dispute. In response to the EU increasing its duty-free import quotas on hormone-free beef, the USA began to remove its import duties on all targeted European luxury foods.

Another public-health-related dispute revolved around genetically modified (GM) foods and the EU's ban on them. In 2006, the WTO responded to a complaint made by the USA, Canada and Argentina, and concluded that the EU's GM ban was illegal as the risks shown by the scientific evidence did not warrant the ban.

The ruling of the WTO Panel set a deadline of November 2007 for the EU to comply with its decision, but this was extended by one year with no request for retaliation by Canada and Argentina. The USA, however, did request authorisation to retaliate, but subsequently reached an agreement with the EU to suspend the request made to the WTO.

In 2010, GM crops were permitted to be grown under strict regulations throughout Europe and President Barack Obama called for a free-trade agreement between the EU and USA. GM crops continue to be tightly regulated across Europe.

> **?** *Why does the WTO appear to be so ineffective in resolving the disputes between the EU and USA?*

> **Q** *Investigate recent developments in any of the above cases and the role of the WTO. Discuss the WTO's arguments in any of the rulings it has made.*

RECAP

1. Reasons for restricting trade that have some validity in a world context include: the infant industry argument; the senile industry argument; the problem of dumping and other unfair trade practices; the danger of the establishment of a foreign-based monopoly; the need to spread the risks of fluctuating export prices; and the problems that free trade may adversely affect consumer tastes and may not take account of externalities.

2. Often, however, the arguments for restricting trade are in the context of one country benefiting even though other countries may lose more. Countries may intervene in trade in order to exploit their monopoly/monopsony power or to protect declining industries.

3. Even if government intervention to protect certain parts of the economy is desirable, restricting trade is unlikely to be the best solution to the problem, since it involves side-effect costs. It will tend to create net costs to society, it may encourage retaliation and reduce global incomes and national and world growth rates.

12.3 THE WORLD TRADING SYSTEM AND THE WTO

In 1947, 23 countries came together and signed the General Agreement on Tariffs and Trade (GATT). By August 2019, there were 164 members of its successor organisation, the World Trade Organization (WTO), which was formed in 1995. Between them, the members of the WTO account for approximately 98 per cent of world trade. The aims of GATT, and now the WTO, are to liberalise trade.

WTO rules

The WTO requires its members to operate according to various principles. These include the following:

- *Non-discrimination.* Under the 'most favoured nations clause', any trade concession that a country makes to one member must be granted to *all* signatories. The exception is free-trade areas and customs unions (such as the EU), where tariffs between members can be abolished, while still being maintained with the rest of the world.
- *Reciprocity.* Any nation benefiting from a tariff reduction made by another country must reciprocate by making similar tariff reductions itself.
- *The general prohibition of quotas.*
- *Fair competition.* If unfair barriers are erected against a particular country, the WTO can sanction retaliatory action by that country. The country is not allowed, however, to take such action without permission.
- *Binding tariffs.* Countries cannot raise existing tariffs without negotiating with their trading partners.

Unlike the GATT, the WTO has the power to impose sanctions on countries breaking trade agreements. If there are disputes between member nations, these will be settled by the WTO, and if an offending country continues to impose trade restrictions, permission can be granted for other countries to retaliate.

For example, in March 2002, the Bush administration imposed tariffs on steel imports into the USA in order to protect the ailing US steel industry (see Box 12.3 and Case Study D.33 on the student website). The EU and other countries referred the case to the WTO, which in December 2003 ruled that they were illegal.[9] This ruling made it legitimate for the EU and other countries to impose retaliatory tariffs on US products. President Bush consequently announced that the steel tariffs would be abolished.

Following tariffs imposed by the Trump administration in January 2018 targeted on Chinese steel and aluminium imports to the USA, China lodged a request with the WTO for consultations with the USA over the issue. Then, following a widespread imposition of tariffs on steels and aluminium by the Trump administration, Canada, Mexico the European Union, which had seen tariffs take effect from June 2018, each launched their own legal challenges at the WTO. Panels have been established to review the tariffs on these countries and also on India and Switzerland.

> ### Pause for thought
>
> *Could US action to protect its steel industry from foreign competition be justified in terms of the interests of the USA as a whole (as opposed to the steel industry in particular)?*

The greater power of the WTO has persuaded many countries to bring their disputes to it. From the time when the WTO replaced GATT in 1995 to August 2019, 586 disputes had been brought to the WTO (compared with 300 to GATT over the whole of its 48 years).

Trade rounds

Periodically, member countries have met to negotiate reductions in tariffs and other trade restrictions. There have been eight 'rounds' of such negotiations since the signing of GATT in 1947. The last major round to be completed was the Uruguay Round, which began in Uruguay in 1986, continued at meetings around the world and culminated in a deal being signed in April 1994. By that time, the average tariff on manufactured products was 4 per cent and falling. In 1947 the figure was nearly 40 per cent. The Uruguay Round agreement also involved a programme of phasing in substantial reductions in tariffs and other restrictions up to the year 2002 (see Case Study D.29 on the student website).

Despite the reduction in tariffs, many countries have still tried to restrict trade by various other means, such as quotas and administrative barriers. Also, barriers have been particularly high on certain non-manufactures. Agricultural protection in particular has come in for sustained criticism by developing countries. High fixed prices and subsidies given to farmers in the EU, the USA and other developed countries mean that the industrialised world continues to export food to many developing countries which have a comparative advantage in food production! Farmers in developing countries often find it impossible to compete with subsidised food imports from the rich countries.

---

[9] 'U.S. tariffs on steel are illegal, World Trade Organization says', *New York Times*, Elizabeth Becker (11 November 2003).

The Doha Round

The most recent round of trade negotiations began in Doha, Qatar, in 2001. The negotiations have focused on both trade liberalisation and measures to encourage development of poorer countries. In particular, the Doha Development Agenda, as it is called, has been concerned with measures to make trade fairer so that its benefits are spread more evenly around the world. This would involve improved access for developing countries to markets in the rich world. The Agenda has also been concerned with the environmental impacts of trade and development.

The talks were originally scheduled for completion by January 2005, but this deadline has been extended numerous times, as agreements have failed to emerge.

The EU and USA blamed larger developing countries, such as Brazil and India, for being unwilling to make reductions in tariffs on manufactured and service-based imports. The developing countries, in turn, blamed the unwillingness of the developed countries, and especially the EU and the USA, to make sufficient cuts in agricultural protection. The EU blamed the USA for subsidising its farmers; the USA blamed the EU for high tariffs on imported food.

> ### Pause for thought
>
> *How can game theory (see section 5.4) help us to understand the difficulty of getting countries to reach and then abide by trade agreements?*

In Geneva 2008, the talks finally appeared to have broken down, despite the willingness of developing countries to reduce industrial tariffs and the EU and USA to cut tariffs and subsidies in agricultural sectors. The sticking point was agricultural protection for developing countries, which China and India wanted to be available as temporary measures should they be required. With the USA objecting to this, the talks collapsed, although commentators suggested that the lack of agreement was no significant loss, as complete trade liberalisation would only boost developing countries' GDP by 1 per cent. Tariffs were already at an all-time low, showing the extent of progress that had already been made. But then with the 2008/9 recession, there were growing concerns that countries would introduce protectionist measures to support domestic industries. In the end, these concerns were unfounded.

There was a pledge at the G20 meeting in London in 2009 to complete the Doha Round, followed by a report from an 'Experts Group'[10] calling for 'one final push' to conclude the Doha Development Agenda. Pascal Lamy, the Director-General in 2011, urged the WTO's members to 'think hard about the consequences of throwing away ten years of solid multilateral work'.[11]

In December 2013, agreement was reached on a range of issues at the WTO's Bali Ministerial Conference and these were adopted in November 2014 by the General Council. The agreement means a streamlining of trade to make it 'easier, faster and cheaper', with particular focus on the promotion of development, boosting the trade of the least developed countries and allowing developing countries more options for providing food security, as long as this does not distort international trade.

This was the first significant agreement of the round and goes some way to achieving around 25 per cent of the goals set for the Doha Round. Then in December 2015 at the Ministerial Conference in Nairobi, another historic agreement was made on various trade initiatives that should provide particular benefits to the WTO's poorest members. This 'Nairobi Package'[12] contains six Ministerial Decisions on agriculture, cotton and issues related to least-developed countries, including a commitment to abolish export subsidies for farm exports. The Director-General said:

> 'Two years ago in Bali we did something that the WTO had never done before – we delivered major, multilaterally-negotiated outcomes . . . This week, here in Nairobi, we saw those same qualities at work. And today, once again, we delivered.'[13]

These sentiments were echoed by the Chair of the Conference, Kenya's Cabinet Secretary for Foreign Affairs and International Trade, Amina Mohamed who said that 'tough calls had to be made', but that in making them 'We have reaffirmed the central role of the WTO in international trade governance'.

While many issues remain outstanding, some progress has been made. However, many governments have indicated that this could well be the end of the road for the Doha Round. Indeed, the Trump presidency was seen to reflect a new wave of protectionism around the world, with populist movements blaming free trade for the decline of many traditional sectors and the resulting loss of jobs and increased social deprivation.

---

[10] Jagdish Bhagwati and Peter Sutherland, *The Doha Round: Setting a deadline, defining a final deal*, WTO Experts Group (12 January 2011).

[11] *Documents from the negotiating chairs*, WTO (21 April 2011).

[12] 'WTO members secure "historic" Nairobi Package for Africa and the world', *WTO News Items*, WTO (19 December 2015).

[13] Ibid.

BOX 12.4   PREFERENTIAL TRADING

The development of trade blocs

We now know that free trade brings many benefits and, to take advantage of these, the world economy has formed into a series of trade blocs, based upon regional groupings of countries. Such trade blocs are examples of *preferential trading arrangements*. These arrangements involve low or zero restrictions between the members, thus encouraging trade between them.

Trade restrictions remain, however, with the rest of the world. This causes complaints that members gain at the expense of the rest of the world. This can be a significant problem for developing nations looking to gain access to the most prosperous nations.

Types of preferential trading arrangement

There are three possible forms of such trading arrangements:

Free-trade area. This is where member countries remove tariffs and quotas between themselves, but retain whatever restrictions *each member chooses* with non-member countries. Some provision will have to be made to prevent imports from outside coming into the area via the country with the lowest external tariff.

Customs union. This is like a free-trade area, but in addition members must adopt *common* external tariffs and quotas with non-member countries.

Common market. This is where member countries operate as a *single* market. Like a customs union there are no tariffs and quotas between member countries and there are common external tariffs and quotas. But a full common market also includes the following features: a common system of taxation; a common system of laws and regulations governing production, employment and trade (e.g. competition law and trade union legislation); the free movement of labour, capital and materials, and of goods and services (e.g. the freedom of workers from one member country to work in any other); and the absence of special treatment by member governments of their own domestic industries.

The effects of preferential trading

By joining a customs union (or free-trade area), a country will find that its trade patterns change. Most of these changes are likely to be beneficial.

Countries will probably benefit from 'trade creation'. The removal of trade barriers allows greater specialisation according to comparative advantage. Instead of consumers having to pay high prices for domestically produced goods in which the country has a comparative disadvantage, the goods can now be obtained more cheaply from other members of the customs union. In return, the country can export to them goods in which it has a comparative advantage.

Other advantages from preferential trading include: competition from companies in other member states, which may stimulate efficiency and reduce monopoly power; economies of scale for firms which now have access to a bigger market; a more rapid spread of technology within the area; the bargaining power of the whole customs union with the rest of the world allowing member countries to gain

better terms of trade; increased trade encouraging improvements in the infrastructure of the members of the union (better roads, railways, financial services, etc.) and so there may also be investment advantages.

There are some dangers, however, of customs unions. The first is that 'trade diversion' could take place. This is where countries that were previously importing from a low-cost country (which does not join the union), now buy from a higher cost country within the customs union, simply because there are no tariffs on this country's products and hence they can be purchased at a lower price, despite their higher cost of production.

Another danger is that resources may flow from the country to more efficient members of the customs union, or to the geographical centre of the union (so as to minimise transport costs). This can be a major problem for a *common market* (where there is free movement of labour and capital). The country could become a depressed 'region' of the community.

Finally, if integration creates co-operation, firms may be encouraged to collude with each other, in order to maintain high prices. In addition, diseconomies of scale could emerge, if companies become too large and thus run into problems of bureaucracy and inefficiency.

The North American Free Trade Agreement (NAFTA)

Along with the EU, NAFTA is one of the two most powerful trading blocs in the world. It came into force in 1994 and consists of the USA, Canada and Mexico. These three countries have agreed to abolish tariffs between themselves in the hope that increased trade and co-operation will follow. Tariffs between the USA and Canada were phased out by 1999 and tariffs between all three countries were eliminated as of 1 January 2008. Many non-tariff restrictions remain, although new ones are not permitted.

Disputes do arise between the members. In 2009, for example, the USA reneged on a pilot scheme that would allow some Mexican trucks to travel over the US border. In response, Mexico imposed tariffs of up to 45 per cent on 90 US agricultural and industrial imports, ranging from strawberries and wine to cordless telephones.

NAFTA members hope that, with a market similar in size to the EU, they will be able to rival the EU's economic power in world trade. NAFTA is, however, at most only a free-trade area and not a common market. Unlike the EU, it does not seek to harmonise laws and regulations, except in very specific areas such as environmental management and labour standards. Member countries are permitted total legal independence, subject to the one proviso that they must treat firms of other member countries equally with their own firms – the principle

Definition

Preferential trading arrangements A trading arrangement whereby trade between the signatories is freer than trade with the rest of the world.

►

of 'fair competition'. Nevertheless, NAFTA has encouraged a growth in trade between its members, most of which is trade creation rather than trade diversion.

The election of Donald Trump as President was pivotal for NAFTA. During his campaign, Trump had described NAFTA as the 'worst trade deal in US history' and shortly after to coming to office, he committed to renegotiating NAFTA. His administration's concerns included the US trade deficit with Mexico, the amount of imported material in goods, such as cars, that qualify under the original NAFTA agreement, and the mechanism to review trade disputes between NAFTA members. The renegotiation talks began in August 2017 and continued throughout 2018, where midway through the year, the USA and Mexico held bilateral talks, while Canada was side-lined.

At the end of August 2018, the USA and Mexico reached an agreement, which included a sunset clause and regular reviews of the arrangement, as well as provisions to boost US car production. In September, Canada joined the talks and at the end of the month, a preliminary deal between Canada and the USA was reached, with the new agreement called the United States-Mexico-Canada Agreement (USMCA). As of May 2019, it had yet to be ratified and there was still uncertainty as to whether any of the three countries would indeed ratify it. Case Study D.32 on the student website examines NAFTA/USMCA in more detail.

Other trade agreements

APEC
Asia-Pacific Economic Cooperation (APEC) is a preferential trading area that was created in 1989 and it links 21 economies of the Pacific Rim, which together account for over half of the world's total output and almost half of world trade. At the 1994 meeting of APEC leaders, it resolved to create a free-trade area across the Pacific by 2010 for the developed industrial countries and by 2020 for the rest.

This preferential trading area is by no means as advanced as NAFTA and is unlikely to move beyond a free-trade area. This is in part because national interests differ significantly across the nations, as do the economic and political problems they face. Nevertheless, freer trade has brought economic benefits to the countries involved.

ECOWAS
In Africa, the Economic Community of West African States (ECOWAS) has been attempting to create a common market between its 15 members, which have a combined population of around 350 million. ECOWAS sees the development of this common market and the accompanying regional integration and economic co-operation as key in increasing the rate of development of its members.

The West African franc is used in the eight French speaking countries and it is planned to introduce a common currency throughout ECOWAS, thereby creating a monetary union. The launch of the common currency has been delayed several times, however, but in April 2019, a working group met to consider the currency name, which ideally will be launched in 2020, as part of the African Union's stipulation that every region in Africa will have a monetary union by 2034.

TPP
The Trans-Pacific Trade Partnership agreement was signed in February 2016 by 12 countries (Australia, Brunei, Canada, Chile, Japan, Malaysia, Mexico, New Zealand, Peru, Singapore, the USA and Vietnam). China was not part of it and on coming into office in January 2017, Donald Trump withdrew the USA from the agreement.

TPP is more than a simple free-trade agreement. In terms of trade, it involves the removal of many non-tariff barriers as well as most tariff barriers. It also includes elements of a single market. For example, it contains many robust and enforceable environmental protection, human rights and labour standards measures. It also allows for the free transfer of capital by investors in most circumstances.

It also established an 'investor–state dispute settlement' (ISDS) mechanism. This allows companies from any of the TPP countries to sue governments of any other countries in the agreement for treaty violations, such as giving favourable treatment to domestic companies, the seizing of companies' assets, or controls over the movement of capital. Critics of ISDS claim that it gives too much power to companies and may prevent governments from protecting their national environment or domestic workers and companies.

In March 2018, the remaining 11 countries signed up to a revised, though largely unchanged, version of TPP and on 30 December 2018, the new agreement, called Comprehensive and Progressive Agreement for Trans-Pacific Partnership (CPTPP), came into force. Other countries, including South Korea, Indonesia, the Philippines, Thailand, Taiwan and Colombia, have expressed an interest in joining. The Japanese Prime Minister, Shinzo Abe, invited the UK to consider joining the CPTPP in the next round of negotiations, saying that Britain would be 'welcomed with open arms'. Once Britain has left the EU, it will certainly be looking to strike trade deals with countries around the world, but it is unclear whether such an arrangement would be advantageous.

There are also trading arrangements in Latin America and the Caribbean. Examples include the Latin American Integration Association (LAIA), the Andean Community, the Central American Integration System (SICA) and the Caribbean Community (CARICOM). In 1991, a Southern Common Market (MerCoSur) was formed, consisting of Argentina, Brazil, Paraguay and Uruguay. Venezuela joined in 2012, but its membership was suspended in 2016. Most of MerCoSur's internal trade is free of tariffs and it also has a common external tariff.

1. *What factors will determine whether a country's joining a customs union will lead to trade creation or trade diversion?*
2. *Using the Internet, identify some other preferential trading arrangements around the world and their various features.*

Investigate uses of the investor–state dispute settlement mechanism. Has the mechanism generally been to the advantage of companies or the state?

RECAP

1. Most countries of the world are members of the WTO and in theory are in favour of moves towards freer trade.

2. The WTO can impose sanctions on countries not abiding by WTO rules.

3. There have been various 'rounds' of trade talks, originally under the auspices of GATT and more recently under the WTO. The Uruguay Round led to substantial reductions in tariffs and other trade restrictions.

4. The latest, the Doha Round, focuses on trade liberalisation and aims to spread the benefits of trade across developing countries. It has yet to be concluded, but progress has been made since 2013. There is some doubt, however, as to whether any further progress will be made and whether the round, therefore, is effectively over. This is especially true since the USA's position on freer trade has changed under the Presidency of Donald Trump.

12.4 THE EUROPEAN UNION AND THE SINGLE MARKET

In recognition of the benefits of free trade within the EU, the member countries signed the Single European Act in 1986. This sought to dismantle all barriers to internal trade within the EU by 1993, and create a genuine 'single market'. Although tariffs between member states had long been abolished, there were all sorts of non-tariff barriers, such as high taxes on wine by non-wine-producing countries, special regulations designed to favour domestic producers, governments giving contracts to domestic producers (e.g. for defence equipment), and so on.

Most of the barriers were removed by 1993, and by the mid-1990s it was clear that the single market was bringing substantial benefits. In 2012, the European Commission published *20 Years of the European Single Market,* noting the following:

> EU27 GDP in 2008 was 2.13 per cent or €233 billion higher than it would have been if the Single Market had not been launched in 1992. In 2008 alone, this amounted to an average of €500 extra in income per person in the EU27. The gains come from the Single Market programme, liberalisation in network industries such as energy and telecommunication, and the enlargement of the EU to 27 member countries.

Although the size of the gains from the single market are difficult to quantify, the following are some of the main benefits:

Trade creation. The expansion of trade within the EU has reduced both prices and costs, as countries have been able to exploit their comparative advantage. Member countries have specialised further in those goods and services that they can produce at a relatively lower opportunity cost.

Reduction in the direct costs of barriers. This category includes administrative costs, border delays and technical regulations. Their abolition or harmonisation has led to substantial cost savings, shorter delivery times and a larger choice of suppliers.

Economies of scale. With industries based on a Europe-wide scale, many firms can now be large enough, and their plants large enough, to gain the full potential economies of scale. Yet the whole European market is large enough for there still to be adequate competition. Such gains have varied from industry to industry, depending on the minimum efficient scale of a plant or firm (see Box 4.4 on page 96). Economies of scale have also been gained from mergers and other forms of industrial restructuring.

Greater competition. Increased competition between firms has led to lower costs, lower prices and a wider range of products available to consumers. This has been particularly so in newly liberalised service sectors such as transport, financial services, telecommunications and broadcasting. In the long run, greater competition can stimulate greater innovation, the greater flow of technical information and the rationalisation of production.

Pause for thought

In what ways would competition be 'unfair' if VAT rates differed widely between member states?

The economic evidence was backed up by the perceptions of business. Firms from across the range of industries felt that the single market project had removed a series of obstacles to trade within the EU and had increased market opportunities.

Despite these gains, the single market has not received a universal welcome within the EU. Its critics argue that, in a Europe of oligopolies, unequal ownership of resources, rapidly changing technologies and industrial practices, and factor immobility, the removal of internal barriers to trade has merely exaggerated the problems of inequality and economic power. More specifically, the following criticisms are made:

Radical economic change is costly. Substantial economic change is necessary to achieve the full economies of scale and efficiency gains from a single European market. These changes necessarily involve redundancies – from bankruptcies, takeovers, rationalisation and the introduction of new technology. The severity of this 'structural' and 'technological' unemployment (see section 10.6) depends on (a) the pace of economic change and (b) the mobility of labour – both occupational and geographical. Clearly, the more integrated markets become across the EU, the lower will be the costs of future change.

Adverse regional effects. Firms are likely to locate as near as possible to the 'centre of gravity' of their markets and sources of supply. If, before barriers are removed, a firm's prime market was the UK, it might well have located in the Midlands or the North of England. If, however, with barriers now removed, its market has become Europe as a whole, it may choose to locate in the South of England or in France, Germany or the Benelux countries instead. The creation of a single European market thus tends to attract capital and jobs away from the edges of the Union and towards its geographical centre.

In an ideal market situation, areas like Cornwall, the south of Italy or Portugal and now parts of Eastern Europe should attract resources from other parts of the Union. They are relatively depressed areas; thus wage rates and land prices are lower. The resulting lower industrial costs should encourage firms to move into those areas. In practice, however, as capital and labour (and especially young and skilled workers) leave the extremities of the Union, so these regions are likely to become more depressed. If, as a result, their infrastructure is neglected, they then become even less attractive to new investment.

The development of monopoly/oligopoly power. The free movement of capital can encourage the development of giant 'Euro-firms' with substantial economic power. Indeed, recent years have seen some very large European mergers. This can lead to higher, not lower prices and less choice for the consumer. It all depends on just how effective competition is, and how effective EU competition policy is in preventing monopolistic and collusive practices.

Trade diversion. It is possible that the internal market has actually diverted trade from those countries with lower costs to those with higher costs. Countries may have been importing from a low-cost country, but if this country does not join the union, then its imports may now become more expensive, because of the tariff. Trade may therefore be diverted away from this country to another country within the union, but as no tariff is imposed on these intra-union imports, they can be purchased at a lower price, despite their higher costs of production.

Perhaps the biggest objection raised against the single European market is a political one: the loss of national sovereignty. Governments find it much more difficult to intervene at a microeconomic level in their own economies and this was one of the main arguments in the debate over Britain's future within Europe, as we discuss in Box 12.5.

Completing the internal market

Despite the reduction in barriers, the internal market is still not 'complete'. In other words, various barriers to trade between member states remain. What is more, national governments have continued to introduce new technical standards, several of which have had the effect of erecting new barriers to trade.

In 1997, an 'Internal Market Scoreboard' was established to monitor the progress in dismantling trade barriers. This shows the percentage of EU single market Directives still to be transposed into national law (see Case Study D.34 on the book's website). To counteract new barriers, the EU periodically issues new Directives. If this process is more rapid than that of the transposition of existing Directives into national law, the transposition deficit increases.

In 2007, an average transposition deficit target of 1 per cent was set and by 2008 this had been reached, following successive falls in it from an average of 6.3 per cent in 1997 to 3.5 per cent by 1999 and 0.7 per cent in 2009. The average deficit did then rise in 2010 and 2011, due to a reduction in the speed with which Directives were being enacted and so began a 'zero tolerance' policy for delays of two years or more in transposing Directives, as this was seen as impairing the functioning of the single market.

In the 2011 Single Market Act, the European Commission proposed a reduction in the target transposition deficit for each Member State from 1 to 0.5 per cent. Subsequently the average transposition deficit began to decline and by November 2014 the EU average had fallen to 0.5 per cent.

It was then to prove difficult to meet the target consistently. In 2015 the transposition deficit had increased to 0.7 per cent, but there was a more substantial increase in 2016 when the deficit rose to 1.5 per cent.

BOX 12.5 | IN OR OUT?

A pre-Brexit assessment

While attention after the Brexit vote was focused on the UK's future relationship with the EU and what this would look like, it is still useful and important to consider the arguments surrounding the Brexit debate.

Views of economists

Economists were strongly in favour of remaining in the EU and in a poll of 100 economists for the *Financial Times*,[1] almost three-quarters thought leaving the EU would damage the country's medium-term outlook. This compared with only 8 per cent who thought the country would benefit from leaving. Most feared damage to financial markets in the UK and to inward foreign direct investment.

Another poll[2] of Royal Economic Society and the Society of Business Economists members was also strongly in favour of remaining, with 72 per cent believing that Brexit would have a negative effect on UK real GDP over the next 10 to 20 years, and 88 per cent believing GDP would be negative in the next five years.

Despite the barrage of pessimistic forecasts by economists about a British exit, there was a group of eight economists in favour of Brexit. They claimed that leaving the EU would lead to a stronger economy, with higher GDP, a faster growth in real wages, lower unemployment and a smaller gap between imports and exports. The main argument to support their claims was that the UK would be more able to pursue trade creation freed from various EU rules and regulations.

Views of organisations

Most national and international organisations were also in favour of Britain remaining part of the EU.

In its 2016 analysis of the long-term implications of Brexit, The Treasury argued that openness to trade and investment had been a crucial factor in Britain's actual and potential growth and hence maintaining this outside of the EU would be crucial. The Treasury's analysis distinguished between three new relationships with the EU and attempted to estimate the average impact on UK households. With a Norwegian-type deal, households would be £2600 worse off each year; a Swiss deal would lead to a £4300 annual loss of GDP per household and a complete exit would create a household loss per annum of £5200. It found that tax receipts would be lower and that the overall benefit to the UK of being in the EU, relative to another arrangement, would be between 3.4 per cent and 9.5 per cent of GDP, depending on the exact 'new deal'.[3]

Similar adverse effects were highlighted by the Governor of the Bank of England, who noted that Brexit would be likely to result in lower growth – possibly a recession – increased unemployment, a fall in the exchange rate, higher prices and that uncertainty would damage investment.

The OECD suggested that Brexit would be like a tax, pushing up the costs and weakening the economy. Its analysis

indicated that by 2020, GDP would be at least 3 per cent lower than it otherwise would have been, making households £2200 worse off. By 2030, these figures would be 5 per cent and £3200. It continued that:

> In the longer term, structural impacts would take hold through the channels of capital, immigration and lower technical progress. In particular, labour productivity would be held back by a drop in foreign direct investment and a smaller pool of skills. The extent of forgone GDP would increase over time . . . The effects would be even larger in a more pessimistic scenario and remain negative even in the optimistic scenario.[4]

The OECD also noted that the UK's membership of the EU had influenced the patterns of trade and investment and hence has provided the framework in which businesses have operated, for example in the development of supply chains across EU members. Structural changes accompanying Brexit, the OECD argued, would have negative supply-side effects.

The IMF also warned of the dangers of Brexit.[5] Its Managing Director, Christine Lagarde, indicated that a leave vote could lead to a stock market crash, falling house prices, rising inflation, unemployment and send the economy into recession, possibly even depressing long-term growth. The UK's large current account deficit and hence its reliance on external financing was also expected to exacerbate the risks.

Open Europe, a think tank, provided a more nuanced assessment.[6] In a best-case scenario, under which the UK manages to enter into favourable trade arrangements with the EU and the rest of the world, while pursuing large-scale deregulation at home, the UK could be better off by 1.6 per cent of GDP a year by 2030. The remain campaign suggested that such a trade arrangement would be unlikely, as the UK would not be allowed a 'pick and mix' approach that leads to a better deal for Britain than that for Germany or France.

Views of business leaders

Another set of arguments focused particularly on the impact on industry. A report for the CBI conducted by PricewaterhouseCoopers[7] analysed the effects of Brexit and estimated that total UK GDP in 2020 could be between around 3 per cent and 5.5 per cent lower under either a free trade agreement or a WTO scenario than if the UK remained in the EU. In light of the report, the CBI argued that Brexit could cost the UK economy £100 billion by 2020, lead to nearly 1 million job losses and would leave the average household between £2100 and £3700 worse off.

The CBI's stance was supported by many individual business leaders. However, in May 2016, 300 business leaders wrote a letter in support of Brexit, outlining the adverse effect that EU membership has on British competitiveness because of

[1] Chris Giles and Emily Cadman, 'Economists' forecasts: Brexit would damage growth', *Financial Times* (3 January 2016).

[2] *Economists' Views on Brexit*, Ipsos Mori (28 May 2016).

[3] *EU Referendum: HM Treasury Analysis Key Facts*, HM Treasury (18 April 2016).

[4] *The Economic Consequences of Brexit: A Taxing Decision*, OECD (27 April 2016).

[5] See: Philip Inman, 'Brexit would prompt stock market and house price crash, says IMF'; *The Guardian* (13 May 2016).

[6] *What if. . . ? The Consequences, Challenges and Opportunities facing Britain Outside the EU*, Open Europe (23 March 2015).

[7] *Leaving the EU: Implications for the UK Economy*, PwC for the CBI (2 March 2016).

▶

rules and regulations.[8] Outside the EU, they maintained, British business would be free to grow faster, expand into new markets and create more jobs.

Clearly Brexit will affect different industries in different ways. Much of the economic impact depends on the terms of their access to the single market and the extent to which they will be governed by single market rules. Also it depends on whether they will still be able to benefit from trade deals with other countries secured by the EU and how any new trade deals will affect their export opportunities. However, the biggest impact of Brexit to date has been the uncertainty from the protracted negotiations, as we discuss on pages 350–2.

---

[8] See: Peter Dominczak, 'EU referendum: More than 300 business leaders back a Brexit', *The Telegraph* (15 May 2016).

?

1. The UK's Chancellor of the Exchequer said that with Brexit, the Bank of England would have to tackle either inflation or unemployment. Use an aggregate demand and aggregate supply diagram to explain this point.
2. Why was there a belief that house prices might fall with a British exit from the EU?
3. Mark Carney suggested that a British exit might cause the pound to fall. Why could this happen? How did Bank of England interest rate decisions in the light of the Brexit vote impact on the exchange rate?

Q

Research two assessments of the effects of a 'no-deal' Brexit that were conducted in 2019. Summarise their arguments. How do they differ from the assessments considered in this Box?

As a result, 20 of the 28 EU member states' deficit exceeded 1 per cent with only one member state (Malta) meeting the 0.5 per cent target proposed by the European Commission as part of the 2011 Act. By December 2017, it had fallen to 0.9 per cent.

In addition to giving each country's 'transposition deficit', the Scoreboard gives their 'conformity deficit' (previously known as their 'compliance deficit'). This identifies the number of infringements of the internal market that have taken place by not correctly transposing Directives into national law. The proposed target for the conformity deficit in the 2011 Single Market Act is also 0.5 per cent and in recent times, this deficit has been relatively stable, with the EU average standing at 0.6 to 0.7 per cent from November 2012 to December 2017.

The hope is that the 'naming and shaming' of countries in the Scoreboard will encourage them to make more rapid progress towards totally free trade within the EU.

> **Pause for thought**
>
> *If there have been clear benefits from the single market programme, why do individual member governments still try to erect barriers, such as new technical standards?*

The effect of the new member states

Given the very different nature of the economies of the new entrants to the EU since 2004 and their lower levels of GDP per head, the potential for gain from membership has been substantial. The gains come through additional trade, increased competition, technological transfer and inward investment, both from other EU countries and from outside the EU.

A European Commission Report produced in April 2009, five years after the enlargement,[14] found that the expansion had been a win–win situation for both old and new members. There had been significant improvements in the standard of living in new member states and they had benefited from modernisation of their economies and more stabilised institutions and laws. In addition, enterprises in old member states had enjoyed opportunities for new investment and exports, and there had been an overall increase in trade and competition between the member states.

While there do remain significant differences between the members of the EU, trade between them is likely to continue to grow as a proportion of GDP. Furthermore, as we discuss in section 13.4, the euro is now used by 19 members, with the possibility of others adopting it at some time. Europe has dealt with many changes in recent years, including the expansion of the EU, the financial crisis and the eurozone debt crisis. But, in 2019, it is in the midst of what may be the biggest political shake-up of the EU in decades: Brexit. We discuss this in section 12.5.

> **Pause for thought**
>
> *Why was it expected that the new members of the EU had the most to gain from the single market, but also the most to lose?*

---

[14] 'Five Years of an Enlarged EU – Economic Achievements and Challenges', *European Economy 1 2009* (Commission of the European Communities).

RECAP

1. The Single European Act of 1986 sought to sweep away various administrative restrictions to free trade in the EU and to establish a genuine free market by 1993.

2. Benefits from completing the internal market have included trade creation, cost savings from no longer having to administer barriers, economies of scale for firms now able to operate on a Europe-wide scale, and greater competition leading to reduced costs and prices, greater flows of technical information and more innovation.

3. Critics of the single market point to the costs of radical changes in industrial structure, the attraction of capital away from the periphery of the EU to its geographical centre, possible problems of market power with the development of giant 'Euro-firms' and the political cost of lost national sovereignty.

4. New members have gained substantially from free trade within the EU. There have also been gains to existing member states.

5. Significant differences exist between members of the EU in terms of their economic performance and uncertainty remains as to how these economies will fare as the region starts to move out of recession.

12.5 BREXIT

On 23 June 2016, the UK held a referendum on whether to remain a member of the EU and by a majority of 51.9 per cent to 48.1 per cent, Britain voted to leave the EU.

In the run-up to the vote there was heated debate on the merits and costs of membership and of leaving ('Brexit'), as we discuss in Box 12.5. Although many of the arguments were concerned with sovereignty, security and other political factors, many of the arguments centred on whether there would be a net *economic* gain from either remaining or leaving.

Forecasting the economic impact of the decision, however, is difficult. First, the effects of either remaining of leaving were likely to be very different in the long run from the short run, and long-run forecasts are highly unreliable as the economy is likely to be affected by so many unpredictable events. Secondly, the costs and benefits will depend on the future trading relationship that Britain has with the EU. Writing at the start of April 2019, this remains a mystery. The British Parliament has rejected the Prime Minister's Withdrawal Deal three times and to date, there has been no majority on any other trading arrangement that has been brought to the House of Commons.

Despite the uncertainty surrounding Britain's future, the tools of economics provide a framework in which we can discuss the *potential* economic benefits and costs of the UK's membership of the European Union as compared with the alternatives outside the EU.

There are broadly three possible types of trading arrangement with the EU post-Brexit:

The 'Norwegian model'.[15] Britain leaves the EU, but joins the European Economic Area (EEA), giving access to the single market, but removing regulation in some key areas, such as fisheries and home affairs.

Bilateral agreements. These fall under three types:

- The 'Swiss model':[16] the UK negotiates a series of bilateral agreements with the EU, including selective or general access to the single market.
- The 'Canadian model':[17] the UK forms a comprehensive trade agreement with the EU to lower customs tariffs and other barriers to trade.
- The 'Turkish model':[18] the UK forms a customs union with the EU. In Turkey's case the agreement relates principally to manufactured goods.

WTO membership. The UK makes a complete break from the EU (known as a 'hard Brexit') and uses its membership of the WTO to make trade agreements.

In a speech in January 2017,[19] the UK Prime Minister, Theresa May, stated that the UK 'cannot possibly' remain in the single market, as that would mean 'not leaving the EU at all. So we do not seek membership of the Single Market. Instead, we seek the greatest possible access to it through a new, comprehensive, bold and ambitious Free Trade Agreement.'

Formal Brexit talks began following the triggering of Article 50[20] in March 2017. The talks would therefore shape a new trading relationship between the UK

---

[15] Damien Gayle, 'The Norway option: what is it and what does it mean for Britain?', *The Guardian* (28 October 2015).

[16] Sabine Jenni, 'Is the Swiss model a Brexit solution?', *The UK in a Changing Europe*, Kings College London, (23 March 2016).

[17] *CETA Chapter by Chapter*, European Commission (January 2017).

[18] 'Turkey', Countries and Regions, EC Trade Directorate (updated 5 June 2019).

[19] *The government's negotiating objectives for exiting the EU: PM speech*, Prime Minister's Office, 10 Downing Street, Department for Exiting the European Union, and The Rt Hon Theresa May MP (17 January 2017).

[20] 'Consolidated version of the Treaty on European Union: Title VI: Final Provisions: Article 50'; *Official Journal of the European Union* (26 October 2012).

and EU. At their heart would be what happened at the 'UK/EU border'. Would firms face tariffs? Would the UK be able to reach an agreement with the EU which would allow it to make trade deals with other countries? Then there was the need to avoid physical border checks between Northern Ireland and the Republic of Ireland.

A historical perspective

While we have already seen many effects of Britain's decision to leave the EU, the long-term impact, for example on long-term economic growth and investment, will obviously take many years to become clear. What is clear, however, is that the ongoing uncertainty surrounding Britain's future relationship with the EU, has had many negative effects on businesses and not just those in the UK.

The UK was due to leave the European Union at 11pm on 29 March 2019. This would have given the country two years from the date when Article 50 was triggered to prepare for leaving and to agree terms of the withdrawal with the EU. Draft negotiating guidelines were unanimously adopted by the European Council and the UK government set out its negotiating objectives, which included:

- A smooth orderly Brexit;
- Certainty;
- Control of its own laws and control of immigration;
- Maintaining the common travel area with Ireland;
- Rights for EU nationals in the UK and British nationals in the EU;
- Protection of workers' rights;
- Free trade with European markets and new trade agreements with other countries.

Negotiation of the Withdrawal Agreement
On 19 June 2017, the negotiations began and over the ensuing months, the Government set out its position on a range of areas, including: trade across the border between Northern Ireland and Ireland, judicial proceedings, nuclear issues, trade, research, funding and data protection. There would be a transition period after the UK left the EU to allow details of future arrangements to be finalised and during which the UK would remain in the single market and customs union. This would enable businesses to adapt to the withdrawal terms and prepare for the time when the new post-Brexit rules came into force.

In November 2017, outline plans were published for the Withdrawal Agreement and Implementation Bill and, in the following month, the first phase of talks was completed. This included agreements on the rights of EU and UK citizens, the arrangements for trade across the border in the island of Ireland, the amount that the UK should pay to honour its previously agreed commitments (the so-called 'divorce bill') and the length of the transition period. The negotiations in phase two then turned to other matters, including trade and the future relationship that the UK would have with the EU.

Throughout the start of 2018, negotiations continued, with the European Commission publishing its draft legal text on transition and the Foreign Secretary 'setting out the path for an outward-facing, liberal and global Britain' after its exit. At the end of February 2018, the draft Withdrawal Agreement[21] was published and in a speech to Parliament on 5 March 2018, Theresa May said:

> First, we are leaving the single market. In certain ways, our access to each other's markets will be less than it is now. We need to strike a new balance. However, we will not accept the rights of Canada and the obligations of Norway . . . We want the freedom to negotiate trade agreements around the world. We want control of our laws. We also want as frictionless a border as possible with the EU, so that we do not damage the integrated supply chains on which our industries depend . . . The Commission has suggested that an 'off the shelf' model is the only option available to the UK.[22]

After various amendments, the Withdrawal Agreement was published with the aim to finalise it by October 2018 and in June 2018, it received Royal Assent, becoming the European Union (Withdrawal) Act, which includes text for a 'meaningful vote'. This means that the UK Parliament would need to vote on and approve the final deal. However, at this point, uncertainty escalated.

Political difficulties
In a meeting at Chequers, in July 2018, the Cabinet agreed on a collective position for the future Brexit negotiations, but David Davis, the Brexit Secretary and key negotiator for the UK, resigned, saying he felt that the UK was 'giving away too much too easily'. Dominic Raab became his replacement. Over the next few months, negotiations continued, but concerns were rising about the possibility of a 'No-deal' Brexit and guidance was given on how the UK was planning for this outcome.

One issue that was a particular cause for concern was the Irish border. Ireland will remain a member of the EU (and eurozone), but Northern Ireland (which did vote to remain) will leave the EU, as it is part of the UK. After Brexit, the land border between Northern Ireland and Ireland will become the land border

---

[21] *Draft Withdrawal Agreement on the withdrawal of the United Kingdom of Great Britain and Northern Ireland from the European Union and the European Atomic Energy Community*, European Commission (28 February 2018).

[22] 'UK/EU Future Economic Partnership: Speech by the Prime Minister, Theresa May to the House of Commons', *Hansard*, vol. 637 (5 March 2018).

between the UK and the EU, but neither part of the island of Ireland want to see a hard border, with checkpoints, etc., as this will prevent the free flow of people (many of whom live on one side of the 'border', but work on the other side) and of trade. However, it was proving difficult to arrive at a solution.

The UK and EU therefore agreed a 'backstop', which means that, whatever the outcome of future talks, there would not be a hard border. However, it would mean that some products going to Northern Ireland from the UK would have to be subject to some checks and controls and so Northern Ireland would remain subject to some EU rules. Furthermore, it also means a temporary single customs territory would be implemented after Brexit, which would apply indefinitely and could only end with the agreement of both the UK and the EU. It is this point, in particular, which caused problems amongst MPs in the UK Parliament and especially those representing the Democratic Unionist Party (from Northern Ireland), who have supported Theresa May's government.

Political tensions continued to grow, with clear divisions over the Agreement, the way forward and the whole Brexit process. Some MPs were in support of the Withdrawal Agreement; others wanted small changes; some wanted significant changes, particularly regarding the backstop. There were many MPs calling for the UK to remain in the single market; some wanted a different Brexit with a customs union arrangement; while others called for the UK to leave with no deal; and others called for a second referendum, with remain on the ballot.

By the end of August 2018, the value of sterling had fallen to an 18-month low in response to the goings on in Parliament, reflecting the uncertainty and instability that this process was creating in the British economy.

Finally on 14 November 2018, the EU and UK reached an agreement on the Withdrawal Agreement for the terms of the UK's exit in March 2019 and the Outline Political Declaration for future relations. However, the following day, Dominic Raab resigned because of his opposition to the Withdrawal Agreement and this triggered other Ministerial resignations.

As 2018 ended, the Attorney General's legal advice on the Withdrawal Agreement was made public and five days of debate on the Withdrawal Agreement occurred prior to the 'meaningful vote'. But, with defeat in the 'meaningful vote' looming, the Prime Minister delayed it until January.

Economic data showed that 2018 had been the UK's weakest year of growth (1.4%) since 2012 and in December 2018 output shrank. Consumer confidence was at its lowest in more than five years and the Bank of England's credit conditions survey indicated that lenders were expecting the weakest three months of borrowing since 2007.

Pause for thought

Why do you think that businesses were so concerned about the ongoing delays to the Brexit process?

As the new year began, the Prime Minister faced further debates and losses in Parliament. On 15 January 2019, the government suffered a massive defeat in the 'meaningful vote'.

Further debates ensued, which indicated that the majority of MPs were unhappy with the 'backstop' in its current form and were against exiting the EU without a deal. In February 2019, the Prime Minister outlined planned changes to the Withdrawal Agreement, but the UK was told by President Junker that the EU-27 would not re-open it, although additional text could be included in the Political Declaration.

Some reassurances were received from the EU regarding the 'backstop' and the PM announced that she has secured 'legally binding' changes to the deal. However, the Attorney General's statement to the House of Commons indicated that in his opinion, the risks to the UK remain unchanged. The Withdrawal Agreement was again put to Parliament and the government suffered a second heavy defeat, clearly indicating that the majority of MPs remained unhappy with the Withdrawal Agreement as it stood. However, MPs also voted to reject a no-deal Brexit.

In response to the defeat in the House of Commons, Michel Barnier made a statement saying it 'prolongs and worsens the major uncertainty that was created . . . by the sovereign decision . . . of the United Kingdom to leave the European Union . . . It is the UK's responsibility to tell us what it wants for our future relationship, what its choice is, what its clear line is.'

The pound fell once more in reaction to the news. Business groups reacted with dismay over the lack of clarity about the future trading relationship that the UK would have with the EU. The Director General of the CBI described the process as 'a circus' and called for an urgent extension to Article 50. Key car manufacturers indicated their plans to shift production from the UK to the EU if the UK left without a deal, prompting serious concerns about the future of the British car industry. There was similar reaction in other sectors.

On 27 March 2019, the Prime Minister announced that she would stand down before the second stage of Brexit and in Parliament a series of indicative votes occurred. This provided a clear picture of just how divided the House of Commons was on the way forward, as not a single 'option' of how to proceed received a majority. The options voted on were:[23]

- No deal
- A comprehensive customs arrangement called 'common market 2.0'
- A proposal that the UK remains within the EEA, re-joins the EFTA, but remains outside of the customs union – the 'EFTA and EEA' proposal
- A permanent and comprehensive UK-wide customs union with the EU
- Labour's alternative plan that proposes a close economic relationship with the EU, including a customs union and elements of the single market
- A 'Revocation to avoid no deal' that required a vote on no-deal before the day of departure, which, if it was not passed, would require the PM to revoke Article 50
- A 'Confirmatory public vote' that requires a public vote to confirm any Brexit deal, with remain on the ballot
- A 'Contingent preferential arrangements' option that called for the government to seek to agree preferential trade arrangements with the EU.

As agreement seemed impossible, an extension to Article 50 was sought by the government. A new leaving date of 12 April was set if no deal had been reached, but this was then further extended to 31 October (or earlier if Parliament voted for the Withdrawal Agreement).

However, while the extension allayed some businesses' fears about a potential no-deal Brexit, it also prolonged the uncertainty. It also meant the UK participating in the EU Parliamentary elections on 22 May 2019, or face leaving with no deal on 1 June. The government and the Labour Party continued to hold talks about a suitable Withdrawal Agreement and Political Declaration for future relations.

Eventually, under extreme pressure from within her party, on 24 May 2019 Theresa May agreed to step down as Conservative Party leader and Prime Minister. She would hand over to her successor as Prime Minister on 24 July 2019. Following her announcement, a leadership campaign was organised and 10 Conservative MPs stood. These were whittled down to two in run-off ballots of Conservative MPs. The final choice was made by Conservative Party members, who chose Boris Johnson over Jeremy Hunt.

On becoming Prime Minister, Boris Johnson selected a cabinet with the major posts given to committed 'Brexiteers', vowing to leave without a deal on October 31 if the EU would not renegotiate a deal more in line with Conservative demands. Various forecasts and studies predicted, however, that there would be considerable costs to the UK economy of a no-deal Brexit: see the news item *The costs of a No-Deal Brexit* on the Sloman Economics News site.

The divisions in Parliament extended to the UK population. Opinion across the country remained deeply divided on how the country should proceed: whether it should leave, and if so how, or whether it should remain, confirmed in a referendum. Perhaps the only thing that can be agreed by the British population, the government and the EU is that the whole Brexit process has been, as the Director General of the CBI described, 'a circus'.

---

[23] Ibid.

RECAP

1. The UK voted to leave the EU on 23 June 2016, with a small majority. Many difficulties were encountered in forecasting the economic impact of the decision, especially as the effects of leaving would be very different in the short and long run and as other unpredictable events would also affect the economy. Furthermore, the costs and benefits would depend on the future trading relationship that the UK has with the EU.

2. Economists have largely argued that the decision to leave would result in negative effects on the economy by impeding cross-border trade with its EU partners and thereby damaging growth. A few economists, however, have argued that outside of the EU the UK would be free of EU rules and regulations and would be able to create trade.

3. The UK was due to leave the EU on 29 March 2019, two years after Article 50 was triggered. Negotiations progressed, but even after various issues had been agreed upon, divisions remained, particularly regarding the 'backstop' which concerned the border on the island of Ireland.

4. A Withdrawal Agreement was eventually published, which outlined the terms of the UK's exit from the EU, but before coming into force, it had to be approved by the UK Parliament. After three 'meaningful votes' and an amendment to the Agreement, it has (as of May 2019) yet to be approved.

5. In 2018, the UK economy saw its weakest year of growth since 2012, caused mainly by the uncertainty over Brexit.

6. The UK requested extensions to Article 50 in order to avoid a 'no-deal' Brexit and these were granted. While this allayed some fears and temporarily averted a 'no-deal' Brexit, divisions in the UK Parliament were significant, but the new Prime Minister, Boris Johnson, was determined to take the UK out of the EU by 31 October 2019, with or without a deal.

QUESTIONS

1. What is likely to be the impact of rising levels of intra-regional trade for the world economy?

2. Imagine that two countries, Richland and Poorland, can produce just two goods, computers and coal. Assume that for a given amount of land and capital, the output of these two products requires the following constant amounts of labour:

	Richland	Poorland
1 computer	2	4
100 tonnes of coal	4	5

Assume that each country has 20 million workers.

(a) If there is no trade, and in each country 12 million workers produce computers and 8 million workers produce coal, how many computers and tonnes of coal will each country produce? What will be the total production of each product?

(b) What is the opportunity cost of a computer in (i) Richland; (ii) Poorland?

(c) What is the opportunity cost of 100 tonnes of coal in (i) Richland; (ii) Poorland?

(d) Which country has a comparative advantage in which product?

(e) Assuming that price equals marginal cost, which of the following would represent possible exchange ratios?
   (i) 1 computer for 40 tonnes of coal;
   (ii) 2 computers for 140 tonnes of coal;
   (iii) 1 computer for 100 tonnes of coal;
   (iv) 1 computer for 60 tonnes of coal;
   (v) 4 computers for 360 tonnes of coal.

(f) Assume that trade now takes place and that 1 computer exchanges for 65 tonnes of coal. Both countries specialise completely in the product in which they have a comparative advantage. How much does each country produce of its respective product?

(g) The country producing computers sells 6 million domestically. How many does it export to the other country?

(h) How much coal does the other country consume?

3. Why doesn't the USA specialise as much as General Motors or Texaco? Why doesn't the UK specialise as much as Unilever? Is the answer to these questions similar to the answer to the questions, 'Why doesn't the USA specialise as much as Luxembourg?' and 'Why doesn't Unilever specialise as much as the local florist?'

4. To what extent are the arguments for countries specialising and then trading with each other the same as those for individuals specialising in doing the jobs to which they are relatively well suited?

5. The following are four items that are traded internationally: wheat; computers; textiles; insurance. In which one of the four is each of the following most likely to have a comparative advantage: India; the UK; Canada; Japan? Give reasons for your answer.

6. It is often argued that if the market fails to develop infant industries, then this is an argument for government intervention, but not necessarily in the form of restricting imports. In what *other* ways could infant industries be given government support?

7. What is fallacious about the following two arguments? Is there any truth in either?
   (a) 'Imports should be reduced because money is going abroad which would be better spent at home.'
   (b) 'We should protect our industries from being undercut by imports produced using cheap labour.'

8. Go through each of the arguments for restricting trade and provide a counter-argument for not restricting trade.

9. If countries are so keen to reduce the barriers to trade, why do many countries frequently attempt to erect barriers?

10. Debate the following: 'All arguments for restricting trade boil down to special pleading for particular interest groups. Ultimately there will be a net social cost from any trade restrictions.'

11. If rich countries stand to gain substantially from freer trade, why have they been so reluctant to reduce the levels of protection for agriculture?

12. Construct a case for restricting trade between the USA and Japan. Are there any arguments here that could not equally apply to a case for restricting trade between Scotland and England or between Berlin and Hamburg?

13. Why is it difficult to estimate the magnitude of the benefits of completing the internal market of the EU?

14. Look through the costs and benefits that we identified from the single European market. Do the same costs and benefits arise from a substantially enlarged EU?

15. Consider the process of Brexit negotiations since the triggering of Article 50 (to leave the EU) in April 2017. What model of trade relations with the EU27 is likely to be/was the end result of the negotiations?

16. Is a 'hard Brexit' (reverting to WTO rules and negotiating bilateral trade deals) necessarily an inferior alternative to remaining in the European single market or, at least, in the customs union?

13 Chapter

The global financial environment

Business issues covered in this chapter

- What is meant by 'the balance of payments' and how do trade and financial movements affect it?
- How are exchange rates determined and what are the implications for business of changes in the exchange rate?
- How do governments and/or central banks seek to influence the exchange rate and what are the implications for other macroeconomic policies and for business?
- How do the vast flows of finance around the world affect business and the countries in which they are located?
- What are the advantages and disadvantages of the euro for members of the eurozone and for businesses inside and outside of the eurozone?
- What threats to the stability of the euro arise from the debt and deficit problems of some member states? How do the major economies of the world seek to coordinate their policies and what difficulties arise in the process?
- What are the causes and effects on business of currency speculation?

When countries sell exports, there is an inflow of money into the economy. When they buy imports, there is an outflow. In this chapter we examine these international financial flows and their implications for business. With an increasingly interdependent world, these financial flows have a significant effect on economic performance.

But such flows are not just from trade. Inward investment leads to an inflow of money, as do deposits of money in this country made by people abroad. Outward investment and deposits of money abroad from people in this country result in an outflow of money.

All these inflows and outflows of money to and from a country are recorded in the 'balance of payments'. We examine this process in section 13.1.

Trade and investment are also influenced by the rates of exchange between currencies. Rates of exchange, in turn, are influenced by the demand and supply of currencies resulting from trade and investment. We will see what causes exchange rate fluctuations – a major cause of concern for many businesses – and how central banks can attempt to reduce these fluctuations. Section 13.2 looks at exchange rates.

The remaining sections look at various aspects of global finance: how global financial flows affect the world economy; whether the global financial environment can be managed; and how the EU has sought to achieve greater financial stability through the adoption of the euro by many of its members. Finally, we consider how the process of globalisation has led to harmonisation of nations' business cycles and whether this means economic policy should also be harmonised.

13.1 THE BALANCE OF PAYMENTS

A country's balance of payments account records all the flows of money between residents of that country and the rest of the world. Receipts of money from abroad are regarded as credits and are entered in the accounts with a positive sign. Outflows of money from the country are regarded as debits and are entered with a negative sign.

The balance of payments account

There are three main parts of the balance of payments account: the current account, the capital account and the financial account. We shall look at each part in turn, and take the UK as an example. Table 13.1 gives a summary of the UK balance of payments for 2018.

The current account

The *current account* records (a) payments for exports (+) and imports (−) of goods and services, plus (b) incomes flowing into (+) and out of (−) the country (wages, profits, dividends on shares), also known as primary income flows, plus (c) net current transfers of money into (+) and out of (−) the country, also known as secondary income flows (e.g. money sent from Greece to a Greek student studying in the UK is an inflow of money and so would be a credit item on the UK balance of payments).

The *current account balance* is the overall balance of all these. A current account surplus is where credits exceed debits. A current account deficit is where debits exceed credits.

If you want to look purely at the balance of imports and exports (i.e. just item (a) above), this is given as the *balance of trade*. Remember that exports are an injection and imports are a withdrawal from the circular flow of income. If exports exceed imports, there is a balance of trade surplus and this represents a net injection for an economy. If imports exceed exports, there is a balance of trade deficit and this represents a net leakage. Both exports and imports are components of aggregate demand and so a trade surplus will act to increase aggregate demand, while a trade deficit will reduce aggregate demand.

The capital account

The *capital account* records the flows of funds, into the country (+) and out of the country (−), associated with the acquisition or disposal of fixed assets (e.g. land or patents/trademarks), the transfer of funds by migrants, and the payment of grants by the government for overseas projects and the receipt of EU money for capital projects. As you can see from Table 13.1, the balance on the capital account is small in comparison with the other two accounts.

The financial account

The *financial account* of the balance of payments records cross-border changes in the holding of shares,

Table 13.1	UK balance of payments, 2018	
CURRENT ACCOUNT	**£m**	**% of GDP**
Balance on trade in goods and services (exports minus imports)	−30 969	−1.2
Net income flows (wages and investment income)	−26 650	−1.3
Net current transfers (government and private)	−24 025	−1.1
Balance on current account	−81 644	−3.9
CAPITAL ACCOUNT		
Net capital transfers	−2 464	−0.1
Balance on capital account	−2 464	−0.1
FINANCIAL ACCOUNT		
Direct investment	+10 949	+0.4
Portfolio investment	+270 760	+10.5
Other investment (mainly short-term flows)	−185 721	−7.2
Financial derivatives (net)	−13 216	−0.5
Reserves	−18 566	−0.7
Balance on financial account	+64 206	+2.5
Net errors and omissions	+19 902	+0.8
Total	0	0

Source: Balance of Payments: 2018 Q4, Office for National Statistics (March 2019)

Definitions

Current account of the balance of payments The record of a country's imports and exports of goods and services, plus incomes and current transfers of money to and from abroad.

Current account balance The balance on trade in goods and services plus net incomes and current transfers: i.e. the sum of the credits on the current account minus the sum of the debits.

Balance of trade Exports of goods and services minus imports of goods and services.

Capital account of the balance of payments The record of transfers of capital to and from abroad.

Financial account of the balance of payments The record of the flows of money into and out of the country for the purpose of investment or as deposits in banks and other financial institutions.

property, bank deposits and loans, government securities, etc. In other words, unlike the current account, which is concerned with money *incomes,* the financial account is concerned with the flows of money for the purchase and sale of *assets.*

Anything that involves an acquisition of assets in this country by overseas residents (e.g. foreign companies investing in the UK) represents an inflow of money and is thus a credit (+) item. Any acquisition of assets abroad by UK residents (e.g. UK companies investing abroad) represents a debit (−) item.

Some of these flows are for long-term investment. This can involve the acquisition of buildings and equipment (direct investment) or paper assets such as shares (portfolio investment).

Some of the flows involve the short-term deposit of money in bank accounts. Such short-term monetary flows are common between international financial centres, to take advantage of differences in countries' interest rates and changes in exchange rates. We saw the importance of this aspect of the financial account in the late 2000s, when there was massive disinvestment by non-UK residents in financial assets with UK financial institutions. Largely due to this, the UK's balance of 'other investment' deteriorated from a surplus of £90 billion in 2007 to a deficit of £185 billion in 2008. It then improved over the next few years. However, as Table 13.1 shows, there was once more a large deficit of £186 billion in 2018. This was in part due to speculators expecting a fall in sterling and the Bank of England keeping interest rates low in the light of Brexit uncertainties.

Further analysis of the UK's financial account is given in Case Study D.38 on the student website.

Pause for thought
Where would interest payments on short-term foreign deposits in UK banks be entered on the balance of payments account?

Flows to and from the reserves

The UK, like all other countries, holds reserves of gold and foreign currencies. From time to time the Bank of England (acting as the government's agent) might release some of these reserves to purchase sterling on the foreign exchange market. It would do so as a means of supporting the rate of exchange (as we shall see in the next section). Drawing on reserves represents a credit item (+) in the balance of payments account: money drawn from the reserves represents an inflow to the balance of payments (albeit an outflow from the reserves account). The reserves can thus be used to support a deficit elsewhere in the balance of payments.

Conversely, if there is a surplus elsewhere in the balance of payments, the Bank of England could use it to build up the reserves. Building up the reserves counts as a debit item (−) in the balance of payments, since it represents an outflow from it (to the reserves).

Does the balance of payments balance?

When all the components of the balance of payments account are taken together, the balance of payments should exactly balance: credits should equal debits. As we shall see in section 13.2, if they were not equal, the rate of exchange would have to adjust until they were, or the government would have to intervene to make them equal.

When the statistics are compiled, however, a number of errors are likely to occur. As a result, there will not be a balance. The main reason for the errors is that the statistics are obtained from a number of sources, and there are often delays before items are recorded and sometimes omissions too. To 'correct' for this, a *net errors and omissions* item is included in the accounts. This ensures that there will be an exact balance.

Countries' statistical authorities recalculate recent years' balance of payments figures as more data become available. Thus, the net errors and omissions term tends to be smaller in more recent estimates. If you look at recent data from the ONS on the UK's 2018 balance of payments, you will find that the net errors and omissions term is smaller than that in Table 13.1, which is based on the first estimates by the ONS made in early 2019.

Does a deficit matter?

If the balance of payments must always balance, then in what sense does the balance of payments matter? The answer is that the individual accounts will not necessarily balance. The UK and the USA have traditionally imported more than they have exported. The resulting deficit on the current accounts of these countries has thus had to be financed by an equal and opposite surplus on the capital-plus-financial accounts. In other words, the UK and USA have had to borrow from abroad or sell assets abroad to finance the excess of imports over exports. This

---

Definition
Net errors and omissions A statistical adjustment to ensure that the two sides of the balance of payments account balance. It is necessary because of errors in compiling the statistics.

Figure 13.1 Current account balance in selected industrial countries

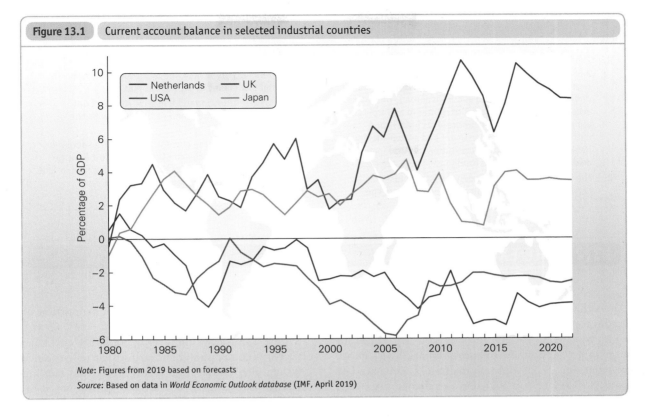

Note: Figures from 2019 based on forecasts

Source: Based on data in *World Economic Outlook database* (IMF, April 2019)

means that higher interest rates have been needed in order to attract deposits from overseas. It also means that there has tended to be an increased ownership of domestic assets over time by residents abroad.

Higher interest rates can have a long-term dampening effect on the economy, by discouraging borrowing and investment. Inward direct investment, on the other hand, although resulting in increased overseas ownership of assets in the UK and USA, will have the effect of stimulating output and employment.

Figure 13.1 shows the current account balances of the UK, the USA, the Netherlands and Japan as a proportion of their GDP.

The UK in most years has had a current account deficit. This deficit, however, has fluctuated with the business cycle. In times of rapid economic growth relative to other countries, expenditure on imports rises rapidly relative to exports and the current account goes deeper into deficit. You can see this in the late 1980s, the late 1990s and from 2005 to 2008. In times of recession, the current account improves, as it did in the early 1980s, the early 1990s and then again from 2008 to 2011. You can also see the effect of oil on the current account. As oil exports have declined in the early 2000s, so this contributed to a deepening of the deficit. The UK's trade and current account deficits are examined further in Case Study D.35 on the student website.

The Netherlands' economy is very different from the UK's. It relies heavily on its large export sector

and has run consistent trade and current account surpluses. It is home to a number of large multinational companies, such as Royal Dutch Shell, Heineken, Philips and ING and many non-Dutch companies are based in the Netherlands, all earning foreign revenues.

The current accounts of the USA and Japan are an approximate mirror image of each other as many of Japan's exports are imported by the USA. Much of Japan's current account surplus is then invested in the USA as direct investment, the acquisition of paper assets, such as shares (portfolio investment), or simply as deposits in US financial institutions. One reflection of this imbalance has been generally much higher interest rates in the USA than in Japan – at least until the financial crisis.

Another consequence of the high US current account deficit is that most of it is paid in US dollars. This increases the supply of dollars in the world banking system, much of it on short-term deposit. These deposits can be rapidly transferred from one country to another, wherever interest rates are higher or where speculators anticipate a rise in the exchange rate (see next section). As we shall see, this movement of 'hot money' tends to lead to considerable instability in exchange rates. The size of the US current account deficit has been one of the concerns of President Trump and has been used as one of the justifications for the increase in protectionism.

RECAP

1. The balance of payments account records all payments to and receipts from other countries. The current account records payments for imports and exports, plus incomes and transfers of money to and from abroad. The capital account records all transfers of capital to and from abroad. The financial account records inflows and outflows of money for investment and as deposits in banks and other financial institutions. It also includes dealings in the country's foreign exchange reserves.

2. The whole account must balance, but surpluses or deficits can be recorded on any specific part of the

   account. Thus the current account could be in deficit, but it would have to be matched by an equal and opposite capital plus financial account surplus.

3. The UK has traditionally had a current account deficit, but this does tend to fluctuate with the business cycle.

4. The US and Japanese current accounts are somewhat of a mirror image of each other. One result of large and persistent US deficits has been an increase in 'hot money', which has aggravated exchange rate instability.

13.2 THE EXCHANGE RATE

An exchange rate is the rate at which one currency trades for another on the foreign exchange market.

If you want to go abroad, you will need to exchange your pounds for euros, dollars, Swiss francs or whatever. To do this you might go to a bank. The bank will quote you that day's exchange rates: e.g. €1.15 to the pound, or $1.25 to the pound. It is similar for firms. If an importer wants to buy, say, some machinery from Japan, it will require yen to pay the Japanese supplier. It will thus ask the foreign exchange section of a bank to quote it a rate of exchange of the pound into yen. Similarly, if you want to buy some foreign stocks and shares, or if companies based in the UK want to invest abroad, sterling will have to be exchanged for the appropriate foreign currency.

Likewise, if Americans want to come on holiday to the UK or to buy UK assets, or American firms want to import UK goods or to invest in the UK, they will require sterling. They will be quoted an exchange rate for the pound in the USA: say, £1 = $1.25. This means that they will have to pay $1.25 to obtain £1 worth of UK goods or assets.

Exchange rates are quoted between each of the major currencies of the world. These exchange rates are constantly changing. Minute by minute, dealers in the foreign exchange dealing rooms of the banks are adjusting the rates of exchange by buying and selling different currencies.

One of the problems, however, in assessing what is happening to a particular currency is that its rate of exchange may rise against some currencies (weak currencies) and fall against others (strong currencies). In order to gain an overall picture of its fluctuations, it is best to look at a weighted average exchange rate against all other currencies. This is known as the *exchange rate index*. The weight given to each

currency in the index depends on the proportion of transactions done with that country.

Figure 13.2 shows the average monthly exchange rates between the pound and various currencies since 1980. It also shows the average monthly sterling exchange rate index over the same period based on January 2005 = 100.

Pause for thought

How did the pound 'fare' compare with the dollar and the yen from 1985 to 2019? What about the euro since it began circulating? What conclusions can be drawn about the relative movements of these currencies?

The determination of the rate of exchange in a free market

In a free foreign exchange market, the rate of exchange is determined by demand and supply. Thus the sterling exchange rate is determined by the demand and supply of pounds. This is illustrated in Figure 13.3.

For simplicity, assume that there are just two countries, the UK and the USA. When UK importers wish to buy goods from the USA, or when UK residents wish to invest in the USA, they will supply pounds on the foreign exchange market in order to obtain dollars. In

Definition

Exchange rate index A weighted average exchange rate expressed as an index, where the value of the index is 100 in a given base year. The weights of the different currencies in the index add up to 1.

Figure 13.2 Sterling exchange rates against selected currencies

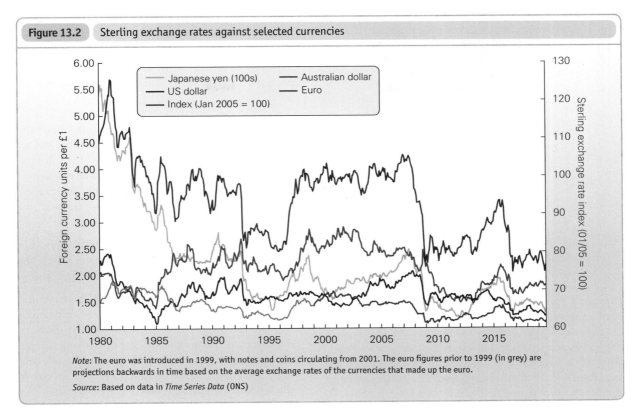

Note: The euro was introduced in 1999, with notes and coins circulating from 2001. The euro figures prior to 1999 (in grey) are projections backwards in time based on the average exchange rates of the currencies that made up the euro.

Source: Based on data in *Time Series Data* (ONS)

Figure 13.3 Determination of the rate of exchange

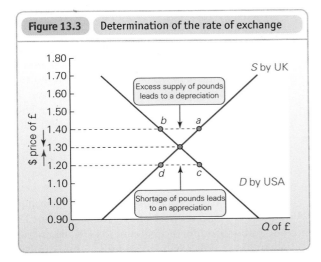

other words, they will go to banks or other foreign exchange dealers to buy dollars in exchange for pounds. The higher the exchange rate, the more dollars they will obtain for their pounds. This will effectively make American goods cheaper to buy and investment more profitable. Thus the higher the exchange rate, the more pounds will be supplied. The supply curve of pounds therefore typically slopes upwards.

When US residents wish to purchase UK goods or to invest in the UK, they will require pounds. They demand pounds by selling dollars on the foreign exchange market. In other words, they will go to banks or other

foreign exchange dealers to buy pounds in exchange for dollars. The lower the dollar price of the pound (the exchange rate), the cheaper it will be for them to obtain UK goods and assets, and hence the more pounds they are likely to demand. The demand curve for pounds, therefore, typically slopes downwards.

The equilibrium exchange rate is where the demand for pounds equals the supply. In Figure 13.3 this is at an exchange rate of £1 = \$1.30. But what is the mechanism that equates demand and supply?

If the current exchange rate were above the equilibrium, the supply of pounds being offered to the banks would exceed the demand. For example, in Figure 13.3, if the exchange rate were \$1.40, there would be an excess supply of pounds of $a - b$. Banks would not have enough dollars to exchange for all these pounds. But the banks make money by exchanging currency, not by holding on to it. They would thus lower the exchange rate in order to encourage a greater demand for pounds and reduce the excessive supply. They would continue lowering the rate until demand equalled supply.

Similarly, if the rate were below the equilibrium, say at \$1.20, there would be a shortage of pounds of $c - d$. The banks would find themselves with too few pounds to meet all the demand. At the same time, they would have an excess supply of dollars. The banks would thus raise the exchange rate until demand equalled supply.

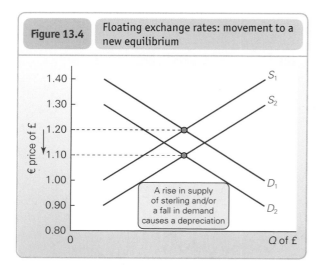

Figure 13.4 Floating exchange rates: movement to a new equilibrium

In practice, the process of reaching equilibrium is extremely rapid. The foreign exchange dealers in the banks are continually adjusting the rate as new customers make new demands for currencies. What is more, the banks have to watch each other's actions closely. They are constantly in competition with each other and thus have to keep their rates in line. The dealers receive minute-by-minute updates on their computer screens of the rates being offered around the world.

Shifts in the currency demand and supply curves

Any shift in the demand or supply curves will cause the exchange rate to change. This is illustrated in Figure 13.4, which this time shows the euro/sterling exchange rate. If the demand and supply curves shift from D_1 and S_1 to D_2 and S_2 respectively, the exchange rate will fall from €1.20 to €1.10. A fall in the exchange rate is called a *depreciation*. A rise in the exchange rate is called an *appreciation*.

A depreciation will make imports more expensive as foreign currencies cost more in domestic currency terms. For example, in February 2016, research showed that the price of roses for Valentine's Day in the UK would be approximately 6 per cent more expensive compared to February 2015 because of the fall in the sterling exchange rate, which meant that flower imports were more expensive.[1] Conversely an appreciation will make imports cheaper.

Definitions

Depreciation A fall in the free-market exchange rate of the domestic currency with foreign currencies.

Appreciation A rise in the free-market exchange rate of the domestic currency with foreign currencies.

On the other hand, a depreciation will tend to make exports cheaper abroad in foreign currency terms and an appreciation will make them more expensive. Exporters thus tend to benefit from a depreciation as it makes their products more competitive abroad.

You can read about changes in sterling exchange rates in early 2016 caused by uncertainty about the outcome of the EU referendum in the blog, *Brexit fears,* on the Sloman Economics News site and how the movements in sterling have reflected the uncertainty over Brexit negotiations in *The Telegraph.*[2] We also consider exchange rate volatility and the impact on business in Box 13.2.

Causes of shifts in currency demand and supply. But why should the demand and supply curves shift? The following are the major possible causes of a depreciation:

- *A fall in domestic interest rates.* UK rates would now be less competitive for savers and other depositors. More UK residents would be likely to deposit their money abroad, thus requiring foreign currency (the supply of sterling would rise), and fewer people abroad would deposit their money in the UK (the demand for sterling would fall).

- *Higher inflation in the domestic economy than abroad.* UK exports will become less competitive. The demand for sterling will fall. At the same time, imports will become relatively cheaper for UK consumers. The supply of sterling will rise.

- *A rise in domestic incomes relative to incomes abroad.* If UK incomes rise, the demand for imports, and hence the supply of sterling, will rise. If incomes in other countries fall, the demand for UK exports, and hence the demand for sterling will fall.

- *Relative investment prospects improving abroad.* If investment prospects become brighter abroad than in the UK, perhaps because of better incentives abroad, or because of uncertainty over key things, such as Britain's future trade relationship with the EU and the rest of the world or worries about an impending recession in the UK, again the demand for sterling will fall and the supply of sterling will rise. Many of the changes in the exchange rate for sterling have been due to uncertainty over investment prospects in the UK post-Brexit.

- *Speculation that the exchange rate will fall.* If businesses involved in importing and exporting, and also banks and other foreign exchange dealers, think that the exchange rate is about to fall, they will sell pounds now before the rate does fall. The supply of sterling will thus rise. People planning to buy sterling will wait until the rate does fall. In the meantime, the demand for sterling will fall.

[1] 'Valentine's Day roses will cost more in the UK this year . . . due to FX rates', *LeapRate* (13 February 2016).

[2] 'How will Brexit impact the pound?', *The Telegraph* (26 March 2019).

Pause for thought

Go through each of the listed causes for shifts in the demand for and supply of sterling and consider what would cause an appreciation of the pound.

Exchange rates and the balance of payments

In a free foreign exchange market, the balance of payments will automatically balance. But why?

The credit side of the balance of payments constitutes the demand for sterling. For example, when people abroad buy UK exports or assets, they will demand sterling in order to pay for them. The debit side constitutes the supply of sterling. For example, when UK residents buy foreign goods or assets, the importers of them will require foreign currency to pay for them. They will thus supply pounds. A *floating exchange rate* will ensure that the demand for pounds is equal to the supply. It will thus also ensure that the credits on the balance of payments are equal to the debits; that the balance of payments balances.

Definition

Floating exchange rate When the government does not intervene in the foreign exchange markets, but simply allows the exchange rate to be freely determined by demand and supply.

This does not mean that each part of the balance of payments account will separately balance, but simply that any current account deficit must be matched by a capital-plus-financial account surplus and vice versa.

For example, suppose initially that each part of the balance of payments did separately balance. Then let us assume that interest rates rise. This will encourage larger short-term financial inflows as people abroad are attracted to deposit money in the UK; the demand for sterling would shift to the right (e.g. from D_2 to D_1 in Figure 13.4). It will also cause smaller short-term financial outflows as UK residents keep more of their money in the country; the supply of sterling shifts to the left (e.g. from S_2 to S_1 in Figure 13.4). The financial account will go into surplus. The exchange rate will appreciate.

As the exchange rate rises, this causes imports to be cheaper and exports to be more expensive. The current account will move into deficit. There is a movement up along the new demand and supply curves until a new equilibrium is reached. At this point, any financial account surplus is matched by an equal current (plus capital) account deficit.

Managing the exchange rate

The government or central bank may be unwilling to let the country's currency float freely. Frequent shifts in the demand and supply curves would cause frequent changes in the exchange rate. This, in turn, might cause uncertainty for businesses, which might curtail

---

BOX 13.1 | THE IMPORTANCE OF INTERNATIONAL FINANCIAL MOVEMENTS

How a current account deficit can coincide with an appreciating exchange rate

Since the early 1970s, most of the major economies of the world have operated with floating exchange rates. The opportunities that this gives for speculative gain have led to a huge increase in short-term international financial movements. Vast amounts of moneys transfer from country to country in search of higher interest rates or a currency that is likely to appreciate. This can have a bizarre effect on exchange rates.

If a country pursues an expansionary fiscal policy (i.e. cutting taxes and/or raising government expenditure), the current account will tend to go into deficit as extra imports are 'sucked in'. What effect will this have on exchange rates? You might think that the answer is obvious: the higher demand for imports will create an extra supply of domestic currency on the foreign exchange market and hence drive down the exchange rate.

In fact, the opposite is likely. The higher interest rates resulting from the higher domestic demand can lead to a massive inflow of short-term finance. The financial account

can thus move sharply into surplus. This is likely to outweigh the current account deficit and cause an appreciation of the exchange rate.

Exchange rate movements, especially in the short term, are largely brought about by changes on the financial rather than the current account. For more on the financial account, see Case D.38 on the student website

? *Why do high international financial mobility and an absence of exchange controls severely limit a country's ability to choose its interest rate?*

🔍 *Download the latest edition of the Triennial Central Bank Survey of foreign exchange markets published by the Bank for International Settlements (BIS). Prepare a PowerPoint presentation summarising the types and levels of activity on the foreign exchange markets, including evidence of any longer-term trends or patterns.*

| BOX 13.2 | EXCHANGE RATE UNCERTAINTY AND THE PLIGHT OF BUSINESS |

One of the perils of international trade

All businesses are affected by the exchange rate, whether directly or indirectly. Even if a business does not export its products, at least some of its inputs are likely to be imported. This means that the exchange rate has an impact on business performance and fluctuations in it can cause uncertainty.

This is particularly difficult for small and medium sized businesses (SMEs), as not only are they trying to find a niche market and compete with large multinationals with all their international connections and resources, but they are also having to manage the uncertainty created by exchange rate fluctuations. In PwC's CEO Surveys of 2018 and 2019,[1] exchange rate volatility was listed as the tenth biggest threat to businesses and it is not just since Brexit that currency volatility has been a concern.

In 2002, when asked to identify the main financial factor causing problems for SMEs, easily topping the list was the high exchange rate of sterling against the euro. Nearly half of the firms in the sample, 47 per cent, said this was very problematic for their business. In addition, more than a quarter responded to the survey by saying it was quite problematic. The survey indicated that when sterling is strong against the euro, it was a problem for more than seven in ten SMEs. But, as we will see, a weak pound can also be problematic.

The impact on business

Between October 2000 and mid-2003, sterling depreciated from £1 = €1.70 to around £1 = €1.43. This meant that in 2000, UK exporters had to sell €1.70 worth of exports to the eurozone in order to earn £1, while in 2003, they only had to sell €1.43. Thus, a depreciating exchange rate is good news for exporters, but what about importers?

Many SMEs rely on key imported components and so a depreciating pound against the euro means businesses have to pay more in sterling to purchase inputs priced in euros. A rise in input prices for UK firms pushes up costs of production and so may force these businesses to pass the higher costs on to their customers. This reduces their competitiveness with firms that are less reliant on imported components and with those based in the eurozone.

There is also an indirect effect. Although higher input prices should reduce consumer demand for imports, some of these products may not be produced in the UK and so demand may be inelastic. Consumers will thus spend more on these imports. This in turn might mean that less is spent on domestically produced goods and so it could harm UK businesses.

With the globalised world in which businesses operate, it is very common for businesses to import inputs from one country and export finished products to another. Thus, businesses are concerned about multiple exchange rates.

In the early 2000s, just as sterling was depreciating against the euro, it was appreciating against the dollar. In June 2001, the exchange rate was £1 = $1.41. By February 2004, it was £1 = $1.86. Then, despite dipping as low as $1.73 in November 2005, in November 2007 it reached $2.07. Thus, if a business was importing inputs from the eurozone and then exporting to

the USA, it would be squeezed in both directions. Input prices from the eurozone were higher in terms of sterling due to the weak pound relative to the euro, while exports earned less sterling due to the strong pound relative to the dollar.

One further consideration is the economic performance of the country to which a firm is exporting. For example, in 2008, with the UK entering recession, the pound plummeted and so British exports were potentially very competitive. Yet, many other developed countries were also in recession and so export demand fell. Furthermore, SMEs typically preferred to keep foreign currency prices much the same and use the lower exchange rate to boost their average revenue and profit in sterling – profit that for many was taking a battering in the recession at home. But keeping foreign currency prices the same resulted in falling sales because of the recession.

This harmonisation of nations' business cycles has emerged from the increasingly globalised world as we discuss in section 13.5.

Exchange rate fluctuations and uncertainty

If the exchange rate is fluctuating, it creates uncertainty for businesses. Their costs and revenues may be incurred in different currencies and, if exchange rates are changing frequently, then firms may experience a high degree of volatility in profits. As we know, businesses do not like uncertainty and so this may reduce their willingness and ability to trade and invest. This, in turn, can have serious implications for both the demand and supply sides of the economy.

Between the financial crisis and the EU referendum, the average exchange rate fluctuations were less severe, but for SMEs in particular, any change in the exchange rate can have considerable effects on business performance and can force such firms to restrict their market size by focusing on domestic sales. Research by Héricourt and Poncet in 2012[2] found that firms cut back on the quantity of their exports to countries with higher exchange rate volatility and that this effect was more pronounced for those firms that were more financially vulnerable – often likely to be SMEs.

Brexit and the exchange rate

The uncertainty surrounding the outcome of the EU referendum created volatility for sterling against the euro, but this time largely being driven by politics. Small things were causing changes in both directions. For example, prior to the EU referendum, an Ipsos Mori poll showing 55 per cent of voters supporting the remain campaign boosted the pound, while a few days later, it fell once more with warnings from the Bank of England of future monetary easing, in part driven by the uncertainty over the 'in-out' referendum.

On the night of the referendum, expectations were that the UK would vote to remain in the EU and the pound appreciated as a result. However, when expectations turned out to be wrong, the pound plummeted and although it did recover somewhat throughout 2017, the uncertainty over the Withdrawal Agreement and whether

[1] 'CEOs' curbed confidence spells caution', *22nd Annual Global CEO Survey*, PwC (2019).

[2] Jérôme Héricourt and Sandra Poncet, 'Exchange rate volatility, financial constraints and trade: empirical evidence from Chinese firms', *FIW Working Paper*, no. 112 (March 2013).

Britain would have a 'hard' or 'soft' Brexit, caused the pound to fall again.

As the date for departure approached, once more, we saw how the politics of Brexit caused currency fluctuations, which, in turn, caused uncertainty for businesses. The Prime Minister's Brexit plan was defeated three times in Parliament and delays to Brexit were requested and granted, as discussed in section 12.5 (see pages 350–2). Whenever something happened to create greater uncertainty about Britain's future within the EU, such as government defeats in Parliament, the pound fell, while discussions about delaying or cancelling Brexit boosted the pound.

As uncertainty about Brexit continues, the currency will continue to fluctuate. Whatever the outcome of Brexit (hard, soft, no deal, no Brexit or some other scenario), once it has been agreed upon, it is likely that sterling will become more

stable. The sterling exchange rate may fall or rise following the announcement, but once currency markets have reacted to the news, businesses will then know what to plan for and this certainty, whatever the outcome, is likely to stabilise markets.

1. *Are SMEs likely to find it easier or harder than large multinational companies to switch the source of their supplies from countries where the pound has depreciated to ones where it has appreciated?*
2. *Use an AD/AS diagram to illustrate the impact on the economy if there is a depreciation in the value of the pound.*

Find out what has happened to the sterling exchange rate against (a) the euro and (b) the dollar since the day that Britain was due to leave the EU (29 March 2019). Explain your findings.

The problem of sovereign risk

Uncertainty over exchange rates creates problems for businesses that trade or invest internationally. This is part of the broader problem of *sovereign risk*. These are the risks associated with locating in or dealing with a particular country. For example, there is the risk that a country may raise business taxes or that its central bank may raise interest rates. Its government might impose new stricter regulatory controls that favour domestic firms, or impose stricter competition or environmental policies. There is a risk that the exchange rate may move adversely or that exchange controls may be imposed. In extreme cases, governments may appropriate a firm's assets or prevent it from trading.

The greater the perceived level of sovereign risk of a particular country, the less willing will firms be to trade with it or locate there. Countries are thus under

pressure to create a more favourable environment for business and reduce sovereign risk.

Pause for thought

Will the pressure on governments to reduce sovereign risk always lead to better outcomes for the citizens of that country?

Definition

Sovereign risk (for business) The risk that a foreign country's government or central bank will make its policies less favourable. Such policies could involve changes in interest rates or tax regimes, the imposition of foreign exchange controls, or even defaulting on loans or the appropriation of a business's assets.

BOX 13.3 THE EURO/DOLLAR SEESAW

What is the impact on business?

For periods of time, world currency markets can be quite peaceful, with only modest changes in exchange rates. But with the ability to move vast sums of money very rapidly from one part of the world to another and from one currency to another, speculators can suddenly turn this relatively peaceful world into one of extreme turmoil, which can be very damaging for business.

In this box we examine the huge swings of the euro against the dollar since the euro's launch in 1999.

First the down . . .

On 1 January 1999, the euro was launched and exchanged for $1.16. By October 2000 the euro had fallen to $0.85. What was the cause of this 27 per cent depreciation? The main one was the growing fear that inflationary pressures were

increasing in the USA and that the Federal Reserve Bank would have to raise interest rates. At the same time, the eurozone economy was growing only slowly and inflation was well below the 2 per cent ceiling set by the ECB. There was thus pressure on the ECB to cut interest rates.

The speculators were not wrong. As the diagram shows, US interest rates rose, and ECB interest rates initially fell, and when eventually they did rise (in October 1999), the gap between US and ECB interest rates soon widened again.

In addition to the differences in interest rates, a lack of confidence in the recovery of the eurozone economy and continued confidence in the US economy encouraged investment to flow to the USA. This inflow of finance (and lack of inflow to the eurozone) further pushed up the dollar relative to the euro.

►

The low value of the euro meant a high value of the pound (and other currencies) relative to the euro. This made it very difficult for companies outside of the eurozone to export to eurozone countries and also for those competing with imports from the eurozone (which had been made cheaper by the fall in the euro).

In October 2000, with the euro trading at around 85¢, the ECB plus the US Federal Reserve Bank, the Bank of England and the Japanese central bank all intervened on the foreign exchange market to buy euros. This arrested the fall, and helped to restore confidence in the currency. People were more willing to hold euros, knowing that central banks would support it.

... Then the up

The position completely changed in 2001. With the US economy slowing rapidly and fears of an impending recession, the Federal Reserve Bank reduced interest rates 11 times during the year, from 6.5 per cent at the beginning of the year to 1.75 per cent at the end (see the chart). Although the ECB also cut interest rates, the cuts were relatively modest, from 4.75 at the beginning of the year to 3.25 at the end. With eurozone interest rates now considerably above US rates, the euro began to rise.

In addition, a massive deficit on the US balance of payments current account, and a budget deficit nearing 4 per cent of GDP, led to investors pulling out of the USA. One estimate suggests that European investors alone sold $70 billion of US assets during 2002. The result was a massive depreciation of the dollar and appreciation of the euro, so that by December 2004 the exchange rate had risen to $1.36, a 60 per cent appreciation since June 2001!

In 2004–5, with the US economy growing strongly again, the Fed raised interest rates several times, from 1 per cent

in early 2004 to 5.25 by June 2006. The ECB kept interest rates constant at 2 per cent until early 2006. The result was that the euro depreciated against the dollar in 2005. But then the rise of the euro began again as US growth slowed and eurozone growth rose and people anticipated a narrowing of the gap between US and eurozone interest rates.

As we saw in Box 11.3, the Fed cut interest rates significantly over a 16-month period from August 2007 to December 2008 to stave off recession. The ECB, in contrast, kept the eurozone rate at around 4 per cent. As a result, short-term finance flooded into the eurozone and the euro appreciated again, from $1.37 in mid-2007 to $1.58 in mid-2008.

... Then down again in a series of steps

Eventually, in September 2008, with the eurozone on the edge of recession and predictions that the ECB would cut interest rates, the euro at last began to fall. It continued to do so as the ECB cut rates. However, with monetary policy in the eurozone remaining tighter than in the USA, the euro began to rise again, only falling once more at the end of 2009 and into 2010 as US growth accelerated and speculators anticipated a tightening of US monetary policy.

Growing worries in 2010 about the level of government deficits and debt in various eurozone countries, such as Greece, Portugal, Spain, Italy and Ireland contributed to speculation and thus growing volatility of the euro (see the blog *FTSE down, euro down with growing debt crisis* on the Sloman Economics News site). Throughout the first part of 2010 investors became increasingly reluctant to hold the euro, as fears of debt default mounted. As such, the euro fell substantially from $1.44 in January 2010 to $1.19 in June. This was a 17 per cent depreciation.

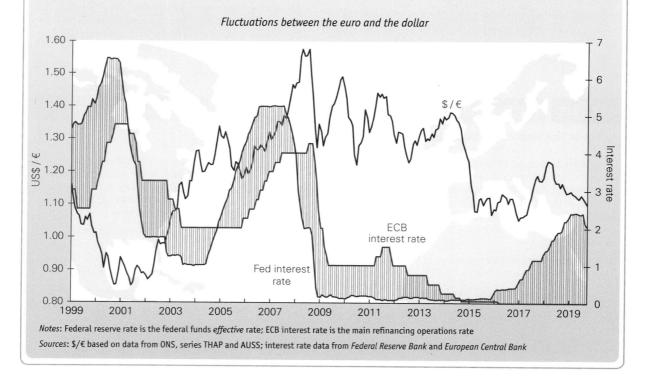

Fluctuations between the euro and the dollar

Notes: Federal reserve rate is the federal funds *effective* rate; ECB interest rate is the main refinancing operations rate

Sources: $/€ based on data from ONS, series THAP and AUSS; interest rate data from *Federal Reserve Bank* and *European Central Bank*

Then, as support was promised by the ECB and IMF to Greece in return for deficit reduction policies, and similar support could be made available to other eurozone countries with severe deficits, fears subsided and the euro rose again. By the end of October 2010, the euro was trading at $1.39 and increased to a high of $1.44 in April 2011.

Then began a dramatic fall in the euro as concerns grew over the eurozone's sluggish recovery and continuing high debt levels. Speculators thus believed that eurozone interest rates would have to continue falling. The ECB cut the main interest rate from 1.5 per cent in October 2011 in a series of steps to 0.05 per cent by September 2014.

With the ECB reducing interest rates and people increasingly predicting the introduction of quantitative easing (QE), the euro depreciated during 2014. Between March and December 2014 it depreciated by 11 per cent against the dollar, while the euro exchange rate index depreciated by 4 per cent. With the announced programme of QE being somewhat larger than markets expected, in the week following the announcement in January 2015, the euro fell a further 2.3 per cent against the dollar, and the euro exchange rate index also fell by 2.3 per cent. The result was that the euro was trading at its lowest level against the US dollar since April 2003 (see the blog *Currency wars – a zero-sum game?* on the Sloman Economics News site).

With the long-awaited rise in US interest rates in December 2015, a fall in the main EU rate to zero per cent in March 2016 and an announcement that the ECB's quantitative easing programme would continue to at least the end of 2017, the euro remained weak against the dollar throughout 2016. Then from 2017, despite a series of increases in the federal funds rate and the delay of the end-point for the ECB's quantitative easing programme being moved to September 2018, the euro began to pick up again. The euro continued to gain momentum through to April 2018, but as growth in the eurozone weakened, particularly in countries such as Germany and uncertainty over Brexit continued, the euro fell in value once more.

The euro's short history shows that interest rate volatility and divergences in interest rates between the USA and the eurozone have been a major factor in exchange rate volatility between the euro and the dollar – itself a cause of uncertainty in international trade and finance. However, more recently concerns over the fiscal health of national eurozone governments have played a particularly important role in explaining fluctuations in the euro.

How important are relative interest rates in the long run in the determination of bilateral exchange rates, such as that between the dollar and the euro?

Find out what has happened to the euro/dollar exchange rate over the past 12 months. (You can find the data from the Bank of England's Statistical Interactive Database.) Explain why the exchange rate has moved the way it has.

RECAP

1. The rate of exchange is the rate at which one currency exchanges for another. Rates of exchange are determined by demand and supply in the foreign exchange market. Demand for the domestic currency consists of all the credit items in the balance of payments account. Supply consists of all the debit items.

2. The exchange rate will depreciate (fall) if the demand for the domestic currency falls or the supply increases. These shifts can be caused by a fall in domestic interest rates, higher inflation in the domestic economy than abroad, a rise in domestic incomes relative to incomes abroad, relative investment prospects improving abroad, or the belief by speculators that the exchange rate will fall. The opposite in each case would cause an appreciation (rise).

3. The government can attempt to prevent the rate of exchange from falling by central bank purchases of the domestic currency in the foreign exchange market, either by selling foreign currency reserves or by using foreign loans. Alternatively, the central bank can raise interest rates. The reverse actions can be taken to prevent the rate from rising.

4. Fixed exchange rates bring the advantage of greater certainty for the business community, which encourages trade and foreign investment. Also, if successful, they reduce speculation.

5. They bring the disadvantages of not being able to use interest rate changes to meet objectives other than a stable exchange rate, the difficulty in responding to shocks and the danger that speculation will be encouraged if speculators believe that the current exchange rate cannot be maintained.

6. There have been various attempts to manage exchange rates, without them being totally fixed. One example was the Bretton Woods system: a system of pegged exchange rates, but where devaluations or revaluations were allowed from time to time. Another was the ERM, which was the forerunner to the euro. Member countries' currencies were allowed to fluctuate against each other within a band.

7. Businesses face sovereign risk when investing in or trading with other countries. These risks relate to unforeseen exchange rate or interest rate movements, or adverse government policies.

13.3 THE GROWTH OF GLOBAL FINANCIAL FLOWS

Financial interdependence

We live in a highly interdependent world, where every country is affected by the economic performance and government policy of other countries. This was illustrated when the sub-prime market in the USA collapsed and spread like a contagion to cause a worldwide recession.

International trade has grown rapidly for many years (see Figure 12.1 on page 326), but international financial flows have grown much more rapidly. Each day, trillions of dollars of assets are traded across the foreign exchanges. Many of the transactions are short-term financial flows, moving to where interest rates are most favourable or to currencies where the exchange rate is likely to appreciate. Countries have thus become increasingly financially dependent on each other. This not only impacts financial institutions but also individual economies.

Assume that the Federal Reserve Bank, worried about rising inflation, decides to raise interest rates. What will be the effect on business in America's trading partners? There are three major effects.

- If aggregate demand in America falls, so will its expenditure on imports from firms abroad, thus directly affecting businesses exporting to the USA. With a decline in their exports, aggregate demand in these other countries falls.
- The higher interest rate in the USA will tend to drive up interest rates in other countries. This will depress investment. Again, aggregate demand will tend to fall in these countries.
- The higher interest rate will attract an inflow of funds from other countries. This will cause the dollar to appreciate relative to other currencies. This will make these other countries' exports to the USA more competitive and imports from the USA relatively more expensive. This will result in an improvement in the current account of the USA's trading partners: their exports rise and imports fall. This represents a rise in aggregate demand in these countries – the opposite from the first two effects.

There is a simple conclusion from the above analysis. The larger the financial flows, the more will interest rate changes in one country affect the economies of other countries; the greater will be the financial interdependence.

> **Pause for thought**
>
> *What will be the effect on the UK economy if the European Central Bank cuts interest rates?*

The impact of capital flows

Large movements of capital into and out of countries can have serious consequences for business. Some of these capital flows are for direct investment; some are for buying shares and other financial assets; some are simply short-term speculative deposits. The global supply of dollars available for such purposes has grown by some 18 per cent per year since the early 2000s. One of the main reasons for this has been the huge current account deficits of the USA. This has led to vast outflows of dollars from the USA into the world economy as Americans have effectively paid for their deficit by creating more dollars.

Capital inflows. Capital flows will be attracted to countries where investment prospects are good or for speculative purposes. When they are, the financial account of the balance of payments will improve, causing the exchange rate to appreciate. This appreciation, if set to continue, will attract further capital inflows in anticipation of a speculative gain from a rising exchange rate. As demand for the domestic currency increases, this will push the exchange rate even higher. Domestic currency will be worth more in dollars and other currencies. In other words, a dollar will buy less of the country's currency.

This will make it harder for firms to export. If exports are priced in foreign currency (e.g. dollars) firms must accept less domestic currency; if exports are priced in the domestic currency, the dollar price must rise. At the same time, imports will be cheaper. This makes it harder for domestic business to compete with imports.

For example, in 2006, capital inflows into the Thai economy pushed up the value of the Thai baht by 16 per cent. As Thai businesses struggled to compete, the Bank of Thailand imposed taxes on inward portfolio investment. But this was not the solution. Share prices fell dramatically, and the tax was hastily withdrawn.

So is the answer to cut interest rates? This would reduce capital inflows and help curb the appreciation of the currency. But it would create another problem. The lower interest rates would encourage more borrowing and hence higher credit growth and higher inflation.

Thus large capital inflows leave countries with an uncomfortable choice: either allow the exchange rate to appreciate, thereby damaging business competitiveness, or cut interest rates, thereby causing higher inflation, which could also damage business competitiveness.

Capital outflows. Just as vast amounts of capital can flow into countries, so they can flow out too. The problem especially concerns money on short-term deposit. If a country's exchange rate is likely to fall, speculators will sell the currency before it does fall. This will then bring about the very depreciation that was anticipated. Such depreciation is likely if the currency had initially appreciated above its long-term equilibrium rate.

From the second half of 2014 and throughout 2015, China experienced significant capital outflows, as expectations of a depreciation of the yuan grew. In 2015 alone there were capital outflows of around $1 trillion.[7] In June 2014, China's reserves had reached a record high of $3.99 trillion, but then started to fall as the central bank drew on them to arrest the downward pressure on the exchange rate. They dropped by $513 billion in 2014 and $300 billion in 2015. However, the need for intervention in 2016 diminished as the exchange rate recovered. Since 2016, China has imposed tough restrictions on capital outflows. This was in the aftermath of a crash on the Chinese stock market in the summer of 2015 and again in January 2016. The new restrictions helped to stem capital outflows, although in 2019 there were signs that they were increasing again.

Capital controls

Excessive capital flows, whether inward or outward, can be highly destabilising for exchange rates. This makes it very difficult for businesses to plan and can rapidly turn a profitable business into a loss-making one. The result is to undermine confidence in long-term investment. And the problem is getting worse as the supply of dollars and other international currencies continues to grow faster than international trade.

So what can be done? Many commentators have called for capital controls. The aim of such controls is not to prevent capital flows. After all, capital flows

are an important source of financing investment. The aim is to prevent short-term speculative flows, based on rumour or herd instinct rather than on economic fundamentals.

Types of control

In what ways, then, can movements of short-term capital be controlled?

Quantitative controls. Here the authorities would restrict the amount of foreign exchange dealing that could take place. Perhaps financial institutions would be allowed to exchange only a certain percentage of their assets. Developed countries and most developing countries have rejected this approach, however, since it is seen to be far too anti-market.

For example, the general principle of the free movement of capital is central to the Single Market of the European Union. The principle of the free movement of capital is defined in Article 63 of the Treaty on the Functioning of the European Union (TFEU). However, Article 66 allows 'safeguard measures' to be taken if 'in exceptional circumstances, movements of capital to or from third countries cause, or threaten to cause, serious difficulties for the operation of economic and monetary union'. Such measures could extend 'for a period not exceeding six months if such measures are strictly necessary'.[8]

Alternatively, certain types of inflow could be restricted. China, for example, restricts portfolio capital inflows. This has held down its exchange rate, thereby increasing its competitiveness. But this, in turn, has reduced the competitiveness of other countries in Asia and around the world.

A Tobin tax. This is named after James Tobin, who in 1972 advocated the imposition of a small tax of 0.1 to 0.5 per cent on all foreign exchange transactions, or on just capital and financial account transactions.[9] This would discourage destabilising speculation (by making it more expensive) and would thus impose some 'friction' in foreign exchange markets, making them less volatile.

In November 2001, the French National Assembly became the first national legislature to incorporate into law a Tobin tax of up to 0.1 per cent. This was followed by Belgium in 2002. In the wake of the 2007/8 banking crisis and the highly risky financial dealings that had led to the crisis, more countries seriously considered introducing Tobin taxes. These, however, would be on speculative financial transactions generally and not just on foreign exchange transactions.

---

[7] 'China capital outflows rise to estimated $1 trillion in 2015', *Bloomberg* (25 January 2016).

[8] Treaty of the Functioning of the European Union (TFEU).

[9] James Tobin, 'A proposal for international monetary reform', *The Eastern Economic Journal*, 4, no. 3–4, pp. 153–9 (1978).

In September 2011, a proposal was made by the European Commission for an EU financial transaction tax to be implemented across the members of the EU by 2014. However, this faced stiff opposition, particularly from non-eurozone nations, including the UK. The UK government argued that the resulting decline in trades would reduce profits for financial institutions, which are a major part of the UK economy.

In October 2012, 11 of the 17 eurozone countries agreed to adopt a harmonised financial transactions tax at rates of 0.1 per cent on trading in bonds and shares and 0.01 per cent on trading in derivatives. However, the implementation of the tax was subsequently delayed as countries struggled to agree on the details of the tax, including the instruments that should be covered, the rates of the tax and the distribution of revenues. You can read about the initial discussions of this type of Tobin tax in the blog,

Rolling out a Tobin tax, on the Sloman Economics News site.

Non-interest-bearing deposits. Here a certain percentage of inflows of finance would have to be deposited with the central bank in a non-interest-bearing account for a set period of time. Chile in the late 1990s used such a system. It required that 30 per cent of all inflows be deposited with Chile's central bank for a year. This clearly amounted to a considerable tax (i.e. in terms of interest sacrificed) and had the effect of discouraging short-term speculative flows. The problem was that it meant that interest rates in Chile had to be higher in order to attract finance.

South Korea operates a similar system and in December 2006 it raised the amount that banks must deposit with the central bank in an attempt to stem speculative capital inflows.

RECAP

1. Countries are increasingly financially interdependent. Changes in interest rates in one country will affect capital flows to and from other countries, and hence their exchange rates, interest rates and GDP. The credit crunch in the late 2000s and sovereign debt crisis in the eurozone are prime examples of this growing interdependence.

2. Capital flows have grown substantially in recent years and can be highly destabilising to an economy. Capital inflows can cause an appreciation, reducing a country's competitiveness.

3. If capital flows could be constrained, however, exchange rates could be stabilised somewhat. Forms of control include: quantitative controls, a tax on exchange transactions (a Tobin tax) and non-interest-bearing deposits with the central bank of a certain percentage of capital inflows.

13.4 ECONOMIC AND MONETARY UNION IN THE EU

Although countries around the world generally operate a system of floating exchange rates, small countries sometimes peg their exchange rates to the dollar or other major currencies. Also, on a regional basis, there have been attempts to create greater exchange rate stability by countries pegging their exchange rates to each other.

Such a system was introduced in Europe in 1979 as the forerunner of the adoption of the euro. The name given to the EU system was the *exchange rate mechanism (ERM)*. The majority of the EU countries at the time were members. The UK initially chose not to join the ERM, but eventually did so in 1990.

Definition

ERM (the exchange rate mechanism) A semi-fixed system whereby participating EU countries allowed fluctuations against each other's currencies only within agreed bands. Collectively they floated freely against all other currencies.

The ERM

Under the ERM, each currency was given a central exchange rate with each of the other member currencies in a grid. However, fluctuations were allowed from the central rate within specified bands. For most countries these bands were set at $\pm 2^{1}/_{4}$ per cent. The central rates could be adjusted from time to time by agreement, thus making the ERM an adjustable peg system (see page 363). All the currencies floated jointly with currencies outside the ERM.

In a system of pegged exchange rates, such as the ERM, countries should harmonise their policies to avoid excessive currency misalignments and hence the need for large devaluations or revaluations. There should be a convergence of their economies – they should be at a similar point on the business cycle and have similar inflation rates and interest rates.

Shortly after the UK joined the ERM in 1990, strains began to show. The reunification of Germany involved considerable reconstruction in the eastern part of the country. Financing this reconstruction was causing a growing budget deficit. The Bundesbank (the German central bank) thus felt obliged to maintain high interest rates in order to keep inflation in check. At the same time, the UK was experiencing a massive current account deficit (partly the result of entering the ERM at what many commentators argued was too high an exchange rate). It was thus obliged to raise interest rates in order to protect the pound, despite the fact that the economy was sliding rapidly into recession. This showed perfectly one of the disadvantages of a fixed exchange rate: having to change interest rates to target the exchange rate in a way that conflicted with other objectives.

The French franc and Italian lira were also perceived to be overvalued, and there were the first signs of worries as to whether their exchange rates within the ERM could be retained. The US had cut interest rates to stimulate the economy and capital flowed from there to Germany, taking advantage of the higher interest rates. This pushed up the value of the German mark and the other ERM currencies.

In September 1992, things reached crisis point. On 'Black Wednesday' (16 September), the UK and Italy were forced to suspend their membership of the ERM; the pound and the lira were floated and depreciated substantially. The following year, in an attempt to rescue the ERM for the remaining countries, EU finance ministers agreed to adopt very wide ± 15 per cent bands.

The old ERM appeared to be at an end. The new ± 15 per cent bands hardly seemed like a 'pegged' system at all. However, the ERM did not die. Within months, the members were again managing to keep fluctuations within a very narrow range (for most of the time, within $\pm 2\frac{1}{4}$ per cent). The scene was being set for the abandonment of separate currencies and the adoption of a single currency: the euro.

Pause for thought

Under what circumstances may a currency bloc like the ERM (a) help to prevent speculation; (b) aggravate the problem of speculation?

With a single currency there can be no exchange rate fluctuations between the member states, any more than there can be fluctuations between the Californian and New York dollar, or between the English, Scottish and Welsh pound.

Birth of the euro

The Maastricht Treaty was signed in February 1992 and it set out the timetable for the adoption of a single currency in Europe. Before joining the currency union, member states had to meet five convergence criteria, to ensure that the economies of the potential members had sufficiently converged. They were:

- Inflation: should be no more than $1\frac{1}{2}$ per cent above the average inflation rate of the three countries in the EU with the lowest inflation.
- Interest rates: the rate on long-term government bonds should be no more than 2 per cent above the average of the three countries with the lowest inflation.
- Budget deficit: should be no more than 3 per cent of GDP.
- General government debt: should be no more than 60 per cent of GDP.
- Exchange rates: the currency should have been within the normal ERM bands for at least two years with no realignments or excessive intervention.

In March 1998, the European Commission ruled that 11 of the 15 member states were eligible to proceed to EMU in January 1999. Their economies were deemed to be sufficiently converged in terms of interest rates, inflation rates and government deficits and debt. The UK and Denmark were to exercise their 'opt out', negotiated at Maastricht back in 1992, and Sweden and Greece failed to meet one or more of the convergence criteria.

The euro finally came into being in January 1999 (although notes and coins did not circulate until January 2002). Greece joined the euro in 2001, Slovenia in 2007, Cyprus and Malta in 2008, Slovakia in 2009, Estonia in 2011, followed by Latvia and Lithuania in 2014 and 2015, respectively, making a total of 19 countries using the euro.

With a single currency, countries must have a single central bank (the European Central Bank for the eurozone) and a common monetary policy, involving common interest rates for all member countries. Such a system is known as *economic and monetary union (EMU)*.

Business and the euro

The adoption of the euro has had a profound effect on business, both within the eurozone and outside it. There are significant advantages in terms of greater

---

Definition

Economic and monetary union (EMU) Where countries adopt a single currency and a single monetary policy. It might also involve other common policies, such as fiscal and supply-side policies.

certainty and greater inward investment, but also various costs in terms of reduced flexibility for governments in managing their economies.

Advantages of a single currency

Elimination of the costs of converting currencies. With separate currencies in each of the EU countries, costs were incurred each time one currency was exchanged into another. The elimination of these costs was, however, probably the least important benefit from the single currency. The European Commission estimated that the effect was to increase the GDP of the countries concerned by an average of only 0.4 per cent. The gains to countries like the UK, which have well-developed financial markets, would be even smaller.

Increased competition and efficiency. Not only has the single currency eliminated the need to convert one currency into another (a barrier to competition), but it has brought more transparency in pricing, and has put greater downward pressure on prices in high-cost firms and countries. This, of course, does not necessarily favour business, which might find its profits squeezed, but it generally benefits consumers. Although there has been some price convergence across the eurozone, it has not been as extensive as many thought it would be, as discussed in *Politico*.[10]

Elimination of exchange rate uncertainty (between the members). The removal of exchange rate uncertainty has helped to encourage more trade between the eurozone countries. Perhaps more importantly, it has encouraged investment by firms that trade between these countries, given the greater certainty in calculating costs and revenues from such trade.

In times of economic uncertainty, such as the credit crunch of 2008 and Brexit in 2019, exchange rate volatility between currencies can be high, creating problems, as we discussed in Box 13.2. However, if the UK had adopted the euro, the uncertainty for the UK in its trade with the eurozone countries would have been eliminated. Furthermore, had the eurozone countries not adopted the euro, the degree of banking turmoil they experienced in 2008 and 2009 may have been even more severe.

Increased inward investment. Investment from the rest of the world is attracted to a eurozone of over 340 million inhabitants, where there is no fear of internal currency movements. By contrast, the UK, by not joining, initially found that inward investment was diverted away to countries within the eurozone; and with Brexit, this trend has the potential to continue.

Lower inflation and interest rates. A single monetary policy forces convergence in inflation rates (just as inflation rates are very similar between the different regions within a country). With the ECB being independent from short-term political manipulation, this has resulted in a lower average inflation rate in the eurozone countries. This, in turn, has helped to convince markets that the euro will be strong relative to other currencies. The result is lower long-term rates of interest. This, in turn, further encourages investment in the eurozone countries, both by member states and by the rest of the world.

Opposition to EMU

There are, however, many criticisms levelled at the monetary union. Many 'Eurosceptics' see it as a surrender of national political and economic sovereignty.

Inability to adjust exchange rates between members. A single currency reduces a country's ability to steer its own economy, as it cannot adjust its exchange rate with other members.

This is a particular problem if a country finds that its economy is at all out of harmony with the rest of the Union. For example, if countries such as Italy, Greece and Spain have higher endemic rates of inflation (due, say, to greater cost-push pressures), then how are they to make their goods competitive with the rest of the Union? With separate currencies these countries could allow their currencies to depreciate, thus increasing competitiveness. Indeed, throughout 2008, sterling depreciated, and this helped to make UK exports more competitive, thereby boosting aggregate demand and helping to soften the recession. With a single currency, however, they could become depressed 'regions' of Europe, with rising unemployment and all the other regional problems of depressed regions within a country. There is some evidence to suggest that this has occurred, especially for countries that are further from the centre of the eurozone.

> ### Pause for thought
>
> *How might multiplier effects (see pages 264 and 267) lead to prosperous regions becoming more prosperous and less prosperous regions falling even further behind?*

The answer given by proponents of EMU is that it is better to tackle the problem of high inflation or unemployment in such countries by the disciplines of competition from other eurozone countries than merely to feed that inflation by keeping separate currencies and allowing continued depreciation, with all the uncertainty that that brings.

[10] Toby Vogel, 'The EU's low-speed price convergence', *Politico* (4 December 2014).

Furthermore, high-inflation countries tend to be the poorer ones, with lower real wage levels. The free movement of labour and capital helps to attract these resources into those countries, which may narrow the gap between the richer and poorer member states. The critics of EMU, however, argue that labour is relatively immobile, especially due to language and cultural differences. As a result, cost differences and unemployment in these countries could persist.

Lack of separate monetary policies. Perhaps the most serious criticism is the loss of an independent monetary policy for individual member countries. This means that the same rate of interest must apply to all eurozone countries: the 'one size fits all' criticism. The trouble is that while one country might require a lower rate of interest in order to ward off recession (such as Portugal, Ireland and Greece in 2010–11), another might require a higher one to prevent inflation.

Furthermore, some countries may be more sensitive to interest changes than others, hence the optimal change in interest rates for one country may represent too much or too little of a change in another. The greater the divergence between economies within the eurozone, the greater this problem becomes.

The problem of asymmetric shocks. A further problem for members of a single currency occurs in adjusting to a shock when that shock affects members to differing degrees. These are known as *asymmetric shocks*. For example, the banking crisis affected the UK more severely than other countries, given that London is a global financial centre.

This problem, however, should not be overstated. Divergences between economies are often the result of a lack of harmony between countries in their demand-management policies. Closer integration and co-ordination between members could help to overcome this criticism.

However, despite harmonised monetary policy and some fiscal integration, even when shocks are uniformly felt in the member states there is still the problem that policies adopted centrally will have different impacts on each country. For example, in the UK, a large proportion of borrowing is at variable interest rates. In Germany, by contrast, much is at fixed rates. Thus if the UK had adopted the euro and the ECB raised interest rates, as it did in July 2008 despite the recession, the contractionary effects would be felt disproportionately in the UK. Of course, were this balance to change – and there is some evidence that types of borrowing are becoming more uniform across the EU – this problem would diminish.

The future of the euro

The need for greater fiscal alignment

Members of the eurozone have a common monetary policy, but not a completely common fiscal policy. Although the Stability and Growth Pact (which applies to the whole of the EU) gives some degree of a common fiscal policy by having rules on public-sector deficits and debts, these rules have not been rigidly enforced, as we discussed in Box 11.1.

Although the Fiscal Compact amended the Stability and Growth Pact and tightened the fiscal rules as from 2013, many argue that this alone is not sufficient for eurozone members to benefit fully from monetary union. Instead, they argue, complete fiscal harmonisation is needed, as one of the key risks to the stability of the eurozone is the deficit and debt levels of member countries.

To date, the eurozone has resisted a centralisation of national budgets. In a more centralised (or federal) system we would see automatic income transfers between different regions and countries. A country, say Greece, affected by a negative economic shock would pay less tax revenues and receive more expenditures from a central eurozone budget, while in a country, say Germany, experiencing a positive shock the opposite would be the case.

Since national budgets in the eurozone remain largely decentralised, fiscal transfers principally take place *within* countries rather than between them. But this severely limits the use of fiscal policy to offset the effects of negative economic shocks in countries which already have large public-sector deficits and high debt-to-GDP ratios.

The state of Greece's public finances brought this issue to the forefront.

The Greek crisis

Following the financial crisis, the Greek economy was in a parlous state, with high and rising deficit and debt levels, structural weakness and an inability to change monetary policy. The resulting Greek debt crisis required three bailouts in 2010, 2012 and 2015 from the IMF, the European Commission and the ECB (the so-called 'Troika') totalling €289 billion. These were conditional on tough austerity measures, involving large cuts in government spending and large tax increases.

Problems arose at the end of 2014 when payments were suspended by the Troika after the Syriza-led Greek government was elected on the back of an anti-austerity platform. A drawn-out set of negotiations between Greece and its international creditors

---

Definition

Asymmetric shocks Shocks (such as an oil price increase or a recession in another part of the world) that have different-sized effects on different industries, regions or countries.

followed and with no agreement on further aid to Greece and the closure of banks across the country, Greece was unable to meet a €1.55 billion repayment to the IMF in June 2015. It became the first developed country to default on an IMF loan.

As conditions continued to deteriorate in Greece, the ECB announced that it would provide emergency liquidity assurance for the Greek financial system, but capital controls were imposed with strict limits on withdrawals from bank accounts.

In August 2015, an agreement was reached for the terms of a third bailout worth €86 billion over three years, but further austerity measures were required and this placed further strains on an already weak economy. However, concerns continued to grow that Greece's current public-sector-debt-to-GDP ratio was unsustainable and so further fiscal austerity and structural reform was needed. In addition, the IMF argued that there must be substantial debt relief to ensure the long-term sustainability of Greece's public finances.

In 2016, to meet the terms of the bailouts, further austerity measures were adopted, including €5.4 billion in pension cuts and tax reforms. These were followed by yet more austerity measures in May 2017. The eurozone issued further credit and loans to Greece and in July 2017, the Greek government set out 21 commitments to the IMF that it intended to meet by June 2018. In June 2018, a 10-year extension was agreed on €96.6 billion of Greece's loans and a 10-year period of grace on interest payments on those loans.

On 20 August 2018, Greece successfully ended its third bailout, and so for the time being at least, Greece's expulsion from the euro has been avoided. Nonetheless, this ongoing crisis raised important questions about the future of the euro and the conditions under which it would be beneficial for other EU member states to join or for existing members to exit. There are various blogs on the Sloman Economics News site that examine the Greek debt crisis at various stages.

Convergence or divergence?

The more similar economies are, the more likely it is that they will face similar or symmetric shocks which can be accommodated by a common monetary policy. Furthermore, greater wage flexibility and mobility of labour provide mechanisms for countries within a single currency to remain internationally competitive.

However, there remain considerable differences in the macroeconomic performance of eurozone countries, reflecting continuing differences in the structures of their economies. Some of these were exacerbated by the financial crisis of the late 2000s and the subsequent deterioration of the macroeconomic environment.

Among the differences is the contrasting trade positions of eurozone economies. This is illustrated in Figure 13.5 which shows the current account balances

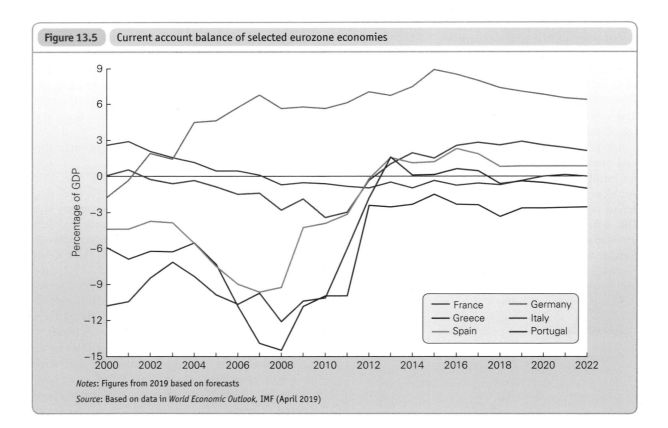

Figure 13.5 Current account balance of selected eurozone economies

Notes: Figures from 2019 based on forecasts

Source: Based on data in *World Economic Outlook*, IMF (April 2019)

of selected eurozone economies since 2000. In the period 2000 to 2008, Greece, Spain and Portugal ran large current account deficits averaging 9, 6 and 10 per cent of GDP respectively. By contrast, Germany ran a current account surplus of around 3 per cent of its GDP. In more recent years, however, the divergences in current account balances have narrowed.

In the absence of nominal exchange rate adjustments, countries such as Greece and Spain looking to a fall in the *real* exchange rate to boost competitiveness need to have relatively lower rates of price inflation. Therefore, in a single currency, productivity growth and wage inflation take on even greater importance in determining a country's competitiveness. The competitive position of countries will deteriorate if wage growth *exceeds* productivity growth.

If this happens, unit labour costs (labour costs per unit of output) will increase.

In the period from 2000 to 2008, labour costs increased at an average of between 3 and 4 per cent per annum in Greece, Spain and Italy compared with close to zero in Germany. This, other things being equal, put these countries at a competitive disadvantage. However, as with current account divergences, increases in unit labour costs have diverged less in recent years.

Greater convergence has been achieved in the eurozone in recent years, but unless there is greater fiscal harmonisation, with moves towards a common fiscal policy, there are dangers that in the future the stability of the eurozone could once more be threatened.

RECAP

1. One means of achieving greater currency stability is for a group of countries to peg their internal exchange rates and yet float jointly with the rest of the world. The exchange rate mechanism of the EU (ERM) was an example. This was seen as an important first stage on the road to complete economic and monetary union (EMU) in the EU.

2. The euro was born on 1 January 1999 with euro notes and coins introduced in 2002. There are now 19 countries using the euro.

3. The advantages claimed for EMU are that it eliminates the costs of converting currencies and the uncertainties associated with possible changes in former inter-EU exchange rates. This encourages more investment, both inward and by domestic firms, and greater trade between EU countries.

4. Critics, however, claim that the loss of independence in policy making might make adjustment to domestic economic problems more difficult, especially when these problems diverge from those of other members. A single monetary policy is claimed to be inappropriate for dealing with asymmetric shocks.

5. The Greek sovereign debt crisis raised concerns about the future of the euro and the sustainability of government deficit and debt levels. It raised important questions about the conditions under which it may be beneficial for EU members to join the eurozone and when existing members might need to exit.

6. It is important in a single currency zone for its members to achieve harmonisation in terms of stable public finances, similar current account positions and similar growth in productivity and unit labour costs. A common fiscal policy helps to smooth divergences.

13.5 INTERNATIONAL ECONOMIC POLICY: MANAGING THE GLOBAL ECONOMY

Global interdependence

We live in an interdependent world, where countries are affected by the economic health of other countries and by their governments' policies. There is an old saying: 'If America sneezes, the world catches a cold' and some have now extended this to include China as well. Viruses of a similar nature regularly infect the world economy. A dramatic example was the global banking crisis of 2007–8. What started largely as a problem of risky mortgage loans in the USA ('subprime' mortgages) rapidly became a global banking crisis, necessitating a global policy response.

The reason why nations are increasingly interdependent is the process of globalisation and, as we have seen, there are two main ways in which this process affects individual economies: trade and financial markets.

World trade flows and world financial flows have both increased significantly and with this has come a greater degree of vulnerability of individual nations to changes elsewhere. For example, if the US administration implements contractionary fiscal and monetary policy, US consumers reduce their consumption of US products, but also reduce their consumption of imported products. But, these are the exports of other countries and as they fall, so it will lead to a multiplier effect in these countries, potentially leading to lower output and employment.

This is particularly significant if countries are very reliant on trade or financial flows. As we saw in section 13.3, trillions of dollars are traded daily across borders and so, as interest rates rise in one country or a country's exchange rate appreciates, so short-term financial flows will move to these countries.

Attempts to co-ordinate global business activity

Individual economies experience business cycles. But so too does the global economy. The greater the degree of global interdependence, though trade and financial flows, the more co-ordinated this international business cycle is likely to be – the more likely that countries will share common problems and concerns at the same time.

For many years now the leaders of the seven or eight major industrialised countries (the G7 or G8), which include the USA, Japan, Germany, France, the UK, Italy, Canada and sometimes Russia, have met once a year (and more frequently if felt necessary) at an economic summit conference.

Since 1999, there have been similar meetings of the much broader G20 group, which also includes major developing countries, such as China and India, and this is now seen as the principal global economic forum. This broader forum recognises the growth and importance of emerging economies and secondly the increasing interdependence of nations through trade and finance, which requires a co-ordinated response from the international community.

A key focus at many G20 and G7 meetings has been how to achieve a *harmonisation* of economic policies between nations to allow worldwide economic growth without major currency fluctuations. In other words, the meetings seek to ensure that all the major countries are pursuing consistent policies aimed at common international goals.

But how can policy harmonisation be achieved? If there are significant domestic differences between the major economies, there is likely to be conflict, not harmony. For example, if some countries are worried about tackling recession, they may be unwilling to respond to demands from other countries for fiscal restraint to tackle the problem of large public-sector deficits and debts. What is more, speculators, seeing differences between countries, are likely to exaggerate them by their actions, causing large changes in exchange rates.

The G7/G20 countries have therefore sought to achieve greater *convergence of their economies*. However, although convergence may be a goal of policy, in practice it has proved elusive, as there are serious difficulties in achieving international policy harmonisation:

■ Countries' budget deficits and accumulated government debts differ substantially as a proportion of their GDP. This puts very different pressures on the interest rates necessary to service these debts.

■ Harmonising rates of monetary growth or inflation targets would involve letting interest rates fluctuate with the demand for money. Without convergence in the demand for money, interest rate fluctuations could be severe.

■ Harmonising interest rates would involve abandoning money, inflation or exchange rate targets (unless interest rate 'harmonisation' meant adjusting interest rates so as to maintain money or inflation targets or a given exchange rate).

■ Countries have different internal structural relationships. A lack of convergence here means that countries with higher endemic cost inflation would require higher interest rates and higher unemployment if international inflation rates were to be harmonised, or higher inflation if interest rates were to be harmonised.

■ Countries have different rates of productivity increase, product development, investment and market penetration. A lack of convergence here means that the growth in exports (relative to imports) will differ for any given level of inflation or growth.

■ Countries may be very unwilling to change their domestic policies to fall into line with other countries. They may prefer the other countries to fall into line with them!

If any one of the five – interest rates, growth rates, inflation rates, current account balance of payments or government deficits – could be harmonised across countries, it is likely that the other four would then not be harmonised.

Pause for thought

If total convergence were achieved, would harmonisation of policies follow automatically?

Total convergence and thus total harmonisation may not be possible. Nevertheless, most governments favour some movement in that direction; some is better than none. A more detailed analysis of global attempts at harmonisation is given in Case Study D.40 on the student website.

Definitions

International harmonisation of economic policies Where countries attempt to co-ordinate their macroeconomic policies so as to achieve common goals.

Convergence of economies When countries achieve similar levels of growth, inflation, budget deficits as a percentage of GDP, balance of payments etc.

BOX 13.4 GLOBAL PROBLEMS. GLOBAL ANSWERS?

IMF and the global response

We don't have to look far to see how much economic and financial interdependence affects our daily lives, from cars built overseas, planes flying overhead and worldwide goods available at the click of a button and in local shops. But, while globalisation and interdependence have brought many benefits, they also mean that problems in one part of the world rapidly spread to others. Just look at what happened when the US sub-prime mortgage market collapsed in 2007–8. America's illness turned into the world's flu!

But, given the now global nature of the problems, who should dish out the medicine? Do we need stronger international institutions to deal with world problems?

The International Monetary Fund (IMF)

The IMF has often been in the news since the financial crisis. It played a major part in organising rescue packages for highly-indebted countries such as Greece, Cyprus, Argentina, Indonesia, Mexico and Ireland. But what is the IMF? And what does it do?

Established in 1944, it is a 'specialised agency' of the United Nations and is financed by all of its 189 member countries (as of 2019), via a system of regularly reviewed quotas, which are largely based on a country's economic position in the world. The role of the IMF 'is to ensure the stability of the international monetary system . . . to include all macroeconomic and financial-sector issues that bear on global stability'.

Another part of the IMF's role is to work with developing nations to alleviate poverty and to do this it is able to offer loans, which to low-income countries are at 0 per cent interest. However, it is also able to provide loans to other countries as part of its objective of helping to achieve economic stability.

IMF to the rescue?

With the financial crisis, the IMF was left in a very difficult position. Many countries were in difficulty, as not only were they (and most of the rest of the world) in recession, but their ability to boost their domestic economies was severely restricted by high levels of debt. The IMF has a limited budget and so had to make choices as to which countries to support.

In November 2008, the IMF approved a $2.1 billion loan to Iceland[1] to support an economic recovery programme. At the same time, the IMF approved a loan of $15.7 billion to Hungary, as the country was struggling to meet external debt obligations and finance its general government deficit. Latvia and Greece were also receiving support as their economies struggled with the recession and their public finances. The IMF committed well over $700 billion in financing to member countries, with a significant amount going to developed economies, especially within the EU. Following crisis talks with finance ministers in Europe in May 2010, the IMF set aside €250 billion to support eurozone countries that were in financial difficulty.

Strengthening the IMF

With the financial crisis raising so many issues and with the subsequent difficulties that so many countries (especially

developed ones) faced in its aftermath, world leaders agreed that there was a need to strengthen global financial institutions. In April 2009, an agreement was reached that IMF resources should be trebled to $750 billion and that a Financial Stability Board should be established to identify potential economic and financial risks. In April 2012, there were further pledges to increase IMF funding by $430 billion.

Furthermore, under the 14th General Quota Review in 2010, various conditions were agreed to increase members' subscriptions. These conditions were met on 26 January 2016, which doubled the total quota of all members to around $663 billion or 477 SDRs ('special drawing rights'). The 15th Review of quotas and hence of IMF funding is due for completion in Spring 2019.

Is the IMF always good?

Although the IMF has had many successes in helping low-income countries and in bringing developed countries back onto more stable financial grounds, it has also been subject to much controversy. One of the reasons is because of the harsh conditions (known as 'conditionality') that it has imposed on loans, especially for some of the most indebted developing countries. For example, in return for the loans, the IMF has sometimes insisted on a country pursuing tough austerity policies and policies of privatisation and market liberalisation.

Critics also suggest that the IMF's conditions often amount to structural changes being required in the economy, which may be politically infeasible. This links to another criticism, which is that the IMF imposes policies on a country without first understanding the country's characteristics that may make the policies difficult to carry out, unnecessary or even counter-productive. In his book, *The White Man's Burden*,[2] William Easterly criticised many of the IMF's interventions, describing the loan conditions and technical advice as out of touch with ground-level realities.

As we discussed in section 13.4, Greece received various loans and bailouts, but was required to implement severe austerity measures, which many argue delayed the nation's recovery and certainly led to much political strife. Nevertheless, the IMF, unlike the other two members of the Troika, was keen to relieve Greece of some of its long-term debt.

Despite the critics, the IMF certainly has a key role to play in the global economy and continuing reforms aim to ensure that this global institution remains equipped to deal with any crisis. Today, it is less rigid in requiring market liberalisation as the major structural requirement of any loans and has been increasingly pressing for more investment in infrastructure.

Do you see any problems arising from a strengthening of global economic and financial institutions?

Examine a recent IMF loan to a particular country. What were the conditions attached to this loan? Do you feel that these conditions were warranted?

---

[1] 'IMF Executive Board approves $2.1 billion stand-by arrangement for Iceland', press release no. 08/296, IMF (19 November 2008).

[2] William Easterly, *The White Man's Burden*, Penguin Random House (27 February 2007).

The problem of speculation

One important lesson of recent years is that concerted speculation has become virtually unstoppable. This was made clear by the expulsion of the UK and Italy from the ERM in 1992, a dramatic fall of the Mexican peso and a rise of the yen in 1995, the collapse of various south-east Asian currencies and the Russian rouble in 1997–8, the collapse of the Argentinean peso in 2002 (see Case Study D.39), the fall in the pound in 2008 and the fall of the euro in 2010 and in 2014–15. In comparison with the vast amounts of short-term finance flowing across the foreign exchanges each day, the reserves of central banks seem trivial.

If there is a consensus in the markets that a currency will depreciate, there is little that central banks can do. For example, if there were a 50 per cent chance of a 10 per cent depreciation in the next week, then selling that currency now would yield an 'expected' return of just over 5 per cent for the week (i.e. 50 per cent of 10 per cent), equivalent to more than 5000 per cent at an annual rate!

For this reason, many commentators have argued that there are only two types of exchange rate system that can work over the long term. The first is a completely free-floating exchange rate, with no attempt by the central bank to support the exchange rate. With no intervention, there is no problem of a shortage of reserves!

The second is to share a common currency with other countries – to join a common currency area, such as the eurozone, and let the common currency float freely. The country would give up independence in its monetary policy, but at least there would be no problem of exchange rate instability within the currency area. A similar alternative is to adopt a major currency of another country, such as the US dollar or the euro. Many smaller states have done this. For example, Kosovo and Montenegro have adopted the euro and Ecuador has adopted the US dollar.

RECAP

1. Currency fluctuations can be lessened if countries harmonise their economic policies. Ideally this would involve achieving common growth rates, inflation rates, balance of payments (as a percentage of GDP), budget deficits and interest rates. The attempt to harmonise one of these goals, however, may bring conflicts with one or more of the other goals.

2. Leaders of the G7 or G20 countries meet regularly to discuss ways of harmonising their policies. Usually, however, domestic issues are more important to the leaders than international ones, and frequently they pursue policies that are not in the interests of the other countries.

3. Many economists argue that, with the huge flows of short-term finance across the foreign exchanges, governments are forced to adopt one of two extreme forms of exchange rate regime: free floating or being a member of a currency union.

QUESTIONS

1. The following are the items in the UK's 2017 balance of payments:

	£ billions
Exports of goods	338.74
Imports of goods	475.77
Exports of services	278.80
Imports of services	165.70
Net income flows	−23.57
Net current transfers	−20.86
Net capital transfers	−1.72
Direct investment	−12.67
Portfolio investment	+104.75
Other financial flows	+4.58
Reserves	−6.80

Calculate the following: (a) the balance on trade in goods; (b) the balance on trade in goods and services; (c) the balance of payments on current account; (d) the financial account balance; (e) the total current plus capital plus financial account balance; (f) net errors and omissions.

Compare your answers with the UK's 2018 balance of payments, which can be found in Table 13.1. What happened to the UK's balance of payments during that period?

2. Assume that there is a free-floating exchange rate. Will the following cause the exchange rate to appreciate or depreciate? In each case you should consider whether there is a shift in the demand or supply curves of sterling (or both) and which way the curve(s) shift(s).

   (a) More electronic goods are imported from Japan.
   Demand curve *shifts left/shifts right/does not shift*.
   Supply curve *shifts left/shifts right/does not shift*.
   Exchange rate *appreciates/depreciates*.
   (b) UK interest rates rise relative to those abroad.
   Demand curve *shifts left/shifts right/does not shift*.
   Supply curve *shifts left/shifts right/does not shift*.
   Exchange rate *appreciates/depreciates*.
   (c) The UK experiences a higher rate of inflation than other countries.
   Demand curve *shifts left/shifts right/does not shift*.
   Supply curve *shifts left/shifts right/does not shift*.
   Exchange rate *appreciates/depreciates*.

   (d) Speculators believe that the rate of exchange will appreciate.
   Demand curve *shifts left/shifts right/does not shift*.
   Supply curve *shifts left/shifts right/does not shift*.
   Exchange rate *appreciates/depreciates*.

3. What is the relationship between the balance of payments and the rate of exchange?

4. Consider the argument that in the modern world of large-scale short-term international financial movements, the ability of individual countries to affect their exchange rate is very limited.

5. What are the main advantages and disadvantages of fixing the exchange rate with a major currency such as the US dollar?

6. Why may capital inflows damage the international competitiveness of a country's businesses?

7. What adverse effects on the domestic economy may follow from (a) a depreciation of the exchange rate and (b) an appreciation of the exchange rate?

8. What are the causes of exchange-rate volatility? Have these problems become greater or lesser in the past 20 years? Explain why.

9. Did the exchange rate difficulties experienced by countries under the ERM strengthen or weaken the arguments for progressing to a single European currency?

10. By what means would a depressed country in an economic union with a single currency be able to recover? Would the market provide a satisfactory solution or would (union) government intervention be necessary and, if so, what form would the intervention take?

11. Assume that just some of the members of a common market like the EU adopt full economic and monetary union, including a common currency. What are the advantages and disadvantages to those members joining the full EMU and to those not joining?

12. What are the economic (as opposed to political) difficulties in achieving an international harmonisation of economic policies so as to avoid damaging currency fluctuations?

13. What are the implications for a country attempting to manage its domestic economy if it is subject to an international business cycle? How might it attempt to overcome such problems?

14. To what extent can international negotiations over economic policy be seen as a game of strategy? Are there any parallels between the behaviour of countries and the behaviour of oligopolies?

ADDITIONAL PART D CASE STUDIES ON THE *ESSENTIAL ECONOMICS FOR BUSINESS* WEBSITE (www.pearsoned.co.uk/sloman)

D.1 **Output gaps.** A way of measuring how far actual output falls short of long-term trend output.

D.2 **The costs of economic growth.** Why economic growth may not be an unmixed blessing.

D.3 **Comparing national income statistics.** The importance of taking the purchasing power of local currencies into account.

D.4 **John Maynard Keynes (1883–1946).** A profile of the great economist.

D.5 **The phases of the business cycle.** A demand-side analysis of the factors contributing to each of the four phases.

D.6 **The GDP deflator.** An examination of how GDP figures are corrected to take inflation into account.

D.7 **How does consumption behave?** This case looks at evidence on the relationship between consumption and disposable income.

D.8 **The multiplier/accelerator interaction.** Numerical example showing how the interaction of the multiplier and accelerator can cause cycles in economic activity.

D.9 **Has there been an accelerator effect since the 1960s?** This case examines GDP and investment data to see whether the evidence points to an accelerator effect.

D.10 **The attributes of money.** What makes something, such as metal, paper or electronic records, suitable as money?

D.11 **UK monetary aggregates.** This examines the various measures of money supply in the UK using both UK and eurozone monetary aggregates.

D.12 **Changes in the banking industry.** This case study looks at mergers and diversification in the banking industry.

D.13 **Bailing out the banks.** An overview of the concerted efforts made to rescue the banking system in the crisis of 2007–9.

D.14 **Credit and the business cycle.** This case traces cycles in the growth of credit and relates them to the business cycle. It also looks at some of the implications of the growth in credit.

D.15 **Technology and unemployment.** Does technological progress destroy jobs?

D.16 **Hyperinflation.** This looks at the extraordinarily high rates of inflation experienced in Germany in the early 1920s Serbia and Montenegro in the 1990s and more recently in Zimbabwe.

D.17 **The national debt.** This explores the question of whether it matters if a country has a high national debt.

D.18 **Trends in public expenditure.** This case examines attempts to control public expenditure in the UK and relates them to the crowding-out debate.

D.19 **The crowding-out effect.** The circumstances in which an increase in public expenditure can replace private expenditure.

D.20 **Central banking and monetary policy in the USA.** This case examines how the Fed conducts monetary policy.

D.21 **Should central banks be independent of government?** An examination of the arguments for and against independent central banks.

D.22 **The modern approach to industrial policy.** This looks at changes in the approach to industrial policy around the world.

D.23 **Productivity performance and the UK economy.** A detailed examination of how the UK's productivity compares with that in other countries.

D.24 **Assessing PFI.** Has this been the perfect solution to funding investment for the public sector without raising taxes?

D.25 **Assistance to small firms in the UK.** An examination of current government measures to assist small firms.

D.26 **Trading patterns.** An examination of the geographical patterns in the trade of merchandise goods and commercial services.

D.27 **Fallacious arguments for restricting trade.** Some of the more common mistaken arguments for protection.

D.28 **Free trade and the environment.** Do whales, the rainforests and the atmosphere gain from free trade?

D.29 **The Uruguay Round.** An examination of the negotiations that led to substantial cuts in trade barriers.

D.30 **The Battle of Seattle.** This looks at the protests against the WTO at Seattle in November 1999 and considers the arguments for and against the free trade policies of the WTO.

D.31 **The World Trade Organization.** This looks at the various opportunities and threats posed by this major international organisation.

D.32 **From NAFTA to USMCA.** The evolution of the North American Free Trade Agreement.

D.33 **Steel barriers.** The use by the USA of tariff protection for its steel industry and the effects of threats of retaliation by other countries.

D.34 **The Single Market Scoreboard.** Keeping a tally on progress to a true single market in the EU.

D.35 **The UK's balance of payments deficit.** An examination of the UK's persistent trade and current account deficits.

D.36 **Dealing in foreign exchange.** The operation of international currency markets.

D.37 **Using interest rates to control both aggregate demand and the exchange rate.** A problem of one instrument and two targets.

D.38 **Making sense of the financial balances on the balance of payments.** An examination of the three main components of the financial account.

D.39 **Argentina in crisis.** An examination of the collapse of the Argentinean economy in 2001/2 and subsequent attempts to tackle its economic problems.

D.40 **Attempts at harmonisation.** A look at the meetings of the G7and G20 economies where the members attempt to come to agreement on means of achieving stable and sustained worldwide economic growth.

D.41 **Oil prices.** What is their effect on the world economy?

D.42 **Optimal currency areas.** What's the best size for a single currency area such as the eurozone?

WEBSITES RELEVANT TO PART D

Numbers and sections refer to websites listed in the Web Appendix and hotlinked from this book's website at **www.pearsoned. co.uk/sloman/**

■ For news articles relevant to Part D, Google the Sloman Economics News site.

■ For general news on macroeconomic issues, both national and international, see websites in section A, and particularly A1–5, 7–9. See also links to newspapers worldwide in A38, 39, 42, 43 and 44 and the news search feature in Google at A41.

■ For general news on money, banking and interest rates, see again websites in section A, particularly A20–23, 25, 35, 36.

■ For macroeconomic data, see links in section B and particularly B1; also see B4 and 35. For UK data, see B2, 3, 5 and 6. For EU data, see B38, 39 and 47. For US data, see B15, 17 and 25. For international data, see B15, 21, 24, 31, 33, 35. For links to data sets, see B1, 4, 28, 33, 35; I13 and 14.

■ For data on UK unemployment, see section B and particularly B3 (search 'unemployment'). For international data on unemployment, see B1, 21, 24, 31, 38, 47, 48; H3.

■ For monetary and financial data (including data for money supply and interest rates), see section F and particularly F2. Note that you can link to central banks worldwide from site F17. See also the links in B1.

■ For information on UK fiscal policy and government borrowing, see section E, sites E18, 30, 36. See also news sites A1–8 at Budget time. For fiscal policy in the eurozone, see Fiscal Governance in the EU Member States in G1 and also see G13. For EU data on government finances, see sites B38 and 47.

■ For monetary policy, see section F. For the UK, see site F1; for the eurozone, see F5 and 6; for the USA, see F8; for other countries, see the respective central banks sites in section F.

■ For inflation targeting in the UK and the eurozone, see section F and particularly sites F1 and 6.

■ For the current approach to UK supply-side policy, see sites in section E and particularly the latest Budget Report (e.g. sections on productivity and training) at site E30. See also sites E5 and 9. For European policy, see section G and particularly sites G5, 7, 9, 12, 14, 19. For support for a market-orientated approach to supply-side policy see C17 and E34. For information on training in the UK and Europe, see section E, sites E5 and 10; and section G, sites G5 and 14. For information on the support for small business in the UK see site E38.

■ For general news on business in the international environment, see section A, and particularly A1–5, 7–9, 20, 23, 24, 25, 35, 36. See also links to newspapers worldwide in A38, 39, 42, 43 and 44, and the news search feature in Google at A41.

■ For international data on imports and exports, see sites B1, 42 and 43. See also trade data in B31 and 35.

■ For international data on balance of payments, see World Economic Outlook in B31 and OECD Economic Outlook in B21. For other sources, see B33.

■ For international data on foreign direct investment (FDI), see UNCTADStat at site B43.

■ For UK data on trade and the balance of payments, see B3 (search International Trade and also Balance of Payments or Pink Book); see also B34. For EU data, see sites B38 and 47.

■ For exchange rates, see F2 > *Statistical Interactive Database*; you can then choose the currencies and the dates to customise an Excel file. See also A1, 3; B34, 45; F2, 6, 8.

■ For discussion papers on trade and the balance of payments, see section H, sites H4 and 7.

■ For trade disputes, see H16.

■ For information on NAFTA and other preferential trading arrangements, see section H, sites H20–23.

■ For various pressure groups critical of the effects of free trade and globalisation, see section H, sites H11, 13, 14.

■ For student resources relevant to Part D, see section C, sites C1–10, 19 and 21.

Websites appendix

All the following websites can be accessed from this book's own website (http://www.pearsoned.co.uk/sloman). When you enter the site, click on **Hot Links.** You will find all the following sites listed. Click on the one you want and the 'hot link' will take you straight to it.

The sections and numbers below refer to the ones used in the websites listed at the end of each chapter. Thus if the list contained the number A21, this would refer to the *Conversation* site.

A General news sources

As the title of this section implies, the websites here can be used for finding material on current news issues or tapping into news archives. Most archives are offered free of charge. However, some do require you to register. As well as key UK and American news sources, you will also notice some slightly different places from where you can get your news, such as *The Moscow Times* and *The Japan Times.* Check out site numbers 38. *Refdesk,* 43. *Guardian World News Guide* and 44. *Online newspapers* for links to newspapers across the world. Try searching for an article on a particular topic by using site number 41. *Google News Search.*

1. BBC news
2. The Economist
3. The Financial Times
4. The Guardian
5. The Independent
6. ITN
7. The Observer
8. The Telegraph
9. Aljazeera
10. The New York Times
11. Fortune
12. Time Magazine
13. The Washington Post
14. The Moscow Times (English)
15. Pravda (English)
16. Straits Times (Singapore)
17. New Straits Times (Malaysia)
18. The Scotsman
19. The Herald
20. Euromoney
21. The Conversation
22. Market News International
23. Bloomberg Businessweek
24. International Business Times
25. CNN Money
26. Vox (economic analysis and commentary)
27. Asia News Network
28. allAfrica.com
29. Greek News Sources (English)
30. France 24 (English)
31. Euronews
32. Australian Financial Review
33. Sydney Morning Herald
34. The Japan Times
35. Reuters
36. Bloomberg
37. David Smith's Economics UK.com
38. Refdesk (links to a whole range of news sources)
39. Newspapers and Magazines on World Wide Web
40. Yahoo News Search
41. Google News Search
42. ABYZ news links
43. Guardian World News Guide
44. Online newspapers

B Sources of economic and business data

Using websites to find up-to-date data is of immense value to the economist. The data sources below offer you a range of specialist and non-specialist data information. Universities have free access to the *UK Data Service* site (site 35 in this set), which is a huge database of statistics. Site 34, the *Treasury Pocket Data Bank,* is a very useful source of key UK and world statistics, and is updated monthly; it can be downloaded as an Excel file. The Economics Network's *Economic data freely available online* (site 1) gives links to various sections in over 40 UK and international sites.

1. Economics Network gateway to economic data
2. Office for Budget Responsibility
3. Office for National Statistics
4. Data Archive (Essex)
5. Bank of England Statistical Interactive Database
6. UK official statistics (GOV.UK)
7. Nationwide House Prices Site
8. House Web (data on housing market)
9. Economist global house price data
10. Halifax House Price Index
11. House prices indices from ONS

12. Penn World Table
13. Economist economic and financial indicators
14. FT market data
15. Economagic
16. Groningen Growth and Development Centre
17. AEAweb: Resources for economists on the Internet (RFE): data
18. Joseph Rowntree Foundation
19. OECD iLibrary statistics
20. Energy Information Administration
21. OECDStat
22. CIA world statistics site (World Factbook)
23. Millennium Development Goal Indicators Database
24. World Bank Data
25. Federal Reserve Bank of St Louis, US Economic Datasets (FRED)
26. Ministry of Economy, Trade and Industry (Japan)
27. Financial data from Yahoo
28. DataMarket
29. Index Mundi
30. Knoema: Economics
31. World Economic Outlook Database (IMF)
32. Telegraph shares and markets
33. Key Indicators (KI) for Asia and the Pacific Series (Asia Development Bank)
34. Open data from data.gov.uk (Business and Economy)
35. UK Data Service (incorporating ESDS)
36. BBC News, market data
37. NationMaster
38. Statistical Annex of the European Economy
39. Business and Consumer Surveys (all EU countries)
40. Gapminder
41. Trading Economics
42. WTO International Trade Statistics database
43. UNCTAD trade, investment and development statistics (UNCTADstat)
44. London Metal Exchange
45. Bank for International Settlements, global nominal and real effective exchange rate indices
46. Vizala (international data)
47. AMECO database
48. The Conference Board data
49. Institute for Fiscal Studies: tools and resources
50. European Central Bank (ECB): statistics

C Sites for students and teachers of economics

The following websites offer useful ideas and resources to those who are studying or teaching economics. It is worth browsing through some just to see what is on offer. Try out the first four sites, for starters. The *Internet for Economics* (site 8) is a very helpful tutorial for economics students on using the Internet.

1. The Economics Network
2. Teaching Resources for Undergraduate Economics (TRUE)
3. Timetric
4. Studying Economics
5. Economics and Business Education Association
6. Tutor2U
7. Council for Economic Education
8. Internet for Economics (tutorial on using the Web)
9. Econoclass: Resources for economics teachers
10. Teaching resources for economists (RFE)
11. METAL – Mathematics for Economics: enhancing Teaching and Learning
12. Federal Reserve Bank of San Francisco: Economics Education
13. Excel in Economics Teaching (from the Economics Network)
14. Beyond the Bike: Economics Lesson Resources
15. Dr. T's EconLinks: Teaching Resources
16. Online Opinion (Economics)
17. Free to Choose TV from the Idea Channel
18. History of Economic Thought
19. Resources For Economists on the Internet (RFE)
20. Games Economists Play (non-computerised classroom games)
21. Bank of England education resources
22. Why Study Economics?
23. Economic Classroom Experiments
24. Veconlab: Charles Holt's classroom experiments
25. Embedding Threshold Concepts
26. MIT Open Courseware in Economics
27. EconPort
28. ThoughtCo. – Economics

D Economic models, simulations and classroom experiments

Economic modelling is an important aspect of economic analysis. There are several sites that offer access to a model or simulation for you to use, e.g. *Virtual Chancellor* (where you can play being Chancellor of the Exchequer). Using such models can be a useful way of finding out how economic theory works within a specific environment. Other sites link to games and experiments, where you can play a particular role, perhaps competing with other students.

1. Virtual Chancellor
2. Virtual Factory
3. Interactive simulation models (Economics Web Institute)
4. Classroom Experiments in Economics (Pedagogy in Action)
5. MobLab
6. Economics Network Handbook, Chapter on Simulations, Games and Role-play
7. Experimental Economics Class Material (David J Cooper)
8. Simulations
9. Experimental economics: Wikipedia
10. Software available on the Economics Network site
11. RFE Software
12. Virtual Worlds
13. Veconlab: Charles Holt's classroom experiments
14. EconPort Experiments
15. Denise Hazlett's Classroom Experiments in Macroeconomics
16. Games Economists Play

17. Finance and Economics Experimental Laboratory at Exeter (FEELE)
18. Classroom Expernomics
19. The Economics Network's Guide to Classroom Experiments and Games
20. Economic Classroom Experiments (Wikiversity)

E UK government and UK organisations' sites

If you want to see what a government department is up to, then look no further than the list below. Government departments' websites are an excellent source of information and data. They are particularly good at offering information on current legislation and policy initiatives.

1. Gateway site (GOV.UK)
2. Department for Communities and Local Government
3. Prime Minister's Office
4. Competition & Markets Authority
5. Department for Education
6. Department for International Development
7. Department for Transport
8. Department of Health
9. Department for Work and Pensions
10. Department for Business, Energy & Industrial Strategy
11. Environment Agency
12. Department of Energy and Climate Change
13. Low Pay Commission
14. Department for Environment, Food & Rural Affairs (Defra)
15. Office of Communications (Ofcom)
16. Office of Gas and Electricity Markets (Ofgem)
17. Official Documents OnLine
18. Office for Budget Responsibility
19. Office of Rail and Road (ORR)
20. The Takeover Panel
21. Sustainable Development Commission
22. Ofwat
23. National Statistics (ONS)
24. List of ONS releases from UK Data Explorer
25. HM Revenue & Customs
26. UK Intellectual Property Office
27. Parliament website
28. Scottish Government
29. Scottish Environment Protection Agency
30. HM Treasury
31. Equality and Human Rights Commission
32. Trades Union Congress (TUC)
33. Confederation of British Industry (CBI)
34. Adam Smith Institute
35. Chatham House
36. Institute for Fiscal Studies
37. Advertising Standards Authority
38. Businesses and Self-employed
39. Campaign for Better Transport
40. New Economics Foundation
41. Financial Conduct Authority
42. Prudential Regulation Authority

F Sources of monetary and financial data

As the title suggests, here are listed useful websites for finding information on financial matters. You will see that the list comprises mainly central banks, both within Europe and further afield. The links will take you to English language versions of non-English speaking countries' sites.

1. Bank of England
2. Bank of England Monetary and Financial Statistics
3. Banque de France (in English)
4. Bundesbank (German central bank)
5. Central Bank of Ireland
6. European Central Bank
7. Eurostat
8. US Federal Reserve Bank
9. Netherlands Central Bank (in English)
10. Bank of Japan (in English)
11. Reserve Bank of Australia
12. Bank Negara Malaysia (in English)
13. Monetary Authority of Singapore
14. Bank of Canada
15. National Bank of Denmark (in English)
16. Reserve Bank of India
17. Links to central bank websites from the Bank for International Settlements
18. The London Stock Exchange

G European Union and related sources

For information on European issues, the following is a wide range of useful sites. The sites maintained by the European Union are an excellent source of information.

1. Business, Economy, Euro: (EC DG)
2. European Central Bank
3. EU official website
4. Eurostat
5. Employment, Social Affairs and Inclusion: (EC DG)
6. Reports, Studies and Booklets on the EU
7. Internal Market, Industry, Entrepreneurship and SMEs: (EC DG)
8. Competition: (EC DG)
9. Agriculture and Rural Development: (EC DG)
10. Energy: (EC DG)
11. Environment: (EC DG)
12. Regional Policy: (EC DG)
13. Taxation and Customs Union: (EC DG)
14. Education, Youth, Sport and Culture: (EC DG)
15. European Patent Office
16. European Commission
17. European Parliament
18. European Council
19. Mobility and Transport: (EC DG)

20. Trade (EC DG)
21. Maritime Affairs and Fisheries: (EC DG)
22. International Cooperation and Development: (EC DG)
23. Financial Stability, Financial Services and Capital Markets Union (EC DG)

H International organisations

This section casts its net beyond Europe and lists the Web addresses of the main international organisations in the global economy. You will notice that some sites are run by charities, such as Oxfam, while others represent organisations set up to manage international affairs, such as the International Monetary Fund and the United Nations.

1. UN Food and Agriculture Organisation (FAO)
2. United Nations Conference on Trade and Development (UNCTAD)
3. International Labour Organisation (ILO)
4. International Monetary Fund (IMF)
5. Organisation for Economic Co-operation and Development (OECD)
6. OPEC
7. World Bank
8. World Health Organization (WHO)
9. United Nations (UN)
10. United Nations Industrial Development Organisation (UNIDO)
11. Friends of the Earth
12. Institute of International Finance
13. Oxfam
14. Christian Aid (reports on development issues)
15. European Bank for Reconstruction and Development (EBRD)
16. World Trade Organisation (WTO)
17. United Nations Development Programme
18. UNICEF
19. EURODAD – European Network on Debt and Development
20. NAFTA
21. South American Free Trade Areas
22. ASEAN
23. APEC

I Economics search and link sites

If you are having difficulty finding what you want from the list of sites above, the following sites offer links to other sites and are a very useful resource when you are looking for something a little bit more specialist. Once again, it is worth having a look at what these sites have to offer in order to judge their usefulness.

1. Gateway for UK official sites
2. Alta Plana
3. Data Archive Search
4. Inomics: information on economics courses and jobs
5. Ideas from RePEc: bibliographic database
6. Wikidata
7. Portal sites with links to other site (Economics Network)
8. 50 Economics Resources for Students and Educators (Value Stock Guide)
9. Global goals 2030 (link to economic development resources)
10. Development Data Hub
11. DMOZ Open Directory: Economics (legacy site)
12. Web links for economists from the Economics Network
13. EconData.uk
14. Yale university: 75 Sources of Economic Data, Statistics, Reports, and Commentary
15. Excite Economics Links
16. Internet Resources for Economists
17. Trade Map (trade statistics)
18. Resources for Economists on the Internet
19. UK University Economics Departments
20. Economics education links
21. Development Gateway
22. Find the Data
23. Portal: Business from Wikipedia
24. National Bureau of Economic Research links to data sources

J Internet search engines

The following search engines have been found to be useful.

1. Google
2. Bing
3. Whoosh UK
4. Excite
5. Zanran (search engine for data and statistics)
6. Search.com
7. MSN
8. Economics search engine (from RFE)
9. Yahoo
10. Ask
11. Lycos
12. Webcrawler
13. Metacrawler: searches several search engines

Key ideas

1. **The principal–agent problem.** Where people (principals), as a result of a lack of knowledge (asymmetric information), cannot ensure that their best interests are served by their agents. Agents may take advantage of this situation to the disadvantage of the principals. (**See page 10.**)

2. **The behaviour and performance of firms is affected by the business environment.** The business environment includes social/cultural (S), technological (T), economic (E), ethical (E), political (P), legal (L) and environmental (E) factors. The mnemonic STEEPLE can be used to remember these. (**See page 12.**)

3. **Opportunity cost.** The opportunity cost of something is what you give up to get it/do it. In other words, it is cost measured in terms of the best alternative foregone. (**See page 22.**)

4. **Rational decision making involves weighing up the marginal benefit and marginal cost of any activity.** If the marginal benefit exceeds the marginal cost, it is rational to do the activity (or to do more of it). If the marginal cost exceeds the marginal benefit, it is rational not to do it (or to do less of it). (**See page 23.**)

5. **People respond to incentives, such as changes in prices or wages.** It is important, therefore, that incentives are appropriate and have the desired effect. (**See page 27.**)

6. **Changes in demand or supply cause markets to adjust.** Whenever such changes occur, the resulting 'disequilibrium' will bring an automatic change in prices, thereby restoring equilibrium (i.e. a balance of demand and supply). (**See page 28.**)

7. **People's actions are influenced by their expectations.** People respond not just to what is happening now (such as a change in price), but to what they anticipate will happen in the future. (**See page 31.**)

8. **Partial analysis: other things remaining equal (*ceteris paribus*).** In economics it is common to look at just one determinant of a variable such as demand or supply and see what happens when the determinant changes. For example, if price is taken as the determinant of demand, we can see what happens to quantity demanded as price changes. In the meantime, we have to assume that other determinants remain unchanged. This is known as the 'other things being equal' assumption (or, using the Latin, the '*ceteris paribus*' assumption). Once we have seen how our chosen determinant affects our variable, we can then see what happens when another determinant changes, and then another, and so on. (**See page 31.**)

9. **Equilibrium is the point where conflicting interests are balanced.** Only at this point is the amount that demanders are willing to purchase the same as the amount that suppliers are willing to supply. It is a point which will be automatically reached in a free market through the operation of the price mechanism. (**See page 35.**)

10. **Elasticity.** The responsiveness of one variable (e.g. demand) to a change in another (e.g. price). This concept is fundamental to understanding how markets work. The more elastic variables are, the more responsive is the market to changing circumstances. (**See page 42.**)

11. **The principle of diminishing marginal utility.** As you consume more of a product, and thus become more satisfied, so your desire for additional units of it will decline. (**See page 56.**)

12. **Adverse selection.** Where information is imperfect, high-risk/poor-quality groups will be attracted to profitable market opportunities to the disadvantage of the average buyer (or seller). (**See page 59.**)

13. **Moral hazard.** Following a deal, if there are information asymmetries (see page 60), it is likely that one party will engage in problematic (immoral and/or hazardous) behaviour to the detriment of the other. In other words, lack of information by one party to the deal may result in the deal not being honoured by the other party. (**See page 60.**)

14. **The law of diminishing marginal returns.** When increasing amounts of a variable input are used with a given amount of a fixed input, there will come a point when each extra unit of the variable input will produce less extra output than the previous unit. (**See page 83.**)

15. **Sunk costs and the 'bygones' principle.** The principle states that sunk (fixed) costs should be ignored when deciding whether to produce or sell more or less of a product. Only variable costs should be taken into account. (**See page 84.**)

16. **Transactions costs.** The costs associated with exchanging products. For buyers it is the costs over and above the price of the product. For sellers it is the costs over and above the costs of production. Transactions costs include search costs, contract costs, monitoring and enforcement costs, and transport and handling costs. (**See page 94.**)

17. **Market power benefits the powerful at the expense of others.** When firms have market power over prices, they can use this to raise prices and profits above the perfectly competitive level. Other things being equal, the firm will gain at the expense of the consumer. Similarly, if consumers or workers have market power they can use this to their own benefit. (**See page 112.**)

18. **People often think and behave strategically.** How you think others will respond to your actions is likely to influence your own behaviour. Firms, for example, when considering a price or product change will often take into account the likely reactions of their rivals. (**See page 121.**)

19. **Nash equilibrium.** The position resulting from everyone making their optimal decision based on their assumptions about their rivals' decisions. Such an outcome, however, is unlikely to maximise the collective benefit. Nevertheless, without collusion in this 'game', whether open or tacit, there is no incentive to move from this position. (**See page 129.**)

20. **Competitive advantage.** The various factors that enable a firm to compete more effectively with its rivals. These can be supply-side factors, such as superior technology, better organisation, or greater power or efficiency in sourcing its supplies – resulting in lower costs; or they could be demand-side

ones, such as producing a superior or better-value product in the eyes of consumers, or being more conveniently located – resulting in higher and/or less elastic demand. (**See page 146.**)

21. **Core competencies.** The areas of specialised expertise within a business that underpin its competitive advantage over its rivals. These competencies could be in production technologies or organisation, in relationships with suppliers, in the nature and specifications of the product, or in the firm's ability to innovate and develop its products and brand image. (**See page 152.**)

22. **Efficient capital markets.** Capital markets are efficient when the prices of shares accurately reflect information about companies' current and expected future performance. (**See page 167.**)

23. **Social efficiency.** This is achieved where no further net social gain can be made by producing more or less of a good. This will occur where marginal social benefit equals marginal social cost. (**See page 222.**)

24. **Externalities are spillover costs or benefits.** Where these exist, even an otherwise perfect market will fail to achieve social efficiency. (**See page 223.**)

25. **The free-rider problem.** People are often unwilling to pay for things if they can make use of things other people have bought. This problem can lead to people not purchasing things which it would be to their benefit and that of other members of society to have. (**See page 225.**)

26. **Economies suffer from inherent instability.** As a result, economic growth and other macroeconomic indicators tend to fluctuate. (**See page 271.**)

27. **The distinction between real and nominal values.** Nominal figures are those using current prices, interest rates, etc. Real figures are figures corrected for inflation. (**See page 285.**)

28. **The law of comparative advantage.** Provided opportunity costs of various goods differ in two countries, both of them can gain from mutual trade if they specialise in producing (and exporting) those goods that have relatively low opportunity costs compared with the other country. (**See page 329.**)

29. **The competitive advantage of nations.** The ability of countries to compete in the market for exports and with potential importers to their country. The competitiveness of any one industry depends on the availability and quality of resources, demand conditions at home in that industry, the strategies and rivalry of firms within the industry and the quality of supporting industries and infrastructure. It also depends on government policies, and there is also an element of chance. (**See page 332.**)

Glossary

Absolute advantage A country has an absolute advantage over another in the production of a good if it can produce it with fewer resources than the other country.

Accelerator The level of investment depends on the rate of increase in consumer demand, and as a result is subject to substantial fluctuations. Increases in investment via the accelerator can compound the multiplier effect.

Adjustable peg A system whereby exchange rates are fixed for a period of time, but may be devalued (or revalued) if a deficit (or surplus) becomes substantial.

Adverse selection Where information is imperfect, high-risk/poor-quality groups will be attracted to profitable market opportunities to the disadvantage of the average buyer (or seller).

Aggregate demand for labour curve A curve showing the total demand for labour in the economy at different average real wage rates.

Aggregate supply of labour curve A curve showing the total number of people willing and able to work at different average real wage rates.

Allocative efficiency A situation where the current combination of goods produced and sold gives the maximum satisfaction for each consumer at their current levels of income.

Appreciation A rise in the free-market exchange rate of the domestic currency with foreign currencies.

Asymmetric information A situation in which one party in an economic relationship knows more than another.

Asymmetric shocks Shocks (such as an oil price increase or a recession in another part of the world) that have different-sized effects on different industries, regions or countries.

Automatic stabilisers Tax revenues that automatically rise and government expenditure that automatically falls as national income rises. The more they change as income changes, the bigger the stabilising effect on national income.

Average cost or mark-up pricing Where firms set the price by adding a profit mark-up to average costs.

Average fixed cost (*AFC*) Total fixed cost per unit of output: $AFC = TFC/Q$.

Average revenue Total revenue per unit of output. When all output is sold at the same price, average revenue will be the same as price: $AR = TR/Q = P$.

Average (total) cost (*AC*) Total cost (fixed plus variable) per unit of output: $AC = TC/Q + AFC + AVC$.

Average variable cost (*AVC*) Total variable cost per unit of output: $AVC = TVC/Q$.

Backward integration Where a firm expands backwards down the supply chain to earlier stages of production.

Backwards induction A process by which firms consider the decision in the last round of the game and then work backwards through the game, thinking through the most likely outcomes in earlier rounds.

Balance of payments account A record of the country's transactions with the rest of the world. It shows the country's payments to or deposits in other countries (debits) and its receipts (credits) from other countries. It also shows the balance between these debits and credits under various headings.

Balance of payments on current account The balance on trade in goods and services plus net incomes and current transfers, i.e. the sum of the credits on the current account minus the sum of the debits.

Balance of trade Exports of goods and services minus imports of goods and services.

Bank (or deposits) multiplier The number of times greater the expansion of bank deposits is than the additional liquidity in banks that caused it: $1/L$ (the inverse of the liquidity ratio).

Barometric forecasting A technique used to predict future economic trends based upon analysing patterns of time-series data.

Bounded rationality When the ability to make rational decisions is limited by lack of information or the time necessary to obtain such information.

Budget deficit The excess of central government's spending over its tax receipts.

Budget surplus The excess of central government's tax receipts over its spending.

Business cluster A geographical concentration of related businesses and institutions.

Business cycle or trade cycle The periodic fluctuations of national output around its long-term trend.

Business ethics The values and principles that shape business behaviour.

Capital All inputs into production that have themselves been produced: e.g. factories, machines and tools.

Capital account of the balance of payments The record of transfers of capital to and from abroad.

Cartel A formal collusive agreement.

Cash in circulation The measure of narrow money in the UK. This is all cash outside the Bank of England: in banks, in people's purses and wallets, in businesses' safes and tills, in government departments, etc.

Change in demand The term used for a shift in the demand curve. It occurs when a determinant of demand *other* than price changes.

Change in supply The term used for a shift in the supply curve. It occurs when a determinant other than price changes.

Change in the quantity demanded The term used for a movement along the demand curve to a new point. It occurs when there is a change in price.

Change in the quantity supplied The term used for a movement along the supply curve to a new point. It occurs when there is a change in price.

Claimant unemployment Those in receipt of unemployment-related benefits.

Cluster (business or industrial) A geographical concentration of related businesses and institutions.

Collusive oligopoly When oligopolists agree (formally or informally) to limit competition between themselves. They may set output quotas, fix prices, limit product promotion or development, or agree not to 'poach' each other's markets.

Collusive tendering Where two or more firms secretly agree on the prices they will tender for a contract. These prices will be above those which would be put in under a genuinely competitive tendering process.

Command-and-control (CAC) systems The use of laws or regulations backed up by inspections and penalties (such as fines) for non-compliance.

Comparative advantage A country has a comparative advantage over another in the production of a good if it can produce it at a lower opportunity cost, i.e. if it has to forego less of other goods in order to produce it.

Competition for corporate control The competition for the control of companies through takeovers.

Competitive advantage The various factors, such as lower costs or a better product, that give a firm an advantage over its rivals.

Competitive advantage of nations The various factors that enable the industries in a particular country to compete more effectively with those in other countries.

Complementary goods A pair of goods consumed together. As the price of one goes up, the demand for both goods will fall.

Complementors Firms producing complementary goods (products that are used together).

Conglomerate merger Where two firms in different industries merge.

Conglomerate multinational A multinational that produces different products in different countries.

Consortium Where two or more firms work together on a specific project and create a separate company to run the project.

Consumer durable A consumer good that lasts a period of time, during which the consumer can continue gaining utility from it.

Consumer surplus The difference between how much a consumer is willing to pay for a good and how much they actually pay for it.

Consumption The act of using goods and services to satisfy wants. This will normally involve purchasing the goods and services.

Consumption of domestically produced goods and services (C_d) The direct flow of money payments from households to firms.

Convergence of economies When countries achieve similar levels of growth, inflation, budget deficits as a percentage of GDP, balance of payments, etc.

Core competencies The key skills of a business that underpin its competitive advantage.

Corporate (social) responsibility Where a business considers the interests and concerns of a community rather than just its shareholders.

Cost-push inflation Inflation caused by persistent rises in costs of production (independently of demand).

Credible threat (or promise) One that is believable to rivals because it is in the threatener's interests to carry it out.

Cross-price elasticity of demand The responsiveness of demand for one good to a change in the price of another: the proportionate change in demand for one good divided by the proportionate change in price of the other.

Crowding out Where increased public expenditure diverts money or resources away from the private sector.

Current account of the balance of payments The record of a country's imports and exports of goods and services, plus incomes and current transfers of money to and from abroad.

Decision tree (or game tree) A diagram showing the sequence of possible decisions by competitor firms and the outcome of each combination of decisions.

Deindustrialisation The decline in the contribution to production of the manufacturing sector of the economy.

Demand curve A graph showing the relationship between the price of a good and the quantity of the good demanded over a given time period. Price is measured on the vertical axis; quantity demanded is measured on the horizontal axis. A demand curve can be for an individual consumer or a group of consumers, or more usually for the whole market.

Demand-deficient or cyclical unemployment Dis-equilibrium unemployment caused by a fall in aggregate demand with no corresponding fall in the real wage rate.

Demand-pull inflation Inflation caused by persistent rises in aggregate demand.

Demand schedule for an individual A table showing the different quantities of a good that a person is willing and able to buy at various prices over a given period of time.

Demand-side or demand management policy Policy to affect aggregate demand (i.e. fiscal or monetary policy).

Depreciation A fall in the free-market exchange rate of the domestic currency with foreign currencies.

Derived demand The demand for a factor of production depends on the demand for the good that uses it.

Destabilising speculation A situation where the actions of speculators cause demand and/or supply curves to shift further in the direction they are currently shifting. This amplifies price changes.

Devaluation Where the government or central bank re-pegs the exchange rate at a lower level.

Discretionary fiscal policy Deliberate changes in tax rates or the level of government expenditure in order to influence the level of aggregate demand.

Diseconomies of scale Where costs per unit of output increase as the scale of production increases.

Disequilibrium unemployment Unemployment resulting from real wages in the economy being above the equilibrium level.

Diversification A business growth strategy in which a business expands into new markets outside of its current interests.

Dominant strategy game Where the firm will choose the same strategy no matter what assumption it makes about its rivals' behaviour.

Downsizing Where a business reorganises and reduces its size, especially in respect to levels of employment, in order to cut costs.

Dumping Where exports are sold at prices below marginal cost – often as a result of government subsidy.

Economic and monetary union (EMU) Where countries adopt a single currency and a single monetary policy. It might also involve other common policies, such as fiscal and supply-side policies.

Economic globalisation The process whereby the economies of the world are becoming increasingly integrated.

Economic growth The rise in GDP. The rate of economic growth is the percentage increase in GDP over a 12-month period.

Economies of scale When increasing the scale of production leads to a lower cost per unit of output.

Economies of scope When increasing the range of products produced by a firm reduces the cost of producing each one.

Efficiency wage hypothesis A hypothesis that states that a worker's productivity is linked to the wage he or she receives.

Efficiency wage rate The profit-maximising wage rate for the firm after taking into account the effects of wage rates on worker motivation, turnover and recruitment.

Efficient (capital) market hypothesis The hypothesis that new information about a company's current or future performance will be quickly and accurately reflected in its share price.

Elastic demand If demand is (price) elastic, then any change in price will cause the quantity demanded to change proportionately more. (Ignoring the negative sign) it will have a value greater than 1.

EMU (see Economic and monetary union).

Environmental scanning Where a business surveys social and political trends in order to take account of changes in its decision-making process.

Equilibrium A position of balance. A position from which there is no inherent tendency to move away.

Equilibrium GDP The level of GDP where injections equal withdrawals and where, therefore, there is no tendency for GDP to rise or fall.

Equilibrium price The price where the quantity demanded equals the quantity supplied; the price where there is no shortage or surplus.

Equilibrium ('natural') unemployment The difference between those who would like employment at the current wage rate and those willing and able to take a job.

ERM (the exchange rate mechanism) A semi-fixed system whereby participating EU countries allowed fluctuations against each other's currencies only within agreed bands. Collectively they floated freely against all other currencies.

Exchange rate The rate at which one national currency exchanges for another. The rate is expressed as the amount of one currency that is necessary to purchase *one unit* of another currency (e.g. €1.20 = £1).

Exchange rate index A weighted average exchange rate expressed as an index, where the value of the index is 100 in a given base year. The weights of the different currencies in the index add up to 1.

Exclusionary abuses Business practices that limit or prevent effective competition from either actual or potential rivals.

Explicit costs The payments to outside suppliers of inputs.

Exploitative abuses Business practices that directly harm the customer. Examples include high prices and poor quality.

External benefits Benefits from production (or consumption) experienced by people other than the producer (or consumer).

External costs Costs of production (or consumption) borne by people other than the producer (or consumer).

External diseconomies of scale Where a firm's costs per unit of output increase as the size of the whole industry increases.

External economies of scale Where a firm's costs per unit of output decrease as the size of the whole industry grows.

External expansion Where business growth is achieved by merging with or taking over businesses within a market or industry.

Externalities Costs or benefits of production or consumption experienced by society but not by the producers or consumers themselves. Sometimes referred to as 'spillover' or 'third-party' costs or benefits.

Factors of production (or resources) The inputs into the production of goods and services: labour, land and raw materials, and capital.

Financial account of the balance of payments The record of the flows of money into and out of the country for the purpose of investment or as deposits in bank and other financial institutions.

Financial flexibility Where employers can vary their wage costs by changing the composition of their workforce or the terms on which workers are employed.

Fine-tuning The use of demand management policy (fiscal or monetary) to smooth out cyclical fluctuations in the economy.

First-mover advantage When a firm gains from being the first to take action.

Fiscal policy Policy to affect aggregate demand by altering government expenditure and/or taxation.

Fiscal stance How expansionary or contractionary fiscal policy is.

Fixed costs Total costs that do not vary with the amount of output produced.

Fixed input An input that cannot be increased in supply within a given time period.

Flat organisation One in which technology enables senior managers to communicate directly with those lower in the organisational structure. Middle managers are bypassed.

Flexible firm A firm that has the flexibility to respond to changing market conditions by changing the composition of its workforce.

Floating exchange rate When the government does not intervene in the foreign exchange markets, but simply allows the exchange rate to be freely determined by demand and supply.

Forward integration Where a firm expands forward up the supply chain towards the sale of the finished product.

Franchise A formal agreement whereby a company uses another company to produce or sell some or all of its product.

Free market One in which there is an absence of government intervention. Individual producers and consumers are free to make their own economic decisions.

Free-rider problem When it is not possible to exclude other people from consuming a good that someone has bought.

Frictional (search) unemployment Unemployment that occurs as a result of imperfect information in the labour market. It often takes time for workers to find jobs (even though there are vacancies) and in the meantime they are unemployed.

Functional flexibility Where employers can switch workers from job to job as requirements change.

Game theory (or the theory of games) The study of alternative strategies that oligopolists may choose to adopt, depending on their assumptions about their rivals' behaviour.

General government debt The accumulated central and local government deficits (less surpluses) over the years, i.e. the total amount owed by central and local government, both to domestic and overseas creditors.

Globalisation The process whereby the world is becoming increasingly interconnected, both economically, technologically, socially, politically, culturally and environmentally.

Globalisation (economic) The process whereby the economies of the world are becoming increasingly integrated.

Goodhart's Law Controlling a symptom or indicator of a problem is unlikely to cure the problem; it will simply mean that what is being controlled now becomes a poor indicator of the problem.

Goods in joint supply These are two goods where the production of more of one leads to the production of more of the other.

Grim trigger strategy Once a player observes that its rival has broken some agreed behaviour, it will never again co-operate with them again

Gross Domestic Product (GDP) The value of output produced within the country over a 12-month period.

Growth maximisation An alternative theory which assumes that managers seek to maximise the growth in sales revenue (or the capital value of the firm) over time.

Growth vector matrix A means by which a business might assess its product/market strategy.

Harmonisation (international) of economic policies Where countries attempt to coordinate their macroeconomic policies so as to achieve common goals.

Heuristics People's use of strategies that draw on simple lessons from past experience when they are faced with similar, although not identical, choices.

Historic costs The original amount the firm paid for inputs it now owns.

Holding company A business organisation in which the parent company holds interests in a number of other companies or subsidiaries.

Horizontally integrated multinational A multi-national that produces the same product in many different countries.

Horizontal merger Where two firms in the same industry at the same stage of the production process merge.

Imperfect competition The collective name for monopolistic competition and oligopoly.

Implicit costs Costs which do not involve a direct payment of money to a third party, but which nevertheless involve a sacrifice of some alternative.

Import substitution The replacement of imports by domestically produced goods or services.

Income effect The effect of a change in price on quantity demanded arising from the consumer becoming better or worse off as a result of the price change.

Income elasticity of demand The responsiveness of demand to a change in consumer incomes: the proportionate change in demand divided by the proportionate change in income.

Independent risks Where two risky events are unconnected. The occurrence of one will not affect the likelihood of the occurrence of the other.

Indivisibilities The impossibility of dividing an input into smaller units.

Industrial cluster A geographical concentration of related businesses and institutions.

Industrial sector A grouping of industries producing similar products or services.

Industry A group of firms producing a particular product or service.

Inelastic demand If demand is (price) inelastic, then any change will cause the quantity demanded to change by a proportionately smaller amount. (Ignoring the negative sign) it will have a value less than 1.

Infant industry An industry which has a potential comparative advantage, but which is as yet too underdeveloped to be able to realise this potential.

Inferior goods Goods whose demand falls as people's incomes rise. Such goods have a negative income elasticity of demand.

Information asymmetry A situation in which one party in an economic relationship knows more than another.

Infrastructure (industry's) The network of supply agents, communications, skills, training facilities, distribution channels, specialised financial services, etc. that support a particular industry.

Injections (J) Expenditure on the production of domestic firms coming from outside the inner flow of the circular flow of income. Injections equal investment (I) plus government expenditure (G) plus expenditure on exports (X).

Interdependence (under oligopoly) One of the two key features of oligopoly. Each firm will be affected by its rivals' decisions. Likewise its decisions will affect its rivals. Firms recognise this interdependence. This recognition will affect their decisions.

Internal expansion Where a business adds to its productive capacity by adding to existing or by building new plant.

International harmonisation of economic policies Where countries attempt to coordinate their macroeconomic policies so as to achieve common goals.

Inter-temporal pricing The practice of charging different prices at different times (of the day, week, year, etc.). It occurs where different groups have different price elasticities of demand for a product at different points in time.

Joint-stock company A company where ownership is distributed between shareholders.

Joint venture Where two or more firms set up and jointly own a new independent firm.

Just-in-time methods Where a firm purchases supplies and produces both components and finished products as they are required. This minimises stock holding and its associated costs.

Kinked demand theory The theory that oligopolists face a demand curve that is kinked at the current price: demand being significantly more elastic above the current price than below. The effect of this is to create a situation of price stability.

Labour All forms of human input, both physical and mental, into current production.

Labour force The number employed plus the number unemployed.

Land and raw materials Inputs into production that are provided by nature: e.g. unimproved land and mineral deposits in the ground.

Law of comparative advantage Trade can benefit all countries if they specialise in the goods in which they have a comparative advantage.

Law of demand The quantity of a good demanded per period of time will fall as the price rises and rise as the price falls, other things being equal (*ceteris paribus*).

Law of diminishing (marginal) returns When one or more inputs are held fixed, there will come a point beyond which the extra output from additional units of the variable input will diminish.

Law of large numbers The larger the number of events of a particular type, the more predictable will be their average outcome.

Leading indicators Indicators that help predict future trends in the economy.

Lender of last resort The role of the Bank of England as the guarantor of sufficient liquidity in the monetary system.

Licensing Where the owner of a patented product allows another firm to produce it for a fee.

Limited liability Where the liability of the owners for the debts of a company is limited to the amount they have invested in it.

Liquidity ratio The ratio of liquid assets (cash and assets that can be readily converted to cash) to total deposits.

Liquidity trap When interest rates are at their floor and thus any further increases in money supply will not be spent but merely be held in bank accounts as people wait for the economy to recover and/or interest rates to rise.

Lock-outs Union members are temporarily laid off until they are prepared to agree to the firm's conditions.

Logistics The business of managing and handling inputs to and outputs from a firm.

Long run The period of time long enough for all inputs to be varied.

Long run under perfect competition The period of time which is long enough for new firms to enter the industry.

Long-run average cost curve A curve that shows how average cost varies with output on the assumption that all factors are variable.

Long-term incentive plan (LTIP) A reward system aimed at improving long-term performance, whereby shares of cash bonuses are paid out if performance meets certain targets/criteria over a longer period of time, typically three years.

Loss-leader A product whose price is cut by a business in order to attract custom.

M0 Cash plus banks' balances with the Bank of England. Note that this definition of narrow money is no longer used (see **cash in circulation** for the current measure of narrow money).

M3 (in eurozone and elsewhere) Cash outside the banks, bank deposits and various other assets that can be relatively easily turned into cash without loss.

M4 (in UK) Cash outside the banks plus all bank and building society deposits (including cash).

M-form business organisation One in which the business is organised into separate departments, such that responsibility for the day-to-day management of the enterprise is separated from the formulation of the business's strategic plan.

Marginal benefits The additional benefits of doing a little bit more (or *1 unit* more if a unit can be measured) of an activity.

Marginal cost (MC) The cost of producing one more unit of output: $MC = \Delta TC/\Delta Q$.

Marginal costs The additional cost of doing a little bit more (or *1 unit* more if a unit can be measured) of an activity.

Marginal revenue (MR) The extra revenue gained by selling one or more unit per time period: $MR = \Delta TR/\Delta Q$.

Marginal revenue product of labour The extra revenue a firm earns from employing one more unit of labour.

Marginal social benefit (MSB) The additional benefit gained by society of producing or consuming one more unit of a good.

Marginal social cost (MSC) The additional cost incurred by society of producing or consuming one more unit of a good.

Marginal utility (MU) The extra satisfaction gained from consuming one extra unit of a good within a given time period.

Market The interaction between buyers and sellers.

Market clearing A market clears when supply matches demand, leaving no shortage or surplus.

Market demand schedule A table showing the different total quantities of a good that consumers are willing and able to buy at various prices over a given period of time.

Market experiments Information gathered about consumers under artificial or simulated conditions. A method used widely in assessing the effects of advertising on consumers.

Market niche A part of a market (or new market) that has not been filled by an existing brand or business.

Market surveys Information gathered about consumers, usually via a questionnaire, that attempts to enhance the business's understanding of consumer behaviour.

Marketing mix The mix of product, price, place (distribution) and promotion that will determine a business's marketing strategy.

Maximum price A price ceiling set by the government or some other agency. The price is not allowed to rise above this level (although it is allowed to fall below it).

Merger The outcome of a mutual agreement made by two firms to combine their business activities.

Merit goods Goods which the government feels that people will underconsume and which therefore ought to be subsidised or provided free.

Minimum price A price floor set by the government or some other agency. The price is not allowed to fall below this level (although it is allowed to rise above it).

Mobility of labour The ease with which labour can either shift between jobs (occupational mobility) or move to other parts of the country in search of work (geographical mobility).

Monetary policy Policy to affect aggregate demand by central bank action to alter interest rates or money supply.

Monopolistic competition A market structure where, like perfect competition, there are many firms and freedom of entry into the industry, but where each firm produces a differentiated product and thus has some control over its price.

Monopoly A market structure where there is only one firm in the industry.

Monopsony A market with a single buyer or employer.

Moral hazard Following a deal, if there are information asymmetries, it is likely that one party will engage in problematic (immoral and/or hazardous) behaviour to the detriment of the other. In other words, lack of information by one party to the deal may result in the deal not being honoured by the other party.

Multinational (or transnational) corporations Businesses that either own or control foreign subsidiaries in more than one country.

Multiplier The number of times a rise in GDP (ΔY) is bigger than the initial rise in aggregate expenditure (ΔE) that caused it. Using the letter k to stand for the multiplier, the multiplier is defined as $k = \Delta Y/\Delta E$.

Multiplier effect An initial increase in aggregate demand of £xm leads to an eventual rise in GDP that is greater than £xm.

Multiplier formula The formula for the multiplier is $k = 1/(1 - mpc_d)$.

Nash equilibrium The position resulting from everyone making their optimal decision based on their assumptions about their rivals' decisions. Without collusion, there is no incentive to move from this position.

Nationalised industries State-owned industries that produce goods or services that are sold in the market.

Natural monopoly A situation where long-run average costs would be lower if an industry were under monopoly than if it were shared between two or more competitors.

Net errors and omissions A statistical adjustment to ensure that the two sides of the balance of payments account balance. It is necessary because of errors in compiling the statistics.

Network An informal arrangement between businesses to work together towards some common goal.

Network economies The benefits to consumers of having a network of other people using the same product or service.

Non-collusive oligopoly When oligopolists have no agreement between themselves – formal, informal or tacit.

Non-excludability Where it is not possible to provide a good or service to one person without it thereby being available for others to enjoy.

Non-price competition Competition in terms of product promotion (advertising, packaging, etc.) or product development.

Non-rivalry Where the consumption of a good or service by one person will not prevent others from enjoying it.

Normal goods Goods whose demand increases as consumer incomes increase. They have a positive income elasticity of demand. Luxury goods will have a higher income elasticity of demand than more basic goods.

Normal profit The opportunity cost of being in business. It consists of the interest that could be earned on a riskless asset, plus a return for risk taking in this particular industry. It is counted as a cost of production.

Number unemployed (economist's definition) Those of working age, who are without work, but who are available for work at current wage rates.

Numerical flexibility Where employers can change the size of their workforce as their labour requirements change.

Observations of market behaviour Information gathered about consumers from the day-to-day activities of the business within the market.

Oligopoly A market structure where there are few enough firms to enable barriers to be erected against the entry of new firms.

Oligopsony A market with just a few buyers. This will give such firms power to drive down the prices they pay to suppliers. It can also refer to employers with market power in employing labour.

Open-market operations The sale (or purchase) by the authorities of government securities in the open market in order to reduce (or increase) money supply.

Opportunity cost The cost of any activity measured in terms of the best alternative foregone.

Organisational slack When managers allow spare capacity to exist, thereby enabling them to respond more easily to changed circumstances.

Overheads Costs arising from the general running of an organisation, and only indirectly related to the level of output.

Peak-load pricing The practice of charging higher prices at times when demand is highest because the demand of many consumers (e.g. commuters) is less elastic and the constraints on capacity lead to higher marginal costs.

Perfectly competitive market A market in which all producers and consumers of the product are price takers.

PEST (or STEEPLE) analysis Where the political, economic, social and technological factors shaping a business environment are assessed by a business so as to devise future business strategy. STEEPLE analysis would also take into account ethical, legal and environmental factors.

Picketing Where people on strike gather at the entrance to the firm and attempt to dissuade workers or delivery vehicles from entering.

Plant economies of scale Economies of scale that arise because of the large size of the factory.

Preferential trading arrangements A trading arrangement whereby trade between the signatories is freer than trade with the rest of the world.

Price-cap regulation Where the regulator puts a ceiling on the amount by which a firm can raise its price.

Price discrimination Where a firm sells the same product at different prices in different markets for reasons unrelated to costs.

Price elasticity of demand A measure of the responsiveness of quantity demanded to a change in price.

Price elasticity of supply   The responsiveness of quantity supplied to a change in price: the proportionate change in quantity supplied divided by the proportionate change in price.

Price leadership   When firms (the followers) choose the same price as that set by one of the firms in the industry (the leader). The leader will normally be the largest firm.

Price mechanism   The system in a market economy whereby changes in price, in response to changes in demand and supply, have the effect of making demand equal to supply.

Price taker   A person or firm with no power to be able to influence the market price.

Primary labour market   The market for permanent full-time core workers.

Primary market in capital   Where shares are sold by the issuer of the shares (i.e. the firm) and where, therefore, finance is channelled directly from the purchasers (i.e. the shareholders) to the firm.

Primary production   The production and extraction of natural resources, plus agriculture.

Principal–agent problem   One where people (principals), as a result of lack of knowledge, cannot ensure that their best interests are served by their agents.

Prisoners' dilemma   Where two or more firms (or people), by attempting independently to choose the best strategy for whatever the other(s) are likely to do, end up in a worse position than if they had co-operated in the first place.

Privatisation   Selling nationalised industries to the private sector. This may be through the public issue of shares, by a management buyout or by selling it to a private company.

Product differentiation   Where a firm's product is in some way distinct from its rivals' products. In the context of growth strategies, this is where a business upgrades existing products or services so as to make them different from those of rival firms.

Production   The transformation of inputs into outputs by firms in order to earn profit (or meet some other objective).

Productive efficiency   A situation where firms are producing the maximum output for a given amount of inputs, or producing a given output at the least cost.

Productivity deal   Where, in return for a wage increase, a union agrees to changes in working practices that will increase output per worker.

Profit-maximising rule   Profit is maximised where marginal revenue equals marginal cost.

Profit satisficing   Where decision makers in a firm aim for a target level of profit rather than the absolute maximum level.

Public good   A good or service which has the features of non-rivalry and non-excludability and as a result would not be provided by the free market.

Public sector net cash requirement (PSNCR)   The (annual) deficit of the public sector (central government, local government and public corporations), and thus the amount that the public sector must borrow.

Pure fiscal policy   Fiscal policy which does not involve any change in money supply.

Quantitative easing   A deliberate attempt by the central bank to increase the money supply by buying large quantities of securities through open-market operations.

Quantity demanded   The amount of a good that a consumer is willing and able to buy at a given price over a given period of time.

Quota (set by a cartel)   The output that a given member of a cartel is allowed to produce (production quota) or sell (sales quota).

Random walk   Where fluctuations in the value of a share away from its 'correct' value are random. When charted over time, these share price movements would appear like a 'random walk' – like the path of someone staggering along drunk!

Rate of economic growth   The percentage increase in output over a 12-month period.

Rate of inflation   The percentage increase in prices over a 12-month period.

Rate of unemployment   The number unemployed expressed as a percentage of the total workforce (i.e. those employed and those unemployed).

Rational choices   Choices that involve weighing up the benefit of any activity against its opportunity cost.

Rational consumer behaviour   When consumers weigh up the marginal utility they expect to gain from a product they are considering purchasing against the product's price (i.e. the marginal cost to them). By buying more of a product whose marginal utility exceeds the price and buying less of a product whose price exceeds marginal utility, the consumer will maximise consumer surplus.

Rationalisation   The reorganising of production (often after a merger) so as to cut out waste and duplication and generally to reduce costs.

Real growth values   Values of the rate of growth in GDP or any other variable after taking inflation into account. The real value of the growth in a variable equals its growth in money (or 'nominal') value minus the rate of inflation.

Real-wage unemployment   Disequilibrium unemployment caused by real wages being driven up above the market-clearing level.

Recession   A period of falling GDP, i.e. of negative economic growth. Officially, a recession is where this occurs for two quarters or more.

Regional unemployment   Structural unemployment occurring in specific regions of the country.

Regulatory capture   Where the regulator is persuaded to operate in the industry's interests rather than those of the consumer.

Repeated or extensive-form games   Games that involve two or more moves. Games can either be repeated an infinite number of times or can be repeated a set number of times.

Replacement costs   What the firm would have to pay to replace inputs it currently owns.

Resale price maintenance   Where the manufacturer of a product (legally) insists that the product should be sold at a specified retail price.

Revaluation   Where the government or central bank re-pegs the exchange rate at a higher level.

Risk   This is when an outcome may or may not occur, but where the probability of its occurring is known.

Sale and repurchase agreement (repo)   An agreement between two financial institutions whereby one in effect borrows from another by selling some of its assets, agreeing to buy them back (repurchase them) at a fixed price and on a fixed date.

Sales revenue maximisation   An alternative theory of the firm which assumes that managers aim to maximise the firm's short-run total revenue.

Scarcity   The excess of human wants over what can actually be produced to fulfil these wants.

Seasonal unemployment   Unemployment associated with industries or regions where the demand for labour is lower at certain times of the year.

Secondary labour market   The market for peripheral workers, usually employed on a temporary or part-time basis, or a less secure 'permanent' basis.

Secondary market in capital   Where shareholders sell shares to others. This is thus a market in 'second-hand' shares.

Secondary production   The production from manufacturing and construction sectors of the economy.

Self-fulfilling speculation   The actions of speculators tend to cause the very effect that they had anticipated.

Senile industry   An industry which has a potential comparative advantage but has become run down and so can no longer compete effectively.

Share (or stock) options   The right to buy shares in the future at a fixed price set today. When granted to senior executives as a reward they do not involve any outlay by the company. They act as an incentive, however, since the better the company performs, the more the market value of its shares is likely to rise above the option price and the more the executive stands to gain by exercising the option to buy shares at the fixed price and then selling them at the market price.

Short run The period of time over which at least one input is fixed.

Short-run shut-down point This is where the *AR* curve is tangential to the *AVC* curve. The firm can only just cover its variable costs. Any fall in revenue below this level will cause a profit-maximising firm to shut down immediately.

Short run under perfect competition The period during which there is too little time for new firms to enter the industry.

Short-termism Where firms and investors take decisions based on the likely short-term performance of a company, rather than on its long-term prospects. Firms may thus sacrifice long-term profits and growth for the sake of quick return.

Simultaneous game Where each player (e.g. each firm) makes its decision at the same time and is therefore unable to respond to other players' moves.

Single-move or one-shot game Where each player (e.g. each firm) makes just one decision (or move) and then the 'game' is over.

Social benefit Private benefit plus externalities in consumption.

Social cost Private cost plus externalities in production.

Social efficiency Production and consumption at the point where $MSB = MSC$.

Sovereign risk (for business) The risk that a foreign country's government or central bank will make its policies less favourable. Such policies could involve changes in interest rates or tax regimes, the imposition of foreign exchange controls, or even defaulting on loans or the appropriation of a business's assets.

Specialisation and division of labour Where production is broken down into a number of simpler, more specialised tasks, thus allowing workers to acquire a high degree of efficiency.

Speculation This is where people make buying or selling decisions based on their anticipations of future prices.

Spreading risks (for an insurance company) The more policies an insurance company issues and the more independent the risks of claims from these policies are, the more predictable will be the number of claims.

Stabilising speculation A situation where the actions of speculators cause demand and/or supply curves to shift in the opposite direction from which they have recently shifted. This causes price to change back again.

Stakeholder An individual affected by the operations of a business.

Stakeholders (in a company) People who are affected by a company's activities and/or performance (customers, employees, owners, creditors, people living in the neighbourhood, etc.). They may or may not be in a position to take decisions, or influence decision taking, in the firm.

Standard Industrial Classification (SIC) The name given to the formal classification of firms into industries used by the government in order to collect data on business and industry trends.

Standardised unemployment rate The measure of the unemployment rate used by the ILO and OECD. The unemployed are defined as people of working age who are without work, available for work and actively seeking employment.

STEEPLE analysis Where the social, technological, economic, ethical, political, legal and environmental factors shaping a business environment are assessed by a business so as to devise future business strategy. (See also **PEST analysis**.)

Stock appreciation rights (SARs) Automatic bonuses linked to rises in the company's stock market price.

Stock (or share) options The right to buy shares in the future at a fixed price set today. When granted to senior executives as a reward they do not involve any outlay by the company. They act as an incentive, however, since the better the company performs, the more the market value of its shares is likely to rise above the option price and the more the executive stands to gain by exercising the option to buy shares at the fixed price and then selling them at the market price.

Strategic alliance Where two firms work together, formally or informally, to achieve a mutually desirable goal.

Strategic management The management of the strategic long-term decisions and activities of the business.

Strategic trade theory The theory that protecting/supporting certain industries can enable them to compete more effectively with large monopolistic rivals abroad. The effect of the protection is to increase long-run competition and may enable the protected firms to exploit a comparative advantage that they could not have done otherwise.

Structural unemployment Unemployment that arises from changes in the pattern of demand or supply in the economy. People made redundant in one part of the economy cannot immediately take up jobs in other parts (even though there are vacancies).

Subcontracting Where a firm employs another firm to produce part of its output or some of its input(s).

Substitute goods A pair of goods which are considered by consumers to be alternatives to each other. As the price of one goes up, the demand for the other rises.

Substitutes in supply These are two goods where an increased production of one means diverting resources away from producing the other.

Substitution effect The effect of a change in price on quantity demanded arising from the consumer switching to or from alternative (substitute) products.

Supernormal profit The excess of total profit above normal profit.

Supply chain The flow of inputs into a finished product from the raw materials stage, through manufacturing and distribution right through to the sale to the final consumer.

Supply curve A graph showing the relationship between the price of a good and the quantity of the good supplied over a given period of time.

Supply schedule A table showing the different quantities of a good that producers are willing and able to supply at various prices over a given time period. A supply schedule can be for an individual producer or group of producers, or for all producers (the market supply schedule).

Supply-side policy Policy to affect aggregate supply directly.

Tacit collusion When oligopolists take care not to engage in price cutting, excessive advertising or other forms of competition. There may be unwritten 'rules' of collusive behaviour such as price leadership.

Takeover (or acquisition) Where one business acquires another. A takeover may not necessarily involve mutual agreement between the two parties. In such cases, the takeover might be viewed as 'hostile'.

Takeover constraint The effect that the fear of being taken over has on a firm's willingness to undertake projects that reduce distributed profits.

Tapered vertical integration Where a firm is partially integrated with an earlier stage of production; where it produces *some* of an input itself and buys some from another firm.

Tariffs Taxes (customs duties) on imports. These could be a percentage of the value of the good (an 'ad valorem' tariff), or a fixed amount per unit (a 'specific' tariff).

Taylor rule A rule adopted by a central bank for setting the rate of interest. It will raise the interest rate if (a) inflation is above target or (b) economic growth is above the sustainable level (or unemployment below the equilibrium rate). The rule states how much interest rates will be changed in each case. In other words a relative weighting is attached to each of these two objectives.

Technological unemployment Structural unemployment that occurs as a result of the introduction of labour-saving technology.

Technology transfer Where a host state benefits from the new technology that an MNC brings with its investment.

Terms of trade The price index of exports divided by the price index of imports and then expressed as a percentage. This means that the terms of trade will be 100 in the base year.

Tertiary production   The production from the service sector of the economy.

Third-degree price discrimination   When a firm divides consumers into different groups and charges a different price to consumers in the different groups, but the same price to all consumers within a group.

Tit-for-tat strategy   A strategy where you copy whatever your rival does. Thus if your rival cuts price, you will too. If your rival does not, neither will you. If the rival knows this, it will be less likely to make an initial aggressive move.

Total consumer expenditure (TE) **(per period)**   The price of the product multiplied by the quantity purchased: $TE = P \times Q$.

Total cost (TC) **(per period)**   The sum of total fixed costs (*TFC*) and total variable costs (*TVC*): $TC = TFC + TVC$.

Total revenue (TR) **(per period)**   The total amount received by firms from the sale of a product, before the deduction of taxes or any other costs. The price multiplied by the quantity sold: $TR = P \times Q$.

Tradable permits   Each firm is given a permit to produce a given level of pollution. If less than the permitted amount is produced, the firm is given a credit. This can then be sold to another firm, allowing it to exceed its original limit. This is known as a 'cap and trade' scheme.

Transactions costs   The costs associated with exchanging products. For buyers it is the costs over and above the price of the product. For sellers it is the costs over and above the costs of production.

Transfer payments   Moneys transferred from one person or group to another (e.g. from the government to individuals) without production taking place.

Transfer pricing   The pricing system used within a business to transfer intermediate products between its various divisions, often in different countries.

Transnational (or multinational) corporations   Businesses that either own or control foreign subsidiaries in more than one country.

U-form business organisation   One in which the central organisation of the firm (the chief executive or a managerial team) is responsible both for the firm's day-to-day administration and for formulating its business strategy.

Uncertainty   This is when an outcome may or may not occur and where its probability of occurring is not known.

Underemployment   Those working fewer hours than they would like to work: e.g. where part-time workers would like to work full time or more part-time hours.

Unemployment rate   The number unemployed expressed as a percentage of the labour force.

Unit elasticity   When the price elasticity of demand is unity, this is where quantity demanded changes by the same proportion as the price. Price elasticity is equal to −1.

Value chain   The stages or activities that help to create product value.

Variable costs   Total costs that do vary with the amount of output produced.

Variable input   An input that can be increased in supply within a given time period.

Vertical integration   A business growth strategy that involves expanding within an existing market, but at a different stage of production. Vertical integration can be 'forward', such as moving into distribution or retail, or 'backward', such as expanding into extracting raw materials or producing components.

Vertical merger   Where two firms in the same industry at different stages in the production process merge.

Vertically integrated firm   A firm that produces at more than one stage in the production and distribution of a product.

Vertically integrated multinational   A multinational that undertakes the various stages of production for a given product in different countries.

Wage taker   The wage rate is determined by market forces.

Withdrawals (W)**(or leakages)**   Incomes of households or firms that are not passed on round the inner flow. Withdrawals equal net saving (*S*) plus net taxes (*T*) plus import expenditure (*M*): $W = S + T + M$.

Working to rule   Workers do no more than they are supposed to, as set out in their job descriptions.

Index

absolute advantage 328
acid test ratio 154
acquisitions. *see* mergers
    and acquisitions
adverse selection 59, 62, 216
advertising 72–4, 76–9
  and developing countries 336
  and the economy 77
  global growth 72
  John Lewis 6
  newspapers 72
Advisory Conciliation and Arbitration
    Service (ACAS) 204
Africa 193–4
  advantages 194
  agent (*see* principal–agent problem)
  connectivity 194
  financial institutions 194
  foreign direct investment 180–1, 183
  GDP 193
  growth 194
  Internet 193–4
  internet penetration 194
  logistics 194
  trade zones 193
  world trade 327–8
African Continental Free Trade Area
    (AfCFTA) 194
aggregate demand 260, 265–6
  labour 281
aggregate supply 266
  of labour 281
agriculture
  protection 342
  subsidies 341
Ahold 189
Airbus Consortium 335–6
aircraft industry 131–2, 339–0
airline industry 13–5, 126–7, 163–4
  Africa 194
  and macroeconomy 289–0
  strikes 205, 206
alcohol 51
Aldi 5
allocative efficiency 106
alternative aims 134–8

Amazon 105, 116, 160
  robotics 117
America first 336
analytical talent 219
animal testing 232
Apple 20, 121
Argentina 297, 340
artificial intelligence 219
Asda 184
Asia 182, 327
Asia-Pacific Economic Co-operation
    (APEC) 344
asset stripping 161
asset turnover ratio 154
assets and the financial account 356
asymmetric information. *see under*
    information
AT&T 159–0
Audi 78
austerity 205
Australia 61, 123
automation 178
  labour substitution 201
average (total) cost 85, 86
average cost of labour 203
average cost pricing 139
average fixed cost (AFC) 85, 86
average revenue 98–0
average variable cost (AVC) 85, 87

B2B and B2C e-commerce 104
backwards induction 132
bailouts 297
balance of payments 191, 259, 355–8
  capital account 355
  current account 355
  deficits 356–7
  errors 356
  financial account 355–6
balance of trade 355
'bandwagon' effects 273
bank (or deposits) multiplier 277
Bank of England
  Inflation Report 308–9
  lender of last resort 306
  quantitative easing 313

bankruptcy 166, 287
banks/banking
  labour-saving technical progress
    (*see also* financial crisis)
barometric forecasting 70
barriers to entry. *see* entry barriers
beef 340
behavioural economics 63–6, 137–8
behavioural theories of the firm 136
Belgium 162, 180, 208, 369
benchmarking 218
bid rigging 245
big data 219
bilateral monopoly 204
biotechnology industry 91
bitcoin 49–0
Black Wednesday 371
Body Shop 232
Boeing 132–3
bonuses 215
borrowing 362
bounded rationality 63–4
BP 7, 49, 205
Bradford and Bingley 313
Brazil 232–3
Bretton Woods system 363
Brexit 347–8, 349–2
  bilateral agreements 349
  circus 352
  divorce bill 350
  Emissions Trading Scheme 240
  hard Brexit 349–0
  inward investment 191, 372
  Irish backstop 350
  mergers and acquisitions 182
  negotiating objectives 350
  Norwegian model 349
  Political Declaration 351
  sterling exchange rate 89, 356, 364–5
  tariffs 186
  UK economy 351
  uncertainty 161–2
  Withdrawal Agreement 350–1
bribes 338
BRICS 327
British Business Bank 171

BT 120
bubbles 49–0
budget deficits and surpluses 295
business
    activity and circular flow of income
        260–4
        determination of 264–0
    cycle 271–5
        fluctuations 272–5
        interest rates 275–0
        and public finances 296
    ethics 228
    and the euro 371–5
    growth 145–4
    organisation 6–1
    strategy and the global economy
        183–9
buy-to-let 41
buyers bargaining power 147
by-products 90
bygones principle 84

Cadbury 164, 175
call centres 185
Canada 51, 169, 331, 340–4 350, 376
capital 21
capital controls 369–0
capital equipment 70, 85, 90, 148, 159, 213,
        273, 298, 328
capital flows 368–9
car industry, Germany 332
carbon trading 239–0
career breaks 213
Caribbean 183
Carrefour 189
cartels 122
cash in circulation 276
Casino 189
casual workers 210
celebrities 64
central banks
    exchange rates 362
    inflation 259
    QE (see quantitative easing)
certainty 362
charities 226, 228
Chile 370
China
    capital inflows 369
    comparative advantage 330
    education 330, 331
    foreign direct investment 183, 189
    labour costs 330
    manufacturing 330
    minimum wages 208
    regulation 234
    steel industry 334
    world trade 327–8

choice, jam tasting 63
choices, economic 22–3
Chrysler 184
circular flow of income 260–4
    injections 262–3
        export expenditure 263
        government expenditure 263
        investment 262–3
    inner flow 261–2
    withdrawals 262–3
        import expenditure 262
        net savings 262
        net taxes 262
        transfer payments 262
climate change 237–8
clothes 330
cloud computing 91
clusters 94–5
co-operatives 7
Coalition government
    austerity policies 300–1
Coca-Cola 190
coffee industry 28
collective bargaining 204
collusion
    factors favourable to 123
    tacit 123
    tendering 245
collusive oligopoly 122
command-and-control (CAC) systems 239
commission 215
commodity prices, Africa 193
common markets 343
companies 7
comparative advantage 329–0
    China, USA, Germany 331
Compare the Meerkat 73
competition 332
    degree of 112
    in EU 345–6
    imperfectly competitive markets 111–6
    perfect (see perfect competition)
    policy and business behaviour 244–0
    price and revenue 47
    substitute goods 30
Competition and Markets Authority
        (CMA) 126, 234, 248–9
competition for corporate control 119
competitive advantage
    five forces model 146–8
    of nations 332
competitive rivalry 147–8
complementary goods 30
complementers 148
conciliation 204, 206
confidence 299
congestion, urban traffic 242–3
Conservative government 302–3

consortia 164
constant returns to scale 89
consumer behaviour 56–2, 230–1
consumer co-operatives 7
consumer prices index (CPI) 284
consumer spending of domestically
        produced goods 260
consumer surplus 57
consumers
    and alternative aims 137
    and the euro 372
    irrational 137–8
    willingness to pay 140
consumption 21
    adjustment delay 44
    proportion of income 43–4
contact costs 93
container principle 90
core competencies 152
corporate responsibility 228–3
cost-based pricing 139
cost leadership 150–1
cost-push inflation 288, 307
costs of production 33
    long-run 82, 89–8
    short-run 82–9
credit cards 276
credit crunch. see financial crisis
creditor days 154
cross-price elasticity of demand 46, 47–8
crowding 225
Cuba 336
cultural factors in business environment 12
currency
    demand and supply 360
    exchange rates (see exchange rates)
current ratio 154
customers
    global businesses 190
customs delays 333
customs unions 341, 343
cyclical fluctuations 70
Cyprus 371

Davies Report 214
de Beers 117
de-industrialisation 15
debt-to-equity ratio 155
debtor days 154
decision trees 133
decline stage of product life cycle 142–3,
        188
decreasing returns to scale 89
deflation 259, 284–5, 287
Dell 148
demand 21–2, 27–2, 55–0, 201
    change in 32
    change in quantity demanded 32

elastic and inelastic 43–6
estimating and predicting 66–1
and the firm 55–6
home market 332
schedule for an individual 29
for shares 38–9
stimulating 71–9
demand and supply curves 35–7
demand curves 28–9
and advertising 76–7
for firm 57
for individual 57
demand management policy 294. *see also*
fiscal policy
demand-pull inflation 285–8
demographics 41
demonstration effect 191
Denmark 371
derived demand 201
design characteristics 74
destabilising speculation 50
devaluation 363
developed countries,
world trade 327
developing countries,
world trade 327
differentiation 150, 151–2
diminishing marginal utility 56
diseconomies of scale 91–2
Disney 9, 140, 163, 229
disposable incomes 298
diversification 75, 157, 159
dividend yield 39
dividends 7, 9, 39, 156, 217
division of labour 90
divorce of ownership from control 9
Doha Round 342
dominant strategy games 128
drip pricing 138
dumping 333–4
Dyson 162

e-commerce 104–5
easyJet 39, 150, 291
eBay 104
economic and monetary union 371
Economic Community of West African
States (ECOWAS) 344
economic factors in business
environment 11
airline industry 14
economic globalisation 176
economic growth 258
rate 258
economies of scale 90–1
multinationals 185
economies of scope 91–2
economist's approach to business 20

Ecuador 378
education
earnings, productivity and 218
strikes 206
efficiency wage hypothesis 215
efficiency wage rate 215
elasticity of demand and supply 42–1
elasticity of market supply of labour 198
electricity generation 87
elimination of waste 212
emotions 63, 65
empire building 161
employees. *see also* labour
reward 138
employers. *see also* labour
flexibility 210–2
multinationals 191
employment
law 199
and unions 203–4
energy sector 126–7
entrepreneurship 169–1
attitudes 170–1
EU policy 171
UK policy 171
entry barriers 112, 116–7
brand loyalty 117
control of inputs 117
control of outlets 117
economies of scope 116–7
lower costs 117
product differentiation 117
supermarkets 125
vertical integration 158
environmental issues 235–3
airline industry 14
in business environment 12
John Lewis 5
multinationals 192
tradeable permits 239–1
environmental scanning 228
equilibrium. *see also* fiscal policy
definition of 27, 35
employment 281
GDP 264
national income 266
price 35–7, 266
rate of interest 279–0
Essilor 160
Estonia 371
ethical factors in business 12
Europe, world trade 327–328
European Central Bank 309, 310, 371
and Fed 313
independence 372
Outright Monetary Transactions 312–3
quantitative easing 313
Securities Market Programme 312

European Commission 120, 240
European Court of Justice 302
European Union
adverse regional effects 346
barrier reductions 345
caps on executive pay 218
carbon trading 239
competition 345
competition law 244–5
credit crunch 301
depressed areas 346
economic and monetary union 370–5
economies of scale 345
Emission Unit Allowances (EAUs)
239–0
environmental regulations 239
euro 181, 348, 371–5
European Stability Mechanism
(ESM) 301
eurozone (*see* eurozone)
exchange rate mechanism (ERM) 363,
370–1
fiscal compact 301
fiscal policy 301–2
GM crops 340
impact of new member states 348
Internal Market Scoreboard 346
International Monetary Fund (IMF) 377
M&A activity 182
Marker Stability Reserve 240
minimum wages 207–8
monopolies 346
oligopolies 346
single market 181, 345–8, 369
sovereignty 346
Stability and Growth Compact
(SGP) 301
tariffs 346
Tobin tax 370
trade creation 345
USA trade disputes 338, 342
eurozone
euro/dollar seesaw 365–7
European Central Bank (*see* European
Central Bank)
exchange controls 319, 365
exchange rate index 358
exchange rates 259, 358–7
and balance of payments 361
Bretton Woods system 363
fixed 362–3
managing 361–3
in practice 363
Tobin tax 369–0
excludability 225
exclusionary abuses 246
executive pay 216–8
exit costs 142, 148

expectations: prices 30, 34, 39
explicit costs 83
exploitation 246
exports 260
external benefits 222, 224
  in consumption 224
external business environment 11–9
external costs 222
  in consumption 224
  produced by business 223
external diseconomies of scale 92
external expansion 155
externalities 222–3, 241–2
  and free trade 336
Exxon Mobil (Esso) 184

Facebook 73
factors of production 20
fairness 235, 341
farming. see agriculture
fast food 114
Fiat 184
film industry 95
finance
  deregulation 126, 181
  sources of business 165–6
Financial Conduct Authority (FCA) 60
financial crisis 260
  credit crunch: cause and responses 311
  and euro 372
  foreign direct investment 179
  government spending 298
  John Lewis 5
  M&A activity 183
  sub-prime market 311–2
financial economies 91
financial flexibility 210
financial stability 260
financial well-being 259–0
fine-tuning of demand 295
fines 231, 239
firms
  aims (see alternative aims; growth of
    firm; profit maximisation)
fiscal policy 293, 295–3
  discretionary 298
  effectiveness of 298–9
  imperfect information 300
  rules 300–3
  stabilisers 297
  time lags 299–0
fiscal stance 295
fixed costs 84, 87
fixed inputs 82
flat organisations 8
flexible firms 19, 210–2
floating exchange rates 361
focus 150, 152

football 120
foreign direct investment (FDI) 179–1
  China 330
  host state 191, 192
  product life cycle 188
  USA 330
foreign markets 190
four Ps 75
Foxconn 330
France
  congestion 243
franchising 164
free markets 26–8
free-rider problem 225
free trade areas 341, 343
functional flexibility 210, 212

G7 376
G8 378
G20 342, 376
game theory 127–4
  in negotiations 204
  prisoners' dilemma 129–0
games consoles 147
Gap 185
gearing ratio 154–5
gender pay gap 212–4
General Agreement on Tariffs and Trade
  (GATT) 341
general government debt 296
Germany
  reunification 370–1
  world trade 327–8
gig economy 199
gilts 278
glass ceiling 214
Global Entrepreneurship Monitor (GEM)
  169–0
global financial environment 354–9
global financial flows, growth of 368–0
global income 338
global trading environment 325–3
global warming 223, 235, 237–9
globalisation 176–7, 375–8
  benefits 176
  costs 176–7
GM crops 340
Goodhart's Law 307
goods
  demand 201
  in joint supply 34
  public 225
  and world trade 326–7
Google 73, 160, 247–8
government
  environmental policy 235–3
  and externalities 223
  macroeconomic policy 260, 293–4

  protecting people's interests 227
  provision 235
government intervention 60, 221–5
government spending (G) 260
Great Depression (1930s) 295
greatest benefit relative to cost 23
Greece 297, 312, 371, 373–4, 377
grim trigger strategy 131
Groceries Code Adjudicator 125
gross domestic product 15–6, 261
gross profit margin 153
groupthink 64
growth of firm 155–3
  maximisation 135
growth stage of product life cycle 142, 188
growth vector matrix 74–5
guarantees 60, 74

Häagen-Dazs ice cream 152
handling costs 94
happiness 270
herding 64
heuristics 63, 137
historic costs 84
historical legacy 213
holding companies 8
Holland 357
Hollywood 94–5
Honda 186
Hong Kong 172, 181, 188, 219
horizontal mergers 159
hot money 357
Hotel Chocolat 172–3
hotel industry 271
house prices 40–1
household income 261
human capital model 218
human resource management 149
Hungary 377
hunger games 132
hyperinflation 287
hypermarkets 189

IBM 150
Iceland 377
Ikea 152
imperfect competition 113
imperfect information. see under
  information
implicit costs 84
import substitution 191
imports, and competition 330–1
incentives
  CEOs 217
  principal–agent relationship 10
income 261
income effect 28, 30, 193
income elasticity of demand 46

income tax 262, 286, 297, 317
increasing returns to scale 89
India 189
indivisibilities 90
industrial action 204–7
industrial classification 15–7
industrial concentration 17
industry's infrastructure 92
inelastic demand 43–6
infant industries 334
inferior goods 30, 46
inflation 259, 284–9
    causes of 285–9
    expectations and 289
    rate 259, 285
    target rate 307
influencers 64
information
    asymmetric 10, 59, 216, 227
    government: provision of 235
    imperfect 58, 227
        advertising 77
    reducing competition by exchange
        of 245
infrastructure, of firm 149
innovation
    advertising 77, 79, 110
    businesses 99, 169, 171, 185, 248, 345
    and economy 19, 219, 321, 323
    location 94, 96
    patents 117
    products 71, 77, 78, 79, 110, 142, 150
insurance 58–2
Intel 148, 152, 332
intellectual property rights, patents 117
inter-temporal pricing 140
interdependence 111, 121
    world trade 326–7
interest rates 278, 306
    central banks (see central banks)
Intergovernmental Panel on Climate
        Change (IPCC) 237
internal expansion 155, 156–9
Internal Market Scoreboard 346
International Monetary Fund (IMF) 377.
        see also exchange rates
    conditionality 377
    Special Drawing Right (SDR) 377
international trade 326–333
Internet
    Africa 193–4
    browsers 114
    consumer knowledge 19, 104–5, 283
    demand 31
    dotcom bubble 49
    job losses 284
    monopolies 247
    and prices 25, 252

recruitment 199
selling 2, 77
social media 19, 73, 104–5, 283
telecommunications 198
investment expenditure (I) 260
Ireland 72, 120, 172, 207, 296, 297, 301, 302
    Brexit 350–2
Italy 312
Ivengar, Sheena 63

Jaguar 184
Japan 315
    balance of payments 357
    deflation 259
    electronics 332
    multinationals 185
    regulation 234
    working practices 185
Japanese model 212
John Lewis Partnership 3–6
joint-stock companies 7
joint ventures 163, 178, 189
JOLED Inc. 184
just-in-time methods 137, 212

Keynesian 45° line 264–5
Keynesian beauty contest 50
kinked demand curve model 124
Kiva 117
knowledge economy 19
Kosovo 378

labelling 237
laboratory shops 68
labour 20. see also employees;
        employers
    marginal productivity theory 200–1
    substitution 201, 210
    supply curve 197–8
    turnover 215
    and wage rates 201
labour force 280
Labour government 300
labour market 196–0
    and incentives 215–9
    perfect 197
    and unemployment 281–4
    wage setters 202
labour turnover 215
land 20
language barriers 190
large passenger aircraft 131–2
Latin America 183
Latvia 371, 377
launch stage of product life cycle 141–2,
        186
law of comparative advantage 328, 329
law of demand 28

law of diminishing (marginal)
        returns 82–3
law of large numbers 61
leading indicators 70
learning by doing 185
Lee, Jae-yong 151
Lee, Yoon-Woo 150
legal factors in business environment 12
legislation 234
Lego 230
Lehman Brothers 312
lender of last resort l
Lepper, Mark 63
licensing 117, 164
limited liability 7
limited liability partnerships 7
liquid assets 277
liquidity ratios, banks 277
liquidity trap 311
Lithuania 371
living wage 208
Lloyds Banking Group 313
loans
    inelastic demand for 307
    unsustainable 177
local communities 136
lock-outs 204
logistics
    inbound 148
    outbound 149
Lomé Convention 338
London
    congestion zone 243
long-run average cost (LRAC) curves
        92–3
long-term finance 165–6
long-term incentive plan (LTIP) 217
L'Oréal 232
loss minimisation 102
low-paid workers 209
Luxottica 160
luxury services 178

M-form (multi-divisional) business
        organisation 8, 9
M3 (in eurozone and elsewhere) 276
M4 (in UK) 276
Maastricht Treaty 371
machine size 90
macroeconomic environment 11, 257–1
macroeconomic objectives 258–0
Malaysia 189, 344
Malta 371
managed trade 335
Manchester United 7
manufacturing 330
marginal benefits 23
marginal cost 23, 85, 86

marginal cost of labour 200, 203
marginal external cost 223
marginal physical product of labour 200
marginal private benefit 223
marginal private cost 223
marginal product of labour 213
marginal productivity theory 200–1
marginal revenue 98–0
marginal revenue product of labour 200
marginal social benefit 222
marginal social cost 222
marginal utility 56–8
    demand curve and 57–8
mark-up pricing 139
market behaviour, observations of 25–4
market clearing 35
market demand
    elasticity 201
    schedule 29
market development 75
market experiments 67–9
market failures 222–8
market intervention 51–2
market observations 67–8
market penetration 74–5
market power 227
market segmentation 74
market structures 110–6
market surveys 67–8
marketing 74–9, 149
marketing mix 75
markets
    foreign 190
    many competitors 111–4
    new entrants 147
Marks & Spencer 71
maternity leave 229
maturity stage of product life cycle
        142, 188
maximum pricing 51
McDonald's 190
medical insurance 62
medium-term finance 165
merger 155
mergers and acquisitions (M&As) 246–9
    competition policy 244
    growth through 159–1
    horizontal 159
    multinational 179–3
    vertical 159
merit goods 227
Metro 189
Mexico 52, 327, 340, 341, 343, 344, 377
microeconomic environment 11, 109–4
Microsoft 114
minimum efficient plant size (MEPS) 96–7
minimum efficient scale (MES) 96–7
minimum pricing 51

minimum reserve ratio 306
minimum wages 207–0
    in a competitive labour market 208–9
    and monopsony employers 209
mission statement 145
mobility of labour 198
mom and pop operations 189
Monarch Airlines 89
monetary policy 294, 304–4
    impact on business and economy
        306–7
    using money
money 261, 276
    demand 278–9, 307
    supply 276–9, 305–6
monitoring
    costs 93
    principal–agent relationship 10, 93
monopolistic competition 111, 113
monopoly 113, 116–1
    airlines 126
    compared with perfect competition
        118–9
    competition policy 244, 245
    and financial markets 119
    protection against foreign-based 334
    Sky 120
monopsony
    and gender inequality 213–4
Monsanto 117
Montenegro 287, 378
moral hazard 59–60, 62, 216
morale 215
Morrisons 111
mortgages 41
most favoured nations 341
multi-stage production 90
multinational corporations 175–5
    access new markets 186
    conglomerates 184
    cost reduction 185, 190
    customers 190
    diversity among 177–9
    downsizing 177
    entrepreneurial and management
        skills 185
    foreign cultures 184
    government policies 186, 190
    headquarters 185
    horizontally integrated 184
    host state 190, 191, 192
    investment 179–3
    joint ventures 184
    problems facing 190
    quality of inputs 185
    subsidiaries 190
    transaction costs 185
    vertically integrated 184

multinational expansion 183–9
multiplier effect 264
    calculation of size of multiplier
        267–8

Nash equilibrium 128
National Living Wage 208
national macroeconomic policy 293–4
natural monopoly 116
nature 34
negative equity 40
Nestlé 3, 232
net profit margin 153
networks 164
New Zealand 155, 188, 344
niches. see market niches
Nike 78, 184–5, 330
Nintendo 147
Nissan 184, 185–6
Nokia 184
non-collusive oligopoly 122
non-price competition 71
normal goods 30, 46
normal profit 100
North America Free Trade Association
        (NAFTA) 343–4
Northern Rock 276, 313
Norway 52, 240
nudge theory 63, 66
numerical flexibility 210, 212

Office for Gas and Electricity Markets
        (Ofgem) 126, 235
oligopoly 111, 113, 121–7
    collusive and non-collusive 121–4
    and consumer 124
    and EU 346
    EU Article 101 245
    fast food 114
    restrictive practices 244
oligopsony 202
Olympics 151, 268–0
OPEC 122–3, 288, 336
Open Europe 347
open-market operations 305–6
operations 149
opportunity costs 22, 83–4
opt-in/opt-out schemes 66
organisation 91
organisational slack 137
output decisions
    imperfectly competitive markets 110–3
outsourcing 158
overheads
    spreading 91
overheating 295
overproduction 223
ownership 178

Panasonic 162, 184
Paraguay 344
Paris Agreement 238
partial analysis 31
partitioned pricing 138
partnerships 7
patents 117, 150
paternity leave 229
peak-load pricing 140–1
pensions 206
Pepsi 47, 159
perfect competition 26–8, 103–6, 112
performance appraisals 216
performance related pay 216–7
PEST analysis 12
petrol prices 123
PG Tips 78
Philippines 72, 344
picketing 204
piece rates 215
place 75
plant economies of scale 91
plastic bags 236
Poland 207, 238
political factors in business environment
    11, 192
pollution 14, 92, 175, 177, 192, 198, 221,
    223, 234–3, 290, 336
Porter, Michael E. 146–8, 150
Portugal 375
predatory pricing 246
present bias 65
price-caps 235
price controls 235
price discrimination 75, 140–1, 246
price elasticity of demand 42–6
    consumer expenditure and 44
price elasticity of supply 48
price-fixing 123, 244
price leadership 123
price mechanism 27
price/pricing 75
    imperfectly competitive markets
        110–3
    profits 99–0
    regulation 250–1
price takers 25
price wars, fast food 114–5
primary activities 148–9
primary labour market 211
primary market in capital 166
primary production 15
principal–agent problem 9–0, 158
    labour market 215, 216
Principles for Responsible Management
    Education (UN) 231
prisoners' dilemma 129, 130
Private Finance Initiative (PFI) 319

private limited companies 7
procurement 149
producer co-operatives 7
producer sovereignty 336
product development 75
product differentiation 71–4
product life cycle
    multinationals and 186–8
    pricing and 141–3
product maintenance 74
product/market strategy 74
production 21
    classification 15
    costs of (see costs of production)
productive efficiency 106
productivity
    of labour 201
profit
    definition 81, 100–1
    normal 100
    satisficing 135
profit maximisation 9, 100–3
    labour 200–1
    monopolies 117–8
profit-maximising rule 100
promotion 75–6
protectionism 177, 182
    problems with 336–8
Prudential Regulation Authority (PRA) 60
Public and Commercial Services Union
    (PCS) 205
public finances 295–7
public goods 224–5
public limited companies 7
public-sector debt
    reduction 296–7
public-sector net borrowing (PSNB)
    278, 295
pubs 117
purchasing power parity 208

quality circles 185
quality standards 71
quantitative easing 278, 306
quantity demanded 28
quotas 333, 341

Rank Xerox 117
rational choices 22–3
rational consumer behaviour 57
rationalisation 91
ratios 153–5
raw materials 20
    extraction 178
real growth values 285
recession and recessionary strategies 182
    definition 271
reciprocity 341

recruitment 199
regulation 234, 250–2, 333
    airline industry 14, 15
relativity 64
rent controls 51–2
repeated games 129–2
replacement costs 84
reputation 60
Reputation Institute 229–0
resale price maintenance 245
reserves 362
resource availability and cost 184, 332
restrictive practices 244, 245
retaliation 153, 338
    (see also price wars)
return on capital employed (ROCE) 153
revaluation 363
revenue 98–0
risks
    definition 58
    dependent 61
    diversification 61
    independent 61
rivalry 225
road pricing 243
Roddick, Anita 232
rogue traders 59
Royal Bank of Scotland 313
Royal Mail 116
Russia 11, 140, 182, 269, 270
Ryanair 327, 376

sale and repurchase agreement
    (repo) 306
sales 149
sales revenue maximisation 135
Samsung 150–1, 179
Sanyo 184
scale of production 89–2, 94
scarcity
    advertising 77
    problem of 20–1
search costs 93
seasonal fluctuations 70
seasonal unemployment 284
secondary labour market 211
secondary market in capital 166
secondary production 15
self-control 65
self-employment 199
senile industry 334
Serious Fraud Office 245
services 74, 149
    and world trade 326–7
Setanta 120
shadow pricing 125
share options 217
share prices 39

shares
  and incomes 39
  substitutes 39
Shell 184
shirking 215
shocks 34, 299, 363
shoes 330
short-run shutdown point 102
short run under perfect competition 100
short-term finance 165
short-termism 166
simultaneous games 128
Singapore 243
single markets 343
single-move games 128
Sky 120
Slovakia 371
Slovenia 371
small and medium-sized enterprises (SMEs) 168–3
  exchange rates 364
  problems facing 169
social benefit 223
social cost 222
social efficiency 222
social factors in business environment 12
social media 73–4
social perceptions 213
socially optimal consumption 224
societal goals 229
software 332
sole proprietors 7
Sony 3, 147, 150, 162, 163, 184
South Korea 370
sovereign risk 365
Spain 312, 375
specialisation 90, 327–8
speculation 41, 49–0, 363, 378
spillover costs or benefits. see also externalities
sporting events 268–0
Spotify 184
stabilising speculation 50
stakeholders 136, 228
Standard Industrial Classification (SIC) 17
Starbucks 99, 318
state ownership
  multinationals 179
staying in business 10
steel industry 334, 339–0, 341
STEEPLE analysis 12
Stern Review 237
stock appreciation rights (SARs) 217
stock market 166–7
  demand and supply in action 38–9
  efficiency 167
stock turnover 154
strategic alliances 155–6, 163–5

strategic analysis
  external business environment 146–9
strategic choice 149–3
strategic management 145
strategic trade theory 334
  Airbus 335–6
strategy 145–4
strikes 205–206
structural unemployment 283–4
structure–conduct–performance paradigm 17–8
sub-prime mortgages 375
subcontracting 164
subsidies 333
  and externalities 233–4
substitutes 34, 147
substitution effect 28, 30, 43
sunk costs 64
  bygones principle 84
supermarkets
  oligopoly 125
  oligopsony 125
supernormal profit 100
suppliers
  bargaining power 146–7
  ethical treatment 229
supply 21–2, 27, 32–5, 81–8
  change in 35
  change in quantity supplied 35
  price taker 81–8
  response time 48
  shares 39
supply chain 95
supply curves 33–4
supply-side policies 294, 314–0
  advice and persuasion 323
  capital movements 319
  competition 318–9
  free trade 319
  government expenditure 317
  infrastructure 320
  interventionist 319–0
  labour costs 318
  market-orientated 314–9
  nationalisation 323
  Private Finance Initiative (PFI) 319
  productivity 321–2
  research and development 320
  small firms 323
  tax cuts 317–8
  training 320–3
support activities 149
Sweden 371

tacit collusion 123
takeover constraint 157
takeovers 155. see also mergers and acquisitions

talent gap 219
tapered vertical integration 158–9
targets 158
tariff walls 186
tariffs 117, 333, 341
  and protectionism 337
tastes 30
Tata Steel 334
taxation
  automatic fiscal stabilisers 298
  effects of 299
  and externalities 233–4
  fat taxes 52
  on goods 52
  green 236–8
  multinational corporations 191
  progressive 297
  sugar taxes 52
Taylor rule 308
teamwork 212
technical standards 71
technological development 149
  and telecommuting 199
technological factors in business environment 12
technology transfer 191
telecommuting 198–9
terms of trade 333
tertiary production 15
Tesco 189
Thailand 170, 171, 189, 344, 368
Thaler, Richard 63
Thurow, Lester 335
tied lease model 117
time consistency 65
time-series analysis 69–0
Time Warner 159–0
tit-for-tat 131
total consumer expenditure 44
total cost 84
total fixed cost 85
total quality management (TQM) 212
total revenue 44, 98
total utility 56
total variable cost 85
Toyota 186
trade
  advantages 327
  restrictions 333–0
trade associations 60
trade blocs. see also European Union
trade cycle. see business cycle
trade unions 203–6
  membership 205, 213
traditional theory of the firm 9
traffic congestion, urban 241–3
training
  new industries 338

Trans-Pacific Trade Paetnership
(TPP) 344
transactions costs 93–5
multinationals 185
vertical integration 158
transfer pricing 192
transnational corporations (TNCs).
see multinational corporations
transport costs 94
multinationals 186
trends in demand 69–0
Trump, Donald 182, 339–0, 344, 357
tulips 49
Turkish Airlines 79
type 1 vulnerability (demand) 87–9
type 2 vulnerability (inputs) 88–9

U-form (unitary) business organisation 8
Uber 184
UK economy
changes 17
uncertainty 34
multinational corporations 192
vertical integration 157
underemployment 259, 282
unemployment 258–9, 280–4
claimant 280
disequilibrium 282
equilibrium 283
and inflation 286–7
and labour market 281–4
natural level 282
number unemployed 280
rate 258–9, 280
standardised 280
Unilever 184
unions. *see* trade unions
unit elastic demand 45–6
United Kingdom. *see also* Brexit
border controls 205

Competition Act 245
Credit Guarantee Scheme 313
disinvestment 356
energy companies 181
Enterprise Act 245
and euro 371, 372
exhaust gases 181
oil exports 357
privatisation 250
reserves 356
water companies 181
United States
America first 336
balance of payments 357
climate change 238
EU trade disputes 338342
Federal Open Market Committee
(FOMC) 309
Federal Reserve 309
and ECB 313
mergers and aquisitions 182
minimum wages 208
quantitive easing 312
regulation 234
special protection 334
steel industry 339, 341
TPP 344
Troubled Asset Relief Program (TARP)
312
world trade 327–8
United States-Mexico-Canada Agreement
(USMCA) 344
university degree and earnings 218–9
utility, definition 56

value chain
analysis 148–9
developing and developed
economies 331
variable costs 84

variable inputs 82
vehicle industry 17
Venezuela 123, 287, 344
vertical integration 94–5, 157
backward 95
forward 95
vertical price-fixing agreements 245
vertical restraints 246
Virgin 159, 229
vocational education 219
Volkswagen 231
vulnerability 87–9

wage rates 201
demand for labour 201
equilibrium 27
perfect competition 27, 201–2
wage setters 202
wage takers 197
Waitrose 3, 4, 5–6
Wal-Mart 179, 184, 189
Wales 191, 284
warrantees 60
wealth 39
white knight' strategy 161
Winter of Discontent (1978-9) 204–5
working to rule 204
world trade
and GDP 326
interdependence 326–7
World Trade Centre 291
World Trade Organization (WTO)
338–9, 341–5
authority 341
Doha Round 342
Nairobi Package 342
Uraguay Round 341

Zambia 336
Zimbabwe 287